KINGS, QUEENS, *and* COURTIERS

ART IN EARLY RENAISSANCE FRANCE

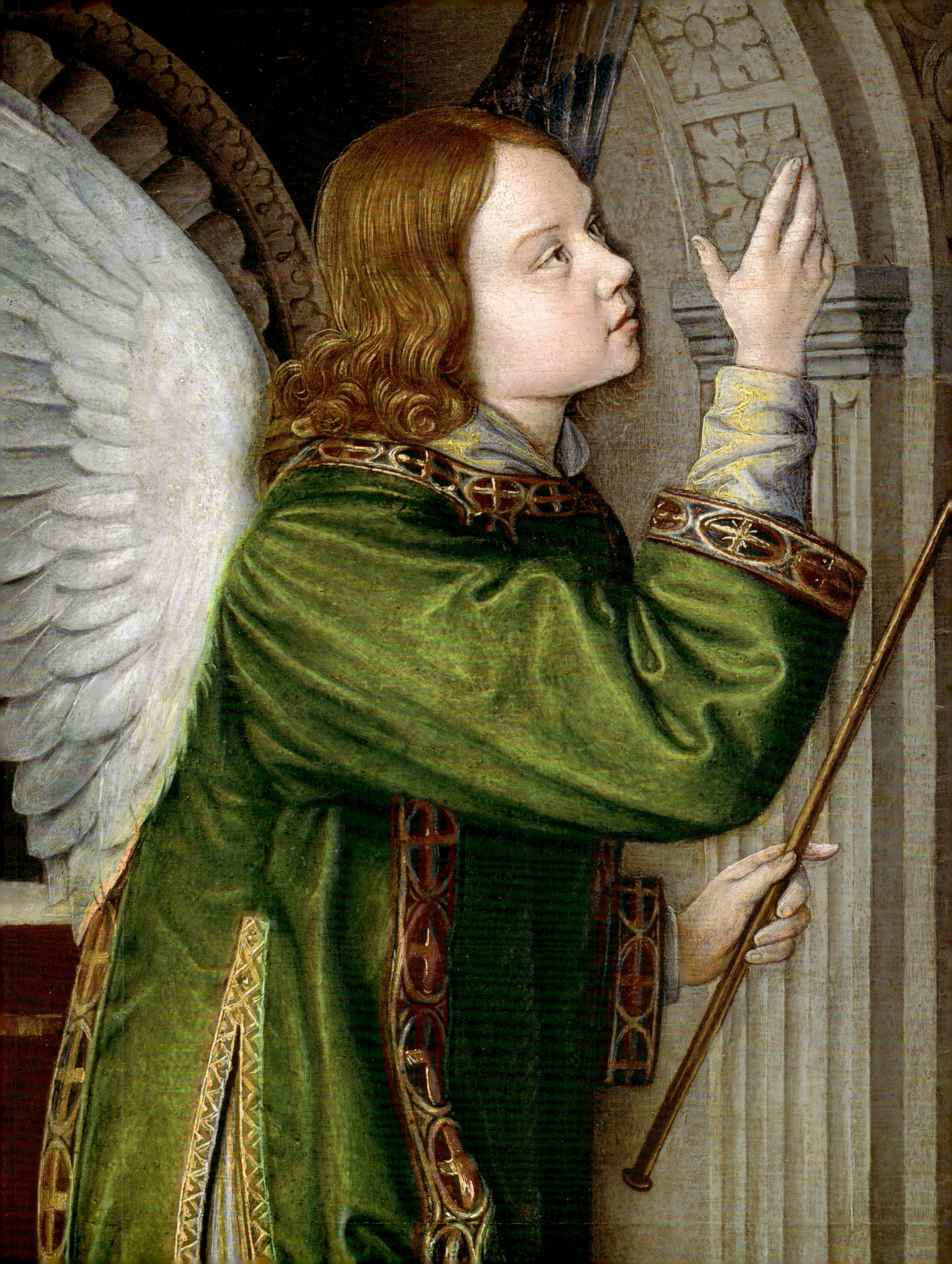

KINGS, QUEENS, *and* COURTIERS

ART IN EARLY RENAISSANCE FRANCE

Martha Wolff, General Editor

The Art Institute of Chicago
Yale University Press, New Haven and London

Organizing Committee

GENEVIÈVE BRESC-BAUTIER, Director, Department of Sculpture, Musée du Louvre, Paris (GB-B)

THIERRY CRÉPIN-LEBLOND, Director, Musée national de la Renaissance, Château d'Ecouen (TC-L)

ÉLISABETH TABURET-DELAHAYE, Director, Musée de Cluny—Musée national du Moyen Age, Paris (ET-D)

MARTHA WOLFF, Eleanor Wood Prince Curator of European Painting and Sculpture before 1750, The Art Institute of Chicago (MW)

Authors

ÉLISABETH ANTOINE, Curator, Department of Decorative Arts, Musée du Louvre, Paris (EA)

AGNÈS BOS, Curator, Department of Decorative Arts, Musée du Louvre, Paris (AB)

GENEVIÈVE BRESC-BAUTIER, Director, Department of Sculpture, Musée du Louvre, Paris (GB-B)

BÉATRICE DE CHANCEL-BARDELOT, Chief Curator, Institut national d'histoire de l'art, Paris (BC-B)

PHILIPPE CONTAMINE, Professor Emeritus, Université de Paris IV (Paris–Sorbonne)

THIERRY CRÉPIN-LEBLOND, Director, Musée national de la Renaissance, Château d'Ecouen (TC-L)

KATE DIMITROVA, Visiting Asssistant Professor, Wells College, Aurora, New York (KD)

FRÉDÉRIC ELSIG, Assistant Professor, Université de Genève

MARK EVANS, Senior Curator of Paintings, Victoria and Albert Museum, London (ME)

ÉTIENNE HAMON, Professor, Université de Picardie, Amiens

MAXENCE HERMANT, Curator, Bibliothèque nationale de France, Paris (MHt)

MICHEL HÉROLD, Chief Curator, Centre André-Chastel, Paris; Director, French Committee, Corpus Vitrearum (MHd)

MARIE JACOB, Adjunct Professor, Université de Paris Ouest–Nanterre La Défense (MJ)

SUZANNE KARR SCHMIDT, Andrew W. Mellon Curatorial Fellow in the Department of Prints and Drawings, The Art Institute of Chicago (SKS)

EBERHARD KÖNIG, Professor, Kunsthistorisches Institut, Freie Universität, Berlin (EK)

THOMAS KREN, Senior Curator of Manuscripts, The J. Paul Getty Museum, Los Angeles (TK)

MARIE-CLAUDE LÉONELLI, Curator of Antiquities and Works of Art, Department of the Vaucluse (M-CL)

SÉVERINE LEPAPE, Curator, Bibliothèque nationale de France, Paris (SL)

PIERRE-YVES LE POGAM, Chief Curator, Department of Sculpture, Musée du Louvre, Paris

PHILIPPE LORENTZ, Professor, Université de Strasbourg, and Lecturer, Ecole pratique des hautes études, Paris (PL)

CHRISTINA NIELSEN, Assistant Curator for Medieval Art, The Art Institute of Chicago (CN)

NICOLAS PETIT, Chief Curator, Bibliothèque nationale de France, Paris (NP)

CHARLOTTE RIOU, Curator of Sculpture, Musée des Augustins, Toulouse (CR)

CÉCILE SCAILLIÉREZ, Chief Curator, Department of Paintings, Musée du Louvre, Paris (CS)

EVE STRAUSSMAN-PFLANZER, Patrick G. and Shirley W. Ryan Associate Curator of European Painting and Sculpture before 1750, The Art Institute of Chicago (ES-P)

ÉLISABETH TABURET-DELAHAYE, Director, Musée de Cluny—Musée national du Moyen Age, Paris (ET-D)

INÈS VILLELA-PETIT, Curator, Bibliothèque nationale de France, Paris (IV-P)

ROGER S. WIECK, Curator of Medieval and Renaissance Manuscripts, The Morgan Library and Museum, New York (RSW)

MARTHA WOLFF, Eleanor Wood Prince Curator of European Painting and Sculpture before 1750, The Art Institute of Chicago (MW)

CAROLINE ZÖHL, Lecturer, Kunsthistorisches Institut, Freie Universität, Berlin (CZ)

CONTENTS

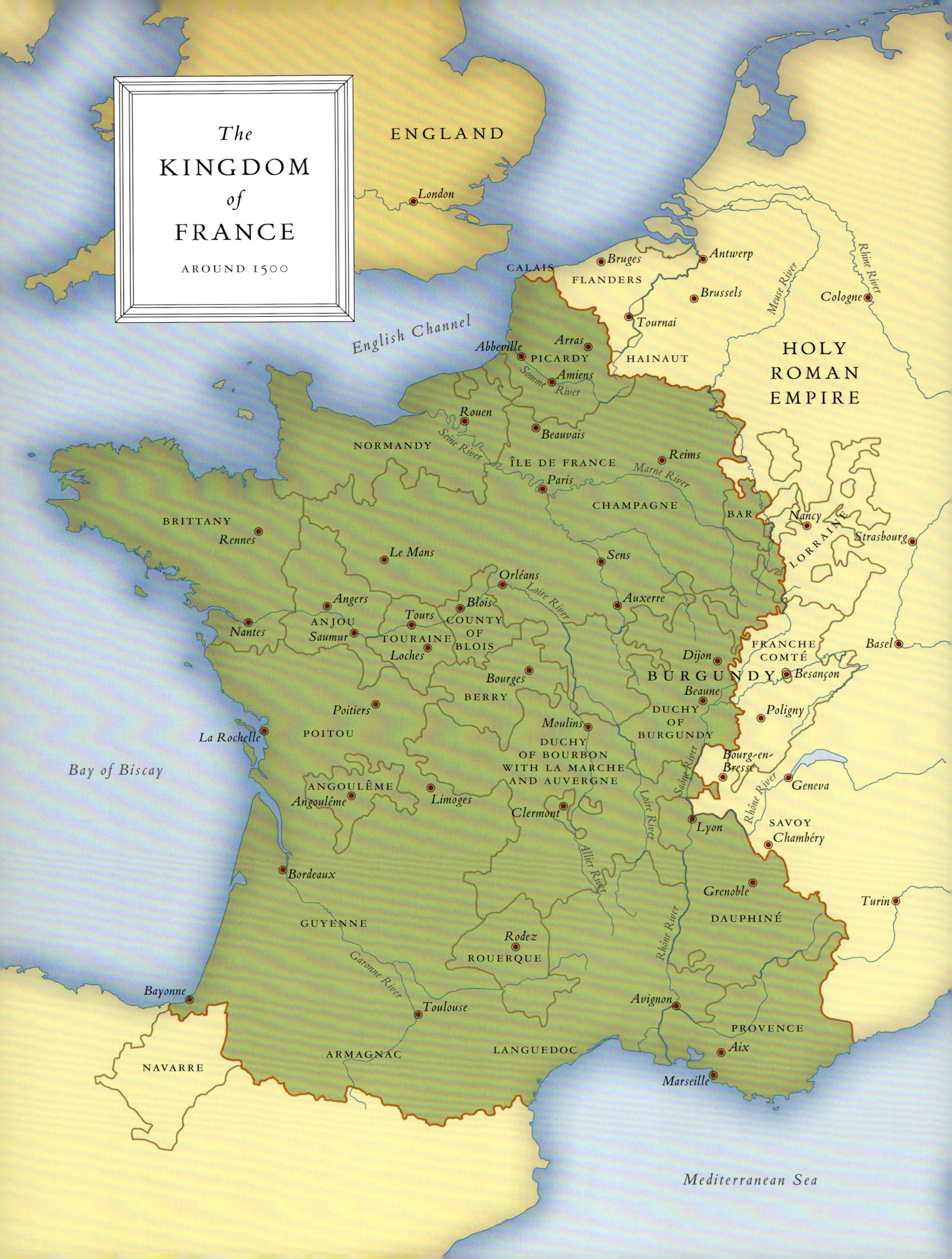

The KINGDOM of FRANCE
AROUND 1500
ENGLAND
London
CALAIS
Bruges
Antwerp
FLANDERS
Brussels
Meuse River
Rhine River
Cologne
Tournai
English Channel
Arras
Abbeville
PICARDY
HAINAUT
HOLY ROMAN EMPIRE
Amiens
Somme River
Rouen
Beauvais
NORMANDY
Seine River
ÎLE DE FRANCE
Reims
Marne River
Paris
CHAMPAGNE
BAR
Nancy
LORRAINE
Strasbourg
BRITTANY
Rennes
Le Mans
Sens
Orléans
Loire River
Auxerre
Angers
Blois
Tours
COUNTY OF BLOIS
Nantes
ANJOU
Saumur
TOURAINE
Loches
FRANCHE COMTÉ
Basel
Dijon
BURGUNDY
Besançon
Bourges
Beaune
BERRY
Poitiers
Poligny
DUCHY OF BURGUNDY
Moulins
La Rochelle
POITOU
DUCHY OF BOURBON WITH LA MARCHE AND AUVERGNE
Saône River
Bourg-en-Bresse
Bay of Biscay
ANGOULÊME
Angoulême
Limoges
Rhône River
Geneva
Clermont
Loire River
Lyon
SAVOY
Chambéry
Allier River
Bordeaux
Grenoble
Turin
GUYENNE
DAUPHINÉ
Rodez
ROUERQUE
Rhône River
Garonne River
Bayonne
Toulouse
Avignon
PROVENCE
Aix
ARMAGNAC
LANGUEDOC
NAVARRE
Marseille
Mediterranean Sea

FOREWORD

The extraordinary quality, variety, and dynamism of the visual arts in France at the dawn of the Renaissance finally receive their due in this stunning exhibition presented at the Grand Palais in Paris and at the Art Institute of Chicago. In the time of Charles VIII and Louis XII, the accomplishments of king, court, and people—united and on the move after the strife of the earlier decades of the fifteenth century—found expression in an exuberant outpouring of activity in all media, including monumental works of sculpture, stained glass, tapestry, refined and intimate illuminated manuscripts, luminous paintings on panel, goldsmithwork, and prints (then an innovative new medium). Open to all new influences, yet retaining a base in the traditions and structures of late medieval art, this period achieved a creative and flexible synthesis of the Flamboyant late Gothic and the new vocabulary *a l'antique*.

It is no accident that the American version of the exhibition should appear in Chicago, for the city has long held a deep appreciation for French art and culture. This is most familiar through Chicagoans' collecting the works of the Impressionists, Post-Impressionists, and the modernist pioneers shortly after they were painted. But one of the founders of the Art Institute, Martin A. Ryerson, who visited Monet at Giverny, was also acquiring "primitives" during the period of the groundbreaking *Exposition des Primitifs Français* mounted in Paris in 1904. Ryerson's acumen brought paintings by Jean Hey and the wings of the Thuison altarpiece to Chicago in the following years, making it possible for the Art Institute to contribute so significantly to this exhibition, which draws deeply on the riches of the French national museums, the Musée du Louvre, the Bibliothèque nationale de France, and on the monuments still preserved in situ in churches throughout France.

In this collaboration with the Réunion des musées nationaux, I am most grateful to Thomas Grenon, General Administrator, and his successor, Jean-Paul Cluzel, and colleagues for mobilizing their resources to help bring together this extraordinary group of loans. This effort was made possible through the knowledge and scholarship of the exhibition's outstanding organizing committee: Geneviève Bresc-Bautier, Director, Department of Sculpture, Musée du Louvre; Thierry Crépin-Leblond, Director, Musée national de la Renaissance, Château d'Ecouen; Elisabeth Taburet-Delahaye, Director, Musée de Cluny—Musée national du Moyen Age; and Martha Wolff, Eleanor Wood Prince Curator of European Painting and Sculpture before 1750, the Art Institute of Chicago. Both this book and the catalogue of the Paris exhibition reflect much new information brought to light, in many cases, by the members of this team and by the distinguished catalogue authors and advisors, as knowledge of this fertile period continues to unfold. We are also deeply indebted to the many institutional, ecclesiastical, and private lenders who have temporarily entrusted us with the rare works in their care.

I acknowledge with gratitude the generous donors who have made possible the realization of this exhibition at the Art Institute. In Chicago major funding was provided by Paul and Melinda Sullivan and the Eloise W. Martin Legacy Fund; by Scott, Lynda, Jonathan, and Lindsey Canel; by an award from the National Endowment for the Arts; and by the Chauncey and Marion Deering McCormick Foundation, the Prince Charitable Trusts, and the Exhibitions Trust, a group of supporters committed to ensuring that the exhibitions at the museum are of the highest quality: Kenneth and Anne Griffin, Thomas and Margot Pritzker, the Earl and Brenda Shapiro Foundation, Donna and Howard Stone, Mr. and Mrs. Paul Sullivan, and an anonymous donor. I am also deeply grateful to Art Institute colleagues, including Martha Wolff, who, as noted, was part of the curatorial team that conceived the exhibition, and who guided its presentation here in Chicago; Robert Sharp, Sarah Guernsey, and Amy R. Peltz of our Publications Department, who prepared the Chicago edition of the exhibition catalogue with characteristic care and skill; Markus Dohner, who devised the exhibition's sensitive and refined installation; Darrell Green, who managed the complex transfer of the exhibition from Paris to Chicago, as well as the addition of loans for Chicago only; and lastly Dorothy Schroeder, Vice President for Exhibitions and Museum Administration, for her sharp oversight of the entire exhibition process. Every such project is a team effort; this one, with its complicated international and national loans, perhaps more than most.

JAMES CUNO
President and Eloise W. Martin Director
The Art Institute of Chicago

LENDERS TO THE EXHIBITION

Abbaye Notre-Dame d'Evron

Alte Pinakothek, Munich

The Art Institute of Chicago

Basiliek Sint-Martinus, Halle

Bibliothèque municipale, Lyon

Bibliothèque nationale de France, Paris

- Département des Estampes et de la Photographie
- Département des Manuscrits
- Département des Monnaies, médailles, et antiques
- Réserve des livres rares

The British Library, London

Cathédrale Notre-Dame de Moulins

Commune de Censeau, église Notre-Dame de l'Assomption

Commune de Montluçon, église Saint-Pierre

Conseil Général de l'Aveyron

The J. Paul Getty Museum, Los Angeles

Kelvingrove Art Gallery and Museum, Glasgow

The Library of Congress, Washington, D.C.

Los Angeles County Museum of Art

The Metropolitan Museum of Art, New York

The Morgan Library and Museum, New York

Musée Anne de Beaujeu, Moulins

Musée Crozatier, Le Puy-en-Velay

Musée de Cluny—Musée national du Moyen Age, Paris

Musée de l'hôtel Sandelin, Saint Omer

Musée départemental des Antiquités de la Seine-Maritime, Rouen

Musée des Augustins, Toulouse

Musée des Beaux-Arts, Tours

Musée Dobrée, Nantes

Musée du Berry, Bourges

Musée du Louvre, Paris

- Département des Arts graphiques
- Département des Objets d'art
- Département des Peintures
- Département des Sculptures

Musée Fabre, Montpellier

Musée national de la Renaissance, Château d'Ecouen

Musée Rolin, Autun

Musées royaux des Beaux-Arts de Belgique, Brussels

Museum of Fine Arts, Boston

The National Gallery, London

National Gallery of Art, Washington, D.C.

North Carolina Museum of Art, Raleigh

Philadelphia Museum of Art

Teylers Museum, Haarlem

Toledo Museum of Art

Trésor de la Cathédrale Saint-Etienne, Sens

Waddesdon Manor, The Rothschild Collection (National Trust)

Worcester Art Museum

And private collections

ACKNOWLEDGMENTS

The extraordinary loans and the synthesis of new scholarship that make up this beautiful exhibition and its catalogue are the work of many individuals, to whom we owe a huge debt of gratitude. The art of France in the years around 1500—between the Middle Ages and the Renaissance—has never before been assembled in America, and even in France it has often been overlooked, in favor of the glamorous reputation of Francis I, the work of the earlier decades of the fifteenth century, or concentration on a single medium, at least in recent exhibitions. Hence the time was right to focus on what is an essential turning point, a newly self-confident moment for king and court, and a tremendously fertile field for discoveries in the careers and interactions of artists and in the use and diffusion of works of art.

To be able to bring together such rare and fragile objects required true collaboration at all levels, but most essentially it was motivated by the vision and energy of the leaders of the two organizing institutions: James Cuno, President and Eloise W. Martin Director of the Art Institute of Chicago, and Thomas Grenon, General Administrator of the Réunion des musées nationaux, followed by Jean-Paul Cluzel, his successor in that position.

The concept and realization of the exhibition in Paris and Chicago were the product of an organizational committee made up of Geneviève Bresc-Bautier, Director, Department of Sculpture, Musée du Louvre; Thierry Crépin-Leblond, Director, Musée national de la Renaissance, Château d'Ecouen; Elisabeth Taburet-Delahaye, Director, Musée Cluny—Musée national du Moyen Age; and Martha Wolff, Eleanor Wood Prince Curator of European Painting and Sculpture before 1750, the Art Institute of Chicago. Elisabeth Taburet-Delahaye gracefully guided and coordinated the work of this committee. On a personal level, it was deeply rewarding to work with these three colleagues on such a challenging project. It is important to acknowledge too that the initial organizing effort for the exhibition came from Hilliard Goldfarb and his colleagues at the Musée des Beaux-Arts, Montréal, led first by Guy Cogeval, then director of the Musée des Beaux-Arts, followed by Nathalie Bondil.

A distinguished Scientific Committee provided invaluable advice and support in shaping the exhibition. Its members were: François Avril, Honorary Head Curator, Bibliothèque nationale de France; Agnès Bos, Curator, Department of Decorative Arts, Musée du Louvre; Béatrice de Chancel-Bardelot, Chief Curator, Institut national d'histoire de l'art; Xavier Dectot, Curator, Musée Cluny—Musée national du Moyen Age; Sophie Guillot de Suduiraut, Chief Curator, Department of Sculpture, Musée du Louvre; Etienne Hamon, Professor, Université de Picardie, Amiens, and Centre André-Chastel, Paris; Maxence Hermant, Curator, Bibliothèque nationale de France; Michel Hérold, Chief Curator, Centre-André Chastel, Paris; Fabienne Joubert, University Professor, Université de Paris IV (Paris–Sorbonne); Séverine Lepape, Curator, Bibliothèque nationale de France; Pierre-Yves Le Pogam, Chief Curator, Department of Sculpture, Musée du Louvre; Philippe Lorentz, Professor, Université de Strasbourg, and Lecturer, Ecole pratiques des hautes-études, Paris; Florian Meunier, Curator, Musée Carnavalet, Paris; Nicolas Petit, Chief Curator, Bibliothèque nationale de France; Nicole Reynaud, Chargée de mission, Musée du Louvre, and Honorary Fellow, Centre national de la recherche scientifique; Cécile Scailliérez, Chief Curator, Department of Paintings, Musée du Louvre; and Inès Villela-Petit, Curator, Bibliothèque nationale de France. They are also to be thanked for their generous participation in the creation of this catalogue, contributing essays, chapter introductions, and entries. The team is listed in full on page four. Among the members of this Scientific Committee, two extraordinary scholars should be singled out for the special contribution that was their advice and support—François Avril and Nicole Reynaud. Their names and work are invoked on almost every page of the book.

Other colleagues contributed in important ways to the realization of this project. They helped locate possible loans, made the direct study of objects possible, and shared their insights, experience, and documentation. Their enthusiastic support is warmly acknowledged: Maryan Ainsworth, Rita Albertson, Jonathan Alexander, Dita Amory, Christopher Apostle, Ronni Baer, Joseph Baillio, Pantxika Beguérie-de Paepe, Rachel Billinge, Till-Holger Borchert, Peter van den Brink, David Alan Brown, Lorne Campbell, Perry Chapman, Julien Chapuis, Justin Clegg, Tarnya Cooper, Alan Darr, Catherine Daunt, Diane De Grazia, Nanne Dekking, Dagmar Eichberger, Molly Faries, Stephen Fliegel, Andreas Fingernagel, Sam Fogg, Françoise Gatouillat, Pierre-Gilles Girault, George Gordon, Michael Gregory, Nica Gutman, John Hand, Dare Hartwell, Nicholas Herman, Sandra Hindman, Juliette Jestaz, Sue Jones, Aurélien Joudrier, Laurence Kanter, Suzanne Karr Schmidt, Guy-Michel Leproux, Catherine Metzger, Amanda Mikolic, Hélène Mund, Audrey Nassieu-Maupas,

Christina Nielsen, Christina Normore, Noelle Ocon, Catherine Reynolds, Hannelore Roemich, Ashok Roy, Amandine Royer, Paul Saenger, Jan Schmidt, Manfred Sellink, Sabine van Sprang, Jochen Sander, Jon Seydl, Joaneath Spicer, Eve Straussman-Pflanzer, Jean-Christophe Ton-That, Laura Weigert, Terri Weisser, Yao-Fen You, and Rebecca Zorach.

Work on an exhibition of this scope relies on a wide range of research institutions and libraries. The organizing committee and authors are deeply grateful to the libraries and the library staffs of their respective institutions. Work on the exhibition could not have gone forward without the resources and help of the Bibliothèque nationale de France and its several branches, especially the Department of Rare Books and the Department of Manuscripts; the Services de documentation of the several departments of the Musée du Louvre; the library of the Institut national d'histoire de l'art; and the library of the Ecole nationale supérieure des Beaux-arts. In Chicago, the Newberry Library and, most especially, the Ryerson Library of the Art Institute were indispensable. Jack Perry Brown, Executive Director of the Art Institute libraries and his staff, including Susan Augustine, Amy Ballmer, Anne Champagne, Melanie Emerson, Christine Fabian, Nancy Ford, Patrice Murtha, and Curtis Osman, provided their usual unstinting support to a lengthy project.

A wide range of public institutions were extraordinarily generous in making their rare objects available for loan to the exhibition and in advising on the care and display of these complex works, a number of them still in situ in the religious foundations for which they were made. We are deeply grateful to the dedicated curators and administrators who made it possible to study and borrow them: Michel Draguet and Veronique Bücken, Musées Royaux des Beaux-Arts de Belgique; Ann Renaux-Veys, Kerkfabriek, Sint-Martinus, Halle; Scot McKendrick, The British Library; Nicholas Penny, Susan Foister, and David Jaffé, The National Gallery; Fabia Bromovsky and Pippa Shirley, Waddesdon Manor (National Trust); Professor Klaus Schrenk, Helga Siefert, and Martin Schawe, Bayerische Staatsgemäldesammlungen; Mark O'Neill and Patricia Collins, Glasgow City Museums and Art Gallery; Marjan Scharloo, Teylers Museum; Patrick Bazin, Bibliothèque municipale de Lyon; Bruno Racine, Bibliothèque national de France, with Michel Amandry and Inès Villela-Petit, Department of Coins, Medals, and Antiquities, Bibliothèque nationale de France; Sylvie Aubenas and Séverine Lepape, Department of Prints and Photographs, Bibliothèque nationale de France; Thierry Delcourt, Marie-Pierre Laffitte, and Maxence Hermant, Department of Manuscripts, Bibliothèque nationale de France; Antoine Coron and Nicolas Petit, Réserve des Livres Rares, Bibliothèque nationale de France; Louis Allemant and Claire Delmas, Conservation régionale des monuments historiques, DRAC Midi-Pyrenées; Jean-Paul Dufrègne, Musée Anne de Beaujeu; Gilles Grandjean, Musée Crozatier; Jacques Philippon, Musée de l'hôtel Sandelin; Nathalie Roy, Musée départemental des Antiquités de la Seine-Maritime; Axel Hémery and Charlotte Riou, Musée des Augustins; Philippe Le Leyzour, Musée des Beaux-Arts de Tours; Jacques Santrot, Musée Dobrée; Béatrice de Chancel-Bardelot and the Musée du Berry; Henri Loyrette, Musée du Louvre, together with Vincent Pomarède, Dominique Thiébaut, Cécile Scailliérez, and Sébastien Allard, Department of Paintings, Musée du Louvre; Marc Bascou, Elisabeth Antoine, and Agnès Bos, Department of Decorative Arts, Musée du Louvre; Carel van Tuyll, Department of Graphic Arts, Musée du Louvre; Michel Hilaire, Musée Fabre; Brigitte Maurice-Chabard, Musée Rolin; Joel Bedouet, Mayor of the town of Evron; Père Trocherie and Luc Caudroy, Basilique Notre-Dame de l'Epine, Evron; Michel Clément and Abbé Pierron, Cathedral of Notre-Dame, Moulins; Pascal Mignerey, Conservation régional des monuments historiques, DRAC Franche-Comté; Daniel Duglery, Mayor of the town of Montluçon; Louis Poulhès, DRAC Bourgogne; Lydwine Saulnier-Pernuit, Musées de Sens; David Bomford, Thomas Kren, and Scott Schaefer, The J. Paul Getty Museum; James H. Billington and Daniel De Simone, Library of Congress; Michael Govan, Wendy Kaplan, and Elizabeth Williams, Los Angeles County Museum of Art; Malcolm Rogers and Pam Parmal, Museum of Fine Arts, Boston; Earl A. Powell III, John Hand, Andrew Robison, and Meg Morgan Grasselli, National Gallery of Art; Lawrence J. Wheeler, Dennis Weller, and David Steel, North Carolina Museum of Art; Timothy Rubb, Joseph Rishel, Carl Strehlke, and Lloyd de Witt, Philadelphia Museum of Art; Thomas Campbell, Peter Barnet, Keith Christiansen, and Ian Wardropper, The Metropolitan Museum of Art; William Griswold, William Voeckle, and Roger S. Wieck, The Morgan Library and Museum; Don Bacigalupi and Jutta Page, Toledo Museum of Art; and James Welu, Worcester Art Museum.

At the Réunion des musées nationaux, the administrative abilities of Marion Mangon, Melanie Gaunelle, Francine Robinson, Barbara Kroher, and Sylvia Linard were instrumental in the realization of the exhibition; Laurence Posselle, aided by Hugues Charreyron and Anne Chapoutot, produced the beautiful catalogue for the exhibition in Paris, at the same time helping immensely with its English iteration. Gaëlle Le-Page's tenacious and good-humored management of a myriad of details was instrumental in moving things forward for both venues.

In Chicago, James Cuno's leadership and enthusiasm were essential from the inception of the exhibition to its realization. We are deeply grateful to the generous donors who came forward to make it possible. In Chicago, major funding was provided by Paul and Melinda Sullivan and the Eloise W. Martin Legacy Fund; by Scott, Lynda, Jonathan, and Lindsey Canel; by a generous award from the National Endowment for the Arts; and by the Chauncey and Marion

Deering McCormick Foundation, the Prince Charitable Trusts, and the Exhibitions Trust: Kenneth and Anne Griffin, Thomas and Margot Pritzker, the Earl and Brenda Shapiro Foundation, Donna and Howard Stone, Mr. and Mrs. Paul Sullivan, and an anonymous donor.

I am also very grateful to Douglas Druick, Searle Curator of Medieval to Modern European Painting and Sculpture and Prince Trust Curator of Prints and Drawings, for his steady support throughout. Sincere thanks are due to David Thurm, Chief Operating Officer; Dorothy Schroeder, Vice President for Exhibitions and Museum Administration; Jeanne M. Ladd, Vice President of Museum Finance; Julie Getzels, Executive Vice President, General Counsel, and Corporate Secretary; and Jennifer Sostaric, Associate General Counsel, for their administrative insight and care. Darrell Green expedited the complex shipping and installation arrangements with aplomb. It was a pleasure to work with Bernice Chu and Markus Dohner on the design of the exhibition; with Jeff Wonderland, Salvador Cruz, and Susanna Kim Vitayaudom on its graphic presentation; and with Bill Foster and Tom Riley to develop the valuable audio-visual component. Associate Vice President William Caddick, Tom Barnes, and the craftsmen of the Physical Plant Department made the installation a reality. Led first by Susan F. Rossen and then by Robert V. Sharp, the staff of the Publications Department—Sarah Guernsey, Amy R. Peltz, Carolyn Ziebarth, Joseph Mohan, Clo Pazera, and intern Laura Schell—worked tirelessly and with inventiveness and humor to produce a beautiful catalogue to the highest standard. The book's design by Maria Grillo and Gabrielle Schubart of the Grillo Group was both elegant and sympathetic, aided by the expertise of Pat Goley and Kirsti Monsen-Kellogg of Professional Graphics. Mary Jane Drews, Patricia White, Kevin Beck, Lawrence DelPilar, and Mary Beth Witte helped find support for the exhibition. Carrie Heinonen, together with Erin Hogan, Gary Stoppelman, Lauren Schultz, and Chai Lee, ably publicized the exhibition, while Robert Eskridge, Mary Sue Glosser, David Stark, Jeff Nigro, Robin Schnur, Karin Jacobson, and Terah Walkup gave it a fitting educational face.

The exhibition benefited greatly from the expertise, diligence, and sensitivity of conservators Frank Zuccari, Faye Wrubel, Allison Langley, Kirk Vuillemot, Barbara Hall, Suzanne Schnepp, Emily Heye, Sarah Moy, Lauren Chang, Isaac Facio, Christine Fabian, Harriet Stratis, Kim Nichols, Christine Conniff-O'Shea, Charles Pietraszewski, and Christopher Brooks. Their expertise made it possible to confidently transport and display such a wide range of objects. I am indebted to colleagues who generously offered the time and talents of their staff for this joint effort, in particular Christopher Monkhouse, Daniel Walker, Douglas Druick, Suzanne Folds McCullagh, Martha Tedeschi, and Jack Perry Brown.

The entire staff of the Department of European Painting and Sculpture was an immense support: Douglas Druick, Geraldine Banik, Gloria Groom, Stephanie D'Alessandro, Christina Nielsen, Eve Straussman-Pflanzer, Adrienne Jeske, Jane Neet, Jill Shaw, Robert Burnier, Aza Quinn-Brauner, George Sferra, and Christina Giles. Jennifer Paoletti's wisdom, care, and attention to detail made it possible to accomplish the many tasks associated with the exhibition. She was helped by Marsely Kehoe and volunteers Kelli Wood, Austin White, and Anastasia Standa. Equally essential was Florence Cazenave's knowledge, tenacity, enthusiasm, and wit. Though she was with us only for a brief internship, Valérie Carpentier made a signal contribution to the representation of architecture and ornament in the exhibition in Chicago.

On another level, I am deeply grateful for David Van Zanten's wonderfully constant support, which sustained me in this effort.

MARTHA WOLFF
Eleanor Wood Prince Curator of European Painting
and Sculpture Before 1750
The Art Institute of Chicago

GENEALOGICAL CHART *of the* KINGS OF FRANCE

FROM THE MID-FOURTEENTH CENTURY TO 1515

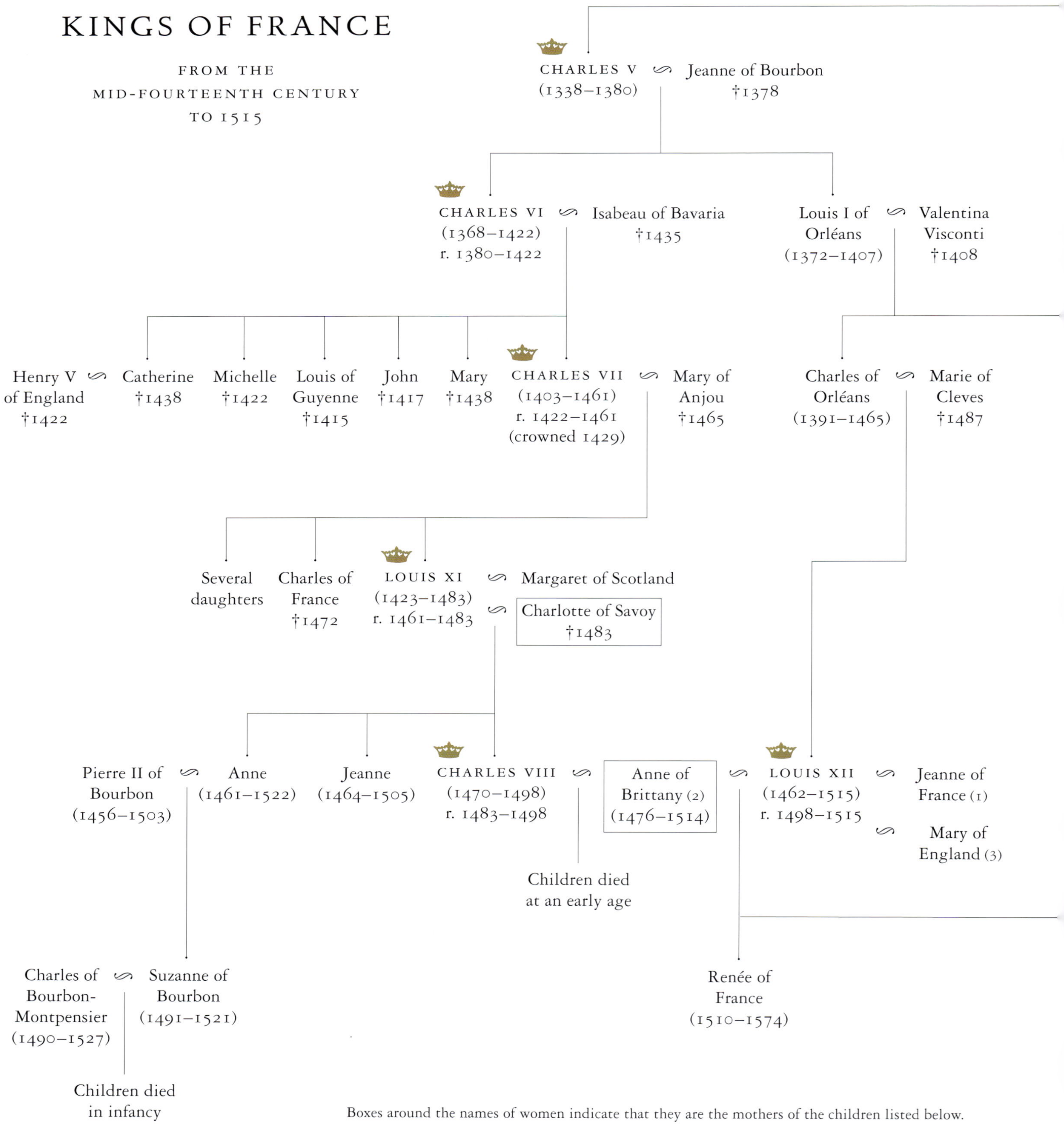

Boxes around the names of women indicate that they are the mothers of the children listed below.

JOHN THE GOOD (1319–1364) r. 1350–1364 ∽ Bonne of Luxembourg †1349
∽ Jeanne of Auvergne

Marie of Blois ∽ Louis I of Anjou (1339–1384)

Jean of Berry (1340–1416)

No male heirs

Phillip the Bold (1342–1404) ∽ Margaret of Flanders

Louis II (1377–1417) ∽ Yolande of Aragon †1443

John the Fearless (1371–1419) ∽ Margaret of Bavaria

John of Angoulême (1399–1467)

Louis III †1434

René of Anjou †1480

Charles of Maine †1463

Phillip the Good (1396–1467) ∽ Michelle of France
∽ Bonne of Artois
∽ Isabelle of Portugal

Charles of Angoulême (1459–1496) ∽ Louise of Savoy (1476–1531)

Charles the Bold (1433–1477) ∽ Catherine of France
∽ Isabelle of Bourbon
∽ Margaret of York

Maximilian of Austria (1459–1519) ∽ Mary of Burgundy (1457–1482)

Claude of France (1499–1524) ∽ FRANCIS I (1494–1547) r. 1515–1547

Joanna of Castile (1479–1555) ∽ Philip the Handsome (1478–1506)

Margaret (1480–1530) ∽ Betrothed to Charles VIII
∽ John of Castile (1478–1497)
∽ Philibert of Savoy (1480–1504)

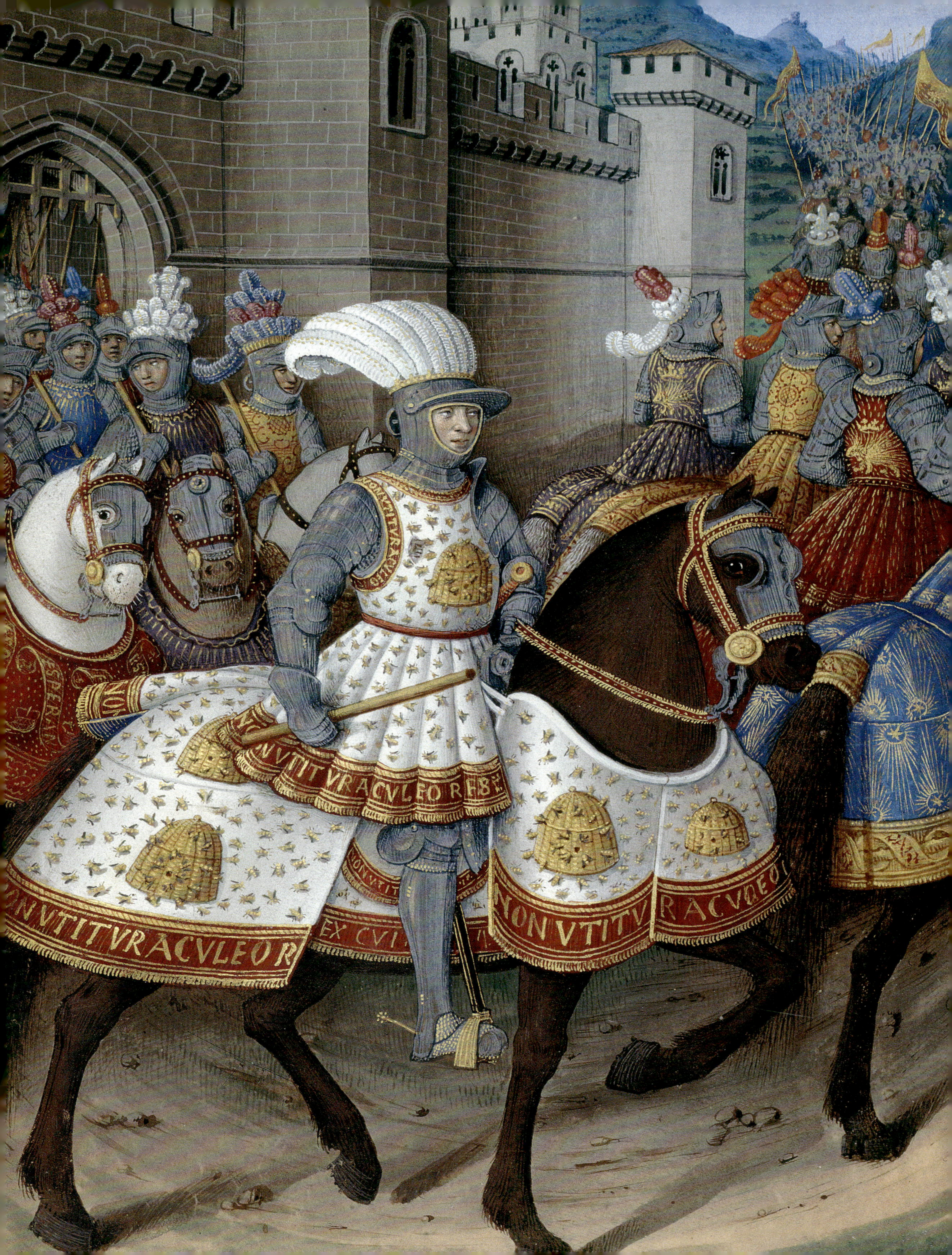
NONVTITVRACVLEOR
EX CVI
NONVTITVRACVLEOREBE

THE FRANCE OF CHARLES VIII AND LOUIS XII: A TURNING POINT?

Philippe Contamine

The history of the West from the 1480s to the 1520s is reputed to have been marked by several original phenomena that, once fully developed, led to an authentic turning point. Hence the widespread notion over at least the last two centuries of international historiography positioning the transition from the Middle Ages to the early modern period: in 1492, when Christopher Columbus discovered the New World; in 1494, when Charles VIII (r. 1483–98) crossed the Alps; in 1517, when Martin Luther posted his theses in Wittenberg; and in 1511, when Raphael painted the *School of Athens* to ornament one of the halls in the Vatican. One could privilege one or another of these four dates, but the basic interpretation remains. The first of these phenomena is known as the Age of Discovery; the second the rise of humanism, understood as a different approach to the legacy of classical civilization; the third as the first stirrings of the Reformation; and the fourth as the renaissance of the arts.

In all these different categories, France, although not absent, was or is alleged to have been a secondary player or latecomer. The discovery of the New World was essentially the work of Castile and Portugal, as no one would deny. In the rise of humanism, Guillaume Budé and Lefèvre d'Étaples certainly have their importance, but they are largely isolated in their own country. In other words, there is no French equivalent to Marsilio Ficino, Pico della Mirandola, Erasmus, or even Thomas More. All things considered, Philippe de Commynes is no Machiavelli. And who would not admit that in the arts, innovation would come from elsewhere, principally the "great studio" across the Alps?[1]

Facing Page
FIGURE 1. Jean Bourdichon. *Louis XII Leaving Alessandria,* in Jean Marot, *Voyage to Genoa.* Tempera and gold on parchment. Bibliothèque nationale de France, Paris, ms. fr.5091, f. 15v.

To this subdued picture, add an economy that was stable but quite traditional—if only in its dominant mode of production (peasant tenures and a multitude of small ateliers and shops). It was an economy based first and foremost on agriculture (cereals, wine, dyestuffs, livestock [horses, cattle, and sheep, hence leathers and hides]), and to a lesser extent fishing and sea salt. These products, often highly regarded, were accompanied in many regions by a craft industry in textiles, including hemp, linen, silk, and wool; a metallurgical craft industry largely working for the domestic market; a very significant construction sector including the labor of masons, stonecutters, carpenters, and tile and slate roofers; the production and working of glass; and the making of precious objects such as reliquaries and jewels (what can be called the artistic trades). France also benefited from a network of weekly markets and annual fairs with local, regional, national, or international reach, authorized by and under the protection of the king. Although all this is far from negligible, there is no equivalent of the banking and trading associations that were springing up elsewhere in Europe, such as the Fuggers of Augsburg, the Great Ravensburg Trading Society, the trading association of the Hanseatic League, the Medici bank with its branches, and the Merchant Adventurers and Wool Staplers of

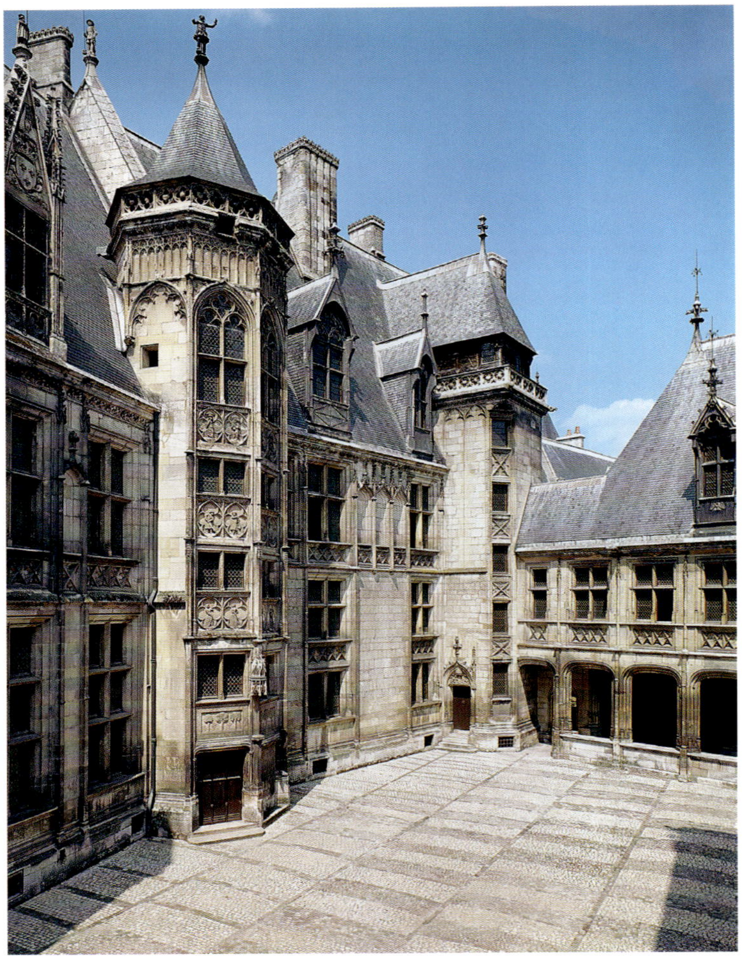

FIGURE 2.
The courtyard of the house of Jacques Cœur, Bourges.

England. Jacques Cœur, trader, financier, and *argentier* to Charles VII (r. 1422–61), who came too early, wanting to go too far and too fast, had no real successor (fig. 2). The end of the fifteenth century saw the real launch of the Lyon fairs, but these very events reveal the French economy's subordinate nature in comparison to those of other nations, which were more dynamic, more conquering: the bankers and merchants came from elsewhere. In addition, recurrent plagues—though nothing like the Black Death of the mid-fourteenth century—and bad harvests due to inevitable meteorological events affected the population numbers, according to a chronology revealed by various urban sources.

Yet this impression of, if perhaps not utter listlessness, then at least of relative inertia, whereby the French chiefly aimed to reproduce, retrieve, and renew models and immemorial formulae through small adaptations in the economy, in technology, and in the complementary nature of the three estates (the clergy, the nobility, and the people), is contradicted in part by the self-perception of the inhabitants of the kingdom. Notwithstanding a diversity rooted as much in geography as in language (of south and north), and as much in social as in cultural factors, the French (at least those who left written traces of their way of thinking) were proud to be French, for they felt that they lived in a Christian kingdom, even a "Very Christian" one (fig. 3), a fertile and populated land that was protected by heaven and enjoyed a moderate climate, and where the values of courtesy, politeness, and civilization were especially widespread, envied, and renowned. The French also saw themselves as governed by a moderate royalty, one that was "well ordered" (*reglée*), and by no means tyrannical, embodied by kings to whom they showed loyalty and affection. Here at the very end of the Middle Ages, relations seemed to be good, not only between the kings and their nobles, between the kings and their church (in the institutional context limiting the powers of the pope within the kingdom set two generations earlier, in 1438, by the Pragmatic Sanction of Bourges),[2] but also between the kings and their *bonnes villes* (it was a joyous occasion for these cities with a privileged connection to the monarch to welcome their king, especially on the occasion of his first entry following his accession), and indeed between the kings and their people. It is no coincidence that Louis XII (r. 1498–1515), after a clever propaganda campaign, was officially dubbed father of the people (*père du peuple*). The French court was already a melting pot.

The actions of the Estates General gathered in Tours in 1484 marked a high point of this unanimity, this concord, as they met to quietly settle the fiscal and other excesses of Louis XI (r. 1461–83), who had died the previous year. Assembled for several weeks were hundreds of deputies from all of the kingdom's administrative districts in addition to those of the nominally independent regions of the Dauphiné and Provence, as well as the "Estates of Flanders." The only absence was the representatives of Brittany, then deliberately on the edge of, or outside, the crown's sphere of influence. While an explosion of anger could have been expected (there were numerous grounds for it), the reality was endless discussions, beautiful verbal jousting, backroom debates, the respectful handing over of lists of grievances, but also and above all reciprocal concessions. The price for everything to return to order was a change in the composition of the king's council, a limitation of the *taille* (a land or personal tax on peasants and non-nobles), and a wise decrease in pensions and military spending. It was agreed that the Estates would come together every two years, but this commitment was almost immediately forgotten. The crown did not leave this skillfully conducted assembly shaken or contested, but rather morally reinforced. As Philippe de Commynes put it in a rightly famous page from his *Memoirs* of his experiences at the courts of Louis XI and Charles VIII, "It might have been thought at the time that such an assembly would be dangerous;" some even said, "It was a crime of lèse-majesté to consider having a meeting of the Estates and that it would only serve to diminish the authority of the king."[3] And yet in this kingdom "so oppressed in many ways" by the levying for years of "great and terrible *tailles*," there was no division against the new king: neither princes nor subjects took arms against him, they did not try to find another in his place, nor restrain him so that he could not "perform his role and issue commands." On the contrary, "All came before him. Both the princes and the lords as well as those of the *bonnes villes* acknowledged him as their king and swore allegiance to him."[4]

The reports of ambassadors, which almost comprise a distinct literary genre, provide valuable testimony to the state of the king and his realm. As diplomacy intensified in the Renaissance, more such reports were written and preserved. Naturally these evaluations, whose worth depends on the quality of the information received and the observational flair of the diplomat in question, emphasize problems of foreign relations and only secondarily internal policy. The reports of the Venetian Zaccaria Contarini are particularly relevant to our subject. He traveled to France in the summer of 1492 in the company of a few high-ranking compatriots to present his credentials to the young Charles VIII, then in Paris with Queen Anne, Duchess of Brittany, who was even younger and whom he had just married, putting an end to a painful military conflict of several years. Like a true diplomat, Contarini is especially sensitive to the quality of the welcome he might receive; he provided information about the king; he was highly critical of his poor physique (despite his taste for jousting and *jeu de paume*, or tennis), his slow elocution, and his limited intelligence. He was distinctly more flattering regarding the queen, whom he described as small, pretty, and vivacious, but with a limp. He did have some admiring words for the relics of the Sainte-Chapelle and the abbey of Saint-Denis, and for the Parlement and the Bois de Vincennes.[5] He also evoked Paris's large size and its great number of students, even if one only counted the "real ones" who "make a profession" in the liberal arts, metaphysics, theology, medicine, or law. But above all, Contarini is interested in the organization and yield of royal finances (the figures he was given were certainly inflated, however). He proves to be astute, noting that taxes are levied in France without the consent of the Estates, thanks to a system put in place by Charles VII, which consisted of sharing receipts between the king on the one hand and the princes and the nobles on the other. A detailed examination of the armed forces then follows. Here, again, he had been provided with figures, sometimes correct and sometimes grotesquely exaggerated (but he does express his incredulity). From all this, Contarini forms and communicates an impression, independent of the actual person of the sovereign (decidedly a sad fellow), of a strong and respected monarchy able to defend itself against any enemy, and of the French united behind Charles VIII, as much the high nobility as the prelates and aldermen of the towns. Contarini was particularly struck by one thing: the growth of royal power following the union of France and Brittany.

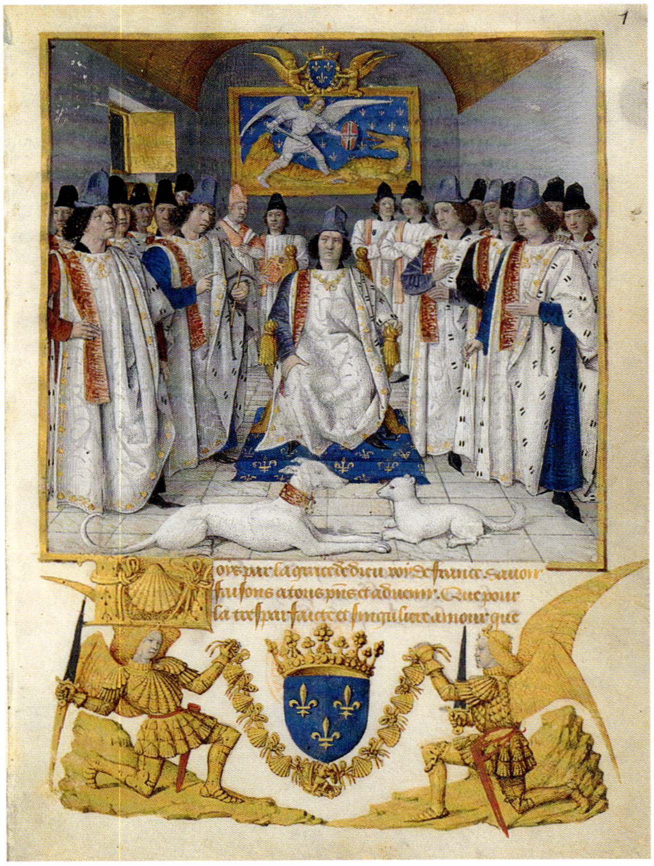

FIGURE 3.
Jean Fouquet. *Louis XI and the Knights of the Order of Saint Michael*, in the *Statutes of the Order of Saint Michael*.
Tempera and gold on parchment. Bibliothèque nationale de France, Paris, ms. fr. 19819, f. 1.

In 1508 Claude de Seyssel, bishop of Marseille and counselor to the king, wrote his *Louenges du roy Louys XII* (In Praise of King Louis XII), a text of open propaganda intended, among other things, to silence criticisms of France's Italian policy made by those who wished for a return to the approach of Louis XI: staying within the bounds of the kingdom and distributing large pensions, even if this meant crushing the people with taxes. Naturally, one cannot take this praise literally; nonetheless, even heavily exaggerated, it says something both about the kingdom's real state and the ideal to which it aspired.[6]

For Seyssel, there was no doubt: the kingdom was "now populated and powerful with people, opulent and full of all goods, fitted with strongholds, peaceful and without any division or bias of peoples, nobles, and princes;" it was consequently prepared "to undertake all great things and sustain all great events." One sees "throughout the kingdom the

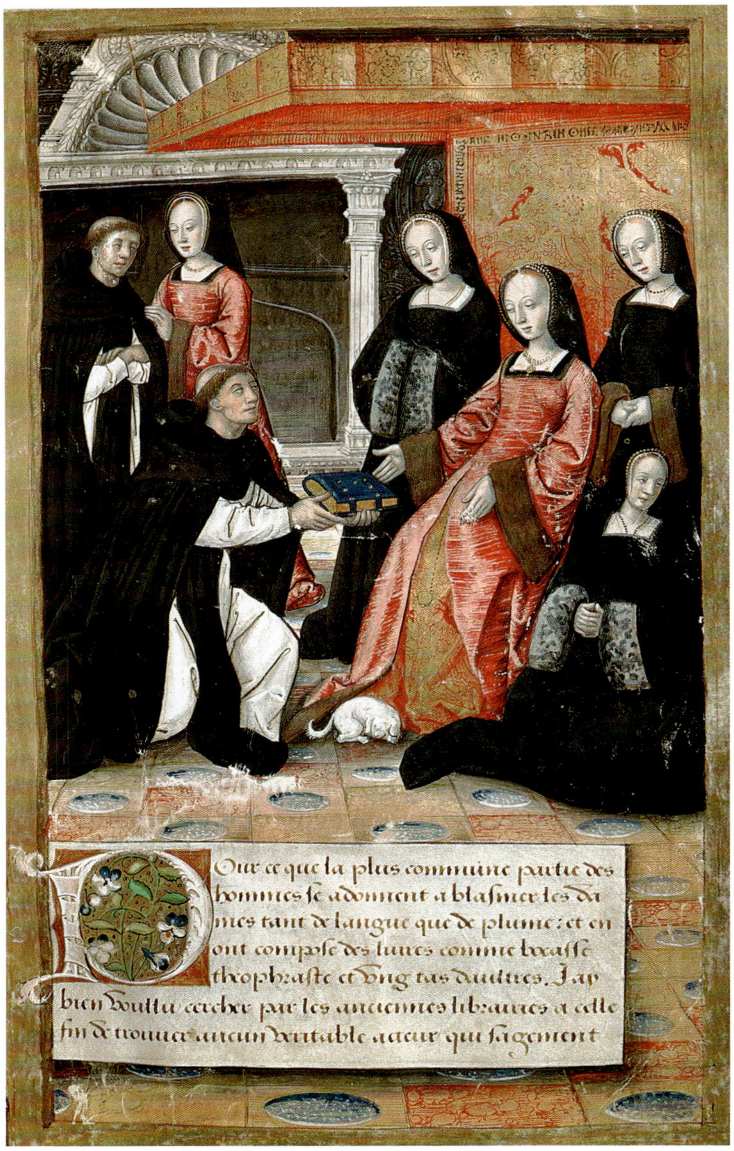

FIGURE 4.
Jean Pichore. *Antoine du Four Presents His Book to Anne of Brittany*, in Antoine du Four, *Vie des Femmes Célèbres*. Tempera and gold on parchment. Musée Dobrée, Nantes, ms. 17, f. 1.

building of large edifices both public and private" with gilding more or less everywhere, including on "the tiles, the roofs, the towers, and the statues that are on the exterior." Next Seyssel vaunted the sumptuousness of the clothing and the richness of the tableware, and affirmed the increase in revenues from land, farms, salt taxes, and tolls.[7]

According to Seyssel, trade was healthy, both on land and on the seas. French merchants, constantly growing in number, were respected abroad. They were less hesitant to go to London, Rome, and Naples than they once were to go to Geneva or Lyon. Even in the small towns, one rarely saw a house opening onto the street "that isn't a shop for goods or mechanical arts." Another indication of the health of France's economy: Seyssel consulted with the king's financial advisers, who told him that taxes are coming in far more easily than before. The explanation is simple: there are more taxpayers, they work more, and they are wealthier.

The king's popularity is not just a facade. If his subjects say they love him, it is the truth, because "the French have always had license and liberty to speak at will of all people and even of their princes." For Seyssel, population growth is obvious, even if he never carried out a real survey—this was scarcely in the spirit of the age. This increase is true across every sector of society, "nobles and merchants and also craftsmen, laborers, and common people." The big cities, formerly "half vacant and empty," are filling up with new construction, including on their outskirts. In the absence of a great plague or famine, the "plenteousness of the people" allowed and indeed made necessary the expansion of cultivated lands. Hence the sentence often quoted by historians of the period: "A third of the kingdom has generally been returned to cultivation in the last thirty years." Despite this, the cost of living remains high because demand is strong, due to the increased number of mouths to feed.

It is against this background that Seyssel returns to the military forces available to Louis XII, like Contarini some fifteen years earlier, but more accurately. Here he slips in an interesting remark: if, since the time of Louis XI, the Swiss have been used as foot soldiers, it is because "the profession of war is so appealing and attractive" that once the peasants and the people have tasted it, they do not easily return to their former activities and, at the end of hostilities, when the payment of wages is stopped, they are transformed into pillagers. Under these conditions, it was better to recruit a kind of foreign legion when the need arises.[8]

All of these military expenditures were made possible thanks to taxes, including *tailles*. And yet these *tailles* are far from weighing on everyone: the exempt include churchmen, "who hold the third part" of the kingdom; the lords, barons, and other noblemen "who live nobly," who hold at least as much; the civil servants, who are more numerous "than in all the kingdoms of Christendom together"; and finally "the inhabitants of all the largest, most powerful, and principal towns and cities of the kingdom." One could be surprised, even angered, at the existence of such a selective tax system that ultimately weighed on the rural population, but this was the order of things for Seyssel, and there is nothing to indicate any disapproval on his part.

A few further points then follow, this time dealing with the king's allies, including the Scots, whose friendship is so old, so faithful, that of the four hundred archers committed to the king's personal guard, one hundred come from that nation, in addition to an ordnance company (one hundred men at arms and two hundred archers) and others spread through other companies. This ancient friendship is so strong that, hearing the rumor of war in Italy, the king of Scotland offered to come serve and assist the king with ten or twenty thousand men. According to Seyssel, the king of Denmark made a similar offer. The dukes of Savoy, Lorraine, and Guelders, the bishop of Liège and his brother Robert de La Marck, a pensioner and knight of the Order of Saint Michael, were also in the French sphere of influence. Given these conditions, one can understand the joking remark attributed to Maximilian I of Habsburg: if he were God and he had several sons "the oldest he would make God after him but the second king of France, knowing that he is the most glorious and most powerful prince in the world."[9]

Of course, there are the Ottoman Turks, whose power could not help but impress, yet is tyrannical; the Grand Turk treats his subjects, notably the Christian Greeks, "like his serfs and slaves," while the rule of the king of France "is politic and gentle" to the point that his subjects love and honor him "almost like God on earth" and would, if need be, practically sacrifice their lives and their goods for him.

All these estimations are idealized and deliberately exaggerated. If we examine the specifics of the economic and demographic situation of a given city (for example, Poitiers or Tours) or province (for instance, Anjou), we discover a darker reality. In particular, in these first years of the sixteenth century, many accounts refer to the growing number of the destitute, who frightened the state and society, leading to repression. The stability of revenue in the face of such heavy expenditures (war, the court, diplomacy) is explained by a growing debt that, a few years later, would result in serious financial jolts. The crown under Louis XII lived beyond its means. Nonetheless, France in about 1500, at the dawn of the "beautiful sixteenth century" (*beau seizième siècle*) was a country on the move, doing so in stability and unity.[10] The great English wars (since called the Hundred Years War), were not forgotten, explaining why the French accepted the constraints of a strong crown. The legend of Joan of Arc (the Maid of Orléans), an expression of the divine protection of the Very Christian king and his kingdom, enjoyed a new vigor in this period due to the accession to the throne of a duke of Orléans, Louis XII, and also due to the prominence of Anne of Brittany. Antoine Du Four, her husband's confessor and an author of strict devotional texts, thought to please the queen with the gift of a beautiful, richly illuminated manuscript describing the lives of ninety-one famous women, from Eve to Joan of Arc (fig. 4).

In all this, we find no material or mental break: thus the chivalric ideal embodied by "the good knight," the Chevalier de Bayard, or the brilliant general Louis II de La Trémoille, remain the order of the day. But there was by no means an overcautious retreat into the past. "Un Dieu, un roi, une foi, une loi," (One God, one king, one faith, one law): the famous formulation of the prolific poet Pierre Gringore was certainly an ideal, but also in large part a reality.[11] Because they were sure of their people, Charles VIII and Louis XII, paving the way for Francis I, dared to embark on the Italian adventure in the name of what they considered their right—Milan, Genoa, and Naples.

NOTES

1. The term was coined in Chastel 1965. For the translation, see Chastel 1966.

2. For the Pragmatic Sanction of 1438, see Stieber 1978, pp. 64–71, 322–30.

3. "L'on pouvoit estimer lors que ceste assemblee estoit dangereuse"; "c'est cryme de leze-majesté que de parler d'assembler estatz et que c'est pour diminuer l'auctorité du Roy." This and ensuing quotations, unless otherwise attributed, are from Commynes 2007, vol. 1, pp. 410–12. For the translation see Commynes 1969, pp. 159–60.

4. "tant foullé en mainte sorte"; "grandes et terribles tailles"; "user d'office de roy et commander"; "tout vint devers luy. Tant les princes et les seigneurs que ceulx des bonnes villes le recongneurent pour Roy, luy feirent serment et homaige."

5. Contarini 1860, vol. 4, pp. 14–26.

6. This and the following quotations are from Seyssel 2009, pp. 216–20, 231–352, 252.

7. "à present peupleé et puissant de gens, opulent et plain de tous biens, garny de lieux fors, paisible et sans aucune division ne parcialité de peuples, de nobles et de princes"; "à entreprendre toutes grans choses et soustenir tous grans faiz"; "L'on voit generallement par tout le royaulme bastir grans ediffices tant publiquez que privez," with gilding on "les couvertes, les toitz, les tours et ymages qui sont par le dehors."

8. "le mestier de la guerre est si friant et attractif."

9. "Et non sans cause le roy des Rommains Maximilien a dit plusieurs fois, en soy jouant, que s'il estoit Dieu et il avoit plusieurs enfans: l'aisné, il le feroit Dieu après loy, mais le second il feroit roy de France, cognoissant que c'est le plus glorieux et le plus puissant prince du monde." Seyssel 2009, p. 352.

10. Quilliet 1998.

11. Gringore 1858, vol. 1, pp. 34–37.

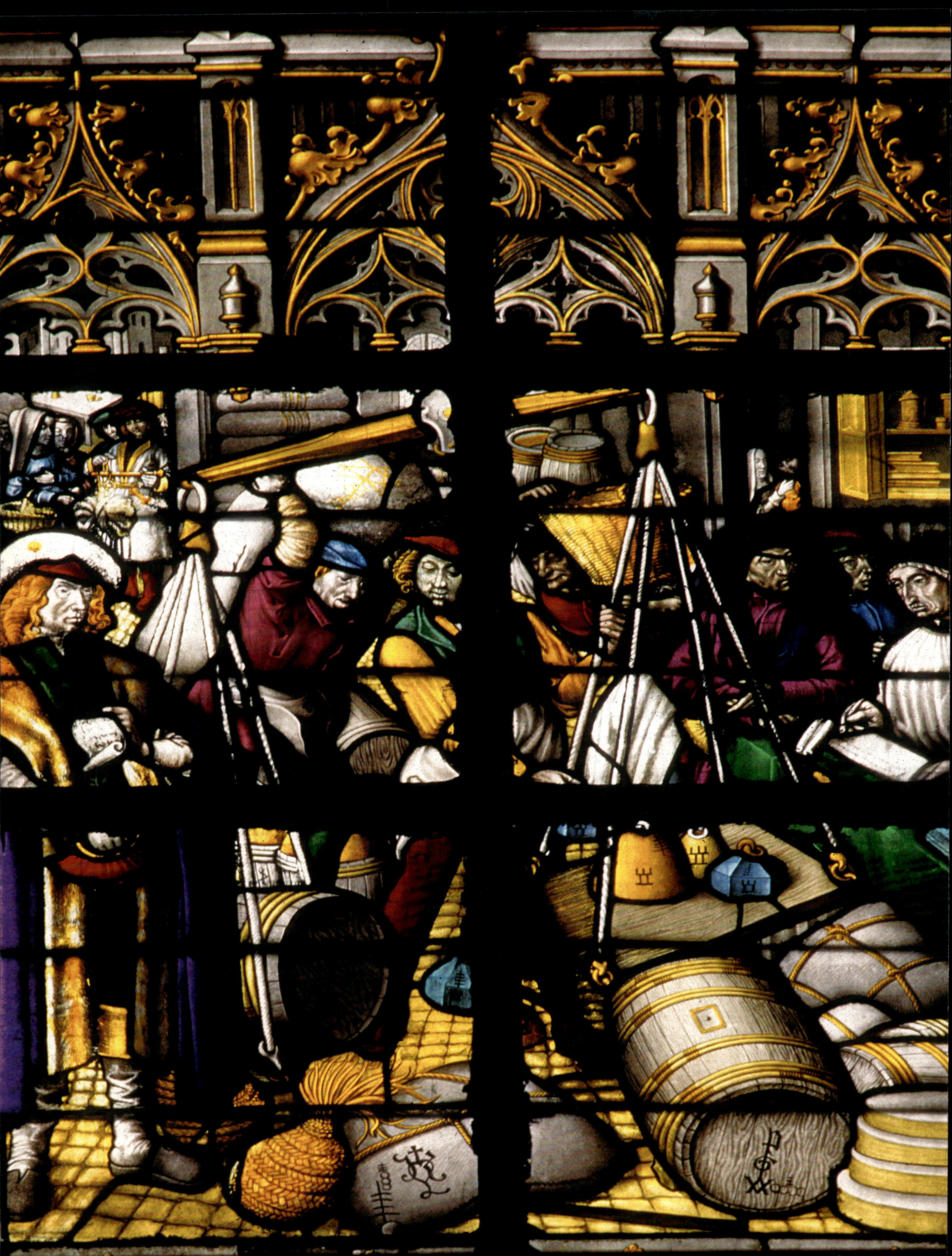

THE GENESIS OF THE WORK OF ART: THE PATRON AND THE ARTIST IN FRANCE AROUND 1500

Philippe Lorentz

In France around 1500, the so-called Renaissance seemed to have become a reality. In the domain of artistic creation, if one views the Renaissance as distinguished by the introduction of forms derived from classical antiquity, the process had already been in motion for half a century, thanks to Jean Fouquet. More generally, the Renaissance is also regarded as the period during which the "modern" artist was born. Thanks to enlightened patrons, the artist would have been able to free himself from the wholly medieval restrictions imposed by the guilds in the towns.[1] Can this phenomenon be observed in the kingdom of France? The genesis and elaboration of a work of art (complex processes stemming from the combination of the patron's needs and aspirations and the artist's capacity to meet them) have left documentary traces that are eloquent enough to attempt to evaluate the role of these two participants in the commission. Where did the artist's creative freedom begin and end? In this respect, did the years around 1500 constitute a turning point? The documentation to which we have access concerns only works that were the subject of commissions. An entire swath of artistic activity therefore escapes the historian: the works executed for the market, a sector that, although flourishing, remains largely unknown because of the lack of sources.

Facing Page
FIGURE 5. Netherlandish artist (Henri de Campes?). *The Privilege of Weighing*. Stained glass. Cathedral of Notre-Dame, Tournai.

¶ CHOOSING AN ARTIST

In the beginning was the patron. When an institution (a parish, a chapter), a group (a guild, a confraternity) or an individual (a prelate, a prince, a nobleman, a prominent citizen) decided to have a work of art made, they needed to select an artist. For sacred art, around 1500 in the large towns of the kingdom of France, the equivalent of what we would today call showrooms was readily available. To make his choice, the patron therefore had only to visit the numerous churches, chapels, and monasteries filled with altarpieces, statues, stained glass, goldsmithwork, and liturgical textiles. All these objects were the product of intense competition to decorate and equip places of worship, which were the motivating engines for artistic commissions.

It was often because the patron had seen and admired a work that he approached an artist. This can be deduced a priori from the contracts in which the notary recorded the sense of the first agreements negotiated between a patron and an artist. They frequently mention a work in place in the immediate vicinity of the signatories to be used as a model to be followed, at least in part. Several contracts (*prix faits*) for Provençal retables permit assessment of the full extent of this phenomenon starting in the early fifteenth century,[2] a phenomenon accentuated by the conventional structure of these works and of the iconography on which they were based, but stimulated above all by the desire to do as well as, if not better, than one's neighbor. Another scenario is equally possible: the patron was initially attracted by the artist's reputation, since this was founded on the success of his work, which was always accessible in the town's religious establishments. In this case, the sought-after painter or sculptor would woo his client by bringing him to see his finished pieces. He had everything to gain: the repetition of a work, even with variations, allowed for optimal productivity because the workshop and its collaborators could reuse the same graphic material (patterns or cartoons).

That the patron sought a copy of a known work goes against our notion of what constitutes an original artistic creation. Based on our criteria, the audience for art about 1500 was conformist. But do we not ourselves submit to a certain routine when we admire, in the museums of modern art that we visit, the selection of often unsurprising and repetitive works of great artists from the twentieth century? Around 1500, the desire to possess a replica of a work was linked to the reputation of its artist and reflected the artistic tastes of the audience of the time, which did not scorn novelty. In Rouen in 1515–16, at Saint-Etienne-la-Grande-Eglise, the church fabric (those responsible for the maintenance of the church's physical structure), wanting to commission a stained-glass window in honor of their patron saint, chose as a model a work that must have been well received in the Norman capital. It was a window depicting the life of Saint Stephen, made a few years before for the church of Saint-Etienne-des-Tonneliers by Arnoult de Nimègue.[3] Settled in Rouen from the early years of the sixteenth century, this Netherlandish painter, who furnished designs for windows and sculptures, had made a name for himself by importing an art that synthesized the great Flemish masters from the end of the fifteenth century. But, by 1515, Arnoult de Nimègue had left Normandy for good. Two years earlier he had joined the painter's guild in Antwerp. The fabric of Saint-Etienne-la-Grande-Eglise bypassed this obstacle by commissioning "a drawn copy" (*pourtrait*) of the stained-glass window at Saint-Etienne-des-Tonneliers from a local painter, whose name has not survived. This *pourtrait*, a simple record of the composition, was then sent to Paris and entrusted to the painter Gauthier de Campes, who was to execute the cartoons (*patrons*) that were then used as a guide for the fabrication of the window. Like Arnoult de Nimègue, Gauthier de Campes was a native of the Low Countries. The two artists in all likelihood knew each other; around 1500, Arnoult and a certain Henri de Campes—related to Gauthier?—made stained-glass windows for Tournai Cathedral (fig. 5).[4] Now absent from the Rouen scene, Arnoult probably recommended his fellow countryman living in Paris, who he knew could faithfully replicate his invention, and probably also its spirit.

¶ THE GRAPHIC DEVELOPMENT OF WORKS

The case of the window of Saint-Etienne-la-Grande-Eglise in Rouen points to the major role that certain artists played in the process of artistic creation and patronage, thanks to their capacity to produce models transferable to all media (painting, stained glass, tapestry, and sculpture). In France, such artists emerged well before 1500, indeed as early as the fourteenth century. Their versatility, sanctioned in Paris by the fact that painters and sculptors belonged to the same guild, justified the generic title of "peintre" (painter) given to artists who were qualified as both painters and sculptors. Although they did not necessarily all wield the chisel, they controlled the graphic conception of a three-dimensional work, and could delegate its execution to a member of their workshop. The elite sought the skills of these artists capable of managing complex and wide-ranging projects. The first artist to be described as painter to the king was Evrard d'Orléans in 1304; paradoxically, we only know him through his sculptures.[5] In the fifteenth century, the painters Jean Fouquet and Nicolas d'Ypres (Colin d'Amiens) belonged to this category of designers. They participated in successive phases of a royal project, the tomb of Louis XI at Notre-Dame-de-Cléry, which featured the gilded bronze statue of

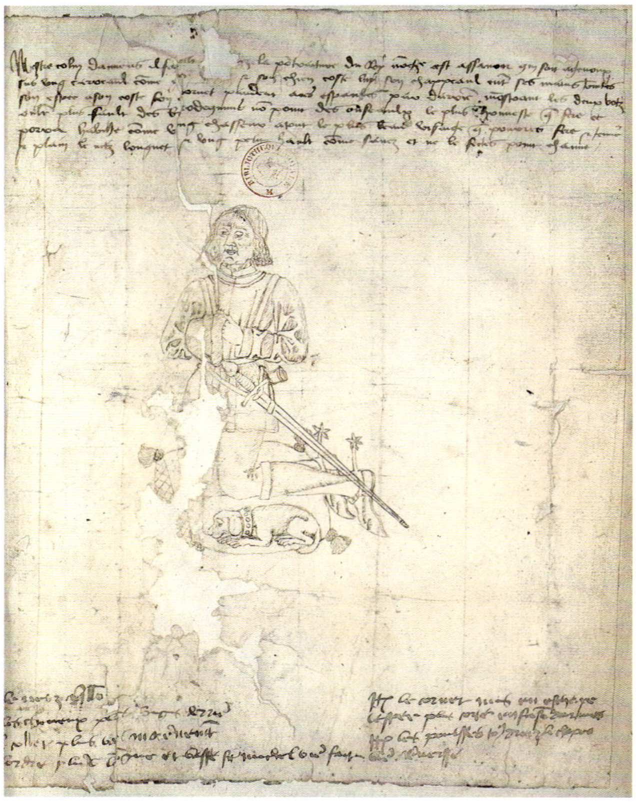

FIGURE 6.
Jean Bourré. *Annotated Drawing with Instruction for the Tomb Effigy of Louis XI at Notre-Dame de Cléry.*
Pen and ink on paper. Bibliothèque nationale de France, Paris, ms. fr. 20493, f. 5.

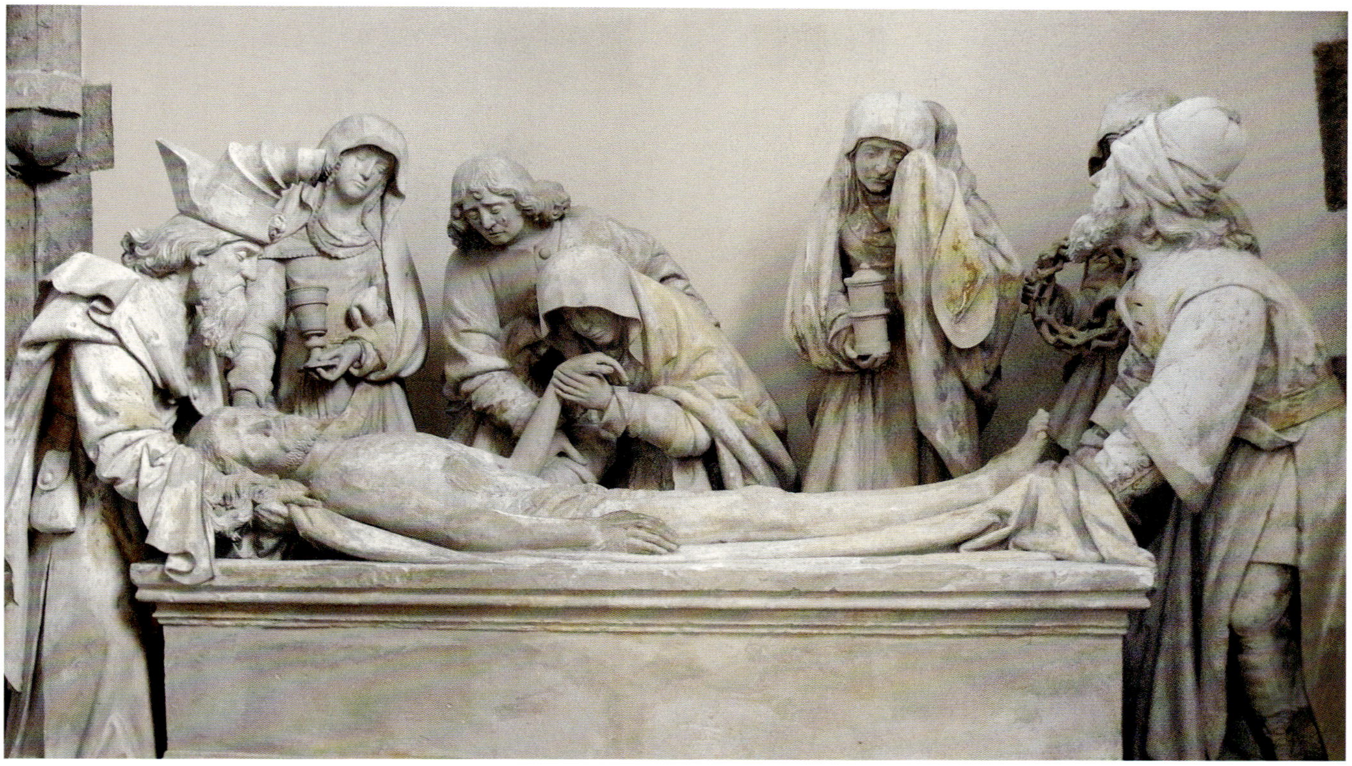

FIGURE 7.
Adrien Wincart, after a design by Colin d'Amiens. *The Entombment of Christ*. Limestone. Church of Saint-Martin, Malesherbes.

the king kneeling in prayer (the monument was destroyed in the sixteenth century).[6] In 1474, Fouquet drew and painted a pattern from which the sculptor (*tailleur d'images*) Michel Colombe made a three-dimensional model. Interrupted for a few years, work on the tomb began again in the early 1480s. The Parisian painter Nicolas d'Amiens was then asked to update the pattern designed in 1474 by Fouquet, who had died in the meantime. The transaction with the artist was conducted by Jean Bourré, a loyal servant and confidante of Louis XI. Bourré was attentive to the dignity of the representation, which was to convey the image of the king for posterity, sending the painter his own summary drawing based on Fouquet's pattern, with notes explaining the modifications to be made to the royal effigy as it had initially been envisioned (fig. 6). Bourré indicated how the physiognomy of the king was to be rendered: "Dressed as a hunter, with the most handsome face that you can make and young and full, the nose long and a little high as you know, and do not make him bald."[7] This was around 1480. Louis XI, who was almost sixty, no longer had a "young and full" face and he was most likely bald! But, for his tomb, his appearance had to be flattering. Such concerns were not new. On the *Parement de Narbonne* (c. 1375, Musée du Louvre), the silhouette of Jeanne of Bourbon, wife of Charles V, was very clearly made more slender,[8] a change that was in all likelihood introduced upon the request of the queen, who hoped to appear younger. Bourré's recommendations to Nicolas d'Amiens shed light on the choice of the artist. They show that the painter knew the king's face well, having probably had the opportunity to study it while executing a portrait. The painted pattern (*patron de painture*) provided by Nicolas d'Amiens was apparently satisfactory, because the goldsmith Conrad de Cologne and the founder Laurent Wrine followed this model when they executed the life-size tomb effigy of Louis XI in 1482.

Nicolas d'Amiens, one of the leading painters working in Paris in the second half of the fifteenth century, did not practice his art within the framework of the court. But as an artist wearing many hats and as a provider of patterns, he was repeatedly offered royal commissions, which indicates that we are not to underestimate the influence of the Parisian artistic scene in comparison to that of the Loire Valley, which historians have tended to overvalue. In any case, his work was also appreciated by the members of the royal entourage, who called upon his talents. In 1495, so eminent a figure as the admiral Louis Malet de Graville asked him to provide the "disposition and pattern" (*ordonnance et patron*) for an Entombment for the chapel at his castle of Bois-Malesherbes in Gâtinais (today in the church of Saint-Martin de Malesherbes, Loiret; fig. 7). In accord with a contract enacted in Paris in 1495, Adrien Wincart, a Flemish sculptor (*tailleur de ymages*) living in the capital, undertook to make this ensemble in Tonnerre stone, following Nicholas d'Amiens's pattern.[9] This drawing was detailed enough to

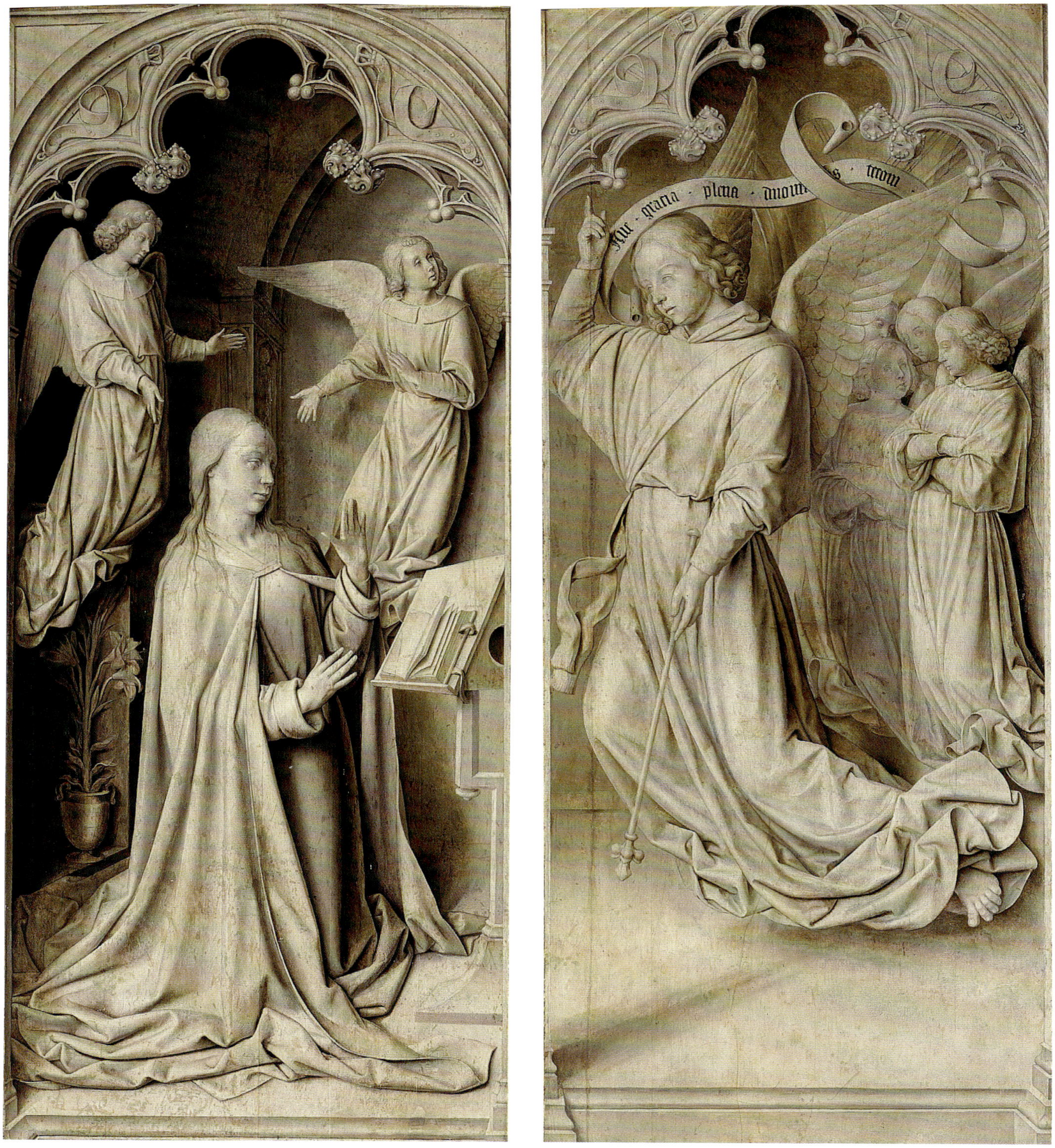

FIGURE 8.
Jean Hey (The Master of Moulins). *The Annunciation* (exterior of the *Virgin in Glory Triptych*, fig. 39). Oil on panel. Cathedral of Notre-Dame, Moulins.

permit the sculptor to transpose the forms invented by the Parisian master into three dimensions.

The painter emblematic of France around 1500, Jean Hey—again of Netherlandish origin!—was also a multitalented artist, serving the dukes of Bourbon in the court of Moulins starting in the 1490s. Although there are no sources mentioning patterns, analysis of the works allows us to credit him with the design of three large statues whose execution is attributed to Jean Guilhomet, known as Jean de Chartres (cat. 66). They come from the chapel of Saint Peter built around 1500–03 in the former château of the dukes of Bourbon in Chantelle, Allier, one of the duke's favorite residences. They are the figures of Saint Peter, of Saint Anne educating the Virgin, and of Saint Suzanne: the patron saints of Pierre II, duke of Bourbon; his wife, Anne of France; and their only daughter, Suzanne. The quality of these works—they are exceptional amid the homogeneous Bourbon production of sculpture at the end of the fifteenth century—and especially their very close formal connection to the figures of the same saints represented in the *Virgin in Glory* triptych (1498/99, Notre-Dame Cathedral, Moulins; fig. 39), suggests that they were conceived by Jean Hey, the painter of this large altarpiece.[10] Moreover, the treatment of the Annunciation in grisaille on the back of the wings of the Moulins triptych (fig. 8) reveals a painter who was particularly attentive to the weight of the drapery enveloping figures carved in stone.

The first graphic stage in the development of a work of art, the one before the full-scale cartoons, involved the artist creating a *petit patron* or *pourtrait*, which was a project drawing giving the patron an idea of the work before the start of its execution. This type of drawing, which was presented

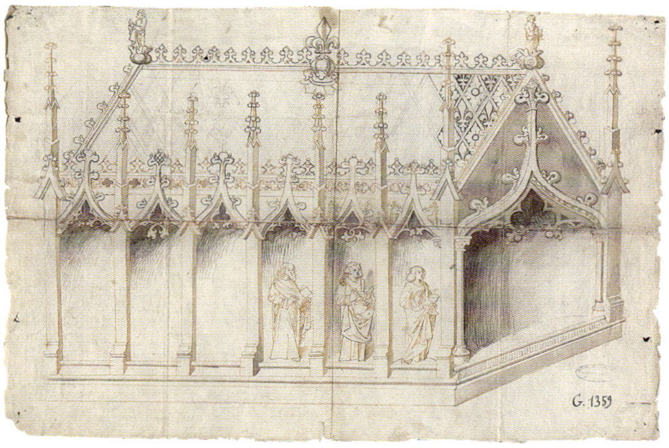

FIGURE 9.
Jean de Graval. *Contract Drawing for the Chasse of Saint Godeberthe.* Black chalk, pen and ink with wash on paper. Archives départementales de l'Oise, Beauvais, G 1359.

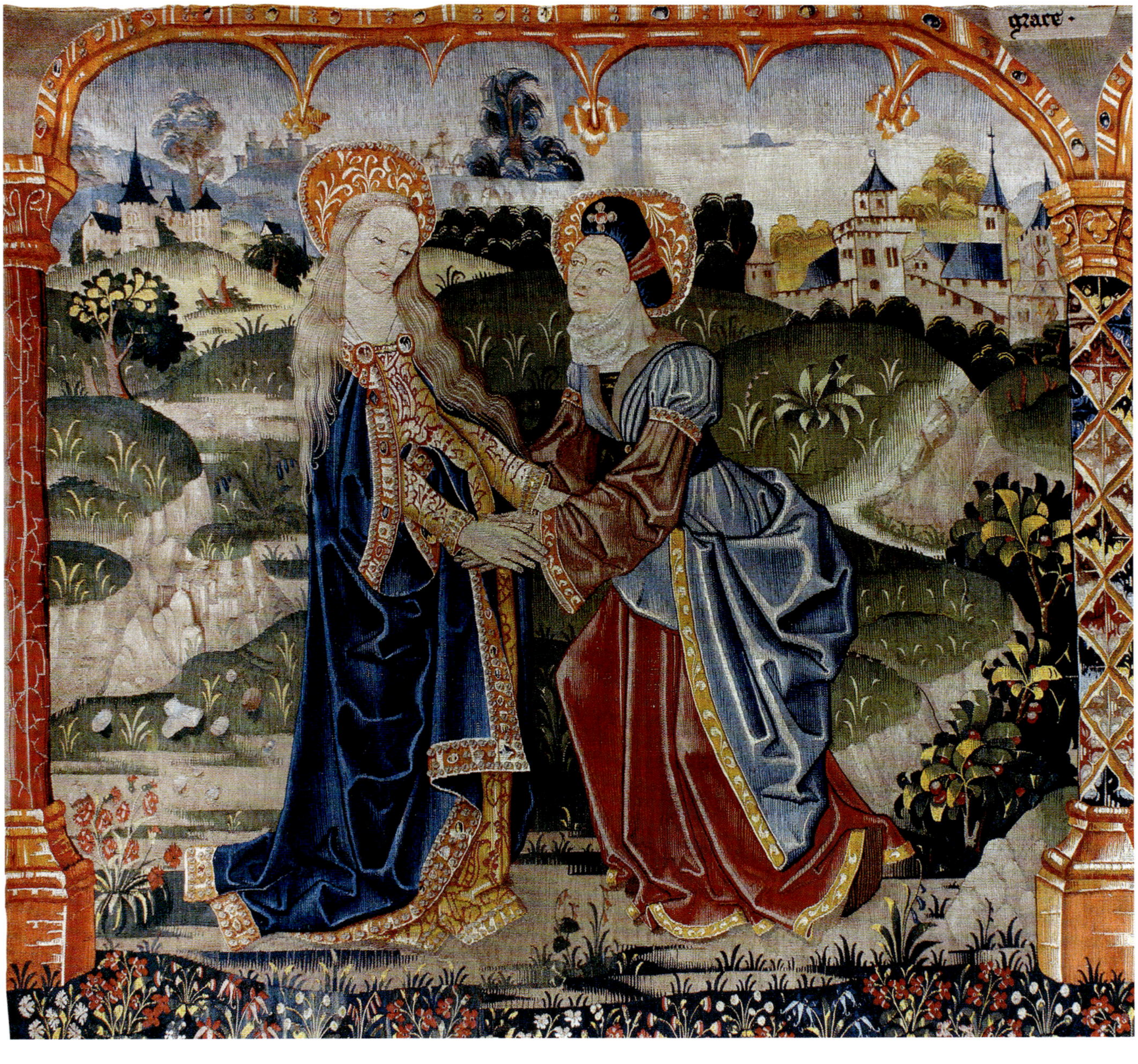

FIGURE 10.
After a design by Pierre Spicre. *The Visitation*, from the *Life of the Virgin.* Tapestry, Church of Notre-Dame, Beaune.

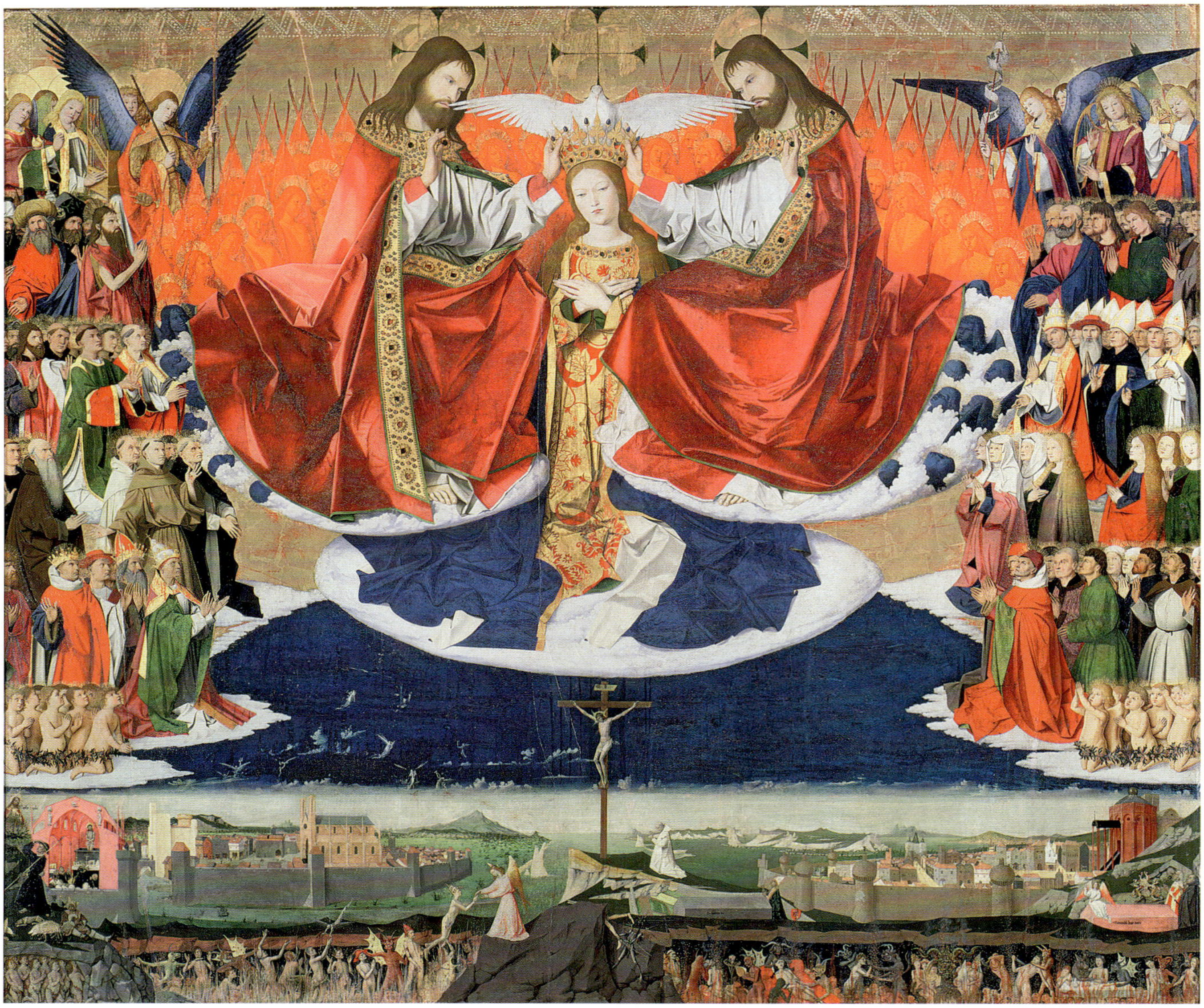

FIGURE 11.
Enguerrand Quarton. *The Coronation of the Virgin.* Musée Pierre-de-Luxembourg, Villeneuve-lès-Avignon.

when the contract was finalized, was rarely saved. The one for the sumptuous silver gilt chasse of Saint Godeberthe, commissioned in 1499 by the fabric of Noyon Cathedral from the Amiens goldsmith Jean de Graval (melted down in 1793), was presented on the reverse of the contract (fig. 9).[11] The draftsman was in all likelihood Jean de Graval himself, who depicted the architecture of the chasse, a small church with a pitched roof. The drawing is far from complete: it includes only a bit of the diamond design on the roof and represented only three of the six apostles that were called for on the side of the chasse shown in the drawing. Among them, Saint John the Evangelist is recognizable; he is duplicated on top of one of the gables solely to indicate that a small statue would also be placed there. In all likelihood, the details of the iconography were not yet defined but, at this stage of the commission, it was important that the patron and the artist agreed on the general arrangement (*ordonnance*) of what was a developing project. The ambition of the *pourtrait* was limited to a first concept.

¶ THE EXCHANGES BETWEEN THE PATRON AND THE ARTIST

The patron who went to a painter or sculptor with the intention of ordering a work communicated his expectations through words. This first exchange produced a written document, the *devise*, which preceded or accompanied the presentation drawing (*pourtrait*). This work order was often mentioned, sometimes summarized and more rarely recopied in full, in the contract. On occasion, the patron was also the author of the devise. In 1477, the painter Nicolas Froment was paid "for certain paintings" (*pour certaines painctures*) made for René d'Anjou, "which the aforementioned lord had drawn up" (*lesquelles ledit seigneur avoit devisées*).[12] We should understand from this that the prince had provided Froment with a handwritten note, describing what he wished to see represented in these paintings. René of Anjou's evident interest in the figurative arts made him an exceptional patron, one who was capable of elaborating an iconographic program himself. Most of the time, the task of writing the *devise* was entrusted to a third party. Between 1425 and 1430, the fabric of the church of the Magdalene in Troyes, in commissioning a hanging depicting the life of Saint Mary Magdalene, paid a Dominican friar, Brother Didier, "for having extracted and put together in writing the story of the said life in the aforementioned tapestry of *haute lisse*" (*pour avoir extrait et baillié par escript l'istoire de la dicte vie dudit drap d'auteliche*).[13] In certain cases, an artist was called upon. In 1503–04, at the cathedral of Sens, assistance was sought from a tapestry weaver for the *devise* for a hanging of the life of Saint Stephen (cat. 78), on the basis of which the Parisian painter Gauthier de Campes executed the cartoons for the cycle, which were then transmitted to another tapestry weaver charged with actually making the work.[14]

The *devise* relates to the domain of iconography. It is above all a description of the stories (*histoires*) that were to be represented and of their proper distribution through the work. This was not, in general, the place to transmit indications regarding the manner of execution. In 1474, the chapter of the collegiate church of Notre-Dame in Beaune negotiated a contract with Pierre Spicre, the Dijon painter—of Flemish origin—for the painting of the cartoons for a suite of tapestries depicting the life of the Virgin that was not woven until 1500 (still on view in the choir of this church; fig. 10).[15] The text of the contract refers to a description of the "stories and personages" (*hystoires et personnaiges*) that has not survived. However, the writer of the document was not stingy with details concerning the way these episodes should be represented. Spicre was required to make "the aforementioned figures similar and resembling one another, where they will appear in different places, true stonework where it will belong, castles, churches, chapels and houses, landscapes, flowers, small flowers, lawns, forests, trees, and other things appropriate to these stories. The draperies in these stories will have good true folds, and strong or gentle faces, as the case requires."[16] At first, we are tempted to interpret this as a meticulous description of the formal restrictions imposed on the painter by the patron. But the degree of precision concerning what should be represented suggests rather that we regard this passage as phrases dictated by the artist, eager to demonstrate his ability. Another famous and often cited contract can be understood in the same way. It is the *prix-fait* for the altarpiece of the *Coronation of the Virgin* commissioned in 1453 in Avignon by Jean de Montagny of the painter Enguerrand Quarton from Picardy (Musée Pierre-de-Luxembourg, Villeneuve-lès-Avignon; fig. 11). The exhaustive description of the arrangement (*ordonnance*) of the altarpiece, from the principal figures to the most minute details, at first seems to highlight the notion of an artist constrained by the demands of his client. But, on closer examination, we realize that the leeway given to the painter is not insignificant. In many of the contract's paragraphs, particulars about what must be painted are punctuated by a small phrase indicating that such a representation will be left to the discretion of Quarton: "according to what will seem better to the aforementioned master Enguerand"; "according to the opinion of the aforementioned master Enguerand"; "to the disposition of said master Enguerand."[17] Furthermore, in the finished product the painter did not respect the patron's express wish to include an exact representation of Rome. Instead he used views of Villeneuve-lès-Avignon, having never visited the Eternal City.

Around 1500, the image of the artist, as far as we can understand it through documents related to commissions of works, was not that of an artisan constrained by the demands of his client. Contracts and financial records point to the importance of the artist's graphic work. His mastery of design was the basis of his versatility. He was capable of conceiving works that were sometimes complex, bringing together several media, such as altarpieces that included sculptures and painted elements. Such skills gave him the authority he needed to impose his aesthetic choices on his patrons. This situation was not new around 1500, however. The mechanisms of the artistic commission were those that already existed, and they had provided the context for several stylistic upheavals before the one that we call the Renaissance.

NOTES

1. Warnke 1985.
2. Robin 1992.
3. Hérold 1998, pp. 51–52.
4. Leproux 2001, pp. 81–85, 171–72.
5. Baron 1971; Schmidt 1992.
6. Sterling 1990, pp. 92–93; Avril in Paris 2003, pp. 138–41.
7. "Habillé comme ung chasseur, atout le plus beau visaige que pourres fere et jeune et plain, le nez longuet et ung petit hault comme savez, et ne le fectes point chauve." Paris 2003, pp. 140–41.
8. Sterling 1987, p. 221, fig. 130.
9. Grodecki 1996.
10. Lorentz 2008.
11. Hérold and Plouvier 1985; Taburet-Delahaye 2006.
12. Pächt 1977, p. 79; Ferré 2009.
13. Guignard 1849–50, pp. 427–31.
14. Hérold 1998, p. 55.
15. Joubert 1999.
16. "les dits personnaiges semblables et ressemblans l'ung l'autre, la ou ils seront en divers lieux, massonerie vraye ou elle appartiendra, chateaulx, eglises, chapelles et maisonnemens, pais, fleurs, fleuretes, sourmance de verdure, bois, arbres et aultres choses convenables esdites hystoires. Les draperies desquelles histoires pourteront bon vray pliz hardiz et doulz visaiges ou le cas le requerra." Joubert 1999, p. 171.
17. "selon qu'il semblera mieulx audit maistre Enguerand"; "selon l'adviz dudit maistre Enguerand"; "à l'ordonnance dudit mestre Enguerand." Sterling 1983, pp. 36–79.

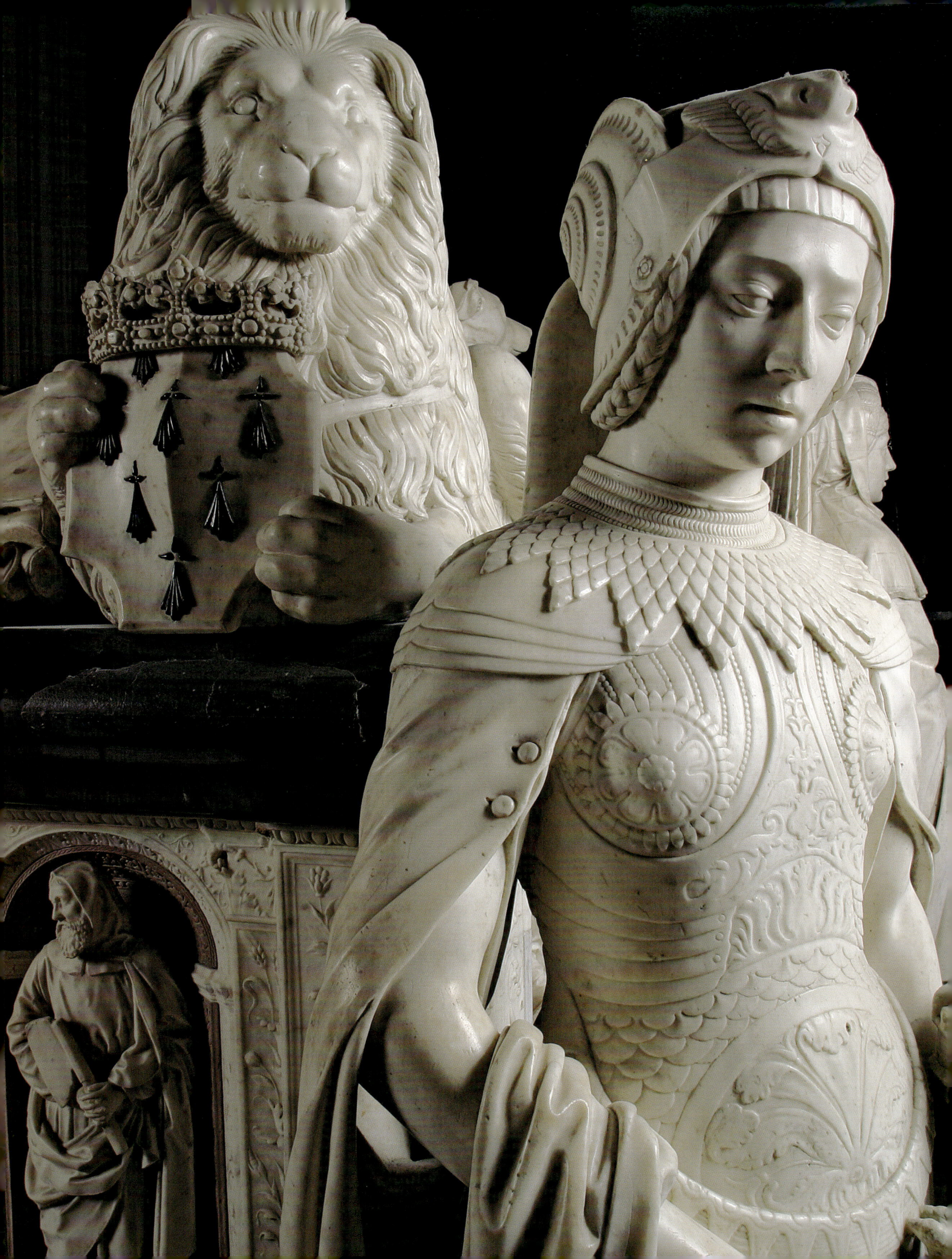

THE ARTISTIC LANDSCAPE AROUND 1500: WORDS AND THINGS

Pierre-Yves Le Pogam

The degree to which art history in the West derives from the vision introduced by Vasari can never be overestimated, for better or for worse. A two-part idea formed the ideological foundation of the *Lives* penned by the Florentine artist and historiographer: first, the artistic primacy of Italy, indeed of Tuscany, and second, the emergence of this superiority through a rupture with the rest of Europe as early as the period of Giotto and certainly during the Quattrocento.[1] Even though it was already challenged, qualified, and rivaled in the sixteenth century, Vasari's model took root. From this perspective, French art around 1500 can only be seen through the lens of the rupture. An art of transition, certainly, but a traumatic transition that tipped France, thanks to the Italian wars, into the camp of the humanist Renaissance, sometimes slowly and with resistance and at the cost of abandoning Gothic ostentation. It was precisely in this intellectual context that there emerged the notions of Gothic and Renaissance, applied to the arts by Vasari himself, who was adopting and transmitting expressions that circulated before his time, especially in Ghiberti's writings. This vision of a dramatic break is particularly debatable, but it has almost always remained dominant in historiography, thanks in part to later voices, like that of Jules Michelet, Romantic chronicler of the history of France, for whom Charles VIII's Italian campaign in 1494 constituted a genuine parting of the waters between the obscure but fascinating Middle Ages and a Renaissance that was radiant, at least at its start. Crossing the Alps was, to Michelet, equivalent to discovering the New World two years earlier; in his words, "Charles VIII's companions were no less stunned than those who accompanied Christopher Columbus."[2]

Facing Page

FIGURE 12. Michel Colombe, Jérôme Pacherot, and workshop, after a design by Jean Perréal. Detail of Fortitude from the *Tomb of Francis II of Brittany and Margaret of Foix*. Cathedral of Saints Peter and Paul, Nantes.

Despite the omnipresence of this point of view, a growing number of voices rose up against this Italocentric and caricatured vision of artistic development as early as the seventeenth and eighteenth centuries, but especially in the nineteenth century, in the context of the nationalist claims of different European countries. According to this interpretation, the Renaissance could also and above all have emerged north of the Alps in the fifteenth century. For some, it was indeed during the final third of the fourteenth century that it surfaced at the Valois court in Paris, but also in Prague, Avignon, and Barcelona, to be developed around 1400 and through the fifteenth century in the splendid Burgundian milieu and beyond, thanks to the international influence of Netherlandish art. Northern inventions were as decisive as those of Italy; the discovery of oil painting and the achievement of a meticulous realism, all conveyed by the name of Van Eyck, countered the perspective and humanism of Brunelleschi, Donatello, Masaccio, and the like. In particular, the Germans (from Friedrich von Schlegel to August Schmarsow) and Belgians (for example, Hippolyte Fiérens-Gevaert) contributed to this historiographical construction that naturally favored northern Europe and their respective homelands.[3] In

France, this vision of northern supremacy was above all embodied in the writings of Louis Courajod,[4] although it had been anticipated to a certain extent by his predecessor at the Louvre, the count de Laborde. Paradoxically, it was in the Anglo-Saxon world in particular (and to a lesser extent in the Germanic world) that this historiographical shift made its mark, since the concept of the Renaissance, or at least of a northern Renaissance, still commonly serves to designate the art of the fifteenth century (or of the fifteenth and sixteenth centuries together) in northern Europe.[5] However, this theoretical construction barely took root elsewhere—not in France and certainly not in Italy. It rests, in fact, on two insoluble contradictions. If it were accurate, one could scarcely distinguish sixteenth-century European art from that of the preceding century, except by a greater measure of Italianism and of the return to antiquity, which the most superficial observation would belie. It would moreover imply that in northern centers during the fifteenth century, there was already an awareness of belonging to a new era, as was the case in Italy during this period.[6] However, north of the Alps, this feeling remained much more tenuous and mixed, despite some indications (the phenomenon of the *devotio* aptly called *moderna*, a spiritual movement often connected to Flemish painting).

It has indeed been noted that fifteenth century northern art presented a strong link to the Gothic past. Furthermore, it has long been clear that this style continued well into the sixteenth century. Different concepts were developed to define this final phase in Gothic art,[7] either by drawing on the language of form (hence the notion of the Flamboyant in France, the Plateresque in Spain, the Perpendicular in England); by simply adding the qualifier *late* to the noun *Gothic*; or by qualifying it as "special" (*Sondergotik*) and emphasizing the regional and national characteristics that emerged, defining them by dynastic names (hence the notion of the Manueline and the Tudor styles for Portugal and England, respectively). To our mind, these last two modes of designation are scarcely convincing, the one being overly neutral, even disparaging, and the other being biased and sacrificing commonalities to bolster geographical differences. For France, at least, we would therefore like to retain the old term "Flamboyant Gothic."[8] But if this label is well suited to the art of the fifteenth century, the problem of 1500 again reappears. Although structures and forms continue well into the sixteenth century, one can certainly not place all artistic production of this period under the rubric "Flamboyant Gothic." Every historiographical construction therefore reaches an impasse. Art around 1500 did not represent an abrupt and total rupture with the medieval past through the adoption of the Italian Renaissance, nor can it be defined as the extension of a northern Renaissance established a century before; and it cannot be considered the imperturbable continuity of an unchanged Flamboyant art.

¶ THE VOCABULARY OF THE PERIOD

For a clearer perspective, it might be wise to turn to the words used by artists, artisans, and patrons around 1500, taking our examples from France or neighboring regions. Nevertheless, one must be aware from the start of two difficulties. The available sources are few and such as remain are rarely even remotely theoretical. Furthermore, the terms used are particularly ambiguous and deceptive, especially when we do not know the objects to which they refer—as is still often the case, although sources and works are more abundant than in earlier periods. Of course, the French terms "gothique," "renaissant," and "flamboyant" did not exist in the sense that interests us here. However, in certain documents, we find the notion of the "antique" and the "modern." How should we interpret these two words? At times, the texts are rather laconic and lend themselves to dispute.[9] Thus, in the early sixteenth century during the reconstruction of part of the west facade of Bourges Cathedral, some "tabernacles" (meaning baldachins) were mentioned as executed "a l'antique." Other baldachins receive no qualifier. The source being incomplete, it is difficult to establish a clear correlation between the texts and the baldachins in question, on the Saint-Guillaume portal and the Virgin portal.[10] For the Augustinian monastery at Brou, in Bourg-en-Bresse, Margaret of Austria commissioned three tombs for her deceased mother-in-law, her husband, and herself (fig. 13). In the second version of this project, the latter two monuments are referred to as a "sepulture moderne" (modern tomb) in a payment document dated July 7, 1516.[11] The interpretation of this text has long been debated, but it is now generally agreed that the Regent of the Habsburg Netherlands was thereby renouncing the earlier idea of an Italianate project and was anticipating work in the spirit of the Flamboyant Gothic from the artists she had engaged (Louis van Boghem, Jan van Roome, later Conrad Meit).[12] Finally, it is evident that in the 1520s the printer Geoffroy Tory used ornament in the Italian taste combined with Roman characters and decoration in the Flemish style along with Gothic batard type. It is of course tempting to identify these two visual languages with the "histoires et vignettes a l'antique, et pareillement unes autres a la moderne" (stories and vignettes in the antique style, and at the same time, others in the modern style) that the printer used, according to a *privilège* published in 1524.[13]

The sources just mentioned could appear ambiguous concerning the meaning of "antique" and "modern." However, several other documents make it possible to dispel any doubt, because they relate to preserved works or because their phrasing eliminates any ambivalence. In his treatise on perspective, one of the rare texts that is not purely practical and that we can bring to bear on this question, Jean Pèlerin, known as Viator, sheds light on his subject through a series of illustrations. In the second edition from 1510, he adds couplets, and the one commenting on a building in the

Italian Renaissance style reads: "Les colunnes et antiquailles / sont magnifiques en murailles" (The columns and antiquities / are magnificent on walls).[14] On November 15, 1509, Jean Perréal wrote to Margaret of Austria regarding the first version of the tomb project mentioned above. He had just been approached for advice by Jean Lemaire de Belges, Margaret's court poet and advisor. He proposed a program realized "by means of antique things that I had had part of in Italy" (*au moien des choses antiques que j'ay eu es parties d'Italie*).[15] Even if the verb used in French—"eu" (had) and not "vu" (seen), as it has often and erroneously been transcribed—might be somewhat surprising, the meaning poses no problem. Furthermore, for the tomb of Francis II of Brittany and his wife Margaret of Foix (fig. 12), commissioned by Anne of Brittany from both Michel Colombe and Italian sculptors including Jérôme Pacherot, we know that the latter were referred to as "carvers of antique Italian masonry" (tailleurs de massonnerie entique italiens).[16] It was the same Jean Perréal who used these terms in a letter addressed to the secretary of Margaret of Austria, on January 4, 1511, when he was still hoping to persuade the regent of the Netherlands to adopt an analogous scheme for the tombs at Brou. A vain effort, as we saw above, since she eventually changed both team and project in favor of the "modern" style of Flemish artists. At the cathedral of Saint-Sauveur in Aix-en-Provence, the doors exhibit a decorative repertoire that combines Gothic and Italianate motifs. In connection with this work, the sources describe "foliage in the new art" (*fulhages a novel art*) and "in the antique style" (*a l'antica*).[17] If there were any question of the equivalence of words and things, a second example from Aix-en-Provence cannot be questioned. At the church of Notre-Dame de Consolation, the repertory of arabesques and the Italianate candelabra on the doors is described in the contract as "a l'antica" (in the antique style).[18] It is therefore correct to give this interpretation to texts where the meaning of antique and modern is ambiguous, as in the cases mentioned earlier.[19]

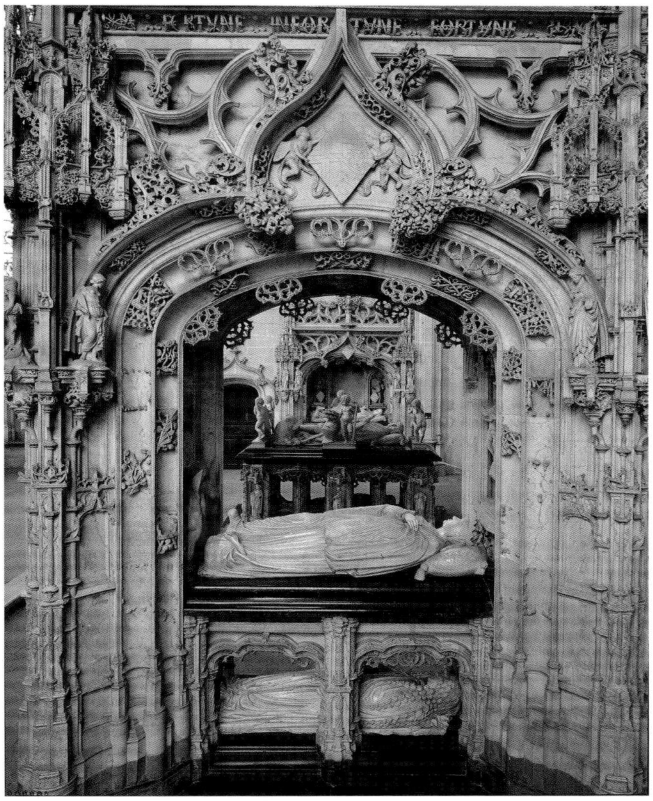

FIGURE 13.
Louis van Boghem, Jan van Roome and Conrad Meit.
Tombs of Margaret of Austria, Philibert of Savoy, and Margaret of Bourbon. Limestone and alabaster. Church of Saint Nicholas of Tolentino, Brou, Bourg-en-Bresse.

Thus, it is evident that around 1500 there was a clear awareness of a specific vocabulary for Italianate decorative motifs, inspired more or less by antiquity and designated with the label "antique," while the term "moderne" was applied to Flamboyant Gothic art. What can we conclude about the work of that period? Are we to designate it by some chaotic term, for example "antique-modern" or "Italian-Flamboyant" art? The adjective "gothico-renaissant" (renaissancizing Gothic) has been used at times, for example to describe Flemish art or the art of Croatia.[20] Matt Kavaler has suggested the similar term "Renaissance Gothic,"[21] but not enough attention has been paid to the fact that, as he admits, this suggestion stems more from irony and an effort to stimulate discussion of this thorny issue.[22] Creating a new label would hardly make sense, therefore, and would only add to the confusion. Furthermore, the combination of two opposing terms would not take into account the totality of artistic production. For example, it would mean disregarding works that are fully Gothic or fully Renaissance, or the process of this alliance, which is by no means a harmonious synthesis of opposites. Moreover, the formula "from Gothic to Renaissance," even if it initially seems more satisfying, risks introducing the idea of a simple evolution from one style to the other, which was far from the case.[23] We must therefore turn to the works themselves to see how the words of the past or of the present might help us define French artistic culture around 1500, between the Middle Ages and the Renaissance, although the debate in large part also applies to the rest of Europe, not just the north.[24]

¶ WHAT THE MONUMENTS AND WORKS TELL US

If we consider artistic activity as a whole, we are first struck by the overall seamlessness of production at the turn of the century: the continuation of the medieval workshop structure (perhaps it was even intensified in this period) with its system of controls (the hierarchy of masters, journeymen, apprentices; admission to the rank of master through a masterpiece; belonging to the guild and its associated confraternity), its internal recruitment process, its firm hand

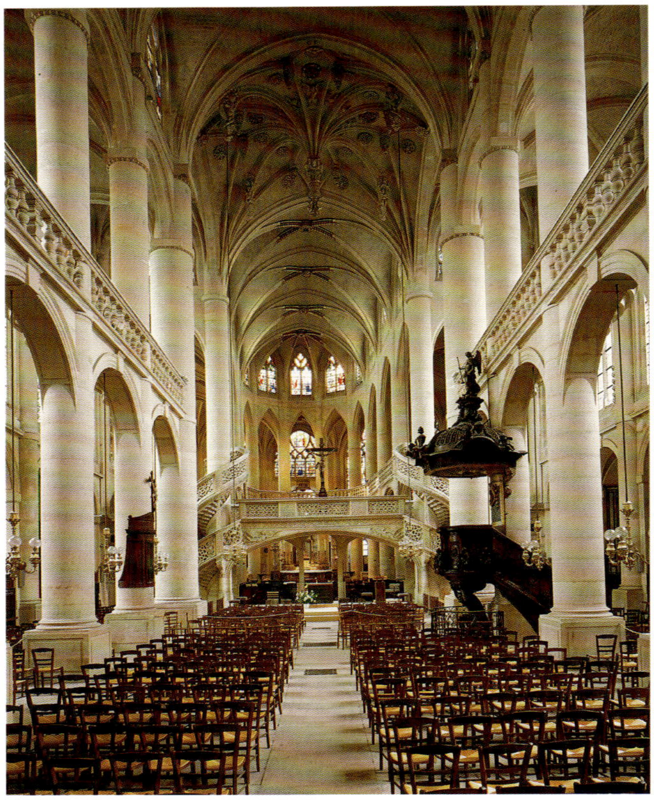

FIGURE 14.
View of the nave facing the choir in the church of Saint-Etienne-du-Mont, Paris.

on the local market. But paradoxically, the art developed in this traditional manner was, in terms of style, the one that contemporaries designated as modern. And the name is fully deserved, for this was not an art that was in any way routine or mediocre: it achieved, in addition to a "median" level of production, the splendor of churches with complex plans and vaults (fig. 14), the luxuriance of religious sculpture, and the remarkable quality of illuminated and printed books of hours. And its modernity was expressed, as has long been noted, not only through decorative exuberance and technical virtuosity, but also through a sometimes exaggerated emotional charge given to the work of art. Hence the profound continuity (to take a category typical of French art) between the dramatic sculpted Entombment groups of the fifteenth century and those of the succeeding century (fig. 15).

But there also exist monuments or works that point to a different direction. At the court of the king and those of the great princes, and in the circles of those close to them, patrons sought to express their superior status by appropriating every innovation or by seeking fashionable works, northern as much as Italian. Importation of objects, commissions to foreign artists transplanted to France, the adoption of innovations by local artists best able to integrate them into their repertory: all were ways of seeming to be and actually staying up to date, and above all of differentiating oneself from those who were not—in short, ways of distinguishing oneself. Parallel to the Italianate character of the château of Gaillon, for example (a monument which moreover was not derivative of any single southern model), was the recourse to northern painters like Jean Hey, who followed the Bourbons from Lyon to Moulins; the importation of retables from Brabant and of "Flemish" tapestries; and the repetition of northern engravings.[25] Beyond the courtiers, their castles, and their chapels, these influences were evidently more generally felt in the regions on the periphery of France in 1500—Picardy, Provence, Artois (the latter province having been shuffled between the kingdom and the Holy Roman Empire)—or in those that belonged only partially to it both politically and culturally—Lorraine, Savoy, Bresse, the Franche-Comté.

Despite this last nuance, this sketch of the French artistic landscape could promote a bias just as harmful as the inappropriate labels criticized above. One might think that there was a neat dichotomy between two levels of patronage (the ordinary as opposed to the exceptional commission) associated with two levels of execution (one good, the other excellent). This vision would be a caricature, firstly because the same artists and workshops could perfectly well practice both manners successively and even at the same time. Above all, the information provided by the contemporary texts cited above (the simultaneous use of the terms "antique" and "modern" with the same degree of appreciation) implies that artists were capable of changing their stylistic language depending on the type of the commission, the subject required, and the monumental or local context. It is not a matter of insincerity on the part of the artist or of the uncertain taste of patrons. In reaction to the rigid categories of evolution that have too often dominated the discipline of art history since its inception, several scholars have little by little argued for the concept of stylistic simultaneity in the same region and time, either because the artists felt the

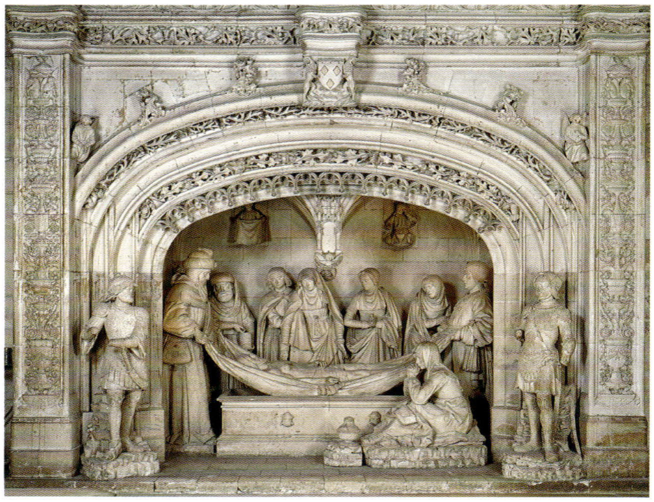

FIGURE 15.
The Entombment of Christ. Limestone. Church of the Abbey of Saint Peter, Solesmes, Sarthe.

need to use varied modes of expression, or due to the simple proximity of workshops with different practices and goals.[26] The possibility applies particularly to art around 1500, as Henri Zerner has emphasized.[27] The musicians and *grands rhétoriqueurs* of this period were masters at changing registers and varying their style to achieve refined effects. In the visual arts as well, this acquired polyphony allows us to understand the complexity and depth of its productions, their lavish, even disconcerting, character in comparison to the more normative aspect of the classic Renaissance at mid-century. Therefore, the formulation "between the Middle Ages and Renaissance" (or perhaps more precisely, "between Gothic and Renaissance") is still the most accurate designation for an attempt to approach artistic reality around 1500, on the condition that it is not made into a hesitant in-between period or a neutral space between two clearly defined moments, but rather is understood as a place of tension between two contradictory forces that were nevertheless sometimes reconcilable.[28]

NOTES

1. Vasari 1550; Vasari 1568.

2. "Les compagnons de Charles VIII ne furent pas moins étonnés que ceux de Christophe Colomb"; Michelet 1893, p. 138; passage correctly underlined by Sankovitch 2000.

3. For example, see Haskell 1993; Bullen 1994; Belozerskaya 2002, chap. 1; and Krul 2005.

4. Gaborit 2003b; Bresc-Bautier 2008b; Vaisse 2008. See also Sénéchal 2008.

5. One could cite many college texts, both old and new, including Belozerskaya 2002; Nash 2008; and Lee et al. 2010, as well as texts meant for the general public, attesting to this usage.

6. These criteria were put forwarded by Burke 2007 for the period in general and by Panofsky 1960 for its artistic manifestations (relying primarily on Weisinger 1944); see, however, the nuances developed by Bullen 1994, p. 8.

7. See the fundamental article by Białostocki 1983.

8. It should be remembered that the expression was coined as early as the start of the nineteenth century by E.H. Langlois; see Lafond 1971. For a similar and well-argued position on this question, see Hamon, forthcoming.

9. On the sometimes ambiguous usage of the words "antico" and "moderno" in Italian texts (even reversed in the end by Vasari), see Panofsky 1960, pp. 21–23, 31–35.

10. But we of course can follow the argument of Hamon 2002, pp. 25–26, when he suggests linking the former with those of the portal of the Virgin, characterized by Italianate decorative motifs.

11. Bruchet 1927, p. 234, no. 124.

12. Thus we note that the great art historian was mistaken in his understanding of this problem. The debate is summarized in, for example, Poiret 1994, pp. 90–92, and Burk 2007.

13. Zerner 2003, pp. 13–15.

14. Pèlerin 1510, f. 20 (1521 ed., f. 23v.).

15. Pradel 1963, letter no. 2, p. 167.

16. Pradel 1963, letter no. 3, pp. 168–75 (see p. 174).

17. Bernardi 1995, p. 405.

18. Gloton 1979, p. 42, quoted in Bernardi 1995, p. 404.

19. Of course, this double equivalence has long been established, both for France and the rest of Europe (see for example Vandevivere and Périer-d'Ieteren 1973, p. 19). In the domain of the southern Netherlands, we can cite a case in Louvain in 1536, where "na den nyeuweren aert" (according to the new manner), referring to a baldachin, must naturally be understood as meaning "with Flamboyant Gothic decoration." Kavaler 2000, p. 233.

20. For its application to Flemish art, see Vandevivere and Périer-d'Ieteren, 1973, pp. 19–23. For its use with respect to Croatian art, see Grujic, forthcoming.

21. Kavaler 2000; and *idem*, *Gothique de la Renaissance*, forthcoming.

22. In particular, see the remarks of Kavaler, De Jonge, and Nussbaum in Chatenet, De Jonge, Kavaler, and Nussbaum 2006.

23. See the brilliant conclusion by Jean Guillaume to the symposium bearing this name, especially "Moyen Âge et Renaissance, le piège des mots" (Esquieu 2003, pp. 313–15).

24. In this regard, the reflections of Borchert 2008 and String and Bull 2008 (on northern Europe, especially the Netherlands, and England, respectively) are, above all, deconstructions of standard historiography.

25. On this latter theme, see for example Gallissot-Ortuno 2003 and Boucherat 2005.

26. Białostocki 1961 mentions the related considerations of Meyer Schapiro as early as 1944, not to mention the whole tradition of the modern era; Schmoll gen. Eisenwerth, 1970. Helpful perspectives can also be found in DaCosta Kaufmann 2008 and Recht 2008 (who also recalls the contributions of Focillon and Panofsky).

27. Zerner 2003.

28. It is not possible to explore here the question of periodization in art history based on the turn of a century, which is expressed for example in the notions of art in 1200 or art in 1900, and which raises many questions about the concept of "century." There are scattered thoughts on these issues in various contributions in *Périodisation* 2008.

Ja ne te vueil par armes guerroyer.
Ne ton plaisir de ioye desuoyer.
Car toute tiēne ie suis & tiēne fuz.
Des mon ieune aaige sās en fē reffus.
Et daultre chose po^r certain nay ēuie
Fors destre tienne le surpl^s de ma vie.

Et aps com
mēce lespit^e
de Ysiphile
a Jason.

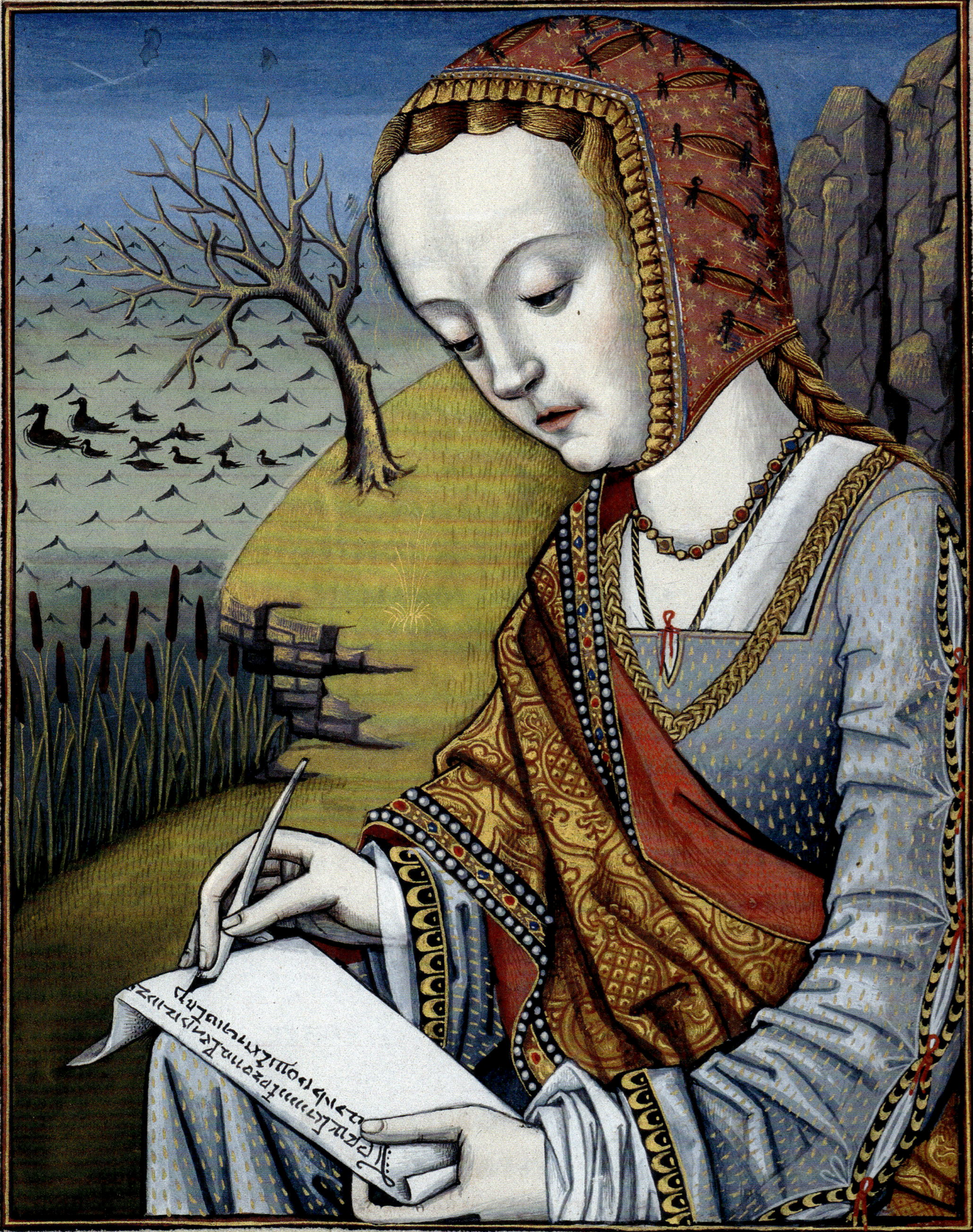

PRINCESSES AS PATRONS

Martha Wolff

In the years around 1500, the French royal family included several princesses who possessed exceptional power, although they could not exercise overt control over the kingdom. Anne of France, Anne of Brittany, and Louise of Savoy were connected by complex ties of kinship, upbringing, and ambition, and were also important patrons. For these princesses the opportunity for artistic patronage seems to be tied to some degree of independent political power.

The daughter of a French king was barred from inheriting the crown or passing it on to her son; in the fourteenth century, to ward off the claim of Edward III of England to the French throne through his mother, Isabelle of France—the basis of the Hundred Years War—lawyers of the French king reaffirmed this provision in the ancient Frankish Salic Law.[1] Toward the end of the fifteenth century, Louis XI, consolidating the power of the monarchy, extended this prohibition against female succession to the inheritance of appanages, those dukedoms or other territories given by a king to his younger sons and their descendants. Making this principle a reality, Louis forced the return of the appanage lands of the duchy of Burgundy to the domain of the French crown after Charles the Bold died in 1477 leaving only a daughter.[2] However, when Louis XI himself died a few years later in 1483, the succession of the French crown from father to son was a matter of some anxiety. Charles VIII, Louis's far from precocious only son, was a mere thirteen years of age when he inherited the throne. Charles's marriage to Anne of Brittany in late 1491 failed to produce surviving children. In 1498, after Charles's sudden death, the next in line to the throne, Charles's distant cousin, Louis of Orléans, inherited the throne as Louis XII and married the widowed queen, but their only surviving children were daughters. In these circumstances, the wives of the king and the princes of the blood were under intense pressure to produce healthy male offspring, and, though denied the throne for themselves, as mothers, wives, and even sisters, they had the chance to exert real power when the king was absent, incapacitated, or too young to actually rule.

Facing Page
FIGURE 16. Robinet Testard. *Hypsipyle*, in Ovid, *Héroïdes*. Tempera and gold on parchment. Bibliothèque nationale de France, Paris, ms. fr. 875, f. 30.

¶ ANNE OF FRANCE: MADAME LA GRANDE

Born in 1461, the eldest surviving child of Louis XI and his second wife, Charlotte of Savoy (fig. 17; genealogical chart, p. 12–13), Anne of France was married in 1474 to Pierre of Bourbon, lord of Beaujeu, a younger brother of Jean II, duke of Bourbon, and an important counselor to her father. Foreseeing trouble when the inexperienced thirteen-year-old dauphin inherited the throne, Louis XI arranged that Anne and her husband would be the governors of Charles VIII. Thus Anne effectively ruled France as regent, but without this title and exercising the greatest discretion to mask the appearance of power, since the regency, while formally allowed to the mother of a king, was not permitted to the sister of a king.[3] From 1488, when her husband inherited the Bourbon dukedom, she turned her attention increasingly to their personal center of power, the duchy's large territories in the center of France, particularly from late 1491, when Charles VIII married Anne, the heiress to the duchy of Brittany, and Anne herself gave birth to a daughter, Suzanne.

Though judgment is hampered by the over-restored or fragmentary state of her building projects, Anne's most active artistic patronage seems have occurred when her husband was duke of Bourbon, from 1488 to his death in 1503, with many projects brought to completion during her widowhood. Her book of hours in the Morgan Library (cat. 53), probably made just before her marriage, is a lavish but not highly personalized production by her mother's favored illuminator, Jean Colombe. As duchess, Anne of France used her patronage to affirm the identity of the Bourbon family and its royal descent from Saint Louis by updating and expanding ducal residences and religious foundations and commissioning sculpture and painted altarpieces that were remarkable for their rhetorical clarity. Beginning in 1490 the ducal castle at Moulins was rebuilt to accommodate visits from the king and court and to adapt it to the latest notions of comfort and symmetry. Anne's leading role in this project is clear from the few surviving accounts, which show her purchases of land for the expansion of the castle and refer to the "large new building of Madame."[4] The same is true for the castle of Chantelle, near Saint-Pourçain, expanded about 1500; little survives from this favored residence, beyond the monumental statues from the adjacent chapel that memorialize the ducal family through their patrons, Saint Peter, Saint Anne, and Saint Suzanne (cat. 66). In taking on the services of Jean Hey, the painter to Pierre's older brother, Cardinal Charles of Bourbon, archbishop of Lyon, the ducal couple used paintings on panel for the aggrandizement of the family. Jean Hey's Moulins triptych of *The Virgin in Glory* (fig. 39) represents a highpoint of this strategy. The ambition of the couple, probably in the first instance that of Anne, may have influenced the development of the painter's style in the 1490s, since it departs from the more private nature of what we know of the painter's earlier work for the cardinal. The wings of about 1492/93 in the Musée du Louvre, in which Pierre and Anne and their infant daughter Suzanne are presented by the heavily draped figures of saints Peter and John the Evangelist before a sun-drenched landscape resembling the Bourbonnais (fig. 18), make bolder, more emphatic use of the painting medium than the cardinal's exquisite private diptych (cat. 56). In these active years, Jean Hey turned to monumental, almost sculptural figures, yet he may have been encouraged to look to other objects belonging to the ducal family, like the diptych from the workshop of Rogier van der Weyden, in which Jeanne of France, first wife of Jean II of Bourbon, kneels before the Virgin enthroned in the sun.[5] The central motif of the Moulins triptych replicates this image of the Immaculate Conception rather closely, despite its much grander scale. Family continuity and prestige are also reflected in the completion of the cardinal's private chapel in Lyon Cathedral, with lavish use of the initials of Pierre, Anne, and Suzanne.[6]

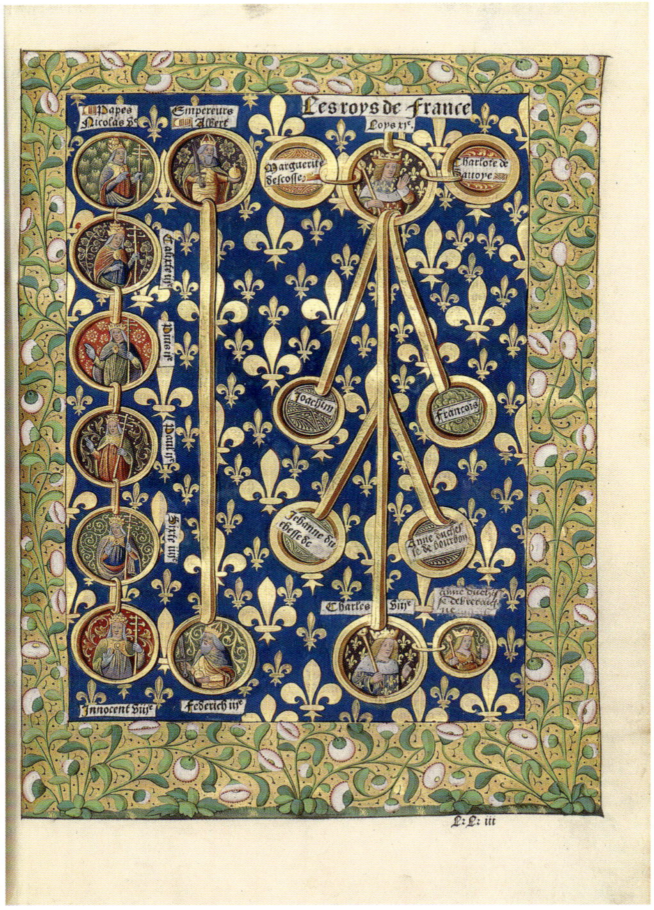

FIGURE 17.
Master of the Chronique Scandaleuse. *Genealogical Chart of the Family of Louis XI.* Illuminated woodcut on vellum. Bibliothèque nationale de France, Paris, Réserve des livres rares, vélins 677, f. KK3.

Significantly, as de facto regent, Anne, with Pierre as her more public face, very ably continued her father's policy of curbing the power of the great nobles and the princes of the blood—particularly of Louis of Orléans, the future Louis XII, who was both her brother-in-law and the heir presumptive to the throne. However, as duchess of Bourbon, she worked against this policy, doing everything possible to maintain control over Bourbon lands, including securing Suzanne's right to succession and insisting on the girl's marriage to Charles of Bourbon-Montpensier—the next male heir to the duchy.[7]

¶ ANNE OF BRITTANY: DUCHESS AND QUEEN

There was no question of Anne of Brittany's right to the duchy of Brittany on the death of her father, Francis II, in 1488. The duchy was a fief, not an appanage. It had pursued independent alliances that were so irksome to Charles VIII (and Anne of France) that, shortly before his death Francis II was forced to sign the treaty of Verger giving the king of France control over the marriage of his daughters. Though only eleven years old when she became duchess of Brittany, Anne fought hard to maintain independence from France, even marrying Maximilian of Austria by proxy in 1490 in

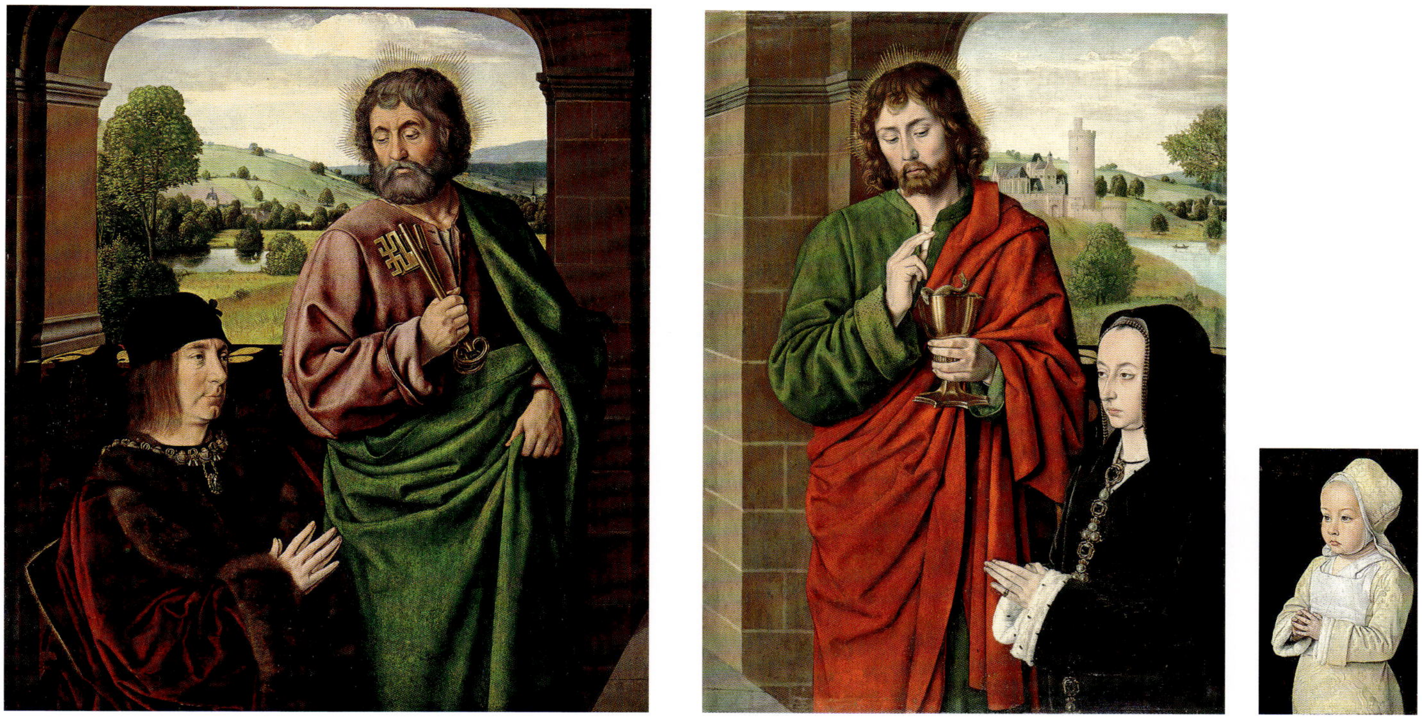

FIGURE 18.
Jean Hey (The Master of Moulins). *Pierre II, Duke of Bourbon, Presented by Saint Peter*; *Anne of France Presented by Saint John the Evangelist*; and *Suzanne of Bourbon* (fragment). Oil on panel. Musée du Louvre, Paris.

the vain hope that he would defend her. But, defeated by the French army, she bowed to what was generally agreed to be political reality and married Charles VIII in late 1491—despite the fact that this action offended Maximilian on two counts: the annulment of their unconsummated marriage and the rupture of Charles's engagement to Maximilian's daughter Margaret of Austria, who had been raised at the French court from the age of three (cat. 57). In 1498, after Charles's sudden death, Anne moved rapidly to reassert control over Brittany as its duchess, minting coins and returning to her capital of Nantes, but at the same time negotiating for a union with Charles's successor, Louis XII. This delicate process was complicated by the fact that Louis had yet to extricate himself from his marriage to the saintly Jeanne of France, sister of Anne of France and Charles VIII.[8] With her second marriage early in 1499, Anne received much more favorable terms, retaining more personal control over Brittany, use of its revenue, and the right of her second son (or in default of a son, her daughter) to inherit the duchy and pass it on, independent of the French crown.

The incomplete documents of her household, surviving more plentifully from her first marriage and the beginning of her second have been analyzed by Vrand (2010); they suggest independent management of her possessions, most strikingly after the death of Charles VIII. While Anne of Brittany was negotiating the terms of her second marriage, she was also engaged in transporting a substantial part of the contents of the château of Amboise, where Charles VIII had died, to her own castle at Nantes or to storage in Tours. These objects included items that were part of Anne's own Breton patrimony, such as ceremonial items used for her first childbed, but also included luxury objects, like tapestries, that had belonged to the king. Vrand demonstrates that these objects were only moved back up the Loire to the royal residences rather slowly following her remarriage in early 1499. Probably not coincidentally, during this same time of transition immediately following the death of Charles VIII, Anne of France petitioned Louis XII for the chattels of her dead brother, as his personal heir, along with other monetary settlements.[9]

Anne of Brittany's most significant act of patronage was the magnificent tomb of her parents for the church of the Carmelites in Nantes, now in Nantes Cathedral, and that for her sons by Charles VIII, formerly in Saint-Martin's, Tours, and now in the church of Saint-Gatien (figs. 12, 49). Her agents sought marble for these complex projects in Italy in late 1599 and early 1500, towards the beginning of her marriage to Louis XII and shortly after she had given birth to Claude of France. The first of these asserted her independent role as duchess of Brittany and the second evoked her role—still hoped for—as the mother of kings of France. Thus the tomb of Charles Orland and his even smaller brother also named Charles use the symbolic dolphins of the heir to the throne on the children's robes and on the rim of the tomb slab, along with Anne's personal and family device, the *cordelière*. Yet the timing and planning of these complex tombs also paralleled Louis XII's own tomb project for his Orléans forebears, celebrating his descent from

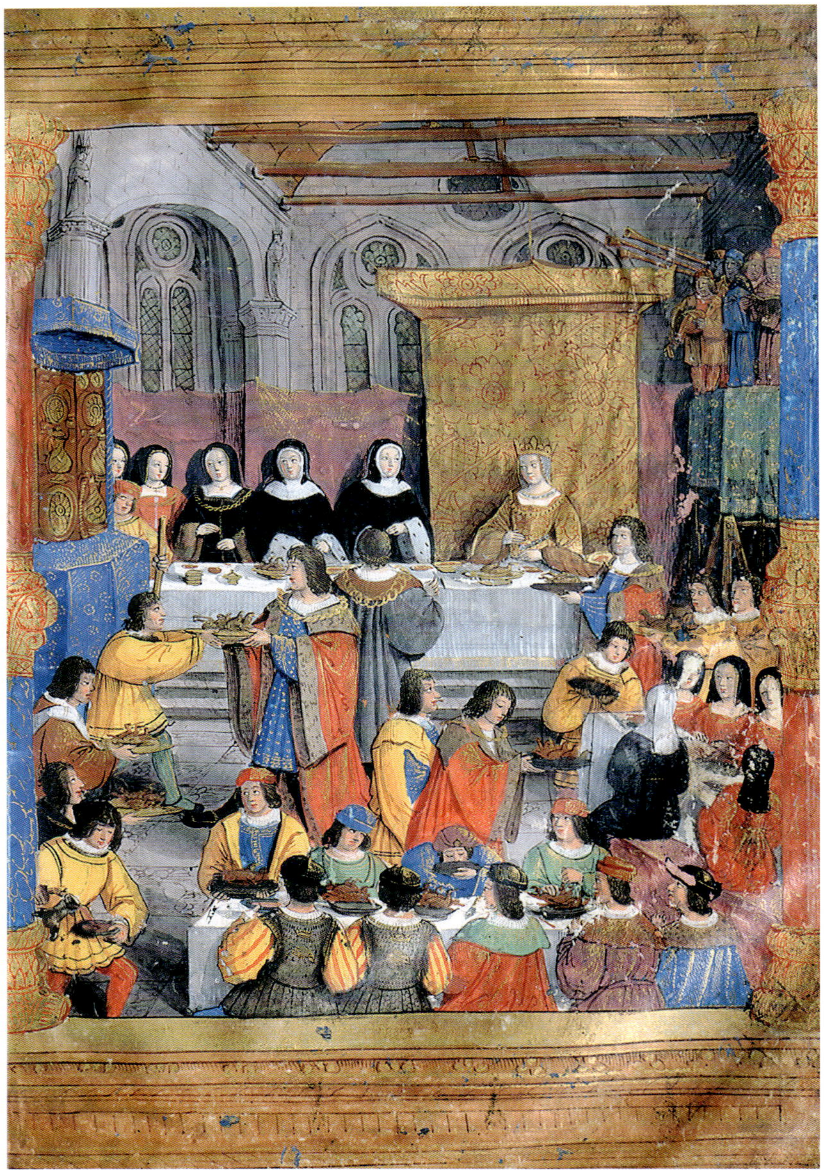

FIGURE 19.
Master of the Chronique Scandaleuse. *Coronation Banquet of Anne of Brittany*, in André de La Vigne, *Description of the Coronation and Entry into Paris of Anne of Brittany*. Tempera and gold on parchment. Waddesdon Manor, Buckinghamshire, The Rothschild Collection, ms. 22, f. 54v.

Charles V, and his claim to Milan through Valentina Visconti, together with what may have been a joint project for the tomb of Charles VIII in Saint-Denis.

In her patronage of illuminated manuscripts, Anne of Brittany supported virtuoso performances: the *Grandes Heures* of Jean Bourdichon—even more lavishly illuminated than his comparable book for Louis XII—and the strikingly tiny *Very Small Hours*.[10] Prayer books reveal her aspirations: the small book illuminated by Jean Poyer intended for use in teaching the dauphin his prayers (cat. 44), or a Florentine prayer book including a petition of Saint Leonard for aid to a queen with difficulties in childbearing.[11] Particularly revealing of her attention to the perception of her role is the illustrated description of her second coronation and entry into Paris written for her by her secretary André de La Vigne (cat. 34). To be twice queen of France was remarkable, but to be crowned twice was even more extraordinary. Indeed, this event did not even take place until late in 1504, almost five years after her marriage to Louis XII. It has been argued that the coronation ceremony in Saint-Denis, and particularly the blessing of her wedding ring by Cardinal Georges d'Amboise, described by de La Vigne, were spurred by the king's serious illness and other constitutional issues earlier in 1504 and reflected the queen's desire to affirm her capacity to act in his stead.[12] In addition to the image of the coronation itself at the high altar of Saint-Denis, the other two episodes illustrated in this manuscript—her entry into Paris and the banquet in the royal palace on the Ile de la Cité (fig. 19)—were public acts of legitimization, mirroring those for the king.

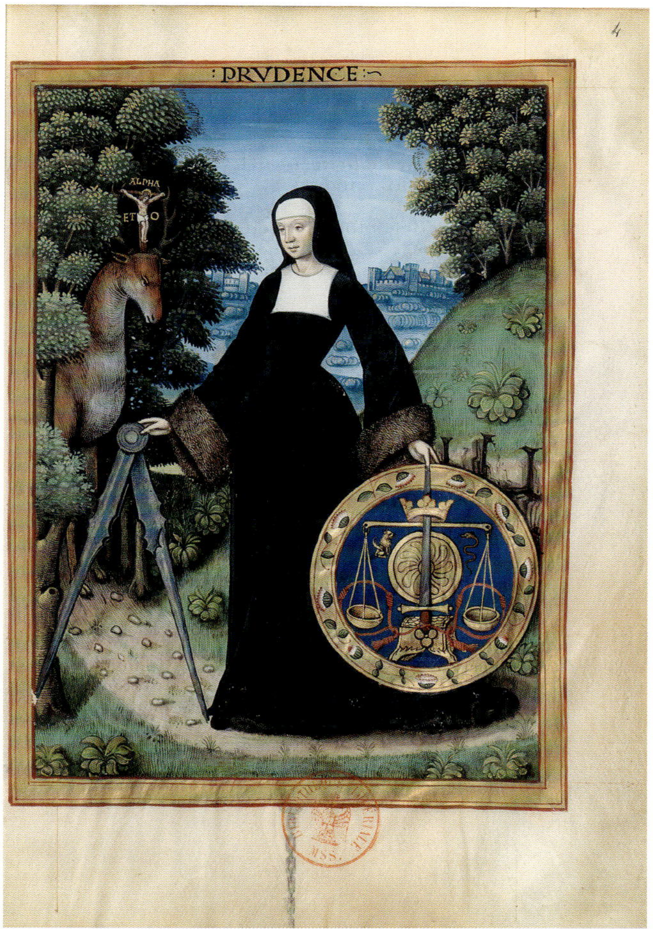

FIGURE 20.
Guillaume Leroy the Younger. *Louise of Savoy as an Allegory of Prudence*, in François Demoulins, *Traité sur les vertus cardinals*. Tempera and gold on parchment. Bibliothèque nationale de France, Paris, ms. fr. 12247, f. 4.

¶ LOUISE OF SAVOY: REGENT IN WAITING

Louise of Savoy had less to spend on art before her son succeeded to the throne as Francis I in 1515; nevertheless, she used texts, emblems, and allegorical imagery very effectively to promote her family's interests. Born in 1476 to a younger son of the duke of Savoy, she and her brother Philibert were sent as children to be raised at the French court, under the supervision of Anne of France. As a poor cousin of the king, Louise was married in 1488 to Charles of Angoulême, who belonged to a junior branch of the Orléans family. When her husband died in 1496, she was still only nineteen, and mother to Margaret, born in 1492, and Francis, born in 1494.

Charles of Angoulême had been a bibliophile (cat. 19), and as a young widow at her court at Cognac, Louise continued an active involvement in the production of innovative books, as attested by her accounts.[13] Many of these books combine traditional courtly themes and humanist elements, as in the translation of Ovid's *Heroïdes* by Octovien de Saint-Gelais, bishop of Angoulême; Louise's copy was illustrated by her court painter, Robinet Testard, with portrait-like images of lovelorn classical heroines writing the epistles that made up the volume (fig. 16). Louise promoted her role as mother and nurturer of the heir to the throne in a series of treatises by François Demoulins, tutor to Francis, in which she is frequently presented in the guise of Prudence. She appears in this role, wearing the modest but still alluring dress of a widow, in Demoulins' *Traité sur les Vertus cardinals* (fig. 20) and probably also on the pages of the moral compendium made to instruct and amuse her son (cat. 98). The salamander and the motto *Notrisco al buono stingo el reo* were first connected with Francis when he was only ten, on a medal of 1504 that must be due to Louise of Savoy's management of her son's image at a time when Louis XII's brush with illness had dramatized the boy's proximity to the throne (cat. 96). Louise had energy and ambition and she also held a trump card that eluded her kinswomen Anne of France and Anne of Brittany—a vigorous son. She knew how to use this advantage and would continue to do so as the closest advisor and frequent regent for Francis I.

NOTES

1. Taylor 2006; Giesey 2007.

2. Saenger 1977.

3. Viennot 2001 analyzes the letters signed by Charles VIII in the early years of the reign in an effort to distinguish Anne's active intervention.

4. Bruand 2001, pp. 58–61 n. 16; Baron d'Heedene 1992, pp. 103–06, for the "batiment neuf du grant corps de maison que ma dite dame a fait pieça commencer."

5. Musée Condé, Chantilly; Comblen-Sonkes 1988, pp. 87–107, pl. 95A.

6. Hamon 2001, pp. 122–26, suggests that the campaign to finish work on the chapel was brought to completion by Anne, perhaps in 1508. The inclusion of Suzanne's initials would support her role as successor to the duchy.

7. This succession was confirmed at the point when Louis XII succeeded Charles VIII; Chombart de Lauwe 1980, pp. 375–76. Confirmation was in response to the situation created by the marriage contract in 1400 of Jean I of Bourbon, Pierre of de Bourbon's grandfather, which had converted the Bourbonnais, the ancient seigneury of the Bourbon family, into an appanage; see Maulde La Clavière 1885, pp. 1145–46.

8. After her divorce from Louis, she founded the order of the Annonciade; she was canonized as Saint Jeanne of Valois in 1950.

9. For Anne of Brittany's removal of objects from Amboise to Nantes, see Vrand 2010, pp. 121–28, 154. Anne of France's claim (Maulde La Clavière 1885, pp. 1154–60) was denied in favor of the concession described in n. 7 above.

10. Reynaud in Paris 1993, pp. 297–300 and 265–67, nos. 164 and 143, respectively.

11. Newberry Library, Chicago, MS. 83; see L'Estrange 2010, pp. 91–93.

12. Scheller 1983; Hochner 2010. During the reign of Charles VIII, Anne of Brittany was not made regent during the king's absence on campaign in 1494/95. Pierre of Bourbon was given this role.

13. Edmunds 1990; Winn 2007.

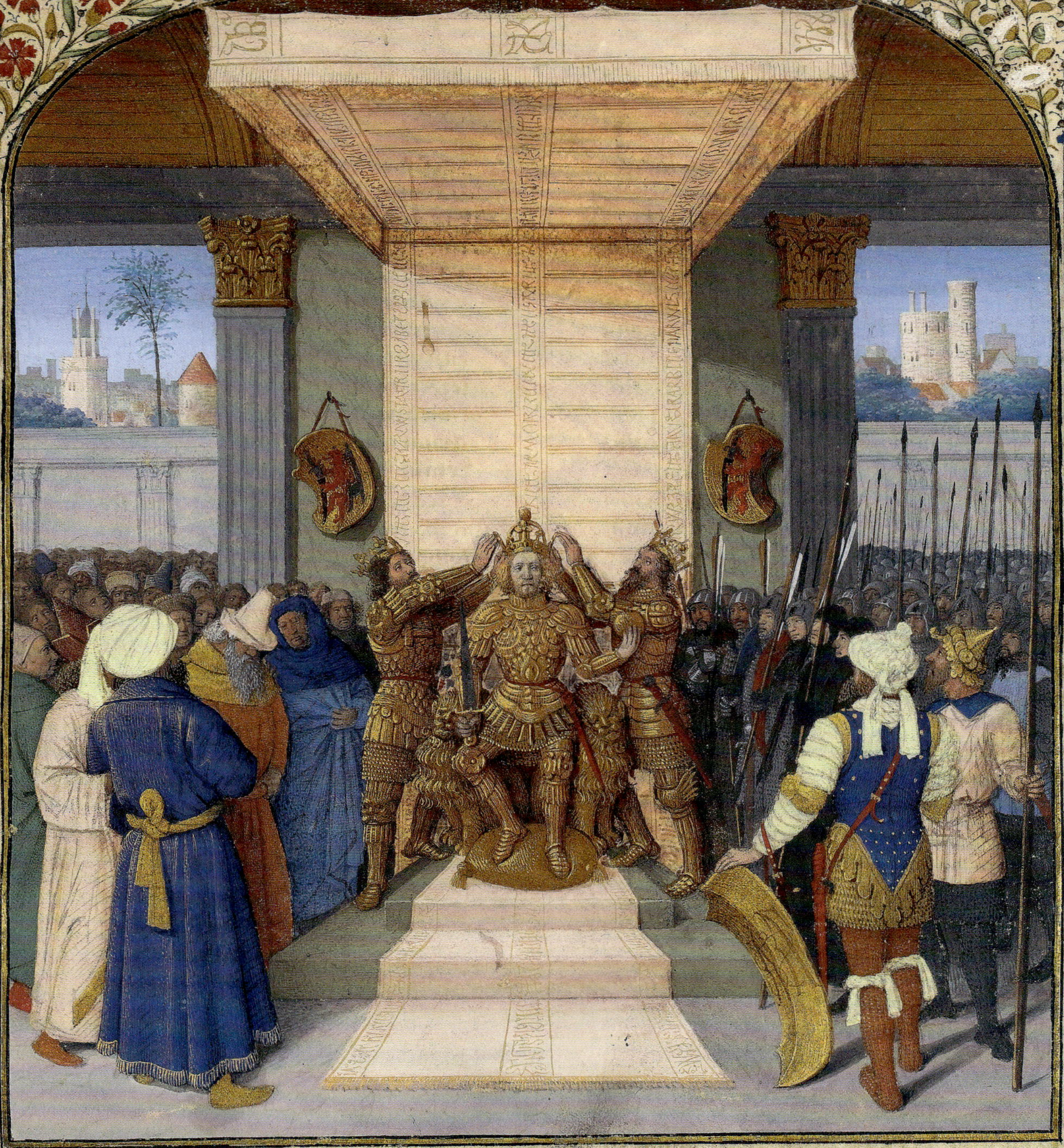

Comment alixandre fut couronne a roy de macedoyne apres la mort le roy phe son pere xvj

Seigneurs quant le roy phe vist ceste merveille il lui vint a lencontre et le salua si haultement comme le seigneur de tout le monde Et quant Alixandre ot .xv. ans il sen ala combatre a ceulx de puille que il vainqui par laide de sa bonne gent et par sa proesse Et apres se combati il au roy Nicolas que il vainqui en bataille si comme vous avez oy plusieurs fois conter et dire Et apres ce mahy il la cite de machome que il soubsmist au commandement de Macedome et si en fist aus gens de la cite jouer le treu a sa voulente et a sa devise.

Apres ce sen retourna il en macedome si racorda sa mere la royne olimpias au roy phelippe qui lavoit laissiee pour ces parens Et lachoison si fu de la laissier pour ce que pausonias amoit olimpiadam et si lavoit ravie et pour ce pausonias en navra le roy phe a mort car il la vouloit avoir et tenir a femme A dans Alixandre en meismes lieux que le roy phe fut navre si come vous avez oy ca arrieres prinst pausonias si le mena devant le roy phe auquel il mist en la main une moult bonne espee toute nue et si lui dist quil sen vengast a sa voulente si comme de celui que lui avoit la mort donnee et le roy phe tantost ocist pausonias si quil perdi la vie. Adonc

THE TRANSFORMATIONS OF THE MID-FIFTEENTH CENTURY

FRÉDÉRIC ELSIG

Around 1400, Paris was a great crossroads of the arts and a source of luxury goods for the French king, the royal princes. and the nobility. This would shift with the gathering disasters of the last phase of the Hundred Years' War, waged between England and France over the succession to the French crown and encouraged by a concurrent civil war among branches of the French royal family and their followers during the reign of the unstable Charles VI (r. 1380–1422). The younger brother of Charles VI, Louis I of Orléans, and his followers were bitterly opposed by the dukes of Burgundy, the descendants of Charles VI's uncle Philip the Bold, whose marriage had added rich possessions in the Low Countries to his lands in eastern France. Taking advantage of the murderous rivalries among the princes of the blood, the young king of England, Henry V, reignited the conflict of the Hundred Years' War, invading France in 1415 and inflicting a decisive defeat at Agincourt. The Burgundians allied themselves with the English, who won favorable terms in the treaty of Troyes in 1420: Henry V of England received Charles VI's daughter Catherine as a bride and became regent of France on behalf of her ailing father, while the succession to the throne of France was assigned to their future children, cutting out the male heir—the dauphin and future Charles VII. When Henry V of England and Charles VI of France both died in 1422, they were succeeded by the dual monarchy of France and England, claimed for the infant Henry VI of England; it was against this claim and the reality of the administration of the boy's uncle, the Duke of Bedford, that the dauphin Charles had to assert himself. With Paris and northern and western France occupied by the English, the dauphin was pushed into the Loire Valley and the center of the country. Only in 1429, bolstered by Joan of Arc, was he able to make his way to Reims to be crowned as Charles VII. Even then the ceremony took place without the normal regalia of French kingship, as these treasures were kept at the royal abbey of Saint-Denis, then in English territory. Though the Burgundians broke with their English allies in 1435, it was not until 1437 that Charles was able to enter Paris in triumph, 1449 before he reclaimed Rouen in Normandy, and 1453 before the conflict was ended.

Even after the departure of the English, the focus of the court was still the Loire Valley, around Bourges and Tours. Although Paris remained an important judicial center—with appeal to the *Parlement de Paris*—as well as an intellectual and religious center with its university, and a great population hub, it was no longer the entry point for the most talented artists seeking court patronage, many of whom had come from the Low Countries and the Rhineland in the preceding decades (for artistic production in Paris during these difficult years, see Reynolds 1989). Instead, these artists found opportunities at home, and the court of the Valois dukes of the Burgundian Netherlands became a model of magnificence. Within their extensive territory, from Dijon to the prosperous cities of French Flanders and the Low Countries—Lille, Valenciennes, Bruges, Ghent, and Brussels—a new taste was launched, breaking with the poetic preciosity of the International Gothic style and defined by a more immediate representation of the physical world, both among men of letters and among sculptors and painters. The complexity of political and cultural allegiances within this sphere is demonstrated by Tournai in the county of Hainaut, part of the territory of Philip the Good of Burgundy (r. 1419–67). It was the seat of a powerful bishop, but the municipality was allied to the king of France and received privileges from him. The city was an important center for textile production, including the manufacture and diffusion of luxury tapestries (cats. 9–10); the Tournai workshop of Robert Campin, the Master of Flémalle, was an incubator for the new Netherlandish painting style (dubbed the *ars nova* by twentieth-century scholars), which was spread through the work of his students and collaborators, among them Jacques Daret and, most successfully, Rogier van der Weyden (Roger de la Pasture).

The Burgundian model spread rapidly through two networks that overlapped and sometimes competed, one economic and the other diplomatic. It thus influenced the cultural identity of the kingdom of France, as it was gradually reconstructed during the period of Charles VII (r. 1422–61), but it truly took root during the next generation, under the reign of Louis XI (r. 1461–83) (see Elsig 2004). The economic network, which connected centers like Bruges, Brussels, Tournai, Amiens, and Paris, determined a flow of influences that extended toward the south of France and disseminated luxury objects as well as artists in search of less competitive markets. In the domain of painting, economic ties were a vehicle for the spread of the inventions of Van der Weyden in particular, rather literally interpreted in Picardy by the Master of 1451 and more subtly by painters like Simon Marmion in Valenciennes and André

Facing Page

FIGURE 21.

Attributed to Jean Fouquet. *The Coronation of Alexander*, a detached leaf from the *Histoire ancienne jusqu'à César* and *Faits des Romains*. Tempera and gold on parchment. Musée du Louvre, Paris, Department of Graphic Arts, RF 4143.

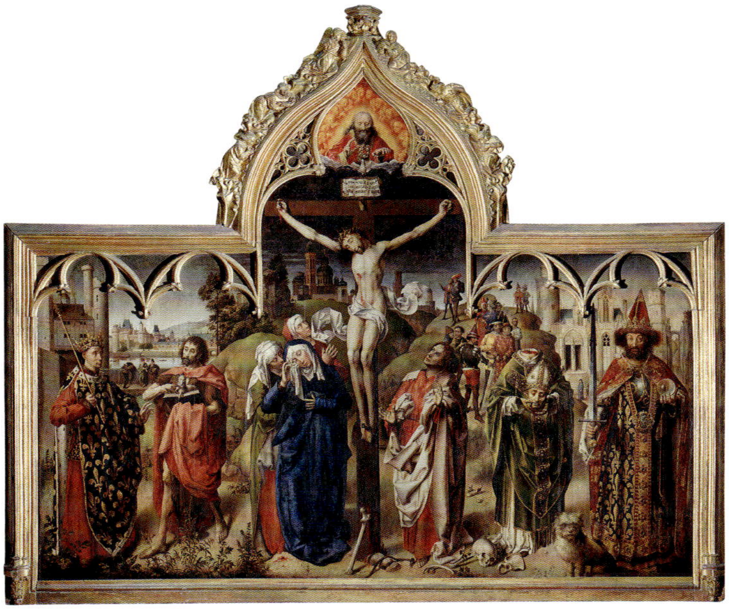

FIGURE 22.
Master of Dreux Budé (André d'Ypres?) and the Coëtivy Master (Colin d'Amiens?). *The Crucifixion of the Parlement of Paris.* Oil on panel. Musée du Louvre, Paris.

d'Ypres, who moved from Amiens to Paris in the mid-1440s (fig. 22; cats. 6–8). His Paris workshop was then taken over by his son Colin d'Amiens, who seems to be identical with the anonymous Master of Coëtivy (Lorentz 2002) and was active from 1450 to about 1497. Colin d'Ypres would be celebrated by Jean Pèlerin, called Viator, in 1521 as one of the most eminent painters of his time. Multitalented, he not only produced altarpieces and illuminations, but also furnished patterns for stained-glass windows (for example for the choir of the church of Saint-Séverin in Paris), for sculptures (like the tomb of Louis XI at Notre-Dame de Cléry), and also for tapestries (notably the cycle depicting the Trojan war, woven through the intermediary of the Tournai merchants Pasquier and Jean Grenier) (Reynaud in Paris 1993, pp. 58–69; fig. 23; cats. 9–10).

In terms of the diplomatic current, the "Good King René" (*Bon Roi René*), duke of Anjou (r. 1434–80), count of Provence, and claimant to the thrones of Naples and Jerusalem, played a role that was as crucial as it was precocious. It was perhaps in the workshop of the painter to Philip the Good of Burgundy, Jan van Eyck, that, as early as 1433, he may have recruited the services of the artist who would become his official painter, Barthélemy d'Eyck. The latter brought Netherlandish models to Provence and Anjou through his output of retables, illuminations, and designs like those for embroideries probably executed in 1444 by his stepfather Pierre du Billant for Saint Martin's in Tours (cat. 14). Also in the mid-1440s, he collaborated in Aix-en-Provence with Enguerrand Quarton (cat. 2), who was originally from the diocese of Laon in northern France, but whose native style had been adapted to the Mediterranean culture of Provence (Thiébaut in Paris 2004). His trajectory overlapped with that of Nicolas Froment (cat. 12), who, having established himself in Uzès around 1465, gradually softened the harshness derived from his training in Picardy, perhaps as a result of the influence of the sculptors

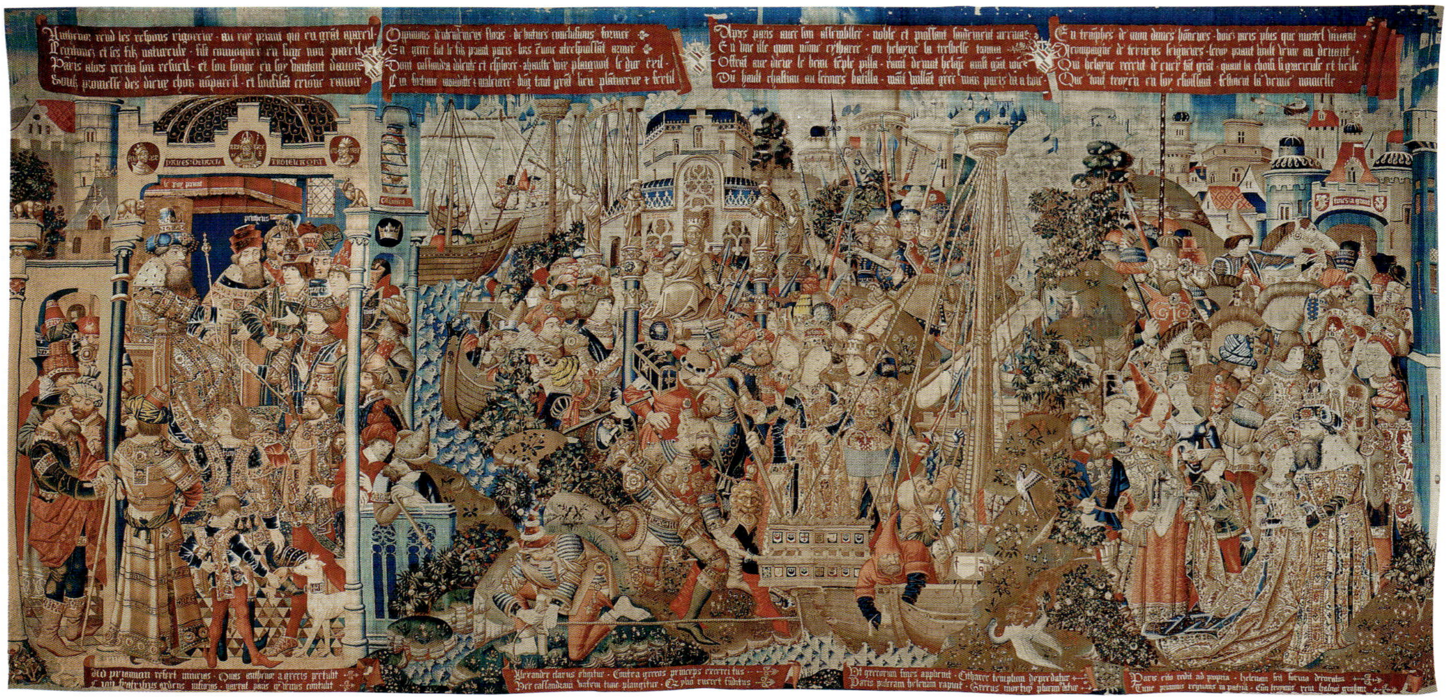

FIGURE 23.
Netherlandish weavers, after a design by the Coëtivy Master (Colin d'Amiens?). *The Abduction of Helen*, from an eleven-piece set of the *History of the Trojan War.* Tapestry. Museo Catedralicio, Zamora, Spain.

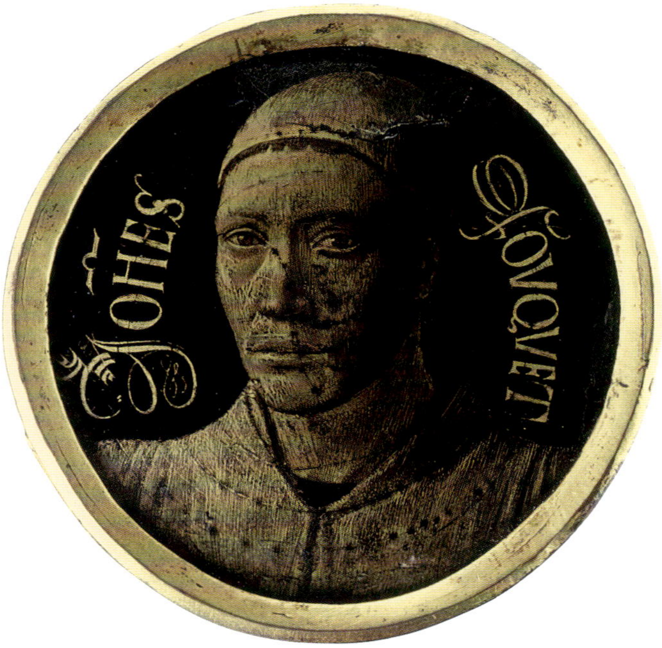

FIGURE 24.
Jean Fouquet. *Self-Portrait Medallion.* Enamel and gold paint on copper. Musée du Louvre, Paris.

and medalists Francesco Laurana and Pietro da Miliano, who began serving René of Anjou in the early 1460s (cats. 13, 22–23). Even if it still remained relatively isolated, René's humanist interest in Italian artists was shared at this time by his former secretary, Guillaume Fillastre, who become the bishop of Tournai and the councilor to Philip the Good; in 1469, he commissioned his own tomb from the Florentine sculptor Andrea della Robbia, to be placed in the monastery of Saint-Bertin in Saint-Omer, of which he was the abbot (cat. 18).

Through such economic and diplomatic networks, the French court forged its cultural identity by means of selective assimilation. It combined the Burgundian model with certain Italian accents, which tempered it. But it also countered this absorption of foreign models in part through a nostalgic attachment to that which was perceived as the French tradition, an attachment that was translated into a predilection for refined techniques (illumination, tapestry, and stained glass) and the persistence of formulae belonging to the glorious period of the International Gothic style around 1400. The innovations of volume and space of the Flemish painters were thus adapted to a more conservative taste in the medium of stained glass in the Annunciation window for the chapel of Jacques Coeur in Bourges cathedral, possibly conceived by Jacob de Littemont, or in the famous tapestry, *The Winged Stags*, in which the elegantly observed and delineated stags are surrounded by heraldic pattern (cat. 1). But these innovations were effectively rejected in works such as the east window of Evreux cathedral, in the tapestry with the arms of Jean de Daillon at Montecute House (National Trust), or in the sculpture of Saint Michael from Toulouse (cat. 21). But these trends were synthesized in a deeply original language developed by Jean Fouquet.

Born in Tours around 1420, Jean Fouquet established himself in a milieu that was dominated by the formulae of the International Gothic style but was also receptive to Flemish innovations (fig. 21). He may have trained in the circle of the Parisian illuminator known as the Master of Jouvenel, perhaps identical with Henri de Vulcop (Elsig 2004, pp. 40–41, pls. 36–37), who could have recommended him very early to the court. Thus at the end of the 1440s he undertook a journey to Rome, perhaps as part of a diplomatic delegation; there he painted the portrait of Pope Eugene IV (now lost) and absorbed the lessons of Fra Angelico (Avril in Paris 2003). He too was called upon to produce designs and works in a range of media, not only manuscript illumination and panel painting, but also very probably for tapestries (see cat. 1) and certainly for sculpture, notably the initial plan for the tomb effigy of Louis XI in the pilgrimage church of Notre-Dame de Cléry, which was, however, not executed. The stained-glass roundel from a domestic context (cat. 5) shows that he was also engaged in designing for this medium. Indeed, the extraordinary self-portrait bust, the only surviving element from the medallions in enamel and gold inserted in the frame of the Melun diptych, shows the degree of his technical experimentation (fig. 24).

Fouquet's stylistic language, which achieved the most balanced synthesis of these different elements intersecting in French art at mid-century, would have an impact on the illumination of Jean Colombe and on the murals in the chapel of canons Jean and Martin du Breuil in Bourges cathedral, perhaps painted around 1470 by the aged Henri de Vulcop (Elsig 2004, p. 40, pl. 37). For the generation that followed, he remained a model, not only for painters like Jean Bourdichon and Jean Poyer, but also for sculptors like Michel Colombe and Guillaume Regnault. He emerged henceforth as the most accomplished expression of a cultural identity proper to the French court, which was diffused down the axis of the Loire.

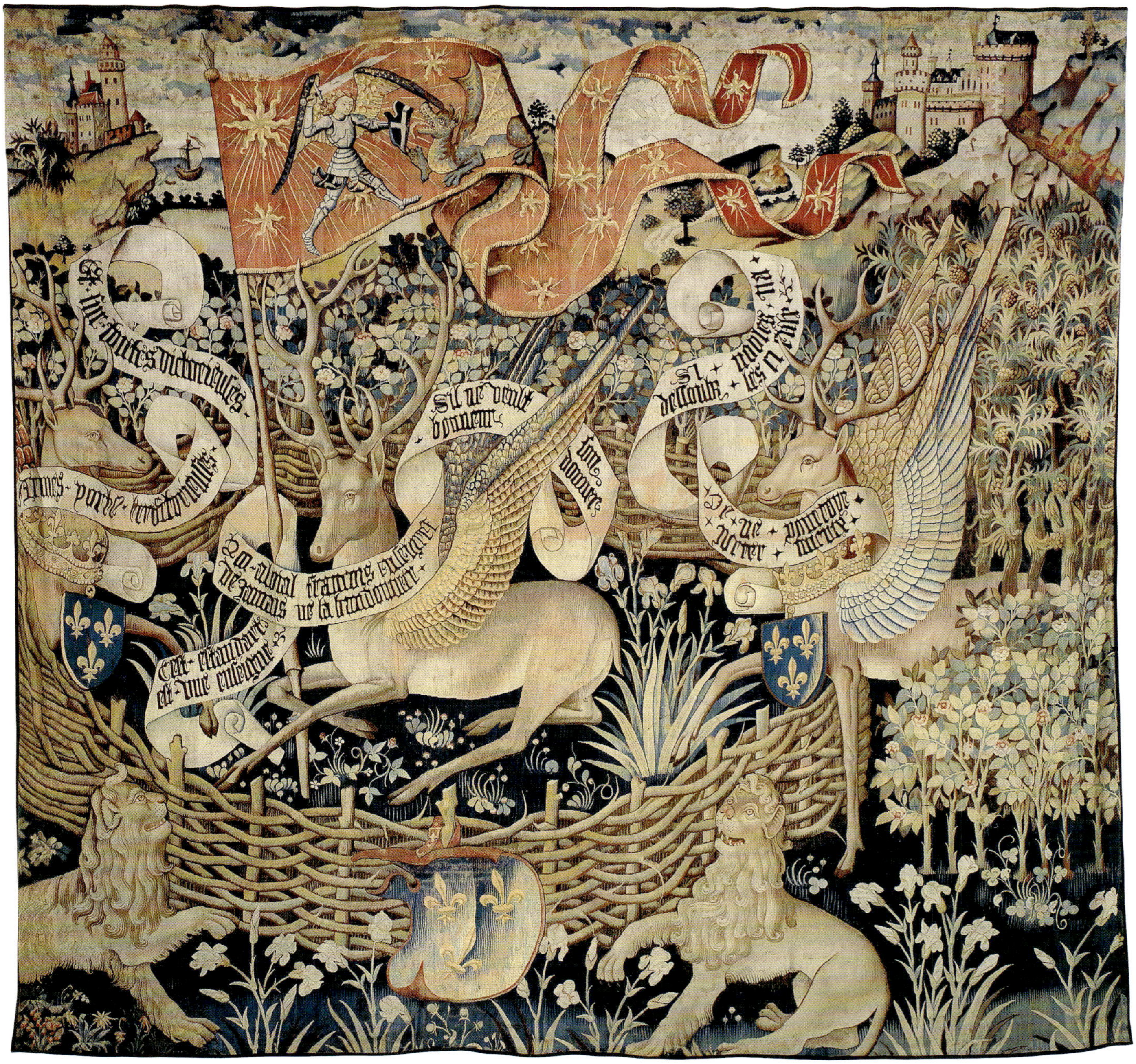

[1]

The Winged Stags

Probably southern Netherlands or northern France, 1453/61

Wool and silk; 347 x 380 cm (136 5/8 x 149 5/8 in.)

Musée des Antiquités de la Seine-Maritime, Rouen, 1854

INSCRIBED: *Cest estandart / est une enseigne / Qui aloial francois enseigne / de jamais ne la bandonner / Sil ne veut son bonneur* [*b* for *h*] *donner* [This standard is the sign that teaches a loyal Frenchman never to abandon it if he does not wish to yield his honor] (on scroll around central stag); *Armes porte* [*tres glo*] *rieuses / Et sur toutes victorieuses* [[I] bear arms [very] glorious / and over all victorious] (on scroll around stag at left); *Si noble na / dessoubz les cieulx* [*je*] *ne pourroye /* [*por*]*ter mieulx* [So noble there is not beneath the heavens [I] cannot carry better] (on scroll around stag at right)

PROVENANCE: Purchased from Raymond Bissieu, 1892.

BIBLIOGRAPHY: Flavigny 1992. Rapp Buri and Stucky-Schürer 2001, pp. 246–52 (with bibliography). Antoine 2010, p. 6.

EXHIBITIONS: Paris 1900, no. 3169. Paris 1973–74, no. 28. New York 1974, no. 31. Caen/Rouen 1999–2000, no. 103.

AT THE CENTER of a garden enclosure, a winged stag is seated, holding between its legs a banner showing Saint Michael slaying the dragon against a bright red background strewn with golden suns. Two more winged stags stand on either side, each wearing a crown around its neck, from which a French royal shield is suspended. The inscriptions on the scrolls unfurling around the stags refer to the arms of France, to the standard of Saint Michael, and their victories. The tapestry was trimmed in the past and rewoven in some areas, particularly at the bottom and on the left side, where the outline of the enclosure, the gesture of the stag, and his red wing are not original.

The heraldic and historic interpretation of this tapestry has been clarified in the course of the twentieth century; it commemorates the reconquest of the kingdom of France by Charles VII "The Victorious" (crowned 1429), who is depicted in the guise of the winged stag holding the banner of Saint Michael within an enclosure symbolizing the kingdom of France. The winged stag was a device of Charles VI, Charles VII and, for a short time, of Louis XI. Under Charles VII, Saint Michael became the protector of the realm, and the standard held by the stag is similar to the banner under which Charles triumphantly entered the recaptured cities of Paris (1437) and Rouen (1449), according to the chronicles of the era. The other devices of Charles VII, irises and roses, decorate the field of the tapestry, which extends to a landscape with a glimpse of the sea. In the foreground, a shield with the arms of France is attached to one of the stakes of the enclosure. The two stags that each place a hoof in the enclosure symbolize the provinces of Normandy and Guyenne, which were recaptured from the English in the battles of Formigny (1450) and Castillon (1453), thereby reentering the kingdom of France, while the two outside the enclosure could be the heraldic leopards of England looking on, powerless in defeat.

The tapestry can be dated to the late 1450s, and is one of the very rare surviving examples of monumental pictorial art from this period, demonstrating the fresh impulse given to the arts by the reconquest of the kingdom. Probably woven for a follower of Charles VII, it is remarkable for the striking contrast between the stylized heraldic treatment and elegant beauty of the stags, whose heads are very subtly modeled with a finesse that some have wanted to attribute to the greatest painter of the era, Jean Fouquet. The penetrating gaze of the central stag is indeed rather strangely evocative of the equally compelling regard of the painter in his self-portrait medallion in the Musée du Louvre. In addition, Nicole Reynaud (Paris 1981, pp. 35–38) has attributed to Fouquet the cartoons for a series of six tapestries celebrating the battle of Formigny, known today only through seventeenth-century drawings, thereby putting forward the artist's activity as a painter of tapestry cartoons. Here one could postulate that Fouquet provided the cartoons for the stags, leaving the rest of the composition to less skilled collaborators who drew on traditional imagery of heraldic tapestries for the lions, the foreground vegetation, and the landscape background. However, the complete absence of any information on the early history of the tapestry prevents us from speculating further on this possible attribution. • EA

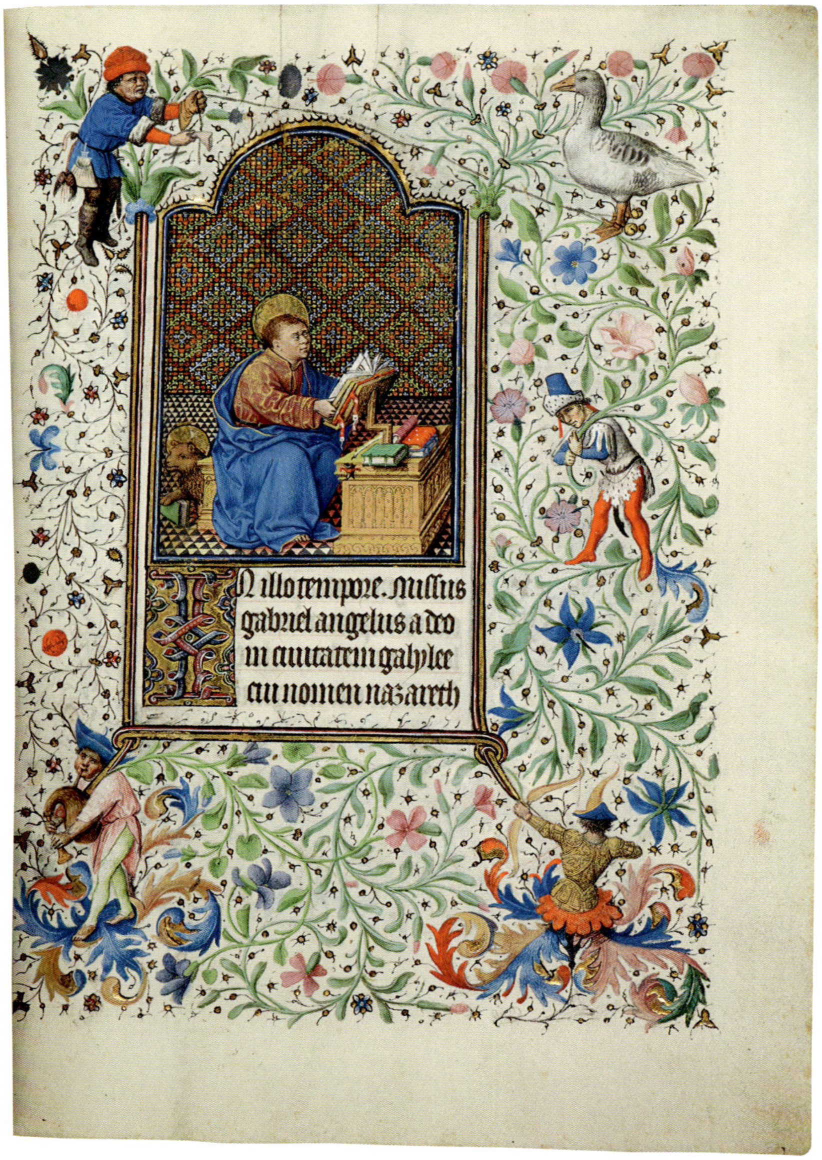

[2]

ENGUERRAND QUARTON
(active 1444–66)

BARTHÉLEMY D'EYCK
(active 1444–71/72)

AND OTHER ARTISTS

Book of Hours for the Use of Rome

Provence, c. 1445–50

Brush drawings, gouache, and gold on parchment; 225 ff; 25 x 18.3 cm (9 13/16 x 7 3/16 in.)

The Morgan Library and Museum, New York, ms. M 358

PROVENANCE: Joseph Barrois; Earl of Ashburnam, from 1849 to 1901; Rodolphe Kann (d. 1905), Paris; J. Pierpont Morgan, by 1909.

BIBLIOGRAPHY: Avril 1977. Sterling 1983, pp. 10–15, 176–77. Avril in Paris 1993, pp. 223–31.

EXHIBITIONS: New York 1934, no. 108. New York/Cleveland/Chicago/San Francisco/San Marino, Calif./Kansas City/Houston/Cambridge, Mass., 1957, no. 32. New York 1982, no. 39. Paris 1993, no. 123. New York 1997, no. 31.

SHOWN: *Saint Mark*, f. 15r

THIS BOOK OF HOURS with ornamentation of the highest quality is incomplete. Only ten of the twenty-four paintings planned for the text divisions of the principal offices were executed. Although all of the borders were decorated with the initial stages of ornamentation, a third of them were never finished.

Such interruptions, occurring at various stages of work, were commonplace for manuscripts executed by the artists in René of Anjou's entourage. Although the volume lacks indications of local liturgical use or marks of ownership, since Avril's memorable article of 1977, it has been associated with Provence, and more precisely with the region of Aix in the 1440s. According to Avril, three of the miniatures—*David at Prayer*, *Saint James*, and *Saint Bartholomew*—were executed by Enguerrand Quarton. We know that Quarton and Barthélemy d'Eyck were working together in Aix in 1444, and as Avril cautiously noted, the seven other paintings, the calendar medallions, and some figures in the margins of the book of hours seem to be from d'Eyck's hand. Both of these proposals have been generally accepted and further explored.

Quarton's very limited contribution poses no problem, nor does the similarity of the miniatures to those of the circle of artists employed by René of Anjou and his court in the first half of the century. When the Morgan Hours includes a landscape, its components (hills, buildings, vegetation) and their rendering are treated in the same manner as in the pages attributed to Barthélemy d'Eyck that were added around 1442–43 to one of René of Anjou's books of hours (British Library, Egerton 1070) and in the paintings on the exterior of the wings of the Aix Annunciation triptych, probably drawn by Barthélemy but painted by a collaborator in 1444–45. For his rendering of *Saint James* (f. 202v), Quarton borrowed from the resurrected Christ on the Aix triptych wings the broad, continuous movement in the drapery of the cloak, as well as the positioning of his staff: exactly parallel to the vertical edge of the fabric and inserted into the narrow fold created by the fall of drapery over the saint's wrist. Conversely, it was from Enguerrand that Barthélemy learned to geometricize forms: the robes stretched in blocky shapes over the knees of figures seated on the ground on folios 11, 13, and 25 are all the more striking because the artist still retained the complex and exaggerated contours and breaking folds.

It is also clear that a single hand was responsible for all of the compositions that structure the 211 decorated pages. With very deft brushwork, the artist outlined the contours of the historiated initials, the plant motifs in the margins, and the figures and whimsical creatures that inhabit them. From one end of the book to the other, we find these nervous strokes, rapid and highly efficient. The line, which is spontaneous and sometimes discontinuous, seems to vibrate with the same sense of movement that animates his figures in their extremely varied poses. The same artist also applied various stages of color for certain motifs in the borders, both scrollwork and figures; he was attentive to the details of his drawings, to their indications of shading, and there is no coarsening of the gestures. Layering color after color, he fully exploited his palette before adding highlights and finishing touches in ink. However, not all of the completed figures in the margins were executed by him: either working under his supervision, or at a later point in time, at least two other hands are evident—one rendering faces that are quite inexpressive despite their down-turned mouths, the other creating a series of birds with rather mechanically hatched feathers.

The book's chief artist and primary illuminator also seems to have been the author of the historiated medallions in the calendar (except for folios 5, 8, and 9 recto and verso) and the illuminations in arched frames on folios 13, 15, 17, 19, 20 verso, 25, and 40. Was this Barthélemy d'Eyck? Analysis of this question is complicated because the book is incomplete and underwent successive interventions, and also by the fact that the illuminator reconstructed under this name in recent decades painted very few religious scenes and almost no representations of young children, while both are abundant in the margins of the *Morgan Hours*. We could compare (among other examples): the seated Virgin of the *Morgan Hours* (f. 25) to the shepherdess in the *Pas de Tarascon* of 1449 (Bibliothèque nationale de France (BnF), ms. fr. 1974); the attention given to differentiating the bakers' peels (fol. 10) and the cooking utensils arrayed in the foreground of the pig-slaughtering scene (f. 12) to the almost documentary detail in the *Livre des Tournois* (BnF, ms. fr. 2695); or the rounded back and crossed legs of the peasant (f. 3) to the stance of the observer in the embroidery of *Saint Martin in front of the Chapel* (Musée Historique des Tissus, Lyon). But we should also note the features that differentiate this manuscript from those of the 1460s: fresher and brighter colors, a more pictorial and pointillist technique, softer contours, more oval facial forms, and more supple bodies with a more varied figural canon. The lively imagination revealed in the figures in the borders (centaurs, hybrid creatures, imaginary combats, wild men) is combined with a certain ironic sensibility (scenes of "the world turned upside down" in the borders and in the calendar: folio 1 showing a lord standing by, waiting for a peasant to finish warming his feet by the hearth; folio 11 with a seated woman with crossed arms watching a hard-laboring sower), of which there is no other evidence in the known works of this painter. He thus demonstrated an impressive ability to evolve, and the presumed dating of his work should be based on this evolution.

In addition to the influence of this manuscript on Provençal illuminators, already amply demonstrated by Avril (Paris 2003), we should add the impact of this stage of Barthélemy's career on Angevin artistic circles between 1450 and 1470. Are not the medallions in the calendar of the *Morgan Hours* the source from which the Master of the Geneva Bocaccio borrowed the foreshortening of an executioner (BnF, ms. lat. 4915, f. 149)? Are not the putti, animals, and mythical creatures in the borders of the New York manuscript the model for those in the Livy commentary made for Charles of Anjou (Biblioteca Nacional, Lisbon, it. 134, f. 1) and of the Frontinus (Bibliothèque Royale, Brussels, ms. 10475, f. 1) also attributed to the Master of the Geneva Bocaccio? He attempted to mimic the way the figures are integrated into the overall border design through their gestures, but he did not match the naturalness and elegance with which the little figures in the *Morgan Hours* cling to or part the branches, and slip through or sit astride the scrollwork. • M-CL

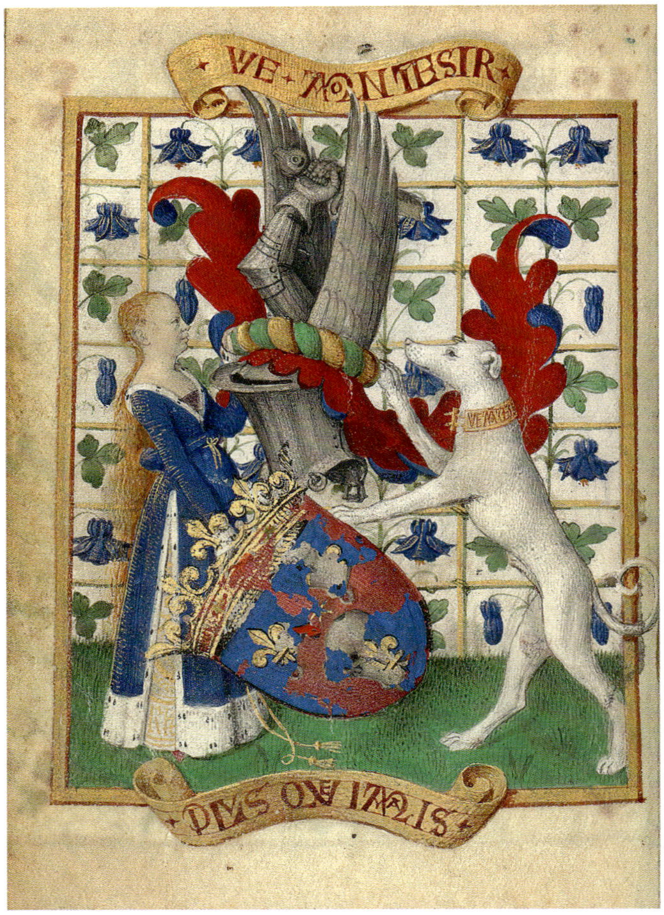

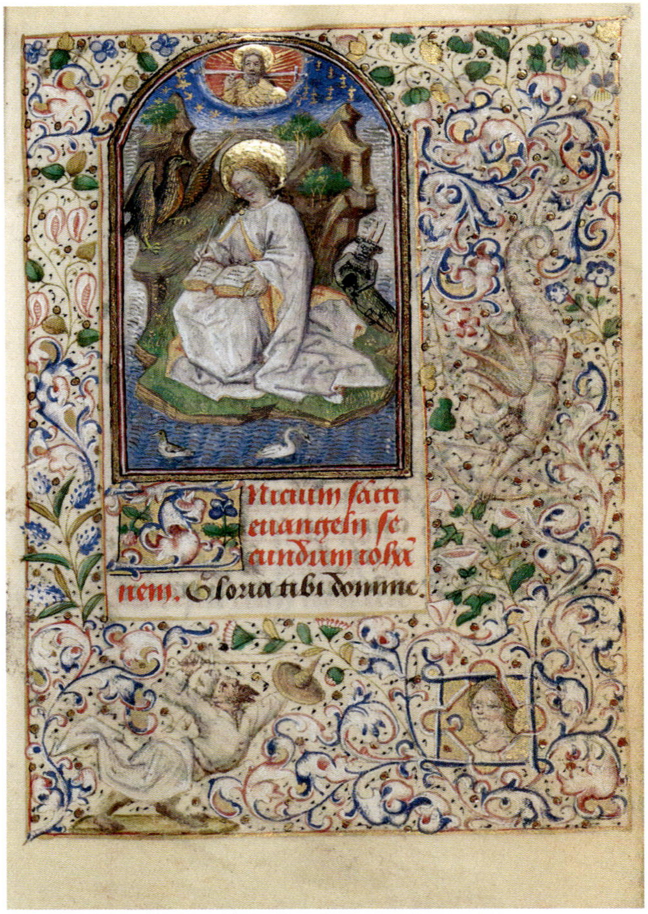

[3]

HOURS OF SIMON DE VARIE

JEAN FOUQUET
(c. 1420–c. 1480)

Escutcheon Supported by a Woman and a Greyhound

CHIEF ASSOCIATE OF THE BEDFORD MASTER
(active c. 1440–66)

Saint John on Patmos

Tours and Paris, 1455

Tempera and painted gold and silver on parchment; 11.4 x 8.3 cm (4½ x 3¼ in.)

The J. Paul Getty Museum, Los Angeles, 85.ML.27 (ms. 7, ff. 2v–3)

PROVENANCE: Made for Simon de Varie, Bourges (d. c. 1463), 1455; Philippe de Béthune (d. 1699). Fletcher, London; sold to Mr. and Mrs. Gerald Borrmann, Lafayette, Calif.; partially given to the J. Paul Getty Museum, 1985.

BIBLIOGRAPHY: Marrow 1985. Avril 1985a. Marrow 1987. Schaefer 1994, pp. 166–69, 310–11. Marrow and Avril 1994. Turner in Los Angeles 2005, pp. 67–69, 71–72, figs. 3.12–.14, 3.18.

EXHIBITIONS: Paris 1993, pp. 43–44, 136–39, no. 69. Paris 2003, pp. 187–92, cat. 23.

THE TWO MINIATURES on view, painted by different artists at separate locations, appear in a private prayer book made for Simon de Varie, a functionary in the royal treasury of Languedoc under Charles VII. The miniature on the left, illuminated by the court painter Jean Fouquet, shows a woman and a greyhound supporting an escutcheon with Varie's arms, visible under seventeenth-century overpainting now partially flaked away. The shield is surmounted by a colorful winged helmet and an arm clad in armor brandishing a broken sword. Varie's personal devices, *Vie a mon desir* (Life according to my wish) and *Plus que jamais* (More than ever), appear at the top and bottom of the image. The elegance and delicacy of the profiles of the maiden and the greyhound anchor the exuberant silhouette of the escutcheon, in front of the perfectly proportioned grid of a trellis of columbine. Such sophisticated and original heraldic formulations remind us that court artists such as Fouquet, who served both Charles VII and Louis XI, were called on not only to illuminate manuscripts and paint portraits, but also to supply a myriad of other kinds of work, including ephemera for court ceremonies and processions, and designs for more lasting pieces, such as Fouquet's stained glass design with similar women supporting the initials of Laurens Girard (cat. 5). Girard, like Varie, was a treasury official. Such works belonged to the elaborate machinery of court propaganda. Thus miniatures such as this one shed light on a substantive aspect of court artists' work that is today nearly entirely lost.

This particular illumination belongs to a suite of six heraldic miniatures that Fouquet supplied as a frontispiece to proclaim the patron's social eminence and devout character. The group also includes a diptych of the handsome Varie kneeling in prayer before the Virgin and Child (ff. 1v–2). Fouquet was one of the first masters of the new art of the individual portrait.

The original book, now divided between the Getty and the Royal Library of the Netherlands in the Hague, opened with these six miniatures by Fouquet, but in fact two older Parisian artists, the Master of Jean Rolin (active c. 1445–65) and the Chief Associate of the Bedford Master, illuminated the rest of the book. They were responsible for a lavish decorative program including twenty-four roundels in the calendar, forty-five half-page devotional miniatures, and six historiated initials. The wholly distinctive idiom of these illuminators is evident in the white hue that dominates the book's overall design, including the bright robes of the figures—such as that of Saint John the Evangelist, shown here—and the dense borders composed of flowers, vines, acanthus, grotesque figures, and drolleries. The heraldic miniature did not originally appear opposite the depiction of Saint John; rather, the present pairing resulted from the shuffling of pages when the manuscript was broken up in the seventeenth century. • TK

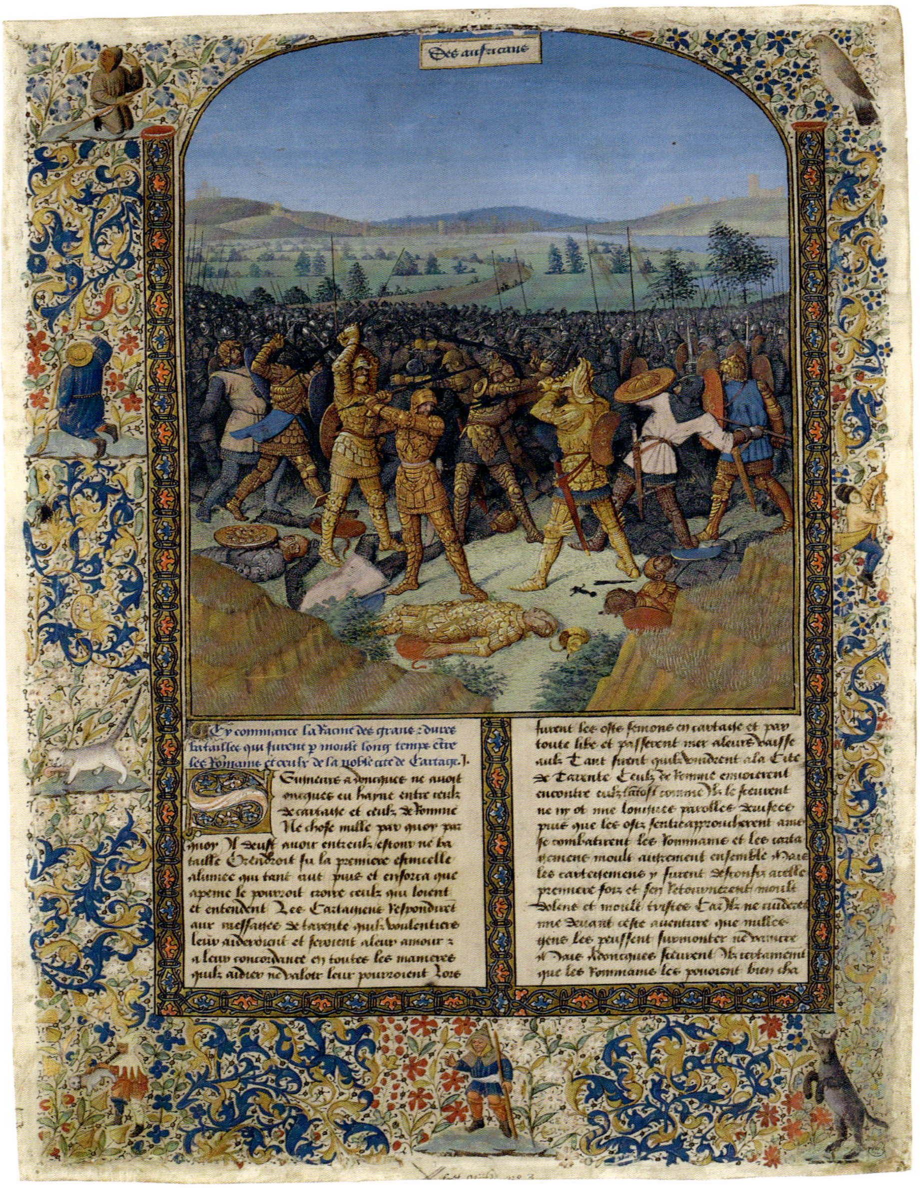

[4]

ATTRIBUTED TO JEAN FOUQUET
(c. 1420–c. 1480)

A Battle between the Romans and the Carthaginians

Removed from a copy of the *Histoire ancienne jusqu'à César* and *Les Faits des Romains*

Tours, 1470/75

Tempera and gold on parchment; 44.8 x 33.4 cm ($17^{5}/_{8}$ x $13^{1}/_{8}$ in.)

Musée du Louvre, Paris, Department of Graphic Arts, RF 5271

PROVENANCE: W. H. Crawford, Lakelands, Cork; sold, Sotheby's, London, March 12, 1891, no. 2113 (with three other pages from the same manuscript, also in the Louvre); sold through Quaritch's to Henry Yates Thompson; sold, Sotheby's, London, June 22, 1921, no. 95, to the Société des Amis du Louvre.

BIBLIOGRAPHY: Thompson 1903. Avril in Paris 2003, no. 30.

EXHIBITIONS: Paris 1904, no. 354. London 1932, no. 747a. Tours 1952, no. 24. Paris 1955–56, no. 252. Paris 1981, no. 22. Paris 1991a, no. 72. Paris 1993–94, no. 72. Washington 1995, no. 44. Paris 2003, no. 29.

WHEN PAINTERS OF THE early Renaissance, such as Jean Fouquet and his workshop, illustrated texts dating from the beginning of the thirteenth century, like the *Histoire ancienne jusqu'à César* and its sequel *Les Faits des Romains*, they could draw upon the Gothic tradition. This battle scene and four other surviving illustrations of major text divisions demonstrate the freedom of an artist securely rooted in the art of his own country, but open to new experiences encountered during a trip to Italy.

The Coronation of Alexander (fig. 21), also in the Louvre, recalls Parisian formulas of around 1415, such as the *Coronation of Hannibal* painted by the Master of Mazarine 469 in a volume of Livy's history of Rome (Bibliothèque nationale de France, ms. fr. 259, f. 253; Meiss 1968, fig. 432). In the placement of the throne between the people on one side and the Roman army on the other, one senses the echo of the tripartite Gothic architectural framework, which was abandoned here in favor of Corinthian pilasters. The baldachin extending from a wall parallel to the picture plane recalls *sacra conversazione* compositions, such as Fra Angelico's 1439 altarpiece of San Marco in Florence. The idea of showing a view of buildings in full daylight beyond the wall recalls the art of Jan van Eyck; on the other hand, the restriction of color around the throne to gold is characteristic of Fouquet.

In his arrangement of heads, the Tours artist follows a strict triangular arrangement. His fascination with this pattern may be why, in *The Battle of the Romans and the Carthaginians*, he did not represent the Carthaginians on elephants. Seen from the vantage point of two small hills, and without any markers of location or date, champions of the two armies confront each other on foot, without cavalry. Painted monochromatically in gold, they are shown as a sea of soldiers whose contour forms a triangle that anticipates the distant horizon, which one reaches through a peaceful landscape that, as always in the art of Fouquet and his workshop, evokes the Loire Valley. • EK

[5]

JEAN FOUQUET
(c. 1420–c. 1480)

Roundel with the Monogram of Laurens Girard

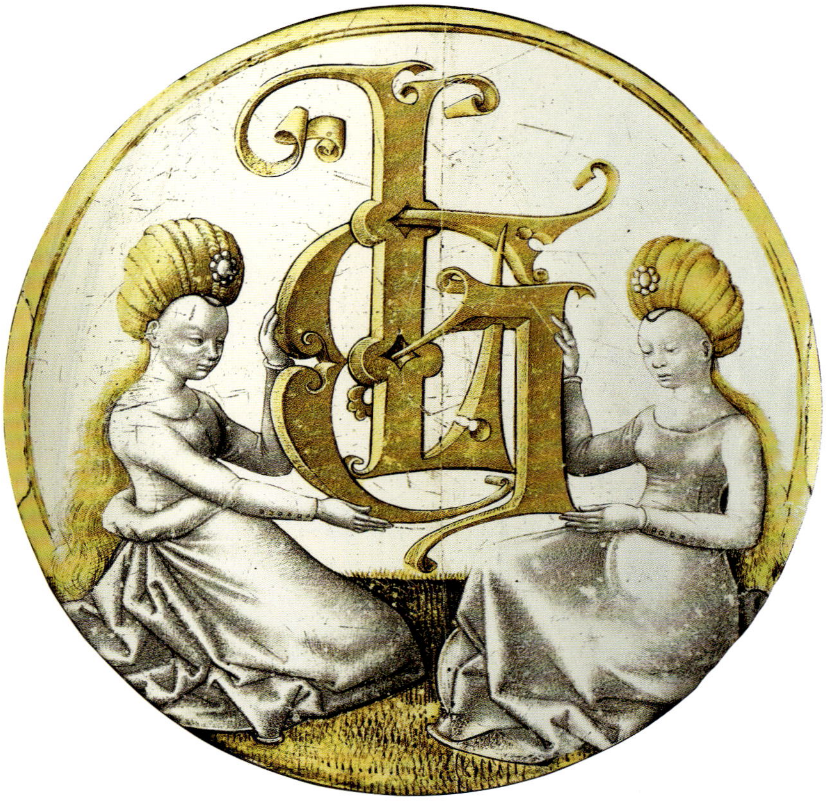

Design: Tours

Glass: Probably Paris, c. 1460

Stained glass; diam. 20 cm (7⅞ in.)

Musée de Cluny—Musée national du Moyen Age, Paris, Cl. 1037 a

PROVENANCE: Found in a later stained glass setting in the Musée national de la Renaissance, Château d'Ecouen, 1992; removed and deposited at the Musée national du Moyen Age, Paris.

BIBLIOGRAPHY: Jacky 1992. Reynaud in Paris 1993, p. 138. Jacky 1993. Perrot 1993–94. Marrow and Avril 1994. Caviness 1995. Lorentz 1999b, no. 4, pp. 36–37. Reynaud 2006, pp. 18, 150.

EXHIBITION: Paris 2003, no. 18, pp. 164–66.

EVER SINCE THE early 1990s, when Jacky identified this roundel in the storage of the Château d'Ecouen, where it had until then been mounted in a stained glass composition with later Renaissance elements, scholars have agreed that it was closely connected to Jean Fouquet. As the only known contribution of this artist or his workshop to stained glass, it may have been executed in Tours or, more probably, in Paris. The monogram *LG* undoubtedly refers to Laurens Girard, and puts this exceptional piece of heraldic imagery in direct relation to the personal circle of Etienne Chevalier, the artist's most important patron: Laurens Girard was a son-in-law of Chevalier, who, as treasurer of Charles VII, may have been instrumental for Fouquet's relations to the royal court in Tours. Girard owned the famous copy of the *Livre des cas de nobles hommes et femmes*, called the Munich Boccaccio (Bayerische Staatsbibliothek, Munich, cod. gall. 6).

Around 1455, Fouquet revived the concept of elegant women presenting heraldic devices on some pages in the *Hours of Simon de Varie* (cat. 3), made for another personality of the same court circle. In costume—especially the huge turban—and style, these figures in the book of hours are perfectly compatible with the two ladies seated holding the letters *L* and *G* in the stained-glass roundel. The identification of the artist, however, has been made somewhat more complicated by a new attribution. In 2003, François Avril split the corpus of painting hitherto widely accepted as by Fouquet into the artist's own oeuvre and that of a close collaborator now called the Master of the Munich Boccaccio. The question, finally, is: Did Laurens Girard distinguish between the master and the collaborator when he ordered the pattern that would be the basis of the stained glass roundel, or did he ask Fouquet himself, who then had it executed in his workshop anyway? In any case, Avril gave to Fouquet himself the most famous painting in the Munich manuscript, the full page miniature of the *Lit de Justice of Vendôme of 1458*.

Apart from this question of the possible differentiation of hands, the roundel proves the involvement of Fouquet's workshop in stained glass production. Of utmost importance for French art at the dawn of Renaissance, this piece witnesses the self-consciousness of a class of rich courtiers and administrators around Charles VII, who displayed their monograms and other heraldic devices lavishly. It renews the idea of women presenting armorials, far removed from a late Gothic sensibility, and it shows a new interest in the design of letters, mixing Gothic and classical traditions. • EK

TRIPTYCH OF DREUX BUDÉ

MASTER OF DREUX BUDÉ (ANDRÉ D'YPRES?)
(active by 1425/26–died 1450)

[6]

The Betrayal of Christ with Dreux Budé and His Son Presented by Saint Christopher

c. 1450

Oil on panel; 48.8 x 30.5 cm (19 3/16 x 12 in.)

Private collection

PROVENANCE: Probably chapel of the Virgin and Saint Christopher, church of Saint-Gervais–Saint-Protais, Paris, with cats. 7–8. H. Becker, Dortmund, by 1954; Heinrich Bischof (d. 2005), Bremen and Berlin; by descent.

BIBLIOGRAPHY, EXHIBITIONS: See cat. 8.

[7]

The Crucifixion

c. 1450

Oil on panel; 47.9 x 71.8 cm (18 7/8 x 28 1/4 in.)

The J. Paul Getty Museum, Los Angeles, 79.PB.177

PROVENANCE: Probably chapel of the Virgin and Saint Christopher, Church of Saint-Gervais–Saint-Protais, Paris, with cats. 7–8. Private collection, France; sold, Palais des Congrès, Versailles, November 19, 1978, no. 88; Galerie Heim, Paris; sold to the museum, 1979.

BIBLIOGRAPHY, EXHIBITIONS: See cat. 8.

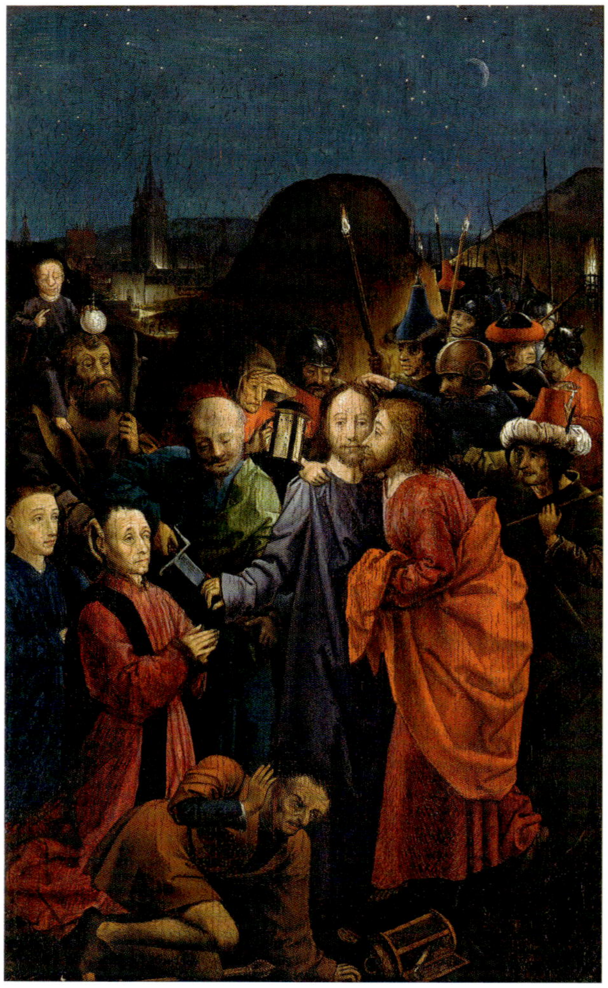

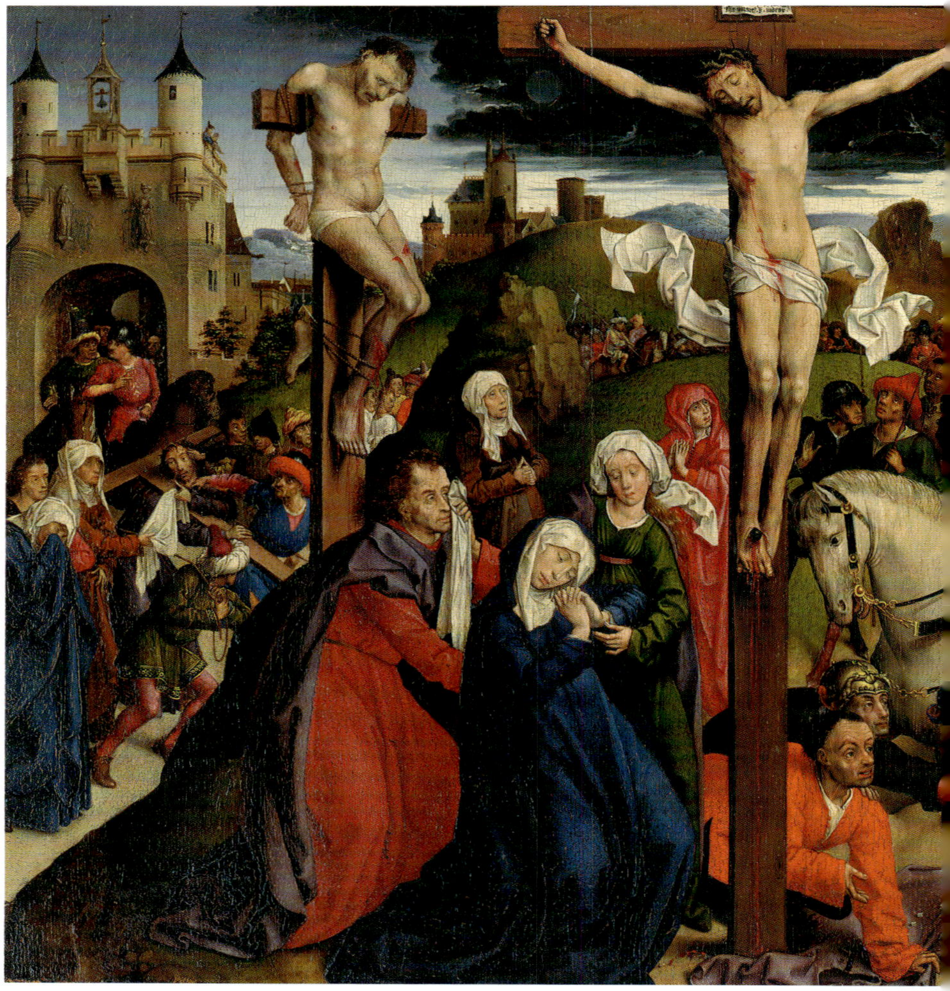

[8]

The Resurrection with Jeanne Peschard and Her Daughters Presented by Saint Catherine

c. 1450

Oil on panel; 48.5 x 30.5 cm (19 1/16 x 12 in.)

Musée Fabre, Montpellier, 892.4.7

PROVENANCE: Probably chapel of the Virgin and Saint Christopher, Church of Saint-Gervais–Saint-Protais, Paris, with cats. 7–8. François Sabatier; given to the museum, 1892.

BIBLIOGRAPHY: Baldass 1920–21, pp. 634–47. Stange 1934–61, vol. 6, p. 67. Fredericksen 1983, pp. 183–96. Sterling 1987–90, vol. 2, pp. 50–75. Reynaud in Paris 1993, pp. 53–58. Dijkstra 1997, pp. 53–59. Lorentz 1998, pp. 101–24. Lorentz and Comblen-Sonkes 2001, pp. 81–132. Lorentz 2004, pp. 40–49. Nettekoven 2004, pp. 34–37.

EXHIBITIONS: London 1927, no. 34 (cat. 8 only). Dortmund 1954, no. 23 (cat. 6 only). Brussels/Delft 1957–58, no. 76 (cat. 6 only). Leuven 1998, no. 84 (cat. 8 only). Bruges 2002, no. 68 (cats. 6 and 8 only).

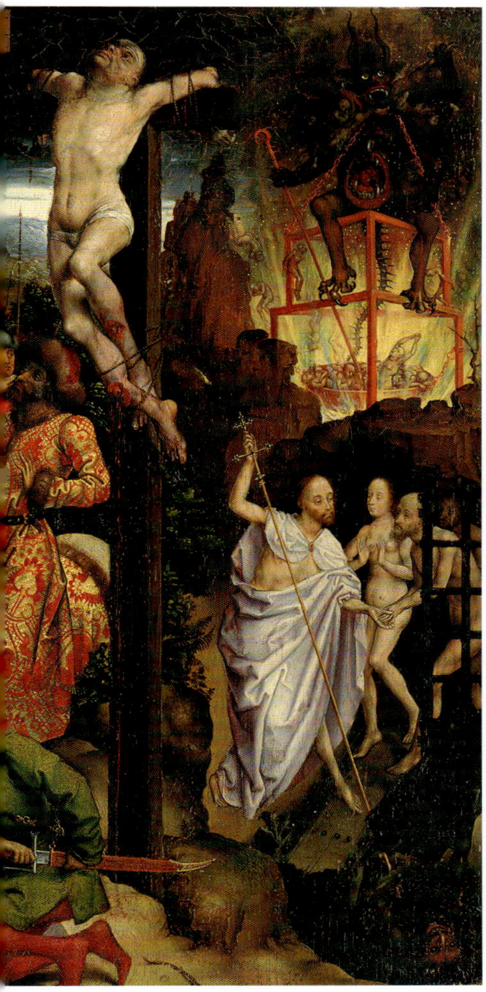

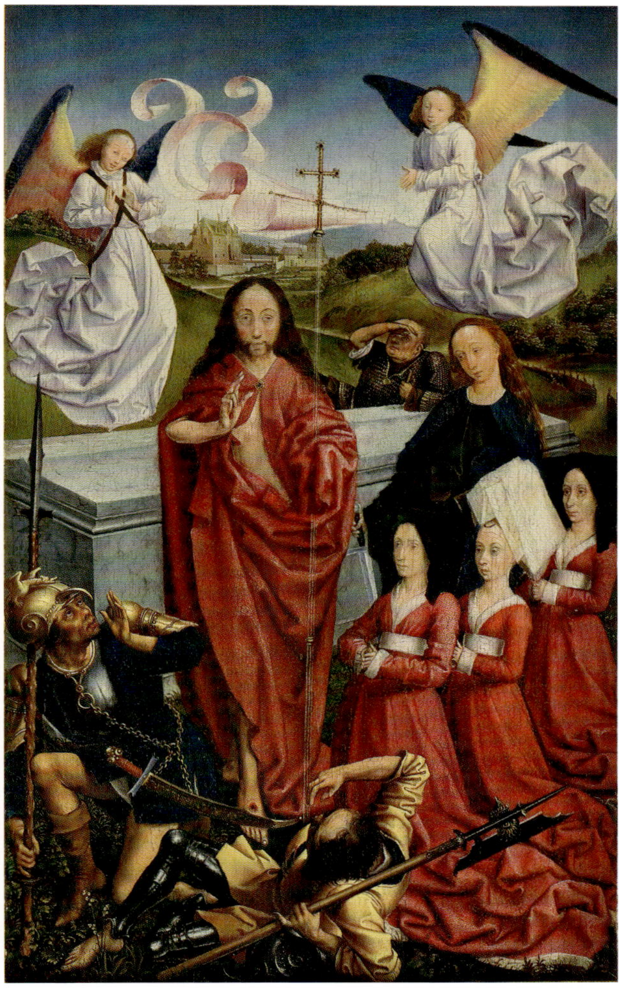

IN 1979, a *Crucifixion* profoundly influenced by Rogier van der Weyden's art entered the collection of the J. Paul Getty Museum, having appeared the previous year in a French auction. Though initially regarded as an independent work, it was actually the central element of a triptych whose wings represented the Betrayal of Christ with two donors presented by Saint Christopher on the left and the Resurrection with three donors presented by Saint Catherine on the right, as Burton Fredericksen demonstrated (1983). Very recently studied by Rachel Billinge, the vigorous underdrawing in the *Betrayal of Christ*, with its abundant use of hatching (fig. 25), is very similar to the underdrawing of the *Crucifixion*, and supports the conclusion that these two panels belong to the same group. The width of the central panel (71.8 cm, or 28¼ in.) corresponds to the dimensions of the altar of a chapel or a secondary altar of a church.

With its scenes of the Arrest of Christ, the Crucifixion, and the Resurrection, the opened triptych displayed to the faithful the key events of the end of Christ's earthly life and the fulfillment of the plan for salvation. Christ sacrificed on the cross dominates the center of the altarpiece; his figure hangs in the location where the priest would have elevated the host while celebrating mass. Jesus is flanked by the crosses of the two thieves. At the foot of his cross are the traditional figures of the Crucifixion drama: on the left, the swooning Virgin, supported by Saint John the Evangelist and a holy woman, and, on the right, Roman soldiers casting dice to decide who gets Christ's robe, together with the centurion mounted on a white horse and dressed in a rich brocade robe. This scene is the culmination of a narrative that includes, on the same panel, Christ Carrying the Cross (left) and his Descent into Limbo (right). This sequence of scenes is customary in narrative treatments of the Crucifixion created in the mid-fifteenth century, as is demonstrated by a number of examples in Westphalia. However, here the painter has introduced some unusual elements. In the Carrying of the Cross, Saint Veronica does not simply display the *sudarium*, the veil on which the image of the Holy Face (*Vera Icon*) has been miraculously imprinted. Rather, she approaches Christ directly, and he returns to her the precious relic, having used it to wipe his face. Even more unusual is the elaborate detail of hell adjacent to the scene of limbo: an enormous pit of fire filled to the brim with damned souls roasting under the supervision of a hideous demon—a terrifying vision of the torments that await those who turn from God.

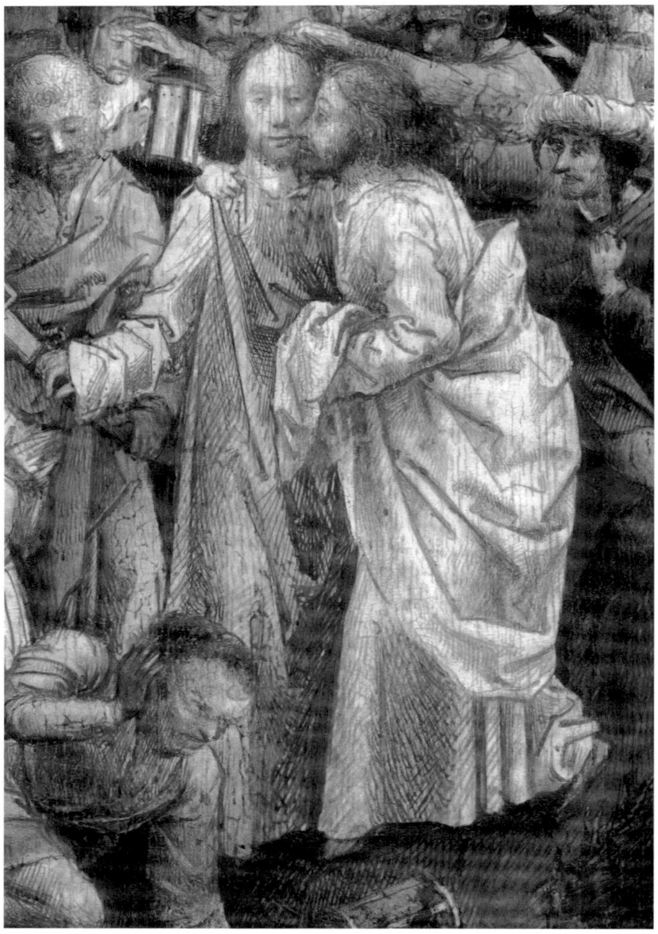

FIGURE 25.
Master of Dreux Budé (André d'Ypres?).
Detail of infrared reflectogram assembly of *The Betrayal of Christ with Dreux Budé and His Son Presented by Saint Christopher*. Courtesy of Rachel Billinge, National Gallery, London.

There is no longer any trace of imagery on the reverse of the wings; they must have originally been painted with scenes that were visible when the triptych was closed. Following a practice that was widespread in the fifteenth century north of the Alps, the exterior of the wings was probably painted in grisaille. The painter used this mode of pictorial representation elsewhere: we know of a grisaille panel by his hand (current location unknown; see Sterling 1990, p. 50, fig. 26), unrelated to this triptych, but representing the same three women as donors. An escutcheon allows us to identify them as Jeanne Peschard, the wife of Dreux Budé, and their two daughters, Jacquette and Catherine. Dreux Budé is represented on the triptych's left wing, with his son Jean. Dreux Budé and Jeanne Peschard were married in 1422; their families were among the most prominent members of the Parisian bourgeoisie. The Budés, who were originally from Auxerre, gained their wealth through the wine trade and were established in Paris by the end of the fourteenth century. Dreux Budé served Charles VII during the darkest days of his monarchy. Notary and secretary to the king, he was named *audiencier* of the royal Chancellery in 1440 and was subsequently keeper of the king's charters. His career as a court official reached its peak in the 1450s, but continued after Charles VII died in 1461, until his own death around 1475/76. Between 1452 and 1456, in his role as dean of merchants, he headed the municipality of Paris. Benefiting from a considerable fortune, he enjoyed a number of seigneuries in the Ile-de-France. In 1444, the younger of the two Budé daughters, Catherine (died 1452), married Étienne Chevalier, who commissioned Fouquet to create a remarkable book of hours (1452/61) and the celebrated Melun Diptych (1452/55; now divided between Berlin and Antwerp).

From the time they first settled in Paris, the Budé family belonged to the parish of Saint-Gervais–Saint-Protais. In the middle of the fifteenth century, Dreux Budé and Jeanne Peschard founded a chapel dedicated to the Virgin and Saint Christopher in the chevet behind the main altar, intending it to house their tombs. The presence of Saint Christopher on the left wing, presenting Dreux Budé, leaves no room for doubt as to the original destination of this triptych: the altar of the Budé family chapel, built around 1450 in the church of Saint-Gervais in Paris.

The painter of the Dreux Budé triptych was none other than the author of the *Crucifixion of the Parlement of Paris* (Musée du Louvre, Paris; fig. 22) who introduced the *ars nova* to the capital of the kingdom of France. Analysis of the two works reveals the same cultural frame of reference—an awareness of models emanating from the workshop of the Master of Flémalle and motifs borrowed from the repertory of Rogier van der Weyden (Sterling 1990, pp. 62–63, 70–71; Dijkstra 1997; Lorentz 1998, pp. 108–11). Comparison of the two works shows the same closely related facial types: the Roman soldiers at the foot of the cross in the Budé *Crucifixion* and the executioners of Saint Denis and his companions in the background of the *Crucifixion of the Parlement de Paris* have the same caricatural, hate-filled faces. Of course the tranquil arrangement of the monumental figures in the *Crucifixion of the Parlement* is absent from the Budé triptych, which is characterized by throngs of small figures in motion. But these differences can be explained by the vast discrepancy in scale between the monumental panel from the hall of justice, intended to be seen from a distance, and the retable, painted for the altar of a private chapel. Despite the disparity in scale, it is striking to observe how the painter prepared his composition in an identical fashion before applying the paint layer. In the *Betrayal of Christ* and the *Crucifixion* of the Budé triptych, as in the *Crucifixion of the Parlement* (Lorentz and Comblen-Sonkes 2001, pls. 62–66), there is a very similar definition of the figures, with highly detailed brush underdrawing to indicate the forms, through a dense network of hatching (sometimes crisscrossed), as is clearly visible in the cloak worn by Judas in the *Betrayal of Christ* (fig. 25).

The Parisian activity of the "Master of Dreux Budé" went beyond the confines of easel painting. He furnished cartoons for stained glass for the nave of the church of Saint-Séverin and produced illuminated manuscripts (Reynaud in Paris 1993, pp. 53–59). His miniatures are so close in style to those of a painter and illuminator active in Paris in the second half of the fifteenth century, the Master of Coëtivy, that some of his works were formerly attributed to the latter, who was younger by a generation than the Master of Dreux Budé. This stylistic relationship could be explained by the existence of a familial relationship between the two artists, that of father and son. Indeed, the Master of Dreux Budé could have been André d'Ypres, a painter mentioned in Amiens from 1425–26, who was admitted as a free master in the Tournai guild on September 13, 1428, and settled in Paris about 1445. His son Nicolas (or Colin) d'Amiens would be the Master of Coëtivy. When André d'Ypres died in 1450, the *Crucifixion of the Parlement* was probably still in progress, and Nicolas d'Amiens would have been able to finish the work after his father's death, based on a quite detailed underdrawing. The Budé triptych, usually dated 1454 (the presumed date of the foundation of the Budé chapel in Saint-Gervais), would initially seem to contradict this proposed attribution (Nettekoven 2004, p. 35). This traditional dating should be reconsidered, however, because in 1453, in the document in which Dreux Budé and Jeanne Peschard established a low mass in their chapel in Saint-Gervais, it is referred to as "newly built" (*de nouvel*; Archives nationales, Paris, L 651). We therefore cannot exclude the possibility that the chapel had already been constructed several years previously and that the Budé triptych was painted slightly before 1450, like the *Crucifixion of the Parlement de Paris*. André d'Ypres therefore remains a strong candidate for identification as the Master of Dreux Budé. • PL

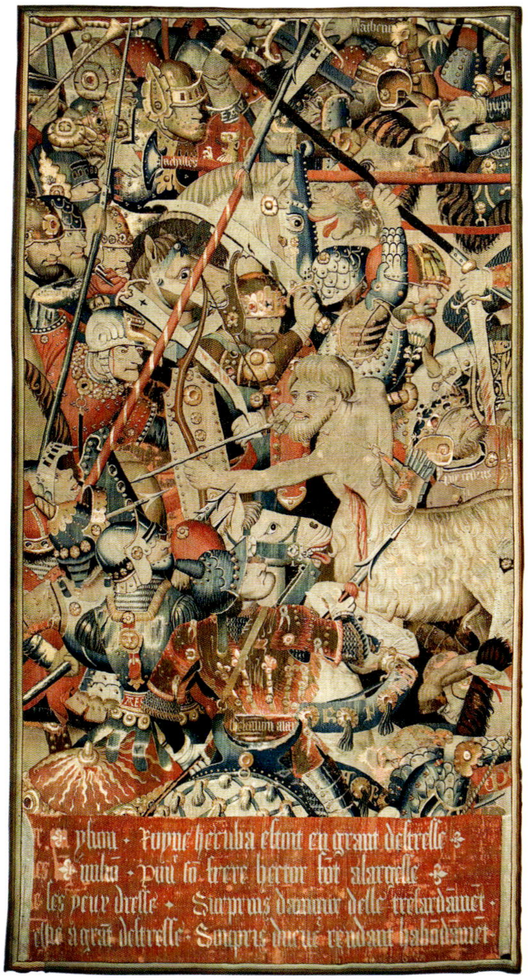

[9]

The Sagittary Fighting the Greeks, a fragment from the sixth tapestry of the Story of the Trojan War

1475/1500

Design: Master of Coëtivy (Colin d'Amiens?) (active c. 1445–died 1497/1500)

Weaving: Southern Netherlands, probably Tournai

Wool and silk; 6 warps per cm; 358.1 x 195.6 cm (141 x 77 in.)

Worcester Art Museum, Massachusetts, gift from the estate of Mrs. Aldus Chapin Higgins, 1970.125

INSCRIBED: *..[n] ❀ ylion ♦ Royne Hecuba estoit en grant destresse / ..[es ❀ unbon] ♦ Pour son frere hector font alargesse / ..[l]es yeux dresse ♦ Surprins [da]mour delle tresardamment / ..elhe [for (reto)urne] a grant destresse ♦ Soupris du cuer rendan[t]habondamment*

PROVENANCE: Château of Sully, Maine-et-Loire, 1860. Amsterdam art market; Otto H. Kahn (d. 1934), New York, by 1925; his widow, Adelaide W. Kahn; sold to Aldus Chapin Higgins with Inglis Griswold as agent, 1937; given to the museum, 1970.

BIBLIOGRAPHY: Hunter 1925, pp. 75–77, pls. S, m. Forsyth 1955, p. 78. Asselberghs 1970, pp. 97–98, 110, 114, 173, 176, 177, fig. 14. Asselberghs 1974, p. 18. Hébert 1976, pp. 109–10. McKendrick 1991, pp. 62–63, 74–75, pl. 15b. Cavallo 1993, pp. 231–49, fig. 108. Delmarcel 2000, p. 30.

EXHIBITION: New York 1974, no. 9.

ANCIENT HISTORY AND MYTH were intertwined with medieval romances and Christian ideals as subjects for art and literature in the mid-fifteenth century. Thus the narrative of the Trojan War was based not on Homer, but on more recent retellings, notably Benoît de Sainte-Maure's *Roman de Troie* (c. 1160) and Guido delle Colonne's *Historia destructionis Troiae* (1280/90), which highlighted the chivalric deeds of heroes such as Hector and Achilles.

In the mid-1460s, Pasquier Grenier, the foremost tapestry merchant of Tournai, began production of an eleven-piece set of tapestries illustrating the *Story of the Trojan War* that would enjoy great success with princely patrons in succeeding decades. Charles VIII, Charles the Bold of Burgundy, Henry VII of England, Ferdinand I of Naples, Federico da Montefeltro of Urbino, and Ludovico Sforza of Milan owned sets. Moreover, with the survival of whole or partial preparatory drawings for nine of the eleven tapestries (cat. 10), as well as seventeen extant tapestries or fragments from various sets, it is possible to reconstruct the order of the series.

This fragment showing the Sagittary, a fierce centaur archer, fighting the Greek cavalry in the fifth battle of the war, was part of the sixth tapestry, which also featured the meeting of Achilles and Hector in Achilles's tent and Hector arming himself for battle. Inscriptions on armor, weapons, and horse trappings permit the identification of the densely packed figures, including Ajax Telamon (center) and Achilles (upper left, aiming a lance).

Though no intact weaving of this tapestry survives, an example missing only the left quarter, which included the battle with the Sagittary, is preserved in the cathedral of Zamora. This tapestry is almost sixteen feet in height, with the figures supplemented by scrolls with explanatory verses in French at the top and narrower scrolls with Latin summaries at the bottom. The Worcester Sagittary fragment and two other fragments (another also in Worcester and one in the Burrell Collection, Glasgow) all share the same recent provenance. The latter two were cut from a weaving of the seventh tapestry in the series, illustrating the commemoration of the anniversary of the death of Hector. The French verses were originally at the top of all three of these fragments; at an unknown date, the inscriptions were removed and transposed. Consequently, the verses on the fragment of the Sagittary refer not to this scene, but to Hector's death, shown in the next tapestry in the series, while verses cut from the sixth tapestry were then joined to the bottom of the other two fragments (Worcester and Glasgow). This transposition of the verses and the common provenance of these three fragments suggest that they may have been part of the same set. Their first patron is unknown, but their adaptation and survival is an indication of the esteem this huge and vivid series enjoyed over many centuries. • KD

[10]

MASTER OF COËTIVY (COLIN D'AMIENS?)
(active c. 1445–died 1497/1500)

The Fourth Battle, the Taking of King Thoas, and the Chamber of Beauty

Paris, c. 1460/65

Pen and brown ink with red, blue, green and ochre washes, white body color on the female faces, on paper; 30.5 x 57.5 cm (12 x 22⅝ in.)

Musée du Louvre, Paris, Department of Graphic Arts, RF 2142

PROVENANCE: Gutbier, Dresden; bought by the Louvre, 1899.

BIBLIOGRAPHY: Lugt 1968, pp. 17–24, pl. 24. Asselberghs 1970, pp. 101, 108–09, fig. 8. Reynaud 1973, p. 7. Hébert 1976, pp. 109–10. McKendrick 1991, pp. 63, 69–73, pl. 19a. Reynaud in Paris 1993, pp. 58–69. Nettekoven 2004, p. 41.

NINE DRAWINGS IN PARIS offer the rare opportunity to compare fragments of tapestry in several collections with an earlier stage of the project. Six nearly complete drawings and fragments of two others are in the Musée du Louvre (RF 2140–2147); one complete drawing is housed in the Bibliothèque nationale de France (Print Room, Ob 62). The complete sequence contained eleven tapestries, forming a narrative more than one hundred meters long (see cat. 9). Possibly conceived in the early 1460s for Charles of France, younger son of Charles VII, the series was much in demand from the merchants Jean and Pasquier Grenier of Tournai for princely patrons throughout Europe.

The Fourth Battle—one of the better-preserved drawings—is a preparation for the fifth tapestry. The battle takes place between the Greek camp, hidden behind hills on the left, and the walls of Troy, on the right. In the lower left corner, Patroclus is shown being dragged away over the bodies of slain Greeks, despite the fact that he should be carried away, slung over the horse of Merion. He is also inaccurately shown as a mature warrior, not a young man. The battle continues: the Greek king Menelaus, on horseback, leads his army, while Paris, who lost his horse, stands beside him. Their names are inscribed on their sword and shield, respectively.

The same characters are shown in more than one episode. Thus King Thoas watches the battle from his prison in a Trojan tower, making him a witness to his own capture. This earlier event occurs below, in front of the city gate, where his enemies lead him into Troy, brandishing his royal helmet on a stick or a lance. Helen and Hecuba watch from the walls of Troy, and they appear again in the door of the Chamber of Beauty. Hecuba, shown young and beautiful, not as a matronly queen, welcomes Aeneas, Antenor, and another warrior, who have come to see Helen.

The best source for the appearance of the tapestry itself, John Carter's late eighteenth-century drawings copying the set then in the British royal collection (Victoria and Albert Museum, London; McKendrick 1991, pl. 11a), indicates that this drawing was not followed precisely. The weavers suppressed the upper level of the battle, rearranged the combat around Paris, and expanded the Chamber of Beauty, among other changes.

Opinion on the role of the drawings in the preparatory process is divided. Nicole Reynaud (1973 and in Paris 1993, pp. 64–66) insists on the happy circumstance that they are the *petits patrons*, sent to the painters who would make the full-scale cartoons, and admires the daring technique of pen drawing that allows no corrections. McKendrick (1991, p. 72), was "inclined to see the Paris drawings as discarded mock-ups of what were to be the *petits patrons*." That they were made in Paris in the 1460s by a painter called the Master of Coëtivy is now commonly accepted. But his identification raises another set of problems: Nicole Reynaud (1973) first identified him with the documented Henri Vulcop (retained by Sterling 1990), but later (Paris 1993, pp. 58–69) advanced the name of Colin d'Amiens (also known as Nicolas d'Ypres), which has been widely accepted. The drawings would then come from the greatest artist working in Paris while Fouquet flourished in Tours, an artist praised by Jean Lemaire de Belges in 1504 as one of the foremost French painters. The dates of the members of this important family of artists of Netherlandish origin are the subject of further study (Nettekoven 2004, pp. 34–35; see also cats. 6–8). • EK

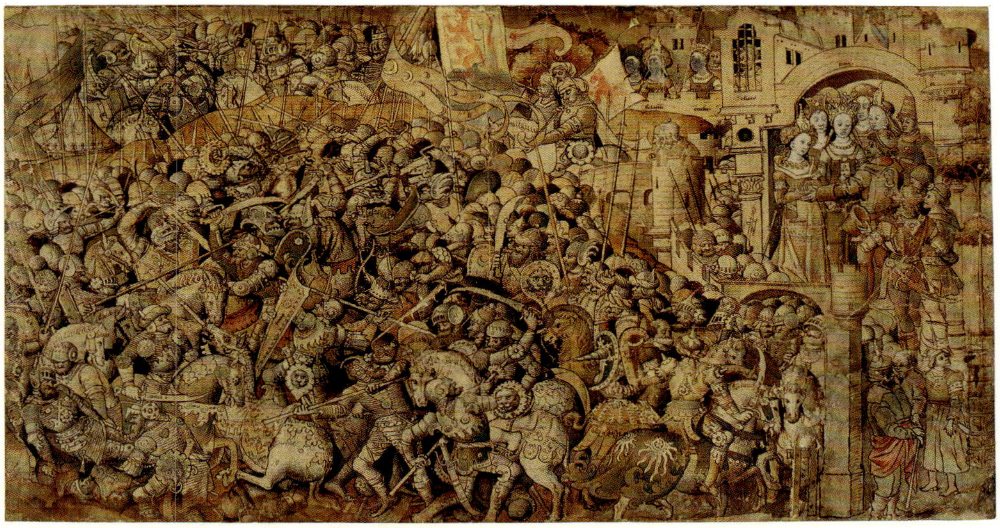

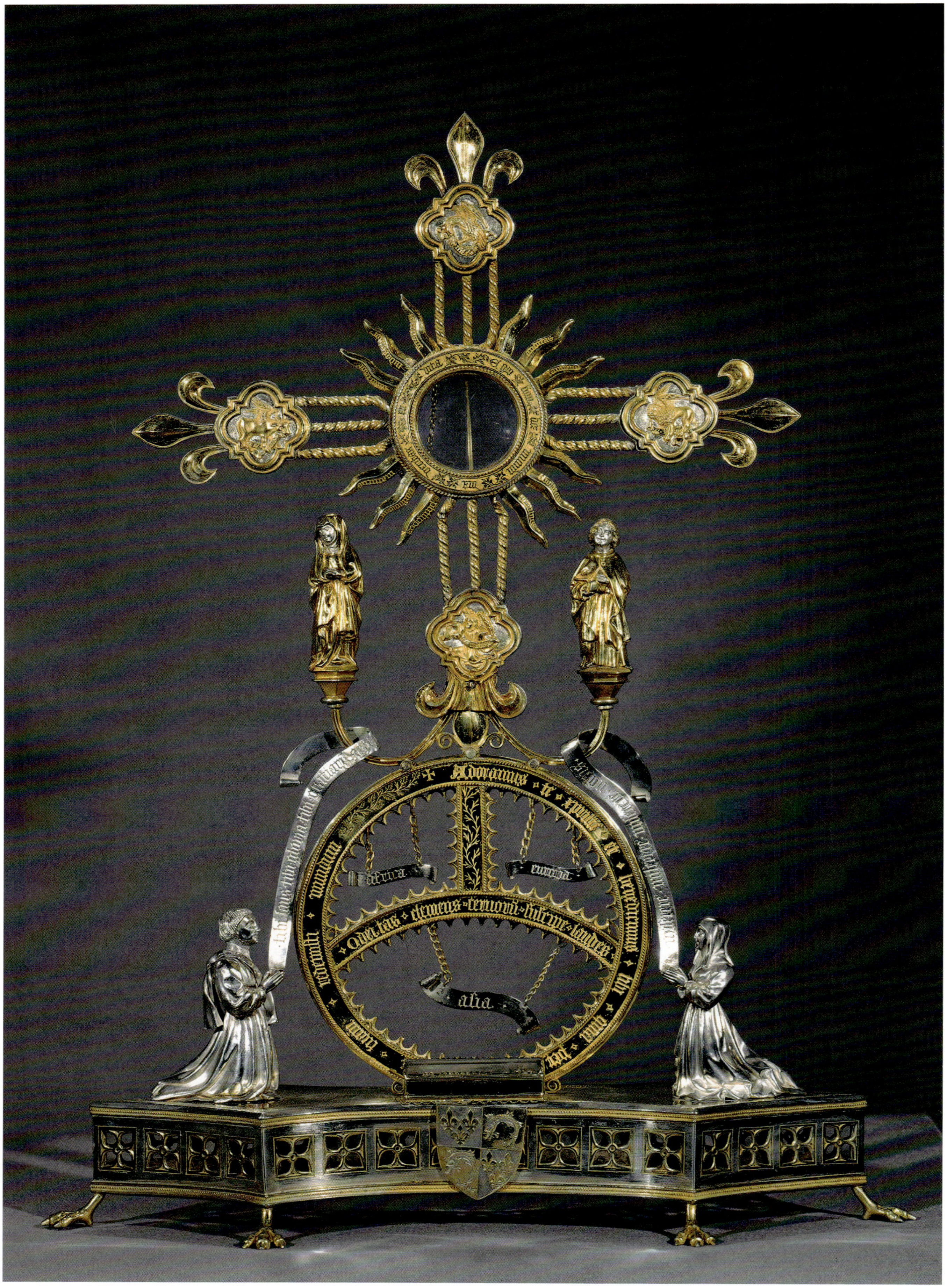

[11]

PIERART RASOIR
(active 1433/64)

Monstrance

Valenciennes, c. 1460

Silver, partially gilded; 54.4 x 41.3 x 15.5 cm (21½ x 16¼ x 6⅛ in.)

Sint-Martinus Basilica, Halle

MARKED: rampant lion (Valenciennes); razor (Pierart Rasoir)

INSCRIBED:

On the pedestal: *Claro paschali gaudio sol mu(n)do mitet radio cu(m) Chr(ist)um iam apostoli visu cernunt corporeo* [The sun shines with a pure ray, bright with paschal joy, while the apostles see Christ again with their eyes of flesh]; *Prietur sicut sol Salvator mundi* [May the Savior of the world arise, like the sun]

Around the large disk: *Adoramus te Christe et benedicimus tibi quia per sanctam crucem tuam redemisti mundum* [We adore you, Christ, and we bless you because by your holy cross you redeemed the world]; *Nos aute[m] Gloria[ri] oportet in cruce D[omi]ni Ihesu Christi in quo est salus vita et resurexio nostra per quem salvati et liberati sumus* [We must be glorified in the cross of Our Lord Jesus Christ, in whom is our salvation, our life, and our resurrection, by whom we are saved and delivered] (on the reverse)

On the internal arc: *O Deitas Clemens cervoru[m] suscipe laudes* [O merciful divinity, receive the praise of your servants]; *Dulce lignu[m] dulces clavos dulcia ferens pondera* [O sweet wood, sweet nails that bear a sweet burden] (on its reverse)

On the pendants: *Europa,* [Afri]*ca, Asia* (in the largest compartment); *Meltior, J*[aspar], *Baltazar* (on the reverse)

On the banderole of the dauphin: *Tibi laus, tibi Gloria tibi [gr]atiaru[m actio]* [To you praise, to you glory, to you thanksgiving]; [...]*f(ac)ti sumus et per s[an]c(t)am cruce(m) liberati [sumus]* [...we have become...and by the holy cross we have been freed] (on the reverse)

On the banderole of Charlotte of Savoy: *Miserere miserere miserere nobis* [Have mercy, have mercy, have mercy on us]; *Fructus arboris seduxi tuos filius dei redemit nos* [I have set aside your fruits of the tree, the son of God has redeemed us] (on its reverse)

On the cross: *Ego sum lux mundi, via, veritas et vita* [I am the light of the world, the way, the truth and the life]; *Panis quem ego dabo caro mea est pro mundi vita* [The bread which I will give you is my flesh for the life of the world] (on the circumference of the disk; *Petrus/Andreas/Jacobus/Johanes/Thomas/Jacobus/Bartholomeus/Matheus/Sim[eonis] Zelot/Judas/Thadeus/Mathias* (on the rays); the symbols of the evangelists, each bearing a banner engraved with his name (in the quatrefoils)

ARMS: Quartered, in 1 and 4 three fleurs-de-lis, in 2 and 3 a dolphin: Dauphin of France (on silver shield; could be a later addition)

BIBLIOGRAPHY: Lipsius 1605. Maillard 1651, p. 353. Crooÿ 1910, pp. 19–30. Lüdke 1983, no. 304. Cartier and Servent 1996, pp. 261–65. Taburet-Delahaye in Prigent 1999, pp. 280–81. Van de Velden 2000, pp. 166–78. Cassagnes-Brouquet 2007, pp. 207–12.

EXHIBITIONS: Bern/Bruges/Vienna 2008–10, no. 65.

THE GIFT OF A silver-gilt cross by the dauphin of France, the future Louis XI, is mentioned as early as the seventeenth century by the historians of the pilgrimage church of Saint Martin in Halle, south of Brussels. The most detailed account, by Maillard (1651), specifies that the object includes the figures of the dauphin and Charlotte of Savoy, married in Namur in January 1457, and that it contains a Holy Thorn. Hence by that date the work was also a reliquary.

The inscriptions indicate the original function and symbolism of this complex work. The large disk divided into three unequal parts represents the earth, with the pendant scrolls bearing the names of the three known continents. The texts engraved around the disk and on its internal arc evoke the redemption of the world through the cross. They are completed by inscriptions on the donors' banderoles: thanksgiving for grace on that of the dauphin, a request for mercy on that of Charlotte of Savoy.

Above this, the cross itself is flanked by freestanding figures of the Virgin and Saint John, and includes at its center a circle surrounded by twelve rays, eleven of them bearing the name of an apostle. The circle served as a monstrance for the display of the Eucharistic host, as revealed by the inscriptions glorifying Christ as light of the world and bread of life. The fleurs-de-lis forming the ends of the cross are preceded by quatrefoils with the four evangelists represented by their symbols on the front and the four fathers of the church on the reverse.

Commissioned by the future Louis XI during his exile in the Low Countries (1457–61) following his quarrel with his father, Charles VII, this object is highly representative not only of a moment in the life of this royal figure and of his precocious interest in sacred goldsmithwork, but also of the development of the cult of Corpus Christi in the fifteenth century. Unique in its form and in the way in which its inscriptions make it a sort of resumé of Christian teaching concerning the cross and the host, this monstrance is also one of the very first examples of the form of a sun surrounded by rays, here made explicit by the inscriptions on the base, which celebrates Christ, the radiant Savior rising like the sun.

Cartier and Servent (1996) identified the hallmark, long confused with that of Brussels, as belonging to the town of Valenciennes, and recognized the stamp of the goldsmith Pierart Rasoir, also the author of the arm-reliquary of Saint George preserved in Lessines, Belgium. The same Valenciennes mark with rampant lion is found on numerous other works from the second half of the fifteenth century, notably the reliquary of the veil of Saint Aldegonde, in the collegiate church of Maubeuge. • ET-D

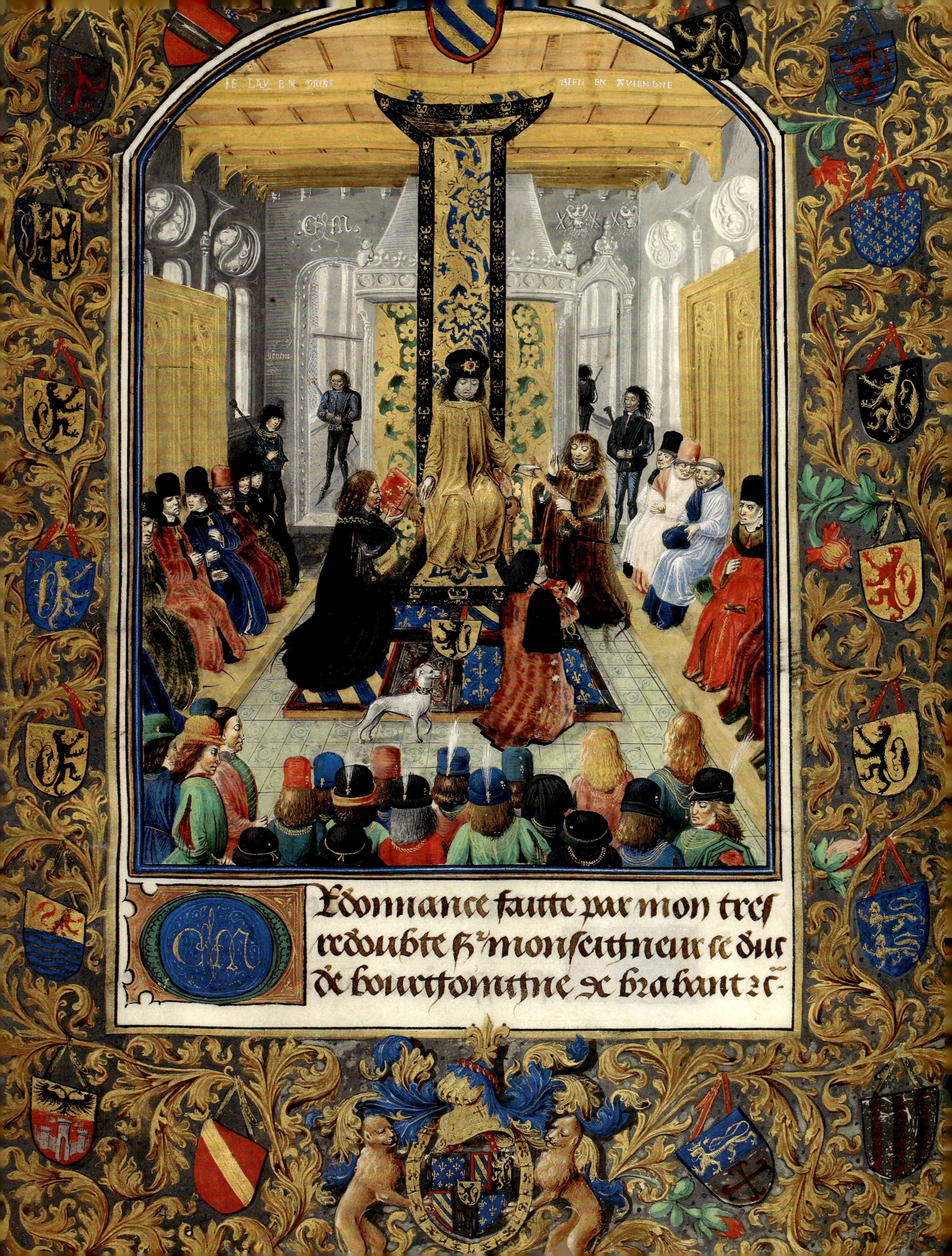
IE LAV EN PRINS
BIEN EN AVIENGNE
Ordonnance faitte par mon tres
redoubte s^r monseigneur le duc
de bourgoingne et brabant &c.

LOUIS XI AND THE PRINCES OF THE BLOOD

MARTHA WOLFF

If the king, his itinerant court, and his administrators located in Tours and in Paris were the source of power and of its visual expression through art, there was another level of royal patronage that was in continuous creative tension with the monarchy. This was the princes of the blood, the younger sons of kings of France and their male descendants, who were in line to succeed to the throne should the king die without a son. To support them in appropriate style, their royal fathers had granted these princes appanages from the royal domain, territories that could, in turn, be passed from father to son and that formed a base of identity and of semi-independent power. The princes of the blood were both a potential support to the monarchy and a threat to royal power through their ambitions, jealousies, and their ability to administer their own territories. They sought to enlarge their power through the same politics of marriage and exchange employed by the kings, even as they built monuments that imitated French royal symbolism. They knew how to draw upon royal prestige in a way that was not open to other great nobles, like the dukes of Brittany, who owed fealty to the king of France, but whose lands were not part of the royal domain.

Before he ascended the throne as Louis XII following Charles VIII's sudden death in 1498 without surviving sons, Louis II of Orléans had been merely a slightly older distant cousin of the king, at once glamorous and intractable. He was the grandson of Louis I of Orléans, the younger son of Charles V (r. 1364–80; see genealogical chart, pp. 12–13), who had given him the duchy of Orléans as an appanage. The Orléans branch of the royal family also included another line, descended from the second son of Louis I of Orléans and his wife Valentina Visconti, the daughter of the first duke of Milan. Given the county of Angoulême in western France, this line would include Francis of Angoulême, the future Francis I; his parents' small but sophisticated court was at Cognac. As king, both Louis of Orléans and Francis of Angoulême would claim the duchy of Milan for France, based on their descent from Valentina Visconti. But, before this turn of events, in the last quarter of the fifteenth century, Louis XI worked to carry forward the consolidation and expansion of the kingdom—begun when the English occupiers were driven out by Charles VII—with a further effort to curb the territory and power of the princes of the blood. Thus, to prevent the young Louis of Orleans from forming an independent marriage alliance, Louis XI had required him to marry his daughter Jeanne of France in 1476, when she was still a child.

Louis XI had to contend with even more long-standing and entrenched lines of princes of the blood, who frequently banded together against the crown, as in the *Ligue du Bien Public* in 1465. These included the descendants of two younger sons of John the Good (r. 1350–1364): Louis I of Anjou and Philip I of Burgundy, known as Philip the Bold. The dukes of Anjou, exploiting the association with earlier, Capetian dukes of Anjou, also acquired the kingdom of Naples and the county of Provence, the first of these remaining more a dream than a reality. Philip of Burgundy, who had been given the duchy of Burgundy as an appanage in 1363, greatly increased his holdings in 1369 when he married Margaret of Flanders, the heiress to rich lands on the northern border of the kingdom. In addition to the continuation of these two royal lines descended from John the Good, a still earlier offshoot of the royal family, the dukes of Bourbon, traced their lineage to the youngest son of Louis IX, canonized as Saint Louis. They built a base of power in the center of France and did not forget the prestige that derived from the revered status of their Capetian ancestor. In addition to the dukes with their court at Moulins, the Bourbon line included the cadet branches of Bourbon-Montpensier and Bourbon-Vendôme.

Of all his cousins, Louis XI found the dukes of Burgundy the most threatening. Through marriage, war, and intimidation they had formed a splendid and powerful domain that could irritate the French monarchy by allying with England or by offering shelter to rebellious French princes—among them Louis XI himself, when he was still dauphin (cat. 11). The possessions of the dukes of Burgundy extended beyond the kingdom of France into the jurisdiction of the Holy Roman Empire. When Charles the Bold, duke of Burgundy, died suddenly in 1477 as he fought to extend his territories further along the Rhine, Louis XI grasped the opportunity to recover the appanage lands of the duchy of Burgundy. Since Charles's only child was a young, unmarried daughter, Mary of Burgundy, Louis used force and a legal argument that applied the principle prohibiting female inheritance (the Salic Law) from the crown of France, by extension, to the appanage lands granted from the royal domain for the use of younger sons (Saenger 1977). The descendants of Mary of Burgundy were no longer considered princes of the blood eligible to become kings of France, and lost the duchy of Burgundy, though they retained the imperial county of Burgundy (the Franche-Comté) and large territories in the

---

Facing Page

FIGURE 26.

Master of Fitzwilliam 268. *Charles the Bold of Burgundy Receives his Military Captains*, in *Military Ordinance of Charles the Bold.* Tempera on parchment. British Library, London, Add. Ms. 36619, f. 5.

Low Countries—and also a long and troubled relation to the French crown. In contrast, the lands granted to Louis I of Anjou as an appanage by John the Good returned more easily into Louis XI's hands, when the death of René of Anjou in 1480 was immediately followed by that of his nephew and heir in 1481, bringing the county of Provence to the crown at the same time.

The ambitions of Louis XI's contemporaries, René of Anjou and the last two Valois dukes of Burgundy, Philip the Good and Charles the Bold, had extended well beyond the kingdom of France. To the fleurs-de-lis of France with the *brisure* mark specific to their cadet, or junior, branch of the family, they had proudly added the bearings of their additional possessions either real or claimed, resulting in coats of arms of striking complexity. Escutcheons with the arms of Charles the Bold's many possessions fill the border of the frontispiece to his copy of his military ordinance, in which he is shown enthroned, giving instructions and authority to his captains (fig. 26). René of Anjou claimed and briefly held the kingdom of Naples, and with it the emotionally powerful, if empty, title of King of Jerusalem, by association with the earlier, Capetian dukes of Anjou and through a complex process of adoption. Adjusting his arms to his changing fortunes, he added to Anjou: Lorraine (inherited through his first wife), Bar, Anjou *ancien* (for the extinct Capetian dukes of Anjou), Hungary, Jerusalem, and, after 1466, Aragon. The splendid della Robbia tondo with René's arms of 1466 or later that decorated the villa of Jacopo Pazzi, a Florentine banker who adhered to René's cause, gives an idea of the very similar lost tondo that once decorated René's palace at Aix (fig. 27; see Mérindol 1987, pp. 75–77). After Anjou reverted to the crown, René's claim to the kingdom of Naples was the basis for Charles VIII's taking of that city in 1494/95, and for Louis XII's later efforts to hold it; this connection is reflected in their use of the motto *Los en crossant* (increasing honor) and the crescent device from the Order of the Crescent founded by René in 1448 (see cat. 27).

Quasi-religious orders of chivalry founded by the princes of the blood, and by other princes and kings, aimed to solidify these nobles' political ambitions and to codify the language of devices and mottos that were signs of identity and loyalty. These foundations continued a practice current from the mid-fourteenth century, though most such orders were short-lived. A notable exception was the Order of the Golden Fleece, established by Philip the Good of Burgundy in 1430, at a time when he was ostensibly a vassal of the double monarchy of England and France. Among its many advantages for Philip was the role of "sovereign" at the head of a select company of the highest nobility of the disparate possessions under his control. As such he could maintain his independence in relation to England's prestigious Order of the Garter (Keen 1984, p. 184; Richard 1996, p. 67). The flint and firestones forming the links of the order's collar became an emblem of Burgundian identity. Subsequently, René of Anjou's Order of the Crescent was an instrument in his effort to unite the even more geographically dispersed Angevin possessions under him, with Saint Maurice, commander of the Theban Legion and titular saint of Angers cathedral, as its patron. It did not survive his death.

It was therefore to some extent in rivalry with the chivalric orders set up by the princes of the blood that Louis XI established the Order of Saint Michael in 1469. Membership in his royal order would forestall the membership of the king's own rebellious younger brother, Charles of France, duke of Guyenne (died 1472) in the Burgundian Order of the Golden Fleece. René of Anjou also accepted the collar of the king's Order of Saint Michael, while remaining the head of his own Order of the Crescent; he is depicted wearing the collar of Saint Michael rather than the Crescent in the Matheron diptych (see cat. 12). The patron of the French royal order, Saint Michael, was associated with victory in the struggle against the English and with the successful resistance of Mont-Saint-Michel to English capture. Though Fouquet's authoritative image of Louis XI in the *Statutes of the Order of Saint Michael* shows him surrounded by the knights of his order and backed by its officers under an image of the saint (fig. 3), as Philippe Contamine (1976) demonstrated, a formal chapter of the order did not take place in Louis's reign, permitting the king to bestow the honor, but avoid sitting in a chapter meeting with his knights.

The rivalries and connections, including marriage alliances, between the crown and the princes of the blood undoubtedly intensified the exchange of artistic influences from North and South. If Burgundy and Anjou had ambitions beyond the current boundaries of the kingdom of France, their revered family monuments were located in their French

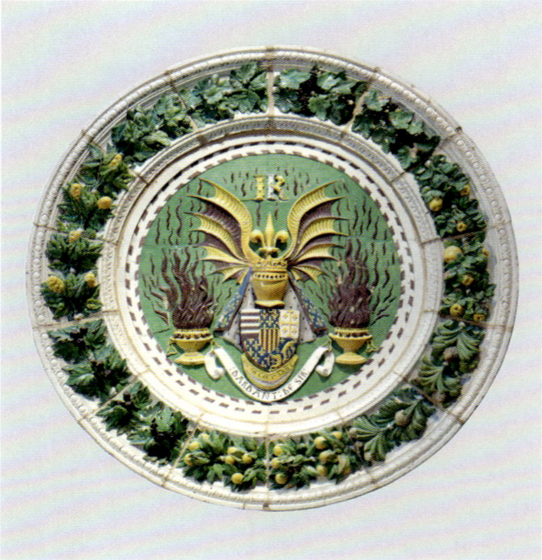

FIGURE 27.
Luca della Robbia and workshop.
Coat of Arms of René of Anjou. Enameled terracotta.
The Victoria and Albert Museum, London.

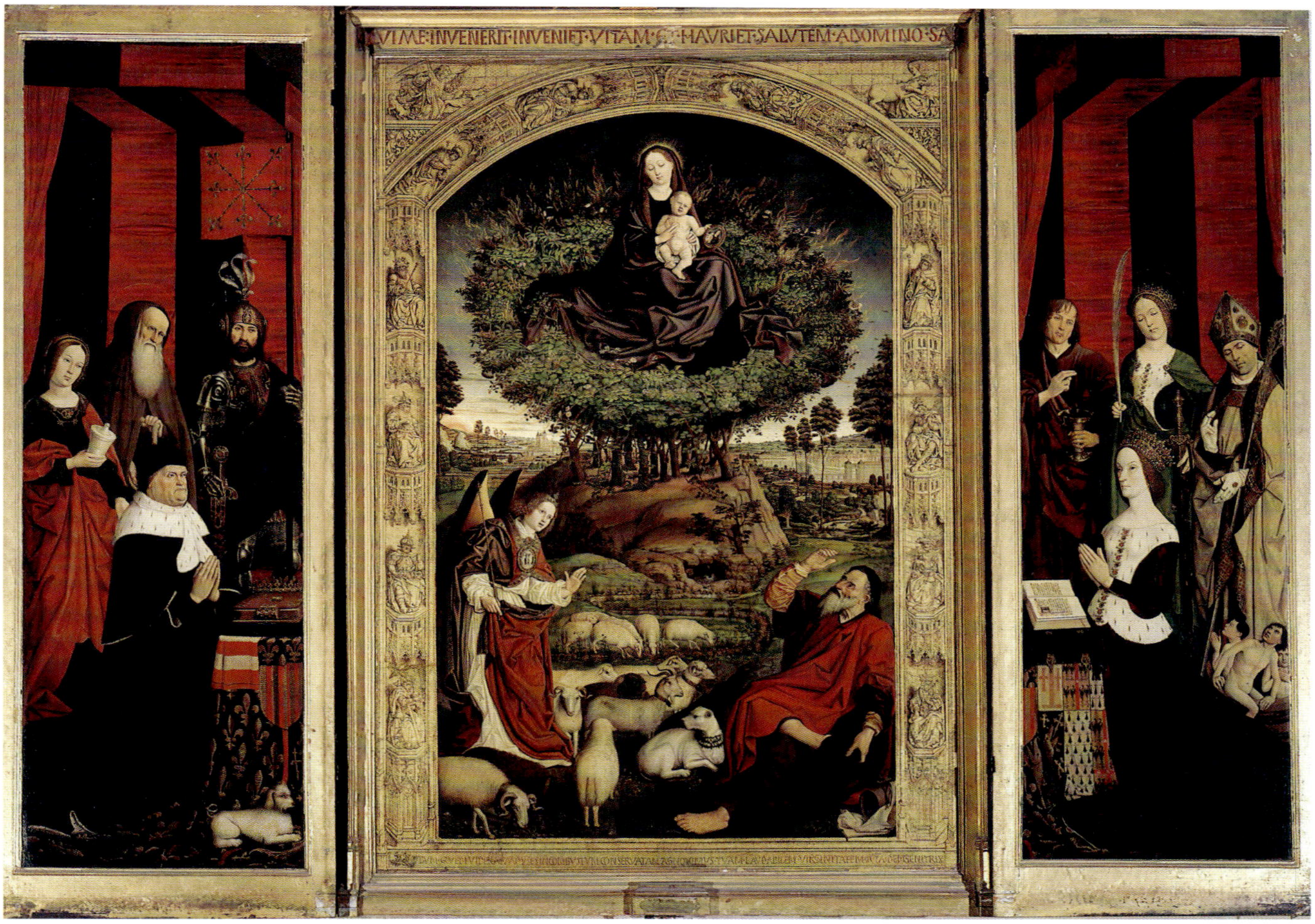

FIGURE 28.
Nicolas Froment. *Triptych of Moses and the Burning Bush, with René of Anjou and Jeanne de Laval.* Oil on panel. Cathedral of the Holy Savior, Aix-en-Provence.

appanages. The Chartreuse of Champmol outside Dijon held the tombs of the Burgundian dukes; a rare journey of Charles the Bold to Burgundy itself took place in 1474 when he brought the remains of his parents, Philip the Good and Isabel of Portugal, there for burial. Likewise, the chapel of the Order of the Golden Fleece was established in the Sainte-Chapelle of the ducal palace in Dijon, though the chapter meetings were mostly held elsewhere. Many of the courtiers and administrators who served the dukes of Burgundy came from their Burgundian rather than Netherlandish territories and themselves commissioned monuments and works of art by Netherlandish artists to be sent back to their native places. Commissions for the collegiate church of Saint-Hippolyte, Poligny, in the Franche-Comté (including Rogier van der Weyden's *Seven Sacraments Altarpiece* now in Antwerp), are outstanding examples of this phenomenon (Nys 2006). Artists, too, might follow this route, as was apparently the case for Jean Hey, the Master of Moulins, who was probably brought to France by Cardinal Jean Rolin of Autun, the son of the powerful chancellor of Philip the Good (cat. 55). Artists who excelled at dynastic representation were shared among the princes of the blood—this must have been the case for Jacques Morel, who sculpted the tombs for Charles I of Bourbon and Agnes of Burgundy at the Bourbon necropolis at Souvigny (following a Burgundian model) as well as those of René of Anjou and his first wife Isabelle of Lorraine in Angers cathedral (destroyed). René of Anjou, an extraordinarily engaged and sophisticated patron, was a vital intermediary for the introduction of foreign artists and works to France, introducing Italian artists and types (cats. 13, 15–16). He also fostered northern artists, whose work he may have first encountered during his early years as a privileged prisoner of Philip the Good of Burgundy (1431/32 and 1435/37). The most brilliant of these northern artists, Barthélemy d'Eyck, is closely associated with René as the illuminator of the prince's remarkable literary production, but he was replaced by another northerner, Nicolas Froment, who, among other works for René, produced the imposing *Triptych of the Burning Bush*, now in Aix cathedral, but painted in 1476 for the tomb of René's entrails in the Carmelite church of Aix (fig. 28). As a grandiose painted statement connecting a prince of the blood to a mystery of the Virgin, it is a forerunner of the Moulins triptych.

[12]

FOLLOWER OF NICOLAS FROMENT
(documented from 1461–died 1483/84)

Matheron Diptych: Portraits of René of Anjou and Jeanne de Laval

Provence, c. 1479–80 and/or c. 1485

Oil on panel; 17.6 x 27 cm (6 15/16 x 10 5/8 in.) (overall)

Musée du Louvre, Paris, Department of Painting, RF 665

PROVENANCE: Matheron family, until 1872; M. Chazaud; acquired by the Louvre, 1891.

BIBLIOGRAPHY: Ruche Provençale 1819, vol. 2, p. 14. Roux-Alphéran 1846–47, vol. 1, p. 477–79. Florisoone 1946, p. 40. Ring 1949, no. 217. Laclotte 1960, pp. 106, 123 n. 73. Sterling and Adhémar 1965, no. 36. Laclotte and Thiébaut 1983, pp. 247–48, no. 72. Robin 1985, pp. 211–12, fig. 129.

EXHIBITIONS: Paris 1878, no. 13. Paris 1904, no. 79. Bruges 2002, no. 71. Washington and Antwerp 2006–07, no. 10.

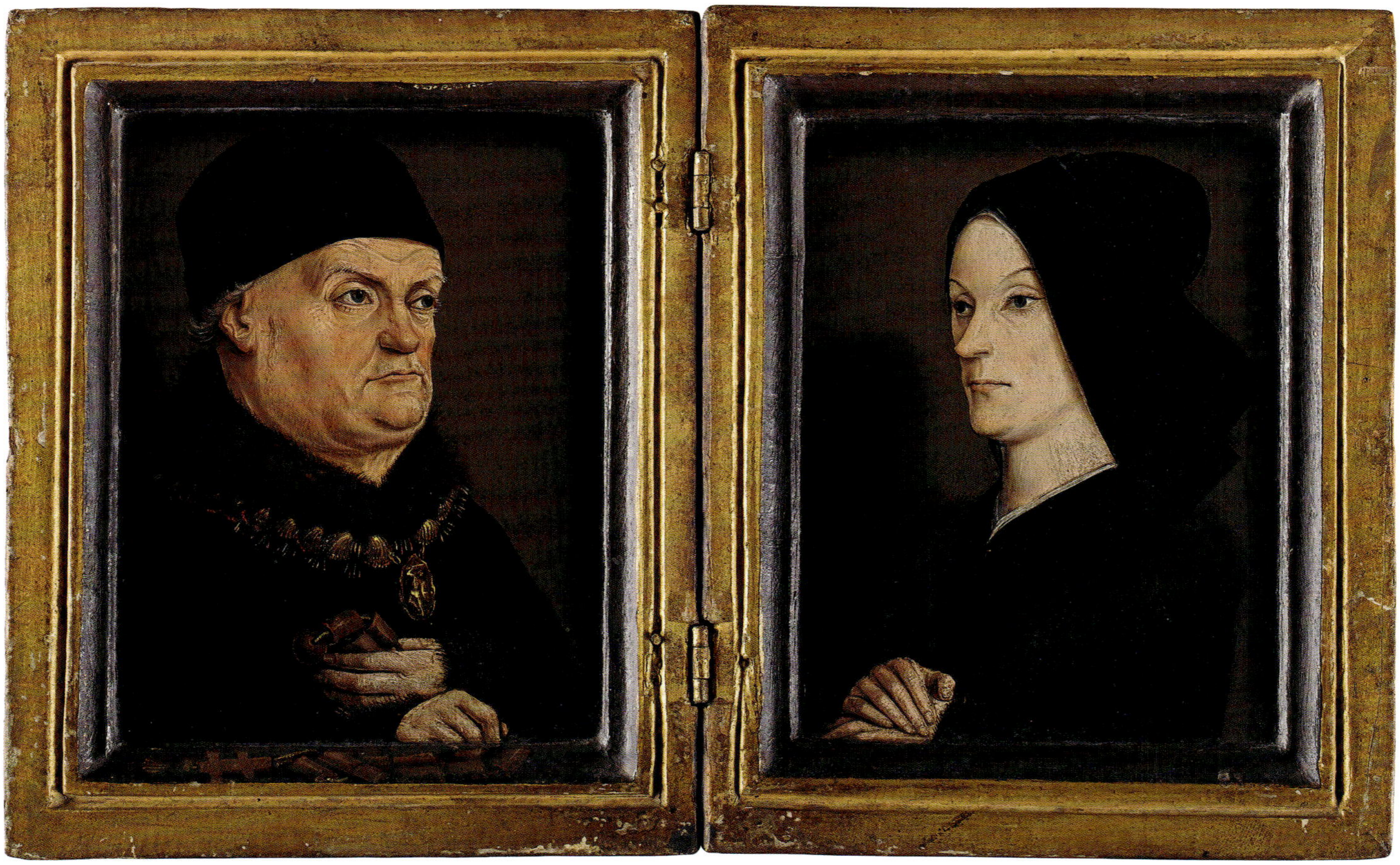

THE TRADITION REGARDING the history of this little diptych was transmitted together with the painting itself through generations of the Matheron family and affirmed by the last heir at the time of its sale in 1872. It was also disseminated by antiquarian residents of Aix from 1819 on (in *La Ruche Provençale* 1819, for example), and subsequently by art historians. No one today believes that René of Anjou, claimant to the throne of Naples and Jerusalem, painted these portraits, but the rest of the family legend has not been questioned. Let us consider its various elements.

René's gift of his own portrait and that of his wife is a possibility, since other instances of gifts of this kind exist. The emblems and devices painted on the back of each small panel are indeed those of the Matheron family. The first of its members to be part of the royal entourage was Michel, enobled by René in 1442, secretary to the king and later counselor in 1453. He was rewarded with the seignury of Peynier in 1463 (Coulet 1986 and 2000). However, it is the name of his son Jean that is associated with the diptych, even if a substantial part of his career was later than René's death. Thus he did not assume the role of president of the Cour des Comptes, a title often associated with his name, until 1487. As master of the accounts and counselor in 1470, he was certainly very close to the king in his last years, and was even said to have been present at his death in late July 1480 (Fabre 1834). But it is impossible to ascertain the circumstances of the gift of the diptych, which nineteenth century texts (particularly Roux-Alphéran 1847) connect to the baptism of one of Jean's sons, named René after his royal godfather. But no mention of a son of Jean Matheron named René has been found in the archives (N. Coulet, written communication); nothing more than a grandson named René, who died in 1552 (Villeneuve-Bargemon 1825). On the other hand, Michel Matheron did choose to give one of his sons this name, in tribute to the king who may have stood as the child's godfather, as he did with other children named after him. But we do not know the child's birth date, nor which of Michel's marriages produced him; he made a will in 1512 (N. Coulet).

Could the diptych's date of execution help in deciding between the two brothers, one new born and the other in his prime? Most writers opt for a date about 1475, based on the example of the *Triptych of the Burning Bush* (fig. 28), commissioned by René of Anjou to hang above his tomb in the Carmelite church in Aix, with portraits of the king and queen on its wings. However, although Jeanne de Laval appears in both images with the same severe features and pallor, the king's appearance is changed. In the diptych, a deep wrinkle creases his brow, gray predominates in his hair, and the wrinkles at the corners of his eyes are more numerous. If we follow other opinions (Ring 1949; Robin 1985) in adopting a later date, the baptismal theory must be rejected. Another indicator could point to Jean Matheron: the family emblem painted on the reverse of the wings is set upon a blue ground covered with a uniform pattern of fleurs-de-lis. The lack of the heraldic label indicating allegiance to René of Anjou leads us to question whether the backs were not painted slightly later, when Jean was energetically and successfully serving Charles VIII of France. In René's lifetime, his counselor Jean was not an advocate of the annexation of Provence by France; in 1481–82, he had supported the duke of Lorraine. Later rallying to the cause of Charles VIII, he was all the more likely to have stamped the diptych with the lilies of France, just as in his own portrait René wears the collar of Saint Michael, the order that Louis XI had founded in August 1469, naming his uncle of Anjou among its first knights (Contamine 1976). Thus, appearing as a loyal servant of the king of France, René anticipated his friend's new choice. Perhaps we should go even farther, and consider the two sides of the diptych as contemporaneous with each other; placing the execution of the entire work around 1485 as a dual homage, post mortem to the king who had enabled the rise of the Matheron family, and here and now to the king who currently supported his position and fortune.

So similar are the faces of René and his wife in the triptych and diptych that one is naturally tempted to attribute them to the same painter. Initially a mere hypothesis, this gradually became an assertion (Laclotte 1960), and the diptych is now considered the work of Nicolas Froment. However, the workmanship is less smooth and the highlights are rougher. The little white touches showing that the king is rough shaven are arranged in a systematic manner by the painter of the diptych; Nicolas Froment placed them randomly, following the relief of the flesh, giving greater life and immediacy to his model. The collar of Saint Michael, summarily treated, lacks the evocative quality of the luminous flashes of the jewelry in the *Triptych of Moses and the Burning Bush* (fig. 28). Finally, the hands of the Matheron king and queen have neither the elegance of design nor the movement of those in the triptych. The painter of the diptych knew how to transpose the official portraits into a more familiar mode, dressing the couple in costumes of somber black, a color that was in vogue in European courts of the fifteenth century, and somewhat softening their expression. Jeanne, although copied very literally, seems less severe. The painter of the diptych also successfully integrated within the frame the two figures turned toward each other with hands posed on the edge. The rosary held by René is painted with a sense of volume, and the cast shadows give a sense of space.

Finally we should note the protective pouch for the object, mentioned since 1819 as being original. It is in any event very old; the red velvet sack in which the closed diptych was kept conveys the portable nature of this object only rarely on view. • M-CL

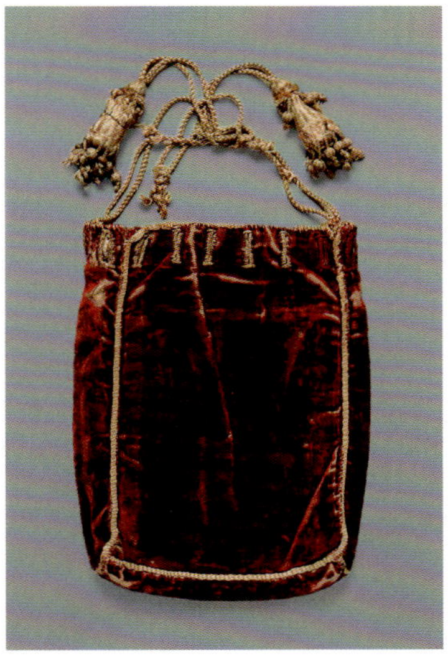

FIGURE 29.
Protective pouch for the *Matheron Diptych*. Velvet, linen, and silk. Musée du Louvre, Paris.

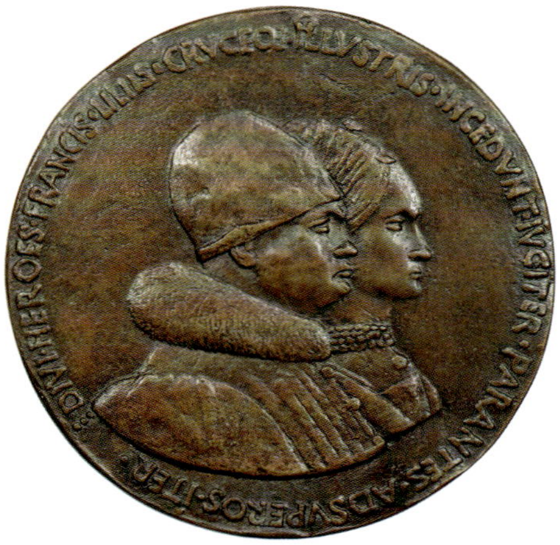

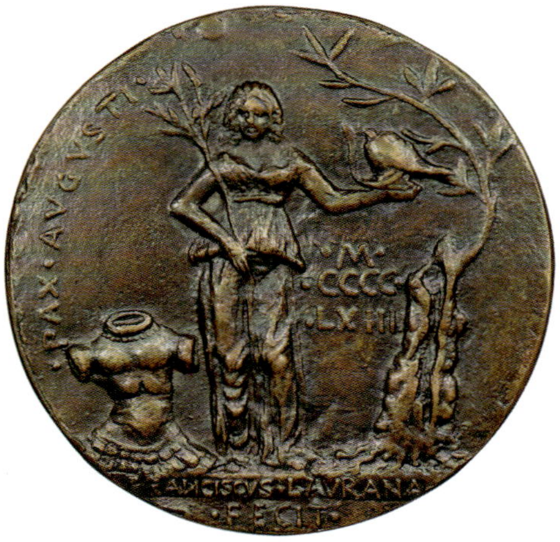

[13]

FRANCESCO LAURANA
(active by 1453–1502)

Medal of René of Anjou and Jeanne de Laval

Provence, 1463

Bronze; diam. 8.7 cm (3 7/16 in.)

Bibliothèque nationale de France, Paris, Department of Coins, Medals, and Antiquities, Armand-Valton 147

INSCRIBED: *DIVI HEROES FRANCIS LILIIS CRVCEQ ILLVSTRIS INCEDVNT IVGITER PARANTES AD SVPEROS ITER* [Divine heroes, glorified by the lilies of France and the cross, advance together, aspiring to the heavens] (obverse); *PAX AVGVSTI MCCCCLXIII FRANCISCVS LAVRANA FECIT* [peace of Augustus 1463 made by Francesco Laurana] (reverse)

PROVENANCE: Bequeathed by Prosper Valton, 1907.

BIBLIOGRAPHY: Hill 1930, no. 59. Kruft 1995, pp. 67–81. Mognetti 1981, pp. 142–45.

IN THIS MEDAL, Francesco Laurana gives his own version of the joined portraits of René of Anjou and Jeanne de Laval made by Pietro da Milano and dated 1462: the relief is thinner and the textures are more clearly differentiated, as in René's fur collar. The more crisply delineated profiles float slightly above the circle formed by the inscription. The same rhymed text—translated as "divine heroes, glorified by the lilies of France and the cross, advance together, aspiring to the heavens" (the lily and the cross refer to the couple's armorial devices) can be found at the château of Tarascon, beneath a niche that shelters the busts of René and Jeanne that are also attributable to Laurana. On the reverse of this medal, an allegorical figure of the Peace of Augustus, inspired by Roman coins, stands holding an olive branch, with a cuirass in the Roman style lying at her feet, while a turtle dove (also interpreted as a helmet), perches on the newly sprouting branch of a withered tree. This composition combines various emblems of René, king of Naples and Jerusalem: the slashed stump of a rosebush he adopted following the death of his first wife, Isabelle of Lorraine; the branch of an orange tree grafted to it, a reference to his marriage to Jeanne de Laval; and the turtle dove, which is also a dove of peace. Like the inscription, the design can be understood in a private, a political, or even a religious sense: the dead tree that is reborn (*rené*)—a pun on the king's given name—is also the Tree of Life. This polysemy is characteristic of René's own writings. He doubtless composed the inscriptions and mottos of these medals himself. • IV-P

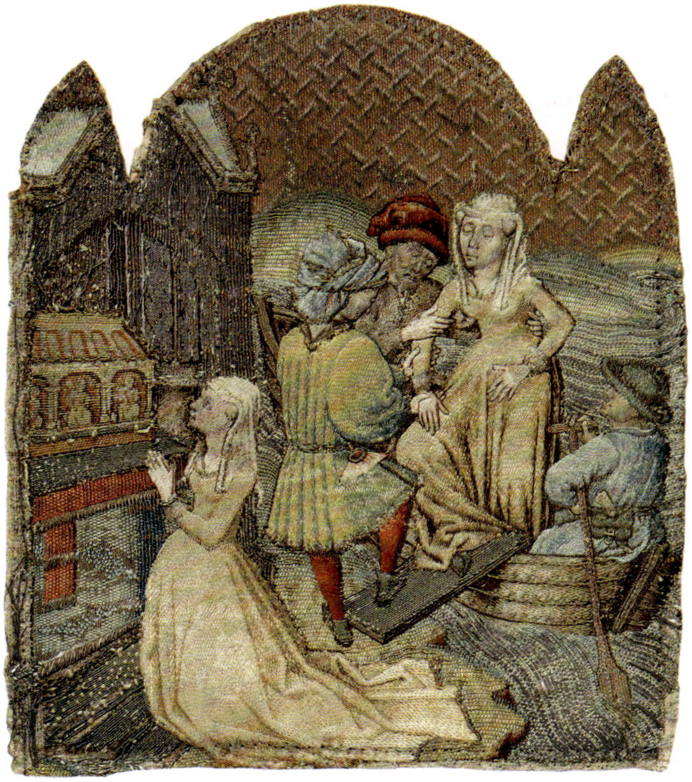

[14]

BARTHÉLEMY D'EYCK
(active 1444–71/72)

PIERRE DU BILLANT
(active 1438–76)

The Healing of the Blind Woman

Probably Angers, c. 1460

Embroidery, colored silks, gold and silver threads; 18.4 x 15.9 cm (7¼ x 6 ¼ in.)

Musée de Cluny—Musée national du Moyen Age, Cl. 23424

PROVENANCE: E.F.A. Münzenberger, Frankfurt-am-Main, 1887 [lent to Krefeld 1887]. Probably the dealer Salvadori, Florence. Baron Heinrich Thyssen-Bornemisza (d. 1947), 1930; by descent to his daughter, Countess M. Batthyany, Lugano; sold, Sotheby's, London, July 8, 1993, no. 147, to the Musée de Cluny.

BIBLIOGRAPHY: Freeman 1968, pp. 96, 125–27, pl. 35. Reynaud 1989, pp. 38–41, fig. 53. Reynaud 1997, pp. 37–50, fig. 1. Zeman 1997, p. 522. Thiébaut in Madrid/Valencia 2001, pp. 367–71.

EXHIBITIONS: Krefeld 1887, no. 24. Fontevraud 2001, no. 199. Paris 2004, no. 41.

THIS EMBROIDERED composition illustrates a posthumous miracle of Saint Martin, recounted by Gregory of Tours: a blind woman named Bella is taken to Tours to pray at the saint's tomb and recovers her sight. It juxtaposes the difficult voyage of the woman, shown setting foot on a narrow gangway supported by two men, with her thanksgiving before Saint Martin's reliquary casket. With remarkable technical virtuosity, the embroiderer has used a great variety of stitches, and the relief of the threads creates textural effects and reinforces their changing spatial nuances. Despite some vivid accents in costume details, the embroidery is now dominated by a harmony of gray and beige tones, probably due to overexposure to light. A drawing copying the embroidery (University Library, Uppsala) supports this.

Stylistic analysis (most recently Thiébaut in Madrid/Valencia 2001) attributes the cartoon of the embroidery to Barthélemy d'Eyck, a painter in the household of René of Anjou for several decades. Comparison with the paintings and illuminations of Barthélemy is very enlightening and need not be repeated here. Archival documents also tell us that René's official embroiderer, Pierre du Billant, was likewise present at the king's side for many years, was from the same region as Barthélemy, and was the second husband of the latter's mother. It is therefore very tempting to consider this piece, and three related ones, as executed by Pierre. Family ties, the same status at court (*valets de chambre* to René), common Netherlandish ancestry, and the same aesthetic, explain the symbiosis between two artists felt in these embroideries. This proposed double attribution (Léonelli 1987; see Reynaud 1989) clearly points to René of Anjou as patron.

The Healing of the Blind Woman belongs to a group of thirty-six scenes of the life of Saint Martin: four small panels of the same format (this one, two in the Musée Historique des Tissus, Lyon, and another in the Metropolitan Museum of Art, New York) and thirty-two circular medallions. In the seventeenth century they were reconstituted as orpheries on a chasuble; their original function is unknown. Such an elaborate cycle devoted to Saint Martin seems unusual; it has been suggested that it was meant for Saint Martin's, in Tours, the location of the saint's tomb. Indeed, René of Anjou's daughter Margaret married Henry VI of England there in 1444, and René's accounts confirm that Pierre du Billant received payment in 1445 for works of embroidery made in Tours on this occasion.

Art historians have dated the embroideries to two different periods: the 1430s for the medallions, the 1440s for the four panels. If the association with the 1445 payment is accepted, the question arises whether the king offered only four pieces as a complement to an adornment that already existed, or was the sole commissioner, reserving certain pieces for his favorite artists, but entrusting the rest to local craftsmen, more traditionally trained or reusing old patterns. This latter practice was commonplace (Tilliet-Haulot 1982), but here it would imply an iconographic development of the cult of Saint Martin for which no evidence has survived. Another possibility remains. Barthélemy d'Eyck's style shows so little chronological development that dating relies on external evidence (archival documents, historical events, costume, and heraldry). Thus the dress in *The Healing of the Blind Woman* has been cited to confirm a date in the 1440s. Yet, the V-neck of the man seen from the back does not appear before the 1460s. This suggests a date close to the *Coeur d'amour épris* in Vienna, which presents the strongest affinities with the embroideries. This second hypothesis seems most likely, as other scholars have also thought (Zeman 1997). • M-CL

[15]

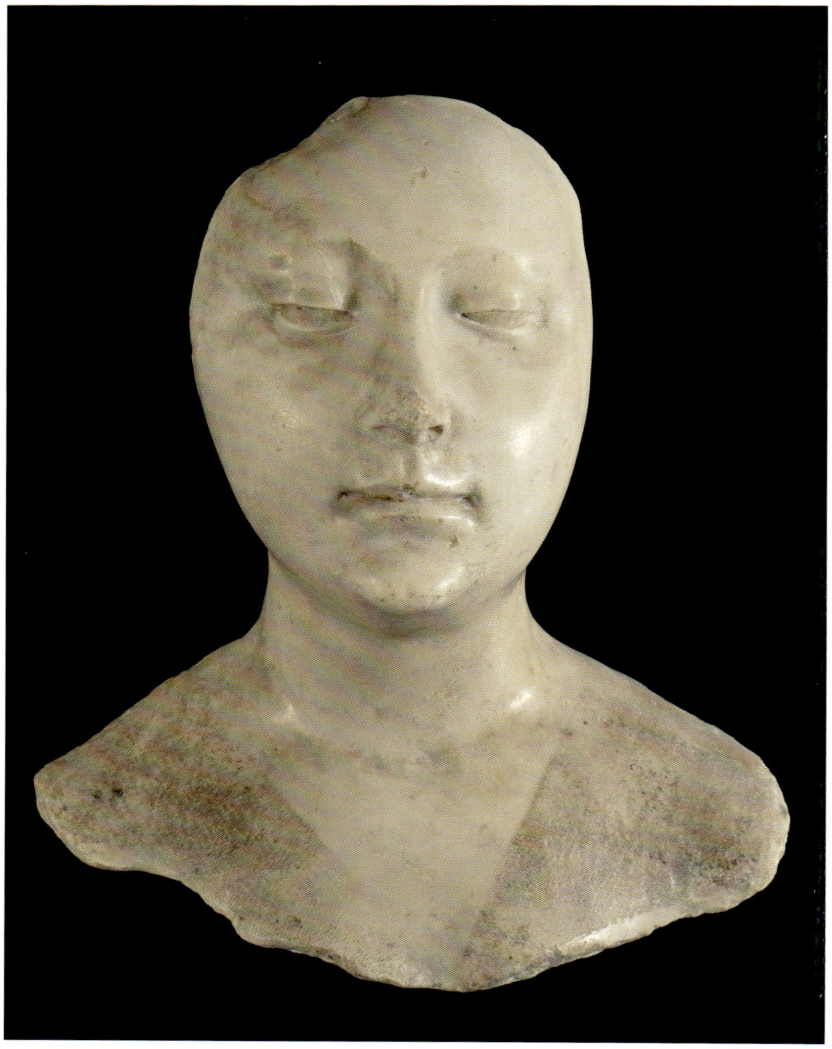

ATTRIBUTED TO
FRANCESCO LAURANA
(active by 1453–1502)

Mask of a Woman

c. 1476–1480

Marble, light traces of polychromy; 29 x 24 x 10 cm (11 7/16 x 9 3/8 x 3 5/16 in.)

Musée du Berry, Bourges, 1836.1.9

PROVENANCE: Labouvrie collection; acquired at auction, 1836.

BIBLIOGRAPHY, EXHIBITIONS: See cat. 16.

THESE TWO MASKS BELONG to an important series of between ten to twelve masks of women executed in marble (except for the example in the Barraco collection in Rome, which is terracotta). All resemble each other despite slight variations in their features, carving, and quality. The similarity between these faces and those of various sculptures documented as by Francesco Laurana, including Madonnas and busts of women, has led scholars to attribute the series to this sculptor of Dalmatian origin, or in some cases to his workshop. The locations where the masks were found in the nineteenth century, on both sides of the Alps, in part reflect the itinerant career of the sculptor, who was active in Naples (1453–58), Provence (1461–66), Sicily and again Naples (1468–75), and finally France (after 1475).

Though the quality of the example in Aix-en-Provence (not exhibited here), has been emphasized (Avignon 1981; Damianaki 2000), the interesting aspects of the mask from Bourges, which is cut at shoulder level, and that from Puy are consistently acknowledged. The incised texture in the garment of the Bourges example appears in several of the Laurana busts (Avignon 1981). The masks from Bourges and Puy were also the first two examples of the series to enter public collections, and did so even before French and German scholarship had reconstructed this sculptor's work in the last third of the nineteenth century. If the mask from Puy was actually discovered in 1789 in this same city, it would also be the first mask to be documented. The execution of this series is usually dated during the sculptor's second period of residence in France, during the time when he was charged with the decoration of the chapel of

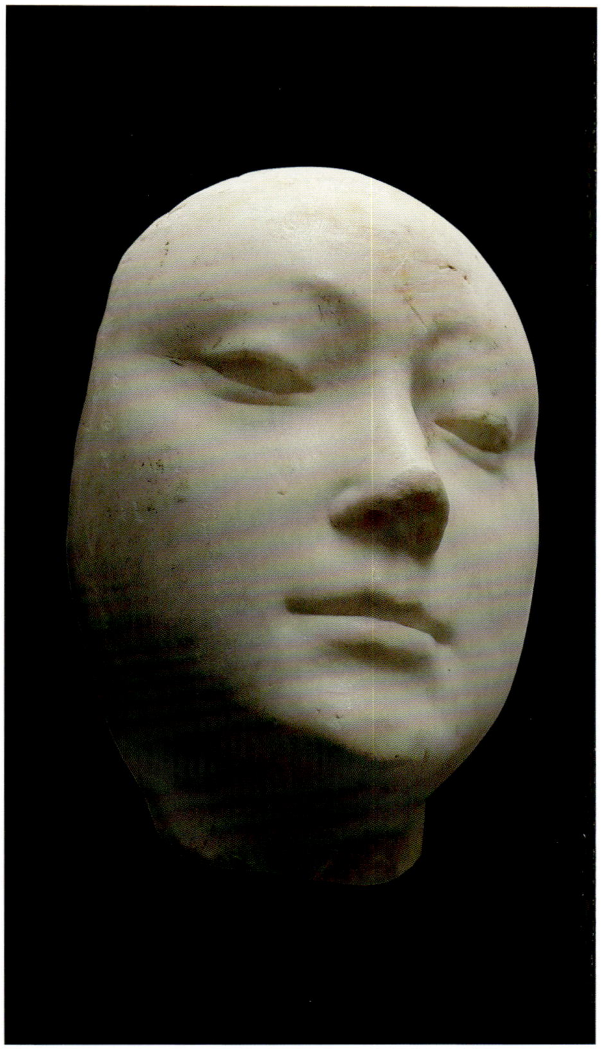

[16]

ATTRIBUTED TO
FRANCESCO LAURANA
(active by 1453–1502)

Mask of a Woman

c. 1476–1480

Marble; 18 x 13.5 x 10 cm (7 1/16 x 5 15/16 x 3 5/16 in.)

Musée Crozatier, Le Puy-en-Velay, 834.7

PROVENANCE: Probably discovered in Rue des Tables, Le Puy, 1789; given by Auguste Aymard, 1834.

BIBLIOGRAPHY: La Guère 1885 (cat. 15 only). Gonse 1904, pp. 119–20, 137–38. Rolfs 1907, p. 408. Gounot 1957, p. 138 (cat. 16 only). Mérindol 1980–81. Beaulieu and Beyer 1992, p. 291. Kruft 1995. Damianaki 2000, pp. 188–89, 191–92. Mognetti 2007. Charlier 2009 (cat. 15 only).

EXHIBITIONS: Paris 1956, nos. 163, 165. Avignon 1981, nos. C28, C30.

Saint Lazarus in the cathedral of Notre-Dame-la-Major in Marseille (1476–83) and also delivered the retable of the *Carrying of the Cross* (1478–81), commissioned by René of Anjou for the church of the Celestines in Avignon.

With their idealized but nonetheless slightly asymmetrical faces (see, for example, the nose in the Bourges mask and the eyes in the Le Puy mask), these remarkable sculptures, found above all in Provence and probably also in Italy, still raise the question of their original purpose. The flat, rough-hewn backs were not intended to be visible or to be attached to another flat surface, which eliminates the possibility that these masks were applied to tomb figures or to a large-scale decoration, where their placement would have required a smooth surface. The similarity to the Virgin in the Museo Civico in Castelvetrano helps us to envision one of the possible uses of these masks: they could have been inserted within marble draperies that would have been executed separately from the faces. According to Mognetti (2007), these masks could also have been made for their own sake, to be displayed independently or within a group, depending on the purchaser's preference. The repeated identification of the Bourges mask with a posthumous portrait of Agnès Sorel (Charlier 2009), which is related to the hypothesis already proposed by La Guère in 1885, relies on a study based on the techniques of forensic medicine from the eighteenth century, when the remains of Charles VII's mistress were transferred to the nave of the collegiate church of Saint-Ours in Loches. There is no documentary evidence to support this proposal. • BC-B

[17]

Coronation of the Virgin with Solomon Crowning Bathsheba and Esther Before Ahaseurus (The Three Coronations)

1476/88

Design and weaving: Southern Netherlands

Wool, silk, and gilt-metal wrapped thread; 11 warps per cm; 170 x 335 cm (66 15/16 x 131 7/8 in.)

Treasury of the Cathedral of Saint Stephen, Sens

INSCRIBED: *SALOMON*, *BERSABEE* (bottom of left scene); *HESTER*, *ASVERRE* (bottom of right scene)

PROVENANCE: Commissioned by Charles II of Bourbon (d. 1488), cardinal and archbishop of Lyon; given to Sens cathedral by a member of the Bourbon family before 1561, perhaps Charles of Bourbon or more likely his distant cousin, Louis de Bourbon-Vendôme, cardinal and archbishop of Sens from 1536 to his death in 1557; listed in inventories, 1561 and 1595.

BIBLIOGRAPHY: Gaussen 1861, p. 3, pl. 11. Montaiglon 1880, pp. 253–59 (ill.). Vaudin 1882, pp. 73–76, pls. 11, 12. Guiffrey 1886, pp. 134–36. Chartraire 1897, pp. 2–5, nos. 2–3. Mâle 1908, pp. 249–54, fig. 115. Chartraire 1925, pp. 7–8, 24–27 (ill.). Migeon 1929, pp. 258–60. Réau 1955–59, vol. 2, pt. 1, p. 288. Bramsen 1957, p. 316, figs. 1, 4, 5, 6. França 1962, p. 540. Weigert 1964, pp. 64–65. Costa 1971, pp. 72–75, figs. 2–5. Naumann 1990, pp. 108–09, fig. 13. Saulnier-Pernuit 1993, pp. 10–99. Franke 1998, p. 21, fig. 1. Châtelet 2001, pp. 67, 73, 173, fig. 34. Elizabeth Cleland in New York 2002, pp. 81–82, under no. 6.

EXHIBITIONS: Paris 1900, no. 3178. Paris 1928, no. 52. London 1932, no. 28. Paris 1937, no. 1286. Paris 1946, no. 35. Paris 1965, no. 826. Paris/New York 1973, no. 70 (no. 75 in New York catalogue).

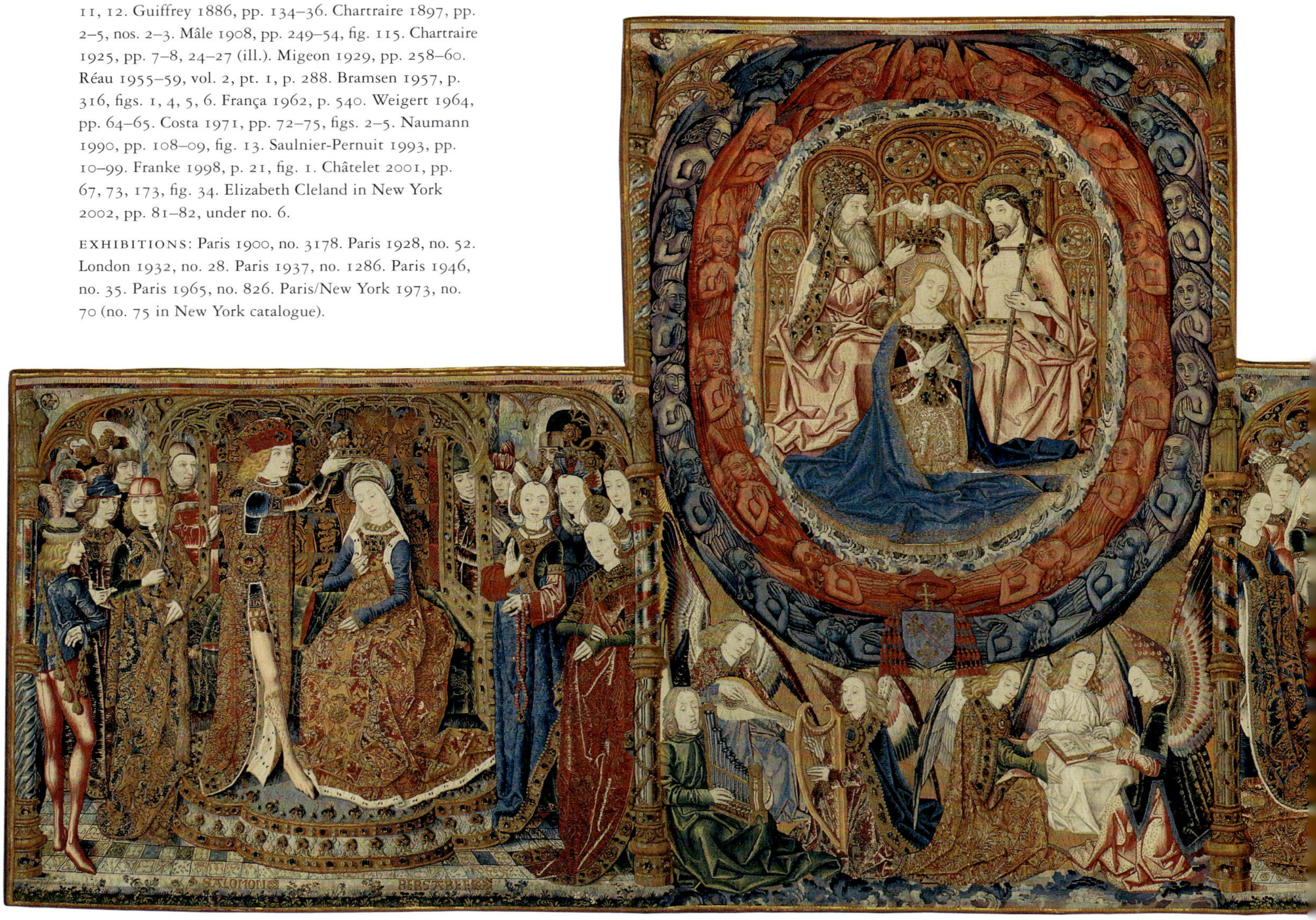

THIS REFINED and richly woven tapestry functioned as an altarpiece; the raised central section devoted to the Coronation of the Virgin gives the hanging the inverted T shape that was common for Netherlandish and French altarpieces of the fifteenth century. The coat of arms and the cardinal's hat indicate that it was made for Charles of Bourbon, cardinal and archbishop of Lyon; another splendid tapestry altarpiece of the Adoration of the Magi, given to Sens cathedral at the same time as this one, has the same arms together with Charles of Bourbon's motto, his initials, and his device of a flaming sword. Since Charles received the cardinal's hat in 1476, this date serves as a terminus post quem for the commission of the tapestry, which would probably have been used as a portable altarpiece by its owner, who traveled widely as a diplomat and member of the council of Louis XI (cat. 56). The praying figure clad in red to the left of Solomon may be a donor portrait of the cardinal.

The traditional title, *The Three Coronations*, is somewhat misleading. The designer of this tapestry drew inspiration from the treatment of the Coronation of the Virgin in the *Biblia Pauperum* (Poor Man's Bible); the subject matter, composition, and shape of the tapestry are all remarkably similar to woodcut editions from the middle of the fifteenth century (Mâle 1908, pp. 249–54; Saulnier-Pernuit 1993, pp. 90–93). As in the *Biblia Pauperum*, the organization of the imagery is typological: the Old Testament heroines Bathsheba and Esther were interpreted in the Middle Ages as prefigurations of the Virgin, who represented the Church, *Ecclesia*. In the center, surrounded by a mandorla of angels, God the Father and Christ crown the Virgin as Queen of Heaven. On the left King Solomon is shown crowning Bathsheba, his mother, who had come to him with a petition, as recounted in 1 Kings 2:19. The scene at right does not represent the moment of Esther's selection and coronation by Ahaseurus, king of Persia, as described in the Bible (Esther 2:17), but rather refers to other sections of the Book of Esther in which the king repeatedly grants her petitions, as signified by the extension of his golden scepter towards her, thereby saving the Jewish people.

Both the design and the weaving of this tapestry are probably from the Southern Netherlands. Stylistically, the designer may be linked with Rogier van der Weyden or one of his followers. Charles of Bourbon had close family ties to the rulers of the Burgundian Netherlands: his mother, Agnes of Burgundy, was the sister of Philip the Good, and Philip's successor as duke, Charles the Bold, had married Charles of Bourbon's sister Isabelle as his second wife. • KD

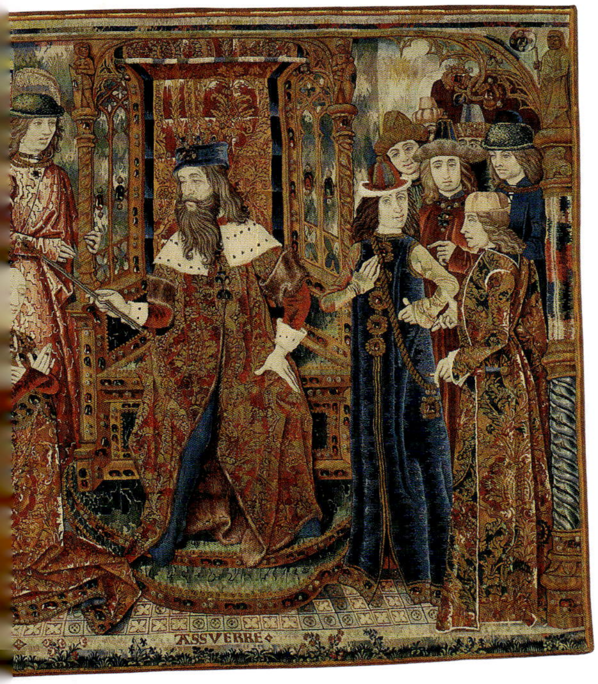

[18]

WORKSHOP OF ANDREA DELLA ROBBIA
(1435–1525)

The Prophet Jeremiah from the Tomb of Guillaume Fillastre, Abbot of Saint Bertin

Florence, 1469

Enameled terracotta; 24.5 x 51 x 9.5 cm ($9^{5}/_{8}$ x 20 x $3^{3}/_{4}$ in.)

Museum of Hôtel Sandelin, Saint Omer, 2796

INSCRIBED: *Mulier circumdabit virum* [The wife will encompass her husband] (on the banderole)

PROVENANCE: Made in Florence for the tomb of Guillaume Fillastre in the abbey church of Saint-Bertin; dismembered during the Revolution; fragment discovered, 1838; given by M. Provost, 1838.

BIBLIOGRAPHY: Blazy in Douai 1986, pp. 102–05. Gaborit 2003a.

EXHIBITIONS: Douai 1986, no. 55. Saint-Omer 1992, no. 64. Nice and Sèvres 2002–03, no. V-11.

GUILLAUME FILLASTRE (1400/07–1473), one of the great prelates of the court of Burgundy, reflects a variety of influences. The illegitimate son of Cardinal Guillaume I Fillastre, he was a Benedictine, a preacher and administrator, but also a statesman and diplomat (Prietzel 2001). A protégé of the Angevin party and secretary to René of Anjou, he entered the service of Philip the Good, duke of Burgundy, for whom he carried out diplomatic missions before becoming head of his council. Successively bishop of Verdun, of Toul, and finally of Tournai, he was abbot of the renowned abbey of Saint-Bertin at Saint-Omer from 1451. There, in 1461, he hosted the tenth chapter meeting of the Order of the Golden Fleece, of which he became chancellor in the same year. For his abbey he commissioned stained glass, goldsmithwork, and a retable for the high altar, whose center of gilded metalwork has disappeared, but whose wings, attributed to Simon Marmion, survive in Berlin and London. This commission to a Valenciennes artist, as well as one for the choir tapestries woven in his episcopal city of Tournai (panels in the Musée de Saint-Omer), show Fillastre's predictable taste for Flemish art.

It was less conventional to commission from Florence a whole ensemble of enameled terracotta reliefs for the abbey church: *The Annunciation* (Church of Saint-Martin-au-Laert), *The Last Supper* (Church of Saint-Denis, Saint-Omer), his epitaph (Museum of Hôtel Sandelin), Jeremiah, and, probably, his arms. In his 1473 will, the abbot specifically alludes to the "sepulcher that I have had brought from Florence" (*sépultre que j'ai fait venir de Florence*), but which was still not installed. In fact, a Tournai record (1469/70) mentions payment to Angelo Tani for transport from Florence to Pisa. Gaborit (2003a) has emphasized that this substantial payment probably also included the execution of the works. Another payment attests to the transport by sea from Pisa to the port of Bruges in the care of Tommaso Portinari. It has been assumed that Fillastre commissioned the tomb in the course of one of his trips to Rome in 1463, 1465, or 1467. But it is equally possible that, impressed by the quality of Florentine art, he ordered the reliefs in 1469 through Portinari, a partner of the Medici in Bruges. Portinari became the preeminent promoter of Flemish art in Florence, via the famous Portinari triptych of Hugo van des Goes.

Gaborit (2003a) also postulated that *The Last Supper* constituted an altar frontal and *The Annunciation* a small retable or the tympanum of a funerary niche associated with the lunette with the prophet Jeremiah shown here. The banderole is inscribed with the prophecy of the Incarnation from Jeremiah 31:22. One cannot help noting the iconographic relationship to the Aix *Annunciation* of Barthélemy d'Eyck, made for the funerary chapel of the merchant Pierre Corpici in 1442; its wings present the figures of Isaiah and Jeremiah. The Incarnation's promise of eternal life is in perfect accord with a funerary function. This resemblance to a work of the circle of René of Anjou, of which Fillastre had been part, is perhaps not coincidental, especially since the abbot was the son of the archbishop of Aix-en-Provence.

Imbued with classical culture, trained in Bologna as well as in Leuven, this great figure of the Burgundian court, patron and bibliophile, knew how to bring together in his abbey the contrasting currents of the Florentine Renaissance and Flemish art. • GB-B

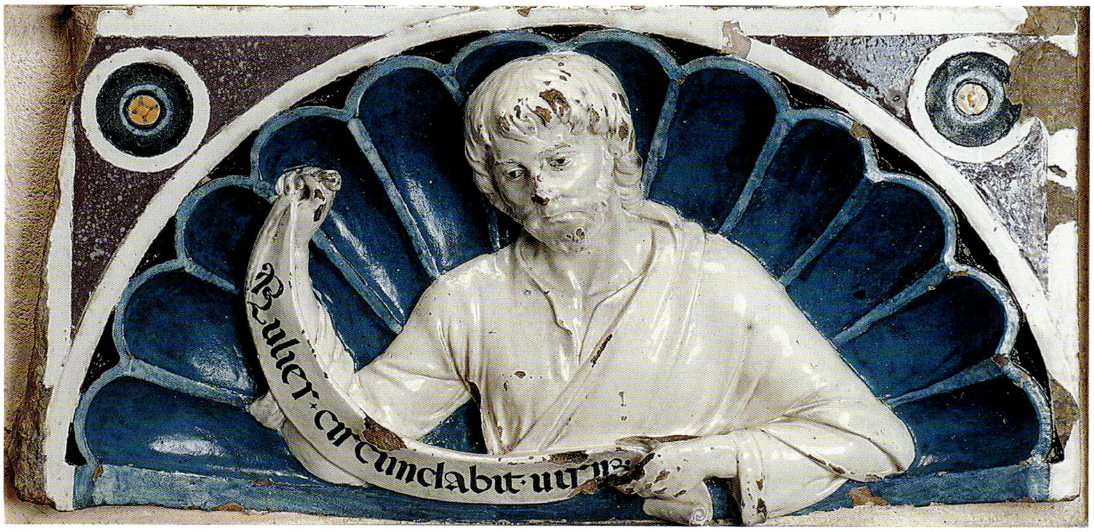

[19]

ROBINET TESTARD
(active 1471–1510)

Hours of Charles of Angoulême

Cognac (or Angoulême?), 1482/85

Tempera and gold on parchment, with an eighteenth-century morocco leather binding with royal arms and monograms; 115 ff.; 21.5 x 15.5 cm (8½ x 6⅛ in.)

Bibliothèque nationale de France, Paris, Department of Manuscripts, ms. lat. 1173

PROVENANCE: Charles, count of Angoulême (d. 1496); Jean Ballesdens (d. 1672) [see Bibliothèque nationale de France, ms. Baluze 100, ff. 178–81v, no. 54; and Brièle 1887, vol. 4, no. 486]; Jean-Baptiste Colbert (d. 1683), no. 4821; by descent until it was sold with Colbert's library to Louis XV, 1732; Bibliothèque du Roi (Regius 44614-4).

BIBLIOGRAPHY: Durrieu 1905, p. 213. Durrieu 1908a, p. 57. Durrieu 1908b, pp. 112–14. Blum 1911, pp. 357–69. Durrieu 1911, pp. 724–25, fig. 495. Delisle 1913, p. 64. Leroquais 1927, vol. 1, pp. 104–08, pls. 92–95. Blum and Lauer 1930, pp. 45, 86–88, pls. 641, 66. MacGibbon 1933, pp. 80, 98–99. Limousin 1954, pp. 59–60, figs. 65–74. Porcher 1959, p. 79. Plummer in New York 1982, pp. 47, 83, 85. Matthews 1986, pp. 4–18. Edmunds and Winn 1987, pp. 295–96. Giogoli and Friedman 2005, pp. 145, 161.

EXHIBITIONS: Paris 1937, no. 191. Tours 1952, no. 35. Paris 1955–56, no. 343. Paris 1993–94, no. 229.

SHOWN: *Presentation in the Temple*, f. 24v

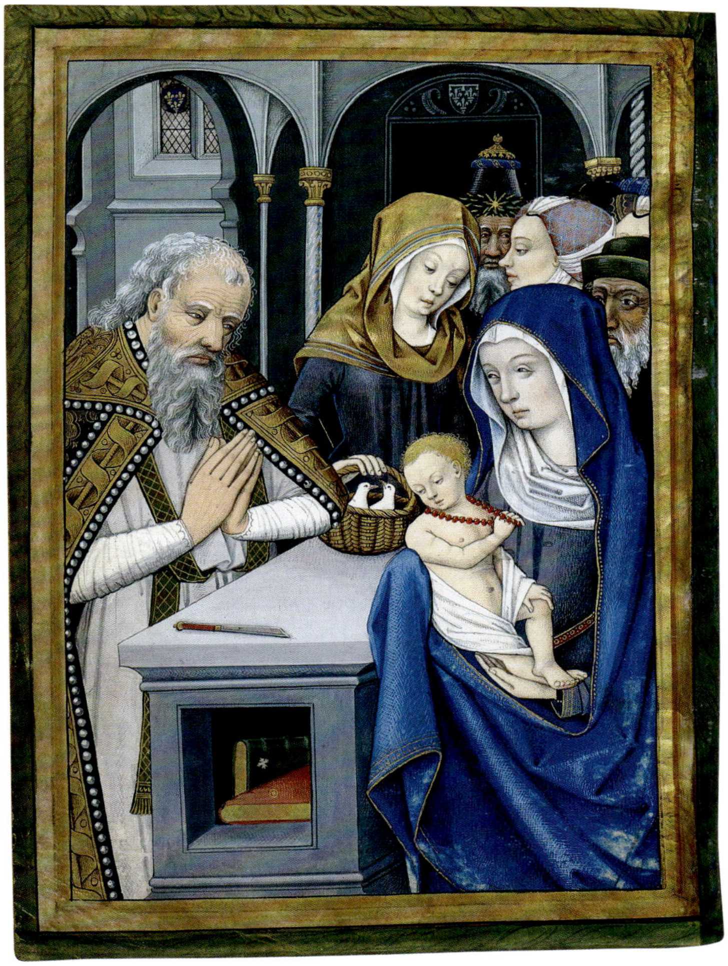

THIS ELABORATE book of hours was certainly commissioned by Charles of Angoulême (1459–1496), the father of the future Francis I, although the volume does not appear in the inventory of books prepared after Charles's death in 1496 (see Sénemaud 1862). His arms, *azure with three fleurs de lis of gold, on a label argent charged with a crescent gules on the central pendant*, appear in the *Annunciation* on folio 9v. and are repeated, in a simplified fashion, in various miniatures. Furthermore, an acrostic poem on folio 53 also spells out his name: *CHARLES DE VALLOYS*.

The manuscript seems to have been designed initially in Tours in the early 1480s. The *Annunciation* and the *Adoration of the Magi* (f. 22v) date from this period, a phase of the manuscript's creation that was connected by Durrieu (1908) to a payment made to Jean Bourdichon between 1482 and 1485. The latter received ten livres tournois "for having painted a story for my aforementioned lord [the Count of Angoulême]" (*pour avoir painct une ystoire pour mondit seigneur*). Moreover, as early as 1905, Durrieu had identified Bourdichon's hand in the manuscript, particularly in the *Annunciation* scene, although he was more reserved in his attribution of the *Adoration of the Magi*. Hence, in 1982, Plummer suggested giving the miniature to one of Bourdichon's assistants, who also seems to have executed a book of hours now at the Morgan Library and Museum in New York (M. 380). Most of the decoration of the manuscript can, however, be attributed to Robinet Testard, the illuminator for the Angoulême court. He created a number of manuscripts for Charles and, beginning in 1488 (the date of their marriage), for Louise of Savoy, his countess. The absence of any references to Louise in the present book of hours would seem to indicate that it was completed before their marriage.

The portion that Testard executed is remarkable and unique in more ways than one. Though the iconography of books of hours was well established, here it is atypical in its creative reliance on engraved models, which has led some scholars to describe the work as "experimental." For some pages, Testard used Netherlandish or German engravings, notably those of Israhel van Meckenem, which he pasted into the volume and illuminated, while introducing significant changes. These engravings can perhaps be explained by Charles of Angoulême's taste for the innovation that was the medium of printing. Absent from the 1496 inventory, the manuscript had probably already left the collections of the Angoulême family by then. • MHt

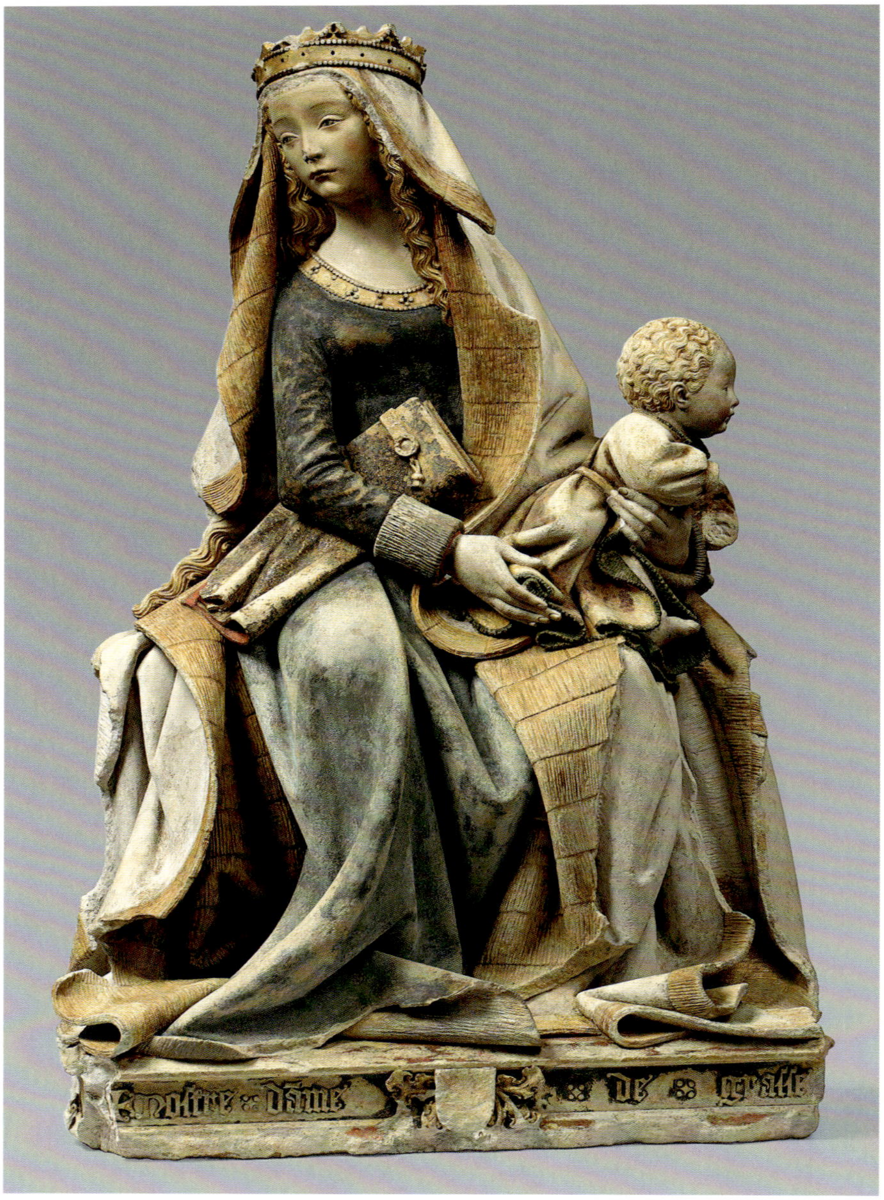

[20]

Our Lady of Grace (Notre Dame de Grasse)

Languedoc, c. 1470

Polychromed limestone; 112 x 75 x 38 cm ($44\frac{1}{8}$ x $29\frac{1}{2}$ x $14\frac{15}{16}$ in.)

Musée des Augustins, Toulouse, RA 788

INSCRIBED: *Nostre dame de grasse* [Our lady of grace] (on base)

PROVENANCE: Probably Toulouse, Church of the Jacobins. Musée des Augustins, by 1805.

BIBLIOGRAPHY: Courajod 1899–1903, p. 46. Vitry 1901, p. 59. Lahondès 1920, p. 160. Bévotte 1936, p. 30. Prin 1952. Ternois 1962, pp. 5–10. Müller 1966, pp. 35, 37. Bousquet 1968, p. 214. Bévotte 1982. Prigent 1999. Prin 2001. Riou 2005–06.

EXHIBITIONS: London 1932, no. 19. Toulouse 2005–06.

THIS MASTERPIECE, restored in 2005 with the aid of the BNP Paribas Foundation, may originally have been part of a larger sculptural group. The pose of the Virgin and Child—turning away from each other, looking in opposite directions—suggests this context. The hypothesis that donors were included on either side of Mary and Jesus, in the context of a funeral monument, seems at present to be the most plausible (Riou in Toulouse 2005–06). The Virgin's pose or the lower part of her drapery were often repeated: in Saint-Alain in Lavaur and Saint-Nicolas in Toulouse, in each of which the Virgin and Child are the central element in an Adoration of the Magi from about 1500 (Toulouse 2005–06, figs. 8–11), and also in Lauzerville, in this instance for the robes of Saint Anne in a later Holy Kinship. If the hypothesis of a funerary context for the present sculpture is correct, it could have come from the axial chapel of the church of the monastery of the Jacobins in Toulouse, granted to the Palays family at the end of the thirteenth century and dedicated to "Notre-Dame-de-Grasse" (Prin 2001). The earlier attribution to the well-traveled sculptor Jacques Morel (died 1459) does not seem tenable to this author, both for stylistic reasons and because of the likely date of *Our Lady of Grace* in the 1470s. The statue's actual creation may perhaps be somewhat later within this framework, in light of the date of most of the works that show its influence, or slightly earlier, if the little *Virgin of the Annunciation* in Inières that so strongly shows its influence can actually be dated before 1480 (Toulouse 2005–06, fig. 19). In any case, *Our Lady of Grace* is certainly a major work from the early stages of the revival of sculpture in Languedoc at the end of the fifteenth century. • CR

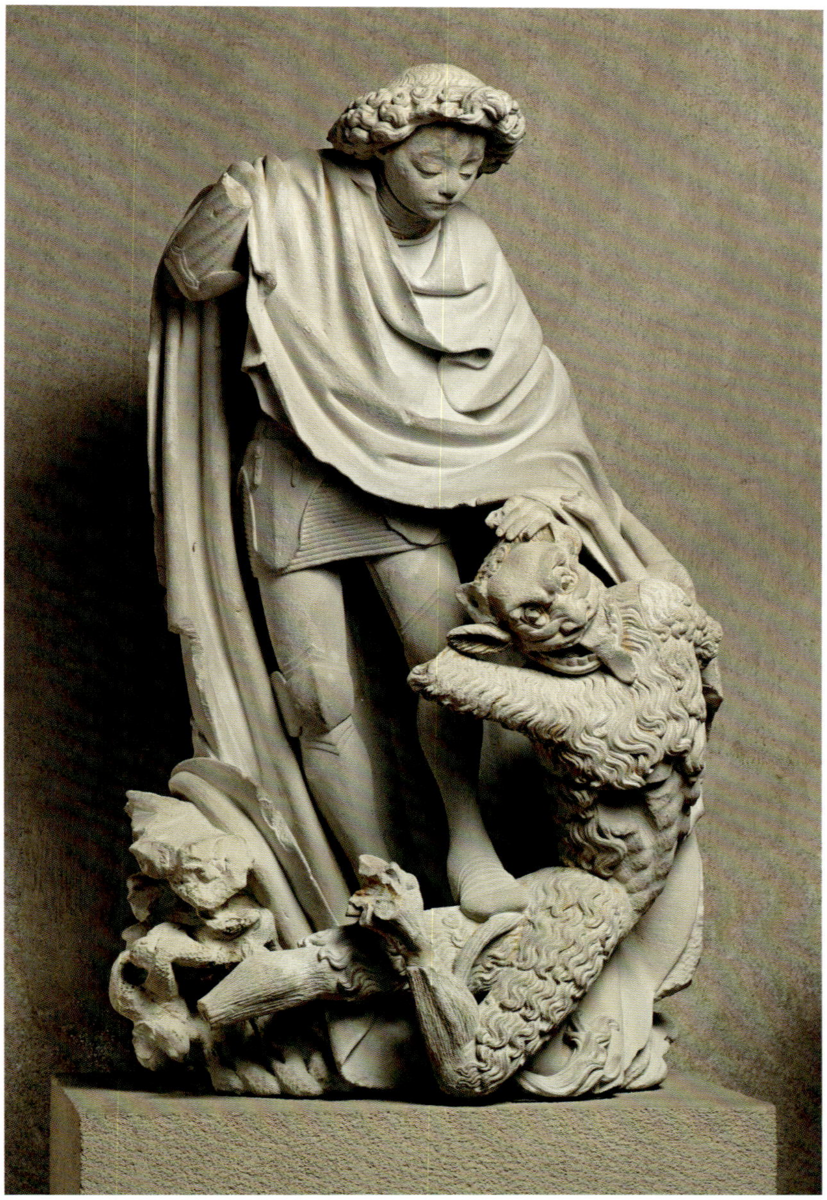

[21]

Saint Michael Defeating the Devil

Languedoc, c. 1500

Limestone, formerly polychromed; 124 x 74 x 48 cm (48 7/8 x 29 1/8 x 18 7/8 in.)

Musée des Augustins, Toulouse, RA 583

PROVENANCE: Probably Toulouse, Church of Saint-Michel. Musée des Augustins, Toulouse, by 1818 or 1820.

BIBLIOGRAPHY: Jacquemin et al. 1818 or 1820, no. 196. Dumège 1828, no. 334. Dumège 1835, no. 477. Roschach 1865, no. 758. Rachou 1912, no. 583. Bévotte 1936, p. 38, pl. VII. Müller 1966, p. 137, fig. 58B. Bousquet 1968, p. 215. Bévotte 1982, pp. 53–54, pl. 6. Chaumet 1998, p. 100 (ill.).

EXHIBITIONS: Paris/Mont-Saint-Michel 1966, no. 42.

THIS WINGLESS Saint Michael fights the devil, from whom he strives to rescue a soul, shown clinging to his cloak with both hands. This iconography is relatively rare, and the overall composition evokes that of the *Saint Michael* in Baume-les-Messieurs, who is also a psychopomp (a guider of souls) and slayer of demons. The childlike face of the *Saint Michael* in Toulouse, with his hair arranged in a crown of generous curls, recalls the angels from Claus Sluter's *Well of Moses* for the charterhouse of Champmol, Dijon. The cloak draped across the front of the torso relates to other works from the beginning of the fifteenth century, such as the *Saint Michael Slaying the Dragon* from Picardy (Musée du Louvre, RF 1342) or another in the château of Pierrefonds. However, the saint's small triangular face, with its expression at once dreamy and childlike, incontestably belongs to the southern French art of Toulouse. The small pouting mouth, together with the sculptor's taste for a graceful silhouette and drapery that falls in broad curves, invite a comparison to the style of the Master of Our Lady of Grace (cat. 20) and also to the face of the *Angel of the Annunciation* from the cathedral of Rodez in Inières, Aveyron (Bévotte 1982, pl. 16). The form of Saint Michael's armor, with its articulated *tassettes* (thigh pieces) and rounded *solerets* (feet), suggest a date of about 1500. • CR

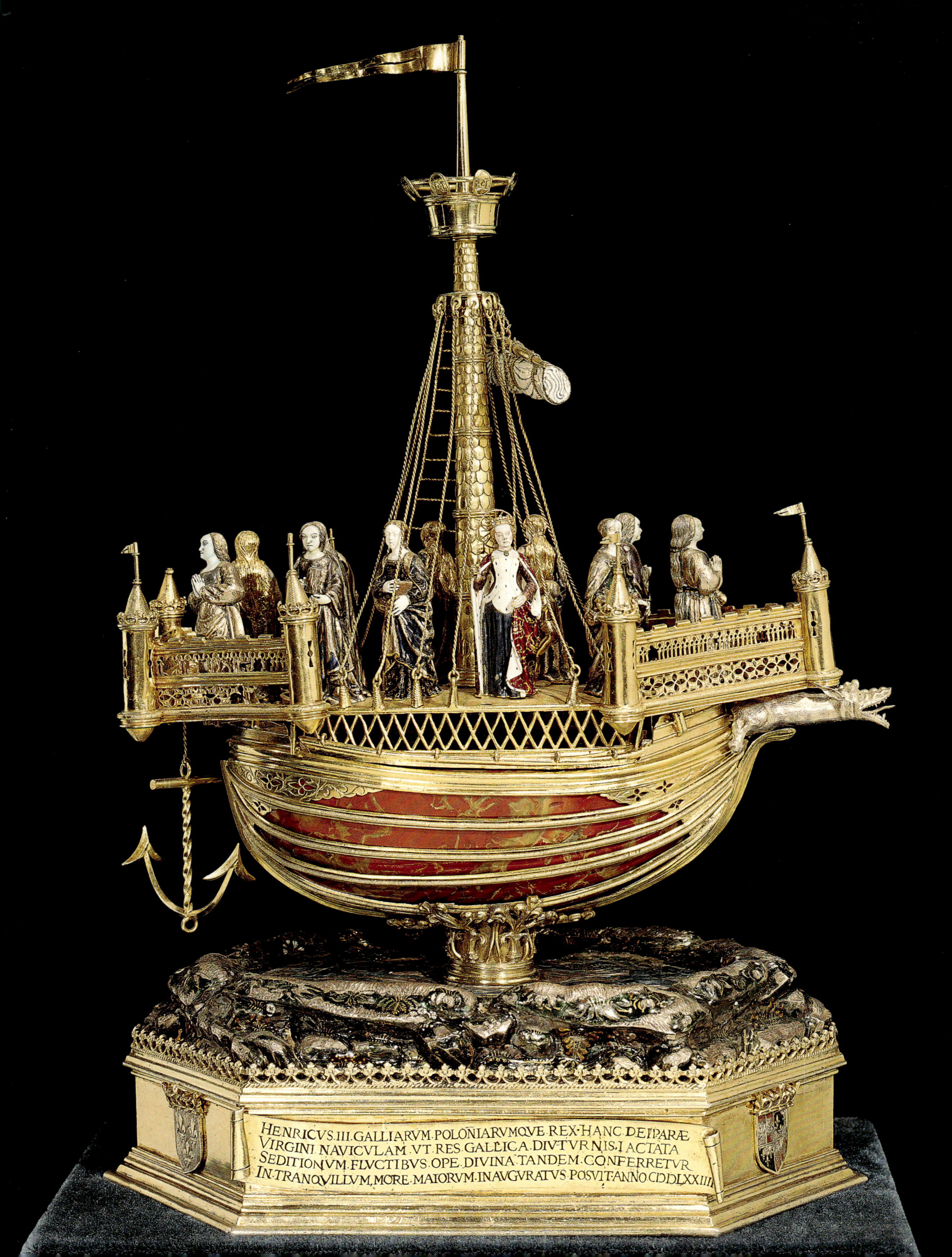
HENRICVS.III.GALLIARVM.POLONIARVMQVE.REX·HANC.DEIPARÆ
VIRGINI.NAVICVLAM.VT.RES.GALLICA.DIVTVRNIS.IACTATA
SEDITIONVM.FLVCTIBVS.OPE.DIVINA.TANDEM.CONFERRETVR
IN.TRANQVILLVM,MORE.MAIORVM.INAVGVRATVS.POSVIT.ANNO.CIƆIƆLXXIIII

THE KINGS AND THEIR ARTISTS

THIERRY CRÉPIN-LEBLOND AND MARTHA WOLFF

The French court remained a model for Europe, even for the Italian princely courts, due to its splendor and opulence as well as the dignity of its ceremonial display. In the years around 1500, it is more difficult to determine the artistic role played by the rulers themselves. Nearly all of the large architectural projects, especially the most innovative ones, for example the châteaux of le Verger or Bury (built by prominent servants of the king, the Marshal de Gyé and Florimond Robertet, respectively), did not develop from a royal decision. But among them are some secular or religious buildings that benefited from the protection of the king and very likely from funding of royal origin. The construction of the Chambre des Comptes and the Pont Notre-Dame in Paris, of the Echiquier in Rouen housing the provincial assembly of Normandy, or of the church of Saint-Aignan in Orléans, were all launched with the approval of the kings and with financial support deriving from taxes.

Nevertheless, certain arrangements at the chateau of Amboise, and later at Blois, correspond to what was clearly a modern vision of the distribution of interior spaces and of their architectural ornamentation. The same was undoubtedly true for their interior decoration, as is suggested by the chamber with a coffered ceiling in the Italian manner in which Anne of Brittany is shown seated with her ladies in the frontispiece of Jean Marot's *Voyage to Genoa* (fig. 31). The detailed account of the reception that Louis XII accorded Philip the Fair and Joanna of Castile at Blois in 1501 includes references to the furnishings of the château and underlines the coexistence of tapestries inherited from Charles VII and Charles VIII with pieces evidently brought back from Naples and Milan (Chatenet and Girault 2010).

It was in fact an explicit wish of the crown of France to thus unite tradition and modernity, in an effort to build on a foundation of legitimacy and exemplarity. The personal taste of Anne of Brittany was for books, and perhaps also for goldsmithwork, even if the earlier destruction of a large number of pieces from the royal treasury during the disasters of the reign of Charles VI undoubtedly explains the use made of her ancestral treasure from the dukes of Brittany to rebuild the royal collection of state jewels and ceremonial goldsmithwork (cat. 38). For lack of an inventory, the existence of a royal painting collection, an innovation in France at this date, is difficult to define precisely, even if certain illustrious works by Leonardo da Vinci, for example *The Virgin of the Rocks* (fig. 32) and *La Belle Ferronnière*, both in the Musée du Louvre, are known to have belonged to the royal collection as early as the reign of Louis XII (Béguin 2004, pp. 64–65).

Painters to the king, like Jean Bourdichon, were charged with disseminating the ruler's portrait and with diverse other tasks, such as making funeral masks, as Bourdichon did of Saint Francis of Paola when the hermit, highly esteemed by the royal family, died in 1507. The portrait of the dauphin Charles Orland painted by Jean Hey, was, in contrast, a private commission, intended to be sent to his father, Charles VIII, who was then campaigning in Italy (fig. 33).

Anne of Brittany played a forceful role in the domain of funerary sculpture, taking advantage of Jean Perréal and Michel Colombe for the tomb of her parents (fig. 12), and supervising the completion of the tomb of her two young sons and probably that of her deceased first husband, Charles VIII. In another example of the combination of traditional and Italian forms, the latter was entrusted to Guido Mazzoni, but was influenced by the kneeling funerary effigy of the king's father, Louis XI, in the collegiate church of Notre-Dame de Cléry, whose design had occupied first Jean Fouquet and then Colin d'Amiens (fig. 6).

It was, however, especially in the domain of the book that royal commissions made their mark: sumptuous manuscripts illuminated by Jean Bourdichon or Jean Poyer; editions printed on vellum by Antoine Vérard and enriched with illuminations and gold decoration; elegant bindings of rich fabric or gilded leather. The royal library truly resonated with the artistic and intellectual evolution of the period, while being enriched by the books captured from the kings of Naples and the dukes of Milan, an additional means for the king of France to claim direct heritage from antiquity, as the new *Imperator* charged with a Christian mission in a direct line from the Emperor Constantine.

Apart from the direct commissions of the sovereigns, a wealth of more indirect evidence attests to the wide-ranging role that art played in the language of royal legitimacy. Whether made for the kings or their subjects, works with reference to the rituals of coronation and royal burial, or to saints viewed as special protectors of the monarchy, drew on the pervasive symbolism of a royal religion, frequently joining it to more personal emblems and devices of individual monarchs.

The story of the conversion and baptism of Clovis, king of the Salian Franks, made him a second Constantine. The Holy Ampule of baptismal chrism (*Sainte Ampoule*),

---

Facing Page

FIGURE 30.
Tours. *Nef of Saint Ursula*, c. 1500. Carnelian and silver, gilded and enameled. Treasury of the Cathedral of Notre-Dame, Reims, on deposit at the Palais du Tau, Centre des monuments nationaux.

thought to have been miraculously delivered for Clovis's baptism and then preserved at Reims to anoint later kings as part of the coronation ritual, supported the notion of sacred kingship. Saint Remy, who baptized Clovis, holds the Holy Ampule on the woodcut frontispiece replete with royal symbols from Robert Gaguin's history (Scheller 1983, fig. 29). The confraternity of the Puy-Notre-Dame d'Amiens used the Holy Ampule as the basis for its annual poetry competition and related painting in 1501. The wings that flanked the lost central mariological allegory expand on the sacred nature of French kingship by pairing the anointing of King David, the ancestor of Christ, with the coronation of Louis XII (cats. 30–31). Louis XII kneels below a baldachin labeled *VNG DIEV. VNG ROI. VNE FOI* (One God, one king, one faith) as the ecclesiastical and secular peers of France support him and bear the articles needed for the coronation of the Very Christian King (*le roi très chrétien*) (for the role of the peers, see Contamine 1988). The *Baptism of Clovis*, set in the Sainte-Chapelle built by Saint Louis, is among the surviving panels from an altarpiece by the Master of Saint Giles that features other royal settings and subjects, including the pardon of Charlemagne set in the royal abbey of Saint-Denis (cats. 32–33; fig. 34).

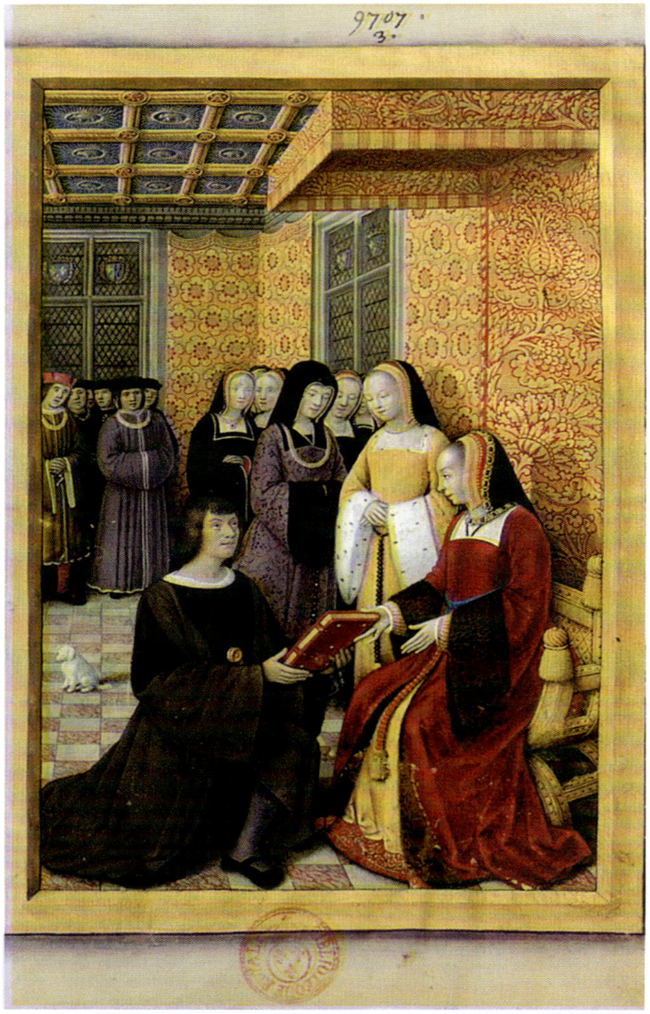

FIGURE 31.
Jean Bourdichon. *Jean Marot Presents His Book to Anne of Brittany*, in Jean Marot, *Voyage to Genoa*. Tempera on parchment. Bibliothèque national de France, Paris, ms. fr. 5091, f. 1.

Louis XII included his sanctified ancestors Saint Charlemagne and Saint Louis among his patrons on the diptych-like presentation bifolio of his book of hours, illuminated by Jean Bourdichon (cat. 40). The other two saints in this miniature are Saint Michael, patron of the royal order and a defender of the kingdom in the recent struggles with the English, and Saint Denis, whose abbey outside Paris safeguarded the regalia, the royal tombs, and the historical record of French kings. Charlemagne was often treated as a saint and paired with Saint Louis, who had reigned as Louis IX; the two were represented on a lost triptych commissioned from Bourdichon by Charles VIII in 1491. Probably in part because of his name, but also due to an atmosphere in the 1490s that encouraged imperial ambitions, Charles VIII associated himself with the emperor Charlemagne. The unusual name of Charles Orland given to the dauphin refers to the exploits of Roland and Charlemagne. The presentation page of Charles VIII's book of hours, now in the Biblioteca Nacional, Madrid, originally showed Charles presented by Saint Charlemagne as two angels hold the paired escutcheons of France and the kingdom of Naples–Sicily–Jerusalem that the king claimed through René of Anjou. This heraldry, together with Charlemagne's attributes—the orb and closed imperial crown—alludes to Charles's VIII Italian project and the appeal to a universal crusading mission that accompanied it (Scheller 1981–82, p. 25, fig. 6). Louis XII's acceptance of these goals is implied in the superimposition of his features on those of Charles VIII on the manuscript page.

The ceremonial entries of the monarchs into the major cities of the kingdom were an occasion for the renewal of a city's privileges, for loyal *tableaux vivants* and the poetry of rhetoricians, and also for the presentation of valuable gifts to the sovereign. For Anne of Brittany's entry in 1494, Lyon commissioned gold medals with images of Charles VIII and Anne, carried by a gold lion emblematic of the city itself (cat. 24). For her first entry as queen to Louis XII in 1499, a less costly vessel of Venetian glass held an imposing, larger medal. Often reissued, it became a signal image of the king and queen. A splendid table ornament, or *nef*, of hardstone, gilded silver, and enamel presented to Anne in 1500, on her first entry to Tours as Louis XII's queen, was sacralized and personalized at her order five years later through the addition of a relic and enameled figures of Saint Ursula, a patron saint of Brittany, with her martyr companions (fig. 30).

Entries and the processions accompanying coronations and funerals made use of the emblems of royal power. The prime symbol of the monarchy and of France itself was

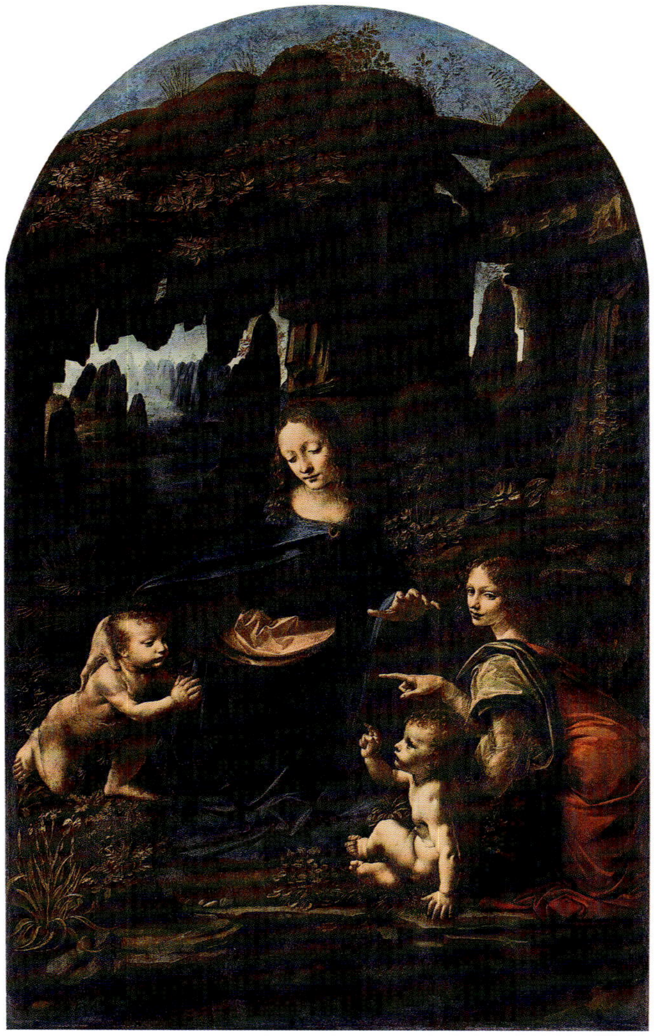

FIGURE 32.
Leonardo da Vinci. *Virgin and Child with Saint John the Baptist and an Angel (The Virgin of the Rocks).*
Oil on panel, transferred to canvas. Musée du Louvre, Paris.

the escutcheon with three gold fleurs-de-lis on a blue field. Others were the crown with fleur-de-lis fleurons above a jeweled band, and the collar of cockle shells with a pendant jewel of Saint Michael belonging to the Order of Saint Michael founded by Louis XI in 1469. More personalized symbols included the crowned initials of the king or of the king and queen linked, as well as their livery colors, the personal colors used on the garments delivered by the king to his retinue (black gold, violet, and silver for Charles VIII; yellow and red for Louis XII). Emblems might be invented to respond to a particular situation, or they might be inherited from an earlier royal ancestor—the golden sun used by Charles VIII had been employed in the time of Charles VII on the Rouen tapestry of the *Winged Stags* and on the newly discovered hanging for that king's throne (cat. 1; Antoine 2010). Radiant suns also decorate the rich gold tabard worn by Louis XII in the presentation miniature of his book of hours (cat. 40) and may reflect his actual attire for his first entry into Paris after his coronation (Backhouse in Los Angeles/London 2005–06). Louis XII's porcupine emblem was inherited from his grandfather, Louis I of Orléans. His subjects included it in the rhetoric of entries—a large mechanical porcupine greeted Louis on the occasion of his 1498 entry into Paris. The creature also decorated the château of Blois, the marble fountain now in the Louvre (cat. 99), the trumpeters' banners in the *Coronation of Louis XII* (cat. 31), and the king's horse trappings in the frontispiece of Rochechouart's Monstrelet (cat. 111). In Bourdichon's illustrations for Marot's *Voyage to Genoa* of about 1508, the porcupine emblem decorates the coffers of the ceiling of the queen's chamber (fig. 31), but on another page the king and his mount sport the new and more magnanimous emblem of a hive and bees (fig. 1), while the porcupine capable of throwing his spines decorates the back of his officers' tabards (Hochner 2001). Anne of Brittany used the emblems of her family; foremost among them were the ermines of the arms of Brittany. The *cordelière*, the knotted rope belt of the Franciscan order that was also associated with her father, Francis II of Brittany, was widely and imaginatively used to tie works of art to her. It appears in the margins of her manuscripts, runs around the edge of the tomb slab for her two small sons (fig. 49), and forms the rim of the vessel containing her heart placed in the tomb of her parents (cat. 39). In this period, the language of royal devices, colors, and heraldry occupies a middle point between its feverish use in the rivalries of the early fifteenth century (Beaune 1981) and the deliberately obscure humanist emblems of the later sixteenth century.

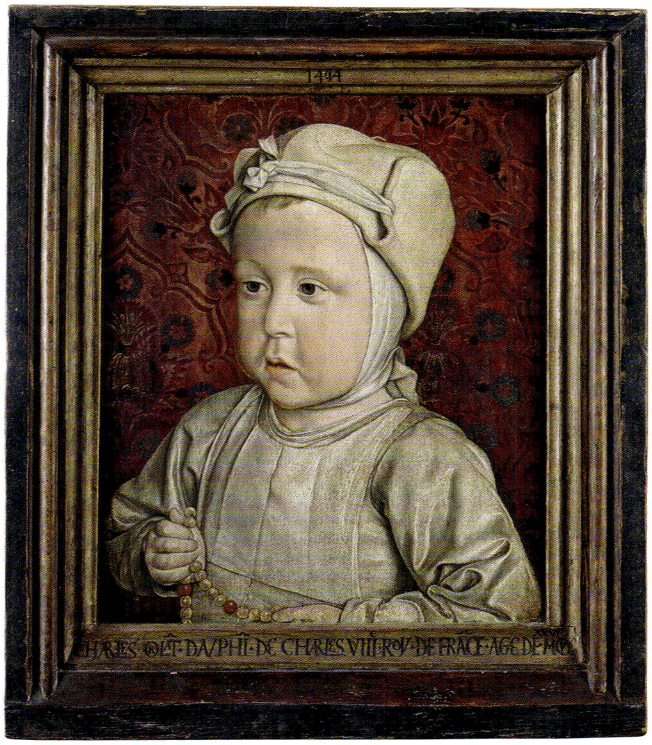

FIGURE 33.
Jean Hey (The Master of Moulins). *Charles Orland, Dauphin of France.* Oil on panel. Musée du Louvre, Paris.

FRANCESCO LAURANA
(active by 1453–1502)

Medal of Louis XI

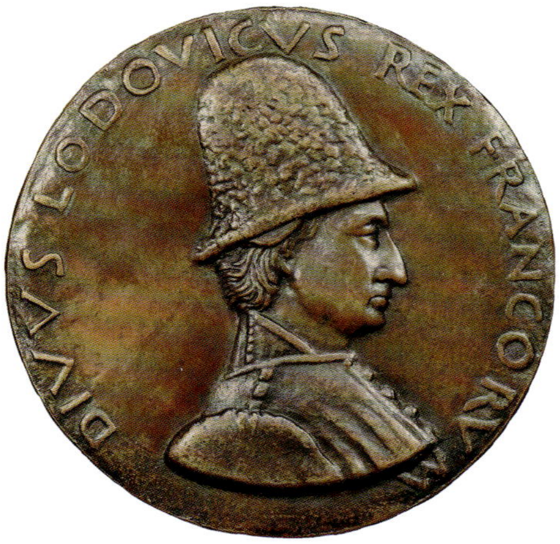

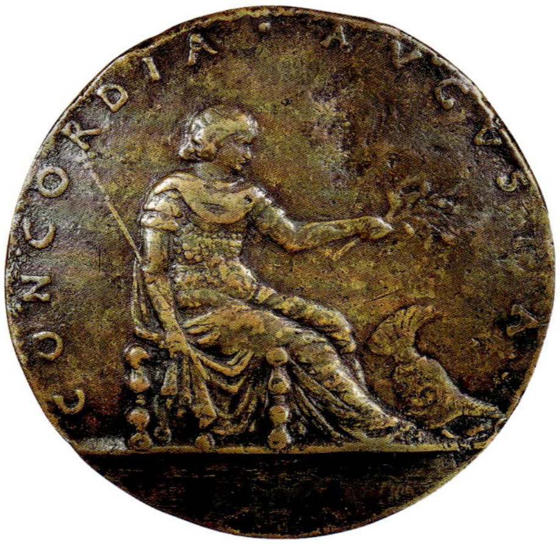

[22]

Provence, c. 1465

Bronze; diam. 8.5 cm (3 3/8 in.)

Bibliothèque nationale de France, Paris, Department of Coins, Medals, and Antiquities, Armand-Valton 144.

INSCRIBED: See below.

PROVENANCE: Bequeathed by Prosper Valton, 1907.

BIBLIOGRAPHY: See below.

EXHIBITIONS: Aix-en-Provence 1981, no. C8.

[23]

Provence, c. 1465

Bronze; diam. 8.5 cm. (3 3/8 in.)

Bibliothèque nationale de France, Paris, Department of Coins, Medals, and Antiquities, série royale 2790

INSCRIBED: *DIVVS LODOVICVS REX FRANCORVM* [Divine Louis, king of France] (on the obverse); *CONCORDIA AVGVSTA* [Concord of Augustus] (on the reverse)

PROVENANCE: Royal collection.

BIBLIOGRAPHY: Hill 1930, no. 65. Kruft 1995, pp. 67–81.

THE MEDAL OF Louis XI, the only one by Francesco Laurana not intended for the court of Anjou, was no doubt designed under the patronage of René of Anjou as a diplomatic gift, perhaps on the occasion of the Peace of October 1465, which put an end to the League of the Public Weal (*Ligue du Bien Publique*), or for the betrothal of his grandson Nicolas of Anjou to Anne of France, daughter of Louis XI, in August 1466. A version signed *FRANCICVS LAVRANA FECIT* on the exergue (that is, below the bust) has been recorded, but is untraced. The portrait of the still youthful king of France with an aquiline profile may have been modeled on a painting or drawing executed at the time of his accession in 1461, when he was 38 years old. He is wearing a buttoned doublet and the beaver hat that he favored. The appellation *divus*, reserved in antiquity for emperors and empresses deified after death, had been adopted as a purely laudatory title in the medals of Pisanello made about 1449/50 for Alphonse V of Aragon, in the lifetime of the king. The reverse borrows the theme of the Peace of Augustus from Roman imperial coins, but the conventional allegorical figure of a woman holding an olive branch and a scepter, like the Roman image of Peace, has been transformed into an idealized representation of the sovereign wearing the cuirass and the cloak of a general, with a Roman helmet at his feet. Thus the medal is a political mate to Francesco Laurana's medal of René of Anjou and Jeanne de Laval (cat. 13) in its reference to the peace so much desired by René, which was to remain only a pious wish. The medal had no artistic successor at the court of Louis XI, but in the seventeenth century, the portrait by Laurana would serve as a model for a reproduction on a commemorative medal honoring the establishment of the Order of Saint Michael, with, on the reverse, the royal shield surrounded by the collar of the order and the inscription *SANCTI MICHAELIS ORDINIS INSTITVTOR, 1469* (Bibliothèque nationale de France, Department of Coins, Medals, and Antiquities, série royale 27). • IV-P

JEAN PERRÉAL
(active 1485–1530)

LOUIS LEPÈRE
(died 1500)

JEAN LEPÈRE
(died after 1534)

NICOLAS OF FLORENCE
(died 1499)

[24]

Medal of Charles VIII and Anne of Brittany

Lyon, 1494

Gold; diam. 4 cm (1 9/16 in.)

Bibliothèque nationale de France, Paris, Department of Coins, Medals and Antiquities, série royale 31

INSCRIBED: *FELIX FORTVNA EXPLORATVM ACTVLIT 1493* [Propitious fortune has brought us that which was long awaited 1493 (old style)] (obverse); *R P LVGDVNEN ANNA REGNANTE CONFLAVIT* (The republic of Lyon had me wrought in the reign of Anne); a lion passant (reverse)

PROVENANCE: Royal collection.

BIBLIOGRAPHY: Rondot 1885. Mazerolle 1902, vol. 1, nos. 1–2, vol. 2, no. 22. Jones 1982, no. 13. Tricou 1958, nos. 2–3. Pollard 1967, no. 526.

EXHIBITIONS: Paris 1971, no. 11.

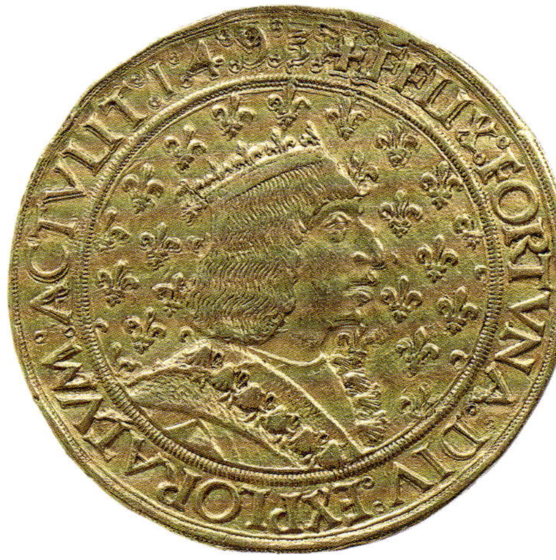

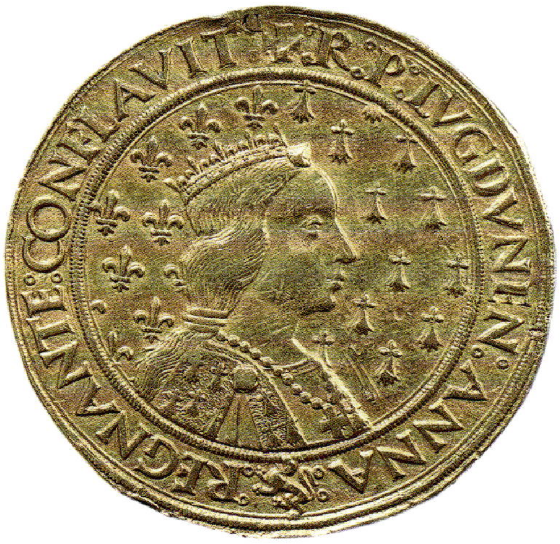

On February 19, 1494, the consuls who governed Lyon deliberated over a present to mark the ceremonial entry of Anne of Brittany into the city, which was to occur in mid-March (Municipal archives, Lyon, BB 21, f. 40). They rejected a "tree of gilded silver with, instead of leaves, several fine gold pieces fashioned like medals, which would be well stamped and portray from life the king on one side and the queen on the other" (*arbre d'argent doré et, en lieu de feulles, quelques belles pièces d'or faictes à façon de metailles, esquelles feussent bien empreinctz et pourtraictz au vif le Roy d'un costé et la Royne de l'autre*); it was judged to be too costly and "of very little beauty" (*de bien petite beaulté*). Instead, they agreed that, as a reference to the name of their city (Lyon/lion), they would have made "a handsome lion of gold, finely made and finely represented, seated on its bottom with its two front paws holding a fine cup of gold in the old fashion, as is painted on the Adoration of the Three Kings, and within the cup a hundred fine pieces of gold made in the fashion of medals, as is specified, and a fine shield belted on his side by a fine belt of gold with the arms of the Queen" (*ung beau lyon d'or bien faict et bien tiré, assiz sur son cul et de ses deux plotes devant tenant une belle coppe d'or à la façon ancienne, telle qu'on la painct ès troys roys, et cent belles pièces d'or faictes en façon de metailles comme dict est dedans la coppe, et une belle terguète çainte sur son costé d'une belle çainture d'or ès armes de la Royne*). For making the coins, the lion, the gadrooned cup, and the shield, Louis Lepère, goldsmith and engraver of the Mint in Lyon, his son Jean, and his son-in-law Nicolas of Florence were paid 55 *livres tournois*, out of a total of 1,940 *livres tournois* (Municipal archives, CC 527). The planning of the ceremonies of the royal entry was assigned to Jean Perréal, who may have supplied the drawings for the profiles of Anne and Charles VIII, the latter wearing the collar of the Order of Saint Michael. The Latin inscriptions on obverse and reverse celebrate the arrival of the king and queen. Although nothing remains of their container, the gold medals worth 7 *écus* each (24 g or 7/8 oz.) and those of silver intended for the queen's entourage became so emblematic of the city that they were re-struck in 1502 and 1514. For the first entry of Charles's successor, Louis XII, into the city in 1499, Jean Lepère and Nicolas of Florence, again following a model by Perréal, created a gift in the form of the king's emblem of a porcupine, in three kilograms (6 5/8 pounds) of gold. • IV-P

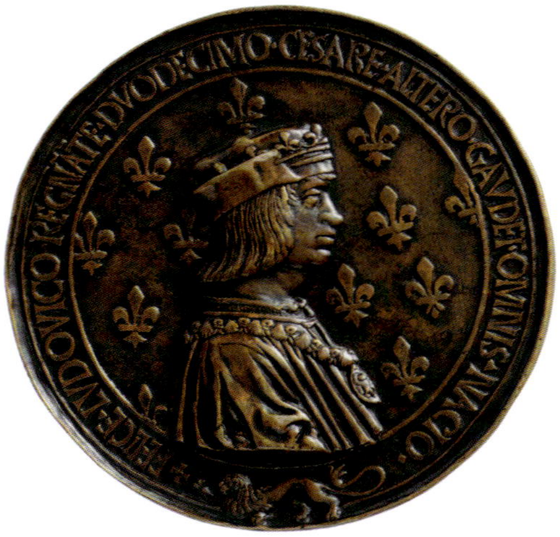

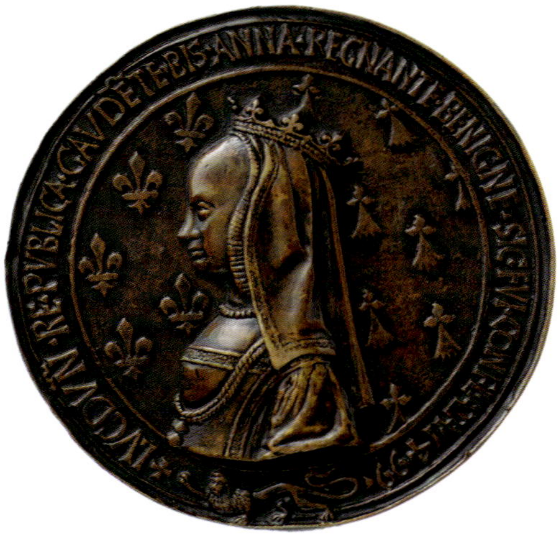

JEAN LEPÈRE
(died after 1534)

NICOLAS LECLERC
(active 1487–1507)

JEAN DE SAINT-PRIEST
(active 1490–1516)

Medal of Louis XII and Anne of Brittany

[25]

Lyon, 1499

Bronze; diam. 17 cm. (6 11/16 in.)

Musée National de la Renaissance, Ecouen, ECl. 477 (obverse exhibited)

INSCRIBED: See below.

PROVENANCE: Alexandre du Sommerard (d. 1842), Hôtel de Cluny, Paris; Musée de Cluny, Paris, opened in 1844; transferred to the Musée National de la Renaissance, 1977.

BIBLIOGRAPHY: See below.

[26]

Lyon, 1499

Bronze; diam. 11.1 cm x 1.6 cm (4 3/8 x 5/8 in.)

The Metropolitan Museum of Art, New York, gift of Ogden Mills, 1925.142.43 (reverse exhibited)

INSCRIBED: *FELICE LVDOVICO REGNATE DVODECIMO CESARE ALTERO GAVDET OMNIS NACIO* [All the nation rejoices under the fortunate reign of Louis XII, the new Caesar] (obverse); *LVGDVN RE PVBLICA GAVDETE BIS ANNA REGNANTE BENIGNE SIC FVI CONGLATA 1499* [I was struck under the second benevolent reign of Anne for which the republic of Lyon rejoices 1499] (reverse)

PROVENANCE: Ogden L. Mills, New York; given to the Metropolitan Museum of Art, 1925.

BIBLIOGRAPHY: Rondot 1885, p. 29. Rondot 1904, p. 77. Mazerolle 1904, vol. 2, no. 27. Tricou 1958, p. 5. Sterling 1963a, p. 5. Pollard 1967, no. 527. Jones 1982, no. 15. New York/Washington 1994, under no. 140.

EXHIBITIONS: New York 1979.

ON MARCH 18, 1499, when the aldermen of Lyon again commissioned a medal to commemorate the joyous entry of Anne of Brittany into their city—her second, following her second marriage, to Louis XII—it was no longer a question of producing multiples (see cat. 24), but of creating a single object on a large scale. The goldsmith and sculptor (*tailleur d'ymaiges*) Jean Lepère and his colleague Nicolas Leclerc, another engraver documented between 1487 and 1507, were commissioned "to make the medal struck to give to the Queen, the King on one side and the Queen on the other, with a background of fleurs-de-lis and ermines as they belong to each, and a lion beneath on each side within the circle of the inscription. Said inscription will be devised and given to them. Said medal to be made as soon as possible" (*de faire la medaille arrestée pour donner à la Royne, le Roy d'un costé et la Royne de l'autre, avec semence de fleurs de liz et armynes, ainsi qu'il s'appartient, et ung lion au-dessoubz de chacun costé dedans le circuit de l'escripture; laquelle escripture sera advisée et à eulx baillée. Laquelle medaille sera faicte le plus tost que possible sera*). The Latin inscriptions are then specified.

Leclerc and another Lyonnais *ymaigeur*, Jean de Saint-Priest, documented from 1490 to 1516, were paid four *écus d'or* "for the carving and fashioning of designs and models to make the medal for the gift and present made for the said lady" (*pour la taille et façon des pourtraictz et molles pour faire la medaille du don et present faict à ladicte dame*) while Jean Lepère received eighteen *écus* "for the fashioning of the gold medal" (*pour la façon de la medaille d'or*), and the merchant Jacques Baronnat three *écus* "for a cup of Venetian glass bought by him to hold and present said medal piece" (*pour une coupe de voirre de Venize, par luy achaptée pour mectre et presenter ladicte pièce medaille*). Jean Lepère, who employed his brother Colin and a founder, also received a commission to make from the same pattern "another medal of plain copper [bronze] to be kept in the city hall" (*une autre medaille de cuyvre brute pour la garder en la maison de la ville*). The version in gold is lost, but the example in bronze was the basis for many re-casts produced up until the nineteenth century, making it one of the best known of French medals. It achieves a felicitous harmony in the melding of traditions (cast medal, elongated bust portrait, and heraldic motifs). The drawing for the king, who wears a crown set into a cloth cap and the collar of the Order of Saint Michael, and that for the queen, who wears a fleur-de-lis crown over her veil, a pearl necklace, and a double chain with a pendant, have sometimes been attributed to Jean Perréal. • IV-P

[27]

Golden Bull of Louis XII

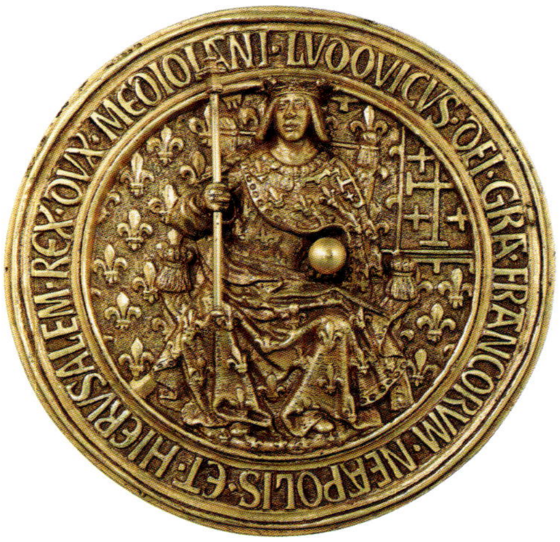

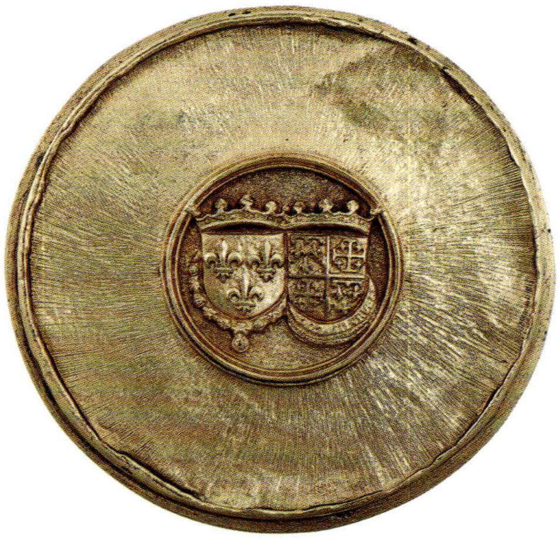

Paris, 1500

Gold, engraved, enameled, and chiseled on a wax core; traces of blue enamel (tunic, lining of the cape, cushion, background), white (arms of Jerusalem), and red (reverse); two holes pierced into the rim; diam. 10 cm (3 5/16 in.); 303.28 g (10 11/16 oz.)

Bibliothèque nationale de France, Paris, Department of Coins, Medals, and Antiquities, 56.439

INSCRIBED: *LVDOVICVS DEI GRA. FRANCORVM NEAPOLIS ET HIERVSALEM REX DVX MEDIOLANI* [Louis, by the grace of God, king of France, Naples and Jerusalem, duke of Milan] (on the obverse)

PROVENANCE: Probably Prince Honoré III of Monaco (d. 1795); acquired by order of Napoleon Bonaparte as First Consul and placed in the Cabinet of Medals on 6 Floréal, Year XI (April 26, 1803); found in the Seine after it was stolen, 1831.

BIBLIOGRAPHY: Millin 1808. Millin 1814. *Trésor de numismatique* 1834, p. 13. De Wailly 1838, pp. 356, 385. Robiano 1853, pp. 32–34. Chabouillet 1858, pp. 483–84. Douët d'Arcq 1863, no. 91. Babelon 1900, pp. 303–04. Pastoureau 1981, pp. 4–6. Dalas 1991, pp. 308–09. Dhénin 1995, pp. 177–78. Dhénin 2002, pp. 107–10.

EXHIBITIONS: Washington 1995, no. 58. Fontevraud 2001, no. 217.

WITH THE secret Treaty of Grenada, signed November 11, 1500, Louis XII of France and Ferdinand of Aragon divided the Kingdom of Naples between them, setting off the Third Italian War (1500–04). The French entered Naples in June 1501, but the alliance with Aragon had fallen apart by 1502, and the defeat of Louis's troops by the Aragonese at Cerignola in April 1503 sounded the call to retreat. This seal is thought to have been used for the official treaty in 1500. Louis XII's claim and that of his predecessor Charles VIII to the throne of Naples was made as heirs of René of Anjou and the tradition of Angevin rulers of Naples; accordingly, Louis XII is shown dressed in a cloak that combines the arms of France and Naples quartered with the emblems of Anjou and Jerusalem, on a background of the same arms. He used the titles King of Naples and Jerusalem and Duke of Milan until 1504. On the reverse, the escutcheon of France, surrounded by the collar of the Order of Saint Michael, is coupled with that of Naples, with the motto *Los en crossant* (Increasing honor) above the Angevin Order of the Crescent.

The craftsmanship has no match among other gold seals, in terms of both weight and technique: the object features four applied elements, detailed regalia, high relief, and polychromy. However, this is not the cover of a casket of a seal (Dhénin 2002), but rather the seal proper that falls within the sigillary tradition of the Angevin kings of Naples. The iconography and dimensions are those of a royal seal, with a counter seal of coats of arms on a smaller scale, similar to the great seal of Louis XII for the kingdom of Naples (Archives of Monte Cassino, VI.1.4) whose die was sent to Italy in 1501 for use by the chamberlain, Etienne de Vesc, and subsequently by the chancellor of Naples, Jean Nicolay. However, the naturalistic portrait of Louis on the bull is unique. • IV-P

[28]

MASTER OF THE CHRONIQUE SCANDALEUSE

La Mer des hystoires. Le Martirologe des sainctz.

Paris, July 1488 (vol. 1); February 1488–1489 (vol. 2)

Printed by Pierre Le Rouge for Vincent Commin

Tempera and gold on vellum, red moroccan long-grained leather binding (by Bradel the Elder); 2 volumes; 270 ff. (vol. 1, not exhibited in Chicago); 310 ff. (vol. 2); 44 x 31 x 12 cm (17 3/8 x 12 3/16 x 4 3/4 in.) (each volume, closed)

Bibliothèque nationale de France, Paris, Department of Rare Books, Réserve Vélins, 677 (vol. 2)

PROVENANCE: Presentation copy made for Charles VIII (d. 1498); royal libraries of Amboise, Blois, and Fontainebleau; Bibliothèque Royale.

BIBLIOGRAPHY: Claudin 1900–14, vol. 1, pp. 458–70. Brun 1968, pp. 191–97. CIBN, no. R-221.

EXHIBITIONS: Lucerne 1949, no. 66. Blois/Paris 1992–93, no. 17. Washington 1995, no. 49.

SHOWN: Frontispiece, ff. A1v–A2r

THIS, THE FIRST PRINTED BOOK to enter the library of Charles VIII, was also one of the most prestigious. It is a luxury copy on vellum of *La Mer des histoires* (The Sea of Histories), the most beautiful—or at least the most ambitious—illustrated French incunabulum. This publication is the French translation of a universal chronicle entitled *Rudimentum novitiorum* (A Handbook of Beginners), compiled in Lübeck and printed there by Lucas Brandis on August 5, 1475. In the French translation there are a number of added features: a geographical dictionary, a description of the Holy Land, a collection of Aesop's *Fables*, and, most significantly, a genealogy of the kings of France extending to the coronation of Charles VIII in 1484. The printer Pierre Le Rouge calls himself "printer to the King" in the colophon (the first known instance of this role). The edition was sold by the bookseller Vincent Commin.

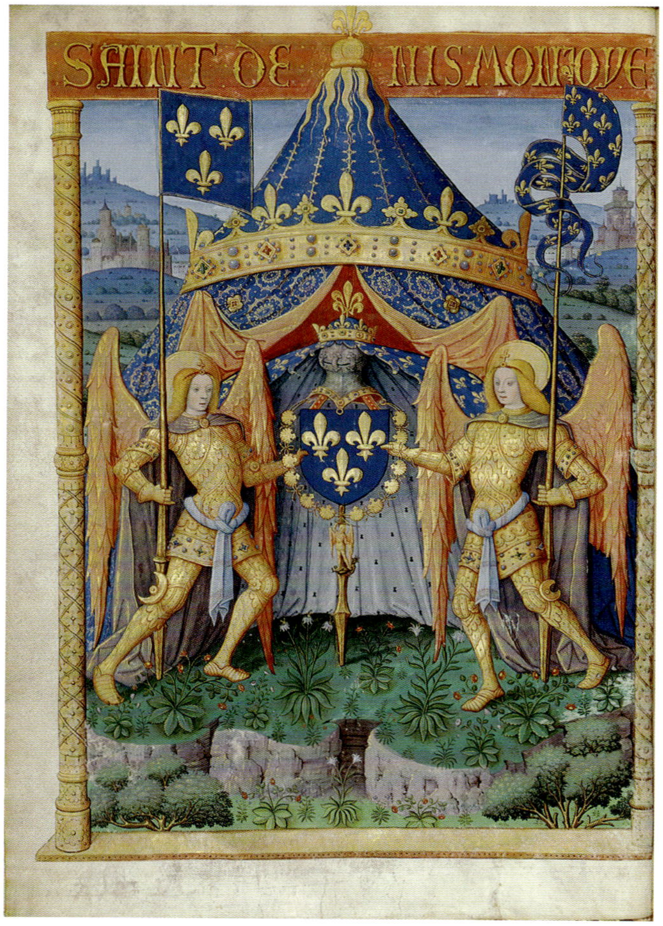

The abundant and ambitious woodcut illustrations include four large historiated initials. Among the plates created especially for this edition are the famous *Baptism of Clovis* juxtaposed with the *Battle of Tolbiac* (cat. 29), as well as genealogical charts (fig. 17). There are also images that show scenes of daily life and episodes from the life of the Virgin; full-page cuts (*The Crossing of the Red Sea*); small illustrations usually found in books of hours; large floriated initials for chapter headings; and many borders featuring scroll-work, birds, and fantastic creatures. Presumably Pierre Le Rouge, who came from a family of calligraphers and illuminators, was the author of some of the woodcuts, of which the bulk later passed into the stock of Antoine Vérard.

Printed on exceptionally fine parchment, this set was fully painted for Charles VIII, with particular care given to the second volume (the one shown here), which includes the genealogy of the kings of France. The 452 miniatures are attributable to several hands; there were at least three different artists, who sometimes only colored in the underlying cuts, and in other cases covered them with original paintings, with lavish use of gold. Two full pages of royal emblems (the arms of France surrounded by the collar of the Order of Saint Michael, the device *Saint Denis Montjoye*, etc.) emphasize the identity of the recipient, who may also have commissioned the work. The borders painted with tendrils of daisies (*marguerites*) and the spectacular painted full page with the daisy stems juxtaposed with the stems of lilies, are a clear allusion to Margaret of Austria, "the little bride." Charles VIII repudiated her in 1491 so that he could wed Anne, duchess of Brittany, whose name appears as a replacement by a second hand over the erased name of Margaret of Austria on the genealogical tree for Louis XI and his children (fig. 17).

This copy deserves deeper analysis. Among the artists responsible for its decoration, only the name of the Master of the Chronique Scandeleuse has so far been advanced (cat. 34). The production quality of this luxury copy elevates a printed book—by its nature commonplace because it is a multiple—to the level of a unique illuminated manuscript worthy of a sovereign. • NP

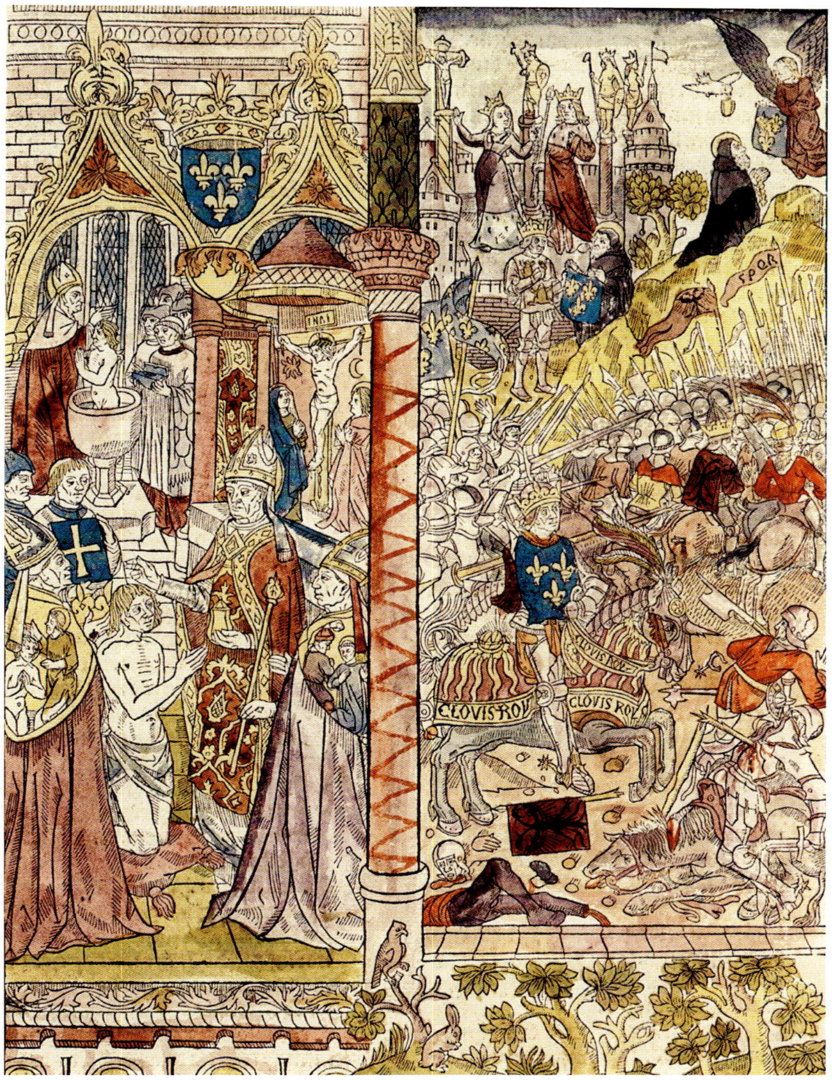

[29]

La Mer des hystoires. Le Martirologe des sainctz.

Paris, July 1488 (vol. 1)–February 1488–89 (vol. 2)

Printed by Pierre Le Rouge for Vincent Commin

Woodcut on paper, handcolored; 41 x 29.2 cm (16⅛ x 11½ in.)

The Library of Congress, Washington, D.C., Thacher Collection, Incun. 1488.R8 (vol. 2)

PROVENANCE: John Boyd Thacher, Albany, N.Y.; by descent to his widow; bequeathed to the Library of Congress, 1926.

BIBLIOGRAPHY: Claudin 1900–14, vol. 1, pp. 458–70. Library of Congress 1915, p. 226, no. 739. Brun 1968 pp. 191–97. CIBN, no. R-221. Hinkle 1991, pp. 38, 95–100.

SHOWN: *Baptism of Clovis and Battle of Tolbiac*, f. S1r

THIS SPECTACULAR full-page woodcut from Pierre Le Rouge's *Mer des hystoires* celebrates the martial and spiritual victories of the Frankish king Clovis (c. 466–511), the first Christian ruler of Gaul. The upper right register details Clovis's conversion. His wife Clothilde first attempts to turn him away from statues of pagan gods to the Crucifixion; then the hermit of Joyenval receives the Holy Ampule (the *Sainte Ampoule* containing coronation oil) and the coat of arms with the fleur-de-lis from an angel. He passes the shield on to Clovis, who is wearing three demonic frogs, an appropriate emblem for the unconverted king who in some early texts was described as a devotee of Satan (Hinkle 1991). The king is said to have finally converted during a pivotal battle against the pagan Alemanni at Tolbiac, around 496, he appears here in the midst of the fray already wearing the fleur-de-lis device. Victory ensued, and he was baptized by Saint Remy, on the left. The entire narrative casts Clovis him as a latter-day Constantine at the Battle of the Milvian Bridge. Traditionally the Holy Ghost is represented bringing the Holy Ampule of chrism for his baptism. Its omission here at Clovis's baptism, as in the St. Giles panel (cat. 32), suggests the elision of the relic with the fleur-de-lis as a symbol of the sacred character of French kingship. Too powerful a monarchic commentary to use only once, the woodcut was reprinted in the same volume to depict Clovis's equally successful later combat against the Goths at Vouillé.

The hand coloring of the Library of Congress exemplar enhances the viewer's understanding of this intricate woodcut without masking its printed lines or the gruesome dead horse and decapitation in the foreground. Five royal shields and a banner have been colored deep blue on this page. They guide the viewer along the story's vertical thrust and also contrast with the dull brown of Clovis's untransformed toads and with the mauve Germanic eagle flags that are trampled into the ground or depicted on the retreating soldiers' backs. The crimson marble veins of the central column unify the divided composition, with red and blue tones applied throughout. The shield in the lower margin of this paper printing is here left blank, awaiting the arms of its purchaser; it was illuminated with Charles VIII's triple fleur-de-lis on an azure ground in his vellum presentation copy (cat. 28). • SKS

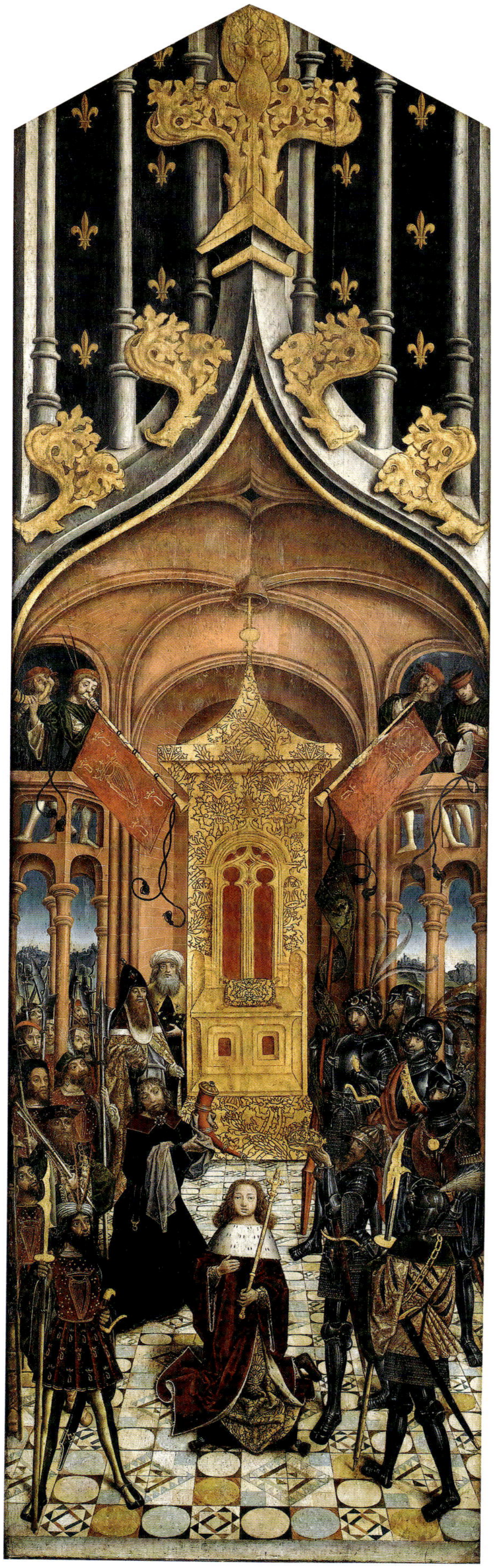

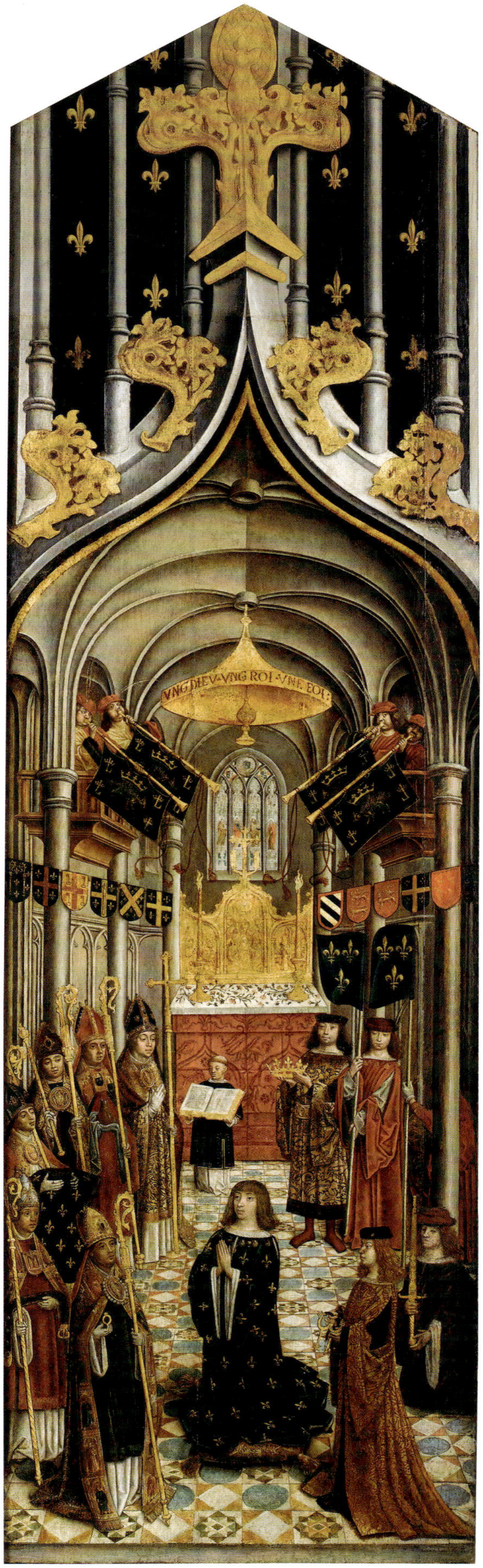
VNG DIEV·VNG ROI·VNE FOI

ATTRIBUTED TO THE MASTER OF ANTOINE CLABAULT

WINGS OF A TRIPTYCH FOR THE PUY NOTRE-DAME D'AMIENS (*THE HOLY AMPULE FOR ROYAL UNCTION*)

[30]

Anointing of David (left wing); *Pietà* (on reverse)

Amiens, 1501

Oil on panel; 194 x 55 cm (76 3/8 x 21 5/8 in.)

Musée de Cluny—Musée national du Moyen Age, Paris, Cl. 822a

PROVENANCE, BIBLIOGRAPHY, EXHIBITIONS: See below.

[31]

Coronation of Louis XII (right wing)

Amiens, 1501

Oil on panel; 194 x 55 cm (76 3/8 x 21 5/8 in)

Musée de Cluny—Musée national du Moyen Age, Paris, Cl. 822 b

PROVENANCE: Executed for the Confraternity of the Puy Notre-Dame d'Amiens in the cathedral of Amiens by order of Jean le Caron du Bouillencourt, 1501. Thieulloy collection, Amiens; acquired by Alexandre du Sommerard (d. 1842), Hôtel de Cluny, Paris, 1839; Musée de Cluny, opened 1844.

BIBLIOGRAPHY: Guilhermy 1844, pp. 21–27, 44–51, 49. Du Sommerard 1838–46, vol. 2, pl. 35, p. 188. Douchet 1862, vol. 2, pp. 136–66. Du Sommerard 1883, no. 1682. Dehaisnes 1890, vol. 33, pp. 183–93. Valet 1902, no. 1682. Durand 1911. Dupont 1933, pp. 6–9. Sterling [Jacques] 1941, pp. 49, 136, no. 119. Ring 1949, no. 161. Marette 1961, p. 189, nos. 206–07. Foucart in Paris 1965, p. 145, no. 185. Richard 1975, pp. 28–33. Sterling 1981, pp. 28–29. Erlande Brandenburg, Pogam, and Sandron 1993, p. 38, no. 9. Reynaud in Paris 1993, pp. 390–91, under no. 220. Leroy 1996, pp. 258–68. Huchard, Lernout, and Mahéo 1995, pp. 67–82. Duvanel, Leroy, and Pinette 1997. Zöhl 2007a, p. 223, fig. 7. Zöhl 2007b.

EXHIBITIONS: Paris 1904, no. 366. Amiens 1951.

THESE NARROW PANELS present the typological juxtaposition of two solemn ceremonies of anointing. The left panel depicts the ritual anointing of King David among his soldiers and court; on the right is the coronation of Louis XII as it took place in Reims Cathedral in 1498, with the king and the attendant peers of France identified by their coats of arms.

These panels were the wings of a triptych whose lost central panel can only be reconstructed on the basis of a copy in a manuscript made in 1517–18 for Louise of Savoy (Bibliothèque nationale de France, ms. fr. 145, fol. 23v), with the help of a description of Amiens Cathedral by Jean Pagès from about 1700. The central panel showed the Virgin enthroned in heaven holding the holy ampule of the title, while angels crown her son, to whom the rulers of Europe, the pope, and the high clergy pay homage from a cloud, joined by a group of earthly supplicants and citizens who are probably the donor's relatives and neighbors (Zöhl 2007a, fig. 7). Since around 1390, Amiens Cathedral had served as the site for the remarkable ritual of the confraternity of the Puy Notre-Dame, which was dedicated to the honor of the Virgin and held regular competitions among rhetoricians (Zöhl 2007b). Comparable competitions of singing and poetry were held elsewhere, but Amiens's confraternity was unique in the special role played by images. Every year at Candlemas, the newly elected master announced a *palinode*, or motto, in praise of the Virgin that would provide the basis for a poetry competition using the form of the *chant royal*. Several weeks earlier, at Christmas, he had unveiled a painting called a *puy* that, as the first artistic interpretation of the *palinode*, inaugurated the annual competition. For one year the painting served as the confraternity's altarpiece; thereafter it was exhibited elsewhere in the cathedral. Most of the Puy panels were still in situ around 1700, including this triptych; however, in February 1723, the cathedral chapter had them removed from the church.

In 1501 the master of the Puy Nôtre-Dame was Jean Le Caron de Bouillencourt; his coat of arms formerly decorated the reverse of the *Coronation of Louis XII*. The triptych's mariological program was completed by a Pietà preserved on the reverse of the *Anointing of King David*. The lost central panel and these surviving wings are striking evidence of the notion of the sanctity of French kingship, with King David, the ancestor of Christ, serving as a prototype of the reigning king of France. The vial of chrism held by the Virgin is the Holy Ampule miraculously delivered at the baptism of Clovis, king of the Franks (cat. 29) and used in the coronation ceremony. The wings are also a rare testament to the high quality of Flemish-influenced panel painting in Picardy at the beginning of the sixteenth century. Nicole Reynaud attributed them to the anonymous Master of Antoine Clabault, who probably also painted the murals in the chapel of Saint Eloy in Amiens Cathedral in 1506 (Paris 1993, under no. 220), and who can be identified hypothetically with the painter and illuminator Riquier Hauroye, documented in Amiens between 1480 and 1504. • CZ

PANELS FROM THE WINGS OF AN ALTARPIECE

[32]

MASTER OF SAINT GILES
Netherlandish, working in Paris c. 1500

The Baptism of Clovis

Oil on panel; 61.5 x 45.5 cm (24 3/16 x 17 7/8 in.)

National Gallery of Art, Washington, D.C., Samuel H. Kress Collection, 1952.2.15

PROVENANCE, BIBLIOGRAPHY: See below.

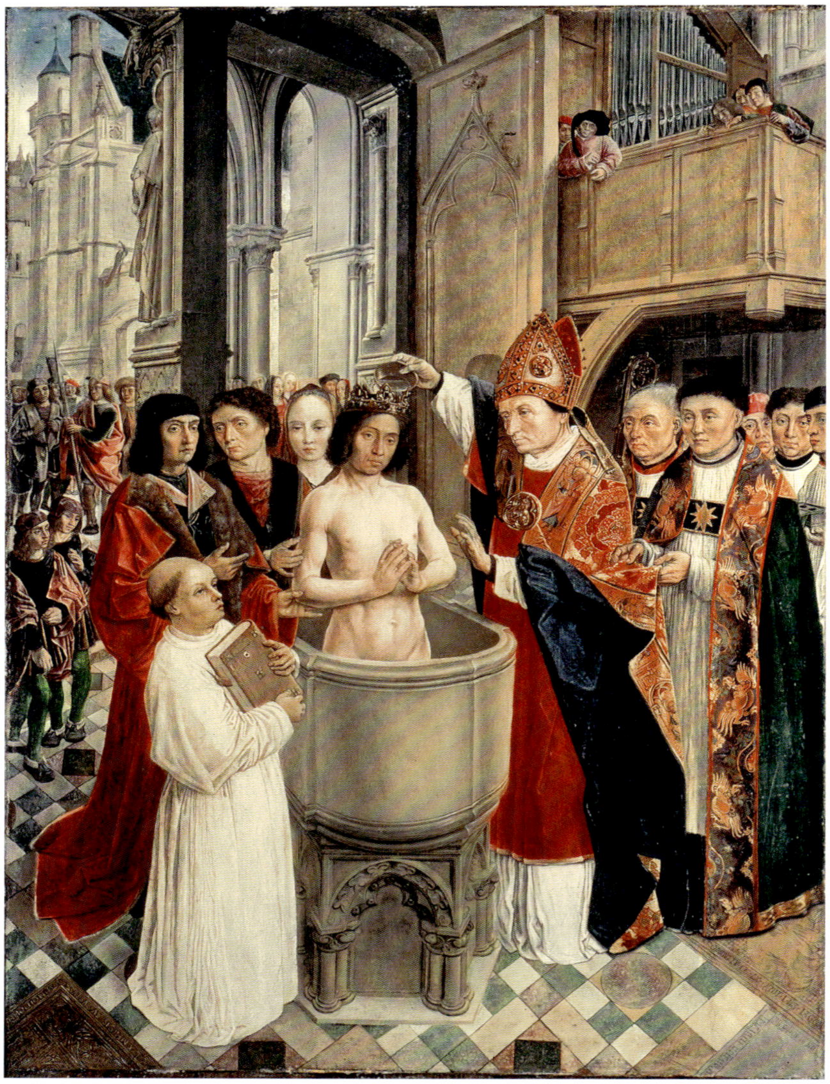

[33]

MASTER OF SAINT GILES AND ASSISTANT
Netherlandish, working in Paris c. 1500

A Bishop (Saint Leu?) Healing the Sick

Oil on panel; 61.5 x 47 cm (24 3/16 x 18 1/2 in.)

National Gallery of Art, Washington, D.C., Samuel H. Kress Collection, 1952.2.14

PROVENANCE: Chevalier Alexandre de Lestang-Parade, Aix, by 1823; Count Melchior de Lestang-Parade; sold, Hôtel Drouot, Paris, May 19–20, 1882, nos. 105–06. Etienne-Edmond Martin, 2nd Baron de Beurnonville, Paris; sold, Hôtel Drouot, Paris, May 21–22, 1883, nos. 43–44. Watel, Paris, 1883. Art market, Paris, 1937. Wildenstein and Company, Paris and New York, 1938; sold to the Samuel H. Kress Foundation, New York, 1946; given to the National Gallery of Art, 1952.

BIBLIOGRAPHY: Champeaux 1883, pp. 186–87. Reinach 1905–23, vol. 2, pp. 665, 744. Friedländer 1913, p. 189. Held 1932, pp. 3–15, figs. 1–2. Friedländer 1937, pp. 221–31, figs. 6, 9–10. Davies 1946, p. xi. Hébert 1949, pp. 199–221, pls. 10–11. Ring 1949, pp. 25, 33, 230, no. 240, fig. 40. Hinkle 1965, pp. 110–44, pls. 19, 21, 22b–c, 25. Davies 1968, pp. 107–13. Montesquiou-Fezensac and Gaborit-Chopin 1973–77, vol. 3, pp. 105–07, pl. 93. Eisler 1977, pp. 239–43, figs. 230–31. Wolff in Hand and Wolff 1986, pp. 163–76. Sterling 1987–90, vol. 2, pp. 235–38, 259–84, nos. 24–27. Sterling and Ainsworth 1996, pp. 18–24. Girault 1997, pp. 151–63. Colenbrander and Girault 1997, pp. 684–89, figs. 24, 26, 28, 30, 32. Châtelet 2001, pp. 144–47, 192–93, figs. 97–98, 110. Leproux 2001, pp. 89–107, figs. 94, 107–08. Girault 2002, pp. 15–23, fig. 2. Lorentz and Sandron 2006, p. 121. Girault 2007a, pp. 161–89, figs. 1–7. Girault 2007b, pp. 135–49, 217–18, fig. 108. Girault 2008, pp. 161–89, figs. 3–4, 16, 20, 23–24. Campbell 2009, pp. 123–27.

THESE TWO PANELS, along with *The Mass of Saint Giles* and *Saint Giles and the Hind* (both National Gallery, London), are the remnants of moveable wings that incorporate multiple references to the sacred nature of French kingship. The panels gave the Master of Saint Giles his name of convenience and are his most significant work.

According to the *Golden Legend*, King Charles, usually identified as either Charles Martel or Charlemagne, sought Saint Giles's aid in connection with a sin he dared not confess. As the saint said mass, an angel appeared with a message of pardon. In *The Mass of Saint Giles*, the king's closed imperial crown suggests that he is meant to be Charlemagne (fig. 34). In *Saint Giles and the Hind* (fig. 35), also part of the legend of Saint Giles, the hind that had nurtured the saint in his hermitage is pursued by the hunting party of the king of the Goths and seeks shelter with the hermit. Both saint and beast are wounded. *The Baptism of Clovis*, shown

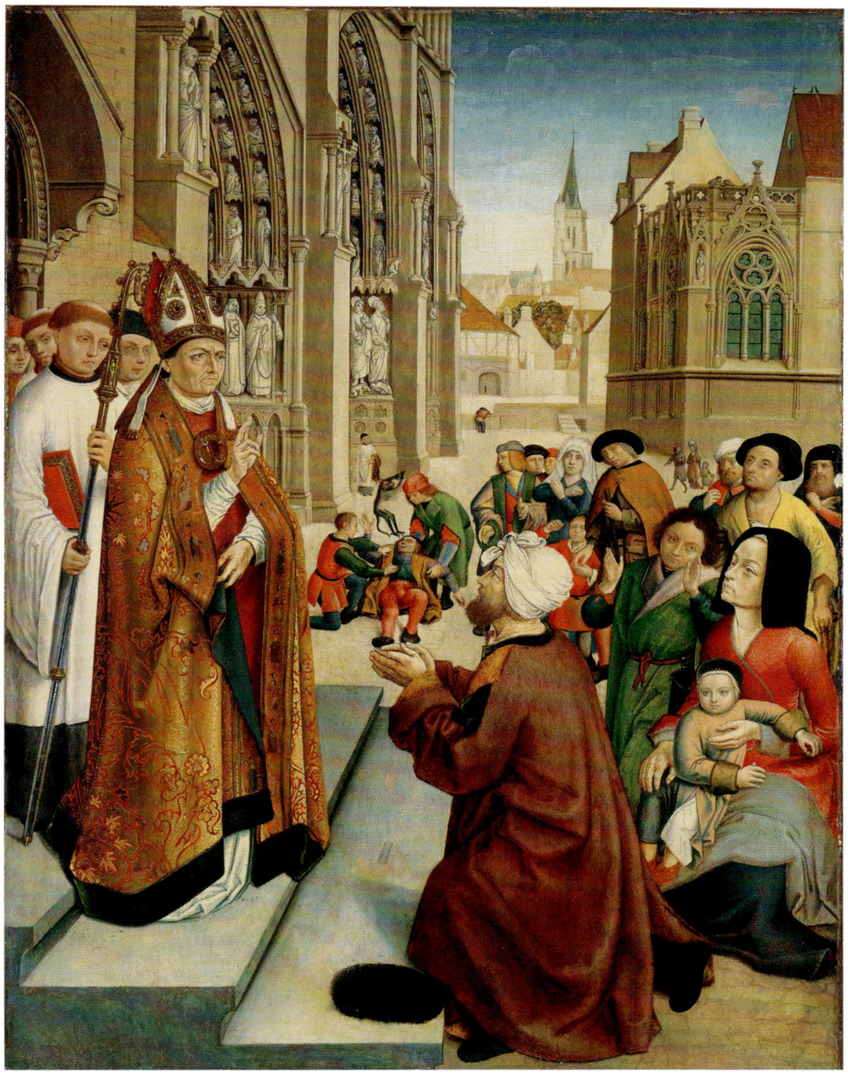

here, depicts the baptism of an adult king of France; the identity of the catechumen has been disputed (Hinkle 1965, Girault 2007a), but he most likely represents Clovis, king of the Franks, who was baptized by Saint Remy, bishop of Reims. The other panel illustrated here shows a bishop saint performing miracles. He has been identified as Saint Remy and, more recently, as Saint Leu (Loup), who shares a feast day with Saint Giles. The settings are accurate architectural portraits, but they do not correspond to the places named in the lives of these saints. Architecture and ecclesiastical furnishings identify the setting for the *Mass* as the choir of Saint Denis, rather than Orléans as stated in the life of Saint Giles. This panel is an extraordinarily important depiction of the abbey church's treasures, including the altar frontal given by Charles the Bald that served as the altarpiece, the structure supporting the chasse with the relics of Saint Louis located behind the altar, and the tomb of Dagobert commissioned by Saint Louis. Although Saint Giles's hermitage was in Provence, near Nîmes, the lush green hills of *Giles and the Hind* may represent the Oise valley to the northwest of Paris. The baptism takes place in the Sainte-Chapelle attached to the royal palace on the Ile de la Cité in the center of Paris. The miracle-working bishop stands in front of Notre-Dame-de-Paris; the left bank of the Seine is visible beyond the corner of the Hôtel-Dieu.

Grisaille paintings simulating standing sculptures of saints on the reverse of each panel indicate that they once formed moveable wings and were part of a complex program. Two saints whose legends are not illustrated on the surviving panels were included on the backs: Saint Denis and Saint Giles were formerly depicted on the backs of the two Washington panels, now thinned and cradled; Saint Peter and a bishop saint resembling the Washington miracle worker are still visible on the backs of the *Mass* and *Giles and the Hind*, respectively. Variations in the niches housing these saints

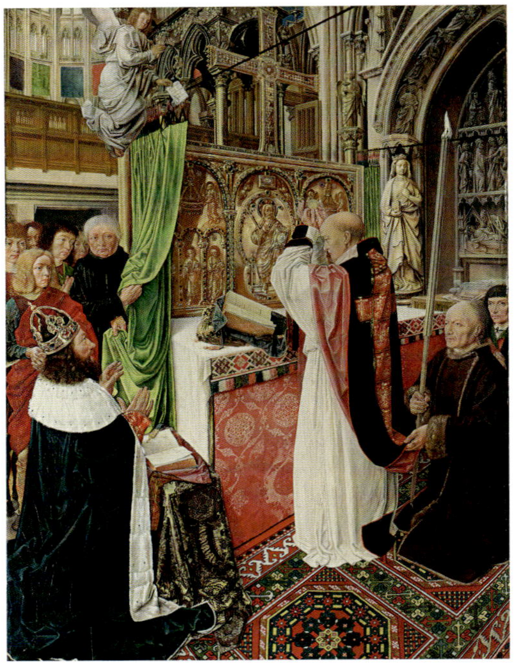

FIGURE 34.
Master of Saint Giles. *The Mass of Saint Giles*. Oil on panel. National Gallery, London.

led to the convincing suggestion (Colenbrander and Girault 1997) that the scenes were arranged in two registers, with four narratives on each wing, hence that four additional narratives—and other grisaille subjects—are now missing. The wings presumably flanked the center of a painted or sculpted altarpiece; the ensemble would have been approximately four meters wide when open.

The dress of the courtiers, their small caps and shoulder-length hair, and the moderate width of their lapels, suggest a date about 1500. The Master of Saint Giles must have been working in Paris at this time, although his Netherlandish origin is clear from other paintings drawing directly on the tradition of Rogier van der Weyden and Dieric Bouts. Whereas Sterling (1990) supposed that he was an essentially Netherlandish painter active in Paris for about a decade before returning to the North, Leproux (2001, followed tentatively by Girault 2002 and 2007a) suggested that he was identical to the Netherlandish painter Wouter or Gauthier de Campes, who settled in Paris by 1500, producing cartoons for tapestries and stained glass until about 1530. The connections to the windows of Tournai Cathedral, associated by Leproux with Gauthier de Campes, are indeed provocative, although attributions are complicated by the collaborative nature of stained glass design and production. However, the three decades of Campes's activity in Paris and the lanky, boneless figures in the tapestries and glass plausibly linked to his cartoons are hard to reconcile with the evidence for a relatively brief period of activity in Paris for the Master of Saint Giles, as well as his preference for small formats and compact figures.

The depiction of Parisian monuments and the appearance of at least two of the panels in private collections in Paris by the mid eighteenth century strongly suggest that the wings were made for a church in the metropolis. Hinkle (1965) was the first to suggest that this was Saint-Leu–Saint-Gilles on the rue Saint-Denis, arguing that the miracle-working bishop in Washington represented this bishop of Sens who shares a feast day with Saint Giles. Hinkle sought an explanation for the saints and sites portrayed in a program of literary sources and believed that the four surviving panels were the entirety of the commission. However, it is clear from the grisailles that other saints must be taken into account—Saint Denis, Saint Peter, and probably others. Moreover, the mentality behind the inclusion of specific sites may not be as literal as Hinkle assumed. Because the miraculous arrival of the Holy Ampule is not depicted in the baptism panel, Hinkle denied that the catechumen was Clovis. He proposed instead that this scene set in the chapel of the city palace was Saint Denis baptizing Lisbius, a nobleman of the Cité. However, given the catechumen's French royal crown, Clovis remains the likely subject, and the Holy Ampule (*Sainte Ampoule*) may have been referenced elsewhere in the altarpiece.

Complicating the interpretation of the narratives is the portrait-like character of many of the figures, both the main actors and the attendant courtiers. Girault (1997 and 2008) saw the king kneeling before the wounded hermit as Louis XII, the cleric accompanying him as Cardinal Georges d'Amboise, and the saint as Saint Francis of Paola, and identified other likenesses on other panels. He viewed the ensemble as a royal commission, with the king appealing to Saint Giles for help with the birth of an heir and to the putative Saint Leu to protect the royal infants. Appeals to Saint Leu on behalf of royal children are documented from the second half of the sixteenth century. While it is possible that the paintings were made for this church on rue Saint-Denis, where a north aisle and small chapels were apparently added in the last decade of the fifteenth century, St-Leu–St-Gilles is by no means the only candidate in a period of vigorous expansion for Parisian churches (see pp. 138–39; Bos 2003). One may wonder whether the evocation of so many touchstones of royal power in the metropolis did not stem from a body of ambitious bourgeois asserting the city's ancient role at a time when the king was only rarely present. • MW

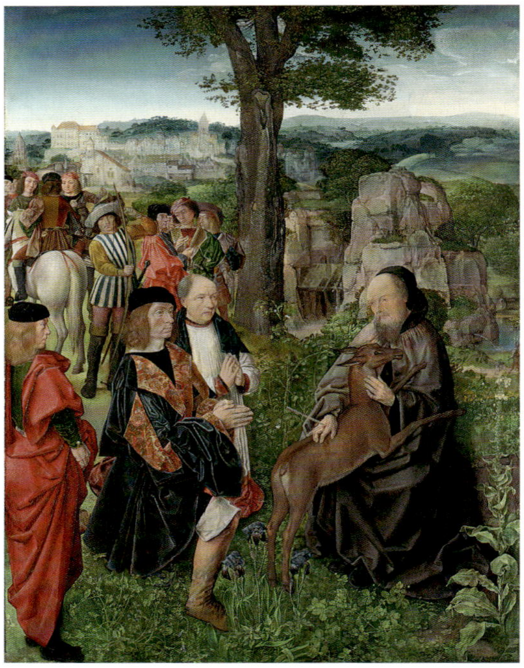

FIGURE 35.
Master of Saint Giles. *Saint Giles and the Hind*. Oil on panel. National Galley, London.

[34]

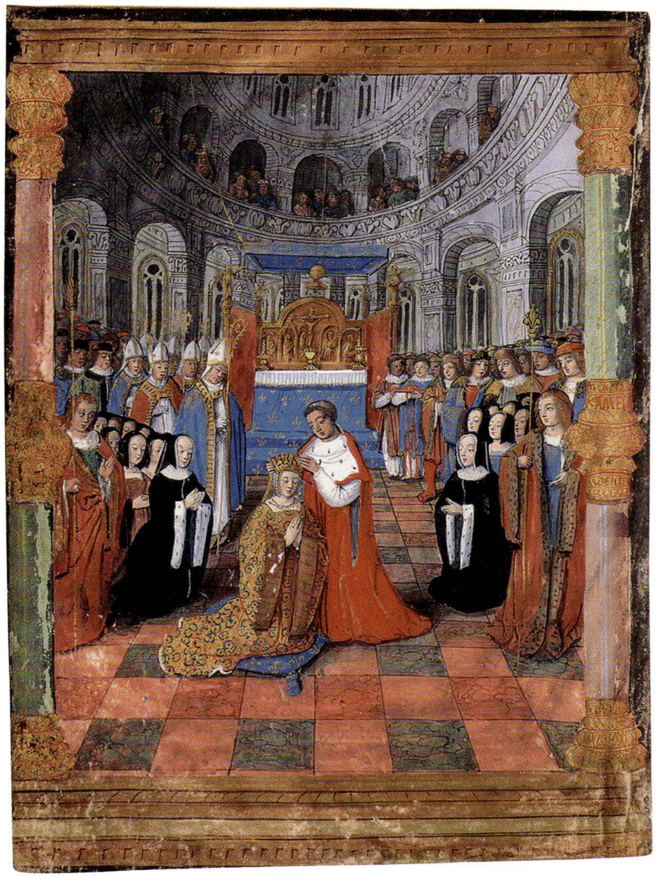

MASTER OF THE CHRONIQUE SCANDALEUSE

André de La Vigne, *Description of the Coronation and Entry into Paris of Anne of Brittany*

Paris, c. 1505

Tempera and gold on vellum; 64 ff. 19.9 x 14.8 cm (7 13/16 x 5 13/16 in.)

Waddesdon Manor, Buckinghamshire, The Rothschild Collection (National Trust), ms. 22

PROVENANCE: Probably Anne of Brittany. Cardinal de Bourbon Condé (d. 1594) [his arms on the binding surmounted by the cardinal's hat, which he received in 1582]. Alexander Hamilton, 10th Duke of Hamilton (d. 1852), by 1819 [Hamilton-Beckford monogram and *inv. no. 63* in pencil]; by descent; sold, Sotheby's, London, June 30–July 13, 1882, no. 393, to the Kupferstichkabinett, Berlin; among the twenty Hamilton manuscripts sold to J. and S. Goldschmidt, Frankfurt am Main, 1887. Baron Edmond de Rothschild (d. 1934), by 1928; his son James de Rothschild, Waddesdon Manor (d. 1957); given to the National Trust by his widow.

BIBLIOGRAPHY: Clarke 1819, p. 257, no. 4. Seidlitz 1884, p. 300, no. 98. Kohler 1896, pp. 379–80. Stein 1902, pp. 268–304. Becker 1928. Boese 1966, p. xix n. 16, no. 393. Delaissé 1977, pp. 471–86. Pächt and Thoss 1977, pp. 81–84. Jones 1978, pp. 59–62, 74, no. 13. Plummer in New York 1982, p. 98. Reynaud in Paris 1993, p. 276. Brown 1995. Brown 2005, pp. 215–56. Brown 2006, pp. 75–91.

EXHIBITION: Nantes 2007, no. 100.

SHOWN: *The Coronation of Anne of Brittany*, f. 1v

THIS SLENDER MANUSCRIPT is the only contemporaneous illuminated copy of André de La Vigne's description of the celebrations surrounding Anne of Brittany's second coronation in 1504, and a significant document of commemoration within the court. In order to keep the duchy of Brittany attached to the crown, the contract for the 1491 marriage of Charles VIII and Anne of Brittany stipulated that, should the king die without an heir, Anne was required to marry the heir to the throne in order to bind her duchy to the crown. Accordingly, after Charles' premature death in 1498, Anne of Brittany became queen for a second time through her marriage to Louis XII in 1499; however, she was not crowned again until five years later.

The manuscript was clearly intended for the queen herself. The three most important text divisions are decorated with her emblems: her crowned initial *A*, her arms, the *cordelière* (a knotted rope associated with Saint Francis), ermine tails, and the motto *non muddra*. The manuscript shows numerous changes in the course of work. It is made up of irregular gatherings with additional inserted leaves and bifolios; the full-page miniatures (ff. 1v, 38v, 54v) were probably also not planned from the outset. Moreover, there are changes and corrections in the text and in the handwriting. Finally, André de La Vigne dedicated the manuscript to the queen in a personal *envoi* including an acrostic of his name; he asks the recipient to preserve this work intended for herself alone and not to forget her humble secretary (fol. 64). These features led Delaissé (1977) to conclude that the queen's secretary had himself supervised its execution and was still working on the text during its production. In contrast to Pierre Choque's illuminated description of Anne of Brittany's funerary ceremonies in 1514, preserved in multiple examples in French noble collections, this is a unique and personal document, not an item of public representation.

The three full-page miniatures (Anne's coronation, her joyous entry into Paris, and the coronation banquet) are each on the verso of their sheet, in accordance with Netherlandish convention; they are enclosed in stylized architectural frames with marble columns, golden plinths, and architraves. Although the illuminator does not give a faithful portrait of the setting of the coronation (the choir of the abbey of Saint-Denis), he is careful to show the attendants holding the scepter and the *main de justice*, symbols of the authority of the king of France. These images featuring protagonists who can be identified from the text were produced by the Master of the Chronique Scandaleuse (Bibliothèque nationale de France, Clair 481). His work, chiefly for high-ranking aristocratic patrons, can be dated between about 1493 and 1510 in Paris. He often collaborated with other painters (cat. 89) and also illuminated printed books (cat. 28). Like Jean Pichore (fig. 4), but probably independent of him, the Master of the Chronique Scandaleuse shows the influence of manuscript illumination in Tours, and of Jean Poyer in particular, as evident in his glowing colors. His facility with multi-figure compositions gives the coronation illuminations a narrative richness. • CZ

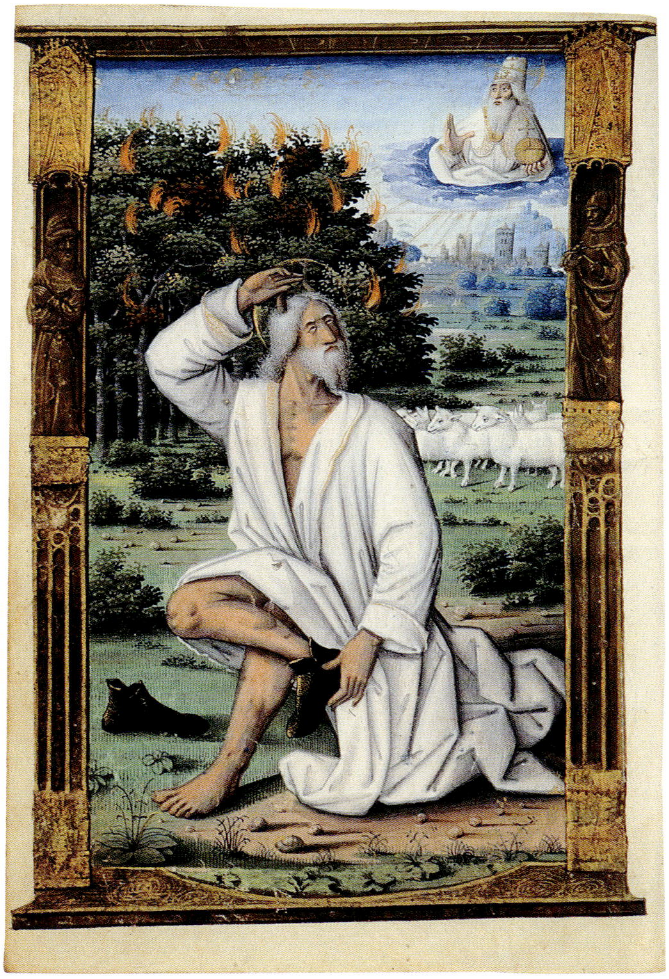

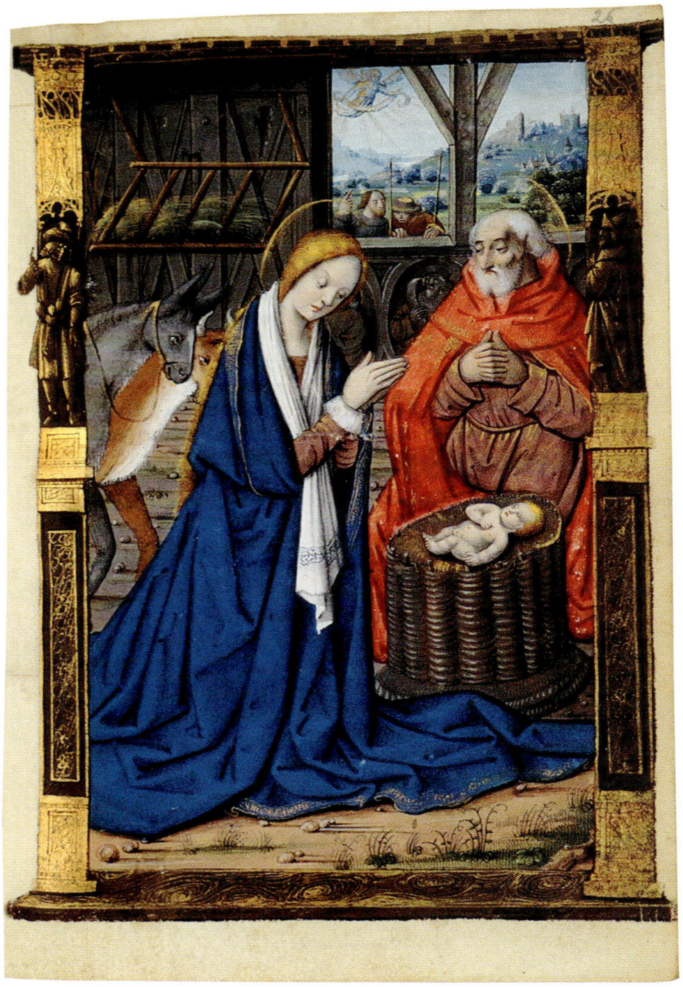

[35]

MASTER OF PETRARCH'S TRIUMPHS

Small Hours of Anne of Brittany

Paris or Rouen, 1500/05

Tempera colors and gold on parchment; II + 78 ff., 17.5 x 13 cm x 2 cm (6⅞ x 5⅛ x ¾ in.)

Bibliothèque nationale de France, Paris, Department of Manuscripts, ms. n. acq. lat. 3027

PROVENANCE: Probably Anne of Brittany. Catherine de Medici [her arms and motto *Adorem extincta testantur vivere flamma* illuminated on an added double page, ff. Av–B]. Norzy collections; Ambroise Firmin Didot; Gaston-Noel des Vergers; by descent to Marquise Hélène de Toulongeon, née des Vergers; bequeathed to the Bibliothèque nationale, 1935.

BIBLIOGRAPHY: Pawlowski 1879, pp. 76–79, no. 28. Delisle 1913, pp. 29–34, 112–15. Leroquais 1943, pp. 1–5, pls. 17–18. König 1978, pp. 163–95, 213, figs. 16–21, 39. König 1984, pp. 72, 88, figs. 9, 13. König 1988, pp. 52–54, 59, 62, 64, 67, figs. 2–3, 6, 10. König 1992, p. 25. Avril in Paris 1993, no. 238. Zöhl 2004, pp. 22, 52–55, 191.

EXHIBITIONS: Paris 1937, no. 194. Tours 1952, no. 41. Paris 1955, no. 358. Nantes 1961, no. 71, pl. 25. Daoulas 1991, no. 200. Paris 1993, no. 238.

SHOWN: *Moses and the Burning Bush* and *The Nativity*, ff. 25v–26

THE ARRANGEMENT of this book of hours for the use of Rouen points to the cultural center that developed at Gaillon near Rouen around 1500 under Cardinal Georges d'Amboise. Its painter takes his name, "Master of Petrarch's Triumphs," from a monumental secular manuscript that Amboise commissioned for Louis XII during the same period. Hence it is tempting to assume that this prayer book was also a gift to the royal family; the letters *NE* and an animal interpreted as an ermine appearing in the border decoration may also support this interpretation; moreover, the emphasis placed on Saint Anne may refer to Anne of Brittany, and the full-page miniature of Saint Louis in the suffrages of the saints could refer to Louis XII. Doubts remain, however, as to why the patron would have given the queen a prayer book for Norman use and omitted the saints she particularly revered. In any case, the manuscript was later in the royal collection, since Catherine de' Medicis had a bifolio with her coat of arms and motto inserted.

This book of hours is captivating for its extremely fine manner of painting, which gives its surprisingly monumental yet calm and impassive foreground figures an intense effect. As in the *Triumphs*, calm rhythm and balanced coloring make even multi-figure compositions appear dreamlike, in contrast to the dramatic and dense ornamental style of Jean Pichore's painting. The latter's work also shows a stronger interest in the Italian Renaissance.

The organizing principle of this book of hours is typological, with traditional New Testament themes alternating with Old Testament subjects. For the major text divisions of the Little Office of the Virgin, related typological pairs are juxtaposed on facing pages, as *Moses and the Burning Bush* and the *Nativity* are on the bifolio for Prime illustrated here. The single images include both Old Testament subjects, such as *Gideon* for Terce, and some from the New Testament, for example the *Ecce Homo* for the Hours of the Cross. There was a change of plan during the execution of the manuscript: in some of the miniatures the text was overpainted and then reinserted within the image's frame, although other images were originally given a full page. It could be that the decision to present the book to the queen was only made during the course of production. Finally, some missing miniatures and recognizable gaps before single images indicate that the richly illuminated codex has been preserved only as a fragment.

In conjunction with this typological organization, the painter used two modes of coloring: in the paired images, the Old Testament types are rendered in grisaille with few accents, while the main subjects from the New Testament are brightly colored. In the single images, however, the coordination of subject and color is not consistent. Subdued black, gray, and brown tones are also used for the remarkably delicate borders with varied geometrical patterns. Both the use of color and the typological pairing of images attest to the formative encounter of the Master of Petrarch's Triumphs with Jean Poyer, who developed a very similar approach for the Briçonnet Hours about 1485 in Tours (cat. 43). • CZ

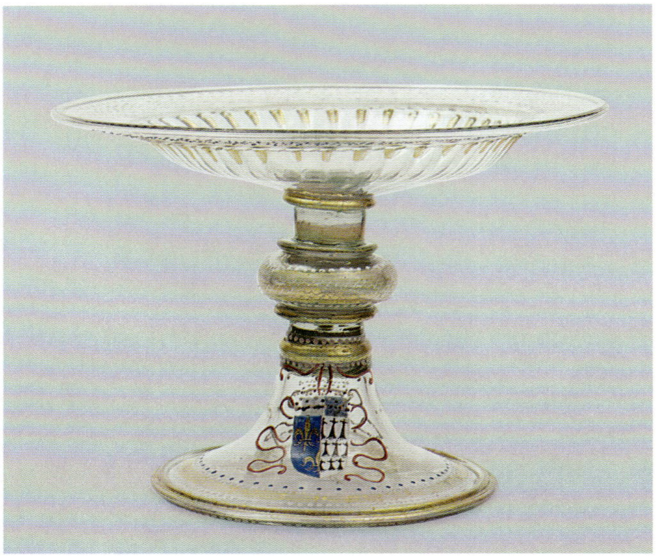

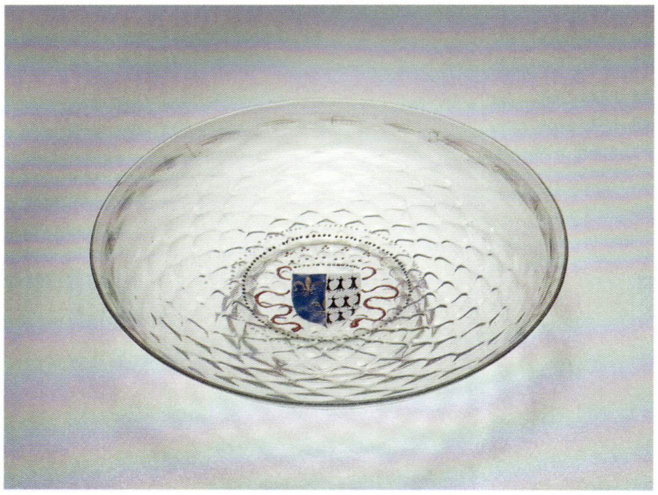

[36]

Tazza with the Arms of Anne of Brittany

Venice, before 1514

Blown glass, pattern-molded, gilded, and enameled; H. 21.2 cm (8 3/8 in.); diam. 28.8 cm (11 3/8 in.)

Musée national de la Renaissance, Ecouen, E.Cl. 1567

PROVENANCE: Brunet-Denon sale, 1846; Musée de Cluny, Paris; transferred to the Musée national de la Renaissance, château of Ecouen, 1985.

BIBLIOGRAPHY: Lanmon 1994, pp. 3–12, fig. 1.2. Rochebrune 2004, pp. 143–45. Thornton in New York/Fort Worth 2008–09, p. 98, under no. 29. Michele Bimbinet-Privat in Ecouen 2009, p. 28.

EXHIBITIONS: Daoulas/Nantes 1991–92, no. 208. Ecouen 1995, no. 45. Nantes 2007, no. 103.

[37]

Bowl with the Arms of Anne of Brittany

Venice, before 1514

Blown glass, pattern-molded, gilded, and enameled; H. 6 cm (2 3/8 in.); diam. 24 cm (9 7/16 in.)

Toledo Museum of Art, Ohio, 1932.1

PROVENANCE: Frédéric Spitzer, Paris, by 1891; sold, 33 rue de Villejust, Paris, April 17–June 16, 1893, no. 2037. Arnold Seligman, Rey and Company, New York; sold to the museum, 1932.

BIBLIOGRAPHY: Spitzer 1891, vol. 3, p. 101, no. 58. Godwin 1952, pp. 1141 (ill.), 1143. Hutton 1963. Toledo Museum of Art 1969, pp. 45, 47 (ill.). Lanmon 1993, pp. 11–12, fig. 1.4. Rochebrune 2004, pp. 143, 144 (ill.), 145, fig. 2. Page 2006, pp. 76, 77, fig. 28C. Thornton in New York/Fort Worth 2008–09, p. 98, under no. 29.

EXHIBITION: Ecouen 1995–96, pp. 87–88, 90, cat. 46.

THIS TAZZA, which is composed of several blown and molded parts, and a related footed bowl both received impressive gilded decoration like that of several Venetian pieces that have survived to this day. They are likewise enriched by enamels, chiefly to represent the escutcheon of Anne of Brittany, which combines the arms of France and Brittany, surmounted by a crown and surrounded by waves of ribbons. These arms are also found on two other pieces, another quite similar tazza in the Robert Lehman Collection at the Metropolitan Museum of Art and a rather large plate at the Victoria and Albert Museum, London. It is tempting to identify these four surviving pieces with the glass objects cited in the queen's household registers of 1499, where they appear with other precious objects for decorative use, and not for table service.

The presence of ribbons around Anne of Brittany's coat of arms, instead of the rope or *cordelière* that was so dear to her as a personal and family device, suggests the pieces were diplomatic gift and not a commission originating in France; the latter would surely have been accompanied by a precise drawing of the royal emblems. Coming from Italy, these glass pieces were incorporated into the ensemble of precious and fragile objects in the royal collection, alongside vessels of hard stone with gold and silver mounts, as attested by comparable objects in inventories of the princely collections of England, Spain, and Flanders. • TC-L

[38]

Angel Bearing a Reliquary

1400/50

Silver gilt; paint (for the flesh); plaquettes with niello on silver (coats of arms); reliquary; set in silver-gilt; 43.5 cm (17 1/8 in.) (including detachable wings); pedestal: 7.3 x 15.5 cm (2 7/8 x 6 1/8 in.)

Musée du Louvre, Paris, Department of Decorative Arts, MR 550

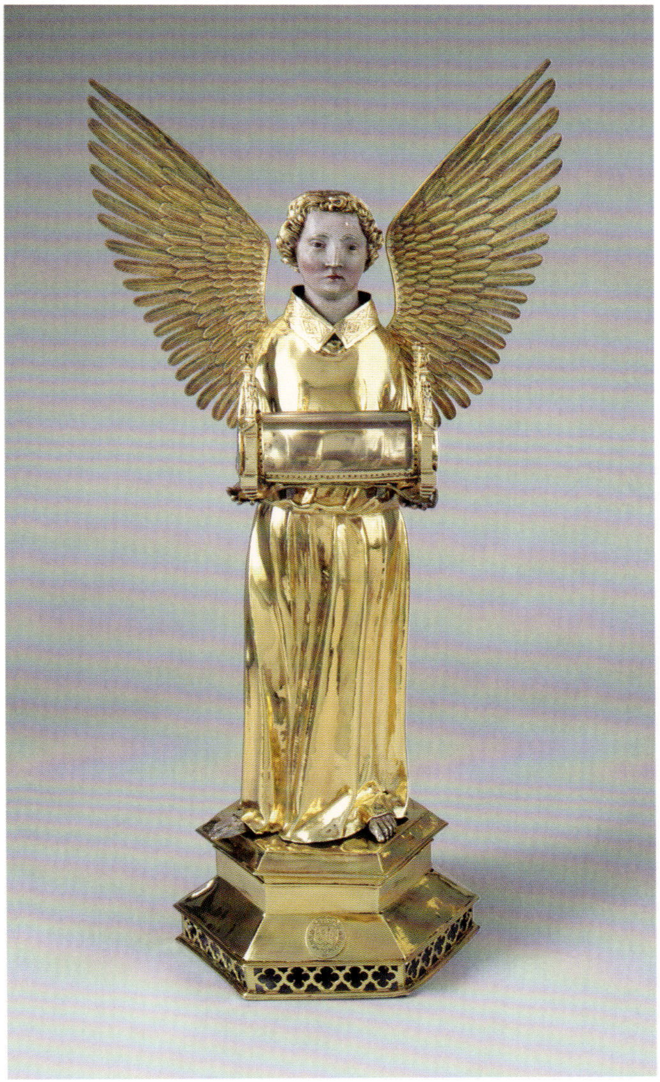

PROVENANCE: Anne of Brittany (d. 1514), by 1491 [cited in inventories of 1491 and 1498]; by descent to her daughter Claude of France; passed to the French royal collections through her marriage to Francis I; mentioned in the inventory of the crown jewels in 1560; given by Henry III to the chapel of the Order of the Holy Spirit in 1578 and mentioned in the inventories of 1593 and 1701; entered the Louvre with the collections of the Order of the Holy Spirit, 1830.

BIBLIOGRAPHY: Gaborit-Chopin 1994 (with complete prior bibliography).

EXHIBITIONS: London 1932, no. 572k (one of the two angels). Nantes/Daoulas/Nantes 1991–92, no. 171. Nantes 2007, no. 61.

THIS AND ANOTHER ANGEL from the collections of the dukes of Brittany form a false pair; only the bases on which they rest are identical. Since the wings are detachable, it is not certain which pair belongs to which statuette. The angel presented here is the better preserved of the two. However, it is the more difficult one to date and localize precisely. It has no hallmark, and the figure, dressed in a long robe with straight pleats gathered at the waist, belongs to a rather generic type of angel. The small, round, relatively inexpressive face is still marked by fourteenth-century conventions, with a straight nose and pinched mouth above a small, slightly pointed chin; the hair, arranged in round curls in two rows above the neck, also recalls the style of that era. The same is true of the orphrey on the collar, decorated with lozenges filled with quatrefoils. Conversely, the little tuft above the forehead formed by a group of curling locks suggests a date later than the fourteenth century.

The two angels belong to a body of goldsmithwork that has survived to this day because the objects passed from the collections of the dukes of Brittany to the French royal collections and were then deposited in several ecclesiastical treasuries. This group includes the *Tableau de la Trinité* given by Jeanne of Navarre to her son John V, duke of Brittany, which, like the two angels, was later given to the treasury of the Order of the Holy Spirit by Henry III and is today preserved in the Musée du Louvre. The group also includes the reliquaries of the Holy Thorn and of the Resurrection given by Henry III to the treasury of Reims Cathedral. In fact, it is due to their successive ownership by Anne of Brittany and her daughter Claude, who married Francis of Angoulême (the future Francis I) in 1514, that these works joined the crown jewels of France. This history of ducal and royal ownership is also evidence of the esteem accorded to examples of Gothic goldsmithwork by the sovereigns of the sixteenth century. • ET-D

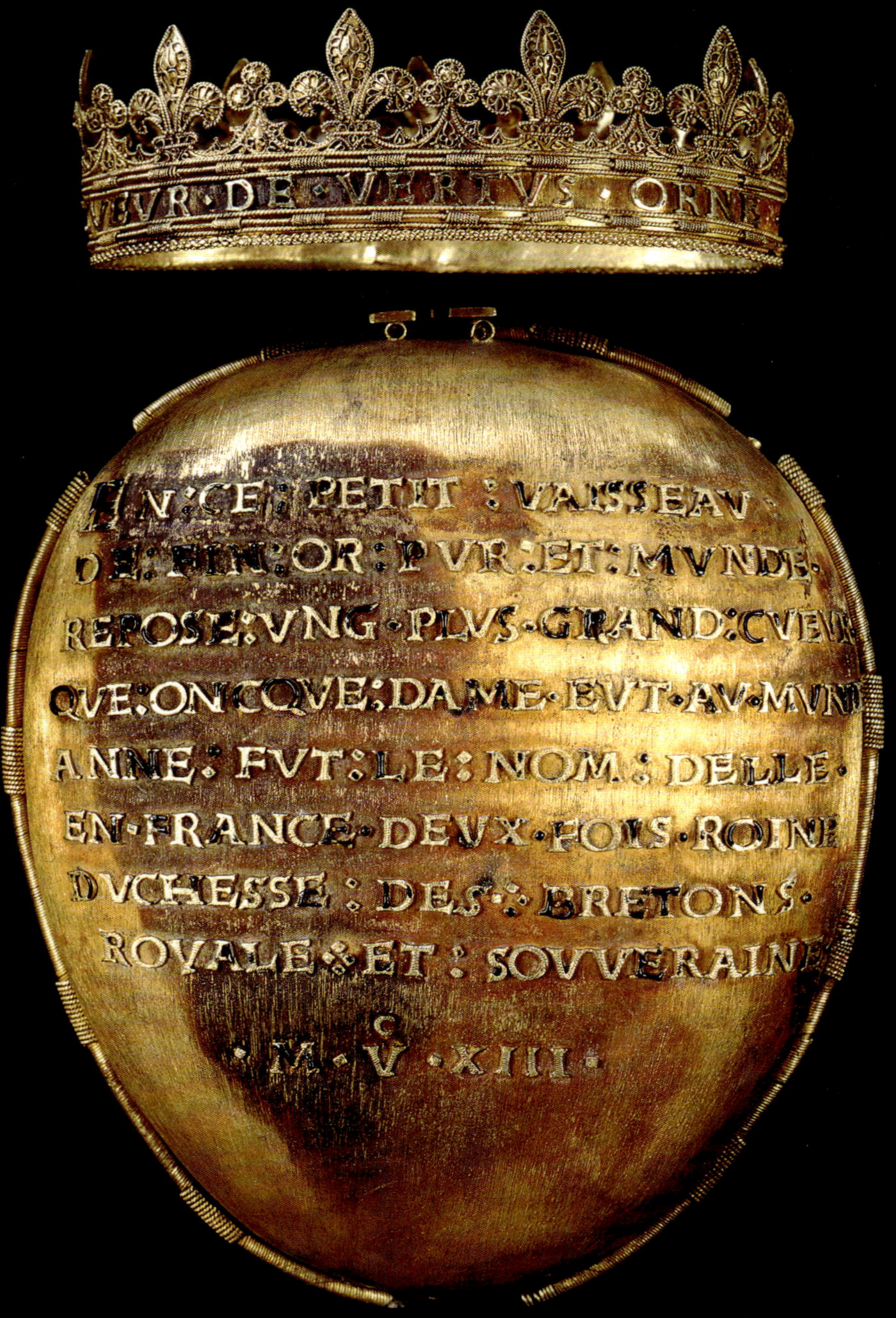
DE · VERTVS · ORNE
EN : CE : PETIT : VAISSEAV
DE : FIN : OR : PVR : ET : MVNDE
REPOSE : VNG · PLVS · GRAND : CVEVR
QVE : ONCQVE : DAME · EVT · AV · MVNDE
ANNE : FVT : LE : NOM : DELLE ·
EN · FRANCE · DEVX · FOIS · ROINE
DVCHESSE : DES : BRETONS ·
ROYALE · ET : SOVVERAINE
· M · V C · XIII ·

[39]

Vessel for the Heart of Anne of Brittany, with Its Crown

Probably Loire Valley or Paris, January 9–March 19, 1514

Musée Dobrée, Nantes, inv. D. 886-1-1

HEART: Gold alloy (6–9% silver, 3–4% copper) with repoussé work on two halves joined by hinges and a clasp; external surfaces with guilloché work; cut-out letters, with guilloché work and enamel (traces of green-black enamel in heavy drops); internal surfaces with guilloché work, enamel (white enamel), inscription highlighted in gold; rope motif of twisted strands on the rim concealing the connection of the two halves; 15 x 12.5 x 6.4 cm (5 7/8 x 4 7/8 x 2 1/2 in.); 407.1 g (14.3 oz.)

CROWN: Gold with guilloché work on the circlet, filigree work on the florets and rope motifs, lattice work on the chain on the lower edge; enameled gold, inscription: red translucent enamel on the letters, green on the punctuation marks; 3.5 x 10.8 x 5.5 cm; 68 g (1 3/8 x 4 1/4 x 2 3/16 in.; 2.4 oz.)

INSCRIBED: Heart: *M* (on the clasp); *S* (which provided the closing at the base, now missing) *EN : CE : PETIT : VAISSEAU. / DE : FIN : OR : PUR : ET : MUNDE. / REPOSE : UNG : PLUS. GRAND : COEUR / que : oncque : dame. eut. au. munde / anne : fut : le : nom : delle. / en. France. deux. fois. roine / duchesse : des+ bretons. / royale+et : souveraine. / mvcxiii.* [In this small vessel of fine pure gold rests the greatest heart that any lady had in the world Anne was her name in France twice queen duchess of the Bretons royal and sovereign 1513 (old style)] (on face); *ce. cueur. fut. si. tres hault. / que de la terre aux cieulx. / sa / vertu+ liberalle~ / accroissoit / mieulx. et miulx. / mais : dieu+ en : areprins. / sa+ portion· meilleure. / et : ceste : part : terrestre. / en. grand. dueil. nous. demeure / .iXe. Ianvier* [This heart was so lofty that from the earth to the heavens her great virtue grew more and more but God has taken back her finest part and this earthly part remains to us in great mourning 9th January] (on back face); *o cueur. caste. et. pudicque. ojuste. et. be(noist) cueur.cueur. magnanime.et.franc.de.tout.vice. vaincqueur. / cueur.digne.entre.tous.de. couronne.celeste.ore.est.ton.cler.esprit.hors.de. paine.et.moleste.* [Oh heart, chaste and modest, oh just and blessed heart, magnanimous and open heart, vanquisher of all vice, heart worthy above all of the celestial crown, your bright spirit is now free from pain and trouble] (interior); Crown: *cueur.de.vertu.orne.dignement.courone.* (Heart, ornamented with virtue, fittingly crowned)

PROVENANCE: Interred in the Carmelite church in Nantes, March 19, 1514; exhumed for examination, October 17, 1727 [large brown blemishes on the exterior of both halves are the products of corrosion during interment and have a high iron and lead content (report of the Centre de recherche et de restauration des musées de France, 1988, and records of 1727 and 1792 describing its placement in nested caskets of lead, iron, and lead, cited in Durville 1915); dents and holes in the lower left third of the back section were incurred when it was exhumed in 1727)]; transferred to the cathedral, February 17, 1792; sent to the Nantes Mint, December 25, 1793; sent to the Paris Mint; found in the Cabinet of Medals of the Bibliothèque Royale, probably 1816; sent to Nantes, 1819; deposited at the departmental archaeological museum, 1886, then at the Musée Dobrée, 1896.

BIBLIOGRAPHY: La Nicollière-Teijeiro 1881. Durville 1915. Ravilly 1977. Caraës 2007. Croix and Guyvarc'h 2007. Bande 2009, pp. 176–81.

EXHIBITION: Daoulas and Nantes 1991–92, no. 221.

ANNE OF BRITTANY requested that her heart be laid to rest in Nantes beside her parents, in the tomb that she herself had commissioned from Michel Colombe (fig. 12). The duchess, who was twice crowned queen, thus honored her lineage, her attachment to her Breton subjects, and also the "rationale for the union" (Bande 2009) of France and Brittany in her person, "royale et souveraine" as underlined by the inscription on the main face of the vessel and by the fleur-de-lis crown.

By separating the burial place of her heart from that of her body, Anne of Brittany wove together French royal traditions and Breton customs (Croix and Guyvarc'h 2007; Bande 2009). The funeral ceremony for her heart, which was brought from Blois to Nantes two months after her death and one month after the burial of her body in Saint-Denis on February 16, 1514, was organized by Pierre Choque, the duchess's king of arms (her chief officer for heraldry and ceremonial). Choque left a precise account of the events that was disseminated in numerous illustrated manuscripts entitled *Trépas de l'hermine regrettée*; Kerssemakers (1992) has counted thirty-four examples. The text includes the description of the "golden heart richly crowned and surrounded by a cord" (*coeur d'or richement couronné et entouré d'une cordelière*), and the transcription of the inscribed poems, including the one on the interior of the vessel, suggests that Choque himself composed or ordered the composition of these verses praising the virtues of the deceased, which are moreover very characteristic of the spirit of the time.

The execution of this golden heart follows the traditions of princely goldsmithwork of the fourteenth and fifteenth centuries; the crown's filigree work is not dissimilar to that of the fifteenth-century saltcellar from the collections of Louis XIV (Musée du Louvre, inv. MR 119); the enamels, which suggest the gold objects enameled with red and white mentioned in Anne of Brittany's accounts (Vrand 2010, pp. 203ff), use techniques that were perfected at the end of the fourteenth century. The refinement of the crown's craftsmanship should be emphasized, in contrast to the coarser treatment of the container. Since the sovereigns primarily patronized goldsmiths who were established in Paris or the Loire Valley, it was probably one of them who received this final commission destined for the queen. • ET-D

This entry benefited from information and comments provided by Jacques Santrot, director of the Musée Dobrée, whose help is acknowledged with sincere thanks.

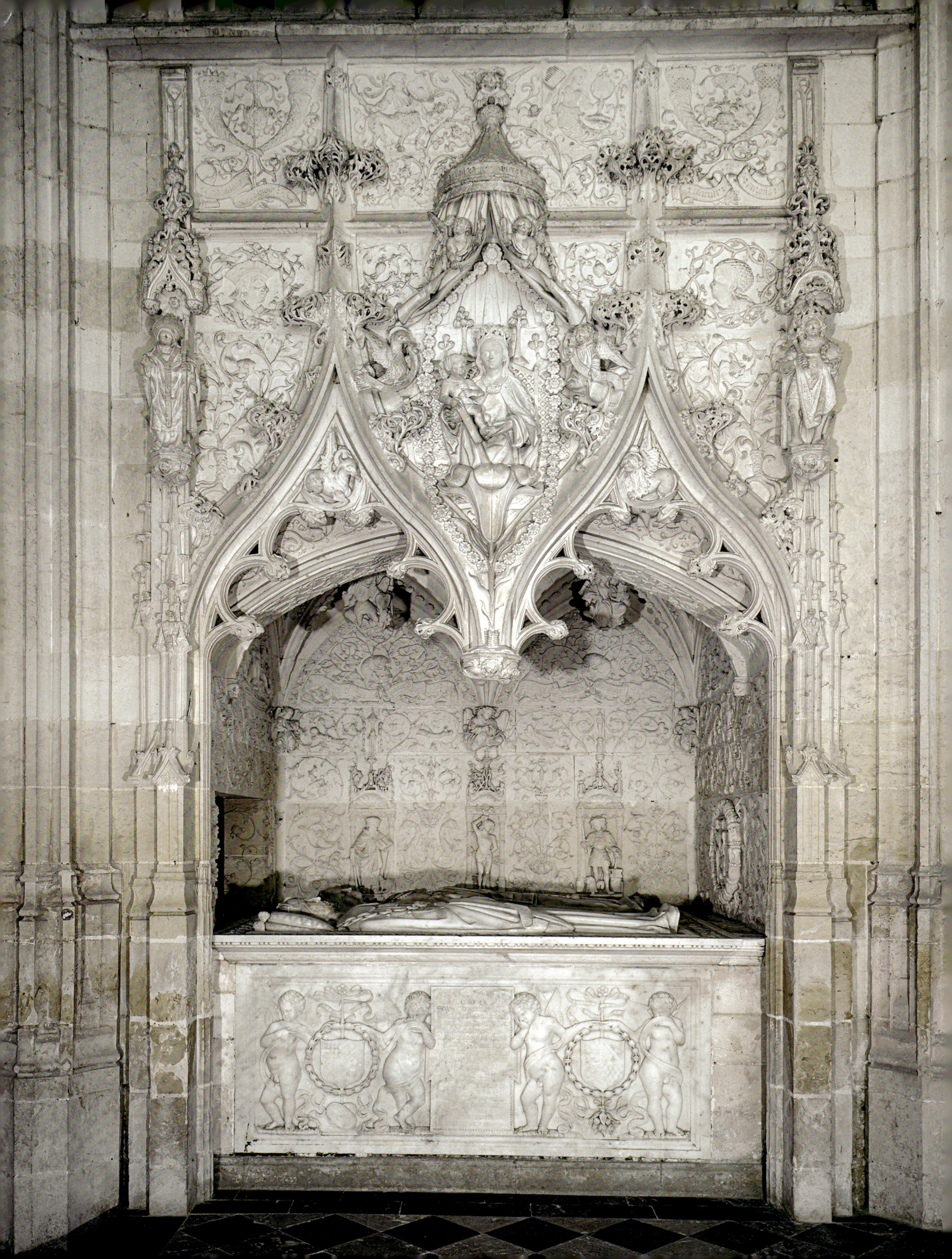

THE SOURCES OF ARTISTIC CREATION: CENTERS AND ARTISTS

GENEVIÈVE BRESC-BAUTIER

In this brief introduction we will not describe the artistic landscape of France around 1500 since, unlike the Romanesque period, for which one can discern a stylistic language characteristic of a region, at this time a multiplicity of styles existed in each area, and their dissemination took place from center to center by "marcottage" (to use a horticultural metaphor), a process of propagation through layering. The movement of artists, the multiple residences of important families, the posting of high-ranking officials across the kingdom, the reassignment of bishops from one see to another, the constant displacements of the itinerant court, even more than the Italian wars, produced a multidirectional cultural and artistic life.

The court was certainly an extraordinary engine. The king wished to recruit the best artists to maintain the decorum necessary for the display of royal power, thereby allowing artists to escape the constraints of urban regulations, and creating conditions that promoted a court idiom. Jean Bourdichon (fig. 3) and Jean Perréal were thus painters and *valets de chambre* to the king; Michel Colombe and Guillaume Regnault, sculptors (*tailleurs d'images*) and *valets de chambre* to the queen. Since the reign of Louis XI, the court spent time at residences in the Loire Valley (first Plessis-lès-Tours, then Amboise or Blois), prompting the recruitment of local officials or the establishment of an administrative elite in the region. Already enriched by the presence of Jean Fouquet in the previous generation, the region of the Loire would foster the development of artists in Tours, like the painters Jean Poyer and Robinet Testard and also the sculptor Michel Colombe, as well as the long-term residence of Italian sculptors such as Jérôme Pacherot and the Juste brothers. For there was an Italian immigration, first in Charles VIII's baggage train following his expedition to Naples in 1494/95, and later through the longer French domination of the duchy of Milan. The residence of such immigrants was often limited and not fixed in Touraine. The sculptor Guido Mazzoni and the architect Fra Giocondo left for Paris; the painter Andrea Solario was in Gaillon in 1507–09.

¶ REGIONAL CENTERS

Short sections will be devoted to the Loire Valley and Berry, to the Bourbonnais, to Paris, and to northern France and the migration of artists. In order to focus on these regions and trends, we must pass over centers that were nevertheless active. Few works came out of Auvergne, even though two enterprising families dominated there: the Bourbon-Monpensier branch of the Bourbon ducal family, to whom we will allude later in terms of their taste for Italian art, so evident in the Sainte-Chapelle of Aigueperse; and the counts of Auvergne from the de La Tour family, who were also active patrons, as the triptych at the North Carolina Museum of Art in Raleigh confirms (cat. 69). But the ecclesiastic authorities should not be forgotten, as their commissions make clear: the mural paintings of the liberal arts at the cathedral of Le Puy; the great tapestry series, probably woven in Flanders, offered by Jean de Saint-Nectaire to his abbey of La Chaise Dieu and still in place.

Provence has also not been given a separate section. Nicolas d'Ypres the Younger, from the d'Ypres dynasty active in Paris, could be mentioned. He was established in Avignon in 1495 and about 1499 painted the retable of the Conception of the Virgin. Only Josse Lieferinxe, a painter originally from Hainaut, will be put forward as an example of a northerner adapting to the local milieu, showing how the language of Flanders could be tinged by the tradition of Provence, thereby renewing itself through fresh contacts. Along with Lieferinxe, we can cite Jean Guiramand, a sculptor from Toulon, who in 1508 executed the ornamentation for the doors of the cathedral of Aix-en-Provence, which were largely inspired by German models taken from engravings by Israel van Meckenem.

Little is known about Gascony. Starting at the end of the fifteenth century, the cathedrals of Lectoure, Condom, and Auch were reconstructed there; and an exceptional glass artist, Arnaud de Moles, one of the few to sign and date his work, was active. His eighteen stained glass windows for Auch Cathedral, where the sibyls appear alongside biblical figures, show his mastery of color, obtained through a unique technical process, as does the window of Fleurance.

For the region of Bordeaux there is the so-called Master of Biron named after the château of Biron, whose chapel was built by Pons de Gontaud starting in 1499. This anonymous sculptor's talent and authority, stemming in part from the art of the Bourbonnais, is evident in the *Pietà* and

Facing Page

FIGURE 36.

Antonio della Porta (known as Tamagnino) and Amiens sculptors. *Tomb of Raoul de Lannoy and Jeanne de Poix*. Marble and limestone. Church of Saint James, Folleville.

the *Entombment* of 1500–10, both today at the Metropolitan Museum of Art, and in comparable works in Carcenac-Salmiech and Bordeaux.

Burgundy, which was undoubtedly less of a guiding light after the death of Charles the Bold in 1477, also does not receive its own section, and is represented largely through the presence of Jean Hey in Autun (cat. 100). Yet sculpture of high quality continued to be produced there, mainly in Autun and Semur.

Because of the geography of French history, we have intentionally excluded the regions that were not yet part of the kingdom: Savoy, the Franche-Comté, and the Dombes. Thus, despite the fact that Margaret of Austria called upon Jean Perréal and Michel Colombe to develop a project for the tomb of her third husband, Philibert of Savoy, at Brou, and despite the marvelous sculptures for this monument eventually executed by the workshop of Louis van Boghem and completed by Conrad Meit, we will not discuss Savoy here, even though it is emblematic of the permeability of styles and the mixing of workshops (fig. 13). Similarly, Lorraine has been passed over, although artists originally from the kingdom of France built their careers there, under the aegis of princes who were themselves of French origin. They included Jacques Bachot and the painter Georges Trubert, who completed his career at the court of René II, duke of Lorraine and grandson of René of Anjou.

¶ BEYOND REGIONAL CENTERS: THE PATRONS

Both works and artists moved around and helped ensure the dissemination of styles. A settled artist could ship his productions elsewhere. For example, Michel Colombe's altarpiece of Saint George and the Dragon (fig. 37) was transported from Tours to Gaillon. Jean Colombe, the miniaturist who remained in Bourges, sent his works as far as Lyon and Champagne.

Many artists, however, led nomadic lives. For some, it was a simple change of location: for the Truberts, from Troyes to Paris; for Lieferinxe, from Hainaut to Provence; for Gauthier de Campes, for the Master of Saint Giles, and for Nicolas d'Ypres the Elder (Colin d'Amiens) from the North to Paris. Others wandered more. Jean Hey went from

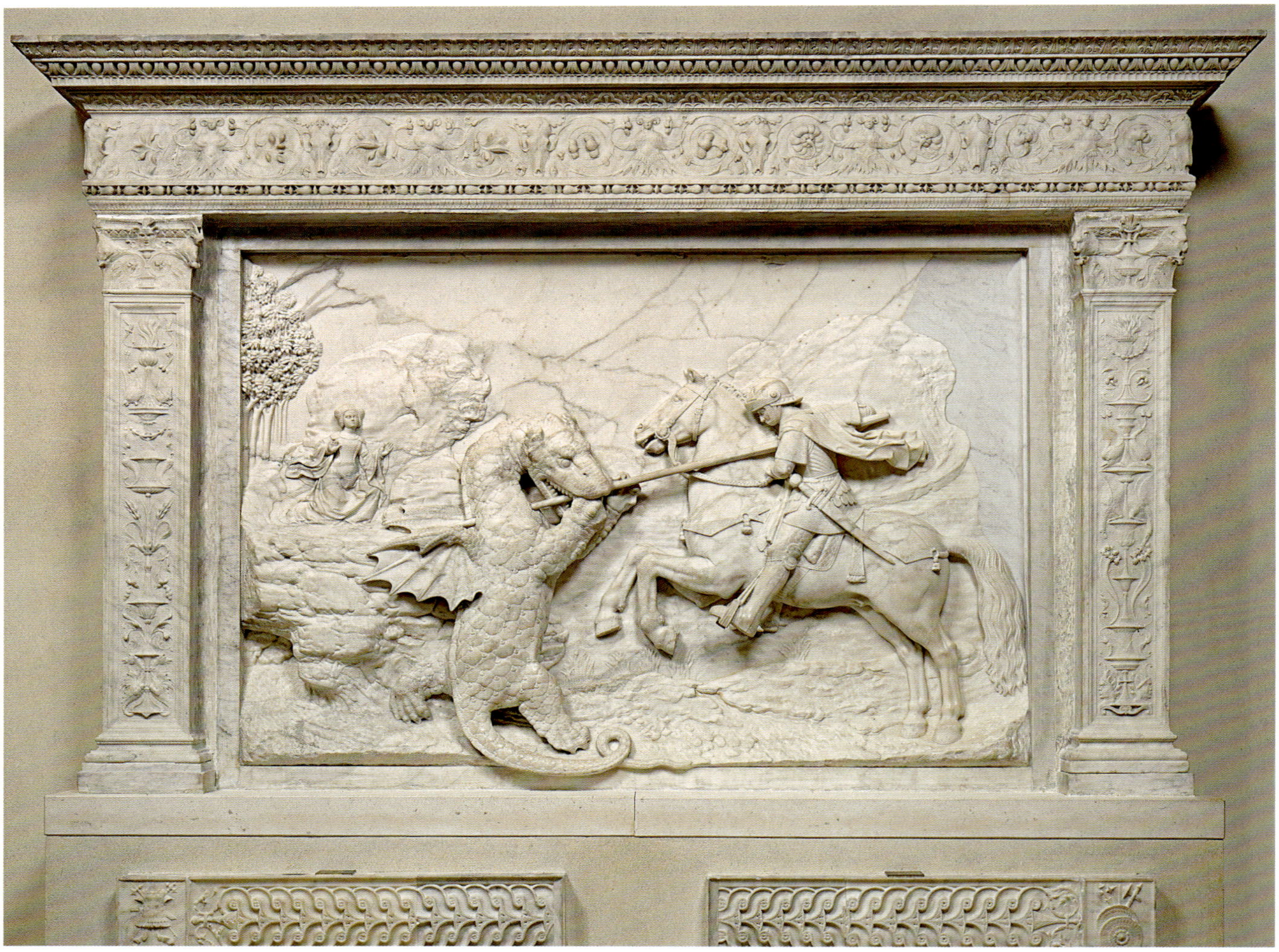

FIGURE 37.
Michel Colombe. *Saint George Slaying the Dragon*, from the château of Gaillon. Marble. Musée du Louvre, Paris.

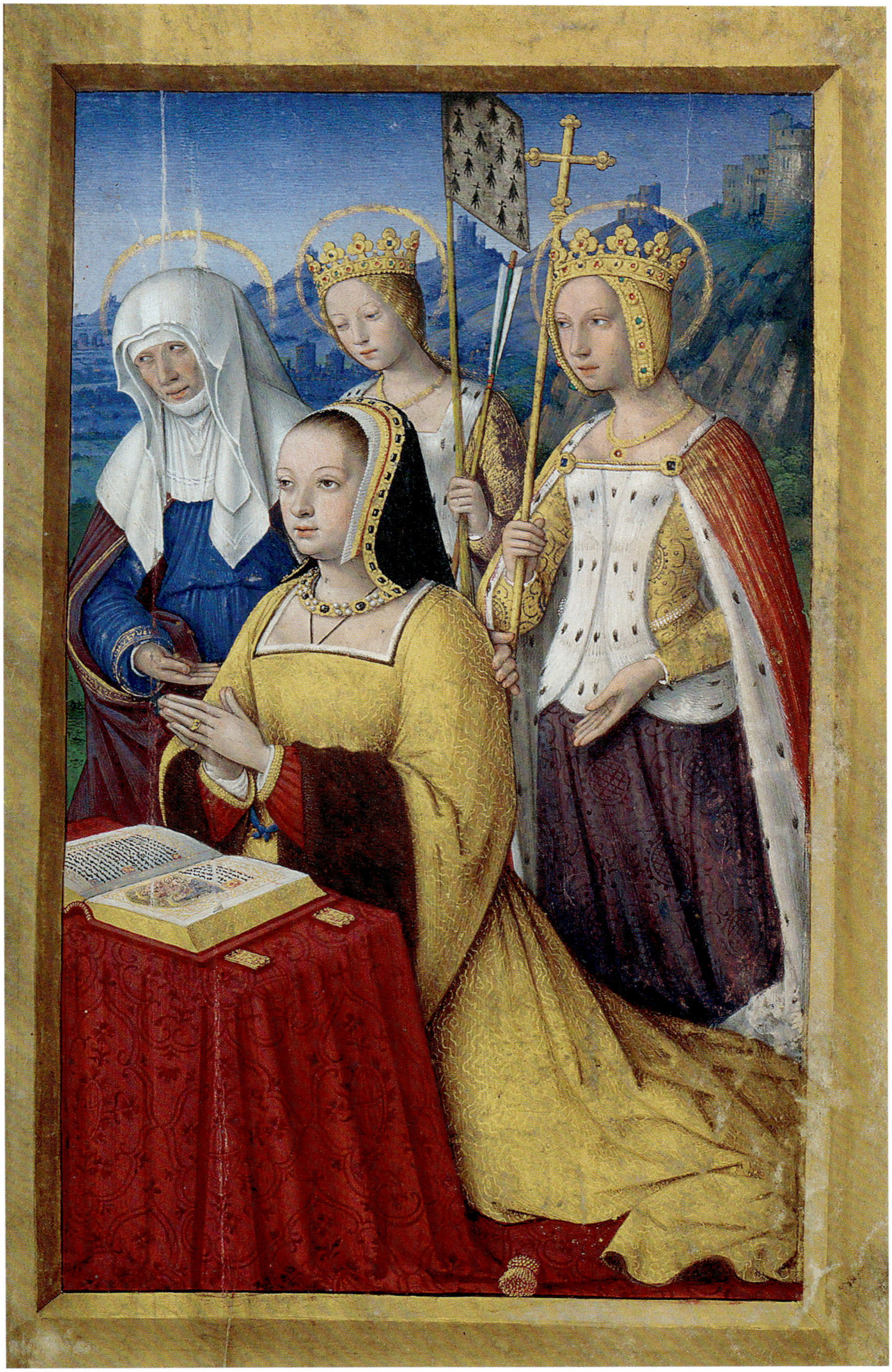

FIGURE 38.
Jean Bourdichon. *Anne of Brittany Presented by Saints Anne, Ursula, and Margaret*, from the *Grandes Heures of Anne of Brittany*. Tempera and gold on parchment. Bibliothèque nationale de France, Paris, ms. lat. 9474, f. 3.

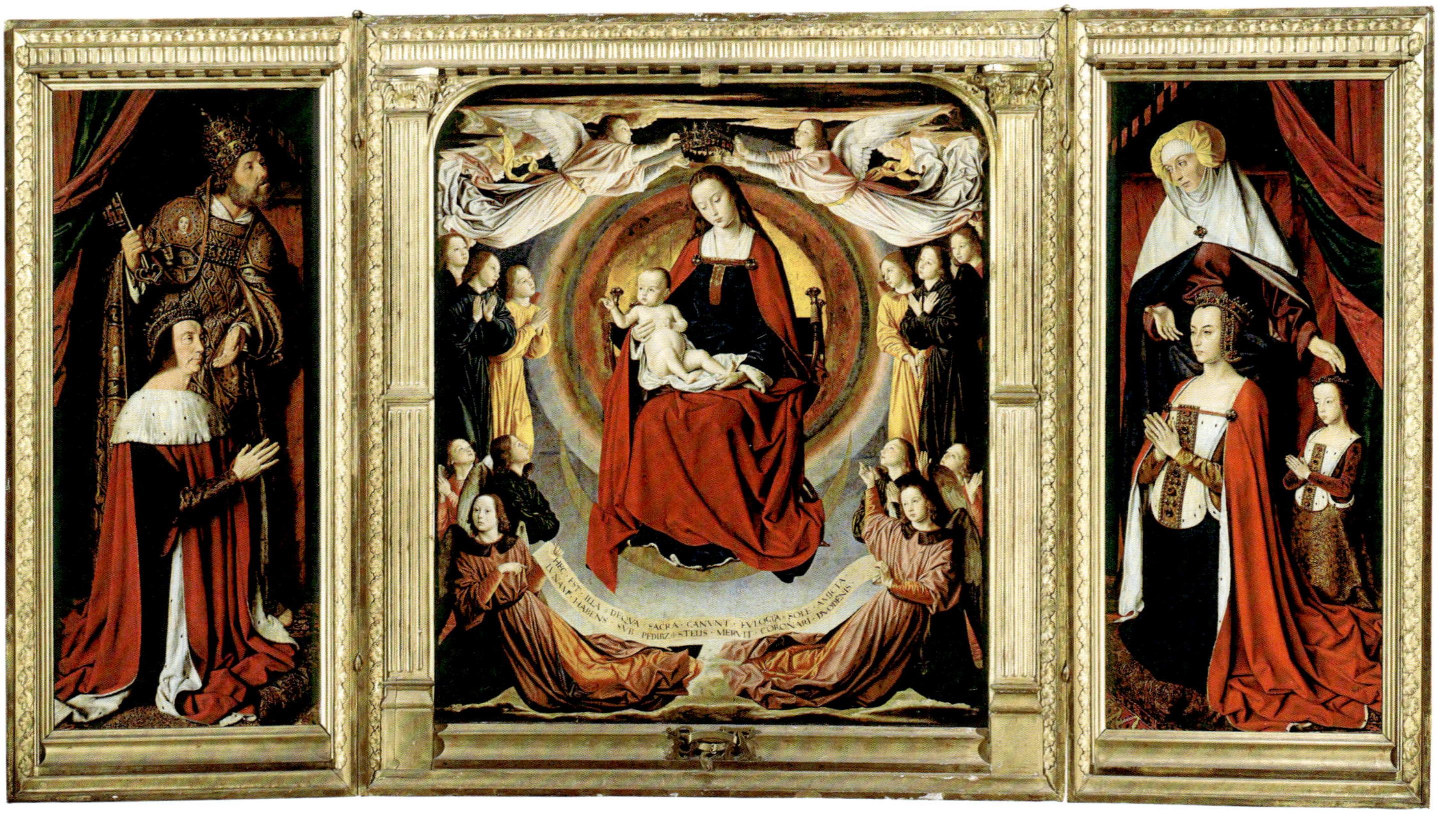

FIGURE 39.
Jean Hey (The Master of Moulins). *Triptych of the Virgin in Glory, with Pierre II, Duke of Bourbon Presented by Saint Peter and Anne of France and Suzanne de Bourbon Presented by Saint Anne.* Oil on panel, Cathedral of Notre-Dame, Moulins.

Autun to Lyon, then to Moulins (fig. 39), at the discretion of his patrons.

It is not surprising to find sculpture in Brou or Albi whose execution suggests the style of the Loire Valley when one learns of the far-flung activity of known sculptors. Michel Colombe practiced his art in Moulins, Tours, and La Rochelle, and installed the tomb of Francis II of Brittany in Nantes. In 1514, Jean Chaleveau, a sculptor born in Sens, executed for Sens Cathedral, at the request of Archbishop Tristan de Salazar, a retable decorated with statues to complement the tomb of Salazar's parents, together with statues of them in prayer. But the figure of the Virgin from this ensemble is the cousin of the Virgins of Mesland and Olivet (cat. 47) in the Loire Valley. In 1523, Chaleveau would settle in Tours and collaborate with Guillaume Regnault, delivering the tomb of Louis de Poncher to Paris for a chapel in the church of Saint-Germain-l'Auxerrois; there, as early as 1507, Jacques Bachot, from Champagne, had installed a retable that included three statues.

Due to their political and ecclesiastical responsibilities, important families were also dispersed across the kingdom, their members sometimes putting down roots far from their home territory. The dukes of Bourbon embellished their domains in Moulins and Souvigny in the Bourbonnais, while a younger son, Charles, enthusiastically decorated his archbishop's seat in Lyon. The large and successful d'Amboise family in particular has been studied for its wide-ranging patronage. In Rouergue, Louis d'Amboise, the bishop of Albi, commissioned a masterpiece of the period, the choir of the cathedral of Saint Cecilia, a total ensemble in which the painted vault and the sculptures of the choir screen form a symphony of form and color executed by artists of diverse yet compatible sensibilities. More restrained in style, his chapel at Combefa in Monestiés, consecrated in 1490, housed a poignant reenactment of the Entombment in a style that is determinedly local. In 1507, Louis d'Amboise's nephew, François de Clermont-Lodève, ambassador to Pope Julius II, took over the diocese of Auch when Arnaud de Moles was installing his first window in its cathedral. Jacques d'Amboise's chapel (fig. 40) in his Paris hôtel (now the Musée de Cluny) and the fountain he had built in his role as bishop of Clermont, Charles d'Amboise's château in Meillant, the *Man of Sorrows* sculpted in the domain of bishop Jean d'Amboise in Mussy, are also marks of the family's taste (Souchal 1976). But it is clearly the activity of Cardinal Georges d'Amboise that is most indicative of an ambitious artistic politics, carried out in Rouen and at his nearby country residence at Gaillon. He called upon the best French masons; the best Norman cabinetmakers; the Italians Andrea Solario, Jérôme Pacherot, and Antoine Juste; and he imported both Michel Colombe's marble masterpiece from Tours and marbles carved in Italy.

Drawing from the centers that were the towns, patrons attracted artists, hired them, and took their works deep into the French countryside. In the Loire Valley, the high officials of the king, the Marshal de Gyé, Florimond Robertet, Guillaume Briçonnet, and Jacques de Beaune transferred art to their châteaux (Le Verger, Bury, Chenonceau, La Carte) as well as to their townhouses in Blois and Tours.

The transport of finished works, sometimes over long distances and in large formats, permitted the diffusion of regional styles but it also mixed these productions with art from other places and points of view. From Rouen, stained glass and retables, sometimes even imported from the Low Countries, filled the surrounding area. In the countryside of Picardy, the chapel of Folleville became, thanks to the patronage of the Lannoy family, a successful compromise between Italian marble sculpture and the virtuoso decorative sculptors from Amiens (fig. 36).

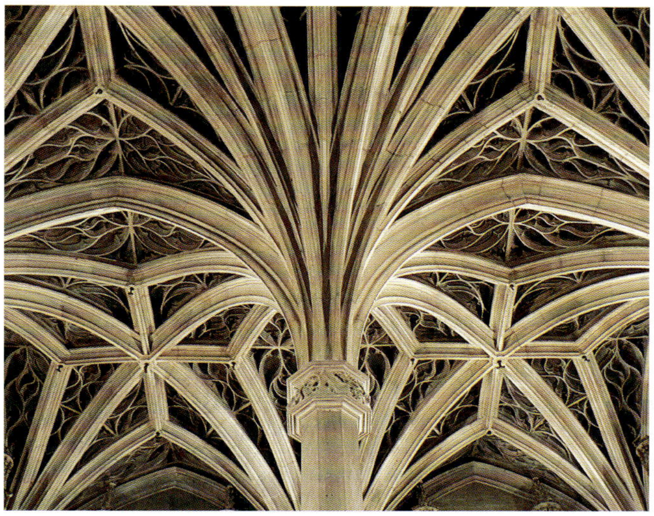

FIGURE 40.
The vault of the chapel of the Hôtel de Cluny. Musée de Cluny—Musée national du Moyen-Age, Paris.

Far from any center, in 1495 the admiral Louis Malet de Graville brought from Paris to Malesherbes an Entombment (fig. 7) by the sculptor Adrien Wincart (probably of northern origin) after a design provided by Nicolas d'Ypres the Elder (Colin d'Amiens). The style, dense and dramatic, is indeed that of the sculptor, as shown by comparison of the female figures and the head of the Virgin in his *Pietà* from the same commission, housed at the château. To the painter, Nicolas d'Ypres, one can only ascribe the overall composition, the costume, and the accessories (restored in 1964).

Rivalries between clients, their eclectic tastes, and the travels of artists, but also the use of media that could easily be transported (albums of drawings and patterns, medals, engravings, tapestries) were therefore the conditions of an artistic life that accessed the totality of the kingdom, and, indeed, all of Europe.

Nevertheless, identifiable regional styles did take root. Fouquet and the Colombe brothers dominated the Loire Valley through their followers, Regnault, Chaleveau, Poyer, and Bourdichon; Picardy revealed its idiosyncratic character through its retables, which were nonetheless inspired by the Netherlands. It is possible to distinguish a true style of the Bourbonnais, of Troyes, of Rouen and of Rouergue, in the numerous statues in the Allier, Champagne, Normandy and Languedoc, respectively. Thus, one can weave a complex reality in which diverse trends were synthesized, overlapped and combined, renewed themselves or became ossified; these trends would persist later in the century, despite the Mannerist revolution that Francis I would bring.

BOURGES AND THE LOIRE VALLEY

BÉATRICE DE CHANCEL-BARDELOT

The growth of Berry, Poitou, and the Auvergne was in part due to Jean, duke of Berry (1340–1416), who received control over these provinces in the second half of the fourteenth century. By establishing a territorial administration there, he laid the foundation that later permitted Charles VII (r. 1422–61), the "little king of Bourges," to embark on the reconquest of the kingdom of France. The cities of the Loire Valley—Nantes, Angers, Tours, Blois, Orléans and, beyond them, Bourges, Riom, and Moulins—developed throughout the fifteenth century, and the kings and their courts gladly spent time in the region. Nantes, Angers, Tours, and Bourges were ancient episcopal centers, with their cathedrals, chapters, and traditions; the administrations of these cities expanded, not without some friction with Louis XI (r. 1461–83). Powerful abbeys like Marmoutier (near Tours), or renowned sanctuaries such as Sainte-Catherine de Fierbois (also in Touraine) and Notre-Dame de Béhuard (near Angers), attracted pilgrims. The administration of the princes and the king, the chapters and abbeys, drew from the pool of local men, while the descendants of the families who had maintained the châteaux during the Hundred Years' War received responsibilities like the post of captain of the château of Tours or accompanied the king on his Italian expeditions. In Blois and Bourges, and to a lesser extent Tours, grand town houses still conjure up the memory of these powerful families: the Beaunes, the Robertets, the Briçonnets, and the Lallemants.

Art collectors were therefore present in these regions of the Loire Valley at the end of the fifteenth century, and many architectural projects were underway for the princes or the bourgeoisie, or, at the beginning of the sixteenth century, the rebuilding of the north tower of the Bourges Cathedral, one of the major enterprises of the period. Goldsmiths, illuminators, and sculptors were busy in the cities of the Loire, responding to patrons. Since the nineteenth century, scholars have sought the traces of these artists in archives: the Marquis de Granges de Surgères for Nantes; Charles de Grandmaison, Jacques Xavier Carré de Busserolle, and Eugène Giraudet for Tours; Célestin Port for Angers; and the Baron de Girardot for Bourges. If many artists are now only known by their name and profession, or at best through the mention of a work, and are linked to a single center, the most talented among them worked in several provinces in succession. Hence, in the nineteenth century, Michel Colombe from Berry was proclaimed to be from Brittany or from Tours, although he also worked in Maine, Normandy, Moulins, and La Rochelle. His brother Jean Colombe, with help from his Bourges workshop, decorated manuscripts for clients living well outside the Loire region, in Lyon and Champagne.

Probably the works that have survived in the largest number are books, especially illuminated manuscripts, compensating for the few remaining panel paintings. Nicole Reynaud has pointed to the dynamism of painters from Tours around 1500, who assimilated pictorial innovations from Italy and the Netherlands to create an elegant style. In addition to the work of Jean Bourdichon, whose talent has long been recognized thanks to the *Grandes Heures* of Anne of Brittany (fig. 38), the work of Jean Poyer, painter and illuminator, can now be better understood. We also know the prolific activity of Jean Colombe, native of Berry, who worked for a local clientele, but also for Louis de Laval, a great Breton lord and governor of Champagne. Besides Colombe and his collaborators, Bourges was home to several other illuminators, including the Montluçon family and the Master of Spencer 6, who contributed to the decoration of several manuscripts for the local Lallemant family. In sculpture, in addition to Michel Colombe, we know that Guillaume Regnault was settled in Tours for the whole first third of the sixteenth century. Also in Tours, the activity of sculptors in wood is well known from archival documents, although perhaps less from surviving work like the angels of Rouziers or the *Saint John* of Loché, long part of the collection of the Louvre.

Glass painters were active in all the cities of the region, but connecting known names to works executed around 1500 has not been possible. Some glass painters also undertook manuscript illumination and the polychromy of sculpture. Goldsmithwork has rarely been spared the melting pot; surviving objects, for example the reliquary of the Virgin in the treasury of the abbey of Evron (c. 1516), are thus all the more precious. This work's hallmark of a bird has given the artist his name of convenience, the Master of the Bird. In Nantes, Tours, and Bourges, goldsmiths are now no more than names, their works only mentions in chapter records and church inventories. Apart from tapestries, textiles have been little studied, and even for tapestries the very existence of the "Loire Valley workshops," formerly presumed to have been important producers of weavings, is not supported by any documentary source. Some artists were multifaceted, like Simon Hayeneufve, active in Maine from the end of the fifteenth century until his death in 1546: the château of Malicorne is attributed to him, as are designs for metalwork and church ornaments (cat. 116).

The milieu of artists of the Loire Valley was open to influences not only from Paris and the provinces, but also from the Netherlands and Italy. Although certain artists, such as Jean Poyer, may have traveled to Italy, Italian sculptors, like Antoine Juste (1479–1519), passing through Bourges and Tours, contributed to the assimilation of new decorative styles and to the creation of works of art that still enhance the reputation of the region.

[40]

JEAN BOURDICHON
(1457/58–1521)

Louis XII Kneeling in Prayer Accompanied by Saint Michael, Saint Charlemagne, Saint Louis, and Saint Denis

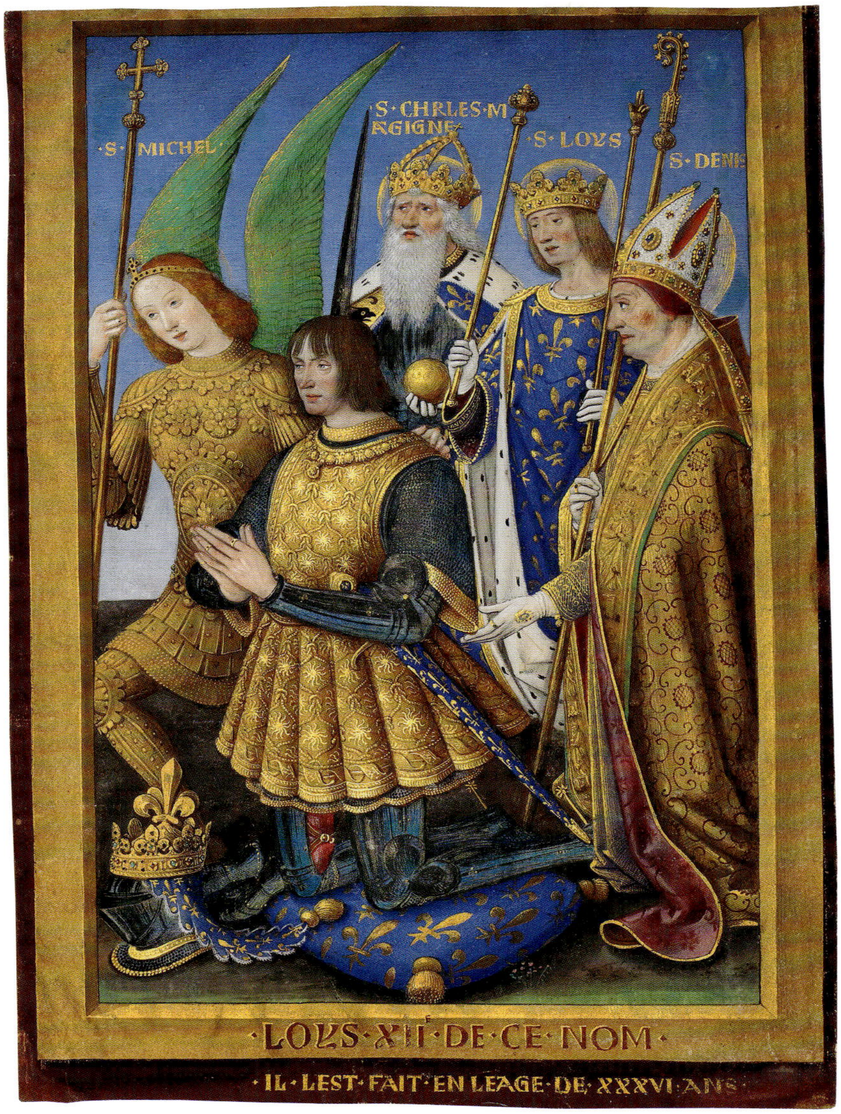

A full-page miniature removed from the *Hours of Louis XII*

Tours, 1498/99

Tempera and painted gold and silver on parchment; 24.3 x 15.7 cm (9⁹⁄₁₆ x 6³⁄₁₆ in.)

The J. Paul Getty Museum, Los Angeles, ms. 79 a, 2004.1

PROVENANCE: Louis XII, king of France (d. 1515); possibly Henry VII, king of England (d. 1509). William Beckford, Fonthill Abbey (d. 1844); sold to Henry Labouchere, later Lord Taunton (d. 1869), 1848; sold, Lord Taunton heirlooms, Sotheby's, July 14, 1920, no. 67, to Edmond de Rothschild (d. 1934), probably his ms. 70 (or possibly ms. 79); by descent to Alexandrine de Rothschild (d. 1965); her executor Maurice Rheims (d. 2003), Switzerland, by 1989.

BIBLIOGRAPHY: Maumené and d'Harcourt 1928, p. 104, no. 103, ill. opp. p. 104. Backhouse 1973, pp. 97–98, 102 n. 12. Reynaud in Paris 1993, pp. 295–96, under no. 162. Backhouse in Los Angeles/London 2005–06, pp. 1–3, 6–7, 18 n. 1, pl. 1. Turner in Los Angeles/London 2005–06, pp. 63–68, figs. 3.4, 3.6, 3.9–.11. Evans in Los Angeles/London 2005–06, pp. 80–90.

EXHIBITIONS: Los Angeles/London 2005–06.

THIS MINIATURE SHOWS Louis XII in dress armor, looking to the left as he kneels on a pillow brocaded with the royal fleur-de-lis, his hands folded in prayer. He is presented, unusually, not by his patron saint alone, but by four male saints, all connected with him personally and to his role as king of France. The image formed the right half of an illuminated diptych, a format popularized in manuscripts by Bourdichon's teacher, Jean Fouquet. The facing miniature, currently untraced, would have represented a devotional image such as the Virgin and Child or the Pietà, and the pair of illuminations would likely have served as a frontispiece. A similar diptych appears, also as a frontispiece, in a manuscript that Bourdichon illuminated about five years later for Louis's consort, Anne of Brittany (Bibliothèque nationale de France, ms. lat. 9474, ff. 2v–3; fig. 38). Indeed, this miniature and its companion were likely removed from a book of hours that was created for Louis not long after he became king of France in April 1498. In addition to the names of the four saints that appear above the figures' heads, the miniature is also inscribed *LOYS.XII.DE.CE NOM* on its painted frame, while the lower margin reads: *IL EST FAIT EN LEAGE DE XXXVI ANS*. The latter statement allows us to date the image precisely: it was painted between Louis's thirty-sixth and thirty-seventh birthdays. The earlier one occurred on June 27, 1498, exactly one month after his coronation at Reims. The book itself survives only in fragments: sixteen large miniatures are scattered in collections around the world, and fifty-one complete pages of text are preserved in the British Library (Royal Ms. 2 D XL).

Both the large dimensions of this miniature and the grand scale of its figures reflect a dramatic development in Bourdichon's style, announcing the monumental scale of much of his illumination thereafter. Since this book represents the court painter's first major commission for the new king, he may have seen fit to inaugurate a fresh artistic vocabulary that would flatter Louis's ambitions and self-image. It enjoyed great success at court. • TK

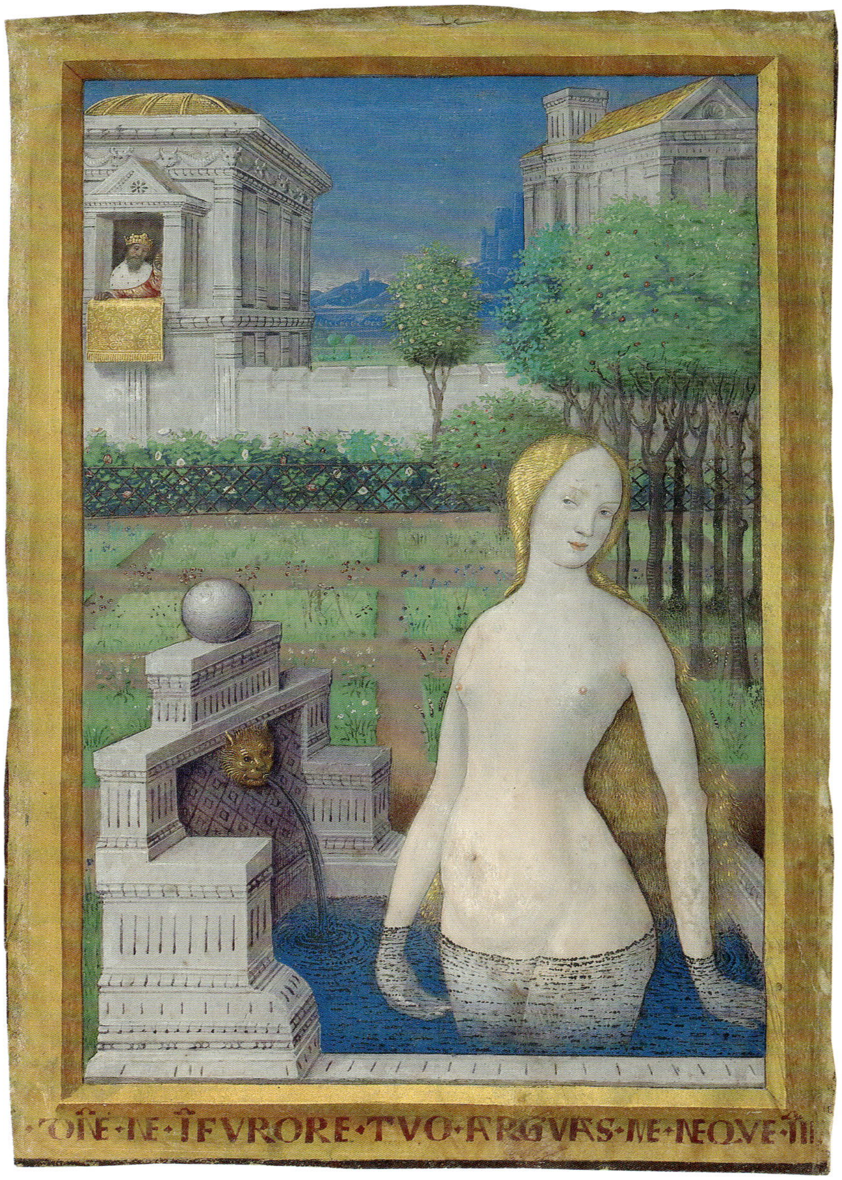

[41]

JEAN BOURDICHON
(1457/58–1521)

Bathsheba Bathing

A full-page miniature removed from the *Hours of Louis XII*

Tours, 1498/99

Tempera and painted gold and silver on parchment; 24.3 x 17 cm ($9\frac{9}{16}$ x $6\frac{11}{16}$ in.)

The J. Paul Getty Museum, Los Angeles, ms. 79, 2003.105

PROVENANCE: Louis XII, king of France (d. 1515); possibly Henry VII, king of England (d. 1509). D. E. Schwabach; sold, Christie's, London, July 11, 1974, lot 7, to Bernard H. Breslauer (d. 2004), London then New York; sold to the Getty.

BIBLIOGRAPHY: Backhouse 1973, pp. 95–96, 101–02, pl. 42. Reynaud in Paris 1993, p. 294, under no. 162. Kren in Los Angeles/London 2005–06, pp. 42–61, fig. 2.1. Turner in Los Angeles/London 2005–06, pp. 63–65, 67, 70, 72–73, fig. 3.16.

EXHIBITIONS: New York 1992, cat. 11. Los Angeles/London 2005–06.

THIS PROVOCATIVE miniature of the naked Bathsheba is one of the masterpieces of the *Hours of Louis XII*, a sumptuous book originally containing a dozen large calendar images and about two dozen full-page miniatures. Today only roughly half of the manuscript's illuminations survive. Bathsheba eyes the viewer coyly as she bathes in a fountain in the garden of King David's palace. David's response attests to Bathsheba's allure; he leans out the palace window, straining to see her. He is so distracted that he must steady himself by holding onto the window jamb. Bathsheba displays herself boldly. Shown in three-quarter view, her naked figure is fully revealed to just above her pubic area, which is submerged but clearly delineated. The silver highlights on the surface of the water, now tarnished to gray, would originally have sparkled and hence focused even stronger attention on this detail.

The story of David and Bathsheba, related in 2 Samuel 11:2–27, emphasizes the king's sinful behavior. Seeing Bathsheba bathing in the garden, he summons her to the palace and commits adultery with her. Upon learning that she has become pregnant, he orders her husband, Uriah, dispatched to battle, where he is killed. The Biblical account does not indicate that Bathsheba was even aware of David while bathing, much less that she enticed him, as shown here. Yet by the twelfth century, Christian theologians began to characterize Bathsheba negatively as a paradigm of feminine shallowness and coquettishness, a seductress to be shunned by women and to make men wary. Bourdichon, however, takes Bathsheba's role as a coquette at face value. He intends for the image's male viewer to *enjoy* her physical attributes rather than *bemoan* her feminine wiles—or perhaps, to enjoy them even as he, nominally, bemoans them. This Bathsheba certainly would have appealed to Louis, who was well-known as a womanizer.

This miniature belongs to a hugely popular French tradition of seductive Bathshebas that appeared discreetly within the pages of private devotional books from the 1480s well into the sixteenth century. Most of these books, it appears, were created for male consumption. Their images of Bathsheba bathing inaugurated the female nude as an enduring pictorial theme in French art. • TK

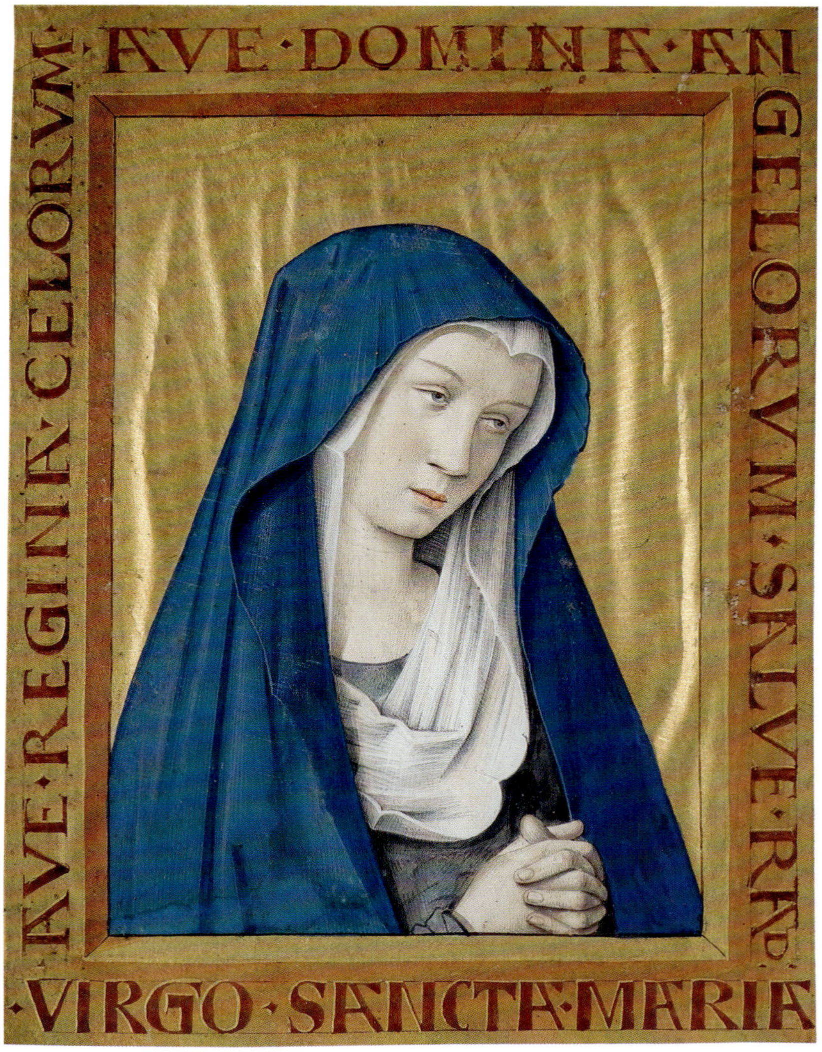

[42]

WORKSHOP OF JEAN BOURDICHON (1457/58–1521)

Virgin Mediatrix

Tours, 1480/90

Vellum pasted to wooden panel; 16.7 x 12.4 cm ($6^{9}/_{16}$ x $4^{7}/_{8}$ in.); with added borders: 19.5 x 15 cm ($7^{11}/_{16}$ x $5^{15}/_{16}$ in.)

Musée de Cluny—Musée national du Moyen Age, Paris, Cl. 23798

PROVENANCE: Perhaps abbey of Sainte-Geneviève, Paris; perhaps a convent of the Order of the Visitation; allocated to the Musée de Cluny, April 2005.

BIBLIOGRAPHY: Cottineau 1937, pp. 2206–07. Marrow and Avril 1994, pp. 77–88. Avril in Taburet-Delahaye 2006, p. 68. Undated typescript report by Marie-Françoise Damongeot.

EXHIBITIONS: Paris 2006, no. 35.

THIS DETACHED MINIATURE is from a book of hours. The Latin text running around its painted inner frame (*AVE . REGINA . C*[A]*OELORVM.AVE. DOMINA ANGELORVM.SALVE.RAD*[IX]) is from the Marian antiphon for compline, the final canonical hour of prayer, for use between the Feast of the Presentation and Easter. The inner border was added to the original leaf around 1510 to 1520. The miniature is pasted to a wooden panel and has been supplemented by an outer floral border, perhaps trimmed from its original manuscript. One of the most celebrated French manuscripts of this era, the *Hours of Etienne Chevalier*, was similarly dismembered during the eighteenth century, its full-page miniatures by Jean Fouquet pasted to panels to serve as devotional images.

The wooden frame, probably of early-nineteenth-century date, incorporates oval cavities containing relics of at least thirty-six identified saints, including Geneviève, the patron saint of Paris. Because of the presence of a relic of Saint Francis de Sales who founded the Order of the Visitation in 1610, Damongeot (curatorial file, Musée de Cluny) suggested that it belonged to a convent of this female order. The uppermost reliquary chamber also contains a cast terracotta medallion, apparently from the eighteenth century, representing saints Clothilde (*clotildis*) and Geneviève (*genovefa*). This suggests that it may perhaps previously have belonged to the major Parisian abbey of Sainte-Geneviève, which was cofounded by Clothilde, Clovis's queen.

The report by Damongeot (ibid.) associated the miniature with the style of Jean Bourdichon and dated it around 1480 to 1490. It was probably originally paired with an image of Christ Blessing, as are a pair of leaves of these subjects in the *Hours of Charles VIII* (Bibliothèque Nationale de France (BnF), ms. lat. 1370, ff. 35v–36; see cat. 52), also attributed to Bourdichon. However, the *Virgin Mediatrix* shown here is more plastic and monumental, recalling Fouquet's *Virgin and Child* from the *Hours of Simon de Varie* (Koninklijke Bibliotheek, The Hague, ms. 74 G 37a, fol. 1v), which has also sometimes been attributed to Bourdichon. Such pairs of half-length sacred portraits of Christ and the Virgin originated as painted diptychs on panel. This origin is made explicit in the present work by the illusionistic inner frame, shaded at the edges to resemble that of a panel painting. This became a characteristic device in Bourdichon's later full-page miniatures, such as those in the *Hours of Louis XII* (cat. 40) and the *Grandes Heures of Anne of Brittany* (BnF, ms. lat. 9474). • ME

[43]

JEAN POYER
(active 1483–1503)

Briçonnet Hours

Tours, c. 1485

Tempera and gold on vellum; 143 ff.; 20.9 x 14.4 cm
(8 1/4 x 5 11/16 in.)

Teylers Museum, Haarlem, ms. 78

Provenance: Guillaume Briçonnet, probably for his wife, Raoulette de Beaune; T. Boendermaker, eighteenth century; presented by George Guffanti of Amsterdam in 1772 to Pierre-Antoine Bolongaro-Crevenna; bought at his sale, 1790.

BIBLIOGRAPHY: New York 1982, p. 85, 87. Wieck et al. 2000, pp. 20–23, 189, fig. 15. Elsig 2004, p. 61. Hofmann 2004, pp. 11, 14–17, 19, 20, 25, 29, 39, 45, 56–57, 60–63, 90–92, 121, 145, 183, 184, figs. 7–31. Paris 2004, pp. 169, 170, fig. 98. Wieck 2004, pp. 249–52, figs. 11.1, 11.3, 11.5. Zöhl 2004, pp. 13, 37–38, 44, 50, 53, 55, 58–59, 91, 95, 97, 106, 111, 115–16, 120, 133–34, 138, 142–43, 150, 158, 172, 174–75, 180, 184, 192, figs. 24, 27, 35, 38, 40, 60, 75, 89. Reynaud 2006, p. 71 n. 5.

EXHIBITIONS: Paris 1993, no. 169. New York 2001. The Hague 2002, no. 74.

SHOWN: *Gideon* and *The Annunciation*, ff. 20v–21

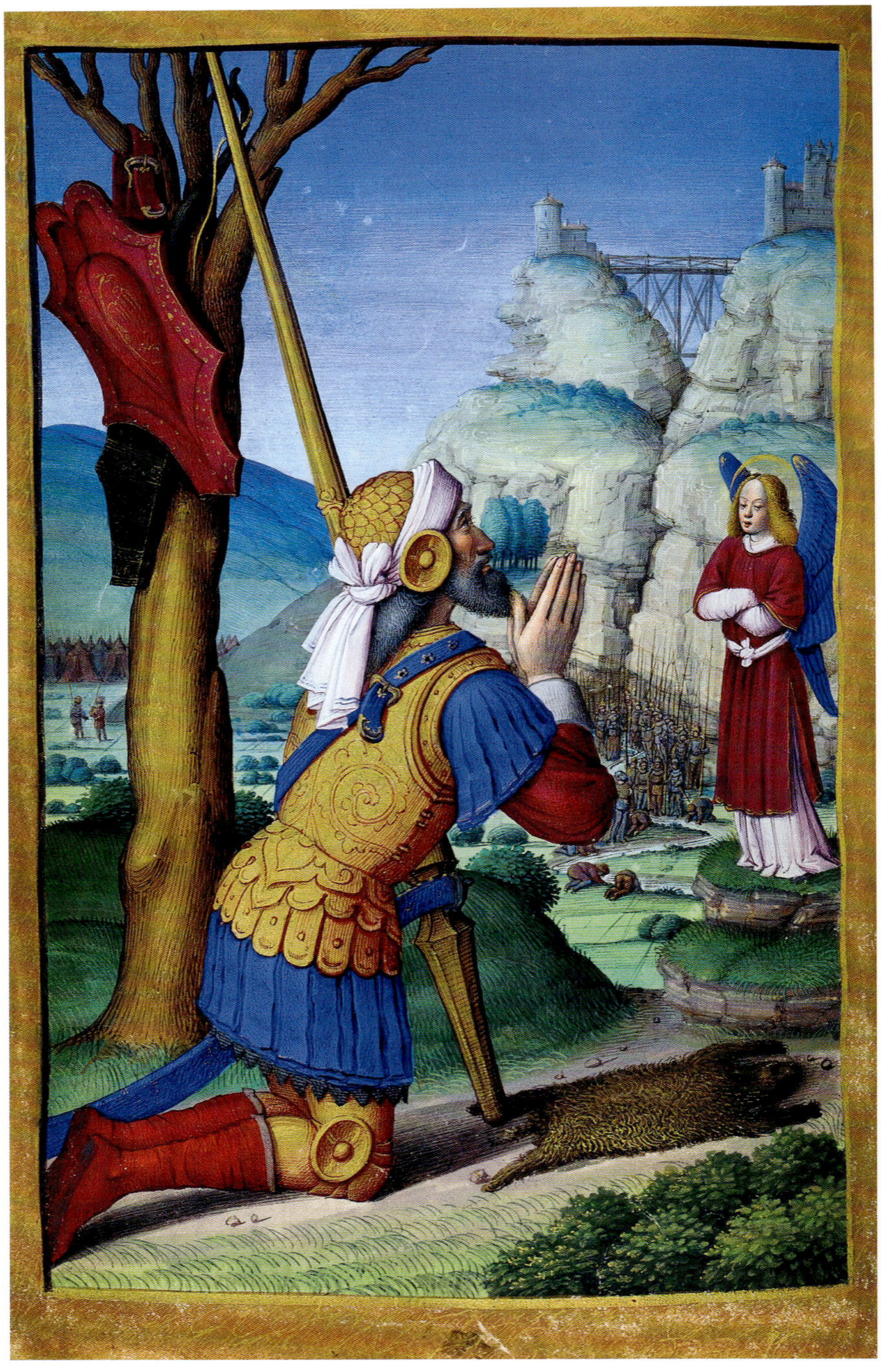

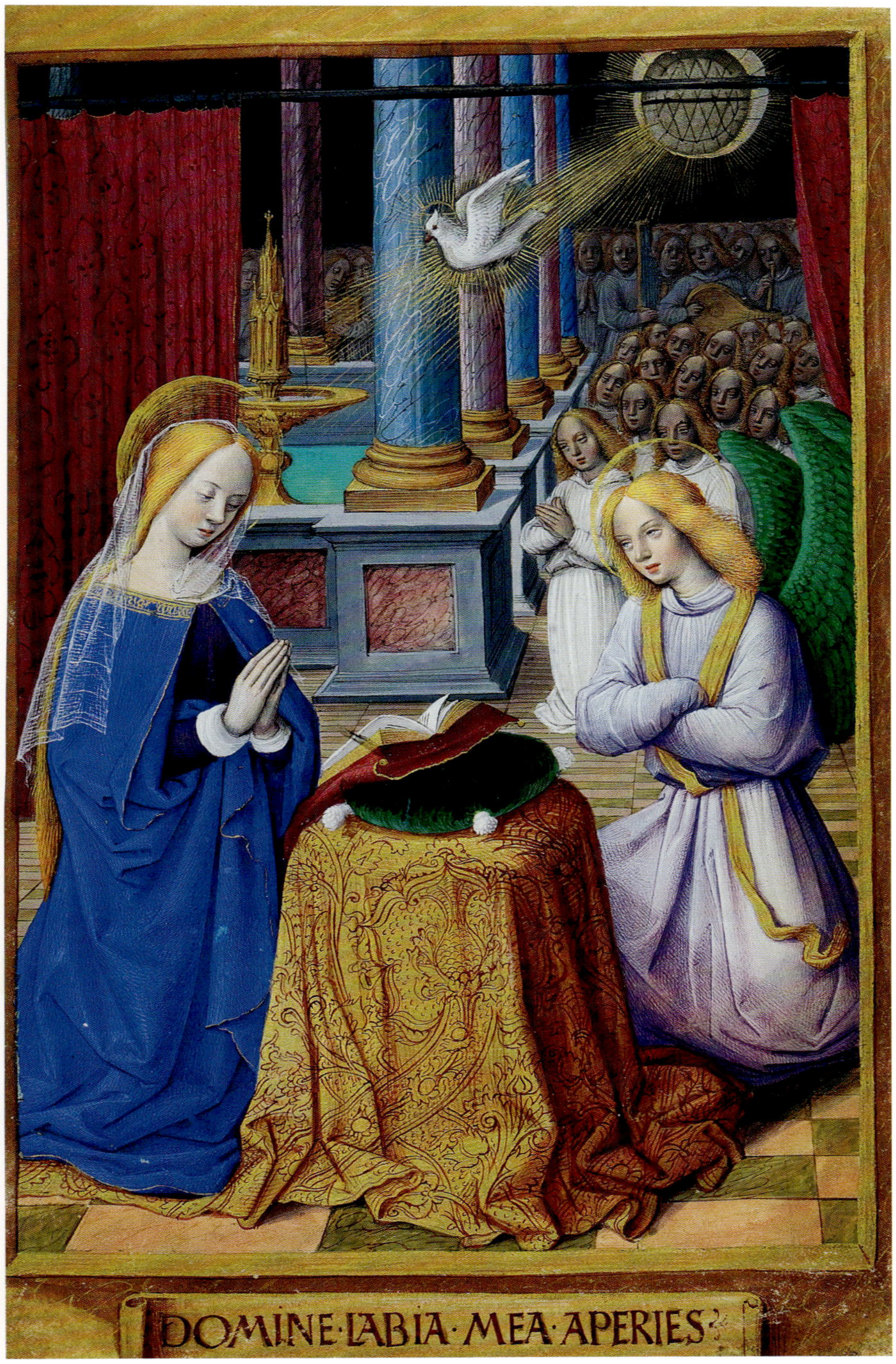

GUILLAUME BRIÇONNET (1445–1514) was superintendent of finance for Languedoc under Louis XI. Recommended by the king on his deathbed in 1483 to his heir, Briçonnet was promoted to France's secretary of the treasury and first place in the council of state when Charles VIII ascended the throne. It was probably upon the occasion of that meteoric promotion that he commissioned—as a kind of celebration—this book of hours as a gift to his wife, Raoulette de Beaune. The Briçonnet arms appear in an initial on folio 10v. In three miniatures the Virgin wears her hair rolled into a burlet under a veil, and in another picture her hair is braided; this attention to fashion, unusual for representations of Mary, hints that these portrayals might be portraits of (or at least allusions to) Raoulette. Historically known as the Cardinal of Saint-Malo, Briçonnet pursued a successful state-ecclesiastical career after the death of his wife in 1491.

Because of its provenance and stylistic affinities to Poyer's monumental Loches Triptych, dated 1485, the *Briçonnet Hours* no doubt dates to that same time. Both works exhibit the hard surfaces and crystalline air of the artist's early style. Although it is the earliest known manuscript illuminated by Poyer, the *Briçonnet Hours*, like the triptych, reveals a stellar mastery of space, volume, and perspective, indicating that its illuminator had already been active for some time. In the background of the miniature of Saint Mark (fol. 11v), Poyer painted the canals of Venice, a pictorial boast that he had traveled to Italy. • RSW

[44]

JEAN POYER
(active 1483–1503)

Prayer Book of Anne of Brittany

Tours, 1492–95

Tempera and gold on vellum; 31 ff.; 12.6 x 8 cm (4 15/16 x 3 1/8 in.)

The Morgan Library and Museum, New York, ms. M.50

PROVENANCE: Commissioned by Anne of Brittany (d. 1514) for herself and the dauphin, Charles Orland (d. 1495). Armand de Crochard, of Fontaine-Milon, c. 1820, and later his son. Théophile Belin, by 1903; sold to J. Pierpont Morgan, 1905.

BIBLIOGRAPHY: Paris 1993, pp. 307, 314, 318, 417. Wieck and Hearne 1999. Wieck et al. 2000, pp. 24–26, fig. 17. Elsig 2004, p. 61. Hofmann 2004, pp. 20–22, 23, 26, 27, 28, 29, 44, 61, 83, 121, 131, 133–36, 166, 180, figs. 50–56. Paris 2004, p. 165. Reynaud 2006, pp. 110 n. 2, 224 n. 5. Wieck 2007, passim.

EXHIBITIONS: New York 1934, no. 118. New York 1982, no. 114. New York 2001.

SHOWN: *St. Anne Instructing the Virgin*, f. 13

THIS CHARMING little prayer book was a personal commission by Anne of Brittany: its miniatures are framed by her personal device, the *cordelière* (the knotted robe of the Franciscans), and by the letters that spell her name. The queen determined the selection and order of the prayers. She evidently commissioned the book to teach her son, the dauphin Charles Orland, his catechism. It starts with the basic prayers every Catholic would memorize as a child: the Our Father, Hail Mary, and Apostles' Creed, as well as Grace Before and After Meals, and the Act of Confession. The pictures, too, had a pedagogical purpose: the miniature illustrating the Confiteor, for example, shows Anne kneeling and confessing her sins (f. 10v). The final miniature depicts Charles Orland at the apparent age of about twelve—an age that the dauphin, who died when he was three, would never reach (f. 31). He is praying for the wisdom to rule. The illustration *Saint Anne Instructing the Virgin* (f. 13) shows how the queen might have used this book to teach her son: while helping Mary hold a book, Anne, the queen's name saint, points to a word in the text and pronounces it.

The thirty-four tiny miniatures in this diminutive manuscript demonstrate that Poyer could work on a small as well as a large scale. Dating about ten years after the extant works in his early style, the Crucifxion triptych in Loches and the *Briçonnet Hours* (cat. 43), this codex is characteristic of the artist's later manner, with its stippled brushwork, atmospheric perspective, and much lighter palette favoring pink, lilac, and white. • RSW

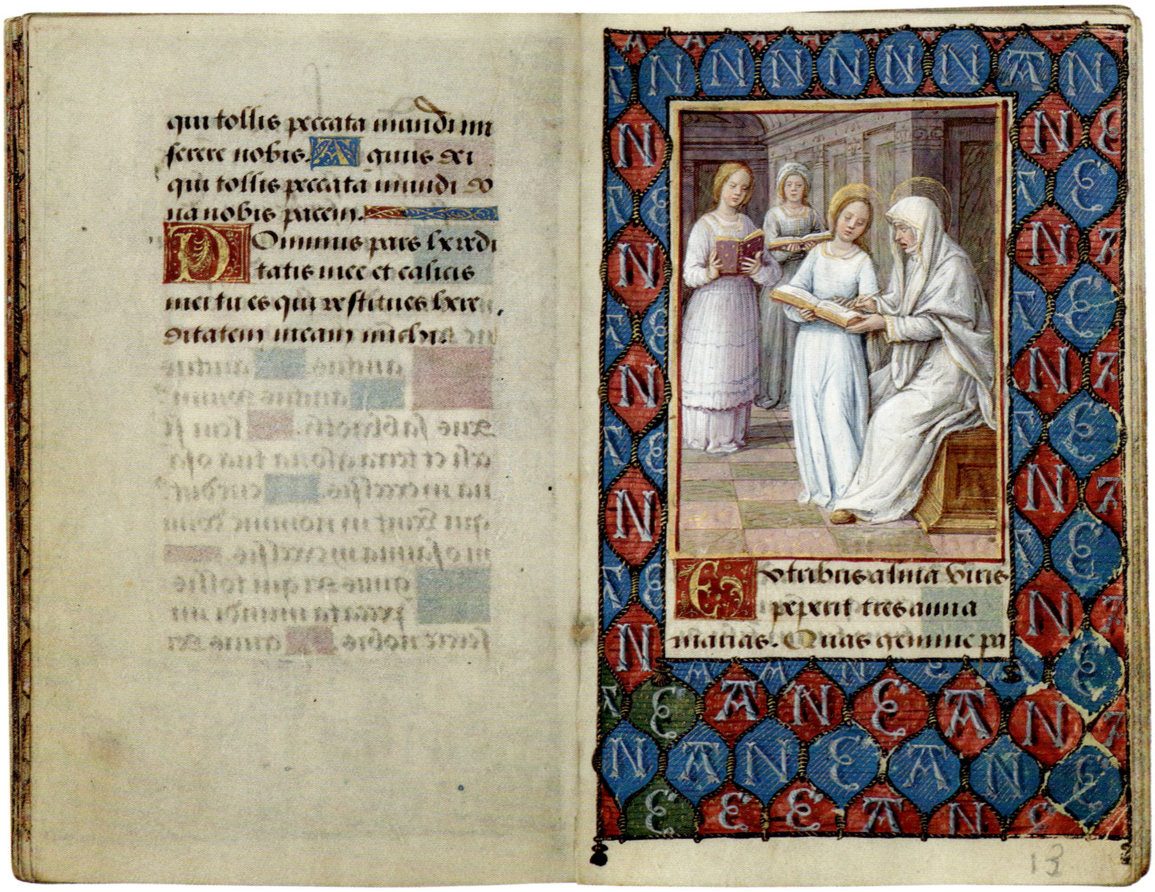

[45]

JEAN POYER
(active 1483–1503)

Hours of Anne of Brittany and Mary of England

Tours, c. 1498 (with additions c. 1514)

Tempera and gold on vellum; 96 ff.; 13.8 x 9.7 x 1.7 cm ($5\frac{7}{16}$ x $3\frac{13}{16}$ x $\frac{5}{8}$ in.)

Bibliothèque municipale, Lyon, ms. 1558

PROVENANCE: Possibly given by Louis XII (d. 1515) as a wedding gift to his second wife, Anne of Brittany (d. 1514), 1498; given by Louis XII as a wedding gift to his third wife, Mary Tudor, 1514; given to her brother Henry VIII of England (d. 1547), 1530. Jean-Baptiste Charvin, by 1842; bequeathed to the Bibliothèque municipale, Lyon, 1842.

BIBLIOGRAPHY: Vingtrinier 1896. Perrat 1926. Blum and Lauer 1930, p. 98, figs. 85–86. Wieck et al. 2000, pp. 26–27, 190, fig. 18. Hofmann 2004, pp. 27–29, 30, 34, 57–58, 117–21, 131, 136, figs. 70–81. Zöhl 2004, pp. 134–35, 173, figs. 33–34. Reynaud 2006, pp. 71, 110 n. 2, 224 n. 5, fig. 11.4.

EXHIBITIONS: Lyon 1920, no. 49. Paris 1993, no. 173. Paris 2004, no. 58.

SHOWN: *The Flight into Egypt*, f. 39v

AS OPPOSED TO THE so-called *Hours of Henry VIII* (cat. 46), this manuscript was indeed owned by this king of England. Inscriptions reveal that Henry received it from his sister Mary Tudor, who was married (for a brief three months) to Louis XII, who had given her the book as a wedding gift. Originally created around 1498, the manuscript was modified by the king at the time of his marriage in 1514; he added two prayers and miniatures by Jean Bourdichon and the Master of Claude of France. It is also possible that the book of hours had originally been a gift from Louis to his previous wife, Anne of Brittany.

Poyer painted his sixteen large and twenty-two small miniatures in a highly restricted palette. The figures wear robes of pale pink, lilac, and blue, the subtle shades of which are nearly grisaille. He rendered the landscapes and interiors in colors that, while not nearly so monochromatic, are also restrained. Architectural elements frame the large miniatures, making them look like Italian Renaissance altarpieces. Putti play at the bottom of many of these structures—another reference to Italian art. • RSW

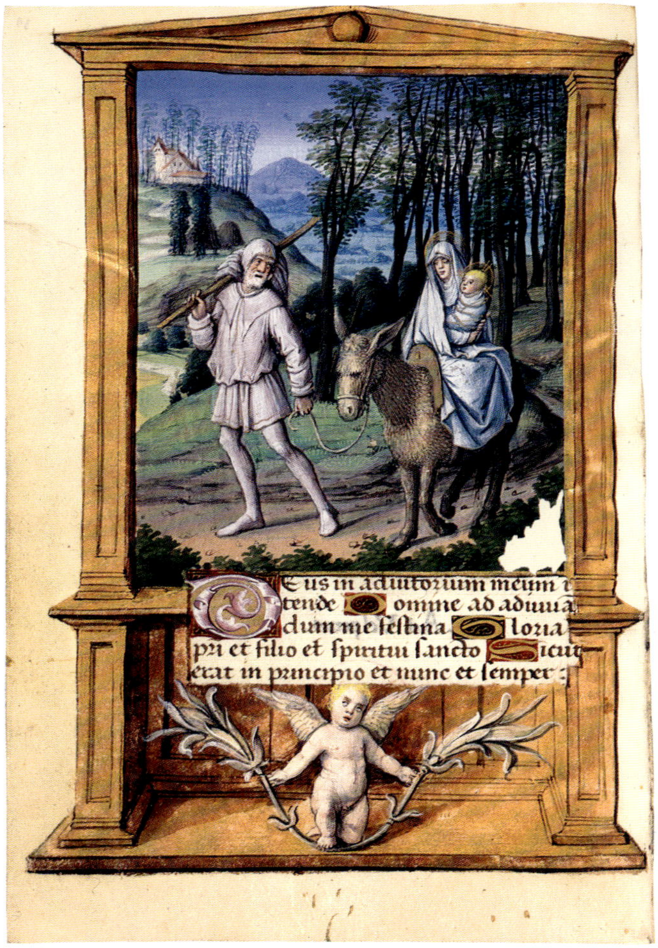

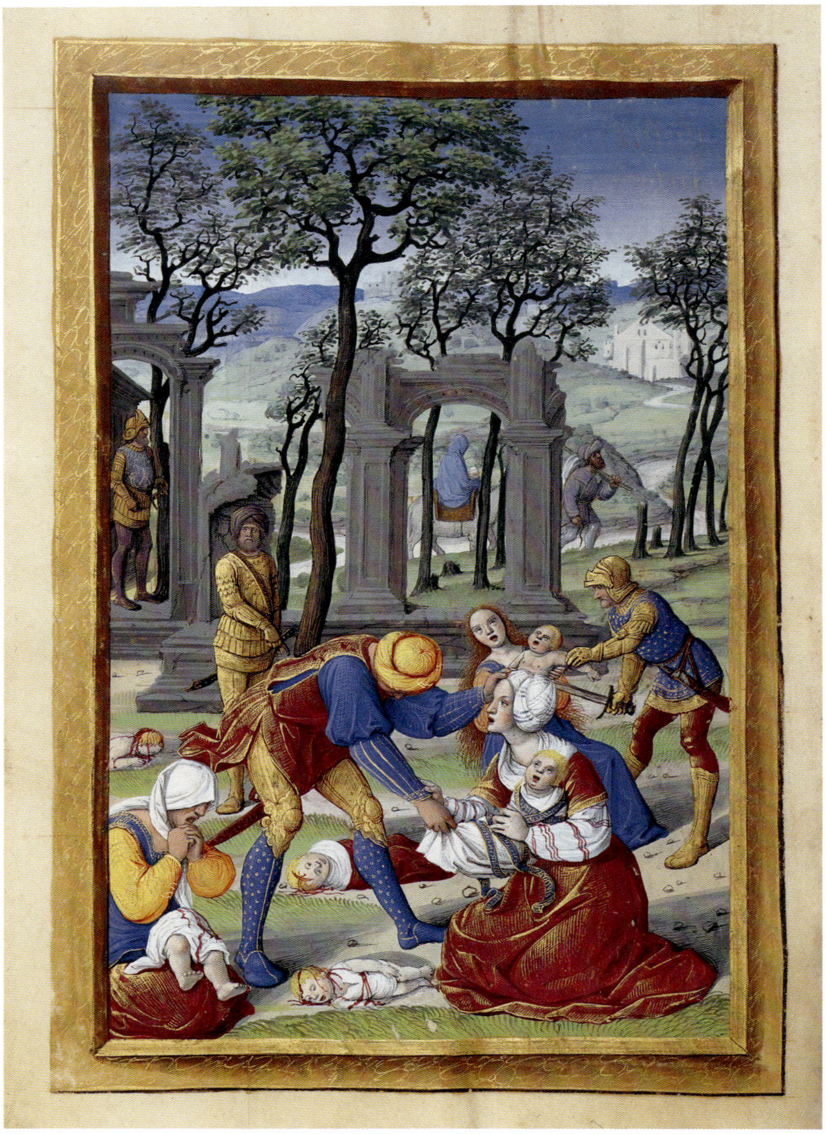

[46]

JEAN POYER
(active 1483–1503)

So-Called Hours of Henry VIII

Tours, c. 1500

Tempera and gold on vellum, 200 ff.; 25.6 x 18 cm (10 1/16 x 7 1/16 in.)

Morgan Library and Museum, New York, ms. H.8

PROVENANCE: Charle Benoit Desmanet, Mons; George Wade (d. 1748); given or sold to King George II of England (d. 1760), by 1740; on deposit at the Royal Library, Hanover; by descent to William IV (d. 1837); by descent to his brother Ernest Augustus, duke of Cumberland and later king of Hanover (d. 1851); by descent to Duke Ernest Augustus II (d. 1953); sold to Dannie H. Heineman (d. 1962); given to his wife, Hettie Heineman (d. 1974); bequeathed to the Heineman Foundation, 1974; donated to the Morgan Library, 1977.

BIBLIOGRAPHY: Paris 1993, pp. 307, 314. Backhouse 1996, p. 405 (ill.). Wieck et al. 2000. Elsig 2004, p. 61. Hofmann 2004, pp. 9, 17, 35–39, 44, 48, 49, 53, 58–59, 63, 87, 93, 97, 106, 108, 117, 126–31, 145, 172, 188, figs. 104–11. Paris 2004, pp. 164, 171. Zöhl 2004, pp. 37, 39, 87, 107–08, 110, 133, 135, 138–39, 145, 158, 173, 175–76, figs. 20, 42, 83, 93. Reynaud 2006, pp. 110 n. 2, 136, 164 n. 1, 202, 208, 224, figs. 28.1, 42.3, 44.3, 47.4. Hourihane 2007, pp. lvii–viii, 7, 20, pls. 18, 49, 84, 125, 160, 192, 209, 244, 270, 292, 323, 355.

EXHIBITIONS: New York 1982, no. 113. New York 2001.

SHOWN: *The Massacre of the Innocents*, f. 69v

THE BINDING of this manuscript has two silver clasps containing the arms, monogram, and motto of Henry VIII, supplying the book with a putative provenance and its nickname. The clasps are not original, however, and the tradition linking the codex to Henry goes back only to the eighteenth century. Although we know that the king once possessed the *Hours of Anne of Brittany and Mary of England* (cat. 45), his ownership of this book is romantic fiction, and the identity of the person who originally commissioned it remains unknown.

With fifty-five (originally fifty-eight) miniatures, this is Poyer's largest and most richly illuminated book of hours. The compositions have a scale, depth, and monumentality, and the figures are endowed with a grandeur of weight and volume not seen in any of his previous work. Spaces are subtly lit, often with a striking use of chiaroscuro, as in the masterful *David and Uriah* (f. 108v). Interiors are also clearly delineated in perspective, a skill for which the artist was famous (Pèlerin 1510–21); the most articulated treatment occurs in the *Annunciation*. Poyer was equally adept at handling landscape, as the half-page calendar miniatures (ff. 1–6v), the full-page *Saint Jerome in Penance* (f. 170), and the *Massacre of the Innocents*, shown here, attest. His palette in this manuscript is not dark and opaque as in the earlier *Briçonnet Hours* (cat. 43) but combines lights and darks as in the *Prayer Book of Anne of Brittany* (cat. 44). Poyer's brushwork, however, is not stippled as in the latter work, this being a much larger codex. When the miniatures occupy half a page, the texts are framed by three-sided borders executed in an unusual range of rich monochrome colors highlighted with gold: brown, blue, green, oxblood, slate, rust, and plum. Executed by assistants, these fine borders reveal something of the training given to, and the rigorous demands put upon, the members of Poyer's workshop. • RSW

[47]

ATTRIBUTED TO GUILLAUME REGNAULT
(active 1502–34)

Virgin and Child

c. 1510–20

Alabaster; 183 x 60 x 41 cm (72 1/16 x 23 5/8 x 16 1/8 in.)

Musée du Louvre, Department of Sculpture, RF 202

PROVENANCE: Jacques de Mainville (d. 1803), owner of the château of Couasnon in Olivet, Loiret; on the Paris market; Jamarin, a dealer in objets d'art; sold to Louis Charles Timbal; sold to the Louvre, May 1875.

BIBLIOGRAPHY: Montaiglon 1875, pp. 385–404. Courajod 1877. Courajod 1888. Grandmaison 1897, pp. 78–96. Bossebœuf 1897–98. Vitry 1901, pp. 426–30. Pradel 1953, pp. 84–85, 93–96. Gaborit 1998, vol. 2, p. 657. Leproux 2000. Le Pogam 2008, pp. 51–52.

BASED ON ITS SCALE and the quality of its materials and execution, the *Virgin and Child* from Olivet is among the major French sculptures of the early Renaissance. Since its acquisition by the Musée du Louvre in 1875, the figure's serene beauty has always impressed observers: the tranquility of the Virgin's expression, the harmonious folds of the drapery, the elegance of the details of her attire (for example, the veil with its ends tied beneath a monogrammed clasp), and the flow of her cloak. The view of the statue from Mary's proper left side, which shows the Christ Child facing front, is just as charming as the frontal view, and demonstrates the artistry of a sculptor who was certainly among the finest of his generation. Although there is no documentary proof, art historians have often thought of Guillaume Regnault, Michel Colombe's nephew and faithful collaborator; the only certain attribution to Regnault is the tomb of Louis de Poncher and Roberte Legendre, formerly in Saint-Germain-l'Auxerrois and now in the Louvre.

The authority of the Olivet Virgin is evident from the fact that it inspired numerous other sculptures of the Virgin, on various scales and in different materials, sometimes with the composition reversed. These include, among others, the stone Virgin from Bourgonnière (commune of Bouzillé, Maine-et-Loire), the marble Virgin from Mesland, the alabaster Virgin from the château of la Verrerie (commune of Oizon, Cher), the Virgin of Ecouen (Louvre) and the Virgin, also in stone, from the altarpiece of Tristan Salazar in the cathedral of Sens. A recently discovered notarized contract establishes the date (1514) and the artist's name for the Sens altarpiece. He was Guillaume Chaleveau, a sculptor born in Sens, doubtless later established in Tours, and known to be a collaborator of Guillaume Regnault on the tomb of Louis de Poncher mentioned above (Leproux 2000). This discovery allows us to put forward the name of Guillaume Regnault as the probable creator of the Olivet Virgin with greater certainty, and makes our continuing ignorance of its patron and original location even more frustrating. • BC-B

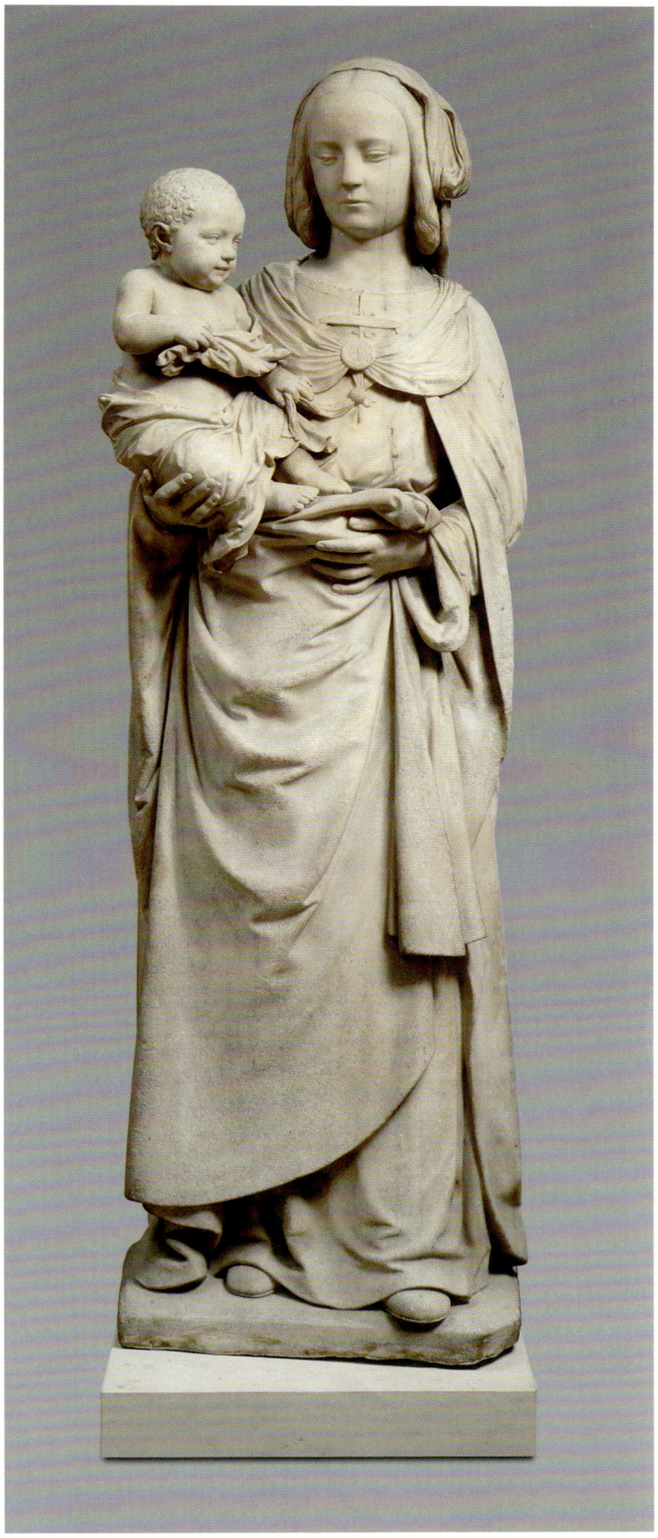

JEAN POYER
(active 1483–1503)
OR A FOLLOWER

WINGS OF A TRIPTYCH OF SAINT MARY MAGDALENE

[48]

Christ Preaching

Tours, 1500–02, or Paris, c. 1515

Oil on wood transferred to canvas; 120 x 92.4 cm (47¼ x 36⅜ in.)

Parish church of Notre-Dame de l'Assomption, Censeau, Jura

PROVENANCE, BIBLIOGRAPHY, EXHIBITIONS: See below.

[49]

Noli me tangere

Tours, 1500–02, or Paris, c. 1515

Oil on wood transferred to canvas; 120 x 92.4 cm (47¼ x 36⅜ in.)

Parish church of Notre-Dame de l'Assomption, Censeau, Jura

PROVENANCE: Possibly commissioned by Jean IV de Chalon, prince of Orange (d. 1502), probably for the church of the Cordeliers at Nozeroy, Jura, as part of a triptych with *Christ in the House of Simon the Pharisee* (Conseil général de Jura, Lons-le-Saunier; now also in the parish church of Censeau, Jura), or commissioned c. 1515 as wings for the triptych. Possibly the Cistercian monastery of Mont-Sainte Marie (diocese of Besançon, destroyed in the French Revolution); transferred to the parish church, Censeau.

BIBLIOGRAPHY: Elsig 2000. Elsig and Avril 2002. Elsig 2004, pp. 61–62, 65. Hofmann 2004, pp. 40–42, 184–85, figs. 127–28.

EXHIBITIONS: Pontarlier 1949, no. 16. Poligny et al., 1972, nos. 230, 231. Paris 2004, nos. 56, 57.

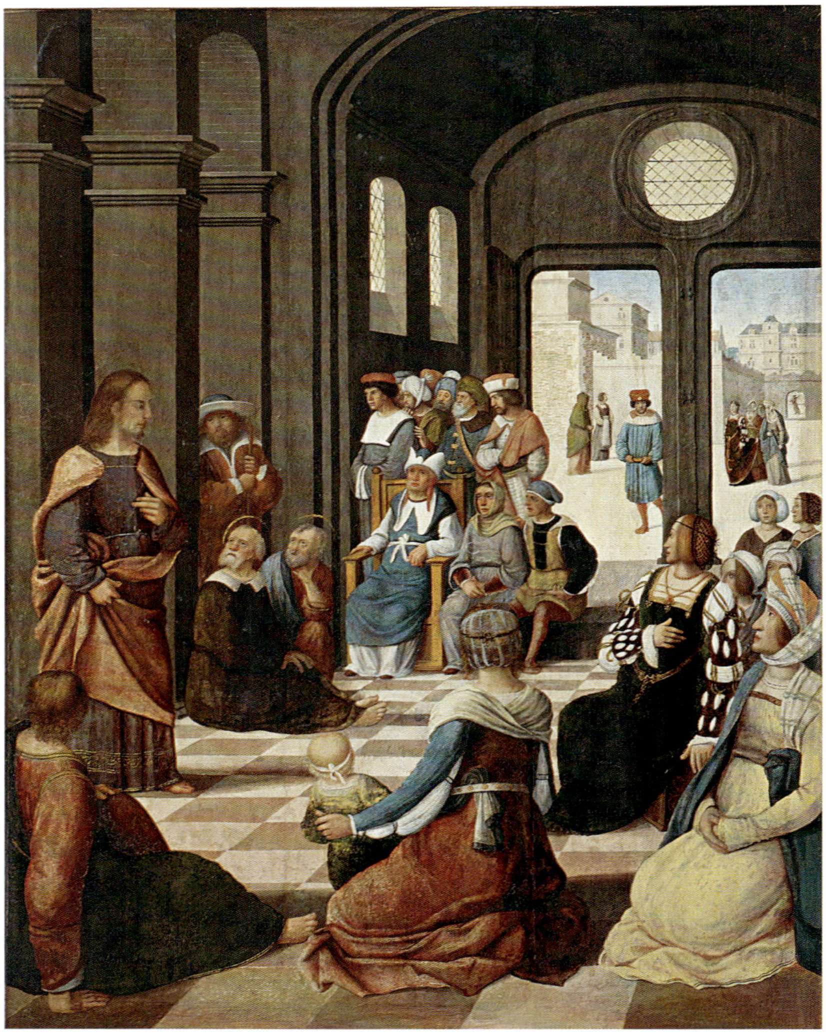

BECAUSE OF THEIR dimensions, subjects, and styles, these two paintings, along with the *Christ in the House of Simon the Pharisee* from Lons-le-Saunier, Jura, are thought to have once formed a triptych. The images show three scenes from the life of Mary Magdalene as it intersected with Christ: the Magdalene hears Christ preach; she visits him in the house of Simon the Pharisee; and, encountering him after the Resurrection, she is admonished not to touch his glorified body. The central panel, although in poor condition, is still eloquent testimony to the talents of Jean Poyer. It shows, at the lower left, the narrative element of the Magdalene washing and anointing the Savior's feet beneath the table, a subject the artist treated in a similar way in the *Prayer Book of Anne of Brittany* (cat. 44) and the so-called *Hours of Henry VIII* (cat. 46). Its narrative is naturally more complex than those of the miniatures. At the left, a disgruntled Judas, gripping a money bag, leaves in disgust while Saint Peter speaks with a group. These are the best-preserved figures

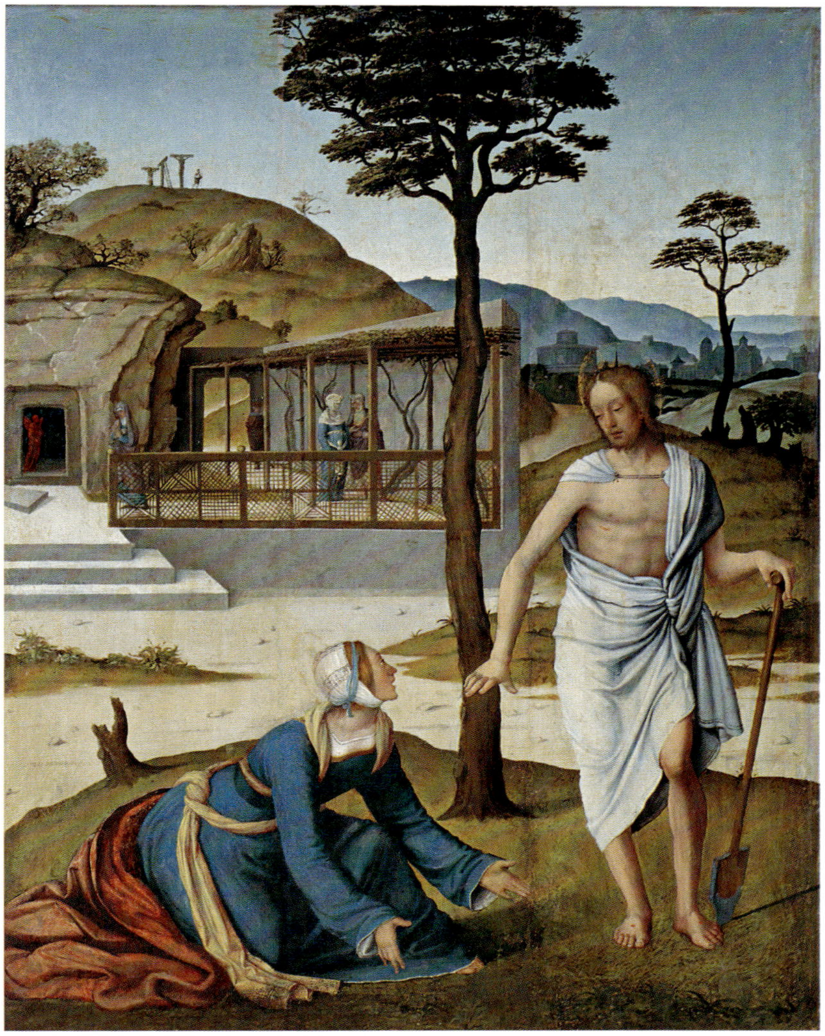

in the painting. The horizontal composition, with the table set parallel to the picture plane, the windows in the background, and the figures interacting in groups, was probably influenced by Leonardo's *Last Supper*, which Poyer could have seen on a visit to Milan. He easily absorbed Italian influences over the course of his career, as seen in two of his earliest works, the *Briçonnet Hours* (cat. 43) and the large triptych in Loches.

While the three paintings might indeed have formed a triptych, it is possible, however, that they were not all executed at the same time or by the same hand. The compositions and figures of the wings are proto-Mannerist in style and could have been painted by a follower of Poyer, possibly around 1515, the date to which Elsig (2000) initially assigned them. The wings share compositional and stylistic quirks of the painter called the pseudo-Poyer who worked under Poyer during his lifetime but, after the master's death, continued his career in Paris. Mannered features include, in the *Noli me tangere*, the Magdalene's long, thin arms and the oddly empty void in the middle ground. In *Christ Preaching*, the foreground women with their backs to the viewer are also Mannerist. Elsig (2002) argued that the Italian style of dress worn by the Magdalene confirms a date in the very early years of the sixteenth century. These Italian fashions, however, provide only a terminus post quem, and it could equally be argued that by the middle of the second decade of the century, when this manner of dress was no longer in vogue, it became appropriately exotic garb for a prostitute in a group of women who are all, incidentally, dressed fantastically. If Jean IV of Chalon (paternal cousin of Anne of Brittany) commissioned these works as a triptych from Poyer in 1500, following a visit to Lons-le-Saunier by Anne of Brittany on the occasion of the baptism of his son, Jean's death in 1502 and Poyer's by 1503 might have interrupted their execution, so that they were only completed later by a follower. • RSW

[50]

JEAN POYER
(active 1483–1503)

The Mocking of Elisha

Tours, c. 1500

Pen and point of brush with black and brown ink and gray, pink, green, blue, and yellow washes; 21 x 14.5 cm ($8^{1}/_{4}$ x $5^{11}/_{16}$ in.)

The Art Institute of Chicago, Everett D. Graff Memorial Fund, 1965.16

PROVENANCE: With cat. 51, Eugène Rodrigues, Paris; sold, still with cat. 51, Frederik Muller, Amsterdam, July 12–13, 1921, no. 114, to H. E. ten Cate, Rotterdam (d. 1955); C. G. Boerner, Düsseldorf, 1964; sold to the Art Institute of Chicago.

BIBLIOGRAPHY, EXHIBITIONS: See cat. 51.

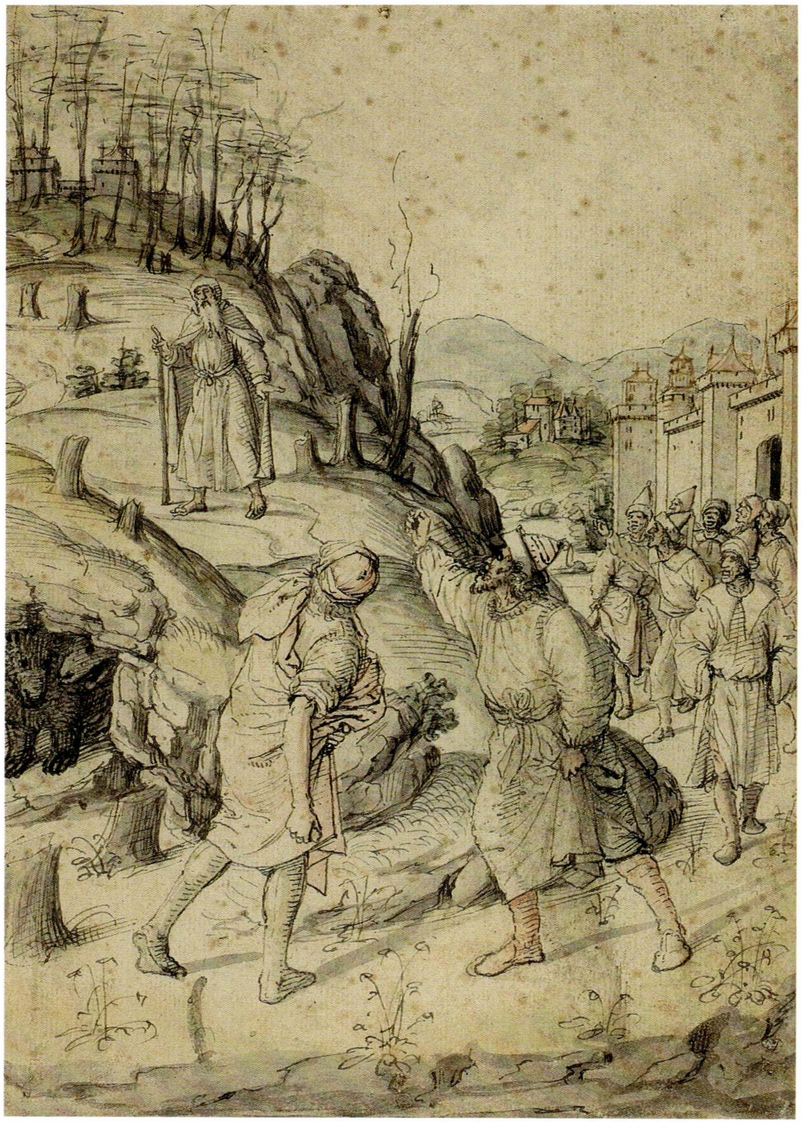

THESE ARE TWO OF FIVE SURVIVING drawings of Old Testament subjects that must once have been part of a larger series. The others are *Cain and Abel* and the *The Sacrifice of Isaac*, which were acquired by the British Museum on the London market in 1874, and *Joseph Sold to the Ishmaelites*, in the Boymans Museum, Rotterdam, first recorded in the Firmin-Didot collection. The present drawings were together in the Rodrigues collection in 1921.

Backhouse (1983 and 1987) first identified the group of drawings, connecting them with manuscripts newly associated with Jean Poyer. The expressive foreground figures, the importance of subordinate narratives, and the way the landscapes are organized all parallel Poyer's illuminations in the *Lyon Hours* (cat. 45), the so-called *Hours of Henry VIII* (cat. 46), and the *Tilliot Hours* in the British Library. Very few independent drawings by French illuminators survive. The format, subjects, and delicate washes of this group have led to speculation concerning their function. Nicole Reynaud (1993) presumed that they were preparations for works other than manuscript illuminations, possibly domestic stained glass.

The Art Institute's drawing depicts the youths who taunt the prophet Elisha, who is shown in the middle ground cursing

[51]

JEAN POYER
(active 1483–1503)

The Coronation of Solomon by the Spring of Gihon

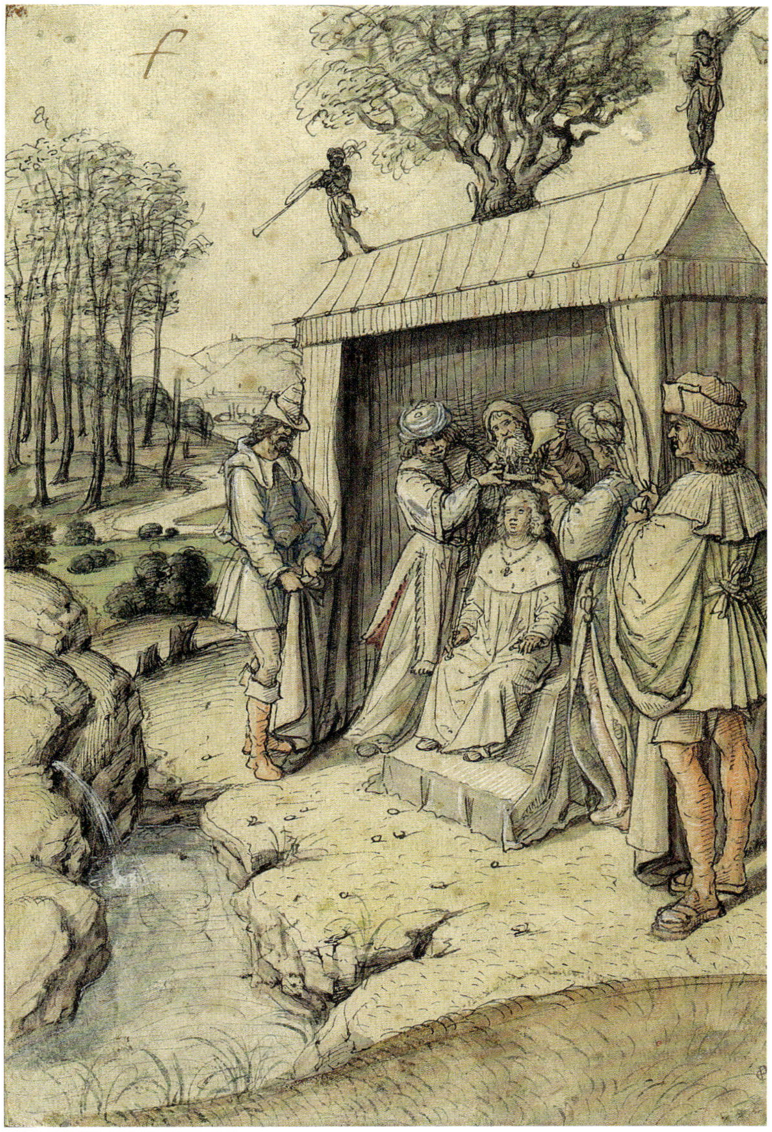

Tours, c. 1500

Pen and point of brush with black and brown ink and gray, pink, green, blue, and yellow washes heightened with white gouache; 21.3 x 14.4 cm (8 3/8 x 5 11/16 in.)

National Gallery of Art, Washington, D.C., Patron's Permanent Fund, 2006.111.3

PROVENANCE: With cat. 50, Eugène Rodrigues, Paris, sold, still with cat. 50, Frederik Muller, Amsterdam, July 12–13, 1921, no. 114, to H. E. ten Cate, Rotterdam (d. 1955); C. G. Boerner, Düsseldorf, 1964. Sold, Sotheby's, London, July 7, 1966, no. 94, to Colnaghi. Private collection. Sold, Sotheby's, New York, January 10, 1996, no. 176, to an American private collection; sold to the National Gallery of Art through Salamander Fine Arts, 2006.

BIBLIOGRAPHY: Hannema 1955, p. 127, no. 219b. Joachim 1977, pp. 27–28, no. 6. Backhouse 1983, p. 180. Backhouse 1987, pp. 224–28, fig. 13. Avril 1993, p. 308. Reynaud 1993, p. 318. Roberts 1996, pp. 120–26, no. 23. Backhouse 1996, p. 406. Wieck 2000, p. 33. Elsig 2002, p. 110. Hofmann 2004, pp. 43–44, fig. 133.

EXHIBITIONS: New York 2001. Washington 2009, no. 1.

his tormentors. This episode was used as a prototype for the Mocking of Christ in the *Biblia Pauperum*, a cycle of typological images expanding on the life of Christ. Similarly, Isaac carrying the wood for his sacrifice was a type of Christ Carrying the Cross, and the Joseph episode prefigured the payment of Judas. The rejection of Cain's offering and the murder of Abel refer to the Betrayal of Christ in another typological cycle, the *Speculum Humanae Salvationis*. The Coronation of Solomon is not part of this typological tradition; rather, the kingship of David and Solomon could have been invoked to amplify the role of French kings (cats. 31–32, and examples cited in Scheller 1981–82, p. 16). The letters *D*, *F*, and *G* in contemporary script, which appear on *Isaac Carrying the Wood*, the *Coronation*, and *Cain and Abel*, respectively, are further evidence that the drawings formed part of a series. Although the context for these vividly imagined narratives remains unclear, it should be remembered that Poyer used Old Testament prototypes in four splendid bifolios at the main text divisions of the *Briçonnet Hours* (cat. 43). • MW

[52]

FOLLOWER OF JEAN FOUQUET (PROBABLY THE MASTER OF THE MUNICH BOCCACCIO)

Diptych of Christ Blessing and The Virgin in Prayer

Tours, c. 1480

Oil on wood; *Christ*: 48.4 x 33.3 cm (19 1/16 x 13 1/8 in.); *The Virgin*: 49.7 x 35.5 cm (19 9/16 x 14 in.)

Musée des Beaux Arts, Tours, 2007-2-1 and 2007-2-2

PROVENANCE: Paul Leprieur (d. 1918); Paul Vitry, Paris (d. 1941); his heirs; acquired with the support of PGA Holding, 2007.

BIBLIOGRAPHY: Dupont 1935–36, pp. 186–88, figs. 5–6. Thiébaut 2008, pp. 28–30.

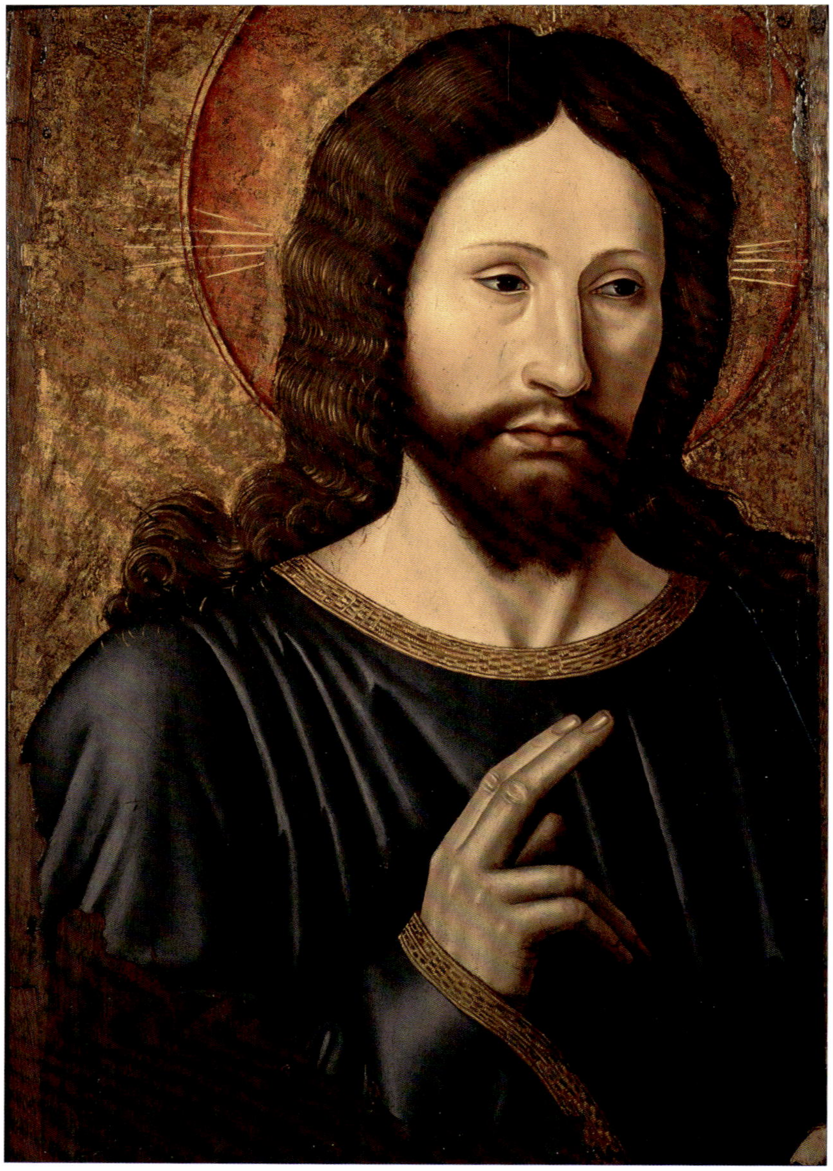

THE RECENT ACQUISITION of these two panels by a public collection is a significant contribution to our understanding of the art of Tours around 1480. They were originally part of a diptych of larger dimensions. Part of Christ's proper left hand has been trimmed; the remnant, visible in the lower right corner, was revealed in a restoration in 2003–05. The two panels were very likely arched at the top like the portraits of the Virgin held by Saint Luke in miniatures by Jean Bourdichon in the *Large Hours of Anne of Brittany* (Bibliothèque nationale de France (BnF), ms. lat. 9474, f. 19v; illustrated in Antoine 2004, p. 26) and in the *Hours of Frederick III of Aragon* (BnF, ms. lat. 10532, f. 152). In both of these miniatures, Saint Luke, the evangelist-painter, holds a wing of our diptych (or its model), proving the exceptional renown of the composition in the artistic circles of Tours around 1500. Another version of the wing showing the Virgin, which was reproduced by Dupont (1935–36) and judged by him to be of higher quality, demonstrates the existence of a replica. This work, formerly in private collections in Riga, Latvia, and in Germany, is also painted on panel, but is smaller in size (44 x 34.5 cm; 17 5/16 x 13 9/16 in.) and more distant from the original design.

The most faithful reproduction of the ensemble was painted by Bourdichon in the *Hours of Charles VIII* (BnF, ms. lat. 1370, ff. 35v–36; illustrated in Antoine 2004, p. 24). The arched format of his miniature diptych is still visible on the reverse of the sheets, although the entire background was ultimately covered by a cloth of honor of gold brocade with white flowers. A reversed version of this composition, in the style of Bourdichon, was studied and reproduced by Antoine in 2004 (Bibliothèque municipale, Saint-Germain-en-Laye, ms. R60 732, f. 92; ibid., p. 26).

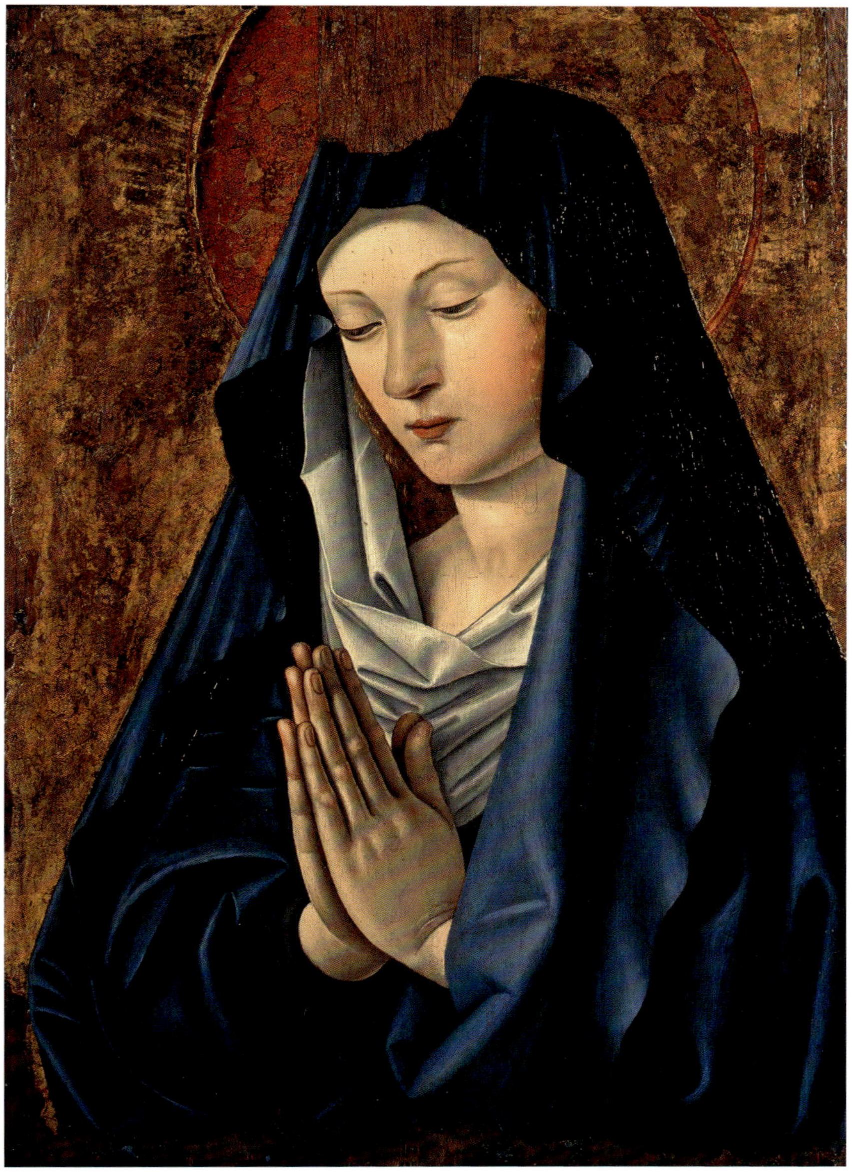

The spiritual concept of the diptych is based on the tradition, derived from the Byzantine world, of paired images of Jesus and the Mother of God, showing them as the Man of Sorrows and Our Lady of Sorrows (cat. 42; see also the double page by Jean Colombe in the *Hours of Anne of France* in the Morgan Library and Museum, New York, M. 677, ff. 37v–38; cat. 53; and Ainsworth in New York 2004, no. 331). It was around 1480 that the variant with a Tours origin appeared, showing the son blessing his mother in an arrangement akin to a Coronation of the Virgin without the crown or the scene of Christ taking leave of his mother. This idea did not originate with Bourdichon, but rather with a painter from the workshop of Jean Fouquet. In general, Bourdichon's versions transform the image of Christ using his own characteristic formula, and a veil covers the Virgin's forehead as in Bourdichon's first version of the *Hours of Charles VIII*. In the Tours diptych, the type of Christ with flowing, wavy hair takes up the iconography that was characteristic of Fouquet, and that still shows an astonishing influence of the face of Adam from Jan van Eyck's altarpiece of the *Adoration of the Mystic Lamb* in Ghent. We find the same facial type in the miniature in the style of Fouquet included in the *Hours of Louis de Laval* (BnF, ms. lat. 920, f. 44; Paris 2003b, p. 391) and in the isolated leaf by the Master of the Munich Boccaccio in the *Hours of Anne of Beaujeu* (BnF, ms. n. acq. lat. 3187; ibid., p. 330). The Tours diptych is also very close to the Nouans *Pietà*, especially the face of Saint John the Evangelist. It is the first known version of this composition of the Son blessing his Mother, perhaps even the prototype for the variants mentioned above. It cannot be attributed to Fouquet himself, but to the Master of the Munich Boccaccio, who was probably identical with one of the master's sons. • EK

[53]

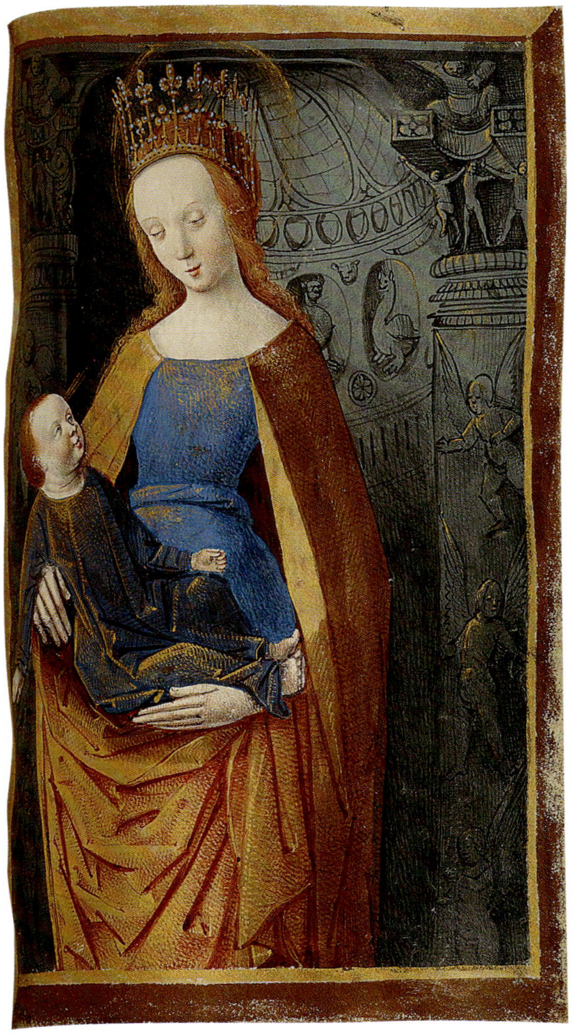

JEAN COLOMBE
(c. 1440–1493)

Hours of Anne of France

Bourges, 1473/74

Tempera and gold on parchment; 333 ff.; 14.7 x 10.9 cm (5¾ x 4¼ in.)

The Morgan Library and Museum, New York, ms. M. 677

PROVENANCE: Probably Anne of France, betrothed to Pierre de Bourbon, lord of Beaujeu, November 3, 1473, and married 1474. Firmin-Didot; sold to Baron de Beurnonville, 1882; Robert Hoe (d. 1909), New York, by 1892; his sale, American Art Association, New York, February 15–March 3, 1911, no. 2137, to Miss Benson; sold to J. P. Morgan, 1923.

BIBLIOGRAPHY: Firmin-Didot 1882, pp. 32–37. Leroquais 1927, vol. 1, no. 6, pp. 15–30. Schaefer 1977, pp. 142–43, 144. Randall 1992, pp. 169, 290–91, 320, 360, 389. Avril and Reynaud in Paris 1993, pp. 294, 336. Jacobs 1993, pp. 61–63, 70, 76. Burin 2001, pp. 18, 20, 21. Legaré 2001, p. 45. Milman 2003, pp. 166, 170–71. Alexander et al. in New York 2005–06, p. 235. Reynaud 2006, pp. 36, 58 n. 10, 71 n. 4. Avril 2007, p. 17. Georgi 2007, pp. 60, 61 n. 110.

EXHIBITIONS: New York 1892, no. 69. New York 1933–34, no. 119. New York 1980, no. 18. New York 1982, no. 70. Baltimore 1988, no. 55. New York 1997–98, no. 81. New York 2004, no. 331.

SHOWN: *Virgin and Child*, f. 98r

THIS BOOK OF HOURS, decorated with twenty-four small miniatures in the calendar and 107 full-page illuminations, is one of the first substantial liturgical commissions given to the celebrated illuminator Jean Colombe of Bourges. The recipient of this precious manuscript was the young woman who appears in folio 42v in prayer before the scene of the Annunciation. Her representation under a canopy and her rich dress show that she is a person of high rank. Historians today agree that she is the princess Anne of France, daughter of Louis XI and his queen, Charlotte of Savoy, given the prominence of the name *Anne* in the text and the presence of the arms of France on the canopy behind her portrait. That the arms of Pierre of Bourbon, lord of Beaujeu, her husband from 1474, are not included suggests that the manuscript was commissioned before that date; stylistic analysis of its illustrations tends to confirm this, as several of Colombe's miniatures still show the dryness of his earliest works, such as the 1472 *Histoire des neuf preux et des neuf preuses* (Österreichische Nationalbibliothek, Vienna, Cod. 2577–78), and the *Passages d'Outremer* (Bibliothèque nationale de France, ms. fr. 5594), which is dated around 1474–75.

Even though he was only at the beginning of his career, the Bourges illuminator already shows a great capacity for invention in this commission. He introduces an original framing formula at the beginning of the *Ave Maria* (f. 7v), consisting of a floral garland decorated with red and white roses for a fine ornamental effect. The opening that shows Christ as the Man of Sorrows with the intercessory Virgin (ff. 37v–38) and the miniature of Death emerging from the tomb (f. 245) are among the most striking. With a bit of regional bias, he introduced in folio 126v a view of the castle of Mehun-sur-Yèvre, the prestigious residence built by Duke Jean de Berry near Bourges. Colombe's tenth vision of Purgatory (f. 329) shows that he was already familiar with the manuscript of the *Divine Comedy* belonging to Charles of France (Bibliothèque nationale de France, ms. Italien 72), illuminated in Paris around 1460–65 by the Master of Coëtivy: from folio 30 of this manuscript he repeated the nude woman stretched out on the grass and attacked by two beasts, as well as the man impaled through the abdomen on a withered tree.

As always when it came to ambitious iconographic cycles, Colombe worked with several collaborators. Two of them can be clearly distinguished. Plummer (in New York 1982) recognized the first of these—who worked chiefly on the Hours of the Virgin (ff. 71v, 82v)—as the principal illuminator of the *Lyon Pontifical* (Bibliothèque municipale, Lyon, ms. 5144), as well as of a manuscript in Paris (Bibliothèque nationale de France, ms. lat. 1198). The second hand created very fine pages in the Hours of the Cross (ff. 192, 194); his style is somewhat closer to the artistic circle of Tours. • MJ

[54]

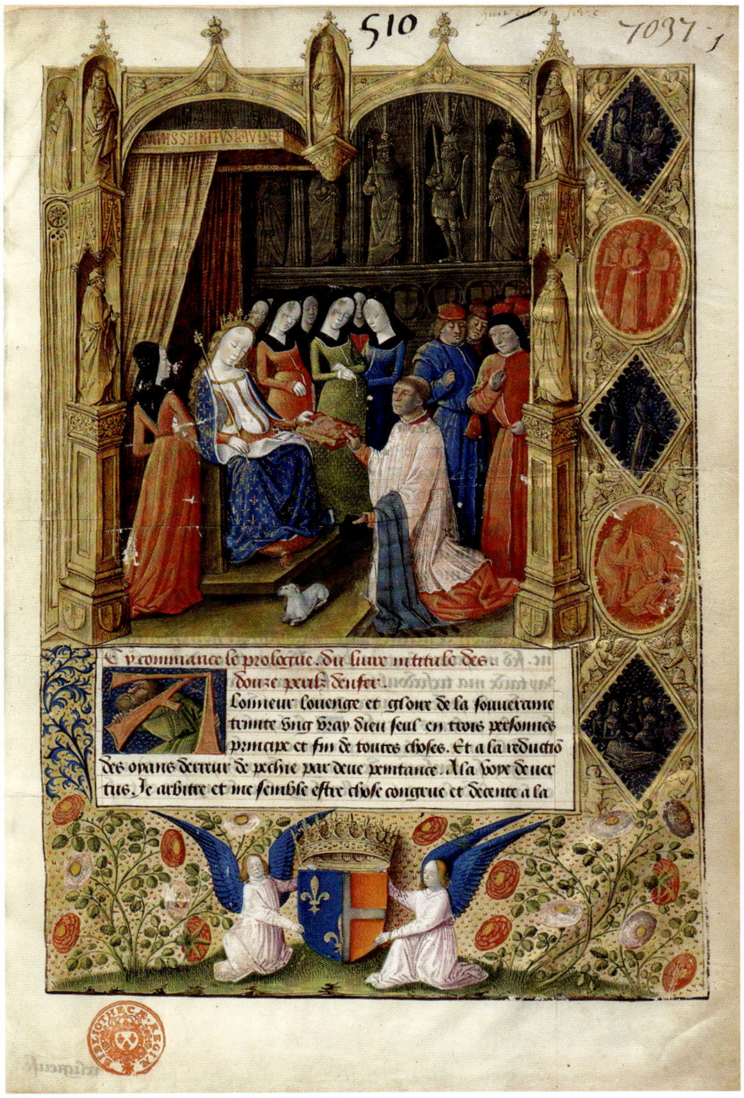

JEAN COLOMBE
(c. 1440–1493)

Des douze périls d'enfer, compiled and translated by Robert Blondel or Pierre de Caillemesnil

Bourges, c. 1480

Tempera and gold on parchment; 112 ff.; 33 x 23 cm (13 x 9 1/16 in.)

Bibliothèque nationale de France, Paris, Department of Manuscripts, ms. fr. 449

PROVENANCE: Charlotte of Savoy (d. 1483), wife of Louis XI [inventory of 1484: "Another book, entitled the book of the twelve perils of Hell, covered in red and well illustrated" (*Ung autre livre, intitulé le livre des douze perilz d'enfer, couvert de roge et bien ystorié*)]; Royal library, château of Blois [inv. 1518: no. 75; inv. 1544: no. 1403].

BIBLIOGRAPHY: Paris 1836–48, vol. 4, pp. 170–71. Valet de Viriville 1852, p. 221 n. 1, p. 224. Durrieu 1904, p. 110. Couderc 1908, pl. 132. Joly 1925, p. 19. Blum and Lauer 1930, p. 68. Porcher in Paris 1955, p. 156. Avril 1985b, pp. 257 n. 5, 260. Avril 1991, pp. 72–73. Baurmeister and Laffitte 1992, pp. 84–85. Avril in Paris 1993, p. 327. Harrouët 1999, p. 191. Delaunay 2000, pp. 59 n. 48, 151 n. 108. Legaré 2001, pp. 33, 44, 45. Cassagnes-Brouquet 2007, p. 57.

EXHIBITIONS: Bourges 1951, no. 29. Paris 1955–56, no. 330. Paris 1991, no. 28. Blois/Paris 1992–93, no. 15.

SHOWN: Frontispiece

IN A LETTER DATING from 1478 or 1479 preserved in the Bibliothèque nationale de France, Charlotte of Savoy, wife of Louis XI, requests that the governor of the Berry, Imbert de Batarnay, exempt her "poor illuminator in Bourges, named Jean Colombe" (*povre enlumineur a Bourges nommé Jehan Coulombe*) from municipal fees, because he "performs many services" (*fait beaucoup de services*) (ms. fr. 2916, f. 3). The services cited by the queen could well include the illustration of this copy of the *Douze périls*, after the text compiled around 1455 for Marie of Anjou, wife of Charles VII and hence the mother-in-law of Charlotte of Savoy. The miniatures in the manuscript correspond to Colombe's stylistic development around 1480. By now aware of his value, the illuminator inscribed his own motto *OMNIS SPIRITUS LAUDET* [*DOMINUM*] (all spirits praise [the Lord]), on the dedication scene of the manuscript's frontispiece—the same page as his protectress's coat of arms. His motto appears on the edge of the canopy above the figure of Marie of Anjou, who is shown receiving the translation that she had commissioned.

In addition to the dedication scene, Jean Colombe executed a total of twelve large images to introduce the chapters of this moral treatise outlining various dangerous spiritual conditions. Each of the thirteen miniatures is surrounded by a rich architectural frame in the form of a gilded double arch, decorated either with statues or naturalistic figures. The decoration of each of these text divisions is completed by a floral border, to which are added small scenes painted in monochrome expanding on the main subject. On folio 77, the Gothic structure that serves as a container for the illustration of the ninth peril of Hell is accompanied by a series of eight bust-length portraits of women inserted into medallions in a rather Italianate style.

The illuminated cycle that Jean Colombe worked out for Charlotte of Savoy met with a certain success; the compositions of the main scenes were repeated a short time later by the Parisian illuminator known as the Master of the Cardinal of Bourbon, in a copy of the *Douze périls* commissioned by Antoine of Chourses and Catherine de Coëtivy (Bibliothèque de l'Arsenal, Paris, ms. 5207). • MJ

THE BOURBONS AND THE BOURBONNAIS

MARTHA WOLFF

Artistic activity in the Bourbonnais was closely tied to the Bourbon ducal family and reached its apogee in the last decades of the fifteenth century with the patronage of Pierre II (died 1503) and his formidable wife, Anne of France (died 1522), eldest child of Louis XI. The Bourbon dukes traced their descent from Louis IX, canonized as Saint Louis, through his youngest son Robert, Count of Clermont-en-Beauvaisis, who married Beatrice of Burgundy, heiress to the barony of Bourbon. Their son Louis I was raised to the rank of duke and made a peer of France. As princes of the blood, the dukes of Bourbon were closely linked through marriage with successive kings of France and with the ducal houses of Burgundy, Savoy, and Berry. By the end of the fifteenth century they had incorporated Auvergne, Forez, Doubs, and other territories into a state within a state that was defined primarily by connection to the ducal family. Three sons of Charles I of Bourbon and Agnes of Burgundy succeeded to the duchy: Jean II (died 1488); Charles II (died 1488), archbishop of Lyon and cardinal; and Pierre II de Beaujeu (died 1503). Even before he inherited the duchy, Pierre and his wife, Anne of France, exercised political power, essentially administering the kingdom as governors of her young brother Charles VIII following his accession to the throne at age thirteen in 1483. When Pierre succeeded as duke in 1488, he and Anne turned their attention to their Bourbon domain and to expressions of dynastic prestige. During Charles VIII's 1494/95 Italian campaign, Pierre was regent and the Bourbon court at Moulins served as a royal administrative center (it would remain an important station on the route from the Loire Valley to Lyon and Italy). After her husband's death, Anne of France continued to guide the administration and artistic patronage of the duchy, even as her only child, Suzanne, was married to the next male heir from the cadet branch of Bourbon-Montpensier, Charles III of Bourbon, the ill-fated Constable of France. Maintaining a more modest court at Aigueperse, the Bourbon-Montpensier had important Italian connections through Charles III's parents, Gilbert, Count of Montpensier (died 1496) and Chiara Gonzaga of Mantua.

As befitted their importance in the kingdom, the Bourbon dukes brought artists from outside the region to work on projects in Moulins and at their other castles and religious foundations. These included the ducal necropolis in the Cluniac priory of Souvigny; the castle and Sainte-Chapelle at Bourbon-l'Archambault, which housed a relic of the True Cross given to Robert de Clermont by Saint Louis; the elegant Flamboyant revision, beginning in the 1470s, of the collegiate church, now cathedral, of Moulins; and the ducal castle at Moulins. The latter was extensively modernized by Pierre and Anne—its chapel dedicated to Saint Louis, with a cupola and central plan, and the surviving symmetrical pavilion and gallery were strikingly innovative expressions of dynastic self-consciousness and a new Renaissance taste (Bruand 2001; Guillaume 2001).

Other princes also sought out the artists working for the ducal family, resulting in a complex network of artistic influences. Thus, the sculptor Jacques Morel, having worked in Lyon and Avignon, was contracted in 1448 to make the tomb of Charles I of Bourbon and Agnes of Burgundy at Souvigny, with the tomb of Philippe the Bold of Burgundy at Champmol stipulated as the model. In 1462, Agnes in turn recommended Morel's nephew Antoine le Moiturier to her brother Philippe the Good for the task of completing their father's tomb at Champmol. Having earlier worked in Berry and collaborated with Jean Fouquet of Tours on commissions for Louis XI, Michel Colombe was established in Moulins in 1484 when he made elements for the entry of Jean II's new wife, Catherine d'Armagnac. Only a few attributions have been ventured for this period of Colombe's activity, among them a small kneeling figure of Jean II in the Walters Art Museum, Baltimore, and a bust of Cardinal Charles of Bourbon in the guise of a Cluniac saint in Moulins. Colombe's legacy is felt in the monumental figures ascribed to his associate Jean Guilhomet, called Jean de Chartres, who worked for Anne of France in the years after 1500, notably on the fragmentary statues presumably from the collegiate church in Moulins (cat. 67) and on the figures of the name saints of Pierre, Anne, and their daughter Suzanne from the castle of Chantelle, now in the Musée du Louvre (cat. 66). The facial types and the calm generalization of the Moulins figures in particular show some affinities to Colombe's masterpiece, the tomb of Francis II of Brittany and Marguerite of Foix at Nantes (fig. 12), and also to what are the most renowned products of Pierre and Anne's patronage in Moulins, the paintings of Jean Hey (see Lorentz 2008). Scholars must proceed with caution in linking the designs of sculptors and painters; early efforts led to much confusion, particularly the erroneous identification of the Master of Moulins with the documented designer of the Nantes tomb, the Lyonnais painter Jean Perréal.

The generally accepted identification of the Master of Moulins as Jean Hey now has additional support from Lyon documents referring to Hey as painter to Cardinal Charles of Bourbon, as a member of his household, and as the recipient of an administrative sinecure in Lyon in the 1480s (Girault and Hamon 2003). The exquisitely refined portrait of *Charles of Bourbon* in Munich (cat. 56) must reflect this relationship. Hey probably first came to France from the Netherlands to work for Cardinal Jean Rolin of Autun (cat. 55), but only when he began to work for Pierre II and Anne of France in Moulins after 1488 did his paintings take on the bolder, more sculptural, and also more public quality most fully expressed in the Moulins *Virgin in Glory* (fig. 39). Through Hey, the ducal couple used the painting medium in support of their dynastic pretensions in a manner rarely seen among the princes of the fleur-de-lis, with the exception of René of Anjou's commission of the triptych *Moses and the Burning Bush* from Nicolas Froment (fig. 28). Skilled at lifelike portraits that also conformed to a courtly ideal, Hey was probably dispatched to the Loire Valley to paint the dauphin Charles-Orland, just as Anne of France sent her goldsmith Arnoul de Viviers to Anne of Brittany. Hey evidently adjusted the finish of his paintings to the circumstances of each commission, the portrait of his master Charles of Bourbon being substantially more refined than the signed Brussels *Ecce Homo* made for the royal secretary Jean Cueillette (cats. 56, 64). Although he must have had the help of assistants, there is little evidence of followers continuing to work in Hey's style. Indeed, unlike the extensive and distinguished production of sculpture made outside the ducal court (the *Virgin and Child* from Longvé in the Louvre, and a *Pietà* still in Varennes-sur-Têche), there are only meager traces of local paintings on panel and these show minimal absorption of larger trends. Thus the outstanding Italian paintings belonging to the Bourbon-Montpensier, Mantegna's *Saint Sebastian* in the Louvre (which was presumably part of Chiara Gonzaga's dowry from Mantua), and Benedetto Ghirlandaio's *Nativity* still in Aigueperse, had a negligible impact on local painting. For the so-called Dreuille Master, author of devotional paintings somewhat reminiscent of Netherlandish models, a loose connection with the design of the east windows of the Moulins collegiate church has been suggested (Elsig 2004). This fine ensemble of windows, largely commissioned by families serving the dukes, suggests an otherwise lost complexity of artistic relationships (cat. 68, fig. 43) during the brief period of flowering in the Bourbonnais before the dukedom was brought down because of the potential of Charles III of Bourbon and Constable of France, to rival the monarchy.

[55]

JEAN HEY, KNOWN AS
THE MASTER OF MOULINS
(active Lyon and Moulins, c. 1480–c. 1505)

Nativity with Cardinal Jean Rolin

c. 1480

Oil on panel; 56.6 x 74.4 cm (22¼ x 29⁵⁄₁₆ in.)

Musée Rolin, Autun, H.U. 87

PROVENANCE: Cathedral of Saint Lazare, Autun, by 1705; transferred to the diocesan palace, Autun, by the mid-nineteenth century; Musée Rolin, 1907.

BIBLIOGRAPHY: Bulliot 1840, p. 1. Courtepée 1847, p. 505. Toulouse-Lautrec 1877, p. 199. Boell 1904, pp. 440–41. Charmasse 1906, p. 176. Winkler 1932, pp. 241–48. Sterling [Jacques] 1941, pp. 20, 44–45, no. 20. Feydy 1957, pp. 166–74. Huillet d'Istria 1961, pp. 16–29. Châtelet 1962, pp. 523–24. Bruyn 1963, p. 370. Sterling 1963b, pp. 9–11, 66. Lorentz 1999a, p. 157. Maurice-Chabard 1999, p. 121. Châtelet 2001, pp. 48–57, 170–71. Campbell 2002, p. 358. Joubert 2006, pp. 115–20. Wolff 2008b, pp. 137–38, 141–42.

EXHIBITIONS: Autun 1876, no. 211. Paris 1904, no. 103. London 1932, no. 67. Paris 1937, no. 22. Dijon 1952, no. 97. La Haye 1966, no. 3. Paris 1966, no. 3.

THE PATRON, Jean Rolin, is identifiable through his arms, cardinal's hat, and motto, *deum time* (fear God), entwined in the ornament in the upper corners. Rolin (1408–1483) was the chief benefactor of the cathedral of Autun during his long tenure as bishop; his likeness and motto were also represented there, on wall paintings and sculptures. This painting was probably once displayed near the cardinal's tomb in the cathedral, near his epitaph plaque. By 1705, it was kept in the sacristy. The inclusion of his lapdog here suggests his worldly and willful spirit; Rolin also required that this pet be included in earlier commissions for Beaune.

The *Nativity* is the earliest known work by the Master of Moulins, now widely identified as Jean Hey and regarded as an associate of the outstanding Ghent painter Hugo van der Goes. The cardinal, as the son of Nicolas Rolin, the powerful chancellor of Burgundy, maintained close ties to the Netherlands and may indeed have brought Hey to France, where he would become painter to members of the Bourbon family. Rolin here appears advanced in age, suggesting a date of about 1480 for the painting, which is supported by its evident debt to Van der Goes's work of the mid-1470s. The distant landscape ending in a relatively flat ribbon of blue hills resembles that in the wing completed by Van der Goes for the triptych of Hippolyte Berthoz of Poligny after the death of the original artist, Dieric Bouts, in 1475. The Virgin's angular features recall the facial type he used in the *Portinari Altarpiece*, while her elegant pallor may follow Jean Fouquet's ideal of beauty.

Hey's *Nativity* is a cleverly calibrated adaption of the half-length format used by Van der Goes to intensify the impact of religious narratives. The cropping of the Virgin, Joseph, and the angels focuses the viewer's attention on their expressive hands and faces and on the vulnerable form of the Christ Child. This group is shifted to the left to make space for Rolin, the only full-length figure, but the painter reasserted the symmetry of the composition by putting the Virgin in the central position and making her more prominent through her slightly larger scale and rich ultramarine garments. • MW

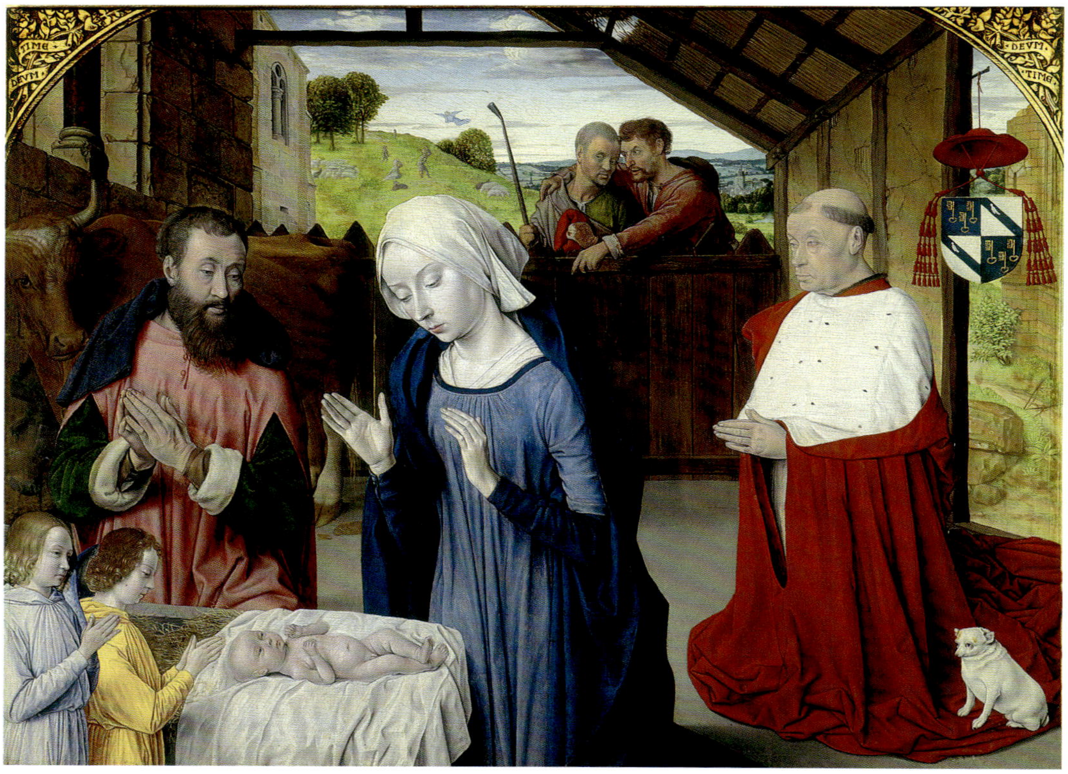

[56]

JEAN HEY, KNOWN AS
THE MASTER OF MOULINS
(active Lyon and Moulins, c. 1480–c. 1505)

Portrait of Cardinal Charles of Bourbon

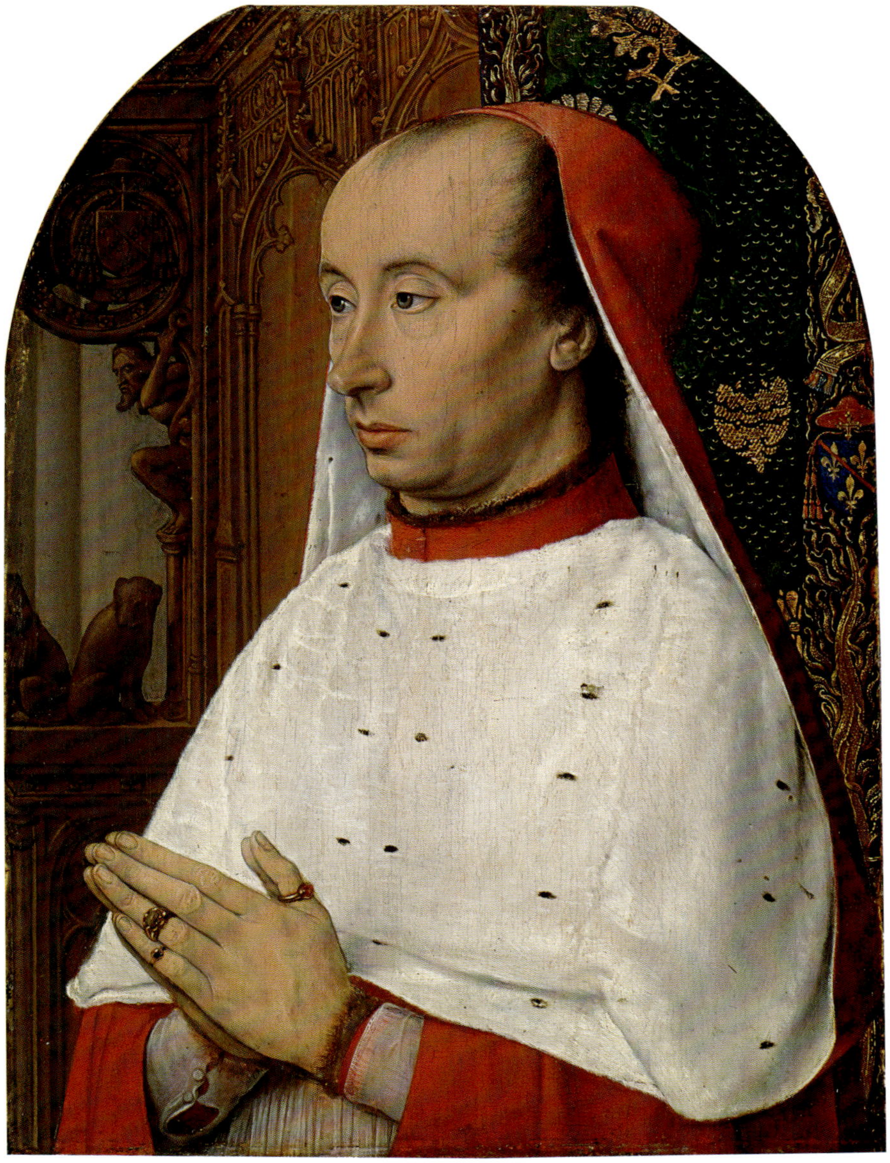

Lyon, c. 1482

Oil on panel; 34 x 25 cm (13 3/8 x 9 13/16 in.) (painted surface)

Alte Pinakothek, Munich, WAF 648

PROVENANCE: Acquired by Sulpiz Boisserée from the dealer Arbeiter in Mainz as by Van Eyck or Memling, 1815; sold with Boisserée collection to King Ludwig I of Bavaria, 1827; in Nuremberg as part of the Königliche Bildersaal in the St. Morizkapelle from 1829, later in the Germanisches Nationalmuseum; transferred to the Alte Pinakothek, 1910.

BIBLIOGRAPHY: Boisserée 1808–54, vol. 1, pp. 245, 255. Hulin de Loo 1902, pp. 52–53. Bode 1903, p. 99. Friedländer 1925, p. 188. Winkler 1932, p. 248. Sterling 1938, p. 21, no. 21. Wescher 1938, p. 8. Ring 1949, p. 239, no. 302, pl. 170. Moisy 1956, pp. 20, 247. Feydy 1957, pp. 165–71. Huillet d'Istria 1961, pp. 16–31. Châtelet 1962, pp. 517, 521. Châtelet 1970, n.pag. Hohenzollern and Soehner 1970, pp. 30–33, fig. 1. Naumann 1990, pp. 99, 110, 118, fig. 9. Châtelet 2001, pp. 59–62, 172, fig. 27. Hamon 2001, p. 124. Châtelet 2003, p. 354. Girault and Hamon 2003, p. 117, fig. 1. Lorentz 2009b, p. 24, fig. 4. Siefert 2009, p. 64.

EXHIBITIONS: Bern 1949–50, no. 15.

THIS ELEGANT portrait, whose back is painted to imitate marble, must have been paired with a devotional image to form a diptych. The Bourbon arms and cardinal's hat displayed on the hanging and on the canopy of the seat identify the subject as Charles of Bourbon, archbishop of Lyon, who was made cardinal in 1476 and died in 1488. Active in the service of Louis XI, Charles of Bourbon was an important patron of the arts who owned exceptional tapestries (cat. 17) and manuscripts and founded a splendid funerary chapel in Lyon Cathedral.

The portrait, long regarded as a relatively early work by the Master of Moulins, takes on particular importance with the recent publication of Lyon documents that name Jean Hey as painter to the cardinal as early as 1482 (or 1472 depending on the interpretation of ambiguities in the documents; Châtelet 2001 and 2003; Girault and Hamon 2003; Lorentz 2009b). Since the cardinal would almost certainly turn to his own painter to provide a devotional diptych, the portrait further supports the identification of the Master of Moulins as Hey, whose name is inscribed on the Brussels *Ecce Homo* (cat. 64) and whose art was praised by the poet Jean Lemaire de Belges.

Hey clearly flattered his sitter through the rich ecclesiastical setting and the extraordinary refinement of the features, dominated by the sinuous line of nose, brows, and forehead. Comparison with the underdrawn preparation shows that the features evolved towards a more idealized, almost feminized representation through subtle exaggeration of the contour of eyes and brow. The cardinal appears younger in the finished state of the painting than in the direct and lively underdrawing. Although some commentators date the portrait as early as 1476, when Charles of Bourbon was made cardinal (Huillet d'Istria 1961; Châtelet 1962 and 2001), it most likely postdates the Autun *Nativity* (cat. 55), the work closest to Hey's Netherlandish roots. The devotional panel associated with the portrait is lost; there are no other paintings securely datable to Jean Hey's years of service to Charles of Bourbon, although the Brussels *Virgin and Child with Angels* has a comparable preciousness and refinement of surface. • MW

[57]

JEAN HEY, KNOWN AS
THE MASTER OF MOULINS
(active Lyon and Moulins, c. 1480–c. 1505)

Margaret of Austria

1490/91

Oil on panel; 32.7 x 23 cm (12 7/8 x 9 1/16 in.)

The Metropolitan Museum of Art, New York, Robert Lehman Collection, 1975.1.130

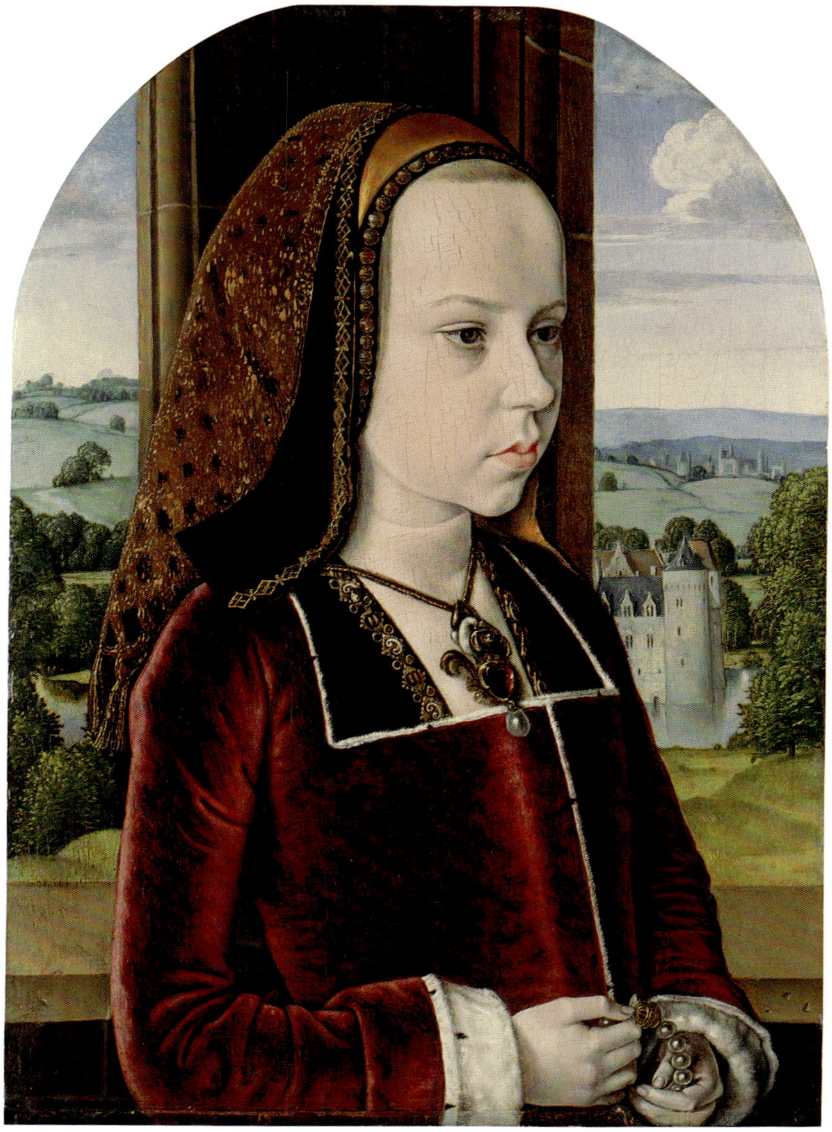

PROVENANCE: Don Sebastián Gabriel de Borbón y Braganza (d. 1874), Madrid and Pau, as *Joanna the Mad* by Holbein; his son Pierre de Bourbon et Bourbon, duke of Dúrcal, Paris, offered for sale, American Art Association, New York, April 10–11, 1889, no. 24, unsold; sold, Hôtel Drouot, Paris, February 3, 1890, no. 23, to Manuel Yturbe, Paris; bequeathed to his granddaughter Princess Yturbe, the Duchess of Parcent, Paris, after 1901; sold to Kleinberger, New York, 1926; Philip Lehman, New York, 1926.

BIBLIOGRAPHY: Maulde La Clavière 1896, p. 370. Benoit 1901, pp. 328–32. Bouchot 1904, pp. 289–94. Durrieu 1911, pp. 744–45. Mayer 1926, pp. 125–26. Lehman 1928, no. 93. Hulin de Loo 1932, p. 63. Winkler 1932, pp. 246–47. Dupont 1937, p. 60. Sterling 1938, pp. 118–19, fig. 145. Sterling [Jacques] 1941, p. 21, no. 24, pl. 65. Ring 1949, p. 239, no. 303, pl. 169. Huillet d'Istria 1961, pp. 80–81, pl. 6. Dupont 1963, pp. 84–85. Sterling 1963b, pp. 65, 67. Reynaud 1968, p. 34. Sterling 1968, p. 30. Labande-Mailfert 1975, pp. 92, 106. Lorentz and Regond 1990, pp. 36–38. Sterling and Ainsworth 1996, pp. 11–18. Châtelet 2001, pp. 93–95, 175–76, pl. 54. Eichberger 2002, pp. 29–42, fig. 6. Lorentz 2005, pp. 120–23.

EXHIBITIONS: Pau 1876, no. 629. Paris 1904, no. 107. Paris 1957, no. 35. Bruges 2002, no. 73.

ONLY PRINCELY CHILDREN, with their special dynastic importance, were subjects for independent portraits about 1500. Although sometimes identified as Suzanne of Bourbon, the only child of Jean Hey's patrons Pierre II of Bourbon and Anne of France, the somber subject of this refined portrait must be the Habsburg princess Margaret of Austria. She was born in 1480 and was raised at the French court as the betrothed queen of Charles VIII from the age of three. The alternating enamel *C*'s and *M*'s that edge her underdress and her large fleur-de-lis pendant support this identification. The scallop shells on her cap probably relate to the French royal Order of Saint Michael. These ornaments also appear in the 1493 inventory of Margaret's possessions when she returned to the Netherlands. Despite her dowry, including Artois and the Franche-Comté, Charles repudiated her in late 1491 to marry Anne of Brittany, thereby binding that recently subdued duchy to the kingdom.

The inclusion of the couple's initials suggests that the portrait was made before Margaret was supplanted by Anne. Margaret had accompanied Charles on a visit to Moulins over Christmas of 1490 and early in the next year (Reynaud 1968; Labande-Mailfert 1975). Hey probably made a likeness of Charles's betrothed queen in a drawing, a drawing from life being the usual preparation for a portrait. The 1494 painting of the dauphin Charles-Orland in the Musée du Louvre shows that the artist's talent as a painter of children was appreciated. While the Louvre portrait has a simple contour underdrawing and must have been made on the basis of a cartoon, the present work is prepared with a direct and incisive underdrawing (Sterling and Ainsworth 1996, fig. 3.1). The princess is presented as a miniature adult, the painting's poignancy resulting from the contrast between the sitter's composure and her slender limbs and small hands. Because other likenesses of Margaret in her childhood and later years survive for comparison, we can see how Hey idealized his sitters. Her heavy lower lip, bowed upper lip, and prominent nose are discernable, but not emphasized. Instead they are subsumed in an elegant linear pattern.

It has been suggested that the picture was paired with a devotional image as part of a diptych (Benoit 1901 and Sterling and Ainsworth 1996); while this is possible, it would have been highly unusual for a portrait of a female subject of such tender years. • MW

[58]

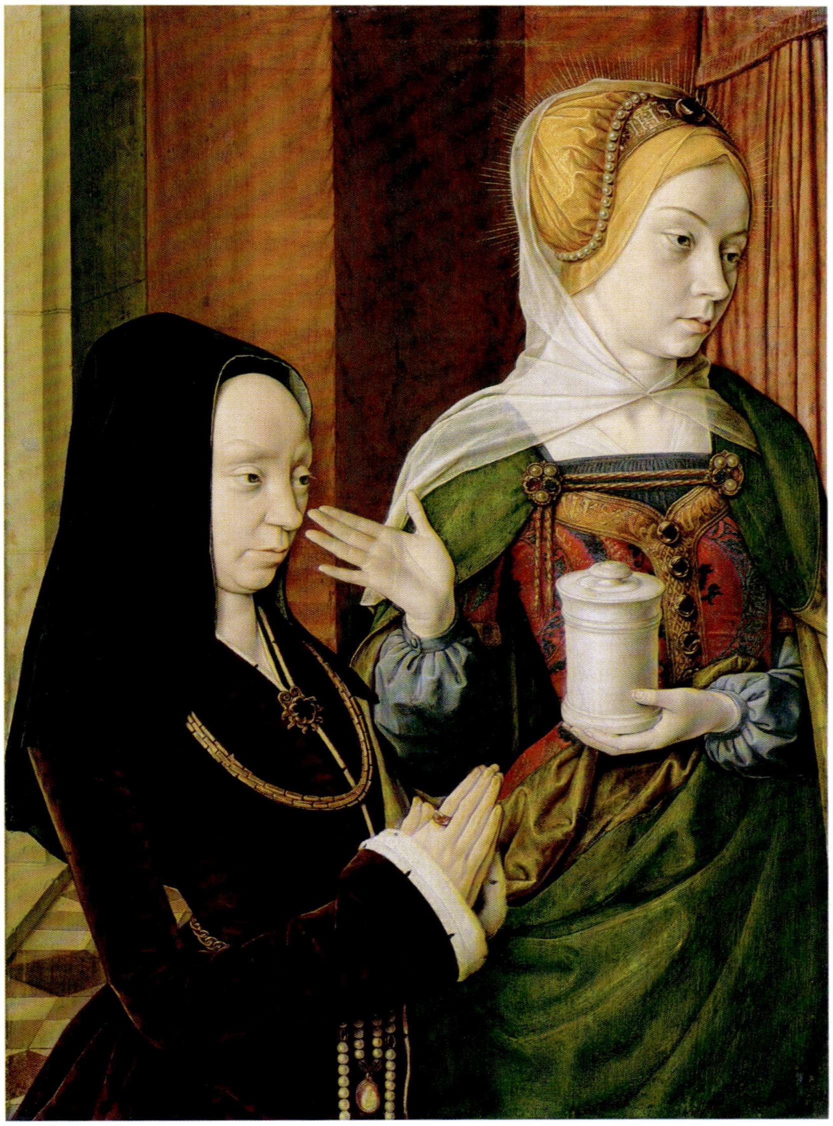

JEAN HEY, KNOWN AS
THE MASTER OF MOULINS
(active Lyon and Moulins, c. 1480–c. 1505)

Madeleine of Burgundy Presented by Saint Mary Magdalene

c. 1490

Oil on panel; 56 x 40 cm (22 1/16 x 15 3/4 in.)

Musée du Louvre, Paris, RF 1521

PROVENANCE: Baron de Laage [according to the catalogue of the Bohn sale, 1885]. Martinengo, Wurzburg; sold, Hôtel Drouot, Paris, May 22, 1861, no lot number, as Van Eyck; Henry G. Bohn, Twickenham (d. 1884), his sale, Christie's, London, March 19, 1885, no. 488, as Hubert and J. van Eyck. Joseph Rushton, Lincoln; his estate sale, Christie's, London, May 21 and 23, 1898, no. 71, as H. van Eyck. C. and G. Somzée, Brussels, by 1902 [lent to Bruges 1902]; sold to Agnew's, London, 1902; sold to the Musée du Louvre, 1904.

BIBLIOGRAPHY: Friedländer 1900, p. 258. Lefenestre 1900, pp. 395–96. Hulin de Loo 1902, p. LVI. Bouchot 1904, pp. 289–94. Huyghe 1935, p. 62, figs. 1–6. Réau 1939, pp. 30–31, 75, 77. Dupont 1939–40, pp. 92–93. Sterling [Jacques] 1941, p. 22, no. 26. Ring 1949, p. 258, no. 299, fig. 164. Huillet d'Istria 1961, pp. 16–31. Dupont 1963, pp. 81–82, figs. 11–12. Hours 1963, pp. 66–69, 72–73. Sterling 1963, p. 67. Sterling and Adhémar 1965, p. 12, no. 29, pls. 81–83. Sterling 1973, pp. 85–86, fig. 16. Reynaud 1978, p. 51, fig. 18. Hackenbroch 1989, pp. 129–30, 132, figs. 4–5. Lorentz and Regond 1990, p. 46, no. 8. Reynolds 1996, p. 732. Châtelet 2001, pp. 80–82, 175, fig. 44. Campbell 2006, p. 38. Lorentz 2008, pp. 133, 135 n. 24, fig. 14. Wolff 2008b, pp. 138–39, 150–51, fig. 5.

EXHIBITIONS: London 1899–1900, no. 27. Bruges 1902, no. 181. Paris 1904, no. 108.

BOTH SAINT MARY MAGDALENE and the plain-featured supplicant are among Jean Hey's most exquisitely observed figures. The saint's dress, with its large jewels and embroidered inscriptions, is at once ostentatious and modest. The donor's wine-colored velvet gown lined with ermine, her gold jewelry, and pearl rosary beads with a pendant cameo of the Virgin and Child all convey high status. The patron has been plausibly identified as Madeleine of Burgundy, one of the numerous illegitimate offspring of Philip the Good of Burgundy; she married Bompart de Laage (or de L'Aage), probably in 1486, and had died by 1495. With lands in the south of France, her husband was a counselor and chamberlain of Jean II of Bourbon, who in negotiations over her dowry referred to her as "sa chiere et amé cousine" (quoted in Kerrebrouck 1990, p. 617). Madeleine of Burgundy was indeed a cousin of dukes Jean II and Pierre II of Bourbon, since their mother, Agnes of Burgundy, was Philip the Good's sister. The identification is based on the combination of the brooch in the form of the Burgundian steel or *briquet* that closes her gown, the painting's provenance from the Laage family, and the protection of Mary Magdalene (Dupont 1939–40 and 1963).

Retaining its original unpainted edges at right, top, and bottom, the painting tightly frames the two women against the background of a chamber richly hung with crimson silk; they approach a sacred space that was represented on the lost adjoining panel, which was probably once the focal point of a diptych rather than a triptych. The apparent anomaly of a female supplicant placed on the more honored right hand of the holy figure (Campbell 2006; Van de Velden 2006), may be explained by the sitter's social pretension, demonstrated by her wearing of the Burgundian emblem and by the richness of her ermine robe, rivaling that of Anne of France on the panel in the Musée du Louvre (fig. 18). The lost devotional image probably represented a Virgin and Child or a Passion figure, undoubtedly shown in a draped, baldachin-like space similar to that of the Brussels *Ecce Homo* (cat. 64), revealed by parted curtains. • MW

JEAN HEY, KNOWN AS
THE MASTER OF MOULINS
(active Lyon and Moulins, c. 1480–c. 1505)

TWO SEGMENTS FROM AN ALTARPIECE

[59]

Charlemagne and the Meeting of Saints Joachim and Anne at the Golden Gate

Moulins, 1490/95

Oil on panel; 73.4 x 60.2 cm (28⅞ x 23¹¹⁄₁₆ in.) (with added strip at top); 71.5 x 59 cm (28⅛ x 23¼ in.) (painted surface; width at bottom)

The National Gallery, London, NG 4092

PROVENANCE: French private collection, until 1903; sold through Kleinberger and Cassirer to Hans Tietje, Amsterdam. Agnew's, London; sold to the National Gallery, 1925.

BIBLIOGRAPHY: See below.

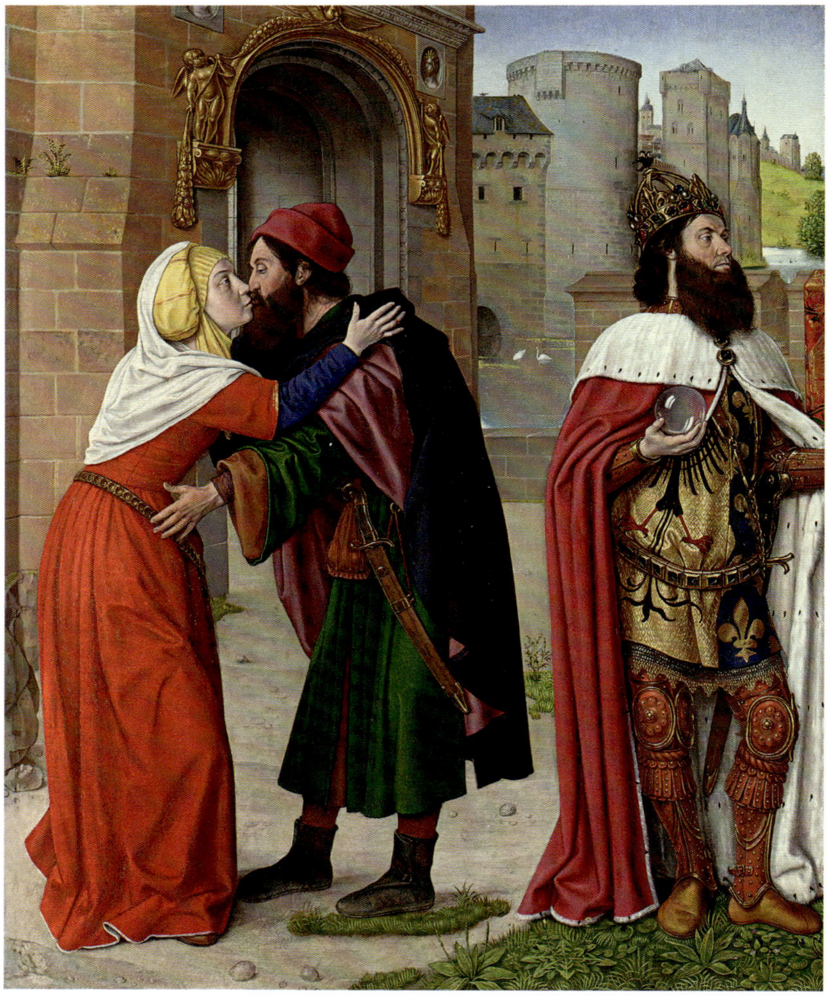

[60]

The Annunciation

Moulins, 1490/95

Oil on panel; 72 x 50.2 cm (28⅜ x 19¾ in.); 71.7 x 49.2 cm (28¼ x 19⅜ in.) (painted surface)

The Art Institute of Chicago, Mr. and Mrs. Martin A. Ryerson Collection, 1933.1062

PROVENANCE: Private collection, Paris, by 1906. Dowdeswell and Dowdeswell, London, 1906–14; sold to Martin A. Ryerson (d. 1932), Chicago, 1914; bequeathed to the Art Institute, 1933.

BIBLIOGRAPHY: Fry 1906, p. 331. Conway 1921, p. 187. Friedländer 1925, pp. 187–88, pls. A, B. Winkler 1933, p. 434. Sterling [Jacques] 1941, pp. 22–23, nos. 29, 30, pl. 72. Dupont 1945–47, p. 226. Davies 1946, pp. 67–68. Ring 1949, p. 238, nos. 297, 298, pls. 165, 166. Davies 1957, pp. 153–55. Huillet d'Istria 1961, pp. 16–18, 31–35, 89, 100, 107, figs. 39, 40, 41, pl. 4. Châtelet 1962, pp. 517–21, figs. 4, 5. Dupont 1963, pp. 78–81, 86, fig. 9. Reynaud 1963, p. 166. Sterling 1963b, pp. 2, 5, 7, 11, 13–15, 66–67, figs. 15, 17, 31. Huillet d'Istria 1964, pp. 43–44. Sterling 1968, pp. 30–31. Gould 1973, p. 440, no. 4092. Lorentz and Regond 1990, pp. 39–40, 49 (ill.), no. 6. Dunkerton, Foister, Gordon and Penny 1991, pp. 105, 358, fig. 139, no. 58, pl. 58. Baker and Henry 1995, p. 434. Reynolds 1996, p. 733. Châtelet 2001, pp. 72–77, 173–75, figs. 39, 105. Elsig 2004, p. 48, pl. 43. Wolff 2005, p. 63, fig. 13. Wolff 2008a, pp. 15–23. Wolff 2008b, pp. 142–51, figs. 10, 11, 13.

EXHIBITIONS: London 1909–10, no. 76. New York 1927, no. 35. Detroit 1928, no. 9. London 1932, no. 63. Chicago 1933, no. 28. Chicago 1934, no. 17.

THE TWO PAINTINGS SHOWN here—*Charlemagne and the Meeting of Saints Joachim and Anne at the Golden Gate* and *The Annunciation*—formed the left and right sides of an altarpiece, as first proposed by Friedländer (1925), who also hypothesized that the figure of Charlemagne flanked a lost central image and was paired with another French royal saint, probably Saint Louis. Recent technical examination confirms these suppositions. The same boards of French oak, aligned horizontally, run through both paintings. The Chicago panel is slightly narrower than its counterpart in London; part of a robed figure was originally painted in the threshold of the Virgin's chamber and has been scraped away and overpainted. The remainder of this figure must have been trimmed off and discarded in an effort to give the fragment the appearance of an independent painting. Analysis of samples taken at its left edge showed traces of ultramarine, suggesting that the discarded figure was indeed Saint Louis, in his characteristic azure robe (Wolff 2008a).

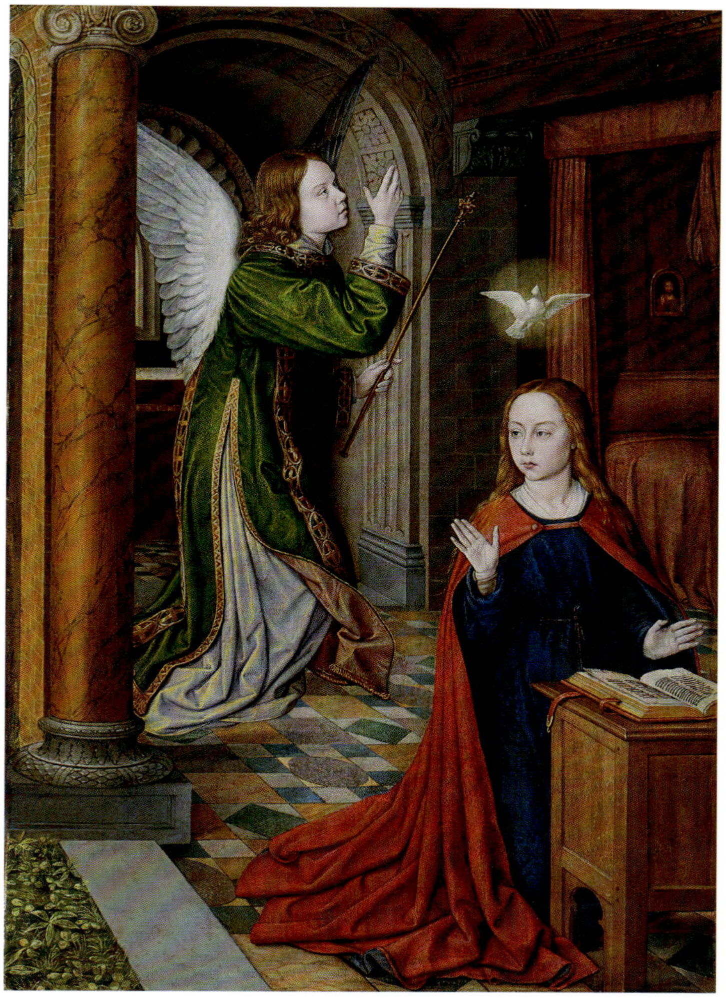

altarpiece with a raised center and a frame overlapping the pictorial space, known from other outstanding French examples: the retable of the Parlement de Paris attributed to André d'Ypres (fig. 22) and the Loches triptych attributed to Jean Poyer. In these works the framing arcade seems to be a vestige of an architectural structure through which a continuous pictorial space is visible.

The contrast between the two surviving segments is exaggerated by their differing conservation histories and the distinction between daylight and shadowed interior. In the London fragment, Hey was attentive to classicizing ornament, including the medallions flanking the gate, and to the combination of imperial and French motifs in Charlemagne's clothing. In the Chicago fragment, Gabriel's garments and the pale faces are painted with exquisite luminous and coloristic effect. The altarpiece's overall subject was presumably the Immaculate Conception and the special role of Saint Anne, here in the context of French royal lineage. Close in date to the 1492/93 panels of Pierre II of Bourbon and Anne of France with their infant daughter Suzanne (Musée du Louvre; fig. 18), the dismembered altarpiece must have been one of the painter's most ambitious works before the Moulins *Virgin in Glory*. It was almost certainly made for members of the ruling family, possibly Anne of France and Pierre of Bourbon, though her brother Charles VIII and his wife Anne of Brittany should not be excluded. For both couples, the possible help of Saint Anne and the Virgin in conceiving and bearing an heir was of vital concern. • MW

The altarpiece's center probably extended above the saints and narratives at the side to accommodate a hieratic image like the Assumption of the Virgin (suggested by Châtelet 2001) or an enthroned Saint Anne with the Virgin and Child. The bright cloth of honor hanging over the crenellated wall behind Charlemagne is a remnant of this central motif. That the altarpiece had an inverted T shape can also be inferred from the right edge of the London panel; the cut that separated the London panel from the center follows the line of a margin of unpainted wood above the arm of Charlemagne. This unpainted edge must originally have been covered by a portion of the engaged frame that would have been a continuation of the moulding extending down from the raised central section. It would have been echoed by a corresponding framing element to the left of the Annuciation. These pendant framing elements must have served to emphasize the raised central section. The work thus belonged to a type of wingless horizontal

JEAN HEY, KNOWN AS
THE MASTER OF MOULINS
(active Lyon and Moulins, c. 1480–c. 1505)

FRAGMENTS FROM *CHRIST CARRYING THE CROSS*

[61]

Saint John the Evangelist

1500/05

Oil on panel; 27.3 x 20 cm (10¾ x 7⅞ in.); image: 26 x 18.8 cm (10¼ x 7 7/16 in.)

The Art Institute of Chicago, Mr. and Mrs. Martin A. Ryerson Collection, 1937.1000

PROVENANCE: M. Guggenheim, Venice, by 1892; sold to Martin A. Ryerson (d. 1932), Chicago; by descent to his widow, bequeathed to the Art Institute, 1937.

BIBLIOGRAPHY: Berenson 1932, p. 141. Hornig 1976, p. 124, no. C4. Wolff 2005, pp. 58–66, figs. 4–6, 11. Wolff 2008a, pp. 23–30.

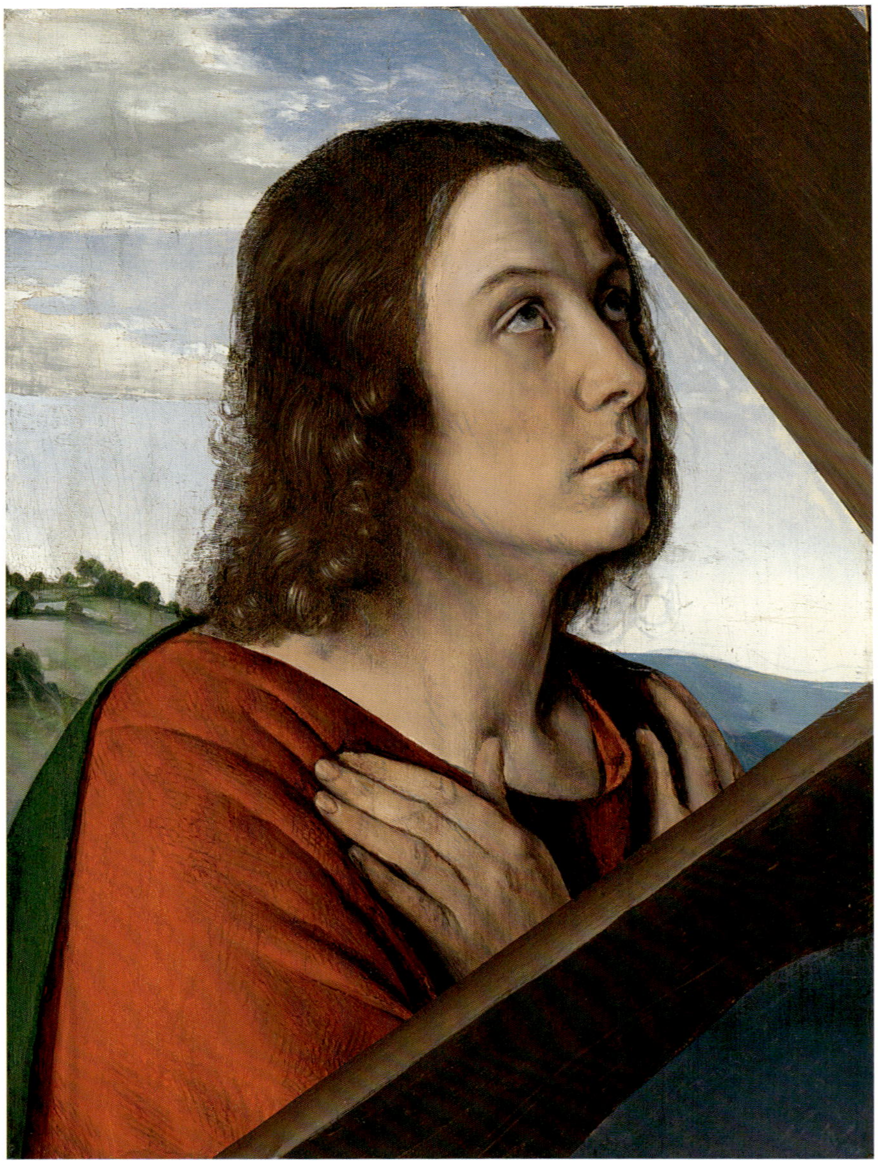

MANY OF JEAN HEY'S surviving works were part of larger, dismembered ensembles, but these heads of Saint John the Evangelist and the mourning Virgin are an especially striking case. Reunited in 2004, they must have been cut apart by the end of the nineteenth century, when the *Saint John* was acquired by Chicago collector Martin A. Ryerson as a work of Francesco Francia. The fragments have the same unusual beveled edges; in both the beam of the cross was scraped away and the loss repainted to make the figure look like an independent subject. For the *Saint John*, this repaint was removed and the upper beam of the cross was reconstructed during a restoration in the 1960s. When the *Virgin* was restored in 2005, the repaint in the lower left corner was retained.

The fragments evidently belonged to a half-length *Christ Carrying the Cross*. In the underdrawing of the *Saint John*, the tendrils of Christ's hair are still visible at the lower right (Wolff 2005). Part of Christ's head most probably overlapped the lower-left corner of the *Virgin* where the design has been scraped away. Apart from this mutilation, the latter fragment is better preserved. It remains uncradled and retains its original edge on the right, as well as its

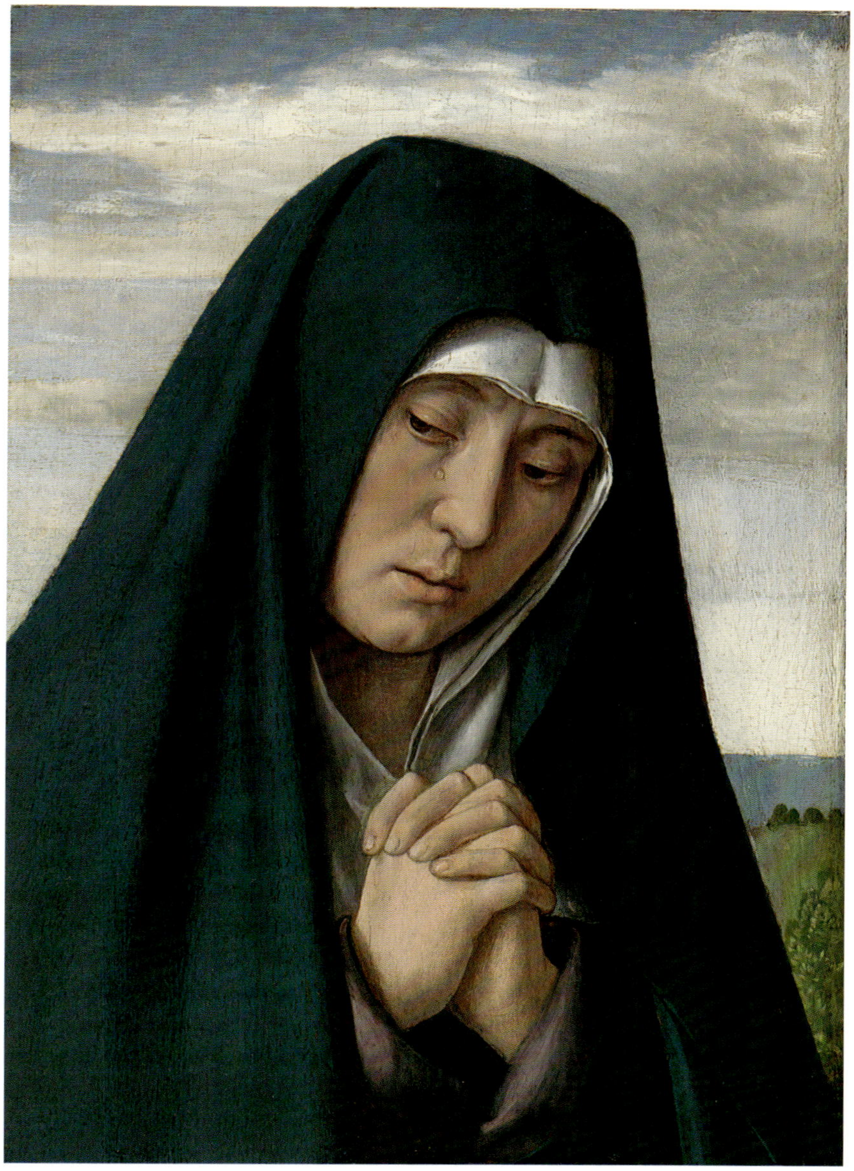

[62]

Mourning Virgin

1500/05

Oil on panel; 27.5 x 19.9 cm (10 13/16 x 7 7/8 in.); image: 26.3 x 18.4 cm (10 3/8 x 7 1/4 in.)

The Art Institute of Chicago, Lacy Withers Armour Fund, restricted gift of the Old Masters Society, the Rhoades Foundation, Marilynn Alsdorf, Barbara Danielson in honor of James Wood, Mr. and Mrs. John W. Madigan, and John and Mary Gedo through the Old Masters Society, through prior gift of the George F. Harding, Mr. and Mrs. Morris I. Kaplan, Charles H. and Mary F. S. Worcester, and Max and Leola Epstein collections, 2004.244

PROVENANCE: Presumably in Italy by the late nineteenth century. Giannino Marchig, Florence, by 1950; sold to Colnaghi, London, July 1, 1952; sold to Sir Thomas Barlow, Bart. (d. 1964), London, July 1, 1952; by descent in the Barlow family, London; sold to the Art Institute of Chicago through Simon Dickinson Ltd., London, 2004.

BIBLIOGRAPHY: Waterhouse 1957, p. 415, fig. 21. Wolff 2005, pp. 58–66, figs. 8–11. Wolff 2008a, pp. 25–30.

EXHIBITIONS: London 1952, no. 6. Manchester 1957, no. 20. Manchester 1968, no. 6. Hampstead 1997–2003.

original marbleized back—an indication that the dismembered painting was a wing of a portable object.

The dismembered *Christ Carrying the Cross* formed a diptych with the Glasgow *Military Saint (Saint Maurice?) and a Donor* (cat. 63). The fragments formed the upper corners of the dismembered panel. When the fragments are aligned so that the outline of the beam of the cross is continuous, the total width equals that of the Glasgow panel, which retains its barbe and has therefore not been cut. The layers of the landscape and clouds appear to extend across the diptych. Moreover, the fragments and the Glasgow painting share a distinctive, economical underdrawing style also found in the donor figures of the Moulins *Virgin in Glory* painted about 1498 to 1500. Although the central figure of Christ carrying the cross is lost and has almost certainly been destroyed, the reconstructed diptych is of particular importance in suggesting the artist's engagement with an empathetic Passion subject. As such it is a significant additional link between the "Master of Moulins," otherwise known as a painter of portraits and mariological subjects, and Jean Hey, the author of the *Ecce Homo* in Brussels (cat. 64). • MW

[63]

JEAN HEY, KNOWN AS
THE MASTER OF MOULINS
(active Lyon and Moulins, c. 1480–c. 1505)

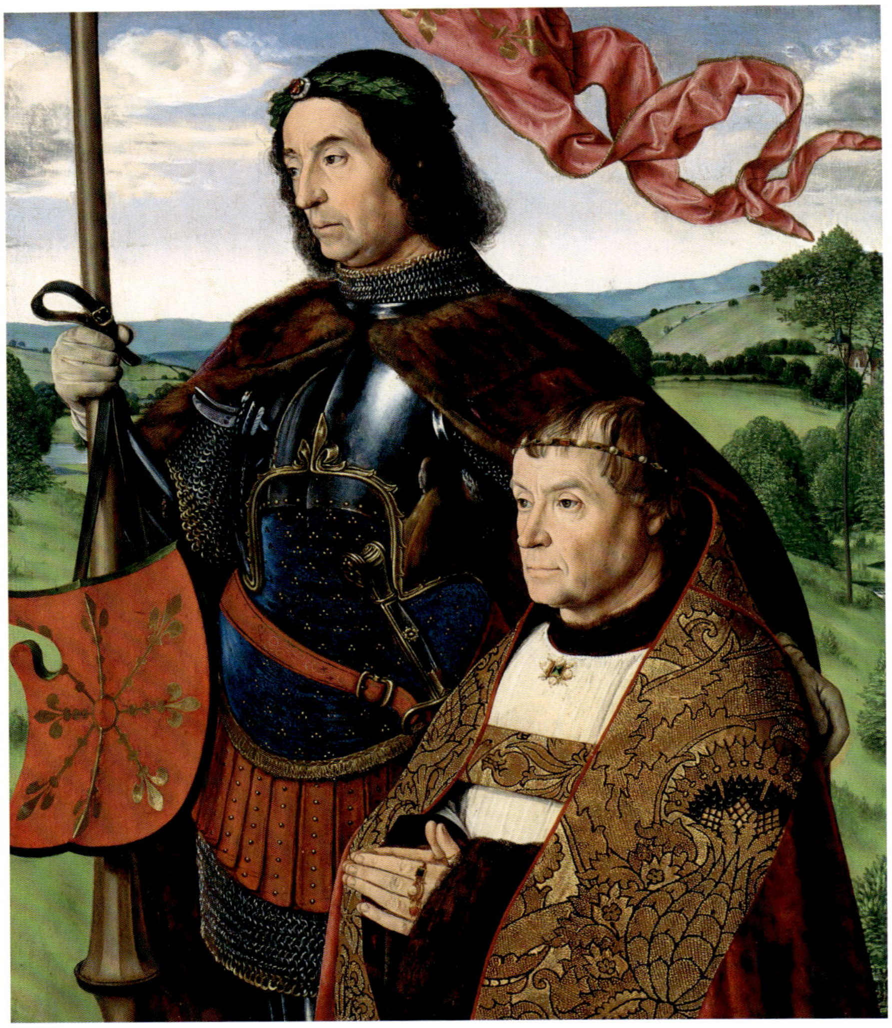

Military Saint (Saint Maurice?) and a Donor

1500/05

Oil on panel; original painted surface: 57.2 x 48.3 cm (22½ x 19 in.); with added edging strips: 58.4 x 49.5 cm (23 x 19½ in.)

Kelvingrove Art Gallery and Museum, Glasgow, acc. no. 203

PROVENANCE: Archibald McLellan (d. 1854), Glasgow, by 1850/51; following his death acquired by the city of Glasgow.

BIBLIOGRAPHY: Waagen 1854, vol. 3, p. 289. Leprieur 1892, pp. 173–74. Friedländer 1900, p. 258. Benoit 1901, pp. 368–73. Hulin de Loo 1902, pp. 22–23, 48, no. 100. Vauloger 1902, pp. 131–32, 147–48, 154–56. Weale 1906, p. 191. Friedländer 1926, pp. 77–79. Winkler 1932, pp. 246–47. Hulin de Loo 1932, pp. 62–63. Sterling [Jacques] 1941, pp. 21–22, 45, no. 25, pl. 66. Ring 1949, p. 238, no. 301. Huillet d'Istria 1961, p. 89. Châtelet 1962, p. 521. Dupont 1963, pp. 85–86. Sterling 1963b, pp. 11, 67. Wells 1981, pp. 148–55, fig. 1. Lorentz and Regond 1990, p. 58, no. 13. Reynolds 1996, p. 733. Châtelet 2001, pp. 95–98, 176–77, fig. 55. Wolff 2005, pp. 58–66, figs. 3, 11, 12. Wolff 2008a, pp. 28–30.

EXHIBITIONS: London 1892b, no. 17. London 1899–1900, no. 51. Bruges 1902, no. 100. Paris 1904, no. 106. London 1906, no. 13. London 1927, no. 67. London 1932, no. 68. Birmingham 1936, no. 878. Paris 1937, no. 24. Bruges 2002, no. 72.

SINCE THE OEUVRE OF the Master of Moulins was first reconstructed about 1900, this painting has been considered one of the artist's most magisterial works. It is usually placed at the end of his career, contemporary with or just after the Moulins *Virgin in Glory*.

Its patron and the saint presenting him remain unidentified, despite numerous suggestions, summarized by Châtelet (2001). The warrior saint carries a jousting shield and a lance with a pennon, both bearing a gold carbuncle on a red ground. These arms are associated with the martyrs of the Theban Legion, particularly saints Maurice and Victor. The prominent fleur-de-lis decorating his cuirass suggests a royal connection. The kneeling patron is generally identified as a canon because of his white rochet and the fur draped over his left wrist, assumed to be a canon's characteristic almuce. However, this fur may instead belong to the sleeves of his cassock, since his right forearm is also heavily draped with a fur lining (compare Gerard David's contemporaneous *Canon Bernardijn Salviati and Three Saints* in the National Gallery, London). His jeweled circlet, claimed to mark fifty years in orders (Weale in Bruges 1902, among others), is not a clue to his identity. This and his other jewelry are apparently later additions, differing from the artist's characteristic boldly painted, oversized jewels, like the one at the center of the saint's laurel wreath. Moreover, the circlet is not present in the donor's reflection in the shiny surface of the cuirass.

This painting formed the right half of a devotional diptych; the left half must have depicted Christ Carrying the Cross, of which only two fragments survive (see cats. 61–62). While the early history of the diptych is unknown, the extant fragments of Saint John the Evangelist and the Virgin both have Italian provenances.

The landscape behind the compact mass of the saint and donor continues onto these fragments. Nevertheless, as with other combinations of supplicant and devotional subject, the space inhabited by the sacred figures is subtly differentiated from the more ample space of the donor. Only a strip of sky and distant hills is visible behind the holy figures, who must have filled the foreground, since Saint John and the Virgin are cropped by the edges of the picture. Their physicality and the half-length or, more properly, three-quarter length format would intensify the pathos of the subject. This choice of format reflects not only Hey's likely training in the art of Hugo van der Goes, but also his openness to Northern Italian treatments of this subject in the work of Mantegna and of Leonardo and his Milanese followers, whose paintings were sought after by the French king and court in the first years of the sixteenth century. • MW

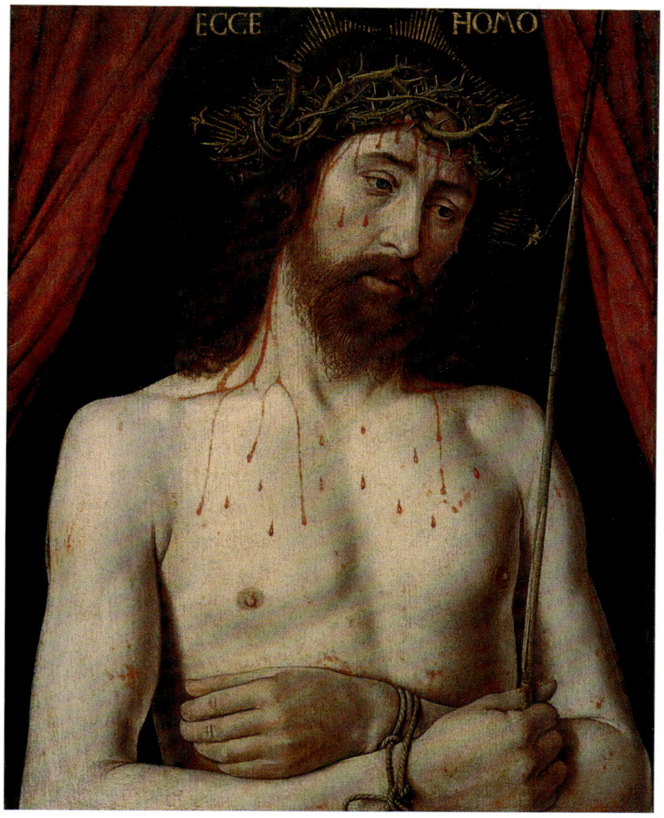

[64]

JEAN HEY, KNOWN AS
THE MASTER OF MOULINS
(active Lyon and Moulins, c. 1480–c. 1505)

Ecce Homo

1494

Oil on panel; 39 x 30 cm (15 3/8 x 11 13/16 in.)

Musées royaux des Beaux-Arts de Belgique, Brussels, 4497

INSCRIBED: *ECCE HOMO* (above Christ); *magr . Jo . cueillete . etat . 04/annor . notari et . secrettari/regis . karoli . octavi . hoc/opus . insigne . fieri . fecit/per . m . Jo . hey . teutoni/ cu . pictorem . egregiu . 14/94* [Master Jean Cueillete age 04 [*sic*] years, notary and secretary to King Charles VIII, had this work made by Master Jean Hey, the outstanding Germanic painter 1494] (on reverse)

PROVENANCE: Piégard collection, Orléans; by descent to M. Michy, Chécy, near Orléans, by 1911; Mme Puyt; Musées Royaux des Beaux-Arts de Belgique, 1923.

BIBLIOGRAPHY: Dumuÿs 1909, pp. 241–42. Durrieu 1911, p. 744. Mély 1911, pp. 315–19, pl. 1. Stein 1913, pp. 1–13, fig. 2. Bautier 1924, p. 60. Hulin de Loo 1932, p. 64. Sterling [Jacques] 1941, p. 21, under no. 20. Dupont 1945–47. Goldblatt 1948, pp. 72–73, no. III. Ring 1949, pp. 235–56, no. 291, figs. 42–43. Panofsky 1956, pp. 95–136, figs. 1, 3. Huillet d'Istria 1961, pp. 87–88, 107. Châtelet 1962, p. 522. Sterling 1963b, pp. 5, 15, 68. Zerner and Katic 1966, n. pag., no. 12. Erlande-Brandenburg 1968, pp. 222–23. Sterling 1968, pp. 27–33, fig. 1. Reynaud 1968, pp. 34–37. Châtelet 1984, pp. 112–14. Brown 1987, pp. 60, 66, fig. 38. Lorentz and Regond 1990, p. 50, no. 10. Reynolds 1996, pp. 733–34. Châtelet 2001, pp. 123–26, 188–89, fig. 78. Campbell 2002, p. 358. Girault and Hamon 2003, pp. 117–25, figs. 2–3. Châtelet 2003, pp. 353–55. Elsig 2004, p. 48, pl. 44. Lorentz 2009, pp. 23–24.

EXHIBITIONS: Nantes 1961, no. 59. Bruges 2002, no. 74.

THE INSCRIPTION ON THE reverse of this powerful devotional image identifies it as the work of Jean Hey for Jean Cueillette, notary and secretary to Charles VIII; as a result the painting has been at the center of the debate over the identification of the artist as the Master of Moulins. By 1909, when it surfaced near Orléans, a body of work had already been grouped around the triptych of *The Virgin in Glory* in Moulins, and the anonymous painter patronized by the Bourbon dukes had been speculatively identified as Jean Perréal (see Hulin de Loo 1902, for example). The well-informed court poet Jean Lemaire de Belges had praised Jean Hey in the same breath as Jean Perréal by 1504. Although Hulin de Loo (1932) was troubled by the appearance of a documented painting by Hey, he declined to change his mind, viewing Hey's career as concentrated in the Loire Valley, not in the Bourbonnais. Dupont (1945–47) put forward an alternate identification of the Master of Moulins as the Lyon glass painter Jean Prévost, which was taken up by Châtelet (1962 and later), while the case for Hey was damaged by the incoherence of its first advocate, Goldblatt (1948). However, the clarification of connections of the Cueillette family to Pierre II of Bourbon and his court at Moulins (Reynaud 1968) and of Hey's role as painter to Cardinal Charles of Bourbon until 1488 (Hamon 2001; Châtelet 2001; Girault and Hamon 2003), removed objections based on documentation and localization, leaving only a comparison of style.

The surface of the *Ecce Homo* is somewhat abraded, particularly in the hair and beard, and disrupted by remnants of yellow varnish and dirt. Nevertheless, it apparently never had the enamel finish of the painter's most refined—and earliest—works, the Autun *Nativity* (cat. 56), the Munich *Charles de Bourbon* (cat. 55), and the *Virgin and Child with Angels* in Brussels. Rather, it shares the broader handling of the Louvre panels of Pierre II of Bourbon and Anne of France in prayer (fig. 18). Christ's facial type and gaze are comparable to the Evangelist who protects Anne of France, and the hands are also strikingly similar, with a soft, generalized contour that rounds the ends of the fingers to minimize the last knuckle. The framing of the half-length figure of Christ, at the front of a shallow space, closely cropped and set off by regal curtains, follows the same compositional principle as *Madeleine of Burgundy Presented by Mary Magdalene* (cat. 58).

The inscription on the *Ecce Homo* includes stubbornly puzzling elements, notably the odd transcription of the patron's age. This text should be understood as a proud statement by the owner, rather than as the signature of the artist. It contains biographical details that suggest a memorial function, as an epitaph, perhaps in conjunction with a portrait. The patron, although a high functionary in the ducal and royal administration, was of lesser rank than the master's other patrons. Very possibly, this innovative treatment of Christ presented to the people, in which the Savior appears without a purple robe, and with a vulnerability and inwardness evocative of the Man of Sorrows (Panofsky 1956), was not invented for Cueillette's painting, but was repeated by the artist in more than one work. • MW

[65]

Mary Magdalene

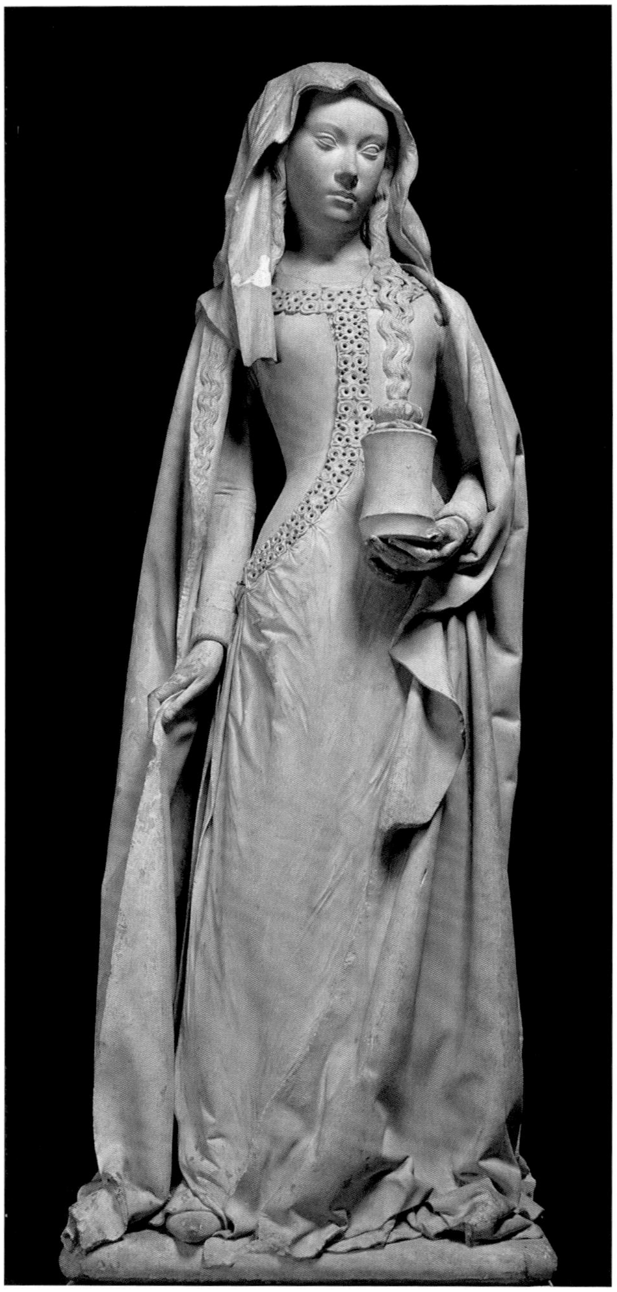

1490/1500

Stone, light application of color in the hair and on the decorated band of the garment; 138 x 51 x 38 cm (54 3/8 x 20 1/8 x 15 in.)

Parish church of Saint-Pierre, Montluçon, Allier

BIBLIOGRAPHY: Vitry 1901, p. 313. Mâle 1908, p. 163. Pradel 1953, pp. 79–80.

AS IN MOULINS, with the impetus of the patronage of the dukes of Bourbon and their circle in the late fifteenth and early sixteenth centuries, the sanctuaries of Montluçon were endowed with many sculptures, tributes to the devotional spirit of the late Middle Ages. This elegant, youthful Mary Magdalene in the church of Saint-Pierre is among the best-known examples, and stands out from other arguably more conventional statues of the incense-bearing saint that still exist in Souvigny, Bourbon-l'Archambault, and Saint-Marien in the Allier, and Saint-Hilaire-la-Croix in Puy-de-Dôme. The shape of the eyes is a distinctive stylistic feature, as noted by Pradel (1953, p. 79), and the elongated silhouette, as well as the delicate gesture of the hand, recall the figures of young women and angels by the Master of Moulins. The very unusual treatment of the fabric of the skirt, stitched to the jeweled border, and the subtle lacing of the bodice beneath this broad decorative band are realistic details that convey the sculptor's sensibility and enhance the charm of the work, which is otherwise quite simple, with the cloak retaining a bit of fullness only beneath the left elbow. Since this piece bears no trace of original polychromy, our attention is focused on the quality of the treatment of the features, the fabrics, and the details. Although Pradel (ibid.) described the figure as the most strongly influenced by the style of Touraine of all the sculpture from the Bourbonnais, and the knotted cloth that seals Mary's pot of incense links her to the Magdalene in Limeray, near Amboise, this saint is certainly among the finest examples of sculpture from the circle of Pierre II of Bourbon and Anne of France. • BC-B

[66]

JEAN GUILHOMET, KNOWN AS JEAN DE CHARTRES
(active c. 1464–died 1515/16)

Saint Peter

1500/10

Limestone, almost certainly from Apremont; 184.5 x 66.5 x 43.5 cm (72 5/8 x 26 3/16 x 17 1/8 in.)

Musée du Louvre, Paris, Department of Sculpture, RF 1159

PROVENANCE: Chapel of Saint Peter in the church of Saint-Vincent in the château of Chantelle; hidden, together with statues of saints Anne and Suzanne, under the sacristy's pavement, almost certainly c. 1633; all three found, February 17, 1845, and placed in the cloister, remaining in place at the installation of the Benedictine monks in 1852; acquired in 1897 from the bishop of Moulins.

BIBLIOGRAPHY: Michel 1899. Vitry 1901b, pp. 307, 417, 462–66. Pradel 1946. Pradel 1953, pp. 75–78. Forsyth 1973. Beaulieu and Beyer 1992, pp. 226–27. Baron 1996, p. 186. Baudoin 1998. Perrot 2001, pp. 76–78. Le Pogam 2008. Lorentz 2008. Lorentz 2009b.

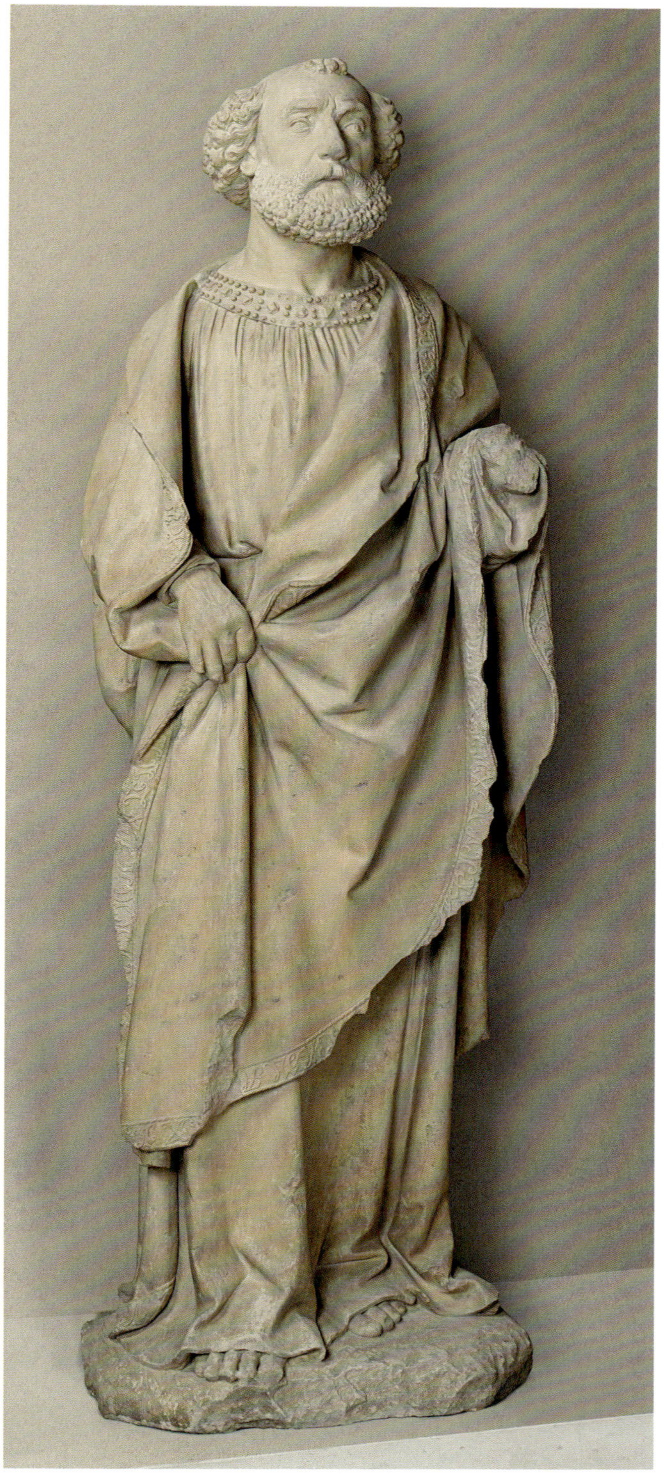

THE CHÂTEAU of Chantelle, in the south of the Bourbonnais near Saint-Pourçain-sur-Sioule, was one of the favorite residences of Pierre II, duke of Bourbon, and his wife Anne of France. This château was served by the nearby church, Saint-Vincent. Around 1500, the master mason Marsault Rodier enlarged the church by adding a chapel dedicated to Saint Peter, one of the ducal couple's patron saints. This chapel was destroyed in 1633 (Hamon 2001, p. 128); it was doubtless at this date that the statue of Saint Peter was buried beneath the floor of the sacristy built by the Jesuits who then had charge of the church. It was found together with two other sculptures. This provenance from the chapel is much more likely than the earlier suggestion that the statues were placed on the castle's towers. The condition of their surfaces, in particular, indicates that they were always kept inside, or at least in a position well-sheltered from the elements.

The three statues, which are slightly over life-size, represent the patron saints of the ducal couple and their daughter Suzanne, who was born in 1491. The sculptures were probably begun between 1500, when work started on the chapel of Saint Peter, and 1503, the date of Pierre II's death. Saint Peter is shown as an apostle, as in Jean Hey's panel in the Musée du Louvre (fig. 18). His face, with its strong features, has been compared to the head of Saint John in the Musée Mandet in Riom (Baudoin 1998; Perrot 2001). The robe, with its fine folds, has a rich border, and the cape, made of heavier fabric, has a border of pseudo-Moorish letters, a simple but imaginative device to emphasize the distance—both chronological and topographical—that separated the apostle from his princely patrons.

A stylistic similarity has been suggested between the figure of the youthful Virgin being educated by Saint Anne from Chantelle, and a sculpted female head in the Musée Anne-de-Beaujeu in Moulins (inv. 1037) said to come from the Carmelite convent for which Jean de Chartres sculpted an Annunciation, according to a payment of 1501. In light of their quality, provenance, and patrons, *Saint Peter* and the two statues accompanying it have been attributed to this sculptor, whose given name was Jean Guilhomet. A disciple of Michel Colombe, he is recorded in Moulins from 1500–01 and from 1511 until his death around 1515/16. Jean de Chartres's only documented work was the *Annunciation* mentioned above, which unfortunately has disappeared. Lorentz (2008 and 2009b) has also suggested that the sculptures were carved based on a design by Jean Hey, a hypothesis that cannot be eliminated a priori, but for which the incomplete ducal documentation does not provide confirmation. • BC-B

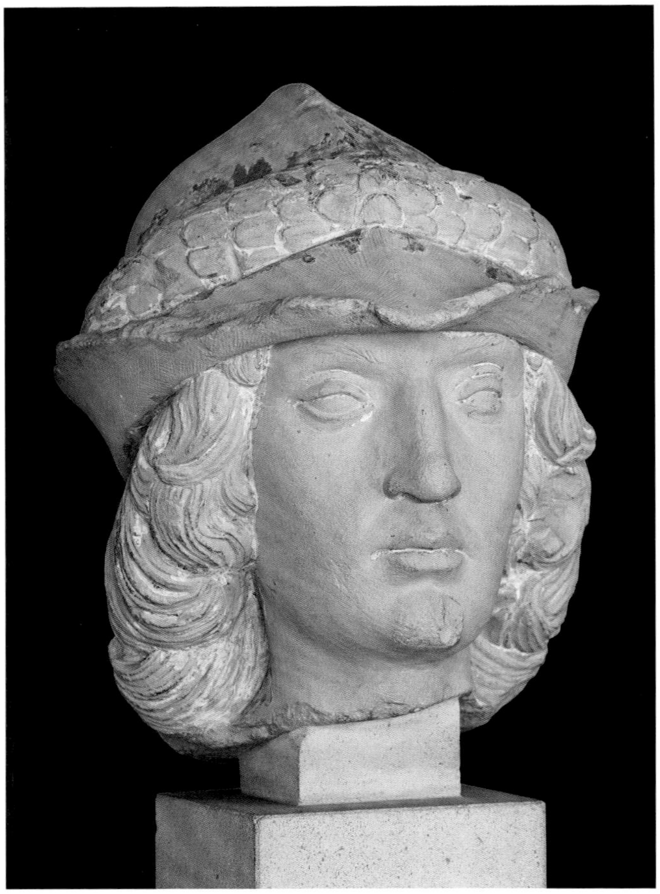

[67]

ATTRIBUTED TO THE WORKSHOP OF JEAN GUILHOMET, KNOWN AS JEAN DE CHARTRES
(active c. 1464–died 1515/16)

Head of a Young Man

c. 1500

Stone, traces of a white preparation; 32 x 20 cm ($12^{5}/_{8}$ x $7^{7}/_{8}$ in.)

Musée Anne-de-Beaujeu, Moulins, 1040

PROVENANCE: Found during work on the extension of the former collegiate church of Notre-Dame, Moulins (elevated to a cathedral in 1822), c. 1850.

BIBLIOGRAPHY: Pradel 1953, p. 78.

EXHIBITIONS: Nantes 1961, no. 91. Paris 1964, no. 57. Tokyo/Auckland 1972–73, no. 80. Nantes 1974–75, no. 95. Tours/Angers 1975, no. 46. Prague/Bratislava 1978–79, no. 107.

THIS IMPOSING head of a young man comes from a life-size statue. Discovered in the middle of the nineteenth century in the course of work on the former collegiate church of Notre-Dame in Moulins, it was undoubtedly part of the decoration of this monument, whose cornerstone was placed by Agnès of Burgundy, widow of Charles I, Duke of Bourbon, in 1468. Its construction, which is poorly documented, did not really begin until 1474, sponsored by Duke Jean II; work continued under Pierre II and Anne of France, although it appears that the church was not completed until 1534. By the 1480s, the decor included stained glass, and subsequently sculptures were added, placed in the church or on the exterior, between the bays of the chapels or ornamenting the buttresses. This head of a young man, found at the same time as three headless statues (two clerics and a Saint Agnes), has always been associated with the patronage of Pierre II, when the sculptor Jean Guilhomet was working in Moulins, around 1500 to 1501. However, there is no document that confirms this attribution (Hamon 2001, p. 130). Scholars have long noted similarities between this youthful face and that of the allegorical figure of Prudence, one of the Virtues from the tomb of Francis II of Brittany in Nantes, despite their different materials. The Nantes tomb was executed by Michel Colombe, Guilhomet's master, after designs by Jean Perréal. Combined with his long hair, the young man's hat, its brim curving upward in back and forming a point in the front, and ringed with a kind of leafy band (perhaps a laurel wreath), does not allow him to be identified precisely. The similarity, previously suggested (Baron in Prague/Bratislava 1978–79), to the cap worn by Donatello's bronze David raises the possibility that a similar iconography was intended for this intense, contemplative young man, who would fit equally well in a cycle of prophets as in a group of saints or heroes. • BC-B

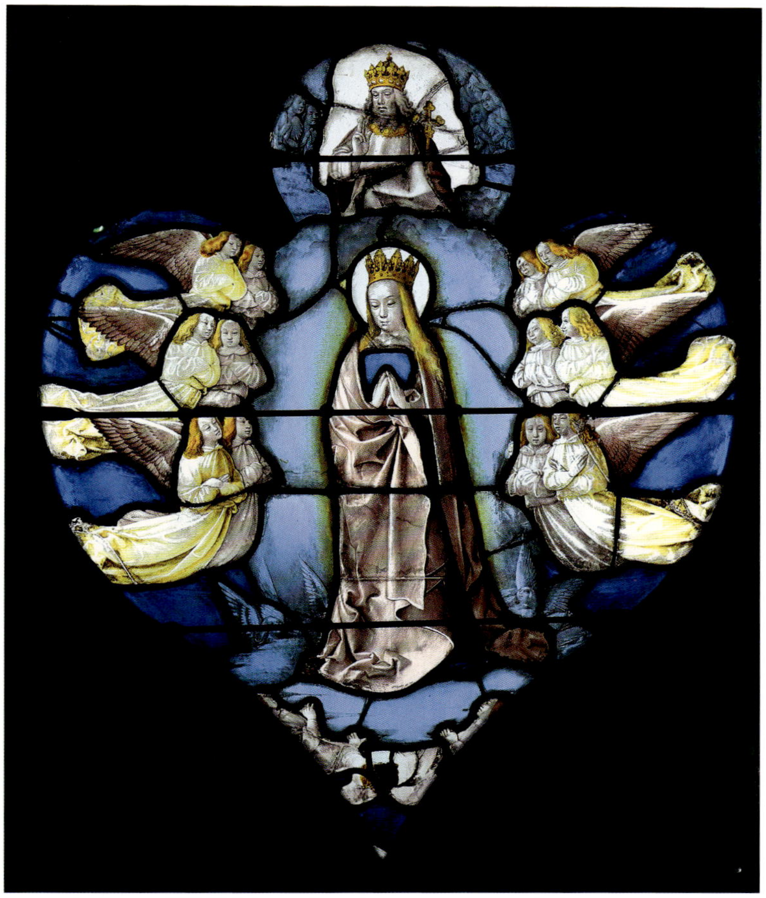

[68]

PROBABLY AFTER JEAN HEY, KNOWN AS THE MASTER OF MOULINS

(active Lyon and Moulins, c. 1480–c. 1505)

The Virgin in Glory

Moulins, c. 1500

Stained glass; 109.5 x 88.2 cm (43 1/8 x 34 11/16 in.)

Former collegiate church of Notre-Dame, now cathedral of Notre-Dame, Moulins

BIBLIOGRAPHY: Grodecki 1951, p. 218. Sterling 1963b, pp. 10, 15. Kurmann-Schwarz 1991, pp. 40–42. Reynaud in Paris 1993, pp. 350–51. Girault and Hamon 2003. Bruel 2005, pp. 415–16. Lorentz 2009a.

THIS SCENE OF THE Virgin in Glory remains the best-preserved part of a window long renowned for its exceptional quality and attributed by Grodecki (1951) to the Master of Moulins. His hypothesis corresponds well with the status of the patron, Charles Popillon (died 1507), president of the chamber of accounts of Moulins and chancellor of Anne of France, duchess of Bourbon, from 1493. One of the most important men of the duchy, Popillon probably had access to the artists who worked for the ducal court.

Numerous points confirm the close similarities between Hey's Moulins triptych (fig. 39) and this Virgin from the Popillon window: the sense of space, the role of the luminous halo around Mary, and many details, even the manner of gathering the fabric of the angels' albs at their necks. At the same time, the clarity of the composition owes much to certain technical characteristics that reveal the craft of the glass painter. Among these is the intelligent choice of a palette of glass for effects at once contrasting and subtle: the light blue glass with an undulating contour surrounding the Virgin detaches itself from a halo of a deeper blue of intense vibrancy. The masterful montage of the two pieces of glass making up her robe are evidence of the skill and virtuousity of which glass painters were capable. Simultaneously, the treatment of painting on glass is strikingly atypical. One notes with interest the connection between the placement of very fine grisaille strokes and the distinctive graphic style of the drawing of the head of a young woman in the Musée du Louvre attributed to Jean Hey (Châtelet 2001, fig. 26). But above all, the rosy brown grisaille with which the Virgin's drapery is so marvelously modeled appears to be a new tonality. If silver-stain is present as expected, applied to the exterior of the glass to make the blond hair of the angels shine, a surprising "painting" in yellow (another form of silver-stain, a colored grisaille, an enamel, or cold painting?) on the interior as a wash or highlight combines with the warm and somber grisaille to make possible the transposition into glass of some of the plastic effects so characteristic of Jean Hey: this color illuminates the reflected light on the angels' robes and is diffused as a halo around the Virgin where it merges with the blue glass. Other deep plum-colored highlights (a colored grisaille? an enamel?), otherwise unknown on glass painting of this date, color the mantle of God the Father and mark the deepest shadows of the Virgin's robe. These astonishing pictorial experiments, which call for technical analysis, are unique and innovative. At what point did the Master of Moulins or another painter working in a closely related style interevene in the working out of the design and perhaps in the execution of the window? • MHd

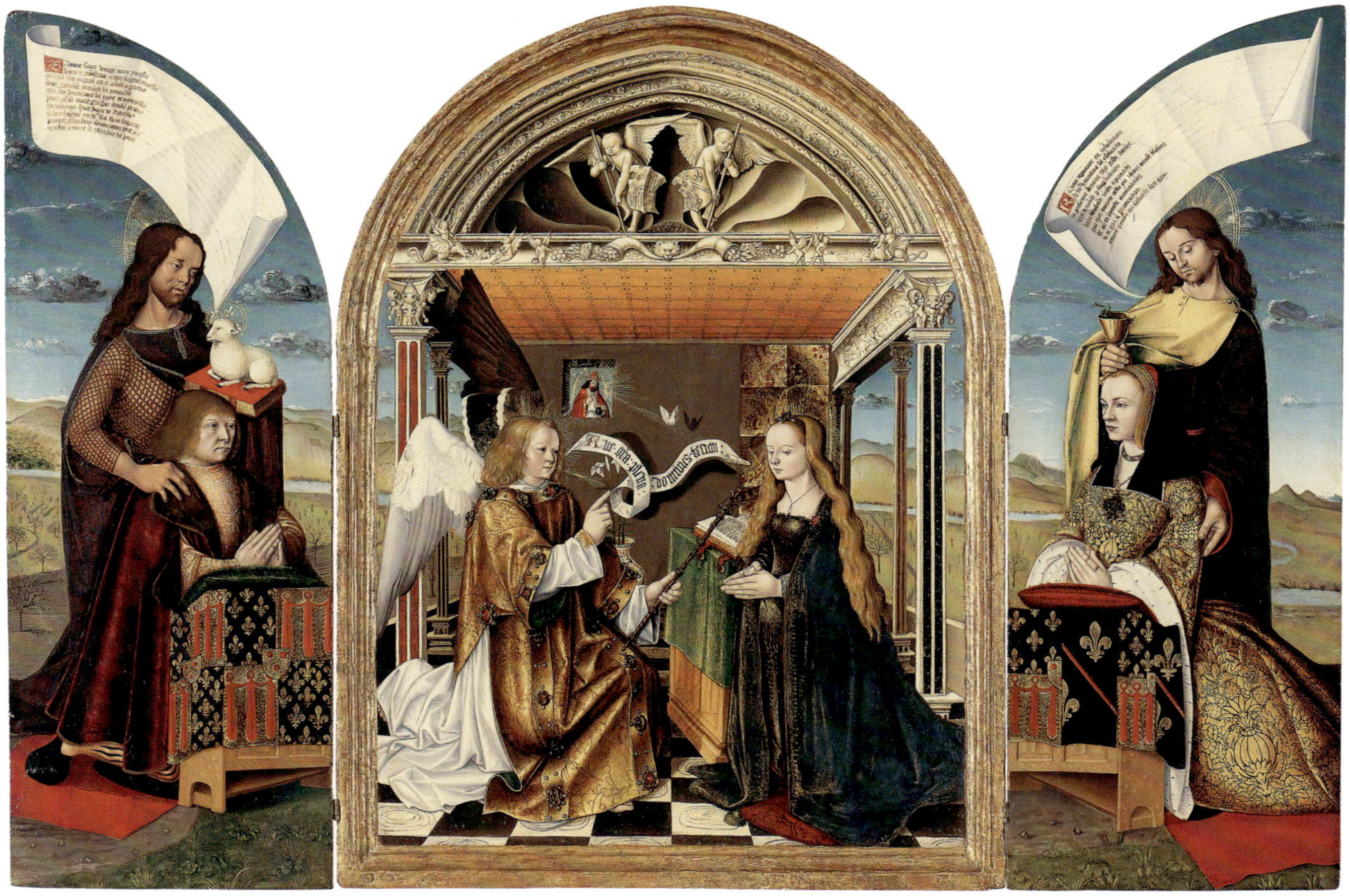

[69]

MASTER OF THE DE LA TOUR D'AUVERGNE TRIPTYCH

The Annunciation with Jean, Count of La Tour d'Auvergne, Presented by Saint John the Baptist and Jeanne de Bourbon-Vendôme Presented by Saint John the Evangelist

1495/97

Tempera and oil on panel; center: 61.8 x 43.5 cm (24 5/16 x 17 1/8 in.), including original frame: 67.8 x 49.3 cm (26 11/16 x 19 7/16 in.); left wing: 67.7 x 24.2 cm (26 5/8 x 9 1/2 in.); right wing: 67.7 x 24.5 cm (26 5/8 x 9 5/8 in.)

North Carolina Museum of Art, Raleigh, gift of Samuel H. Kress Foundation, GL.60.17.61

INSCRIBED: *Sacraire saint Vierge mere pucelle / bien te mõstras a ton seignẽ ancelle / quand ton aignel en ce mõde apportas / dont Gabriel d'annũca la nouvelle / qui des humains la joye renouvelle /* pu[is] *põ sa mort greifve doulẽ portas /en ton ame dont beau te deportas / ce bon seignẽ en tõ ses fais supporte / priant celui dont souverain port as / qui lui oevere de paradis la porte* [Sanctuary, holy Virgin, maiden mother, well did you show yourself the handmaid of the Lord when you brought forth into the world your Lamb, of whom Gabriel announced the news, who renews the joy of humankind; then you bore bitter grief in your soul for his death, in whose beauty you rejoiced; support this good lord [the donor] in all his deeds, praying to his sovereign whom you bore, that he open the gate of paradise.] (on a scroll on the left wing); *Royne regnante en iubilacion / de to humains la consolacion / je presente devant toy cette dame / qui demãde p supplicacion / faire tousjõs juste operacion / par ton moyen celle ou jamez neust blasme / et põ ta saincte annũciacion / je te prie q̄ generacion / avoir puisse au salut de son ame* [Queen, reigning in jubilation, consolation of all humanity, I present to you this lady who asks you in prayer always to have fair dealing [with her] through your instrumentality, by your blamelessness, and by your holy Annunciation I pray you that the bearing of offspring will be effective for the salvation of her soul.] (on the right wing); *Ave grã plena dominus tecum* (on banderole on center)

PROVENANCE: Jean III de La Tour d'Auvergne (d. 1501) and his wife Jeanne de Bourbon-Vendôme (d. 1512); placed near her tomb in the church of the Cordeliers, Vic-le Comte; given to Emmanuel Theodosius de La Tour d'Auvergne, cardinal of Bouillon, 1703 (according to inscription on the reverse of the wings). Reacquired by the La Tour d'Auvergne family at a public sale between 1872 and 1874 [Fournier-Salovèze 1909]. Knoedler and Company, New York, by 1956; sold to the Samuel H. Kress Foundation, New York; given to the North Carolina Museum of Art, 1960.

BIBLIOGRAPHY: Baluze 1708, vol. 1, p. 351. Fournier-Sarlovèze 1909, pp. 184–91. Sterling [Jacques] 1941, p. 23, no. 33. Shapley 1960, pp. 124–25. Wescher 1963, p. 12, fig. 6. Sterling 1966, pp. 10–16, figs. 2, 10–11. Friedmann 1966, pp. 3–15, figs. 1–17. Eisler 1977, pp. 49–51, no. K2157, fig. 234. Scott 1980, p. 205, figs. 148–49. Courtillé 1983, p. 190. Sterling 1991, p. 35, fig. 7. Bussac 1993, pp. 283–96. Reynaud in Paris 1993, p. 352, under no. 195. Luneau 1995, p. 24, n. 4. Wheeler 1998, pp. 72–74. Elsig 2004, pp. 49–50.

EXHIBITION: Washington 1961, no. 30.

THIS TRIPTYCH IS remarkable as a clear statement of its patrons' identity and aspirations. It was made for Jean III de La Tour d'Auvergne and his wife Jeanne de Bourbon-Vendôme, identified by their arms and an early-eighteenth-century inscription on the reverse of the wings. It must have been made between their marriage in early 1495 and May 1498, when Louis XII awarded La Tour d'Auvergne the Order of Saint Michael, whose collar he does not wear in this portrait. Jeanne had previously been the third wife of Jean II, duke of Bourbon (died 1488), but failed to supply him with an heir. Here, through the words of her patron, Saint John the Evangelist, she asks for offspring "for the salvation of her soul," while her second husband requests support in all his deeds. The couple did indeed produce two daughters; the younger, Madeleine, became the mother of Catherine de' Medicis.

Princely families' urgent desire for male heirs also manifested itself in pilgrimages, prayers in books of hours, and medical texts like the *Tractatus de conceptione et generatione praecipue filiorum* (Treatise on Conception and Generation, Especially of Sons), written by Bernard de Chaussade for Anne of France in 1488. The directness of this triptych's petition is reinforced by its somewhat naive realism. The bright early spring landscape extending through all three panels suggests the season of the Feast of the Annunciation (March 25). Cast shadows on the wall and on the speech scrolls have a distinctive literalness also found in the treatment of the small figure of God the Father that appears in the window and of the truncated cloth of honor behind the Virgin. Only one other panel painting has been linked to this artist, a small Virgin and Child in a private collection (Sterling 1991, fig. 6), although he may well have worked in or designed for other media. A connection to the Master of Moulins and painting in the Bourbonnais has been put forward by, for example, Sterling (1941), who later changed his mind (1966), and Elsig (2004). It is not supported by the triptych's style, although the work does reflect a dynastic impulse that parallels, on a less sophisticated level, the great Bourbon commissions. • MW

PARIS, CAPITAL OF THE ARTS

ÉTIENNE HAMON

The largest city in Europe in terms of population, and also the political and economic capital of a prosperous and peaceful kingdom, Paris, after a generation compelled to wait for a better day (1420–40), then another engaged in slow renewal (1450–70), could once again, around 1500, retrieve its status as the leading French center for the arts in terms of diversity and quality of production. This reality still struggles to take root in the minds of those who, having forgotten the idealized image of the Paris of 1482 constructed by Victor Hugo in his *Hunchback of Notre Dame* (1832), were conditioned by a century and a half of rhetoric about a capital without a king and therefore without the great patrons capable of promoting artistic creativity. The inadequacy of medieval primary sources and the scarcity of art historical studies focusing on the capital and on the period have long seemed to validate this perspective. However, reexamination of the texts and the works shows instead the tremendous fecundity and appeal of Paris and its surrounding region for the political elite—for the kings above all (as the splendor of royal entries shows)—as well as for the financial, merchant, and religious elites, and for artists from the periphery of the kingdom, especially the north (Hamon 2008).

Close to two thousand of the probable one hundred and fifty thousand inhabitants of Paris were employed in an artistic profession, which they practiced rather freely except for the approximately three hundred goldsmiths, heirs of a local tradition of excellence spanning many centuries. The goldsmiths' competitors for the first rank among artists and artisans were the members of the building trades, for, between the launch of the 1480s and the sudden halt of the 1520s (which coincided with a true stylistic rupture in all the arts), the city filled with building projects that produced most of the monumental Gothic heritage that remains in the capital, despite huge losses in the area of civil and monastic architecture. Churches, aristocratic and bourgeois town houses, outlying manor houses, and the domestic and collegiate architecture now standing, are, for the most part, Flamboyant, and all were crowded with sculptures, paintings, wall hangings, stained-glass windows, paneling, and liturgical furnishings, now almost totally dispersed. This architecture is gradually emerging from anonymity. The celebrated Jean de Felin, the city's Master of the Works (the Filles-Dieu in 1500, the Tour Saint-Jacques in 1509, the church of Saint-Aspais in Melun in 1517) competed with some dozen architects of the first order, who were also potential collaborators for extraordinary projects, such as the bridge of Notre-Dame. Like the dating of the unprecedented spatial layout of Saint-Etienne-du-Mont, conceived not in 1491, as long assumed, but by Jean Turbillon in 1510 (fig. 14), the chronology of major stages of creativity has been reevaluated as new building projects have been identified. Many of these appear to be related to attempts at reform by the church and the University of Paris, for example Anne of Brittany's foundation of a monastery of the Minimes at Chaillot in 1494. This new evaluation confirms the impression of a veritable frenzy of construction around 1500. A few irksome mysteries remain: What role did the most prominent architect in France around 1500, the Parisian Martin Chambiges, play in the capital, where scholars have been tempted to attribute to him the rose window of the Sainte-Chapelle and the church of Saint-Gervais? Who were the creators, evidently open to multiple influences, of the masterpieces that are the Hôtels de Cluny (fig. 40) and Le Gendre? What is the profile of the authors behind the first Italianate architecture, whose Parisian manifestation has long been overshadowed by monuments from Normandy and the Loire Valley? What role did the Italians Fra Giocondo, Guido Mazzoni, and Domenico da Cortona, installed in Paris under Louis XII, play in this movement?

The panorama of the figurative arts has also become more coherent thanks to the attention paid over the last three decades to new media that emerged during the course of this period (for example, printing) and to the established media (including manuscript illumination, stained glass, and tapestry) for which the capital once again became the primary supplier to provincial centers such as Rouen, Sens, and Auxerre. However, many artists have still not emerged from anonymity. For one newly clarified artist like Jean Pichore (fig. 4), there are dozens of modern names of convenience and as many names of painters known from the archives whose work is not preserved or even described. A few promising linkages of painters with works still await the evidence that will prove them valid, especially with regard to the principal figures of the current of migration from the North, which was the most innovative. Nicolas d'Ypres, also known as Colin d'Amiens, who died after 1497, and one of his sons, either Jean or Louis, are today the best candidates for being, among other names of convenience, the Master of Coëtivy and the Master of the Very Small Hours of Anne of Brittany, respectively (cats. 10, 70–75). Gauthier de Campes, who emerged from obscurity in 1499–1500 with the documentation of his plans for the bridge of Notre-Dame and the portrait of Robert Gaguin—his name figures on a tapestry portrait of the humanist at the monastery of the Mathurins—is likely to be identical to the most sought-after painter of full-scale cartoons for stained glass and tapestry in the years that followed (Leproux 2001). But the many inflections and variants in their proposed work suggests prudence, especially since we know nothing about painters whose recorded commissions tell us that they were well regarded. For example, Henri Ploumion, apprenticed as a painter in Tournai in 1466 and later, in Paris in the 1480s, an *historieur*—a title given to the best illuminators—was called upon to decorate the walls of the royal castle of Amboise in 1495. To this instance of the polyvalence and mobility characteristic of the most talented specialists in the figurative arts, one might add the name of Oudart Trubert, originally from Troyes in Champagne, the brother of Georges Trubert, who was at once a sculptor, a painter, and an engraver (*graveur d'images de taille*), a specialty of which he is, at present, the only known French representative for the fifteenth century.

Uncertainty reigns when it comes to choosing from the short list of recorded names those who wove the most handsome hangings commissioned in Paris from dealers and craftsmen often of Tournai origin (cat. 78), painted the finest stained-glass windows (fig. 41), and produced the most beautiful sculptures. The patience of scholars can sometimes be rewarded, as was the case for the Entombment group in Malesherbes, discovered to be the fruit of the collaboration between a painter, Nicolas d'Ypres (Colin d'Amiens), and a sculptor, Adrien Wincart, surely from the North (Grodecki 1996, pp. 329–34; see fig. 7). The production of objets d'art remains to be discovered, despite the emergence of names of specialists recognized far beyond the city's boundaries. The several dozen metalwork shops established on Rue Saint-Martin—an extreme example of professional concentration—flooded the country with religious objects in brass, none of which have survived in situ. Thus in 1485 Jean and Adam Morant decorated the choir of Albi Cathedral, then probably in the midst of a campaign to furnish the walls and roodscreen with sculptures, and then in 1497 they decorated the choir of Bourges Cathedral. The work of the goldsmiths also remains unidentified. A tiny minority were in a position to fulfill the most elaborate commissions—characterized by a revival of enamel decoration for the tables and the churches of the capital and elsewhere. Emerging from this group are François de Resnes, the goldsmith of Notre-Dame and, in 1499–1502, the maker of a large reliquary for the church of Gisors, and also Lambert Hotman, who, based on a drawing by Guido Mazzoni, executed the gold vessel that was presented by the city to Anne of Brittany in 1504 on the occasion of her entry following her second coronation (Hamon 2007, p. 53 n. 48). The *Nef of Saint Ursula* in the Reims treasury reflects the sophistication and inventiveness of such objects (fig. 30). Without a record of individual maker's marks from this period, attributing the scarce remains of what is presumed to be Paris production has proved to be almost impossible. Finally, three or four cabinetmakers dominated the enormous market for choir stalls for the churches of the Ile-de-France, including Geoffroy Ducloux, to whom we owe the now-dispersed stalls of Saint-Victor (c. 1530) in an antiquated style from a Parisian who started his career at the peak of the Flamboyant Gothic adventure, around 1500.

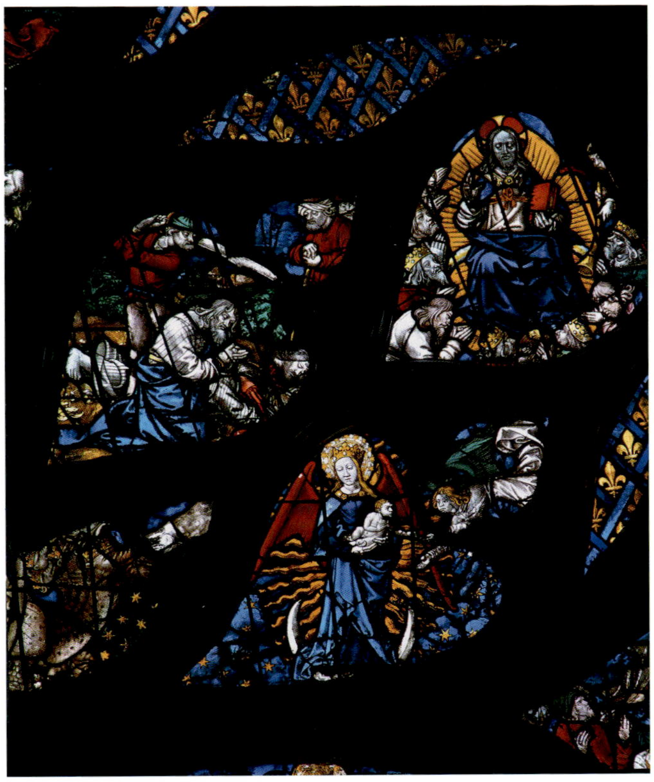

FIGURE 41.
After a design attributed to the Master of the Very Small Hours of Anne of Brittany (Jean d'Ypres?). Detail of the *Rose Window of the Apocalypse*. Sainte-Chapelle, Paris.

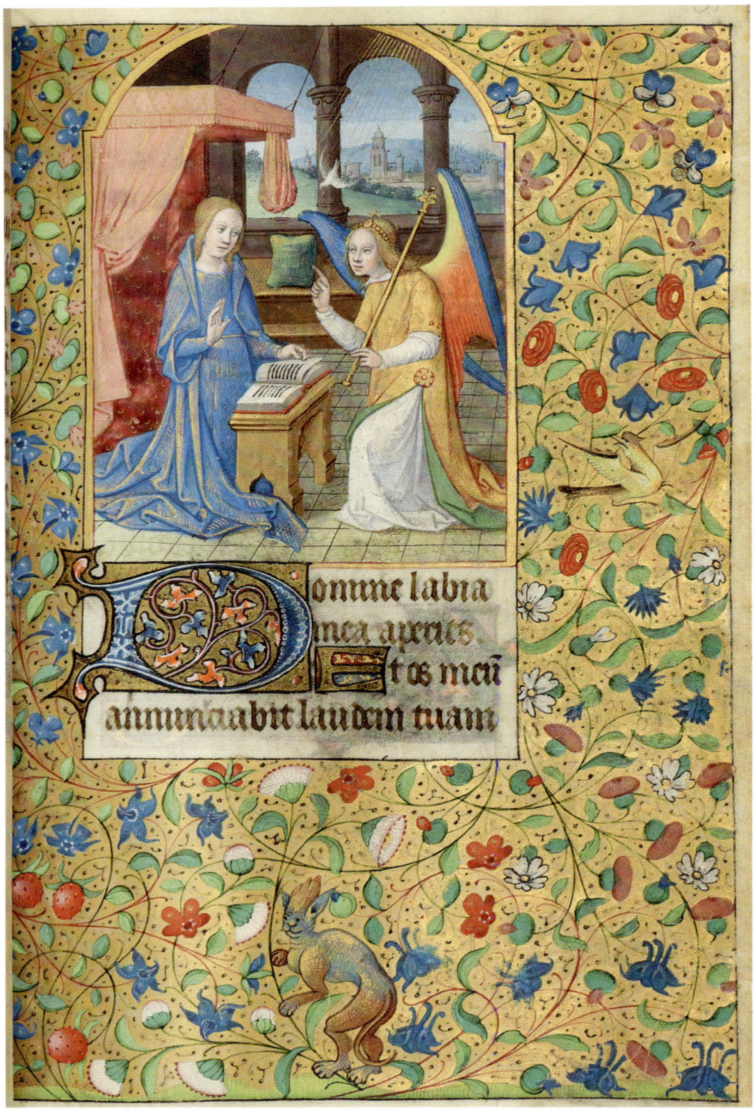

[70]

MASTER OF THE VERY SMALL HOURS OF ANNE OF BRITTANY (JEAN D'YPRES?) AND AN ASSOCIATE
(active c. 1490–1508)

Book of Hours, called the Hours of Anne of Austria

Paris, c. 1500

Tempera and gold on parchment; 262 ff.; 15.3 x 10.2 cm (6 x 4 in.)

The Morgan Library and Museum, New York, ms. M. 1110

PROVENANCE: Anne of Austria, queen of France (d.1666) [her arms on early seventeenth century binding]. Maurice Johnson, Spalding, Lincolnshire; sold, Sotheby's, London, March 21, 1898, no. 573; Michael Tomkinson, Franche Hall, Kidderminster; sold, Sotheby's, London, July 3, 1922, no. 1521; A. Chester Beatty, Dublin, Western MS 84; sold, Sotheby's, London, June 24, 1969, no. 69; Neil F. Phillips; gift of Sharon G. Phillips and her children to the Morgan Library, New York, 1997.

BIBLIOGRAPHY: Reynaud in Paris 1993, p. 267. Wieck 2000, pp. 10–11, fig. 10. Nettekoven 2004, pp. 54–55, 112, figs. 120, 121, 122.

SHOWN: *Annunciation*, f. 37.

THIS MANUSCRIPT bound with the coat of arms of Anne of Austria is evidence of the activity of the Master of the Very Small Hours of Anne of Brittany as an illuminator. Like the *Le Camus Hours* today at Chantilly, this book of hours probably originally included five miniatures, but only three have survived: *The Annunciation* for Matins of the Hours of the Virgin, *The Crucifixion* for the Hours of the Cross, and *The Virgin and Apostles Receiving the Holy Spirit* for the Hours of the Holy Spirit. Judging by the gaps in the text in the body of the manuscript, the other two miniatures probably decorated the beginning of the Penitential Psalms and of the Office of the Dead (Nettekoven 2004). The poses and expression of the figures (the head of the angel jutting in front of his shoulders, the restrained gestures of the Virgin in *The Annunciation* or of the apostles in *The Pentecost*) are characteristic of the repertory used by Jean d'Ypres, although the compositions of the Crucifixion and the Pentecost are somewhat simplified in comparison to those of other illuminated or printed books of hours attributed to the master. The direct face-to-face dialogue of Gabriel and Mary, on the other hand, is novel; the artist usually preferred to emphasize the surprise of the Virgin by representing her with her back turned toward the angel. Nettekoven (2004) has likewise shown that the color palette and the very marked use of gold in the three miniatures were rather unusual in the oeuvre of the Master of the Very Small Hours, a sign that he was here assisted by another artist of his circle, perhaps the Master of the Hours of Charles VIII. • SL

[71]

AFTER THE MASTER OF THE VERY SMALL HOURS OF ANNE OF BRITTANY (JEAN D'YPRES?)
(active c. 1490–1508)

Book of Hours for the Use of Rome

Paris, April 17, 1497

Printed by Philippe Pigouchet for Simon Vostre

Metalcut and letterpress on vellum with initials illuminated in red and blue, 21 x 14.9 cm (8¼ x 5⅞ in.)

The Library of Congress, Washington, D.C., Rosenwald Collection, 442A, Incun. 1497.C28

PROVENANCE: Fritz Kreisler [from Library of Congress catalogue]; Lessing J. Rosenwald, Jenkintown, Penn.; given to the Library of Congress, 1946.

BIBLIOGRAPHY: Library of Congress 1954, p. 73, no. 363. Febvre and Martin 1958, p. 248. Goff 1973, no. H383. Library of Congress 1977, p. 86, no. 438.

SHOWN: *The Annunciation*

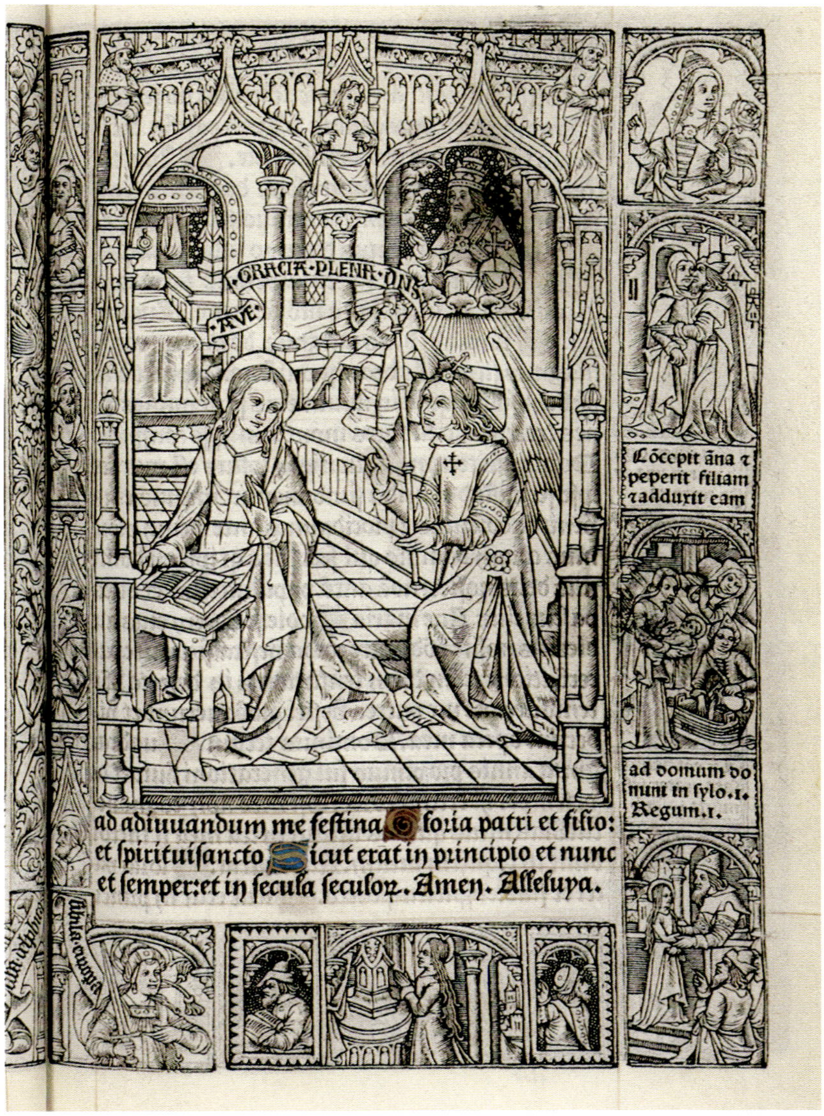

MANUSCRIPT BOOKS OF HOURS became the bestsellers of the Middle Ages by making private worship for the wealthy lay reader an aesthetically pleasing devotional experience. These small volumes were as eminently personal as they were portable. In the late fifteenth and the beginning of the sixteenth centuries, enterprising Paris publishers such as Philippe Pigouchet, Antoine Vérard, and Thielmann Kervier printed many thousands of books of hours with lavish metalcut or woodcut illustrations on fine vellum. These delicate octavo volumes served much the same market as their manuscript predecessors, and they too could be illuminated and personalized as their owners saw fit. Just as the manuscripts widely produced for the uses of Rome, Paris, or Sarum (England) were localized with minor saints days, the mass-produced printed books of hours were almost equally adaptable and remained in high demand.

Many cycles of the life of Christ for these volumes were copied from the Paris workshop of the Master of the Very Small Hours of Anne of Brittany. His metalcut *Annunciation*, included in this 1497 Phillipe Pigouchet printing for Simon Vostre, was part of a series so popular that the publisher opened a second printing house in 1498 to meet demand (Nettekoven 2004, pp. 89–90). The *Annunciation* particularly resembles this painter's style in other media, including the same scene from a manuscript book of hours in the Morgan Library and Museum, New York (M. 1100; cat. 70). While the printed image remains black and white, the translucency of the vellum and the glow of the tiny rubricated initials impart a richness equaling illumination. The ornate border vignettes repeated throughout the volume—here showing other scenes in Mary's life—also contribute to the manuscript-like format. The *Annunciation* marks Matins, at the beginning of the Hours of the Virgin, a sequence that furnished the core of the book of hours following the expansion of the cult of the Virgin in the 1300s (Wieck in New York 1988, pp. 60–61, 159). Gabriel's banderole greeting to the Virgin begins with *Ave*, reminding the viewer to recite the *Ave Maria* at this time. • SKS

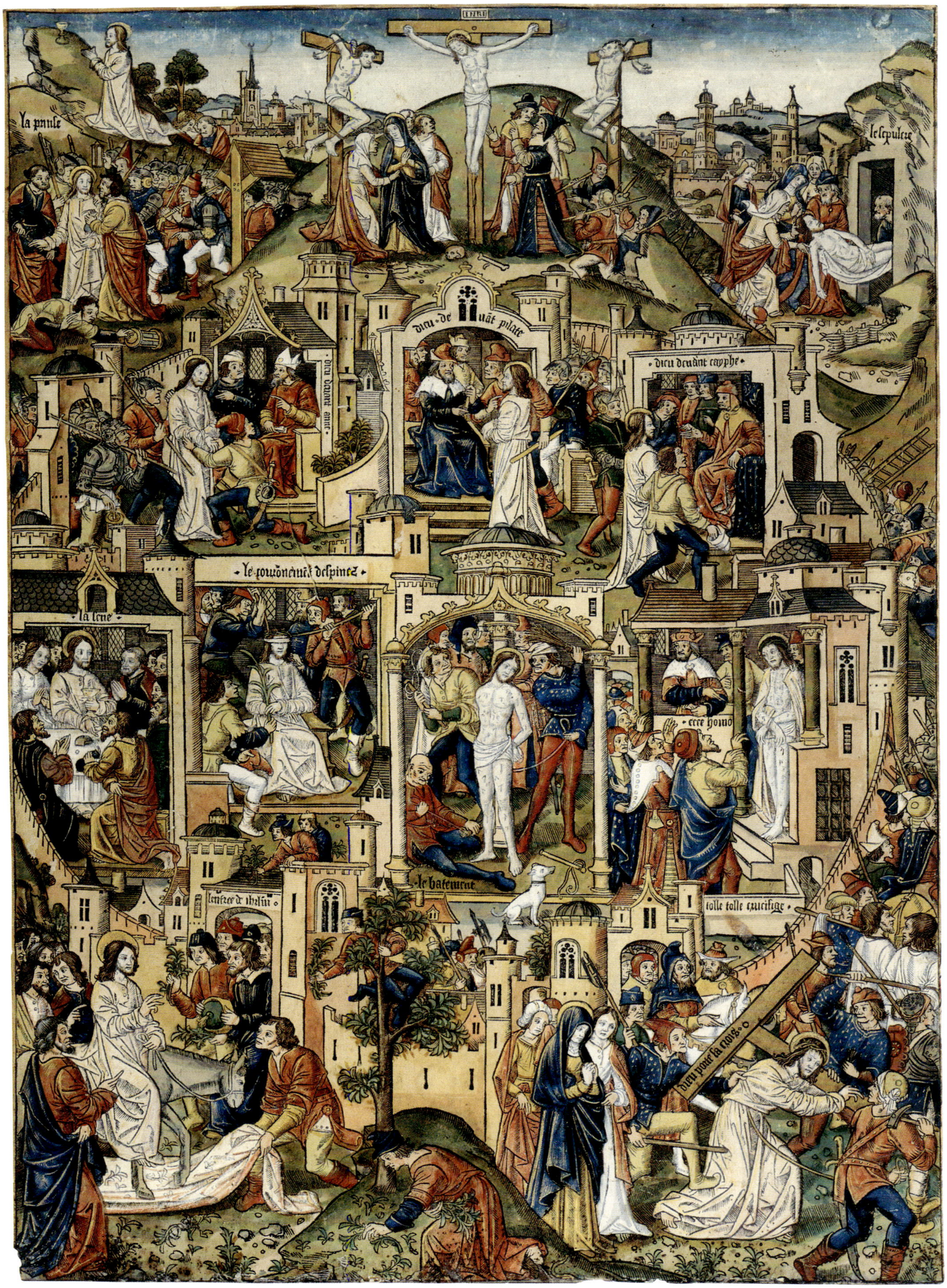
la prinse
dieu deuant cayphe
la cene
ecce homo
tolle tolle crucifige

[72]

GROUP OF THE MASTER OF THE VERY SMALL HOURS OF ANNE OF BRITTANY (JEAN D'YPRES?)
(active 1490–1508)

The Large Passion

Probably Paris, c. 1500

Woodcut printed on paper, handcolored; 50.2 x 35.7 cm ($19^{3}/_{4}$ x $14^{1}/_{16}$ in.)

Bibliothèque nationale de France, Paris, Department of Prints, Rés. Ea-5 (13)

PROVENANCE: Acquired September 10, 1902, acquisition 6435.

BIBLIOGRAPHY: Bouchot 1902, no. 191. Schreiber 1926–30, vol. 1, no. 21a. Courboin 1923, no. 149. Lemoisne 1930, vol. 2, no. cxxviii, 137–38. Souchal 1973, pp. 24, 27, fig. 6. Sterling 1990, p. 196. Jammes and Saffrey 1994, pp. 3–23. Nettekoven 2004, pp. 74–75, fig. 128.

EXHIBITIONS: Los Angeles/New York/Paris 1994–95, no. 2, pl. 1. Paris/Ecouen 2007–08.

THIS WOODCUT, CALLED the *Large Passion* because of its unusually imposing dimensions for the period, is a major work of the d'Ypres group. The careful execution of this colored and illuminated print, only known in this single impression, suggests an artist's direct involvement, rather than a reproduction or adaptation from an existing work. It has not, however, been precisely dated and it is thus difficult to determine whether to assign its authorship to Nicolas d'Ypres (Colin d'Amiens) or to his son Jean d'Ypres. The episodes of the Passion are represented here in a composition that is original for French art of the end of the fifteenth century because it includes both interior and exterior scenes in an urban setting. This arrangement is found in Hans Memling's *Passion*, painted in 1470 (Galleria Saubada, Turin; Souchal 1973; Sterling 1990; Nettekoven 2004), a debt that confirms the northern sources of this family of artists of Flemish origin. The *Large Passion* should also be linked to a series of single-leaf woodcuts of Passion scenes, with the same compositions as appear in this print, but executed with varying degrees of refinement.

This *Large Passion* was most likely used in the same way as its smaller-scale relatives: as a devotional image before which one prayed and meditated. It was probably attached to a wall, perhaps even glued to a wooden panel. A typical image of the *devotio moderna*, it invites the believer to participate in the Passion of Christ, allowing him to internally recreate the road to Calvary in a space that seeks to free itself from the constraints of the two-dimensional sheet. Except for *Ecce Homo*, an expression that at the period had probably passed into the common vocabulary, and the *tolle, tolle, crucifige* of liturgical usage, all the captions are in the vernacular, a sign that the woodcut was not meant exclusively for clerics. It could also have served as a substitute pilgrimage for the faithful unable to travel to Rome or Jerusalem (Nettekoven 2004; Jammes and Saffrey 1994).

A previously unnoticed element is the appearance, on the reverse of the sheet, of printed designs: coins of various sizes, each decorated with a cross at its center and with tooth-like notches along its edge. This is clearly the imprint of a sheet of uncut printed playing cards, each measuring three-and-a-half inches (nine centimeters) long, probably used to back the sheet of the *Large Passion* at an unknown date. The printed side of the backing sheet containing these designs was glued to the reverse of the woodcut and its ink was thereby transferred to the paper, with the glue acting as an intermediary. The backing paper was later removed, as the few fragments still visible indicate.

Coins were long used as suit symbols for playing cards, so unfortunately the date of this backing cannot be determined with certainty. Nonetheless, coins in dimensions identical to those on the reverse of the *Large Passion* are found on a few sheets of printed playing cards from the sixteenth century: sheets used as binding filler with the mark of Martial Gué, a Limoges cardmaker of the 1530s (Bibliothèque nationale de France (BnF), Print Department, Rés. Kh-34-Folio). Moreover, a fragment of a sheet of playing cards, found in the binding of a sixteenth-century register of notaries (BnF, Print Department, Rés. KH-34-Folio) includes a star formed by two inverted triangles with a shield set in its center, a motif that is also found, in the same size, in the upper left corner of the reverse of the *Large Passion*. The backing may therefore be contemporaneous with the execution of the *Large Passion*. It could have served to strengthen the sheet for gluing to a wall or panel. If this hypothesis is correct, the presence of such an element would permit a more precise definition of the milieu that produced the *Large Passion*: that of the "image makers" (*tailleurs d'images*), who printed and sold playing cards as well as single-leaf prints. • SL

[73]

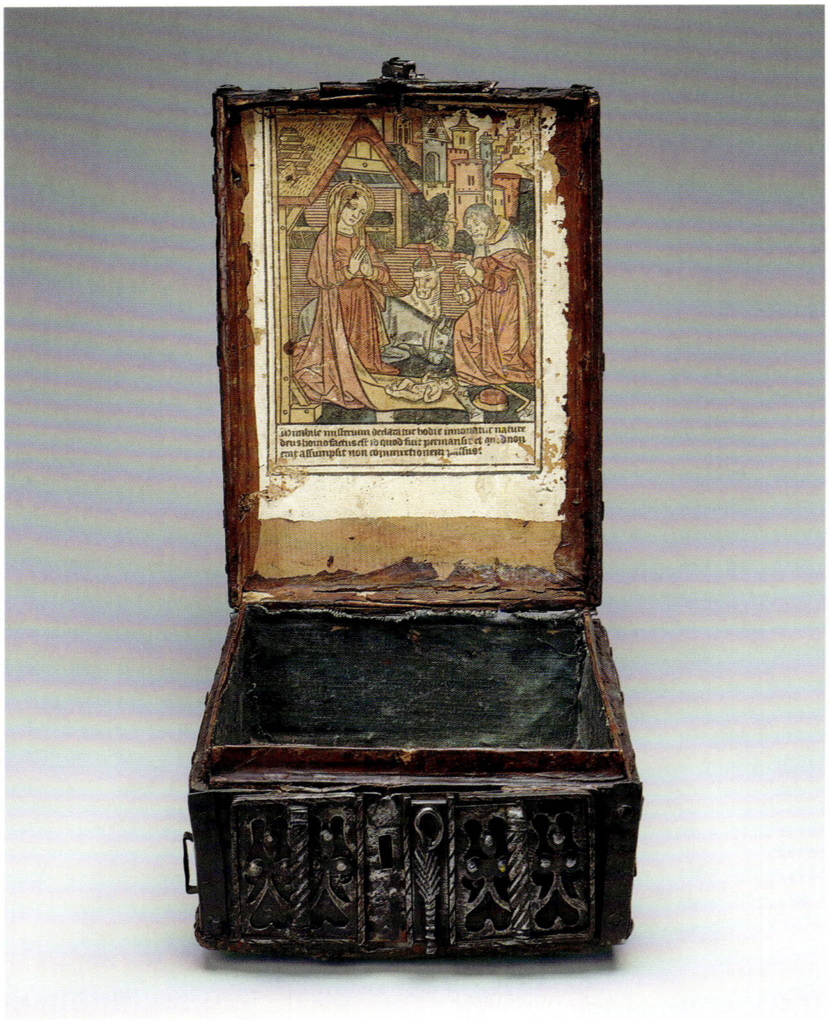

AFTER THE MASTER OF THE VERY SMALL HOURS OF ANNE OF BRITTANY (JEAN D'YPRES?) (active 1490–1508)

Coffer with a Print of the Nativity

Paris, c. 1490

Print: Woodcut, hand colored with brush, stencil, and watercolor on paper; image: 23.1 x 16.4 cm ($9\frac{1}{8}$ x $6\frac{7}{16}$ in.)

Coffer: Wood, iron, leather, linen, and horsehair; 15 x 22 x 33 cm ($5\frac{15}{16}$ x $8\frac{5}{8}$ x 13 in.) (closed)

The Art Institute of Chicago, George F. Harding Deaccessions Fund; Restricted gift of Mr. and Mrs. William Vance; The Amanda S. Johnson and Marion J. Livingston Fund, 2009.49

PROVENANCE: Marie-Thérèse and André Jammes, Paris; sold, Drouot Richelieu, Pierre Bergé, Paris, November 7, 2007, no. 17, to C.G. Boerner; sold to the museum, 2009.

BIBLIOGRAPHY: Hindman 2009, pp. 54–55. Tedeschi 2009, pp. 80–81. Huynh and Lepape 2010.

THIS COFFER with a print of the Nativity demonstrates the rare survival of a late-fifteenth-century devotional French woodcut in its original context. About a hundred similar coffers survive; they were produced near Paris and decorated with woodcuts from Parisian workshops. Though these objects were previously known as "messenger" boxes, recent research by Huynh and Lepape (2010) has shown that their construction was too flimsy for them to serve as strong boxes for long trips on pack animals. Nonetheless, the intricate locking metalwork on the front, metal loops for leather straps on the sides, and horsehair-stuffed cushion on the bottom of the well-preserved Art Institute example suggest local portability, perhaps for merchants, or priests transporting vestments, holy books, or even the Eucharist. The cushion allowed the box to be used as a backpack, and could stabilize it when open on the owner's lap, maybe for contemplation of the image within. Like many such coffers, the lid of this one hides a shallow compartment that may have contained relics or other talismans to protect the contents of the box and its bearer. Once filled, these secret compartments were often nailed shut, but unfortunately no known boxes have retained their fifteenth-century contents.

The Nativity woodcut survives in eleven colored impressions, at least eight of which remain pasted into similar coffers. The print is part of a series of the life of Christ known almost exclusively from these boxes, and also relating to the oversize *Passion* woodcut (cat. 72) from the circle of the Master of the Very Small Hours of Anne of Brittany. This painter, illuminator, and tapestry and stained-glass designer, named for a celebrated manuscript book of hours at the Bibliothèque nationale de France (ms. n. acq. lat. 3120), actively contributed designs to the burgeoning book trade in Paris, especially for printed books of hours. The *Nativity* woodcut was likely simplified from his drawing for a cycle of illustrations for a printed book of hours that Nettekoven (2004) notes appeared in at least four editions printed for Simon Vostre between May 1496 and August 1498. The particularly fine metalcuts on vellum of the Library of Congress's 1497 copy (cat. 71) offer a different audience slightly more luxurious and intimate renditions of nearly identical devotional images. • SKS

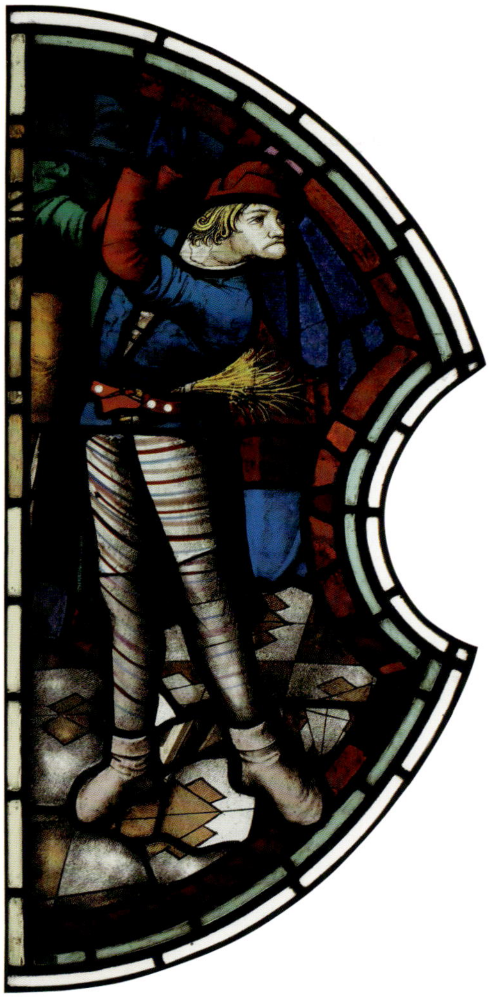

[74]

STYLE OF THE MASTER OF THE VERY SMALL HOURS OF ANNE OF BRITTANY (JEAN D'YPRES?)
(active 1490–1508)

Executioner from the Flagellation of Christ

Paris, c. 1490

Stained glass; 88 x 44 cm ($34^{5}/_{8}$ x $17^{3}/_{8}$ in.)

Musée de Cluny—Musée national du Moyen Age, Paris, Cl. 14476

PROVENANCE: Removed from a Parisian church before 1752; adapted for use as a replacement panel in the *Genesis* window of the Sainte-Chapelle, Paris, 1752; removed from this window, 1852.

BIBLIOGRAPHY: Charenton-le-Pont, Médiathèque d'Architecture et du Patrimoine, cote 0080/151, *Travaux publics, Sainte-Chapelle*, Album *Anciens panneaux*, pls. 24, 17. Lasteyrie 1857, p. 162. Grodecki 1959, pp. 84–85. Souchal 1973, p. 38. Leniaud and Perrot 1991, p. 223. Reynaud in Paris 1993, pp. 265–70. Delaunay 2000, pp. 220–27. Lorentz in Paris 2004, pp. 102–07. Lagabrielle 2006, pp. 78–79, 81 (ill.).

EXHIBITION: Paris 1993a, pp. 45–46.

THIS DEPICTION OF an executioner now in the Musée de Cluny was part of a scene of the Flagellation that was removed in the middle of the eighteenth century from the stained glass window of a Parisian church, at a time when many of the city's buildings were being reglazed to be opened up to the light. In 1752, the glazier responsible for repairing the Genesis window in the Sainte-Chapelle made use of this panel of the Flagellation as a replacement element. The scene, once in a rectangular format, was cut to match the shape of the missing thirteenth-century piece. This surviving part shows the marks of mutilation and also has other misplaced pieces and replacements. The lower part of the man's leggings is a modern reconstruction.

The original sections of this much-altered panel are striking in their meticulous execution, which is just as brilliant as that of the Sainte-Chapelle's west rose window: red glass is etched to show the switch thrust through the executioner's belt and the beaded ornamentation of the belt itself; glass in colored strands, known as the "Venetian" technique, is used for the leggings. The latter type of glass demonstrates that this was a costly commission and also expresses the iconographic convention attributing multicolored garb to executioners.

The figure is a distinctive physical type: wavy locks of hair tumble down over a thick neck; his head is thrust forward, covered with a large cap; and his features are dominated by a protruding chin and sunken lips, as if he had lost all his teeth. This type is not unique in fifteenth-century Parisian art. Souchal (1973) has compared it to another figure traced in 1852 among the replacement pieces removed from the windows of the Sainte-Chapelle and to figures in tapestries of the *Unicorn Hunt*, particularly *The Attack on the Unicorn* (Metropolitan Museum of Art). Comparable types also exist among the windows illustrating the lives of Saint Sixtus and Saint Vincent from Saint-Germain l'Auxerrois, Paris (bay 121). Other images in a similar style can be found in illustrations for Parisian books, notably the book of hours printed by Philippe Pigouchet for Simon Vostre on September 16, 1498.

All of these works belong to a trend in Parisian art whose major personality may have been Colin d'Amiens, followed by his son Jean d'Ypres, the Master of the Very Small Hours of Anne of Brittany. However, in view of its complex ramifications, and because it is no longer possible to attribute the entire production to a single painter, this trend should now be referred to by the generic label of the d'Ypres style (Delaunay 2000). The group of works to which the executioner from the Musée de Cluny belongs is itself far from homogeneous and is marked by considerable variations in scale and handling. These characteristics can be tied, at least in part, to the individual personalities of the craftsmen—tapestry weavers, glass painters, and printmakers—who executed the designs: a nervous, refined drawing style and virtuoso execution in the Cluny window, a broader drawing style with fleshy figures in the scenes from the life of Saint Vincent in Saint-Germain l'Auxerrois, and figures sometimes based on a very different canon in the Unicorn Tapestries. • MHd

[75]

AFTER A CARTOON BY THE MASTER OF THE VERY SMALL HOURS OF ANNE OF BRITTANY (JEAN D'YPRES?)
(active c. 1490–1508)

Carrying of the Cross

Paris, c. 1500

Stained glass; 73 x 41 cm (28 7/8 x 16 1/8 in.)

Musée de Cluny—Musée national du Moyen Age, Paris, Cl. 22391

PROVENANCE: Commissioned by Jacques d'Amboise, abbot of Cluny, for the chapel of the Hôtel de Cluny, Paris. Collection of Alexandre Lenoir, Paris; sold to Alexandre du Sommerard, who had it remounted in its original location before 1834.

BIBLIOGRAPHY: Perrot 1970, pp. 66–72. Souchal 1976, p. 595. Avril and Reynaud in Paris 1993, pp. 265–70. Leproux in Paris 1993a, pp. 44–45. Grodecki 1996. Paris 2004, pp. 102–07. Paris/Ecouen 2007–08, pp. 48–55.

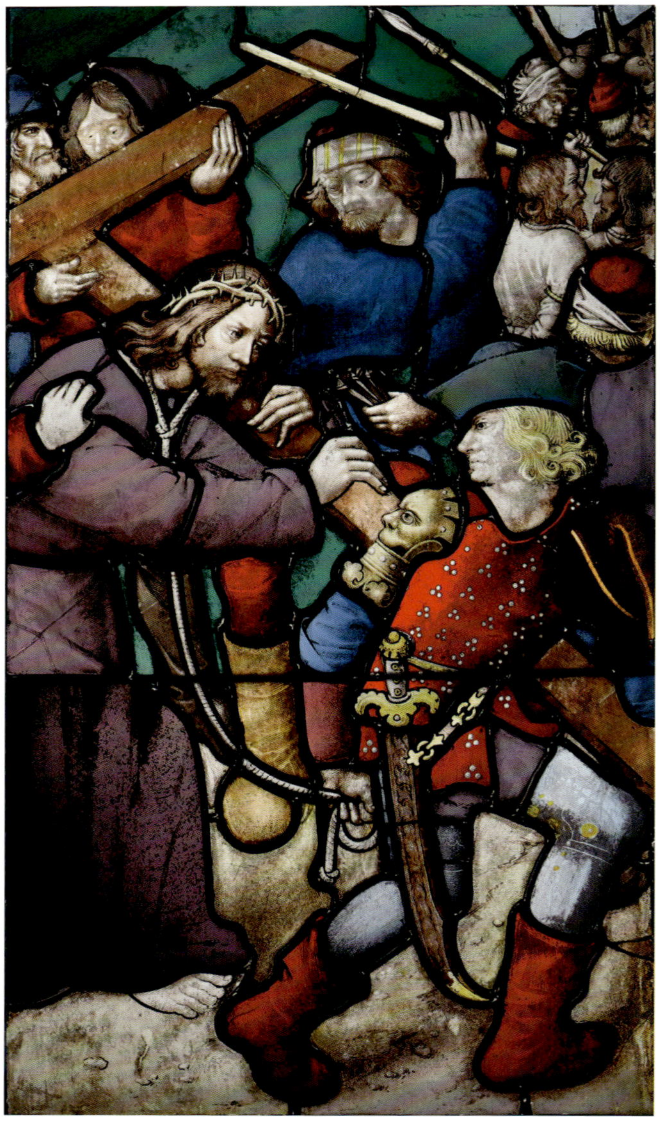

THERE IS NO DOUBT regarding the origin of this panel: the axial bay of the chapel built around 1500 on the second floor of the Hôtel de Cluny for Jacques d'Amboise, abbot of Cluny, for this, his Paris residence. It formed the right portion of a scene of the Carrying of the Cross that originally occupied two lancet windows as part of a Passion cycle, of which a few fragments from the upper register were discovered in 2007.

For decades, this work has been recognized as one of the finest examples of the art of the Master of the Very Small Hours of Anne of Brittany, perhaps Jean d'Ypres (Paris 1993). Given the abundance of, and lack of consistency in, the works attributed to this painter, it is now evident that he, although the initiator of this style and one of its foremost exponents, was not its exclusive purveyor. However, the quality of the Cluny panel is exceptional within this group. It could not have been taken directly from a printed model, such as the woodcut of the same theme in the Bibliothèque Nationale de France (Réserve. Ea-5(11)). While the print does indeed present a closely related composition, its execution points to another aspect of artistic activity in Paris and, more importantly, to another, less demanding, type of clientele. Remarkable for its extremely refined painting, the Cluny window was apparently based on a cartoon provided by a painter, possibly especially for this commission, since no precise equivalent is known. Although the painter cannot be conclusively identified, the patron, Jacques d'Amboise, abbot of Cluny, was a member of an elite social group with access to court artists: his nephew, Charles de Chaumont, married the daughter of the admiral Louis Malet de Graville, who had commissioned an Entombment (fig. 7) on March 28, 1495, based on a pattern by the Paris painter Nicolas d'Amiens. Around 1500, Jacques d'Amboise may have called on the latter's son, Jean d'Ypres, for the design of the window. On the other hand, nothing clearly identifies the glassmaker. We have the name of Amé Pierre, a "painter and glassmaker" documented as having carried out work for Thomas de Riou, who was close to the queen, Anne of Brittany. The similarity of glass painting technique of this panel and the panels of the equally brilliant and virtuosic west rose window of the Sainte-Chapelle in Paris (fig. 41), commissioned by the king, attests to Amboise's ambitions and resources. • MHd

[76]

Panel from a Monumental Window of the Heavenly Court

Paris, 1510/15

Stained glass; 61 x 71 cm (24 x 28 in.)

The Art Institute of Chicago, gift of the Antiquarian Society, 1930.947

PROVENANCE: A church in Paris (Saint-Merry?). Lord Carrington, Wycombe Abbey, Buckinghamshire, before 1896. Jacques Seligmann, Paris and New York, 1909. Colonel Ambrose Monell; sold, American Art Association, New York, November 28, 1930, no. 50. The Antiquarian Society; given to the Art Institute of Chicago, 1930.

BIBLIOGRAPHY: Gatouillat et al. 1997. Raguin et al. 2001, vol. 1, pp. 114–16. Gatouillat 2005.

THIS GROUP OF FIGURES has sometimes been described as an assemblage of miscellaneous pieces, for example by Raguin (2001). To understand the work properly, it is necessary to consider its relationship to five other panels from a series dispersed in 1930 at the Ambrose Monell sale in New York. Three were recognized by Françoise Gatouillat in the Museo Nacional de Bellas Artes in Havana, and two others have not yet been located, while a sixth panel of the same origin but with a different history is in the chapel of the château of Lux in Burgundy. All belonged to a large composition on the theme of the celestial court, where saints and angels, surrounded by clouds, direct their gaze toward the divine apparition. The presumed origin of these dispersed components is the large west bay of the church of Saint-Merry in Paris. As this bay was stripped of its glass between 1646 and 1649, this hypothesis is based not on archaeological evidence, but on the attribution of the panels to glassworkers active in the church's nave, where the glass is still in place. However, the fabrication and style of the pieces of the heavenly court and the glass still in situ are not consistent. The fragments combine obvious references to the d'Ypres style (for example, the bearded man visible here) with an interpretation on a monumental scale of new models, also northern in origin, which is not surprising for Paris at that time. These new models were closely related to the early works of Lucas van Leyden, including the painting *The Fortune Teller* (Musée du Louvre), as well as the work of the Absalom Master. From these sources come the heavy-featured facial types and the half-length presentation of the figures, densely layered in a cramped space, with a background filled by silhouettes. • MHd

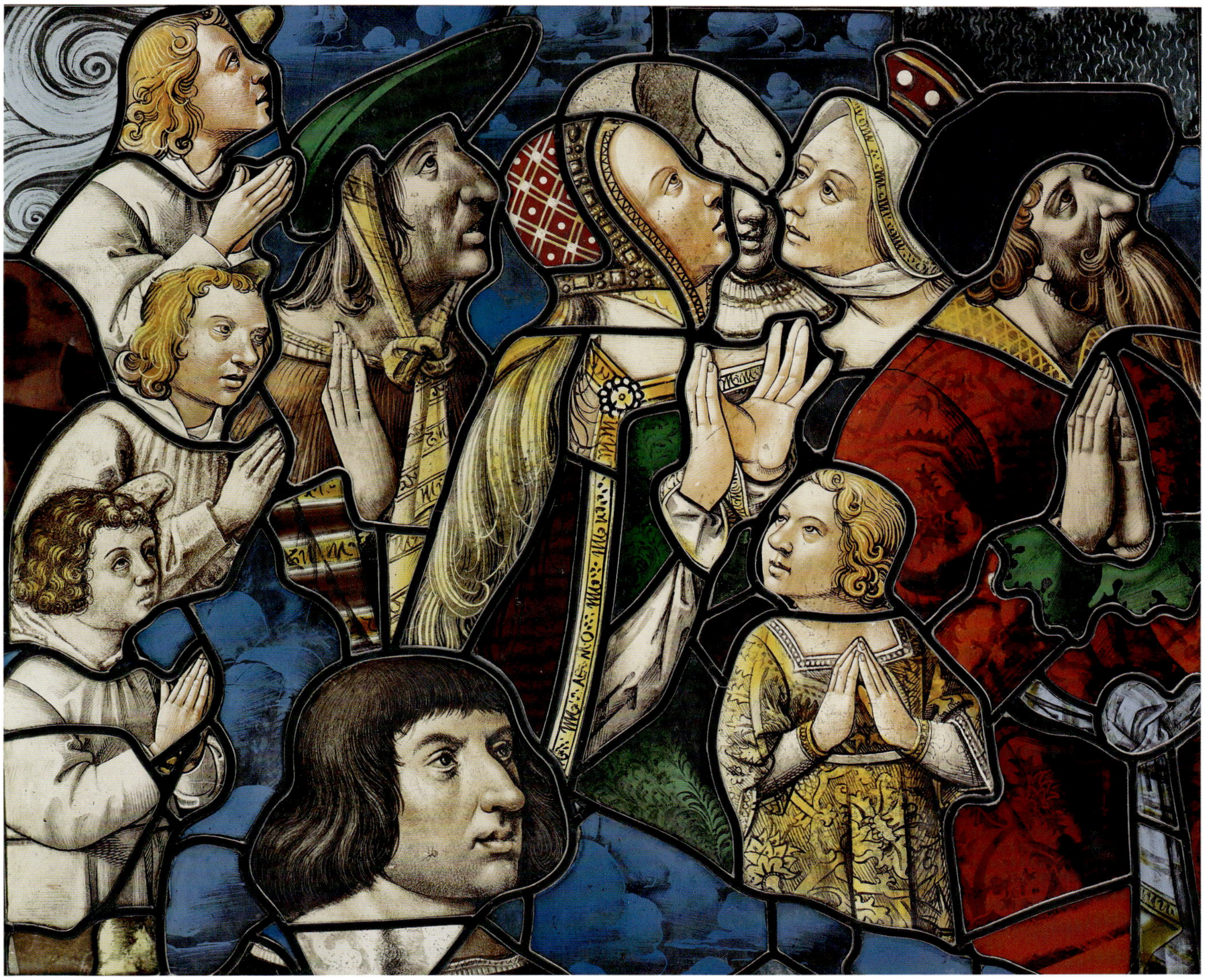

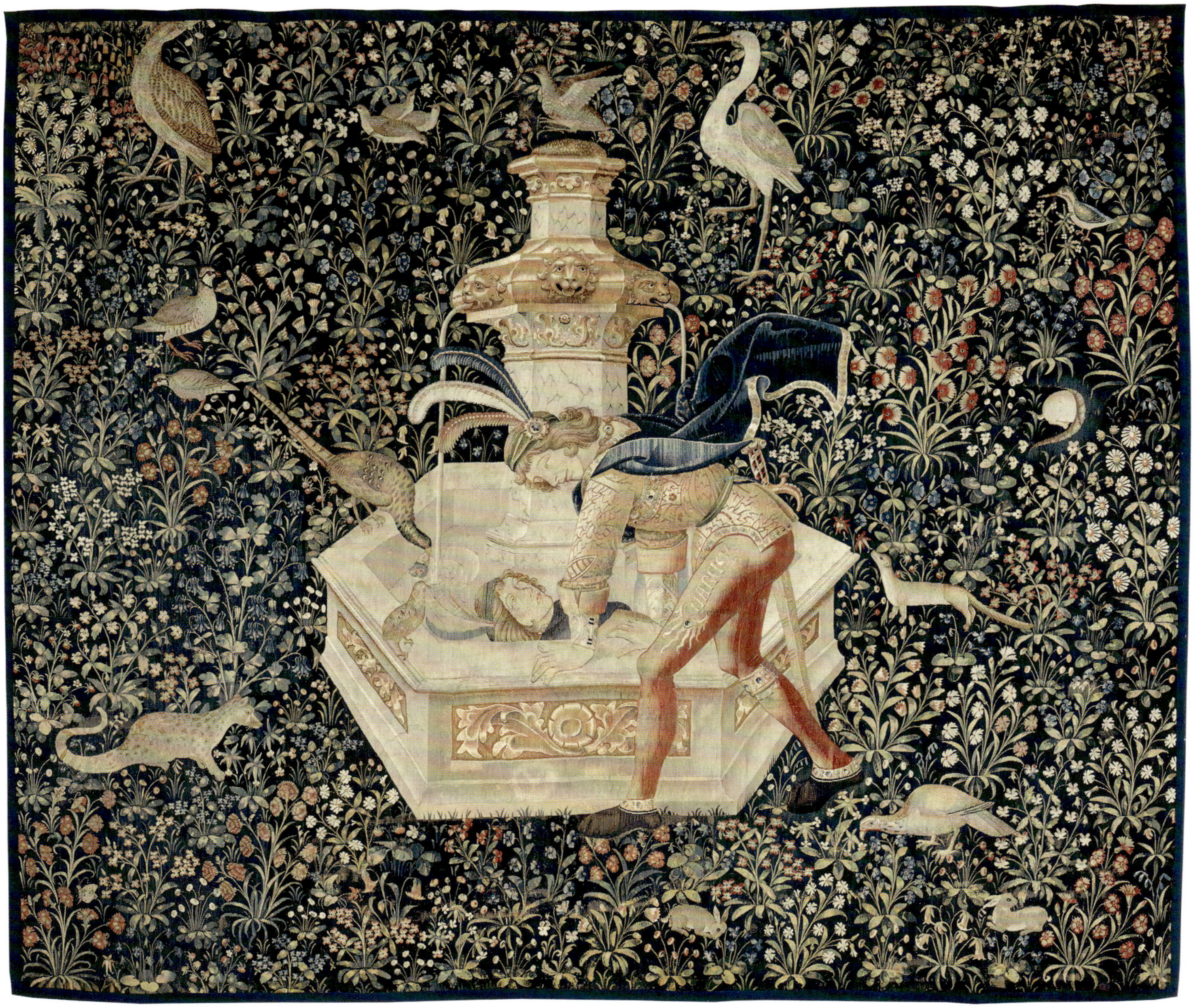

[77]

Narcissus at the Fountain

Cartoon: Paris, c. 1500

Weaving: Probably Paris or Flanders

Wool and silk thread; 282 x 311 cm (111 x 122 7/16 in.)

Museum of Fine Arts, Boston, Charles Potter Kling Fund, 68.114

INSCRIBED: *Narcisus* (on the figure's thigh)

PROVENANCE: Toulgouët collection, Château de Rozay, Saint-Georges-sur-la-Prée, Cher, by 1882; Lady Baillie, Leeds Castle. Wildenstein and Company, New York, 1968; sold to the Museum of Fine Arts.

BIBLIOGRAPHY: Siple 1928. Sterling 1990, pp. 390–93.

EXHIBITIONS: Boston 1972–73, no. 7. Paris 1973–74, no. 30. Paris 2002, no. 29 (note by E. Antoine).

NARCISSUS, who had scorned all of the hearts that were smitten by his beauty, was himself seduced by the reflection of his own image in the water of a fountain; unable to embrace this object, he perished in the attempt and was transformed into the flower that bears his name. This story, told in Ovid's *Metamorphoses*, is repeated at the beginning of the *Roman de la Rose* (line 1435ff), where it is placed in the garden of love. In this long allegorical poem, the story of Narcissus provides the pretext for a commentary on the dreadful fate reserved for ladies who permit their suitors to die of love. This synthesis between the classical theme and its medieval interpretation is continued here: the hexagonal basin, lion spouts, and foliate decoration inspired by acanthus leaves are part of the classical repertoire adopted throughout the Middle Ages.

The medieval garden is evoked by the millefleurs ground, where more than thirty species have been identified (Paris 2002a). Although these flora are generally similar to those in the *Lady and the Unicorn* tapestries, the stylistic connections to this series, and to other works associated with the circle of the Master of the Very Small Hours of Anne of Brittany (cats. 70–75), are not close enough to enable us to attribute the design of the *Narcissus* to him. The elegant youth with his plumed hat is closer to various figures in other tapestries made around 1500, particularly the *Story of Saint Stephen* woven for the cathedral of Auxerre (cat. 78). This confirms that the millefleurs plants and foliage belonged to the workshop stock of cartoon painters or tapestry weavers, and above all demonstrates the complexity of the Parisian artistic milieu around 1500.

The hypothesis that the *Narcissus* may have been part of a series of hangings based on the *Roman de la Rose* (Guy Delmarcel, written communication, Musée de Cluny, G. Souchal archives) is all the more plausible because such hangings were very much in style around 1500—Anne of Brittany, for example, had a sumptuous series of four, woven with gold and silk thread (Vrand 2010). • ET-D

[78]

The Election and Consecration of Seven Deacons

The first two scenes of the *Life of Saint Stephen* for the cathedral of Auxerre

Paris, 1500/03

Cartoon: Probably Gauthier de Campes (active Paris, 1500/30)

Weaving: Workshop of Guillaume de Rasse, Paris (active Paris, 1497–1516)

Silk and wool thread; 167 x 553 cm (66 x 217¾ in.)

Musée de Cluny—Musée national du Moyen Age, Paris, Cl. 20200

INSCRIBED: First scene: *Comment les apostres et disciples de Jhesucrist tindrent conseil pour faire sept diacres et terminer le discord / estant entre les ebreux et les grecs nouvellement convertis a la foi chretienne* [How the apostles and disciples of Jesus Christ took council to elect seven deacons and end the discord between the Hebrews and Greeks newly converted to the Christian faith] (at the bottom); Second scene: *Comment saint estienne avec six autres furent eslus diacres et c(on) sacres par / limposicion des mains des apostres pour regir lesnouveaux chr(e)tiens es choses temporelles* [How Saint Stephen with six others was elected deacons and consecrated by the imposition of hands of the apostles to rule over the new Christians and temporal matters] (at the bottom); *Accipe spm̄ sancteum* [Receive the Holy Spirit] (Saint Peter laying hands on the head of Saint Stephen); *S estienne / Philippus / Procorus / Ethimon / Nicol(aus) / Parmenas* (on the individual deacons)

ARMS: Azure with a bar of gules accompanied by two winged dragons of gold: Baillet, surmounted by the episcopal cross, for Jean III Baillet, bishop of Auxerre (1477–1513).

PROVENANCE: Cathedral of Auxerre, by 1569 [first mentioned in the inventory of the treasury compiled in that year]; sold to the Hôtel-Dieu, 1777; gift to Dr. Maurache (in gratitude for his refusal of fees), about 1830; sold to the Louvre, 1838 (inv. L.P. 3496); given to the Musée de Cluny in 1897.

BIBLIOGRAPHY: Lebeuf 1723, pp. xxxix, 137–38. Lebeuf 1743, vol. 2, p. 94. Joubert 2002, no. 1. Leproux 2001, pp. 39–107. Nassieu-Maupas 2004.

EXHIBITIONS: Paris 1878. Paris 1946. Paris/New York 1973–74. Avignon 1997. Auxerre 2000.

ONE OF THE MOST complete and best preserved, as well as among the finest, of the choir tapestries woven around 1500, the Auxerre series is also one of the most important for understanding the artistic centers and creative processes of this era. The twenty-three scenes, now divided across twelve pieces with a total length of about forty-five meters, were reunited in the Musée de Cluny in 1897, when the two pieces acquired by the Musée du Louvre in 1838 joined the ten others purchased by the museum in 1880. The set illustrates the life, martyrdom, and history of the relics of

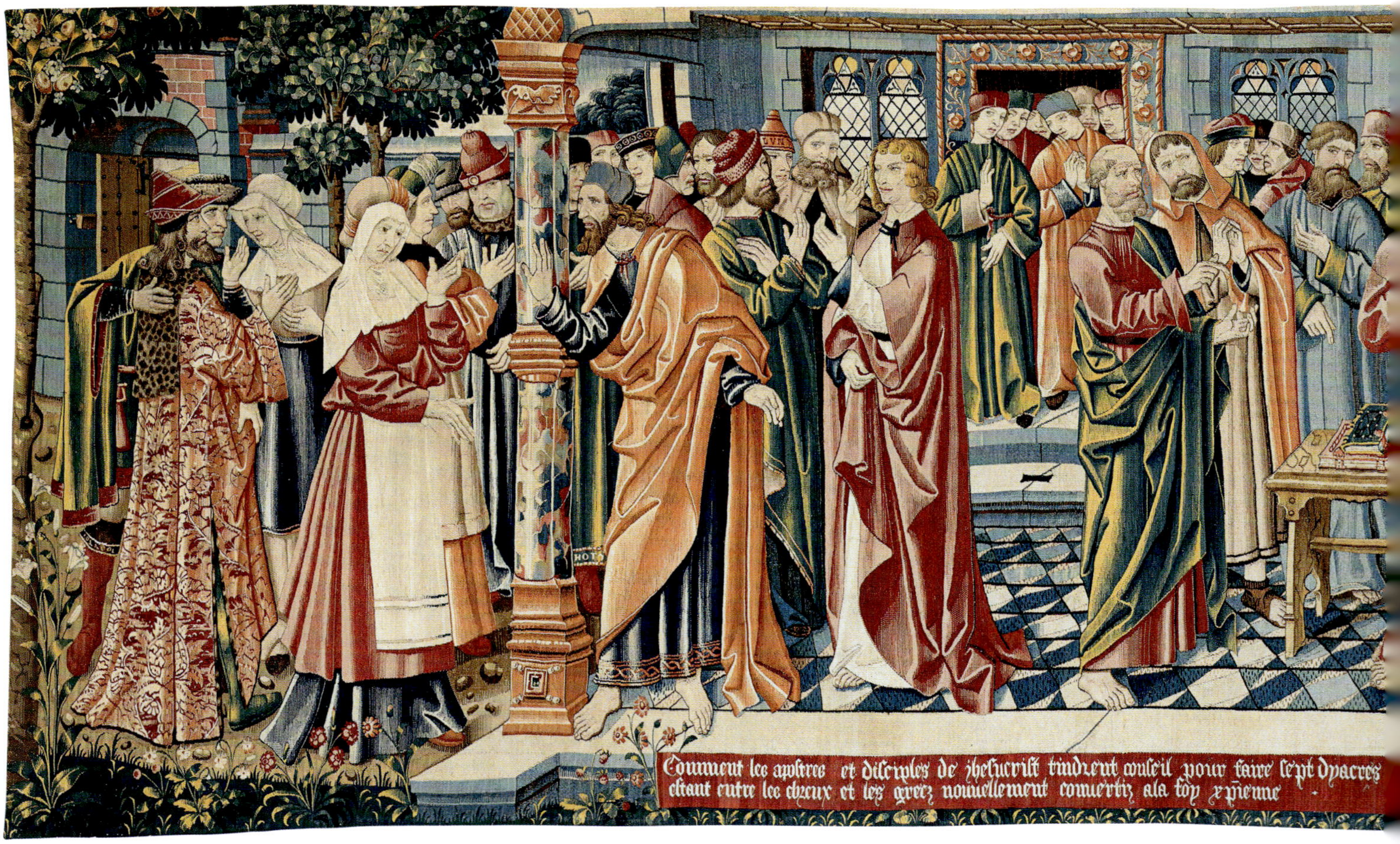

the cathedral's patron saint, according to the text of chapter six of the Acts of the Apostles and Jacobus de Voragine's *Golden Legend*.

There is no doubt that the creator of the cartoons was trained in the Low Countries, probably in Brussels (Joubert 1987). The style, garments, hairstyles, and decorative elements date these models incontestably to the years around 1500, for example, the heavy fabrics breaking into crumpled folds, next to slashed hose and beribboned hats set at an angle (scenes four and six). The locks of hair forming heavy masses that fall over the shoulders, the solid faces with their varied and often intense expressions, the demonstrative gestures, and the compositions organized in the service of narrative clarity—all identify a distinctive artistic personality. This artist could well have been Gauthier de Campes. The contract signed in 1503 between the chapter of Sens Cathedral and the Parisian master tapestry weaver and merchant Guillaume de Rasse for a series of tapestries of the life of Saint Stephen calls for the reuse of patterns that had been the model for a series on a smaller scale: the Sens tapestries were larger by an eighth (*un demi quartier*) at the top, at the bottom, and at the beginning, and a quarter (*un quartier*) at the end; the weaver was to supply the greenery (*verdure*) for the lower part. Two pieces of the series serving as a model had already come off the loom (contract of May 8, 1503; see Leproux 2001, pp. 190–91). Campes was paid for the cartoons for this tapestry in Sens (Hérold 1998, pp. 50–51, 55–57). This strong circumstantial evidence led Leproux (2001) to suppose that the first series was the one commissioned by Jean III Baillet for Auxerre, which has survived, while the one for Sens has disappeared, an identification that coincides with the tradition, admittedly unproven, that places the delivery date of the Auxerre *Life of Saint Stephen* in 1502. • ET-D

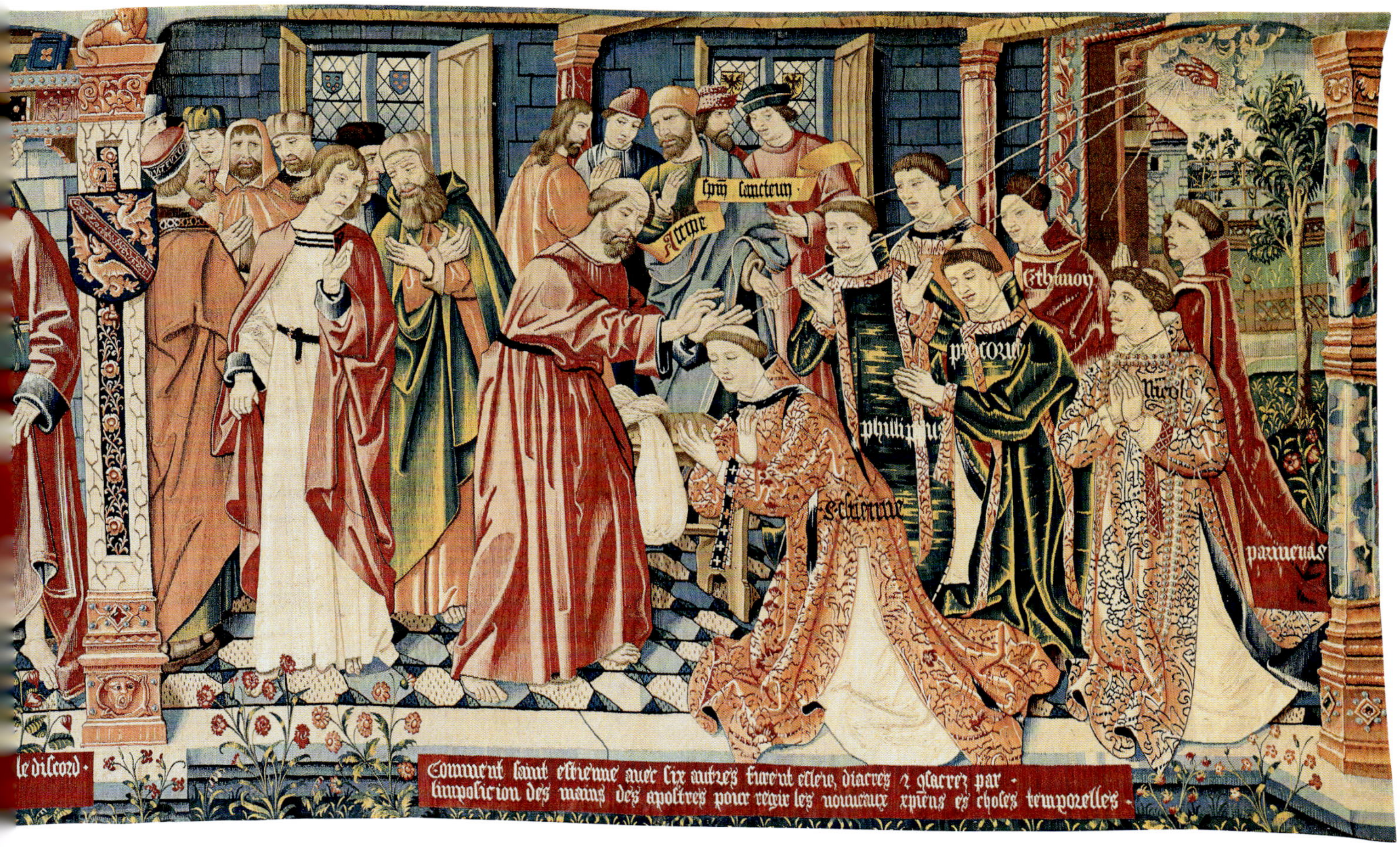

THE NORTH AND THE MIGRATION OF ARTISTS

FRÉDÉRIC ELSIG

During the era of Charles VIII and Louis XII, the artistic landscape that had been established at mid-century did not seem to be affected by the political transformations that followed the deaths of Charles the Bold, duke of Burgundy, in 1477, and of René of Anjou in 1480: namely the annexation of the territories of Picardy, Burgundy, and Provence to the kingdom of France. The cities of the Low Countries remained the principal sources of artistic models, which were transmitted along essentially two axes. One, which we associate with the region of Picardy, connected centers like Tournai, Amiens, Abbeville, and Paris. The other axis, which could be described as Burgundian, followed a commercial route through Châlons-en-Champagne, Troyes, and Dijon to Lyon and from there to Provence, along the Rhone.

The northern French or Picard axis promoted two trends, one conservative, the other more innovative. The former was linked to a phenomenon of regionalism, characteristic of this period, in which local production tended to rely on the inventions of the preceding generation. In Abbeville, the painter of the Thuison altarpiece (cats. 79–82) carried on and hardened the models of Rogier van der Weyden, employing a dry and incisive language that differed from the relative exuberance of the sculptors with whom he collaborated. This painting style was influential until around 1510, as panels of the life of Christ at the Musée des Beaux-Arts in Lyon confirm. In Paris, Nicolas d'Ypres (Colin d'Amiens) continued his long career and his multifaceted activity, as exemplified by the *Entombment* for the château of Malesherbes (today in the parish church; fig. 7) for which he supplied the pattern in 1495 (Grodecki 1996, pp. 329–34). His son Jean d'Ypres must be one and the same as the Master of the Very Small Hours of Anne of Brittany, whose production includes the cartoons for important tapestries like *The Lady and the Unicorn* (Musée national du Moyen Age, Paris), as well as designs for prints for books published by Philippe Pigouchet and Antoine Vérard (Reynaud in Paris 1993, p. 265). The conservative trend seemed to heighten around 1500, as if to better resist the attempts at modernization that were being made in this region of northern France, for example through the patronage of the *puys*, influential lay bodies in Abbeville and Amiens. The surviving wings from the Puy Notre-Dame d'Amiens establishing a parallel between the anointing of David and the coronation of Louis XII (cats. 30–31) interpret the experiences of the generation of Hugo van der Goes and Hans Memling on a simplified level, in reaction to the growing standardization of pictorial production, and perhaps mediated by the crossroads of influences that was the city of Tournai. But did Tournai still play the role it had in the mid-fifteenth century? The Master of Saint Giles, in all likelihood trained in Bruges, has recently been identified hypothetically by Guy-Michel Leproux with Gauthier de Campes, who seems to have made some of the stained-glass windows for Tournai Cathedral (fig. 5). Around 1500, he was established in Paris, where his serene vision dominated until a more tormented language arrived from the North, one devised in Antwerp in the circle of Jan de Beer and imported to Paris around 1512 by Noël Bellemare (Leproux 2001).

At the same time, the "Burgundian" axis presented an analogous dynamic. The conservative and regional trend is represented by the painters of stained glass windows active in Châlons-en-Champagne and in Troyes in particular, who extended and exaggerated the stylistic rigidity of the preceding generation. In certain respects, this trend can also be illustrated by Josse Lieferinxe. Originally from the northern border region of Hainaut, he fully adapted to the tradition of Provence, primed in the mid-fifteenth century by Enguerrand

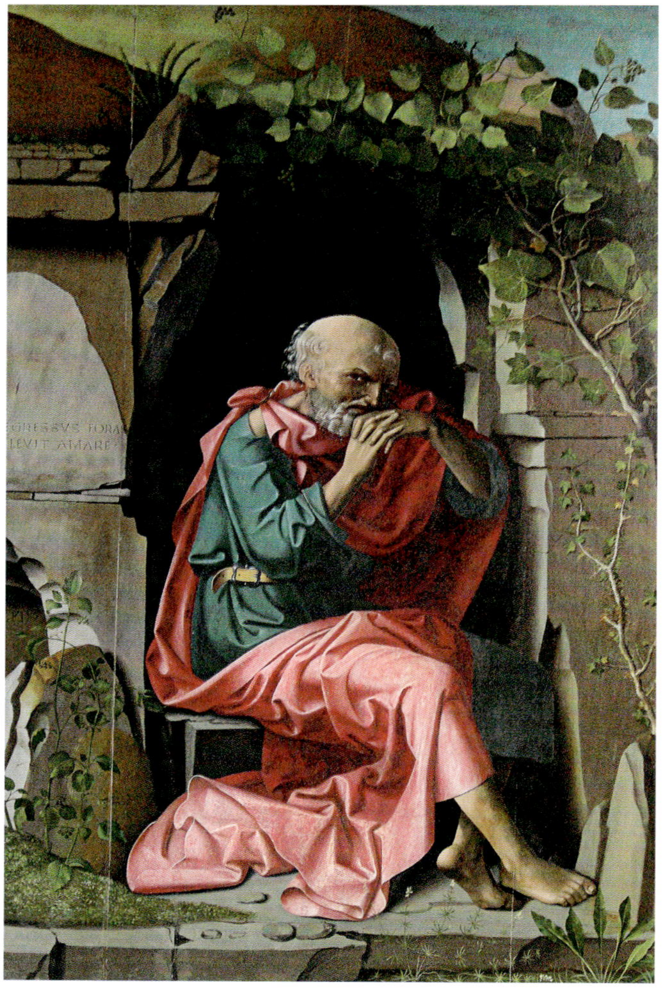

FIGURE 42.
Grégoire Guérard. *Saint Peter Penitent*. Church of Saint Mary Magdalene, Troyes.

Quarton, likewise from the Northeast. Lieferinxe's artistic intelligence nevertheless drove him, around 1500, to integrate new northern influences and to soften his style (Thiébaut in Paris 2004).

We can distinguish three successive waves that, promoted by this Burgundian axis and assimilated at different rhythms, bring forward new Netherlandish models. The first coincides with the activity of Jean Hey, who, receptive to the clarity of Hugo van der Goes, worked for Cardinal Jean Rolin (1408–1483) in Autun, and was then in the service of Cardinal Charles of Bourbon (died 1488) in Lyon, before becoming the court painter of the Bourbons in Moulins (Lorentz 2009b). The second wave, around 1500, is defined by a stylistic softening translated into a more fluid and dilute handling of paint and a more atmospheric treatment of light, as illustrated by the *Adoration of the Child* at the Musée du Petit Palais, Avignon, that resembles the work of Ayne Bru (active in Gerona and Albi, 1500/10; Laclotte and Thiébaut 1983, pp. 114, 272, no. 102). Finally, the third, starting in the second decade of the sixteenth century, corresponds with a transformation of the accustomed artistic landscape and with the influence of a new economic center—Antwerp.

Merchants of all nationalities converged in the port of Antwerp, which exported its production throughout Europe, particularly its carved and painted retables in an agitated style. What we have called the Burgundian axis did not escape from Antwerp's cultural impact. But this time period also saw the advance of a calmer trend originating in the northern provinces of the Netherlands and dominated by Grégoire Guérard. Related to Erasmus of Rotterdam, Guérard first lived in Troyes, where in 1512 he painted an extraordinary *Saint Peter Penitent* (fig. 42) showing the influence of northern Italy (Cécile Scailliérez concurs in the attribution; on Guérard, see Elsig 2005). Then he settled in southern Burgundy, where he produced several retables, imbued with the influence of Filippino Lippi and Leonardo and later by the inventions of Raphael as spread by engravings. Hence he embodied an Italianate northern style that, as early as the end of Louis XII's reign, coexisted with a more direct Italian current that was propelled by the importation of Italian works and artists.

PANELS FROM THE HIGH ALTAR OF THE CHARTERHOUSE OF SAINT-HONORÉ, THUISON-LES-ABBEVILLE

[79]

Virgin and Child

1490/1500

Oil on panel; 117.3 x 50.8 cm (46 3/16 x 20 in.); painted surface 116 x 49.5 cm (45 11/16 x 19 1/2 in.)

The Art Institute of Chicago, Mr. and Mrs. Martin A. Ryerson Collection, 1933.1054

[80]

Saint John the Baptist

1490/1500

Oil on panel; 117 x 52 cm (46 1/16 x 20 7/16 in.); painted surface 115.3 x 49.5 cm (45 3/8 x 19 1/2 in.)

The Art Institute of Chicago, Mr. and Mrs. Martin A. Ryerson Collection, 1933.1055

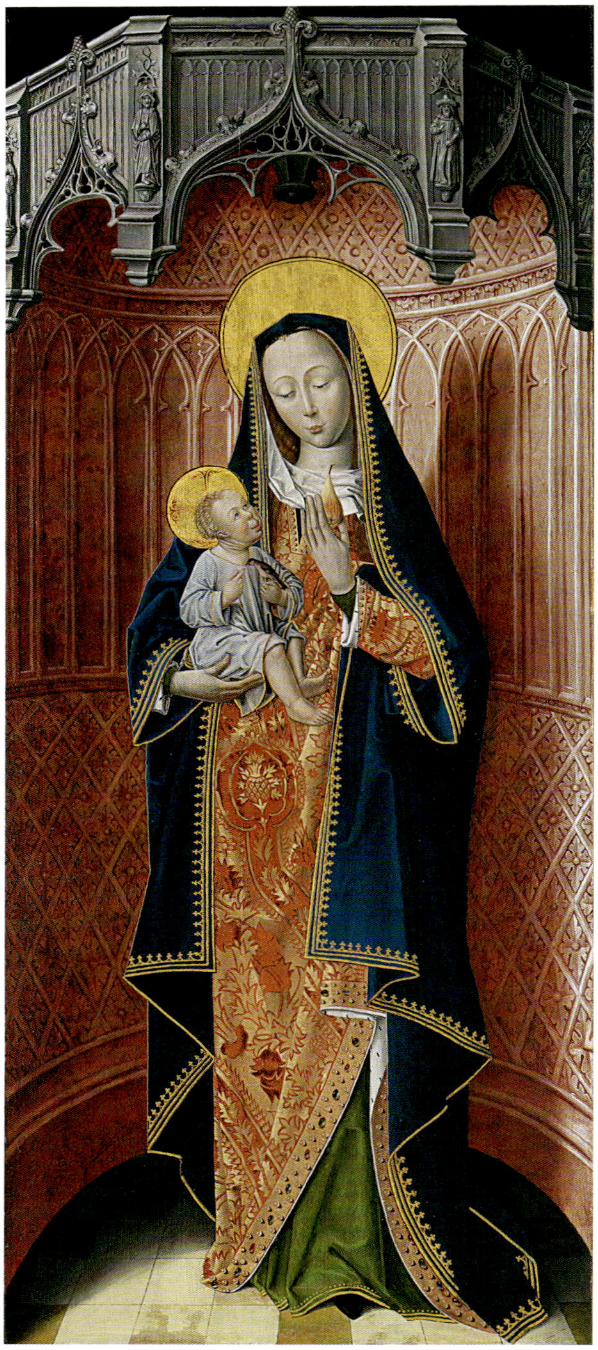

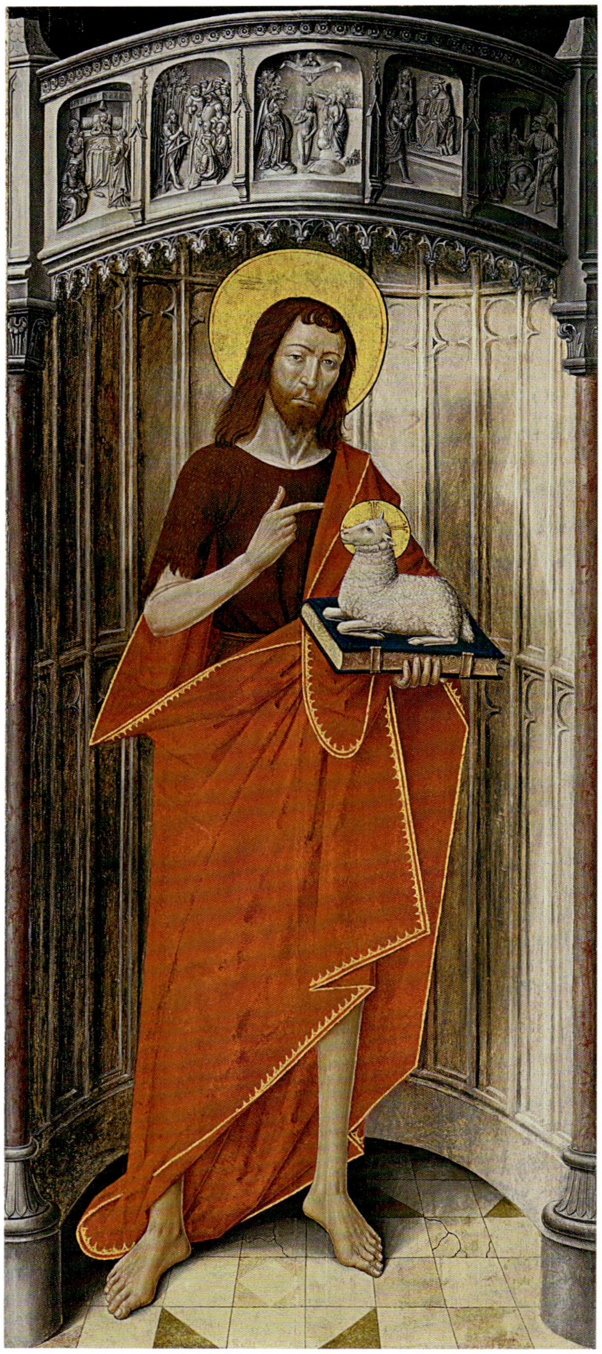

[81]

The Last Supper

1490/1500

Oil on panel; 117.2 x 50.9 cm (46 1/8 x 20 1/16 in.); painted surface 115.6 x 49.7 cm (45 1/2 x 19 9/16 in.)

The Art Institute of Chicago, Mr. and Mrs. Martin A. Ryerson Collection, 1933.1056

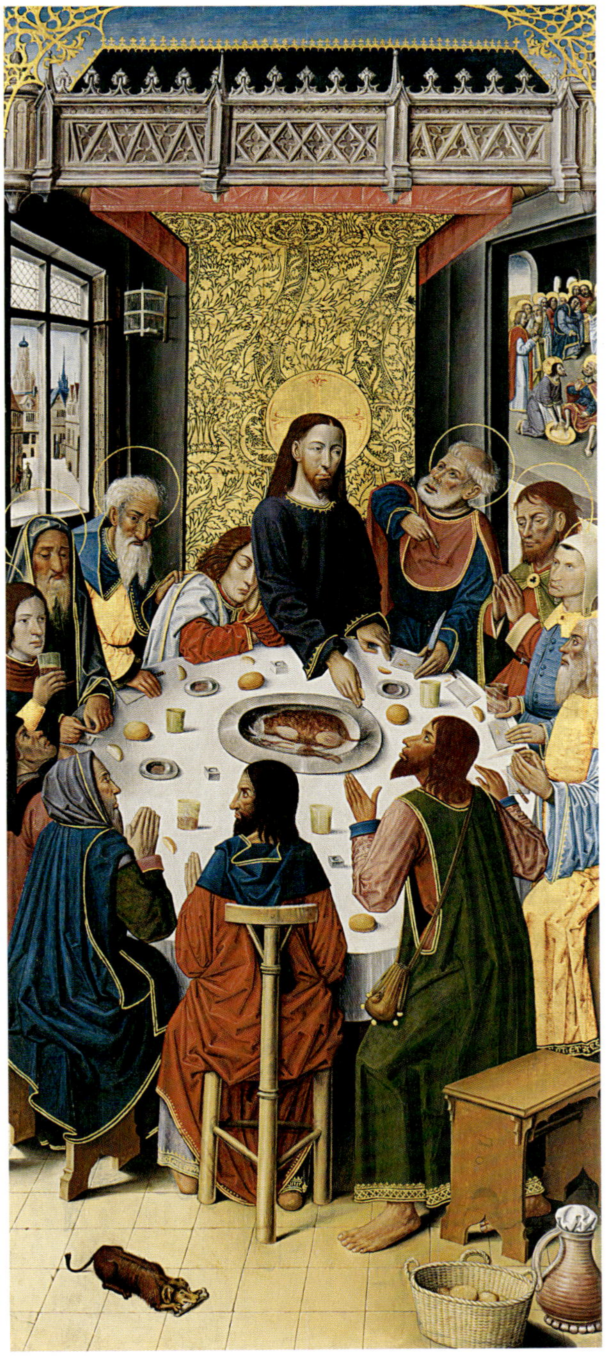

[82]

Pentecost

1490/1500

Oil on panel; 117 x 51.1 cm (46 1/16 x 20 1/8 in.); painted surface 115.1 x 49.4 cm (45 5/16 x 19 7/16 in.)

The Art Institute of Chicago, Mr. and Mrs. Martin A. Ryerson Collection, 1933.1058

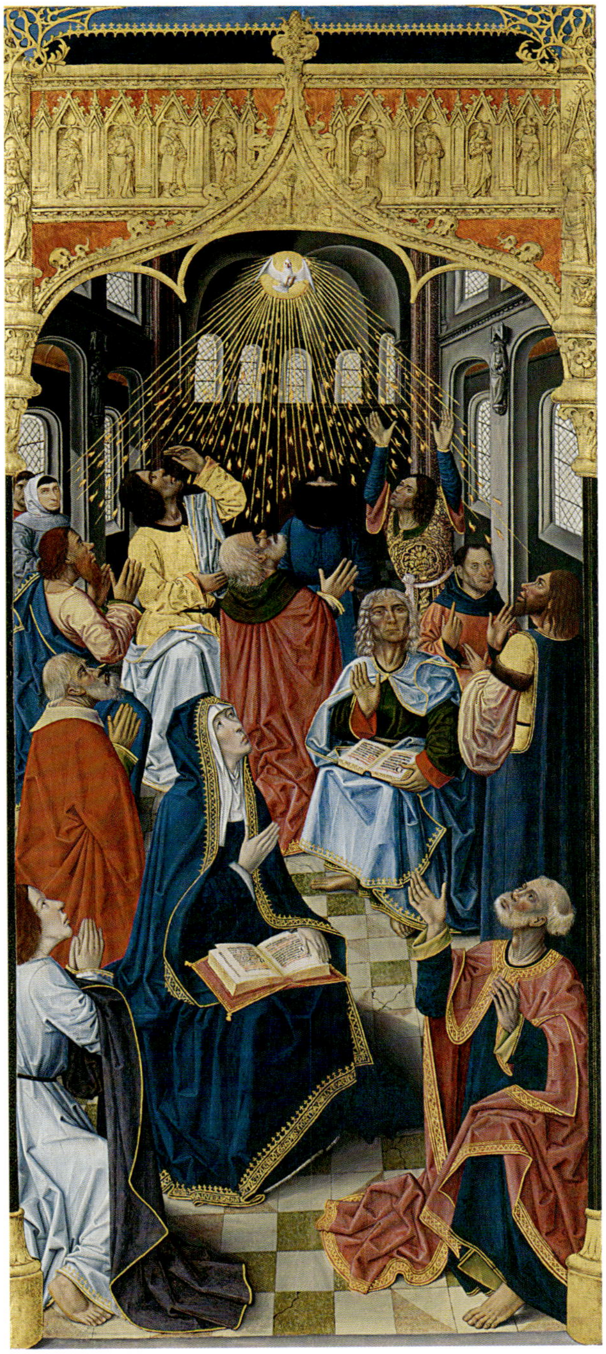

PROVENANCE: High altar, church of the charterhouse of Saint Honoré, Thuison-les-Abbeville, Picardy; sold, probably 1790/91; altarpiece wings acquired by Abbé Louis-Victor Cauchy (d. 1828), Abbeville; private collection, Abbeville; Convent of the Ursulines, Abbeville, 1873; Émile Delignières, Abbeville, by 1898 to 1902; Edmond Soyez, Amiens, 1902–04; Eugène Kraemer, Paris; sold, Galerie Georges Petit, Paris, June 2, 1913, nos. 17, 19, 20, 21, with three other panels, to Kleinberger, Paris, as agent for Martin A. Ryerson (d. 1932), Chicago; bequeathed to the Art Institute of Chicago.

BIBLIOGRAPHY: Prarond 1871–84, vol. 1, p. 356. Corblet 1868/75, vol. 3, p. 74, vol. 4, p. 321. Lefebvre 1885, pp. 166–67. Delignières 1898, pp. 5–43. Hulin de Loo 1902, pp. 84–85. Friedländer 1903, pp. 66–91, 147–75. Delignières 1905, pp. 18–28. Reinach 1905–23, vol. 5, p. 168. Dupont 1937, p. 37. Hoogewerff 1937–47, vol. 2, pp. 32–43, figs. 11, 14, 16. Sterling 1938, pp. 136–37, fig. 175. Sterling [Jacques] 1941, p. 62, no. 112. Ring 1949, pp. 105, 219, no. 169. Sterling 1970, pp. 31–32. Grössinger 1979, pp. 9–10, pl. 24B. Reynaud 1979, pp. 360–61. Sterling 1979, pp. 16–24, 42, figs. 11b–13d. Reynaud 1980, pp. 25–26. Châtelet 1985, p. 227. Bonnet-Laborderie 1986, pp. 34–39, figs. 24, 26. Bangs 1999, pp. 86–92, figs. 18, 22, 25. Béguerie-de Paepe 1999, pp. 67–68. Thiébaut 1999, p. 335. Gil 2000, p. 47. Béguerie-de Paepe in Abbeville 2001, pp. 48, 56, 66, 100–02, 147–50. Guillot de Suduiraut in Abbeville 2001, pp. 33, 35, 37, 43. Béguerie-de Paepe 2002, p. 82. Guillot de Suduiraut 2007, pp. 109, 119. Susan Jones in Wolff 2008, pp. 30–42.

EXHIBITIONS: Bruges 1902, no. 319 (*The Last Supper*). Paris 1904, no. 353. New York 1927, nos. 25, 26, 28, 29. Chicago 1933, no. 3. Chicago 1934, no. 3. Toledo 1935, nos. 37, 38 (*Pentecost*, *Virgin and Child*).

THE WINGS FROM THE high altar of the charterhouse of Saint-Honoré at Thuison-les-Abbeville are important evidence of the conservative painting style that flourished in Picardy about 1500. The Abbeville provenance of the paintings, the representations of the Carthusian saints Honoré and Hugh, and, most importantly, the connection of the sequence to descriptions and diagrams in Jean-François Boitel's late-eighteenth-century manuscript history of Abbeville (Bibliothèque municipale, Abbeville, ms. 447; Abbeville 2001, pp. 147–50), establish their presence on the high altar of the church of the charterhouse. The front and back of the panels were separated in the mid-nineteenth century, freeing the standing images of saints on the exterior from the narrative scenes of *The Entry into Jerusalem*, *The Last Supper*, *The Ascension*, and *Pentecost*. When the altarpiece was open on feast days, these narratives formed a sequence with the carved and gilded wooden reliefs of the Passion in the lost central shrine, which undoubtedly focused on the Crucifixion. Smaller paintings of Gabriel and the Virgin Annunciate, also now lost, were attached at the end of the wings to cover the shrine's raised center. When closed, the altarpiece showed, from left to right, Saint Honoré, the Virgin and Child, Saint John the Baptist, and Saint Hugh of Lincoln. This order, given in Boitel's manuscript, has been confirmed by examination of the panel structure. Except for *The Entry into Jerusalem*, which is in the Hermitage, Saint Petersburg, all the panels are preserved in the Art Institute of Chicago.

The sculpted centers from two smaller altarpieces from the charterhouse survive, but without their painted wings: the altarpiece of the Virgin (Abbeville 2001, no. 6) and the altarpiece of Saint Honoré (Le Crotoy). All three altarpieces were part of a program to refurbish the monastery following damage by the troops of Charles the Bold, duke of Burgundy; contributions towards this effort were solicited from 1478 into the 1490s and the portrait-like heads in the crowd watching Christ's entry into Jerusalem probably represent donors.

The surviving reliefs from Thuison and the painted wings in Chicago and Saint Petersburg share the same lack of concern for spatial recession and a preference for elongated figures and women with smooth, oval faces. In the painted narratives visible when the altarpiece was open, the abundant use of gold, the tracery elements in the upper corners, the brittle angularity of the figures, and the prominence of flat architectural decoration serve to integrate the pictorial vocabulary into the frieze-like treatment of a sculpted narrative. As Sue Jones demonstrated, the painted wings presumably date to the early 1490s, based on the headgear worn by the onlookers in the Saint Petersburg *Entry into Jerusalem* and the dating of the oak boards imported from the Baltic (Jones in Wolff 2008a, pp. 38–39).

The Thuison panels are closely related to other paintings from the region around Abbeville, including a votive panel from Ochancourt and wings in Saint-Riquier (Sterling 1979, figs. 7, 10). At the same time, the features and pose of the *Virgin and Child* are a distant reflection of the inventions of Rogier van der Weyden, although imbued with the somewhat bland naiveté of the local idiom; in *The Last Supper*, this style is applied to a composition made available through a print by the Dutch engraver IAM of Zwolle, which may itself have reproduced a sculptural model. The paintings from Thuison cannot be characterized as the work of a distinct hand, but reflect a workshop style that must have found ample expression in a period of flourishing activity for the many churches of this city at the estuary of the Somme. This local manner was at once conservative and open to influences from the urban centers in the Low Countries, with which the region had so many ties of history and trade. • MW

[83]

Virgin and Child

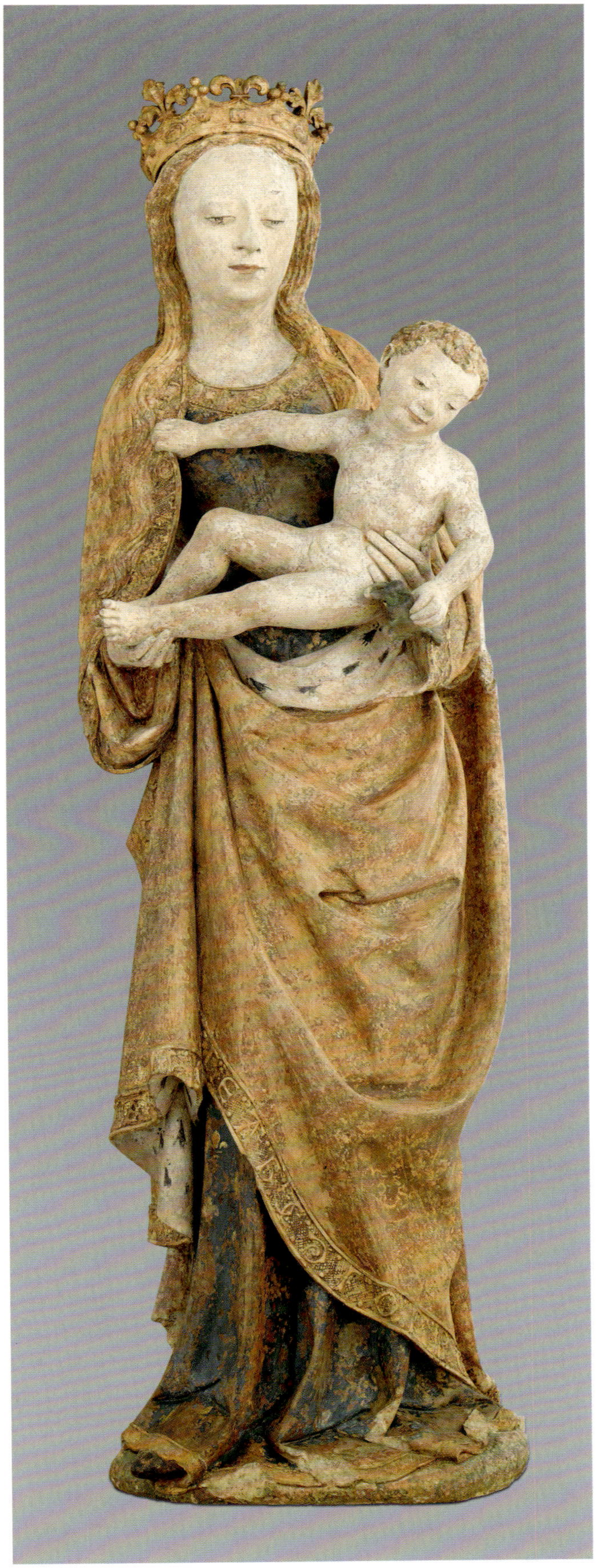

Normandy, c. 1500

White chalk with flint inclusions (Vernon limestone), polychromed; 162 x 51 x 42.5 cm (63¹³/16 x 20¹/16 x 16³/4 in.)

Musée du Louvre, Paris, Department of Sculpture, RF 2201

PROVENANCE: Collection of Charles and Georges Lormier, Rouen; sold, Lormier sale, Hôtel Drouot, Paris, April 8–9, 1921, no. 154; George and Florence Blumenthal, Paris and New York; gift of George Blumenthal, in his name and that of his wife (d. 1930), 1932.

BIBLIOGRAPHY: Beaulieu 1950, no. 373. Baron 1996, p. 198.

THIS *Virgin and Child* is one of a group of large-scale statues originating from Normandy. Here the powerful stability of the figure of Mary contrasts with the joyful movement of the baby Jesus, who is turned toward the faithful. The most obvious resemblances are to several statues of the Virgin and Child, those of Saint-Martin d'Hamelin, Saint-Germain-sur-Ay, Orglandes, and Vrétot, which are situated largely on the Cotentin peninsula, as well as to other statues located further east in the Eure, in particular those at Tilleul-Dame-Agnès, or to the *Entombment* of Verneuil. There too the highly decorative detail of the sculpted orphery bands appears, embellished with letters in relief, with no significance except as ornament. Probably the closest comparison is to the statue of Maucomble, Seine-Maritime, in which the Child—again naked, in contrast to older examples—has the same gangly, almost awkward look. It is evident that an iconographic type was in circulation in the extensive territory of the Norman dioceses, and that different sculptors adapted it according to their own style. The iconographic variants differ in their ways of indicating the role of the future Savior. At times, he holds the orb of the ruler of the world; elsewhere, including the present example, he holds a bird that may represent the clay sparrows that he will bring to life, according to a passage from the Apocryphal Gospels. Following Julie André Madjlessi's examination of the work and the subsequent restoration she undertook in collaboration with Agnès Le Boudec, the sculpture has recovered something of its original appearance. This includes polychromy of a surprising quality, laid over a red preparation that is clearly evident in the numerous losses. The Child holds a bird of an extraordinary vivid green. The Virgin wears a blue dress with a pattern of gold fleurs-de-lis and gold edging. Her cloak, decorated with mordant gilding, is further embellished with a pattern painted with a maroon glaze. The cloak's lining is represented as ermine fur. This insistence on royal emblems, further reinforced by the tall crown with fleur-de-lis fleurons, may indicate a prestigious origin, perhaps from a Norman abbey enjoying royal patronage. • GB-B

JOSSE LIEFERINXE
(active 1493–1508)

PANELS FROM AN ALTARPIECE OF SAINT SEBASTIAN, SAINT ANTHONY, AND SAINT ROCH

[84]

Saint Sebastian Destroying the Idols

Marseille, 1497/98

Oil on wood; 81.3 x 54.8 cm (32 x 21 9/16 in.)

Philadelphia Museum of Art, The John G. Johnson Collection, 1917, cat. 765

PROVENANCE, BIBLIOGRAPHY: See below.

EXHIBITION: Pittsburgh 1951, no. 40.

[85]

Saint Sebastian Tended by Irene

Marseille, 1497/98

Oil on wood; 81.3 x 54.8 cm (32 x 21 9/16 in.)

Philadelphia Museum of Art, The John G. Johnson Collection, 1917, cat. 767

PROVENANCE: Church of Notre-Dame-des-Accoules, Marseille; probably among the six panels of the life of Saint Stephen in the collection of Queen Christina of Sweden, Rome, at the time of her death in 1689, as Mantegna, and the seven panels cited in the 1721 inventory of the remains of her collection (Sterling 1968, p. 9 n. 18); Haskard, Florence, until 1899; Agnew, London; sold to John G. Johnson, 1900; bequeathed to the Philadelphia Museum of Art, 1917.

BIBLIOGRAPHY: Albanès 1884. Sterling [Jacques] 1941. Sterling 1942. Haverkamp Begemann 1958, pp. 19–27, fig. 4. Johnson Collection 1953, pp. 222, 224. Sterling 1964a. Laclotte and Thiébaut 1983, pp. 256–60, no. 86. Gozzano 1994. Léandri-Morin 1997. Paris 2004, pp. 142–53.

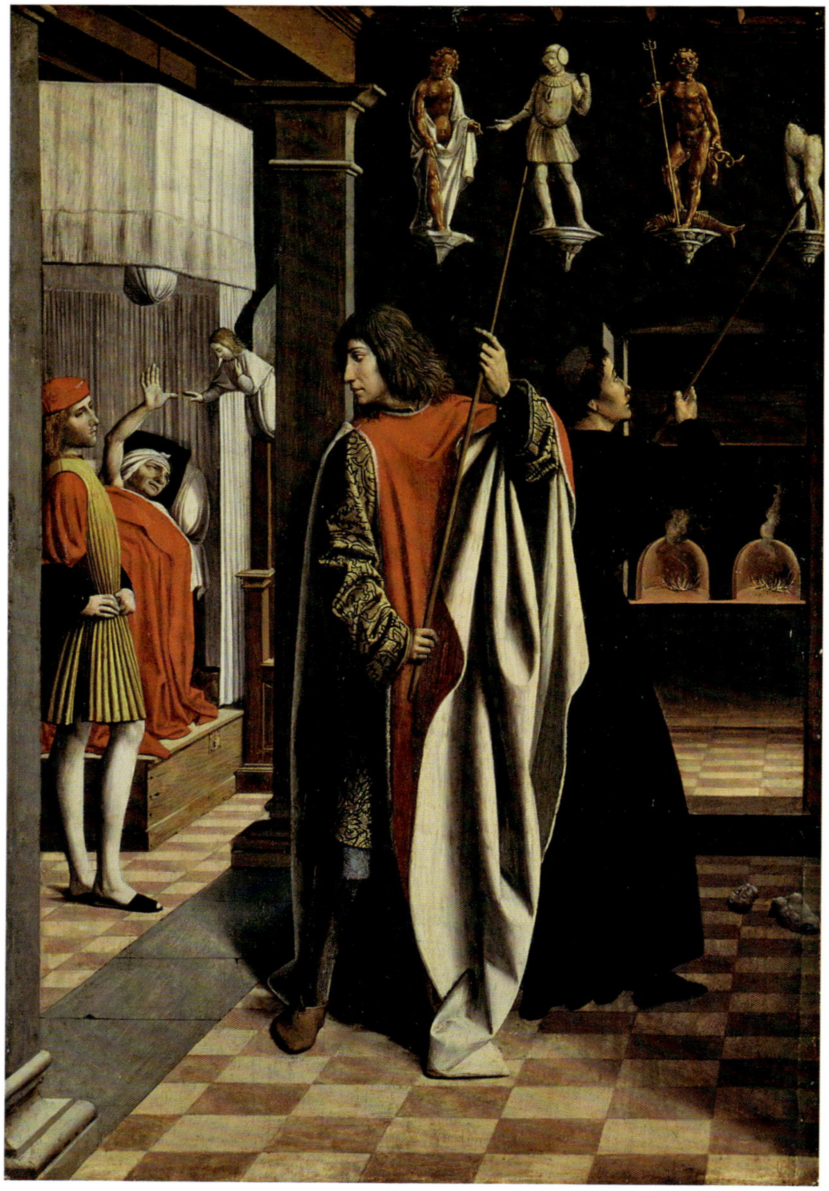

IN JULY 1497, the confraternity of Saint Sebastian of Marseille, which met in the church of Notre-Dame-des-Accoules, commissioned a large retable that showed three saints who protected against the plague as its center—Saint Sebastian appearing between saints Anthony and Roch—as well as eight lateral scenes from the life of Sebastian. Preserved in Philadelphia, Baltimore, Rome, and Saint Petersburg, seven of these side panels had been attributed to the Master of Saint Sebastian, whom critics have now identified as Josse Lieferinxe, after Sterling (1941) connected the paintings with the 1497 contract. This document involved two associated painters, Bernardo Simondi from Piedmont and Josse Lieferinxe. Simondi died in 1498, and the tendency has been to credit him only with the designs and with the Piedmontese influences evident in the panels, while attributing their execution to Lieferinxe alone, along with other related works. Faced with the historical evidence, it seems possible to distinguish two different hands at work on five of the seven panels. One is that of a painter who used more crowded, anecdotal compositions, and whose emotional tenor and certain iconographic details can be linked to Piedmont, whether this was Bernardo himself or one of the numerous painters from that region who were active in lower Provence, and whom Josse could have called on for help when he needed to finish the

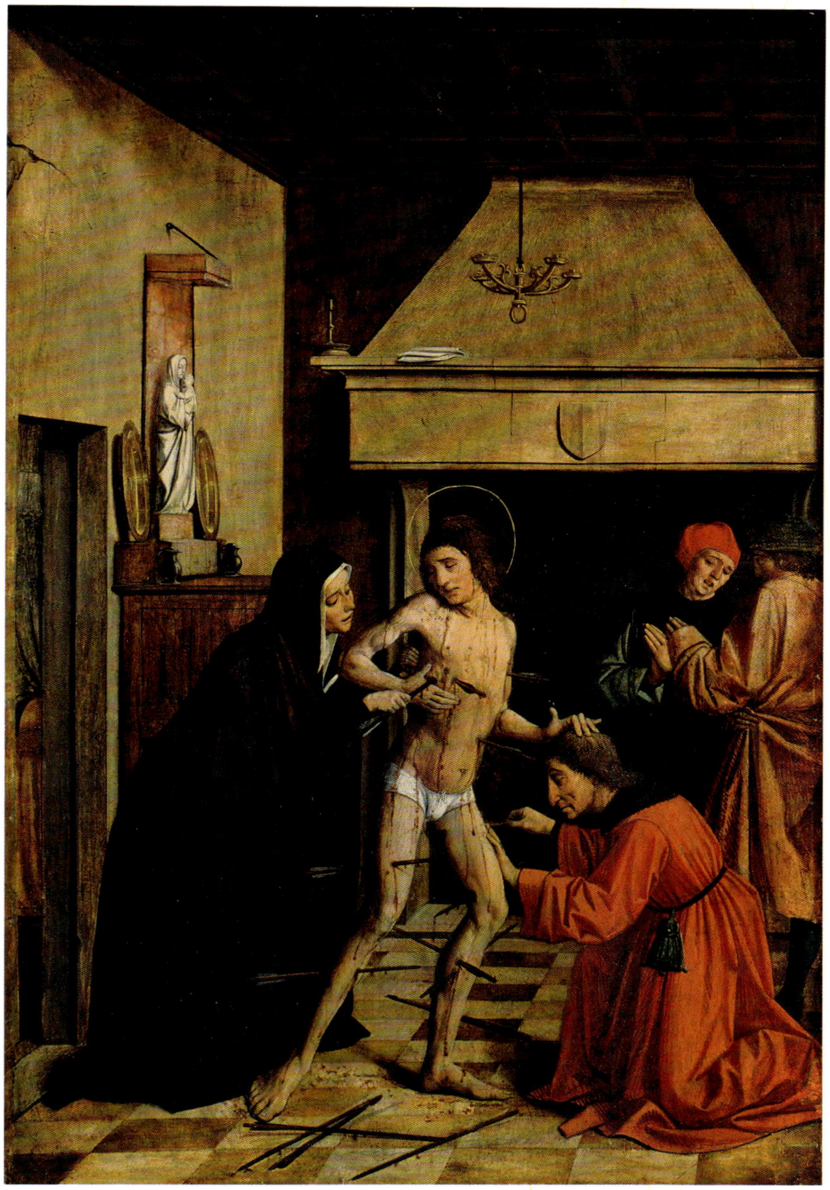

retable. The other is that of a painter of Flemish origin, as even the name Lieferinxe suggests, close as it is to Lieferinghe, a village near Enghien in Hainaut on the border of France and Flanders.

The two panels exhibited here are typical of the style of Lieferinxe. In *Saint Sebastian Destroying the Idols*, the saint and his companion, Polycarp, cure a Roman official of gout by destroying the idols he worshipped. The eye is drawn to the great white swath of the lining of the saint's cape, the pivot point between the two principal groups of figures. Josse often introduced a long counterpoint of light color, white or yellow, that both provides luminosity, forming a contrast with an adjacent saturated or dark color, and emphasizes a line of force in the composition. The elegant young man at the left is the official's son; he keeps an eye on his suffering father, on the two Christians, and on the flames of the ovens that have been prepared for them should their efforts fail. His watchfulness is indicated by the inclination of his head and his hands grasping his belt, while the strong light striking his legs and the patterned pleats of his doublet emphasize his stillness. The folds of the bed curtains form equally strong verticals, contrasting with the more dynamic draperies of Sebastian and Polycarp.

The scene of *Saint Sebastian Tended by Irene* is set in an architectural framework that is just as rigorously constructed, but depicted in a more intimate manner, as the subject requires. Sebastian has survived an attempt at execution and is nursed back to health by Irene. A brass candlestick stands on the mantelpiece and the dresser is decorated—even the hook that secures the canopy over the statue of the Virgin and Child is shown. Lieferinxe's figures exhibit characteristic restraint: Sebastian's pain is revealed only by the clenching of his hand, and the two figures caring for him are deeply attentive but show no emotion.

The cult of Saint Sebastian, reinforced by recurrent outbreaks of the plague, was widespread in the south of France and, in contrast to what has often been written, images of the saint are not rare. In western Provence alone, over twenty commissions for such paintings are documented between 1451 and 1530, six of them coming, as at Marseille, from confraternities named after the saint. They are often small altarpieces, with Sebastian presented as a standing figure, as in the panels in Saint-Maximin, Pertuis, and Pélissane. To find the equivalent of the narrative richness of the retable from Notre-Dame-des-Accoules, it is necessary to look to wall paintings and to a neighboring region: nine Sebastian cycles from the end of the fifteenth and the beginning of the sixteenth century exist in eastern Provence, while seven other painted chapels can be found in neighboring regions of Italy (Léandri-Morin 1997). However, the selection of episodes varies from one cycle to another. The destruction of pagan idols appears in Lanslevillard, Venanson, and Ceillac, although the subject is treated in different ways. The scene of Irene tending Sebastian is not found elsewhere. The written versions of the Passion of Saint Sebastian that circulated in the Alpine areas must have differed from that available to the members of the Marseille confraternity. • MC-L

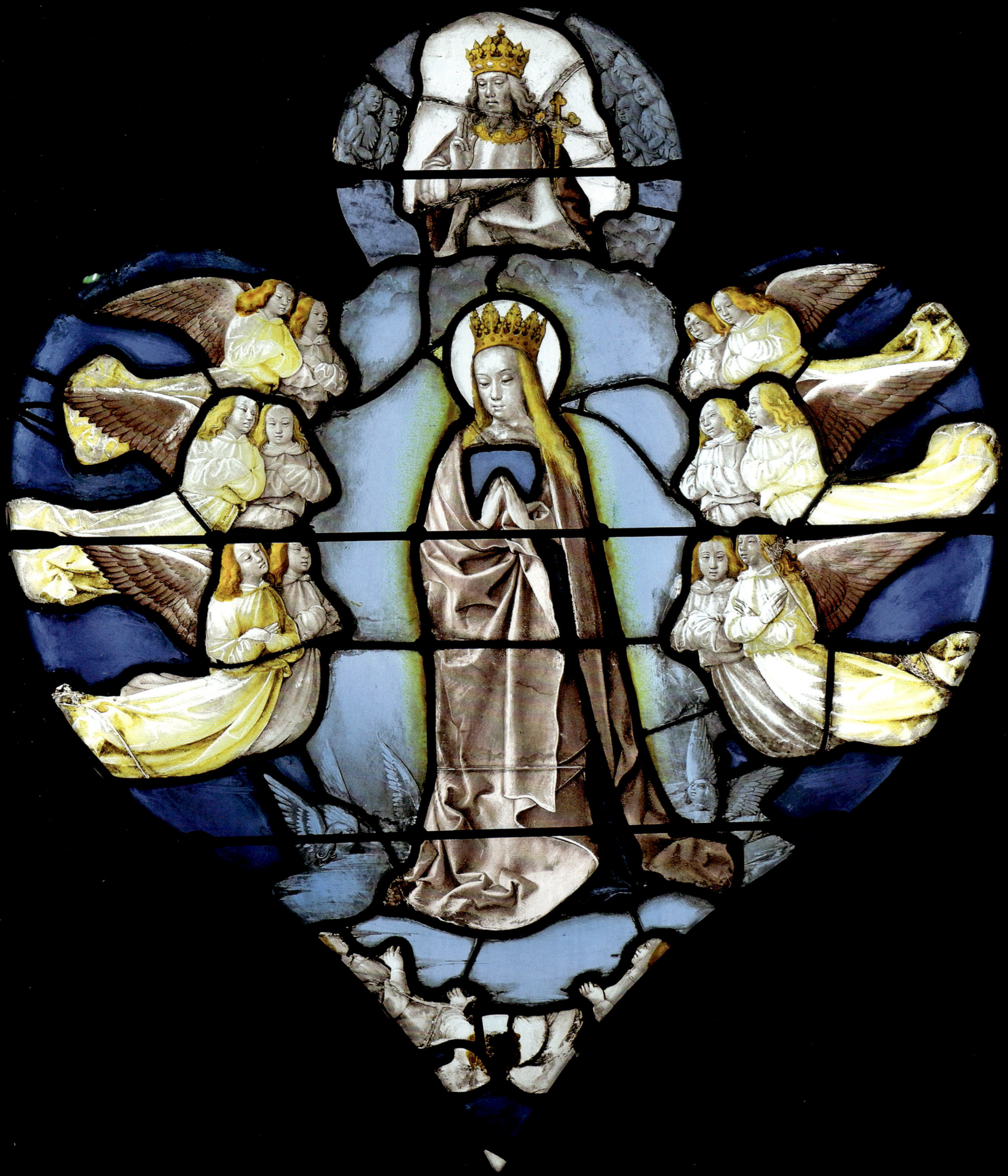

THE DIFFUSION OF THE WORK OF ART

ÉLISABETH TABURET-DELAHAYE AND SÉVERINE LEPAPE

The impetus to create images in multiples and the corollary effect, the tendency to break up the creation of the work of art into a series of steps, were among the most significant developments in the period around 1500, the date generally accepted as the transition from the Middle Ages to the Renaissance in northern Europe. Paradoxically, this period of transition was also defined by an emerging awareness of the dignity of the individual artist.

Admittedly, the reuse of models was not a novelty. Nor was it new for painters to provide models for stained glass windows, tapestries, embroideries, and even sculptures. But in this period this phenomenon took on an unprecedented scope. This was certainly due in part to the success of relatively new forms of artistic expression, such as medals, and above all to the revolution of printing. These technical factors, however, were accompanied by other developments: the evolution of the taste of the public, the need to respond to a demand that was not always directed toward unique, original works, and the organization of printers, booksellers, and other merchants and intermediaries. Thus the graphic arts rapidly assumed a dominant position, with the book playing a major role. Yet the advent of printmaking and the printed book, far from supplanting the activities of the illuminators, gave them greater prominence and offered new outlets for their work. Often the same artists illuminated manuscript pages and contributed to the production of printed books. They responded to the most prestigious commissions, but also provided a significant output for the market stalls that were the purview of booksellers, especially in Paris. Some of them, including the Parisian artists known as the Master of the Chronique Scandeleuse, the Master of Robert Gaguin, and the Master of Jacques de Besançon, as well as Guillaume Leroy of Lyon (both elder and younger), developed lucrative and multifaceted businesses, being well able to adapt a book for a particular clientele (fig. 44; cats. 28–29).

Others became true entrepreneurs. Having inherited or acquired a stock of models from the previous generation, they developed a broad range of artistic production, extending their activities beyond the domain of books to tapestry and stained glass, where they sometimes employed the same compositions, motifs, and ornamentation. The best-known example is certainly the Master of the Very Small Hours of Anne of Brittany. The reconstruction of the body of work of this artist, who was a member of the third generation of a family of painters active in Paris, has been the result of research over the the last forty years (primarily by Souchal 1973; Avril and Reynaud 1993; Delaunay 2000; Nettekoven 2004; and Lorentz in Paris 2004). Nicole Reynaud proposed the identification of these painters with members of the same family, originally from Ypres, who are mentioned in notarized documents: the Master of Dreux Budé with André d'Ypres, active between 1428 and 1450; the Coëtivy Master as his son Colin d'Amiens, also known as Nicolas d'Ypres (active before 1450–died 1497/1500); and the Master of the Very Small Hours of Anne of Brittany as Jean d'Ypres, one of the sons of Colin d'Amiens, active between 1490 and 1508. The grouping of works provided in this exhibition is not intended to verify the accuracy of these attributions, but rather to help us understand the varied means by which stylistic elements were disseminated, extending

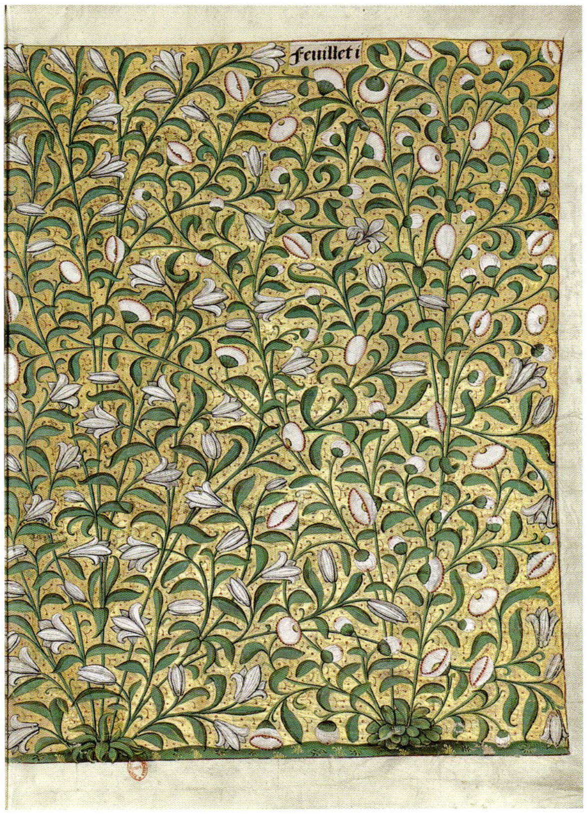

FIGURE 44.
Master of the Chronique Scandaleuse.
Page of Intertwined Lilies and Daisies, in *La Mer des hystoires* (cat. 28).
Tempera and gold on vellum. Bibliothèque nationale de France, Department of Rare Books, Réserve Vélins 677, f. A2r.

Facing Page

FIGURE 43.
Probably after Jean Hey (The Master of Moulin). *The Virgin in Glory*, from the window of the Popillon family (cat. 68). Stained glass. Cathedral of Notre-Dame, Moulins.

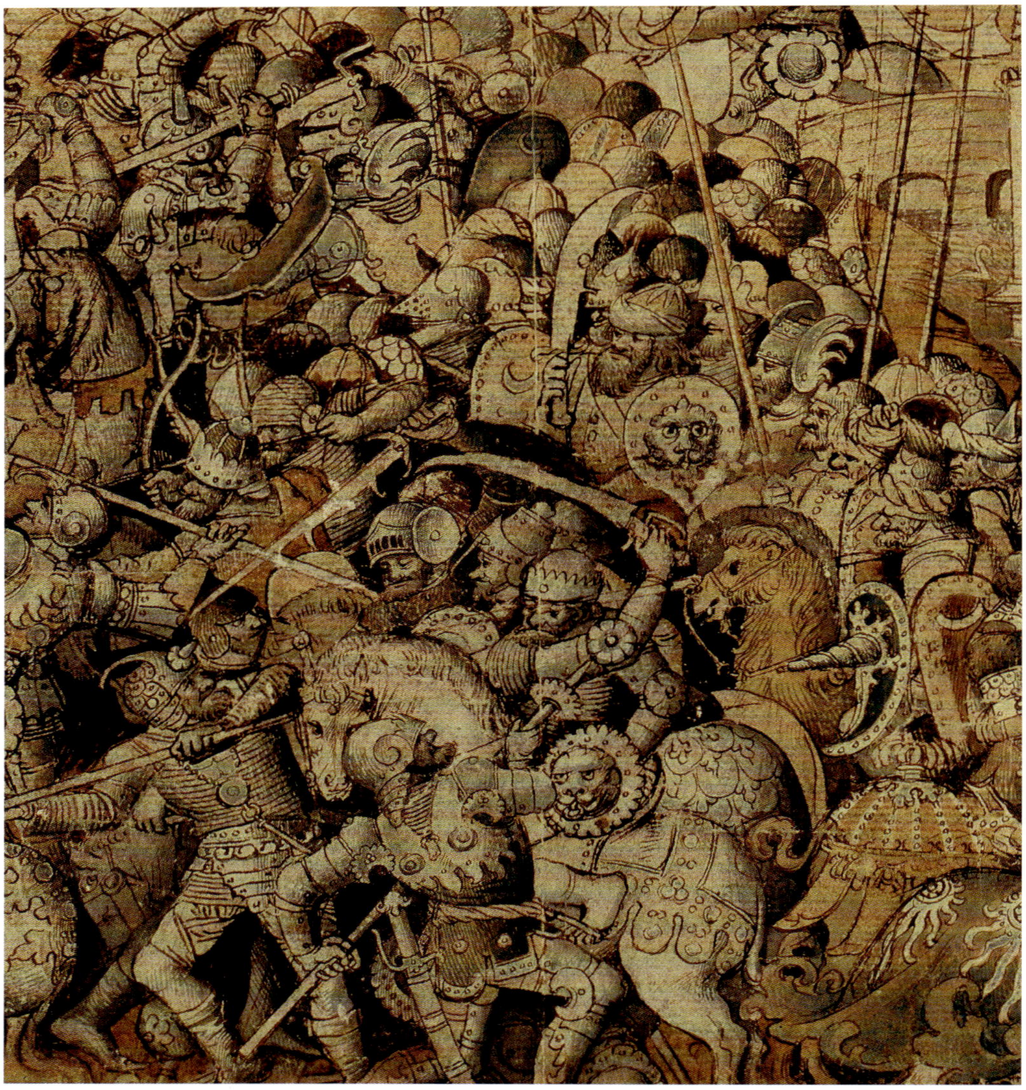

FIGURE 45.
Master of Coëtivy (Colin d'Amiens?). Detail of *The Fourth Battle, the Taking of King Thoas, and the Chamber of Beauty* (cat. 10).
Musée du Louvre, Paris, Department of Graphic Arts, RF 2142.

beyond the notion of the workshop. The absence of homogeneity among works in the so-called Ypres style, as well as their production in quantity over an extended period of time, leads to the supposition that several other Parisian painters adopted this style. Furthermore, the transposition of a design to a glass painting, a tapestry, or an engraving raises the possibility of an intermediary, whose interpretation would be reflected in the design as it was passed on, while the long life of motifs and compositions is evidence that models were transmitted across several generations and proof of the complexity of their circulation (fig. 45).

The development of new avenues of artistic expression also facilitated the dissemination of particular themes and types of ornamentation. The taste for *exempla* characteristic of medieval thought inspired depictions of renowned women of antiquity and female allegorical figures (figs. 46–47) or of scenes in the mode of "triumphs" like those in Petrarch's writings, which had been recently translated into French and illustrated *à l'antique*. One taste did not necessarily supplant another. Symmetrical or asymmetrical window tracery, and the gables and pinnacles of the flamboyant Gothic style, appeared side by side with putti, profiles set within medallions, and masks and classical candelabra in the ornamentation on architecture and furniture. The art of the book was again one of the principal stimulants: ornamentation in manuscript borders sometimes featured traditional vegetal scrollwork, sometimes naturalistic representations of plant and animal specimens—Jean Bourdichon was one of the foremost exponents of the latter approach—and sometimes a classicizing vocabulary. But if Ferdinand of Aragon recruited the Italian Todeschino to paint the trompe l'oeil borders of his book of hours, it was a Netherlandish artist who, in Genoa, decorated the borders of the *Chroniques* of Enguerrand Monstrelet made for François de Rochechouart with profiles of Roman emperors surrounded by rich Italianate ornament (cat. 111). Meanwhile, during the same period,

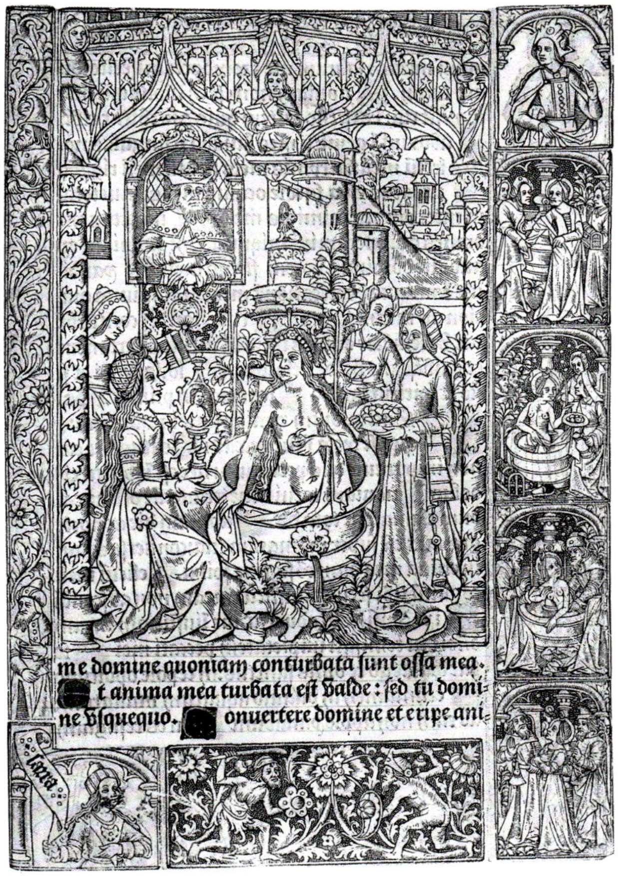

FIGURE 46.
After the Master of the Very Small Hours of Anne of Brittany (Jean d'Ypres?). *Bathsheba at Her Bath*, from a book of hours for the use of Paris. Metalcuts on vellum. Bibliothèque nationale de France, Department of Rare Books, Réserve Vélins 2912, f. F7r.

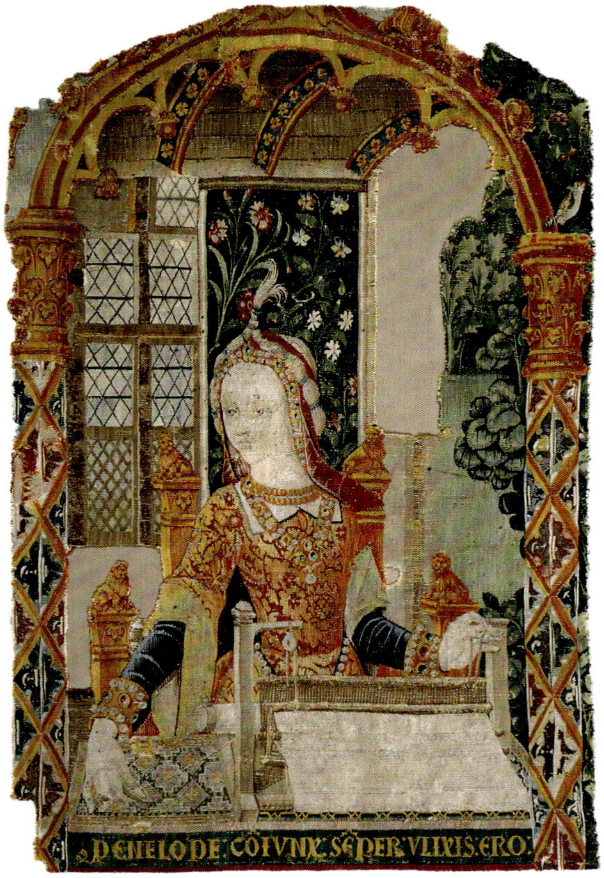

FIGURE 47.
After the Master of the Very Small Hours of Anne of Brittany (Jean d'Ypres?). *Penelope*, a fragment from a suite of tapestries of *Virtuous Women*. Tapestry. Museum of Fine Arts, Boston, Maria Antoinette Evans Fund, 1926.54.

the Norman Jean Serpin was concocting a lively blend of decorative languages for Georges d'Amboise's manuscripts.

The artistic exuberance of the late fifteenth and early sixteenth centuries was also evident in the variety of materials employed and the way they were used. The appearance of the new technique of painted enamel, and the success of the new methods for producing multiple images, including medals and printed books, did not overshadow more traditional art forms, such as tapestry and stained glass, which experienced innovations as well. Stained glass adopted a layering technique, which permitted a play of colors between two superimposed pieces of glass by cutting or engraving a design into the upper layer (see cat. 75). Workshops were capable of supplying very large windows for the numerous religious structures built or renovated during this period, but they also produced smaller panels, usually roundels, intended as decoration for the windows of secular buildings (see cat. 5). The art of tapestry weaving, which had flourished since the second half of the fourteenth century, responded to the desire of princes, the administrative class, and the wealthy bourgeoisie to endow the interiors of their castles or town houses with luxury in the taste of the day (cat. 77). It also responded to the demands of a religious clientele, particularly bishops and chapters of canons, who wanted large hangings to drape over their choir enclosures on feast days (see cat. 78). Tapestries with millefleurs backgrounds, which were very popular from about 1480 to 1530, were a response to the need to provide, rapidly and at a lower cost, pieces that were much in demand for their themes and decorative qualities. If it is impossible to attribute a given hanging to a particular weaver with certainty in the absence of documentary evidence, the models, on the other hand, can often be associated with a center or even an individual painter through comparison with other pictorial arts.

Whether for stained glass or for tapestry, the creative process usually involved several steps. The *petit patron* or model was provided by a painter (fig. 45), then the cartoon, a drawing in the scale of the finished work was made, as the basis for the glass painting or weaving itself. But there were many variations in this process, depending on the complexity of the theme, the prestige of the patron, the urgency for completion, and most importantly the financial means available.

[86]

Book of Hours for the Use of Limoges

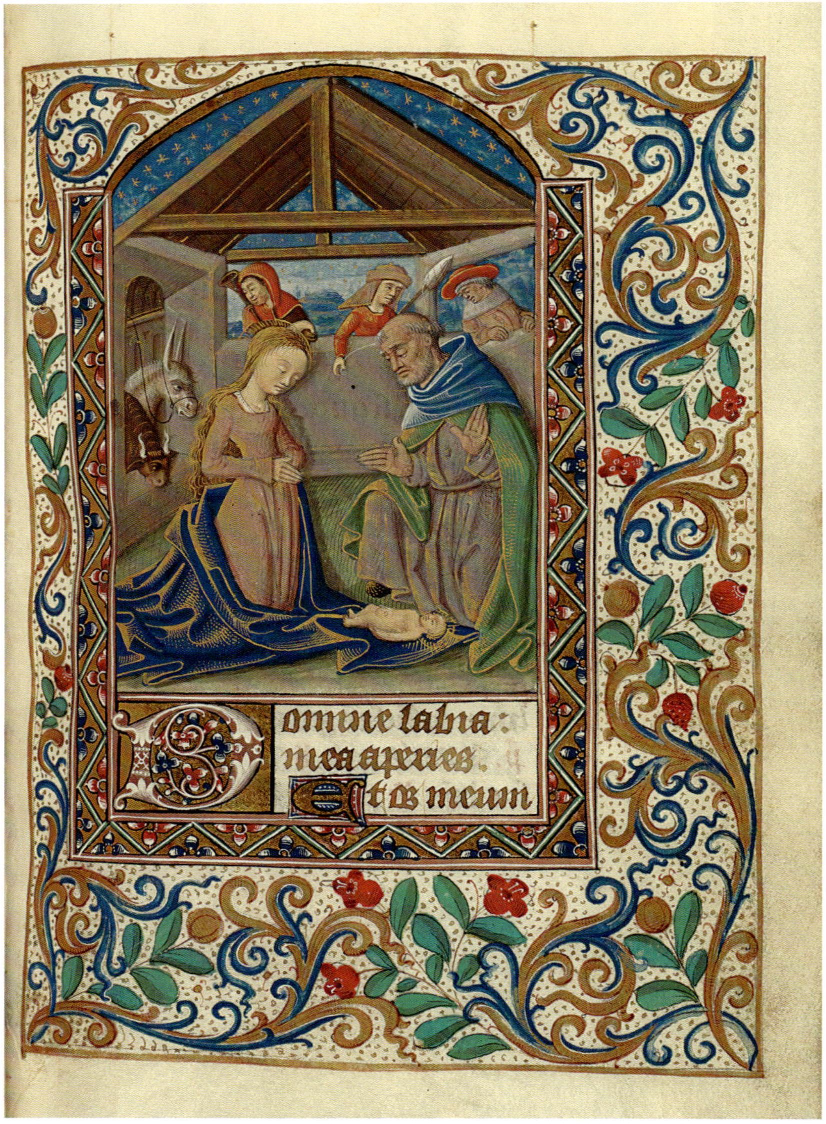

Limoges, 1480/1500

Tempera and gold on parchment; 182 ff.; 21.5 x 14 cm (8 7/16 x 5 1/2 in.) (leaf)

The Art Institute of Chicago, gift of Mrs. John J. Borland and Friends, 1915.540

INSCRIBED: *Ex libris*, repeated on front flyleaf: *Aquestas mandinas sont. Katarine Gentille Molh(er) de Marsau deubost demorant en la rue de las Taulas oupres de St. Marsau.* [These hours belong to Katherine Gentille, wife of Martial Dubois, living in the rue De Taulas near the abbey of Saint-Martial.]

PROVENANCE: Katherine Gentille, wife of Martial Dubois, Limoges, France, late fifteenth century [according to inscription on flyleaf]. Wilfrid F. Voynich, London, by 1915; sold to the museum, 1915.

BIBLIOGRAPHY: Bulletin 1916, p. 144. De Ricci 1935–40, vol. 1, p. 515. Ross 1941, pp. 9–25. Verdier 1967, pp. xvii, 27, 29. Caroselli 1993, p. 72. Baratte 2000, p. 38. Hindman 2008, p. 20.

EXHIBITIONS: Chicago 1969, no. 20. De Ricci 1935–40, vol. 1, p. 515. Ross 1941, pp. 9–25. Verdier 1967, pp. xvii, 27.

SHOWN: *The Nativity*, f. 83

IN 1941, ROSS was the first scholar to associate the miniatures in this book of hours from Limoges with the style of early painted enamels, particularly those attributed to the Master of the Baltimore and Orléans Triptychs. He suggested that this master was in fact both an "enameller and painter," an argument that successive scholars have generally reaffirmed (Kessler in Chicago 1969; Caroselli 1993). Verdier (1967) stopped short of attributing these miniatures directly to him, but claimed that it was indeed plausible that they came from the workshop of an artist who worked on enamels and illuminations.

In fact, many points of comparison can be drawn between the distinctive style of the book's miniatures and that of early painted enamels in general. Particularly striking are the numerous gold highlights that add definition to the architectural elements and give texture to the figures' clothing in each image. The figures themselves also reference the work of other anonymous enamellers: their individualized, sometimes even awkward, physiognomy brings to mind the Monvaerni Master, while the highly stylized and sweet facial type of the Virgin evokes that of the Master of the Large Foreheads. Further archival research, along with input from conservation science, may eventually provide us with a more comprehensive understanding of the different enamellers and other artists' workshops in Limoges, and could allow for a more precise attribution.

While the exact identity of the artists responsible for the illuminations remains unclear, we know the identity of its owner at the turn of the sixteenth century. An ex libris and another inscription repeated on the front flyleaf announce that it belonged to Katherine Gentille of Limoges. She was the wife of Martial Dubois the Younger, who was named consul, a leading civic position, in 1510, and was a counselor and assessor of taxes in 1515 (Verdier 1967). • CN

[87]

MASTER OF THE BALTIMORE AND ORLÉANS TRIPTYCHS

The Nativity and Annunciation to the Shepherds

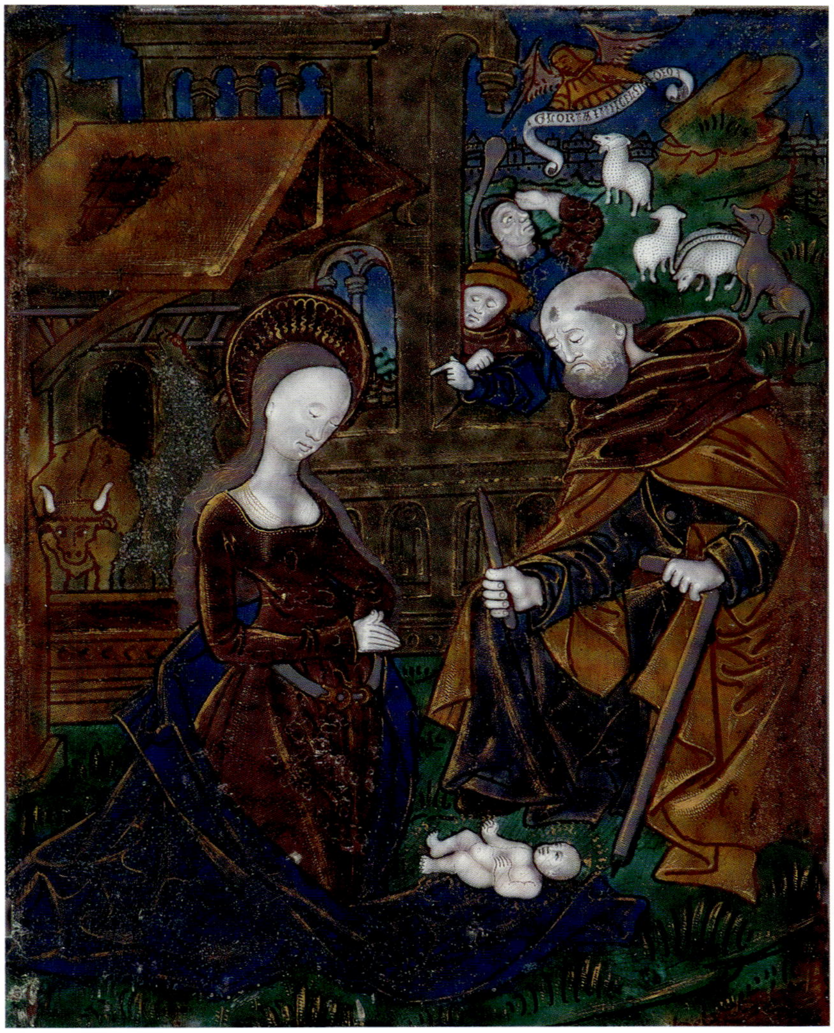

Limoges, 1480/90

Polychrome enamel and gold on copper; 20.6 x 16 cm (8 1/8 x 6 5/16 in.)

Los Angeles County Museum of Art, William Randolph Hearst Collection, 51.13.4

PROVENANCE: Possibly Charles Ducatel; sold, Hôtel Drouot, Paris, April 21–26, 1890, no. 3. Possibly A. Tollin, sold, Chevallier et Mannheim, Paris, May 18–19, 1897, no. 59. Charles Séguin; sold, Hôtel Drouot, Paris, December 12–15, 1910, no. 282. Seligmann and Company, New York, 1910. Thomas Fortune Ryan (d. 1928), Baltimore then New York; sold, American Art Association/Anderson Galleries, New York, November 23–25, 1933, no. 382. William Randolph Hearst (d. 1951), San Francisco then New York, San Simeon, and Santa Monica; given to the Los Angeles County Museum of Art, 1951.

BIBLIOGRAPHY: Marquet de Vasselot 1921, p. 92, no. 71. Caroselli 1993, pp. 69–72.

THE REMARKABLY close stylistic affinities between painted enamels such as this one and works in other media show how dependent early enamellers were on images drawn from a variety of sources, including illuminated manuscripts, printed books, paintings, prints, sculptures, and stained glass. In this case, the striking similarity of this image of the Nativity and one found in a late-fifteenth-century book of hours (cat. 86) at the Art Institute of Chicago has led some scholars to believe that the same artist was responsible for both the enamel and the illuminations (Ross 1941; Caroselli 1993); Ross even suggested that a shift in the market drew illuminators to enamels. However, the leap from miniature painting to metalwork seems unlikely. More probably, the stylistic convergence between the two media is due to manuscripts such as this one serving as models for early enamels.

Closely allied in their aesthetics, the images used for enamels and books of hours also served similar devotional functions, since both were aids to prayer and reflection. The size of enameled images invites close inspection, as do the minute painted details found in personal prayer books. They also would have been made for the same clientele. It is quite probable that Katherine Gentille—the wife of Martial Dubois, consul of Limoges, whose ex libris appears in the Chicago book of hours—would have owned enameled plaques like this one.

Marquet de Vasselot (1921) was the first scholar to attribute this piece to the anonymous master responsible for nearly thirty known enamels, including two Annunciation triptychs in Baltimore and Orléans from which his modern name derives. The same workshop also produced two other extant Nativity plaques, now in the British Museum and the Musée des Beaux-Arts, Lyon. • CN

[88]

Triptych with the Crucifixion, the Flagellation, and the Lamentation

Limoges, c. 1500

Polychrome enamel and gold on copper; central plaque: 18.9 x 17.2 cm (7 7/16 x 6 3/4 in.), wings: 18.9 x 7.4 cm (7 7/16 x 2 15/16 in.)

The Art Institute of Chicago, Mr. and Mrs. Martin A. Ryerson Collection, 1937.822

INSCRIBED: *MARCV[S]* (on the border of the garment of the figure to the left of Christ in the central panel; *MARCVS ES ALES OTE NR.* (on the hose of a soldier on the left wing); *INRI* (at top of cross)

PROVENANCE: Samuel Addington (d. 1886), England, by 1863. Frédéric Spitzer (d. 1890), Paris; sold, Chevallier et Mannheim, Paris, April 17–June 16, 1893, no. 417, as by Nardon Pénicaud; to Durand-Ruel as agent for Martin A. Ryerson (d. 1932), Chicago; by descent to his widow (d. 1937); bequeathed to the Art Institute of Chicago.

BIBLIOGRAPHY: Popelin in Spitzer 1890–93, vol. 2, p. 19, no. 1. Marquet de Vasselot 1921, pp. 69, 77, 240, no. 48. Bennett 1933, pp. 98–99. Monroe 1977, pp. 10–14, fig. 1. Caroselli 1993, p. 66.

EXHIBITIONS: London 1862, no. 1652. New York 1959, no. 1. Chicago 1987, no. 22.

BECAUSE EARLY PAINTED ENAMELS before 1530 were mostly unsigned and undocumented, modern scholars have struggled to assign them to various masters' hands. This effort is complicated by the fact that they were essentially the collective endeavor of workshops, overseen by guild masters from families that had been granted special privileges by Louis XI. This striking devotional triptych was first published with an attribution to Nardon Pénicaud in the mid-nineteenth century, and its attribution has been revised several times (Robinson in London 1862, rev. 1863, p. 142; Popelin in Spitzer 1890–93). Nardon Pénicaud, a member of one such family of enamellers in Limoges, signed and dated a Crucifixion plaque from 1503 now in the Musée national du Moyen Age, Paris, and he therefore became the attribution of choice, irrespective of style.

When Marquet de Vasselot published this triptych in 1921, he attributed it—and two similar plaques in Paris and St. Petersburg—to the so-called Monvaerni Master. Dobroklonskaia (1969) and Rappé and Boulkina (2005) have unconvincingly reaffirmed this attribution for the Hermitage triptych. In the Chicago triptych, certain physiognomic features of some figures recall the unflattering realism of the Monvaerni Master; most, however, are too idealized to confirm this association. Moreover, as Monroe (1977) has rightly pointed out, the technique employed here of fusing two layers (white and lilac) to the ground is more advanced than that of Monvaerni enamels (see also Michaels 1964–65); however, Monroe's attribution of this work to the Master of the Triptych of Louis XII cannot be supported. This enamel should instead be understood as the work of an anonymous artist or group of artists, as Baratte (2000, p. 47) has suggested for the Paris triptych.

Although produced by an unknown workshop, presumably for the market, this triptych displays great refinement in its technique. This is particularly evident in the treatment of flesh tones, which are finely modeled through enlevage, the removal of the top layer of white enamel before firing to reveal darker tones underneath. It is also apparent in the profusion of colorful round "jewels," enhanced with silver foil under drops of enamel, that decorate clothing, halos, horse trappings, and flowers. • CN

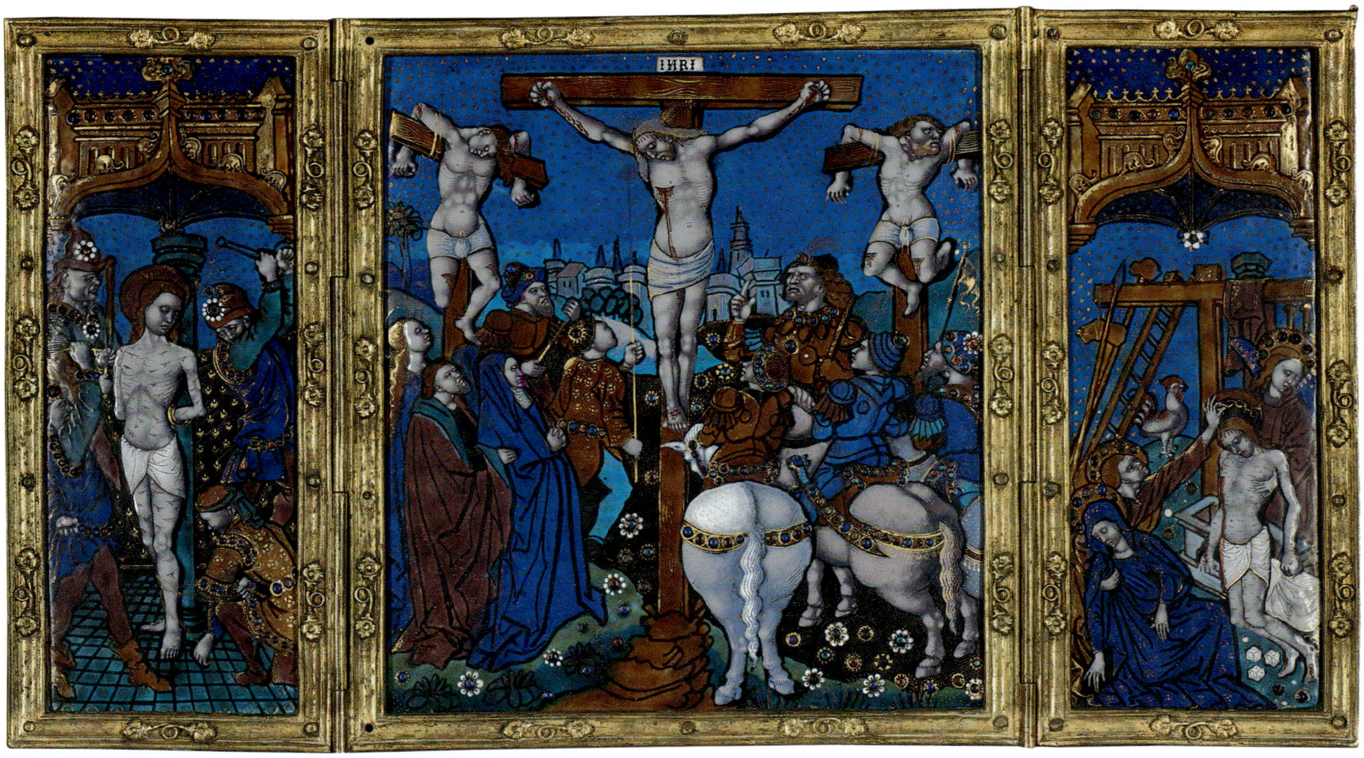

[89]

JEAN PERRÉAL
(active 1485–1530)

Pierre Sala, *Little Book of Love*

Paris and Lyon, c. 1510

Tempera and gold on parchment, with original carrying case of wood covered in tooled, painted, and gilded leather; 13 x 9.5 cm (5 1/8 x 3 3/4 in.)

The British Library, London, Stowe 955

PROVENANCE: Marguerite Builloud, Lyon, later wife of Pierre Sala. Probably Eléonore de Guilhens, his niece. General Andoche Junot, duke of Abrantes (d. 1813). Richard Temple-Nugent-Brydges-Chandos-Grenville, 1st duke of Buckingham and Chandos (d. 1839), Stowe House; by descent to the 2nd duke of Buckingham and Chandos; sold by him with other Stowe manuscripts to Bertram Ashburnham, 4th Earl of Ashburnham (d. 1878), 1849; by descent to the 5th earl, who sold the Stowe manuscripts to the British Museum, 1883.

BIBLIOGRAPHY: British Museum 1895, pp. 638–39, no. 955. Parry 1908, pp. 214–20. Durrieu 1919, pp. 166–67. Fabia 1934, pp. 39–40, 47–48, 56, 64–69. Perls 1935, p. 99, fig. 8. Ring 1949, no. 331, fig. 48. Ring 1950, pp. 258–60, fig. 12. Huillet d'Istria 1952, pp. 57–63, fig. 4. Sterling 1963, p. 12, fig. 4. Burin 1988, pp. 1–3, 19, fig. 1. King 1988, pp. 173–84. Backhouse 1989, pp. 3, 12–13, pl. 1. Backhouse and Giraud 1994. Colenbrander 1994, p. 214. Massing 1995, pp. 13–14. Reynaud 1996, pp. 42–45, figs. 6, 14. Burin 2001, pp. 38–39, 281, fig. 184. Châtelet 2001, pp. 132–35, fig. 84.

EXHIBITIONS: London/New York/Los Angeles 1983, no. 22. Paris 1993, no. 208.

SHOWN: *Portrait of Pierre Sala*, ff. 16v–17

PRESERVED WITH the original case that enabled its owner to carry it with her at all times, this book of poetry is an enchanting token of daily life in early Renaissance France. An old inscription identifies the book's author and the sitter in this portrait as Pierre Sala of Lyon (before 1457–1529), a courtier and amateur poet. Given to Marguerite Builloud, whom Sala married between 1515 and 1519 (it was each spouse's second marriage), it is decorated throughout with their initials, *M* and *P*, composed of dividers. Other clever visual effects include the purple-toned vellum evoking luxurious Roman books and the trompe l'oeil painted tablets that appear to be attached by cords as a support for Sala's verses on many pages. Each tablet bears a quatrain that comments on an image on the right side of the page opening. These amorous or moral texts are adapted from established sources, notably Henri Baude's *Dits moraux*. The accompanying lively but stereotypical images are now recognized as by the Parisian illuminator known as the Master of the Chronique Scandaleuse, and by his workshop (cat. 34; Reynaud in Paris 1993).

What especially distinguishes the book, however, is the brilliantly incisive portrait of Sala by another hand, that of his friend Jean Perréal, also from Lyon and attached to the court as *valet de chambre* and painter to the king. Rapidly and delicately executed over a pen sketch, this bust is linked stylistically to other small-scale portraits of the 1490s and 1510s that can be associated with Perréal, probably the most renowned French painter of his day. As has often been pointed out, the portrait was not made from the live model, since Sala was well into middle age when it was painted (for example Burin 1988 and Backhouse in Backhouse and Giraud 1994). Usually dated about 1500/05, it is probably a little later; the gathered shirt and square bodice worn here and in the image of the lover depositing his heart within a marguerite (f. 6) date from about 1510 or shortly thereafter—compare the figure of Fastus from the moral compendium for Francis of Angoulême (cat. 98). This date is in closer accord with the couple's life, Marguerite having been widowed by 1506. But it is not impossible that the book was to some extent repurposed. The Leonardesque mirror writing of this page is painted over one of the trompe l'oeil tablets, and elements of the dedicatory text that begins the book are erased and rewritten (Giraud in Backhouse and Giraud 1994, p. 245; for Leonardo and Perréal, see Durrieu 1919). • MW

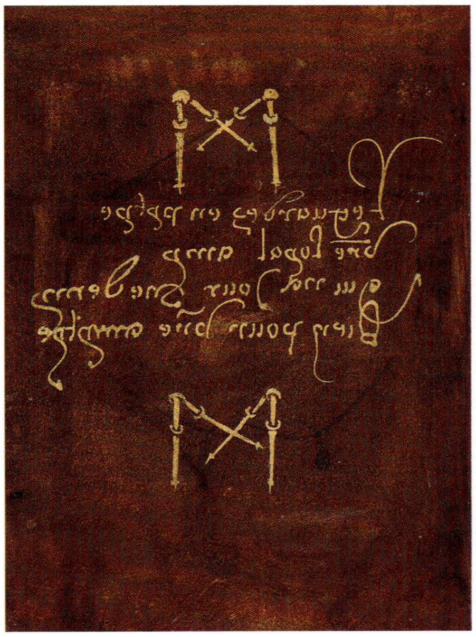

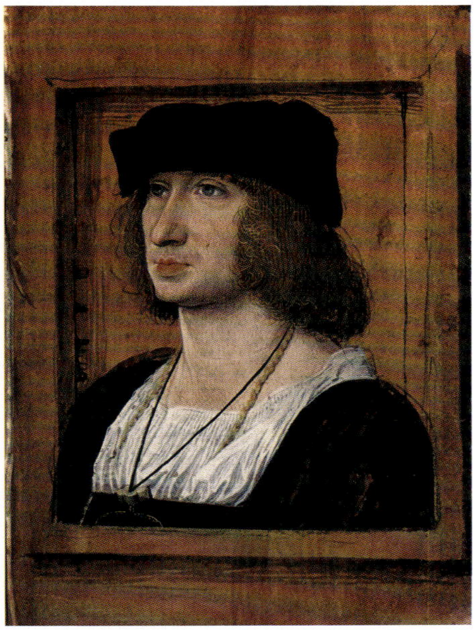

[90]

MASTER OF THE CLUB FEET

The Comedies of Terence

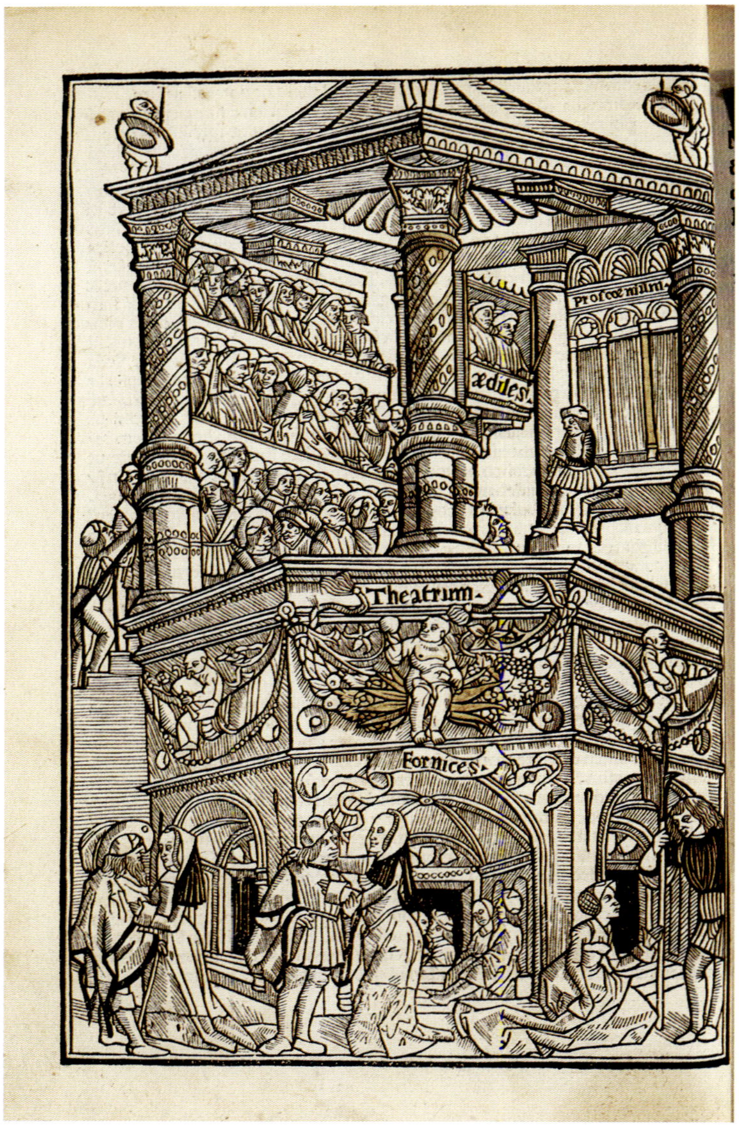

Lyon, August 29, 1493

Printed by Johann Trechsel

Woodcut and letterpress on paper; annotated in brown ink; 25.4 x 18.4 cm (10 x 7¼ in.)

The Library of Congress, Washington, D.C., Incun 1493.J682

PROVENANCE: John Boyd Thacher, Albany, N.Y.; by descent to his widow; bequeathed to the Library of Congress, 1926.

BIBLIOGRAPHY: Claudin 1914, vol. 4, pp. 67–77. Library of Congress 1915, p. 237, no. 773. Huillet d'Istria 1952, pp. 57–63. Sterling 1963, pp. 2–15, 64–65. Woodner Collection 1971, n.pag. Rhodes 1988, pp. 185–296. Colenbrander 1992, pp. 211–20. Massing 1995. Müller in Schongauer 1999, p. 120. Peters 2000, p. 316, no. 16.

SHOWN: *A Theater* (frontispiece)

ILLUSTRATED MANUSCRIPTS of Terence's six comic plays (c. 170–160 B.C.) are known from the ninth century A.D. This 1493 Lyon edition illustrates his complete oeuvre, with 151 woodcuts detailing the games of mistaken identity and ribald sexual innuendo of his works, including *The Eunuch* ("He was, they say, No Eunuch"). The woodcut designer, who remains unidentified, was apparently also responsible for the designs of the cuts in the *Vigilles de la mort du feu Roy Charles septiesme*, printed in Lyon, possibly by Claude Dayne, circa 1500, and an edition of *Les Quatre filz Aymon* printed by Jean de Vingle in Lyon in the 1490s. He has been associated with Jean Perréal and his workshop (cat. 89). The full-page frontispiece shown here displays three tiers of an open, pseudo-Vitruvian theater structure with decorative touches suggesting Italian Renaissance rather than classical influences. The lower level, bluntly labeled *Fornices*, or brothel, offers its own charming amenities; patrons climb past putti and flowery swags on the more respectable *Theatrum* level; while a box near the *Proscenium* stage called *Aediles* houses officials. The play has not yet begun; a lone flutist entertains the audience before the closed curtains that will form the backdrop for the subsequent illustrations of the plays. Terence's comedies invited responses from their audiences through prologues and speeches directed at them; a contemporary reader of this copy responded by underlining, playfully inking in patches of the frontispiece, and caricaturing a man's head later in the volume.

Terence's plays were performed throughout Europe, greatly influencing Renaissance drama. As Peters (2000) pointed out, Jodocus Badius Ascensius, a scholar possibly involved in productions of these works at Ferrara, may have commissioned this 1493 book, for he edited the commentary and married the publisher's daughter. Despite the Lyonnais woodcut artist's anonymity, his Terence was evidently successful. Indeed, according to Müller (1999), the edition was so popular that it may have prevented the publication of a Basel edition for which the young Albrecht Dürer prepared illustrations around 1492. Due in part to the 1493 woodcuts, Terence remained popular in France through Montaigne's time and into the era of Molière as the aristocratic comedian of choice. • SKS

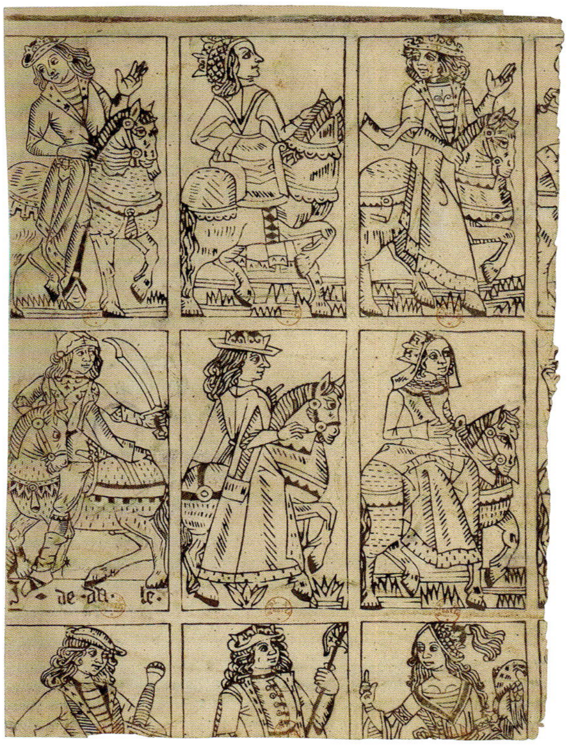

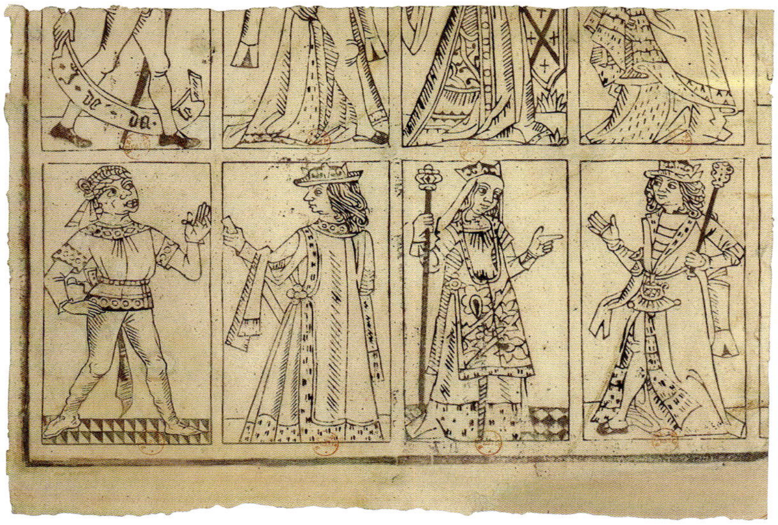

[91]

JEAN DE DALE
(active Lyon and Avignon, 1477–1524)

Two Reunited Fragments from a Woodblock Sheet of Playing Cards

Lyon, 1475/1500

Woodcut; 9.5 x 4.5 cm (3¾ x 1¾ in.) (each card)

Bibliothèque nationale de France, Paris, Department of Prints, Rés. Kh-30 a Pet. Fol.

PROVENANCE: Leclerc Bookseller, by 1902; sold to Henri Bouchot, 1902; given to the Bibliothèque nationale (Acq. 6414).

BIBLIOGRAPHY: Rondot 1896, p. 133. Bouchot 1903, p. 296. D'Allemagne 1906, vol. 1, p. 70. Schreiber 1937, pp. 111–12. Seguin 1968, p. 35. Hoffmann 1972, no. 43b, p. 30.

EXHIBITION: Paris 1963, no. 126.

THESE PLAYING CARDS constitute one of the first known printed card games in France. They were found in the covers of the binding of a book of sermons by Bernardino of Siena and were purchased in 1902 from the bookseller Leclerc by Henri Bouchot, who donated the object to the Bibliothèque nationale de France; the book is now in the Réserve des livres rares there (Rés. m. D.24). A number of duplicate sheets were ceded at the time of the acquisition to Jean Masson, a renowned Amiens bibliophile, who later gave them, with his collection, to the École Nationale Supérieure des Beaux-Arts, Paris (Est. Mas. 322).

Court figures for several games were printed on this one sheet. It was then the practice to print as many figures as were needed on the same sheet, using a block or a die, irrespective of the coherence of the game. The juxtaposition of the two fragments shows that the original block had four rows of five cards. The knave in the third row bears a scroll with the name *J. de Dale*, identified with Jean de Dale, a cardmaker originally from Bourg-en-Bresse, who was active in Lyon and Avignon between 1477 and 1524. The style of the figures and the known dates for this printmaker, who specialized in playing cards, permit these sheets to be dated to the last quarter of the fifteenth century. At the time, Lyon was famed for its production of printed playing cards; the city's archives have revealed the names of almost sixty cardmakers active in the city between 1444 and 1493. Lyon's very lively fair provided an important outlet for the trade in playing cards and allowed for their extensive distribution.

The cards have neither suits (symbols allowing them to be arranged by series, like today's hearts, diamonds, spades, and clubs) nor names. Given the scarcity of comparable works, it is difficult to state with certainty the date when suits first appeared in France and when they became fixed. • SL

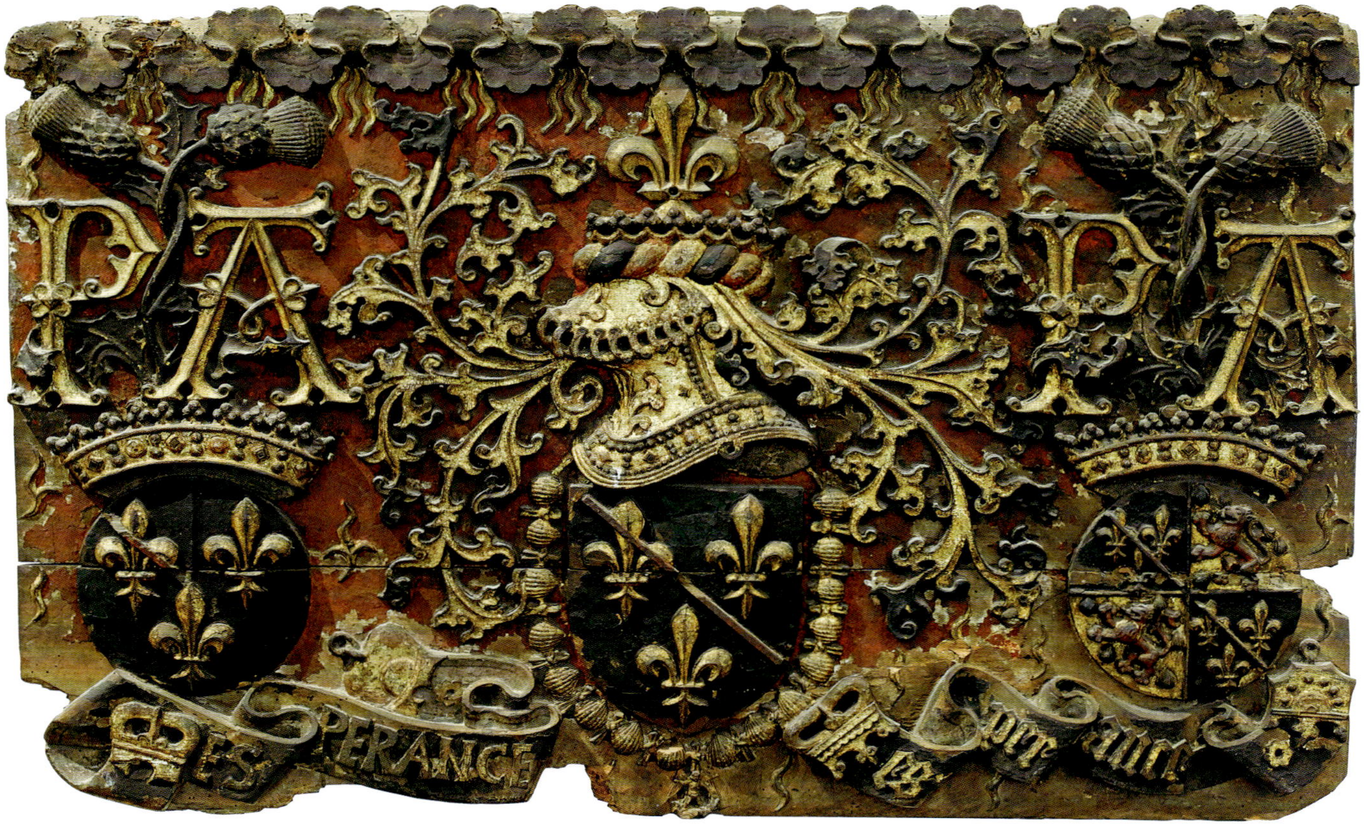

[92]

Panel with the Arms of Pierre II of Bourbon and Anne of France

1488–1503

Fruitwood, showing two successive applications of polychromy; 58 x 91 x 3.5 cm (22 13/16 x 35 13/16 x 1 3/8 in.)

Musée Anne-de-Beaujeu, Moulins, 95.112.1

PROVENANCE: Veauce family; given to the Musée Anne de Beaujeu, 1995.

EXHIBITION: Moulins 1955, no. 31.

LIKE MANY LATE medieval princes, Pierre II of Bourbon and Anne of France, as heads of the Bourbon ducal house, used their arms, initials, and devices (a figurative emblem, sometimes accompanied by a brief phrase) on the monuments and artworks they commissioned. Thus the north wing of the château of Moulins, built between 1500 and 1503 (Bruand 2001), was decorated with the Bourbon device of a belt bearing the word *Espérance* (Hope), originally adopted by duke Louis II on Christmas Day in 1366 (Hablot 2001), and the initials *P* and *A*, the first letters of the ducal couple's given names. This panel, displaying an array of Bourbon emblems, is datable between the accession of Pierre II to the dukedom in 1488 and his death in 1503. There are three escutcheons. In the center is the Bourbon escutcheon, composed of the arms of France (*azure, three fleurs-de-lis or*), with a diagonal band of red indicating a cadet branch of the royal family. It is surrounded by the collar of the Order of Saint Michael and topped by a helmet crowned with a fleur-de-lis; decorative foliage sprouts from its mantling. It is flanked by two other escutcheons, each surmounted by a ducal crown. Beneath them are two unfurled belts, one with the motto *Espérance* in classical capital letters, and the other with the same word in gothic letters. Above the escutcheons, the letters *P* and *A*, intertwined with thistles, repeat twice. The thistle, originally a Burgundian emblem, was adopted by the Bourbons when Charles I married Agnes of Burgundy in 1425; here it may serve both as an emblem and as a symbol of love, based on the analogy between the words *chardon* (thistle) and *cher don* (dear gift).

A band of stylized clouds giving off rays of light marks the upper edge. The ribbonlike forms between the escutcheons are interrupted by the present edges of the panel, indicating that it was once wider. Whether it was once part of a wainscot or a piece of furniture is hard to determine, given its fragmentary condition and the absence of any indication of how it was attached. Another fragmentary emblematic panel in the Musée Anne-de-Beaujeu (inv. 1055) combines Bourbon emblems on a different scale and without polychromy. • BC-B

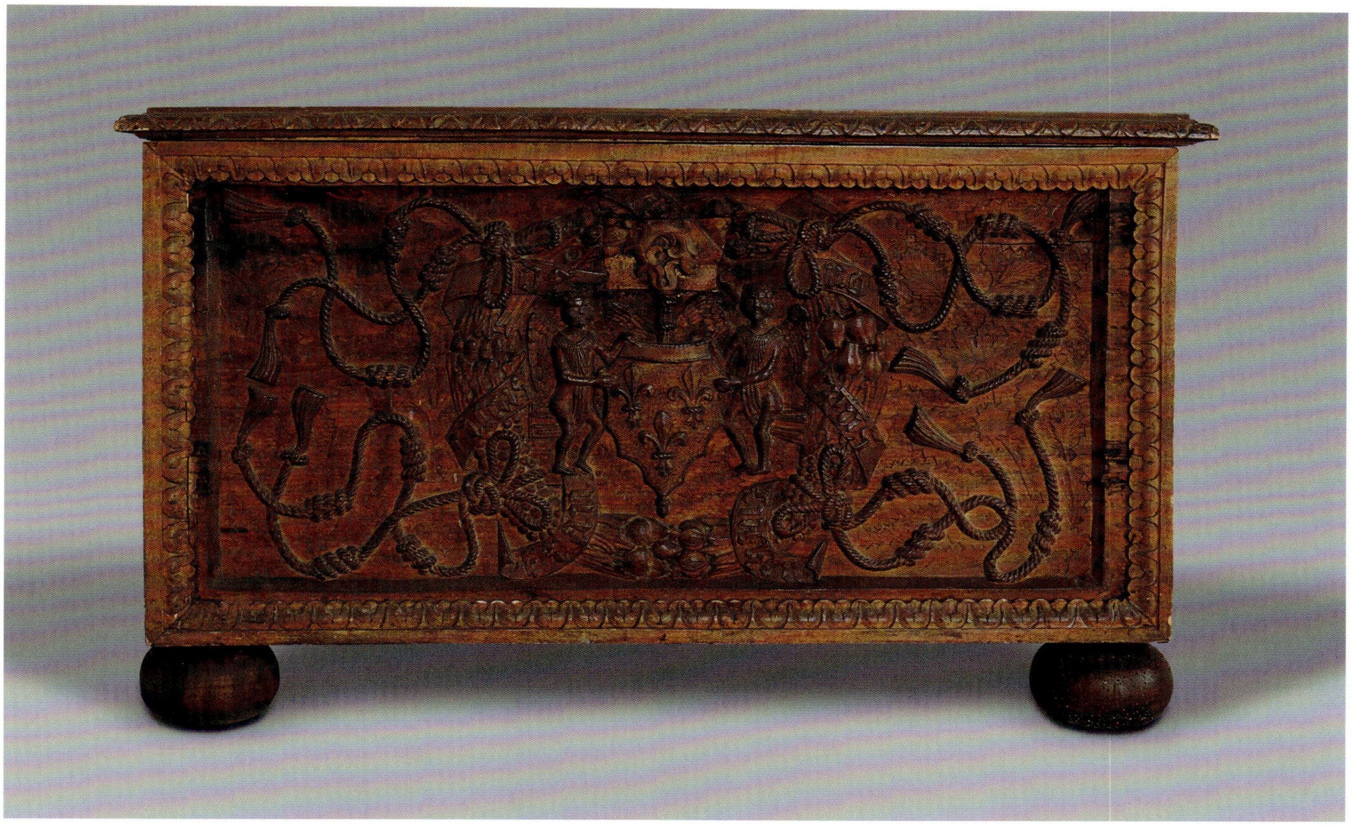

[93]

Chest of François d'Estaing, Bishop of Rodez

Probably Rodez, 1501/29

Lindenwood, carved, with traces of polychromy; 42 x 83 x 47 cm ($16\frac{1}{2}$ x $32\frac{5}{8}$ x $18\frac{1}{2}$ in.)

Diocese of Rodez (on deposit from the Conseil général de l'Aveyron)

PROVENANCE: François d'Estaing (d. 1529); episcopal palace of Rodez.

BIBLIOGRAPHY: Bonnaffé 1887, pp. 112–18. Thirion 1998, pp. 78–79.

EXHIBITIONS: Rodez 1979, p. 166. Blois 2002, no. 3.

DESPITE THE ADDITION of reinforcements and the replacement of the feet and lid, this chest has retained its original panels; its interior compartments are those of a chest used for transporting a *chapelle* and permitted the organization and safe storage of liturgical vessels and ornaments. François d'Estaing, bishop of Rodez, very probably brought this chest along with him when he made his pastoral visits in the diocese. Member of a family closely allied to the crown, trusted counselor to the king, and respected theologian, he fulfilled his duties as bishop with diligence and care, in contrast to the reputation for frivolousness and absenteeism that generally attached to courtier-prelates. He initiated important artistic projects at Rodez and at the diocesan collegiate church of Salles-Curan. The visible panels are ornamented with heraldic decoration showing his arms supported by two rather coarsely rendered angels, set within a garland of foliage (called a *chapeau de triomphe* in contemporary documents), with further decorative elaborations based on the Franciscan rope girdle. The latter is both a reference to the bishop's patron saint and, more generally, a symbol of piety.

Similar heraldic decoration is found on the woodwork of the choir screen and the bishop's throne of the episcopal collegiate church of Salles-Curan, the traditional seat of the bishops of Rodez. But this piece of portable furniture is also a reminder of the degree to which heraldic motifs were ubiquitous in wooden decorative schemes, both for furniture and paneling, echoing their usage in architecture, wall paintings, and tapestry. Used for both storage and transport, François d'Estaing's chest also illustrates a type basic to the history of furniture, whose omnipresence within the framework of secular and religious architecture as both utilitarian and decorative objects is evident from written records and from inventories in particular. • TC-L

[94]

Dish with the Arms of Louis de Villiers de l'Isle-Adam

Beauvais or region, 1497/1521

Stoneware with lead glaze; diam. 43 cm (16$^{15}/_{16}$ in.)

Musée du Louvre, Paris, Department of Decorative Arts, OA 447

PROVENANCE: Sauvageot collection; given to the Louvre, 1856.

BIBLIOGRAPHY: Sauzay 1861, cat. 943. Clément de Ris 1875, cat. 229. Migeon [1901], cat. 13. Ennès 1983, p. 2.

EXHIBITIONS: Sèvres 1861, cat. 136. Ecouen 1996, cat. 43. L'Isle-Adam 2004, p. 78.

THIS LARGE circular dish is one of the rare surviving pieces that can be attributed to potters from the region around Beauvais and linked to an identifiable patron. The arms at its center are those of the Villiers de l'Isle-Adam family, based since the Middle Ages in the Ile-de-France. They are quartered with the arms of the Nesle family and thus correspond to the generation of the children of Jacques de Villiers and Jeanne de Nesle, in particular Philippe, grand master of the Order of Malta (died 1534), and Louis, bishop of Beauvais from 1497 until his death in 1521. The name *Ludovicus* at the top of the escutcheon permits the dish to be connected to the latter dignitary. The absence of any episcopal attribute has led to the hypothesis that the dish was made for the bishop's private use (Ecouen 1996). It seems to have been part of a service, as suggested by two other fragments with identical heraldic decoration (Musée national de Céramique, Sèvres, inv. MNC 5986; private collection), which come from serving vessels.

This dish is important evidence of the success of glazed ceramics from Beauvais, which were widely distributed through the nearby Paris market. It shows the interest of the wealthiest patrons of the era in blue-glazed stoneware with subtle cool tones, as in this dish, although the products of Beauvais potteries were equally appreciated at lower levels of society. • AB

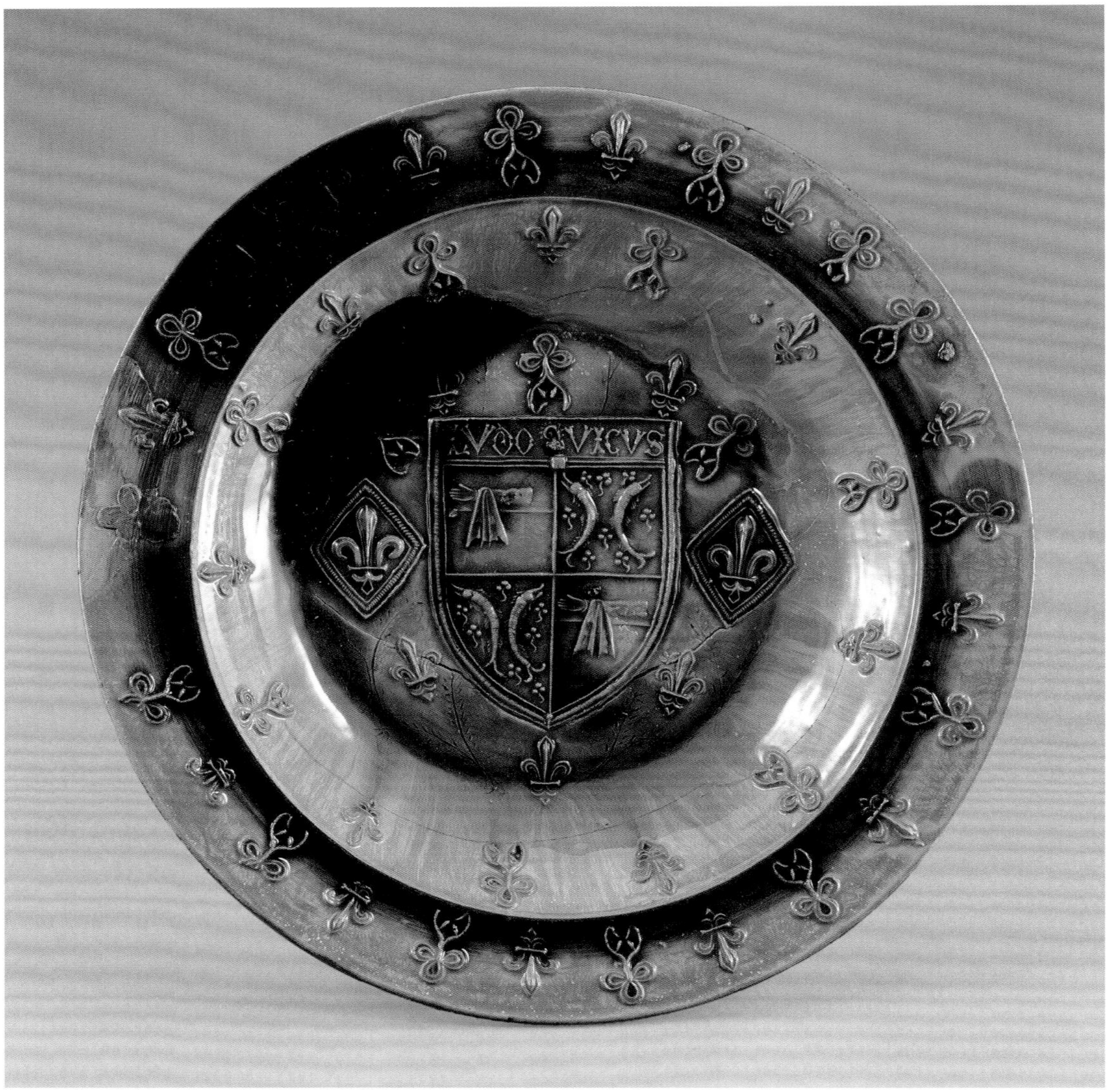

[95]

Tapestry with the Arms and Emblems of a Member of the Robertet Family

c. 1500

Wool and silk; 176 x 161 cm ($69\frac{1}{4}$ x $63\frac{3}{8}$ in.)

Musée de Cluny—Musée National du Moyen Age, Paris, inv. Cl. 22613

INSCRIBED: *ΚΕΡΑΣ ΑΜΑΛΘΕΙΑΣ / ΑΜΑΛΘΕΙΑ ΚΕΡΑΣ / AVREA MEDIOCRITAS* [Horns of Amaltheus / Golden Mean] (on banderoles)

PROVENANCE: Purchased from M. Salman, antique dealer, Paris, 1953.

BIBLIOGRAPHY: Verlet 1955, p. 54. Souchal 1973. Joubert 2002, no. 13.

EXHIBITION: Edinburgh 1992, no. 24.

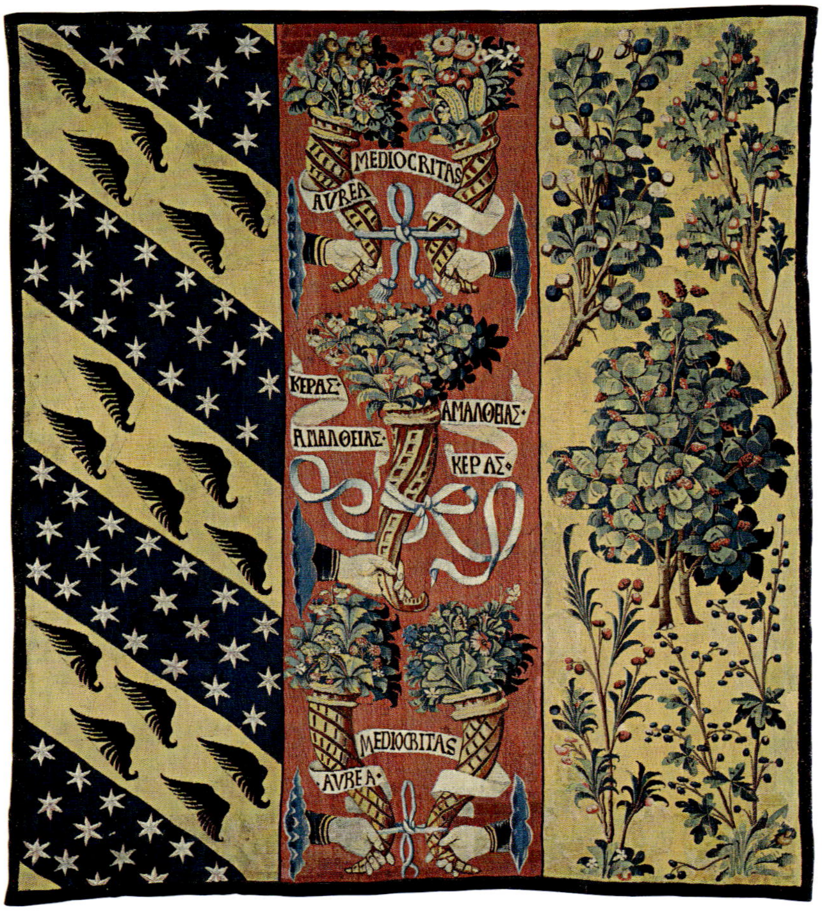

THIS TAPESTRY belongs to the emblematic genre in vogue around 1500, of which the piece with the arms of Angoulême and the emblems of Louise of Savoy and of her son Francis of Angoulême (Museum of Fine Arts, Boston) is one of the most prestigious examples. On the left, the alternating bands repeat the charges of the armorial bearings of the Robertet family: blue with a band of gold overlaid with a sable wing, accompanied by three silver stars, one in the top left quarter and the other two at the bottom. The central section displays a device (or emblem in more modern usage), the horn of plenty, accompanied by banderoles with its Greek name, and a motto (*mot*), *AVREA MEDIOCRITAS* (the golden mean), inspired by the poetry of Horace (Carmina 2.10.5). The poet saw in this rule of life a promise of security and moderation. The formula finds an echo in a metaphor used by Clément Marot to comment on the Robertet arms in his *Déploration sur le trépas de feu messier Florimond Robertet*: "the black wing in the golden band who thus flew as he must between two currents of air, neither too high nor too low" (*l'esle noire en la bende dorée qui a vollé ainsi que voller fault / entre deux aers, ni trop haut ni trop bas*; Mayer and Bentley-Cranch 1994, p. 119).

All the elements of the tapestry would seem to point to Florimond Robertet (c. 1459–1527), who was one of the most important statesmen, men of letters, and patrons of his time (cat. 114) and who had inscriptions in Greek placed around the dormer windows of his château of Bury—apart from the fact that he adopted another motto, "Except one" (*Fors ungne*). While a personal motto was not necessarily unique and immutable, the possibility cannot be excluded that this one, *AVREA MEDIOCRITAS*, was used by another member of this distinguished family, in particular one of Florimond's brothers. • ET-D

[96]

Medal of Francis of Angoulême

Probably Amboise, 1504

Bronze; diam. 6.5 cm (2 9/16 in.)

The Metropolitan Museum of Art, New York, gift of James Hazen Hyde, 1948.90.5

INSCRIBED: *FRANCOIS DVC DE VALOIS COMTE DANGOLESME AV X AN D S EA* [Francis duke of Valois count of Angoulême at ten years of age] (obverse); *NOTRISCO AL BVONO STINGO EL REO MCCCCCIIII* [I feed on the good, I extinguish the evil 1504] (reverse)

PROVENANCE: James Hazen Hyde; given to the Metropolitan Museum of Art, 1948.

BIBLIOGRAPHY: Hill 1930, no. 848. Lecoq 1987, pp. 35–52. New York and Washington 1994, p. 307, under no. 138. Blois 2006, no. 27.

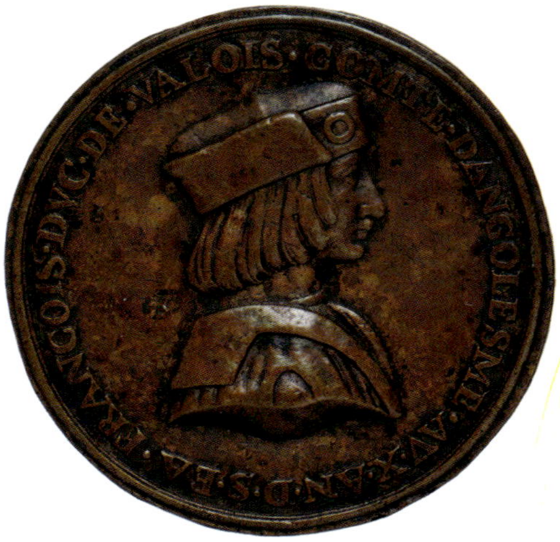

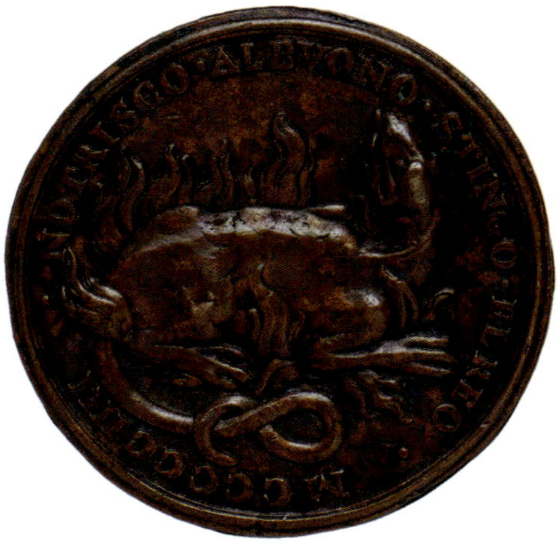

THE FIRST MEDAL of the future Francis I, who was born in Cognac in 1494, is well-known for its use of the handsome device of the salamander that originated with his father, Charles of Valois, or perhaps even with his grandfather, Jean of Angoulême; this medal is the earliest known image of the symbol. It appears with the motto "I feed on the good, I extinguish the evil" in Italian. In the *Devises héroïques* (Lyon, 1557 edition), Claude Paradin, who translated the phrase as the Latin *Nutrisco & extinguo*, recalled "having seen a medal in bronze of the said late king, shown as a young adolescent, on the reverse of which was this Device of the Salamander in flames" (*avoir vu une médaille en bronze dudit feu roy, peint en jeune adolescent, au revers de laquelle estoit cette Devise de la Salemandre enflammée*). The salamander, believed to live in fire and to feed on its flames, was a symbol of justice; it is shown here as a dragon whose tail forms a knot or interlace, the emblem of the ducal house of Savoy. Louise of Savoy was certainly the force behind the creation of this work that puts forward her son; he was a young prince ten years of age, as the inscription states, when, in January 1504, the serious illness of Louis XII, who still lacked a male heir, gave his young cousin hope of attaining the crown. The boy's governor, Pierre de Rohan, Marshal de Gyé, urged the betrothal of Francis and Claude of France, daughter of Louis XII and Anne of Brittany, which would take place in 1506.

Though still influenced by Jean de Candida, the medal is in higher relief, with the bust cut in the same manner as in the medal of Thomas Bohier (Bibliothèque nationale de France, Department of Coins, Medals, and Antiquities, série iconographique no. 2020). A still more ambitious medal was designed in 1512, when Francis had just been appointed lieutenant general of the king; an attribution to the Lombard goldsmith Cristoforo Foppa, known as Caradosso, has recently been proposed for the latter medal (Blois 2006, no. 28). This laurel-crowned portrait shows Francis as a young emperor; indeed, his mother called him "my Caesar" (journal of Louise of Savoy). The medals track the stages of his ascent to power. • IV-P

[97]

Medal of Louise of Savoy and Marguerite of Angoulême

Probably Amboise, c. 1505

Bronze; diam. 6 cm (2 3/8 in.)

The Metropolitan Museum of Art, New York, Harris Brisbane Dick Fund, 1936.110.8

INSCRIBED: *LOYSE DVCHESSE DEVALOIS COMTESSE DANGOLESME* (obverse); *MARGVERITE FILLE DE CHARLES COMTE DANGOLESME* (reverse)

PROVENANCE: Henry Oppenheimer (d. 1932), London; his sale, Christie's, London, July 27, 1936, no. 82; sold to the Metropolitan Museum of Art.

BIBLIOGRAPHY: D'Espézel 1925, pp. 1–10. Hill 1930, no. 852. Philips 1938, p. 273. Waldman in New York and Washington 1994, no. 138. Rouhette and Tuzio 2008, no. 13.

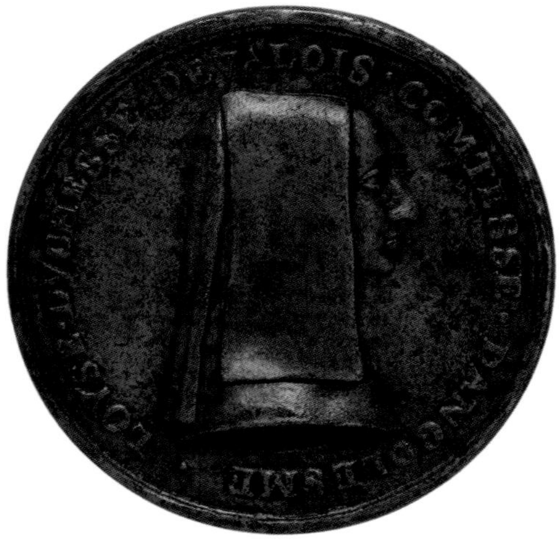

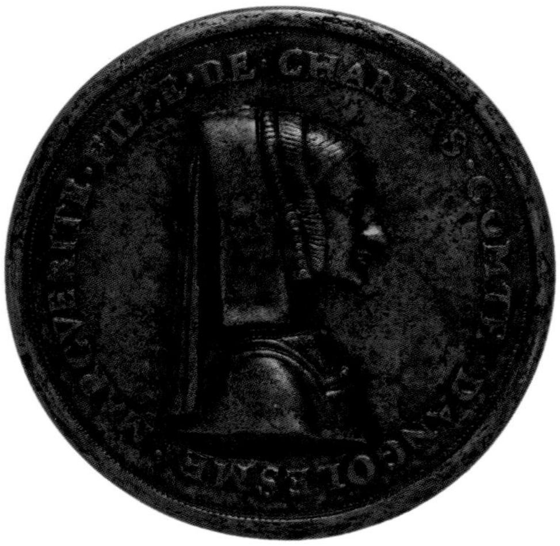

WIDOWED WHEN Charles of Valois died in 1496, Louise of Savoy (1476–1531) took over the administration of the duchy of Valois and the county of Angoulême during the minority of her son Francis. She retired to her château of Cognac in Angoumois, but was recalled by Louis XII, who installed her and her children at the royal castle of Amboise: Francis of Angoulême was the presumptive heir to the throne since the marriage of Louis XII and Anne of Brittany had not produced a son. A pendant to the medal of Francis of Angoulême (cat. 96) by the same artist, this double portrait of Louise and Marguerite of Angoulême (1492–1549) must be from the same period. The duchess was then twenty-eight years old, but her depiction in a starched veil seems as youthful as that of her twelve-year-old daughter, who wears a headdress in a style then fashionable at court and a gown with a square neckline. The medal is certainly earlier than Marguerite's marriage to Charles, duke of Alençon, in 1509. Was it made for Francis of Angoulême, who left Amboise for the court in August 1508, in order to remind him through this small portable object of the features of the two women who were most dear to him? Perhaps it was part of a gallery of family portrait medals, celebrating the growing influence of the Valois-Angoulême branch of the royal family and a mother's pride. The medal maker, who may have been trained as a sculptor, worked with volume and broad, smooth surfaces that contrast with the more minutely detailed style of the royal medals (cat. 26). • IV-P

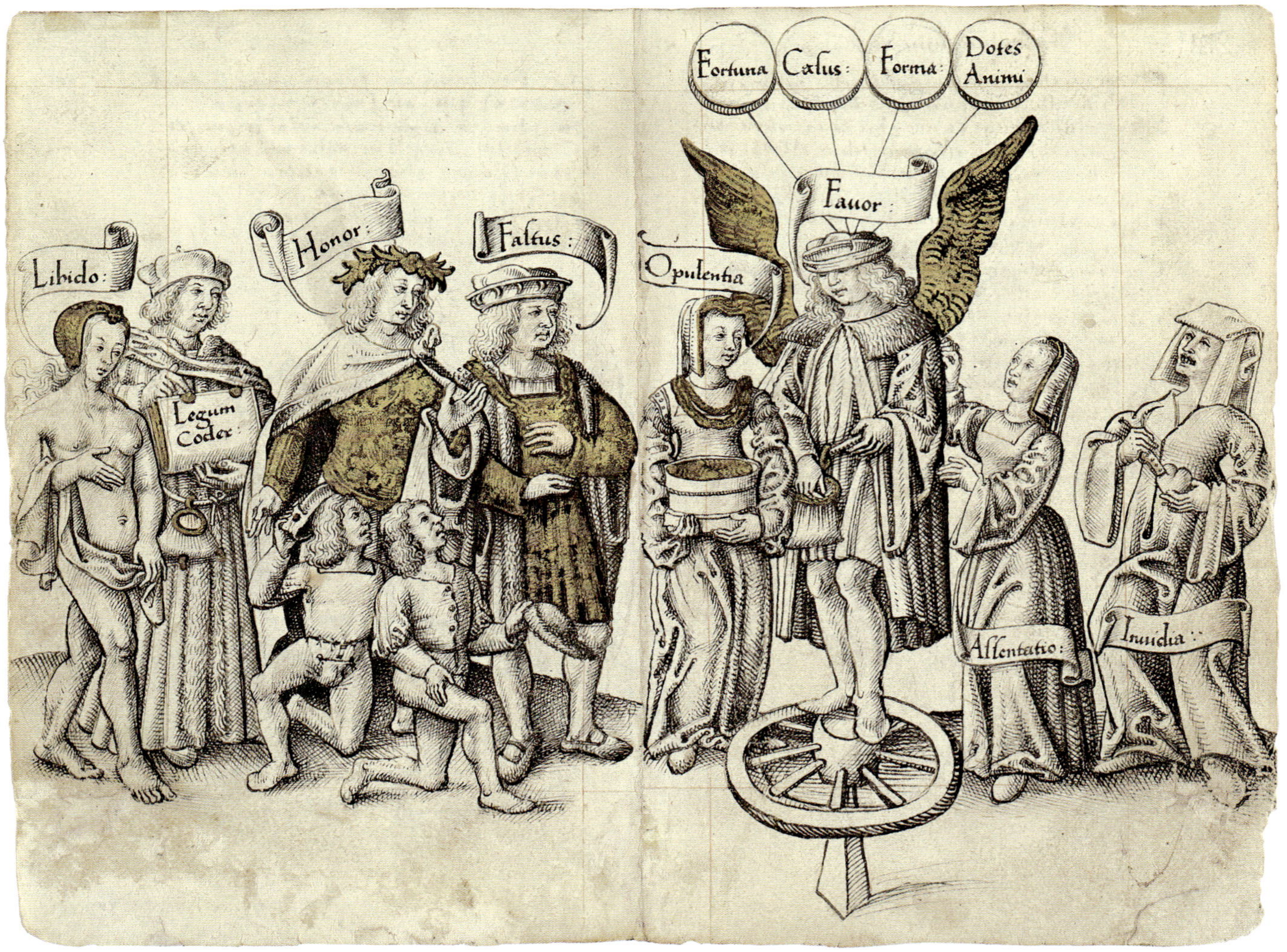
Fortuna
Casus:
Forma:
Dotes
Animi
Fauor:
Libido:
Honor:
Fastus:
Opulentia
Legum
Codex:
Assentatio:
Inuidia:

[98]

Illustration of "A Dialogue on Human Favor" from a Moral Compendium

1512–15

Two leaves from a dismembered manuscript, joined as a single sheet; pen and brown and black ink, and gold paint on paper; 16.3 x 21.4 cm (6 7/16 x 8 7/16 in.)

National Gallery of Art, Washington, D. C., Woodner Collection, gift of Andrea Woodner, 2006.11.34.a

INSCRIBED: *Libido*, *Legem Codex*, *Honor*, *Fastus*, *Opulentia*, *Fauor*, *Assentatio*, *Inuidia* [Lust, Codes of Laws, Honor, Haughtiness, Favor, Ostentation, Envy] (on banderoles); *Fortuna*, *Casius*, *Forma*, *Dotus / Animi* [Fortune, Chance, Beauty, Mental Gifts] (above Favor)

PROVENANCE: Probably made for Francis of Angoulême, later Francis I. Offered for sale, Sotheby's, London, July 13, 1937, no. 64, bought in; sold, Sotheby's, London, November 15–17, 1937, no. 546. Maggs Brothers, London, by 1941; sold through Paul Graupe to William H. Schab Gallery, New York, when the book was dismembered; sold with other drawings from the book to Ian Woodner (d. 1990), New York, by 1973; by descent to his daughter Andrea Woodner, New York; given to the National Gallery of Art, 2006.

BIBLIOGRAPHY: Massing 1983. Hackenbroch 1986, p. 77, fig. 7. Massing 1990, p. 236, under no. 90. Colenbrander 1994, fig. 1. Massing 1995. Châtelet 2001, pp. 132–33.

EXHIBITIONS: New York/Los Angeles/Indianapolis 1973, no. 3. Washington 2009, no. 2c.

THIS DRAWING ILLUSTRATES a Latin poem written by Bernardino Dardano that purportedly describes an allegorical image of Favor; he is the winged young man blinded by his good luck and perched on an unstable wheel like the one traditionally associated with Fortune. Both poem and illustration were part of a moral compendium that included other ekphrastic poems and several sayings from the 1508 edition of Erasmus's *Adagiorum chiliades*. It was bound with an edition of Guillaume de Conques's *Dogma moralium philosophorum* printed in 1511. The book was disassembled after 1941 and many of the accompanying texts were erased, giving the sheets the appearance of independent drawings; most of the drawings are now in the National Gallery of Art. Fortunately, its previous state and binding were documented in photographs. Although the manuscript compilation apparently bore no clear signs of royal ownership, it seems to have been made to amuse and guide the young Francis of Angoulême, who became Francis I in 1515. The heir presumptive in the absence of a direct male heir for Louis XII, he was being groomed for his eventual role as king by his ambitious mother, Louise of Savoy. The protagonist in many of the images is a young man, sometimes shown with a ducal crown; in one instance he is seated on a throne ornamented with dolphins, evoking the role of the dauphin, heir to the throne, that Louise of Savoy was quick to appropriate for her son (Massing 1995, pp. 9–11, 87, 163). The features and widow's garments of Prudence in the illustration of the Pythagorian adage "Do not eat your heart out" resemble those of Louise, who associated herself with the allegorical figure of Prudence as part of her carefully crafted image. Moreover, Massing identified the handwriting as that of François Demoulins, the prince's tutor, and the lost binding showed striking similarities to that of books in the young prince's personal library (Laffitte 1998, p. 66).

The compendium is less a *speculum principis* (mirror of princes) than a witty guide for a young man surrounded by the temptations of life at court. It provides excerpts from recent neo-Latin texts while referencing the earlier tradition of vernacular books of proverbs. The illustrations were apparently designed for this compendium, but their author remains unidentified. The proposal (New York/Los Angeles/Indianapolis 1973; also Châtelet 2001 and Colenbrander 1994) connecting him to the exceptional designer of woodcuts for Lyon books, the so-called Master of the Club Feet or Maître aux Pieds-Bots, is untenable. He is more likely to be found among the anonymous artists illustrating books for Louise of Savoy about 1515 (compare Orth 1999, fig. 4). • MW

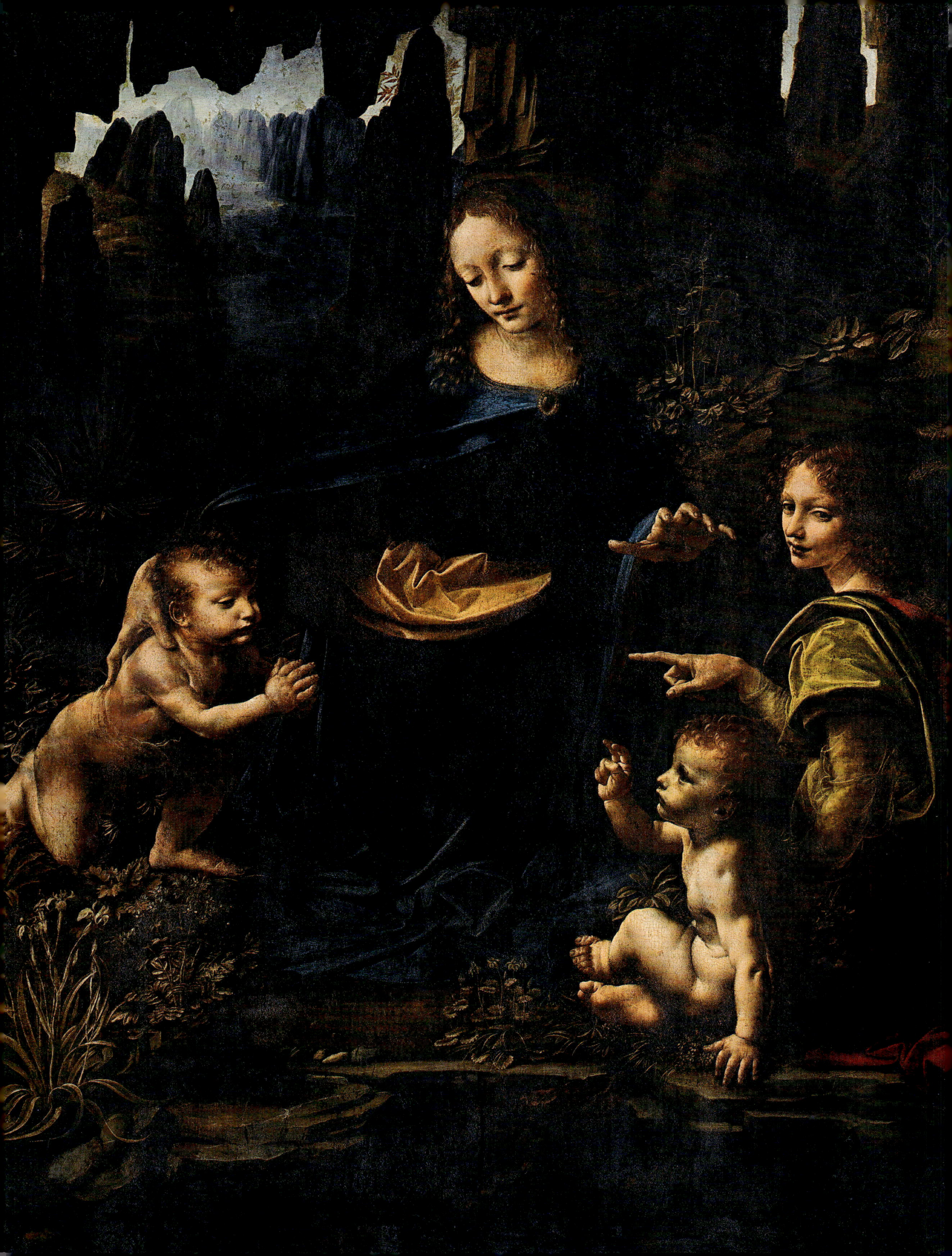

THE FASCINATION OF ITALY: MYTH AND REALITY

GENEVIÈVE BRESC-BAUTIER

Every traditional history of art repeats over and over again how, as if by the touch of a magic wand, the rough French knights, moved by the grace of Italian art and captivated by the ornamentation of the charterhouse of Pavia, were converted to the Italian "Renaissance." Things are not that simple, however: first, because Italian art and artists were indeed present in France during the fifteenth century; further, because such a radical conversion did not take place in a country that still remained firmly anchored in the atmosphere of the North; and finally, because Italy itself was not monolithic, but divided into states, and still heavily swayed by the Gothic style, as the architecture of the cathedral of Milan and certain Venetian palaces confirms. Moreover, northern art was admired in Italy. Jean Fouquet was very well received for having painted the portrait of Pope Eugene IV, and a Sicilian chronicler and humanist, Pietro Ranzano, writing a historical account around 1480, named the French painter Jean together with Roger de Bruges (presumably Fouquet and Rogier van der Weyden) as remarkable figures in the year 1447. And Rome, followed by Arezzo, were very welcoming to the stained glass painter Guillaume de Marcillat, who had come to make a career in Italy.

It is true, however, as Louis Courajod had underlined by 1884, that the influence of Italy was not negligible in France. The king and queen were drawn to the lure of utter novelty. Charles VIII, the "scourge of God" according to Savonarola, had pranced effortlessly all the way to Florence and then Naples. Although stopped at the battle of Fornova, the "French fury" had had time to negotiate the export to the court of artists, designers of buildings (*deviseurs de bastiments*), weavers of cut velvet, keepers of parrots, embroiderers, etcetera, and above all of the gardener Marcoliano, the architect and antiquary Fra Giocondo, and the sculptor Guido Mazzoni. But their activity remains mysterious. Giocondo builds the Pont Notre-Dame in Paris. Mazzoni executes the tomb of Charles VIII and a statue about which we know little at the château of Blois, both destroyed. Of his time in France, there will remain only the frescoes in the chapel of the Hôtel de Cluny, according to a recent suggested attribution (Scailliérez in Paris/Ecouen 2007–08, pp. 43–47). No sculpture in France can claim to take its inspiration from this great specialist in life-size representations of the Lamentation over the body of Christ.

The influence of Jérôme Pacherot is more extensive, partly because he settled in Tours permanently. A native of Naples, he was charged with finding the marble to make the tomb of the sons of Charles VIII and Anne of Brittany (fig. 49). For Cardinal Georges d'Amboise, he worked on the arch of the château of Gaillon, which was perhaps influenced by the arch of Alfonso the Magnanimous at the Castelnuovo in Naples (Bardati 2007). And he directed the team of ornamental sculptors who carved the marble decoration of Gaillon's upper chapel (cats. 108–09).

In 1507–09 the cardinal also had Andrea Solario working for him—painting the frescoes of the Gaillon chapel and the large panel of *The Lamentation* (Musée du Louvre)—as well as Antoine Juste, who provided a large relief of the triumphant entry of Louis XII into Genoa and a series of Christ and the apostles (cat. 101). Juste and his brother Jean (Antonio and Giovanni di Giusto Betti) came from Florence. While Jean was responsible for the tomb of Thomas James, bishop of Dol, in Brittany (1507), Antoine worked at Gaillon, before starting on his great work, the tomb of Louis XII and Anne of Brittany.

Ecclesiastics and ambassadors did not wait for the Italian wars to provide themselves with works of art. Just as Guillaume Fillastre commissioned Andrea della Robbia's workshop to execute his tomb (cat. 18) in 1469, in 1484 Thomas James, bishop of Dol, had his missal illuminated by the Florentine miniaturist Attavante. It is nevertheless clear that the glimpse of an "earthly paradise," as Charles VIII described it in his letters from Naples, whetted appetites. First there were the spoils of war that would enrich the royal collections, such as the Greek manuscripts of the Aragonese kings of Naples, which were transferred to Amboise, and the relocation of entire collections from the duchy of Milan. But other acquisitions made by the king were more peaceful. Anne of Brittany's inventory indicates the presence of paintings from Naples or in the Italian or Lombard manner. In all probability, masterpieces by Leonardo—*La Belle Ferronnière* (in reality the portrait of a Lombard lady) and *The Virgin of the Rocks* (figs. 32, 48)—belonged to Louis XII.

The possession of the duchy of Milan by Louis XII between 1502 and 1515 produced fruitful artistic relationships. Indeed, it was there that the French discovered a passion for Leonardo's art. By 1501, Florimond Robertet commissioned Leonardo to create the *Madonna of the Yarnwinder*; (see cat. 114). Gabriel Gouffier, an apostolic prothonotary, had Marco d'Oggiono make a copy of *The Last Supper* in

---

Facing Page

FIGURE 48.
Leonardo da Vinci. *Virgin and Child with Saint John the Baptist and an Angel (The Virgin of the Rocks)* (detail; fig. 32). Oil on panel, transferred to canvas. Musée du Louvre, Paris.

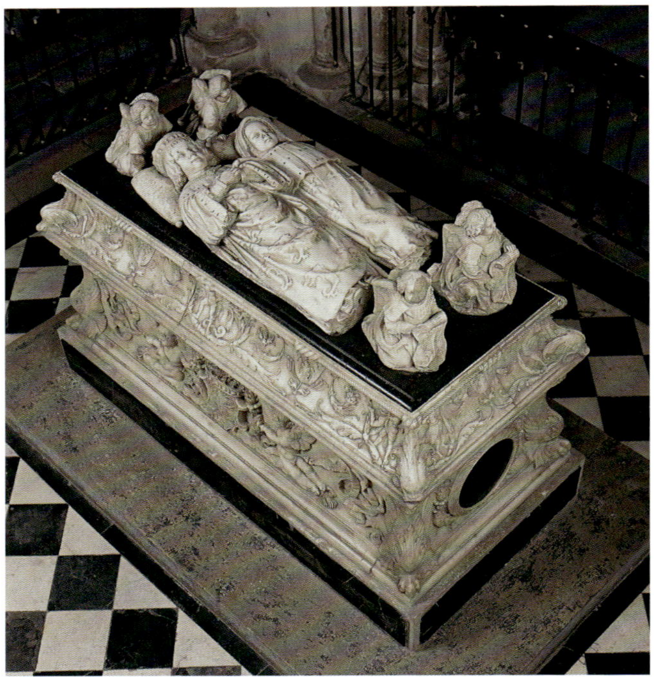

FIGURE 49.
Jérôme Pacherot (Girolamo Paciarotto) and Tours workshop. *Tomb of the Children of Charles VIII*. Marble, with traces of gilding on the sarcophagus. Cathedral of Saint-Gatien, Tours (formerly in the abbey church of Saint Martin, Tours).

1506; it was later brought to the chapel of the château of Ecouen, where it remains to this day (fig. 50). On the same occasion, he commissioned an altarpiece of the Passion from d'Oggiono, which has not survived.

Especially in demand were works in Carrara marble sculpted in Genoa or Milan. The most prestigious undertakings were destined for Louis XII, who asked his treasurer in Milan, Jean Hérouet, to organize the production of the tombs for his grandparents, Louis d'Orléans and Valentina Visconti (the latter providing the basis for his claim to the duchy of Milan); for his father, the poet Charles d'Orléans; and for his uncle, Philippe, Count de Vertus. The contract, executed in August 1502, provided details concerning the marbles—recumbent tomb figures, bases, and statuettes—sculpted by two partnerships active on the Genoese scene, that of the Lombards Michele d'Aria and Girolamo Viscardo and that of the Florentines Benedetto da Rovezzano and Donato Benti. Two of the sculptors came to install the monument at the convent of the Celestines in Paris (now in Saint-Denis).

Emulating the king, his counselors in Italy had marble sent for their own residences. The most acquisitive among them was Cardinal Georges d'Amboise, who transformed the château of Gaillon, his country palace near Rouen, into a center of the early Renaissance in France. He paid to rent a shed on the port of Genoa for the work of the sculptor Pace Gagini. This was how the large Genoese fountains were transported (one to Rouen, and two to Gaillon) and installed by the Genoese Bertrand de Meynal; one of them had been commissioned in 1506 from the sculptors Agostino Solario and Antonio della Porta in association with Pace Gagini. In Milan, where his nephew Charles II d'Amboise was governor, the cardinal also commissioned the statue of the king (cat. 100) from Lorenzo da Muzzano and imported medallions in the antique style with Guido Mazzoni and the admiral Prégent as his agents (cats. 103–05).

Indeed, marble medallions, a more or less artisanal type of production like holy water fonts (examples in Tours, Bourges, etc.), could easily be imported by sea. As early as 1502, the fabric of Milan Cathedral had authorized Cristoforo Solari to make six medallions for a "maréchal de France," who was either Gian Giacomo Trivulzio or the Marshal de Gyé. Eight medallions and applied busts, signed by Lorenzo da Muzzano, decorated the Palais de Justice in Grenoble (Musée de Grenoble); sixteen others were integrated into the decor of the château of Meillant, which was the property of Charles II d'Amboise; and still others were installed at the château of Nançay, the property of Gabriel de La Châtre (cats. 106–07).

At the same time, Raoul de Lannoy, French governor of Genoa after the 1507 revolt, commissioned Antonio della Porta, known as Tamagnino, who had made a name for himself with his work on the charterhouse of Pavia, to produce his funerary monument in white marble for the chapel at his property in Folleville in Picardy. The sculptor executed the works in Genoa and entrusted the transport of the marbles to his nephew Pace Gagini. Thus it was that Gagini came to install the beautiful tombstone representing the couple, as well as a relief decorated with two small funerary putti, in a niche in the French style, carved by local workshops (fig. 36). To this were added the figures of an Entombment, later transferred to Joigny in Burgundy, the only surviving group of this type in marble. It is likely that the medallion of Antoine de Lannoy (Musée de Picardie, Abbeville) arrived under similar circumstances.

Antoine Bohier, abbot of Fécamp and counselor to the king, was also particularly ambitious during his time in Genoa in May 1507. He contracted with Girolamo Viscardo for three marble monuments, consisting of architectural structures with ornamental pilasters, statuettes, and reliefs: a shrine with virtuoso decoration for the relic of the Holy Blood; an altar of the Savior, from which five bas-reliefs survive; and a reliquary casket decorated with small figures of the apostles and two statues, Saint Suzanne and Saint Taurin (Bottineau-Fuchs 2003B).

Other, less known monuments deserve to be mentioned, including the large alabaster *Virgin with Child*, given in 1510 to François de Rochechouart, governor of Genoa from 1508 to 1512, who had it installed at his château of La Motte-Chandenier (now in Poitiers Cathedral). In Auvergne, two statues from the Sainte-Chapelle of Aigueperse, the *Virgin* and *Saint Louis*, were probably sculpted from Italian marble. At the château of Cordés, also in Auvergne, a whole

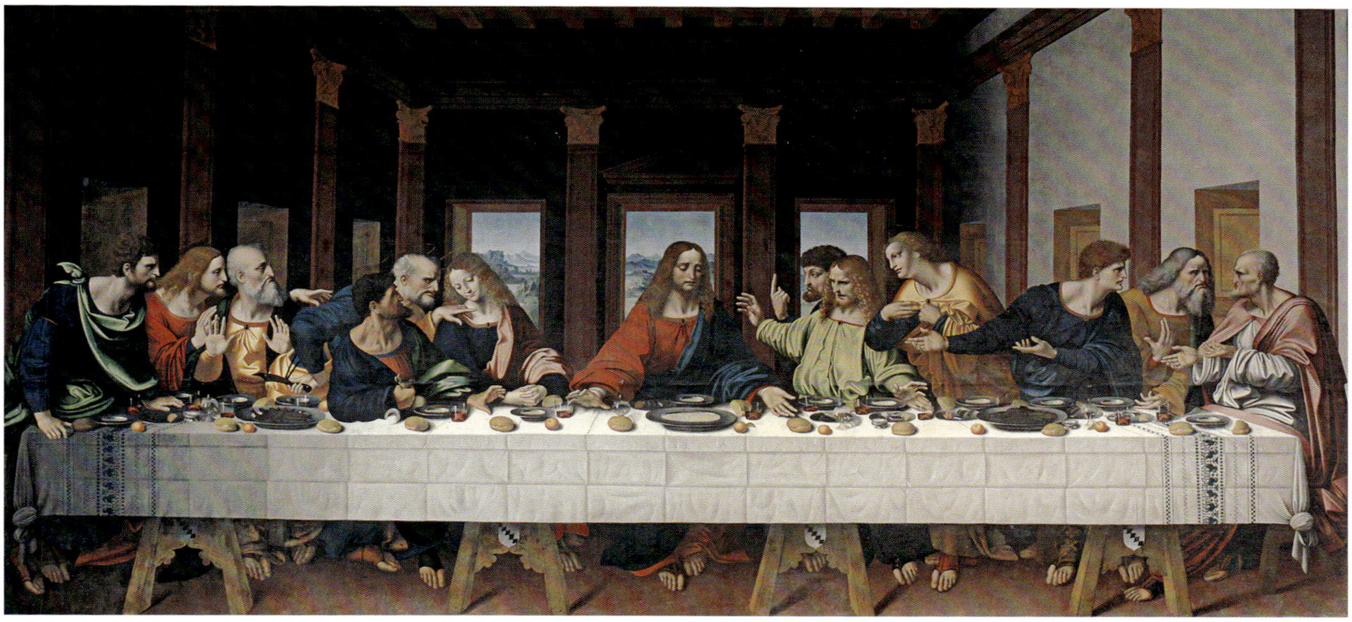

FIGURE 50.
Marco d'Oggiono, after Leonardo da Vinci. *The Last Supper*. Oil on panel. Musée national de la Renaissance, Château d'Ecouen.

group has recently been studied: an altarpiece, a holy water font, and the funerary monument for Yves II d'Allègre, killed at the battle of Ravenna in 1512 and a companion of the almost legendary Chevalier de Bayard (Durin-Tercelin 2004); and we must add a holy water font signed *Jehan de la Barda, 1512* in the church of Meilhaud near Issoire.

From outside those parts of Italy dominated by the French king, importations were less common. From Venice came only a few pieces of glass (cats. 36–37). But Florence, which made a strong impression at the time of Charles VIII's passage to Naples, sent a few handsome pieces. *The Nativity* (1490), signed by Benedetto Ghirlandaio, the brother of the great Domenico, landed at the Sainte-Chapelle d'Aigueperse. In 1496, the Signoria of Florence gave Jean de Ganay, the future chancellor of France, a mosaic altarpiece by David Ghirlandaio, and in 1512 they gave Jacques Hurault, bishop of Autun, the *Mystic Marriage of Saint Catherine* by Fra Bartolomeo (fig. 51). Two other works by Fra Bartolomeo arrived in France before 1516, the *Nativity* (cat. 115) and, probably, the *Noli me tangere* from the royal collection (Louvre). As for the insatiable Marshal de Gyé, who had obtained from the Signoria seven marble heads and two bronze ones, he insisted on having a rendering of Donatello's bronze *David* made by Michelangelo himself. But the piece (now lost), completed in 1508 by Benedetto da Rovezzano, finally ended up at the Blois town house of Florimond Robertet. In the meantime, the Marshal de Gyé had received a bronze *Vulcan* from Mantua in 1503, for the art of the court of the Gonzagas of Mantua was also solicited. Already the Sainte-Chapelle of Aigueperse had received, perhaps as part of the dowry of Chiara Gonzaga, the wife of Gilbert de Bourbon-Montpensier, whom she married in 1481, the superb *Saint Sebastian* by Andrea Mantegna. From that point on, everyone sought out Mantegna: Cardinal Georges d'Amboise in 1499, Louis II de La Trémoille in 1502, the young Francis of Angoulême in 1504. When the great painter died in 1506, his successor at the Gonzaga court, Lorenzo Costa, also took his place in the hearts of the French: in 1508, Florimond Robertet obtained the *Saint Veronica*, and in 1510 the queen received the *Holy Family*.

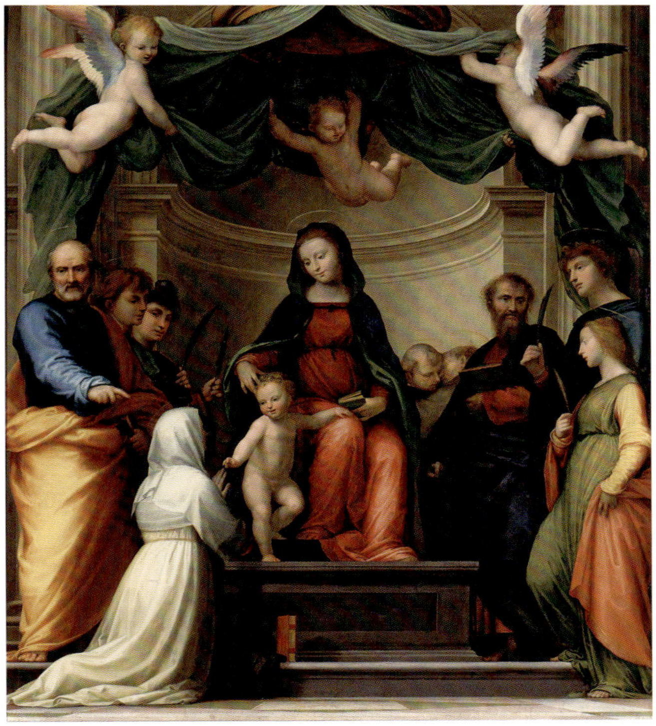

FIGURE 51.
Fra Bartolommeo (Baccio della Porta). *The Mystic Marriage of Saint Catherine*. Oil on panel. Musée du Louvre, Paris.

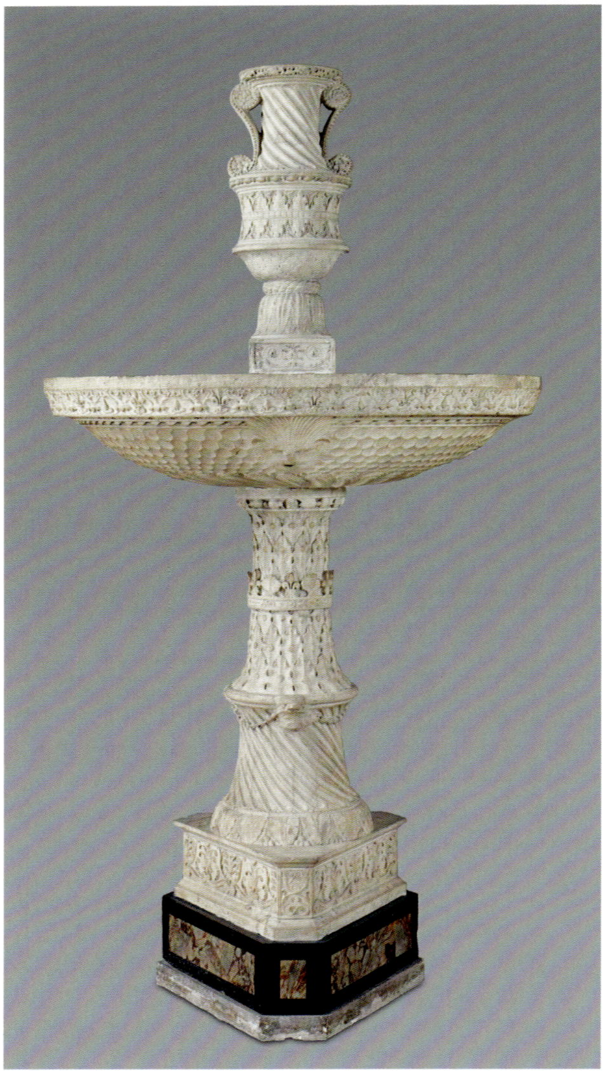

[99]

Fountain

Loire Valley, 1500/10

Marble; H. 235 cm (92½ in.); diam. 122 cm (48 in.)

Musée du Louvre, Paris, Department of Sculpture, MR 1660

PROVENANCE: Acquired as an exchange with the marble mason Mazetti in November 1800 by Alexandre Lenoir for the Musée des Monuments Français; entered the Louvre, 1818.

BIBLIOGRAPHY: Vitry 1901b, p. 149. Lesueur 1937, pp. 75–76. Chirol 1952, pp. 219–22. Miller 1977, pp. 71–72. Beaulieu 1978, no. 69. Bresc-Bautier 1998, pp. 196–200. Gaborit 1998, p. 618.

THIS FOUNTAIN was acquired by Alexandre Lenoir from a marble mason who did not participate in the dismantling of the château of Gaillon. Lenoir later spread the idea that it came from Gaillon. This traditional identification with one of the fountains of Cardinal Georges d'Amboise is not tenable, since the engraving in Jacques Androuet du Cerceau's *Les Plus Excellent Bastiments de France* (1576–79) recorded the two fountains that did come from Italy, allowing them to be identified, and there is no evidence for a third. From the point of view of technique, iconography, and style, this fountain is related to the basin that is still at the château of Blois, a vestige of one of the fountains that could have been acquired in Tours in 1503. A Blois provenance is thus a possibility, particularly since the work does not bear the emblems of Cardinal d'Amboise—in contrast to the fountains from Gaillon. The style of the ornamentation is also related to the fountain of the Hôtel de Beaune in Tours. The emblems are those of the royal couple, Louis XII and Anne of Brittany. We can distinguish the crown ornamented with fleurs-de-lis encircling the base, the porcupine heads used as a symbol by Louis XII on the underside of the basin, and a frieze on its edge with the lilies of France alternating with the ermine tails of Brittany.

The fountain consists of three pieces of marble: a cylindrical base resting on a triangular plinth, a basin, and a shaft in the form of a vase-baluster. It originally had two basins, but only the upper one has survived. The water rose up to the top through the shaft and flowed down into the basins, escaping through the holes in the porcupine heads on the upper basin.

The decorative vocabulary is largely borrowed from classical art, but has been enriched and transformed: *feuille d'eau, rai-de-coeur* with little flowers interspersed, a twisting gadroon border, and spiral fluting. Bird heads hold a garland suspended from their beaks. The curve of the two basins was decorated with concave scales. In contrast, one detail suggests a decorative sculptor still working in the Gothic tradition: the upper edge of the vase has a narrow border carved with acanthus leaves.

The use of fine white marble suggests that the raw material was transported from Carrara and Genoa, perhaps in a semi-finished state, but not as a completed work. It may have been carved in Tours, like the fountains for Blois or like the fountain of the Hôtel de Beaune in Tours, the work of Martin and Bastien François. This hypothesis was advanced by Vitry (1901B), Lesueur (1977), and Miller (1977). • GB-B

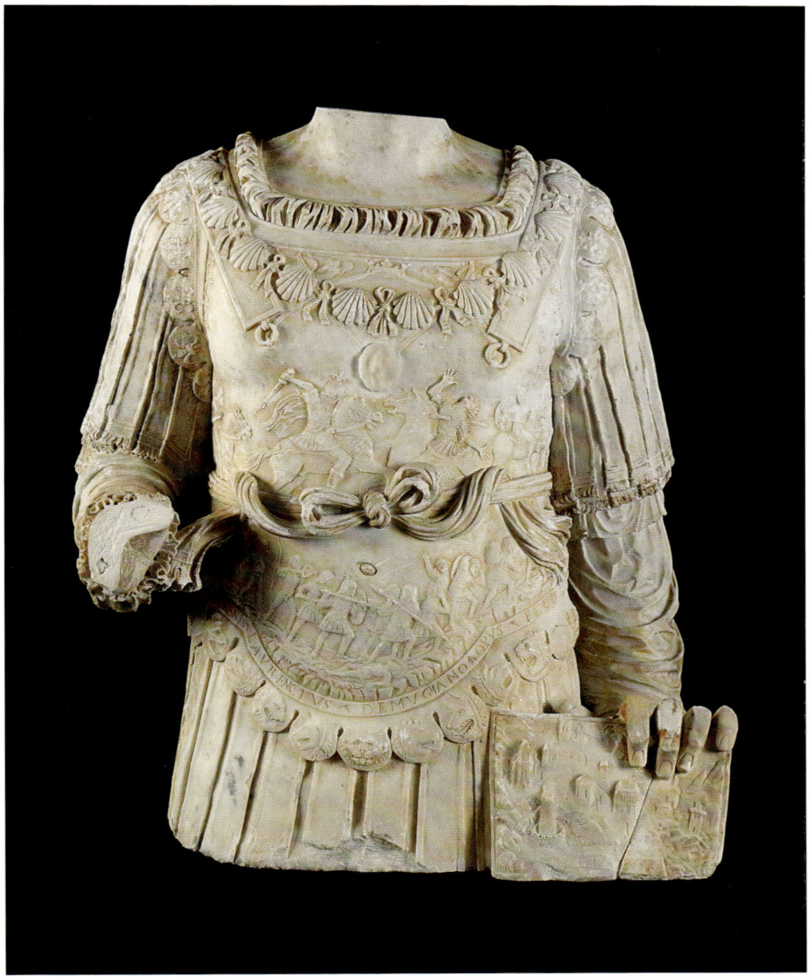

[100]

LORENZO DA MUZZANO
(active 1490–1510)

Louis XII

Milan, 1508

Marble; 70.4 x 70 x 38 cm ($27\frac{11}{16}$ x $27\frac{9}{16}$ x $14\frac{15}{16}$ in.)

Musée du Louvre, Paris, Department of Sculpture, MR 1596 A

SIGNED AND DATED: *MEDIOLANENSIS LAVRENCIVS DEMUGIANO OPVS FECIT 1508* (on the cuirass)

PROVENANCE: Executed in Milan; château of Gaillon; sold by the marble mason Corbel to Alexandre Lenoir for the Musée des Monuments Français, 1796–98; entered the Louvre, 1818.

BIBLIOGRAPHY: Vitry 1901b, pp. 150–51. Chirol 1952, pp. 173–75. Scheller 1985, pp. 56–57. Zani 2000, p. 35. Le Pogam 2008, pp. 46–47.

EXHIBITIONS: Rouen 1980–81, no. 60. Paris 1985, no. 34. Blois 1987–88, no. 29. Paris/Frankfurt 1990.

THIS HALF-LENGTH STATUE of Louis XII, the first great royal sculpture in the Roman style, is signed by Lorenzo da Muzzano and dated 1508. It was commissioned in Milan after the king had conquered that duchy and when Charles II d'Amboise, nephew of Cardinal Georges d'Amboise, was its governor. The cardinal's accounts include payments for wine and ropes for the carters who carried the "*portraictures*" of the king, the cardinal, and his nephew, as well as the cost of river transport from Paris to Rouen on July 19, 1508 (Deville 1850, pp. 286–87). Decapitated at the time of the French Revolution, the figure wears the collar of the Order of Saint Michael and a cuirass in the antique style. If the king's lost right hand once held a royal scepter, this might explain why it was broken off; the left hand displays a plaque with a schematic map of northern Italy. Abbreviated inscriptions and stylized monuments identify the cities: Milan, Cremona, Verona (or Venice), Florence and its baptistery, Rome and the Coliseum, and Genoa. The delicacy of the relief and sophistication of details like the knotted belt are entirely consistent with the Lombard school of the 1500s. Traces of preparation suggest that the marble was extensively gilded.

Muzzano's career has recently been reassessed. Apprenticed to Giovanni Antonio Amadeo (1447–1522), he participated under that master's direction in the vast project of Milan Cathedral. Also in that city, he worked with Andrea da Saronno on the tomb of Ernesto Brasca in Sant'Eufemia and on the ornamentation of Santa Maria presso San Celso, executing sculptures in terracotta and stone, including a Saint Gregory that he signed in 1503. He probably specialized in works for the export market, signing four of the twelve applied portraits of Roman emperors that decorated the Palais de Justice in Grenoble (Musée de Grenoble) as well as executing this marble statue for Gaillon, and perhaps the two others mentioned above.

Three images of Louis XII embellished the château of Gaillon. This half-length figure, and sculptures of the cardinal and his nephew were displayed on the facade overlooking the courtyard of the Grand'Maison, where it was described in 1678. Another image of Louis in the antique style appeared with that of the cardinal on the entry gate. The king also appeared in a series of terracotta portraits that included Charles VIII, Anne of Brittany, Georges I d'Amboise, Charles and Suzanne of Bourbon, Charles II d'Amboise, Jeanne Malet de Graville, Eleanor of Aragon, Cardinal Sanseverino, and the wife of the superintendent of finance. The existence of this series at Gaillon based on the accounts of Jacopo Probo d'Atri in March 1509 and Antonio de Beatis in 1517, should nevertheless be treated with caution. It could also refer to busts from the château of La Péraudière. All that remains of these is a half-length statue of a woman, truncated in the same way as the one of Louis XII, and transformed into a figure of Joan of Arc by the sculptor Pierre-Nicolas Beauvallet in 1800 (Musée d'Orléans). • GB-B

[101]

ANTONIO DI GIUSTO BETTI, KNOWN AS ANTOINE JUSTE
(1479–1519)

Head of an Apostle (Saint Peter?)

1508/09

Terracotta; 30 x 28 x 19.9 cm (11 13/16 x 11 x 7 7/8 in.)

Musée du Louvre, Paris, Department of Sculpture, RF 2574

PROVENANCE: Fragment of one of the statues of the apostles made for the upper chapel of the château of Gaillon; damaged during the Revolution. Found in excavations in the town and noted as being in the office of the prison director, 1888; Louvre, 1901; given by Paul Vitry, 1940.

BIBLIOGRAPHY: Vitry 1901a. Vitry 1901b, pp. 213–15.Chirol 1952, p. 199, no. 98, pl. 24. Beaulieu 1978, no. 57, p. 50. Gaborit 1998, p. 449. Crépin-Leblond in Paris/Ecouen 2007–08, pp. 103–04.

EXHIBITIONS: Rouen 1980–81, no. 68. Paris/Ecouen 2007–08.

ANTOINE JUSTE received ten payments between November 1, 1508, and October 23, 1509, totaling 297 livres, "for the images in the chapel" (*pour les ymages de la chapel*) of the château of Gaillon (Deville 1850, pp. 419–20). Although their subject is not specified,

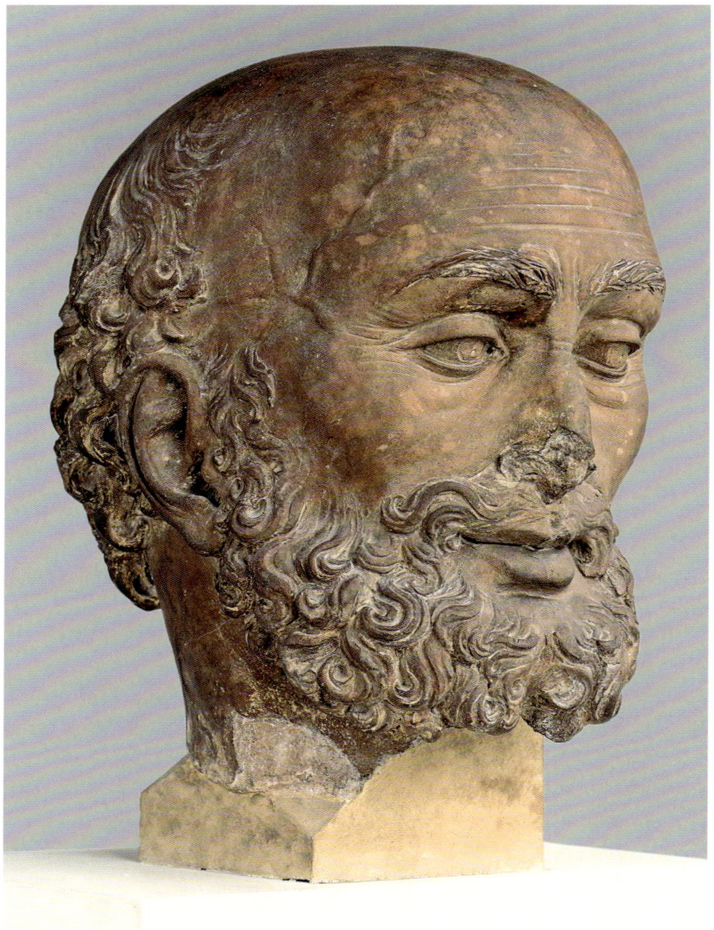

these "images" must correspond to a solidly attested apostolic procession surrounding Christ: "the figures of twelve apostles in relief" (*les figures de douze apôtres en relief*) are cited by Thomas Corneille in 1750. During the French Revolution, the statues of Christ and a saint were moved to the parish church of Gaillon; this head of an apostle ended up at the Musée du Louvre by 1901. A 1996 restoration revealed the polychromy of the full-length figures and the inscription on the surviving apostle, identifying him as Saint James. The polychromy was fully consistent with the decor of the Gaillon chapel painted by Andrea Solario. The length of time that the execution of the series took (averaging less than a month per figure) suggests that the modeling as well as the firing occurred on site, the figures having first been hollowed out and cut at mid-body to avoid problems with drying, heating, and cooling in the production process.

The twelve apostles are the twelve pillars of the church; they also symbolize the creed, which they were considered to have written. They sometimes carried the crosses of consecration of the building. Here they may also reference the conclave that could have elected Georges d'Amboise to the papacy. Such apostolic processions, like the one Saint Louis (Louis IX) chose for the Sainte-Chapelle in Paris, for example, also appear in other saintes-chapelles: in Bourges for Jean, duke of Berry, and in Vic-le-Comte for Jean Stuart. These series also evoke the terracotta medallions of the apostles in the chapel of the château of Cognac.

Antoine Juste worked extensively at Gaillon. In the same year, 1508, he was paid 240 livres for the bas-relief of Louis XII's entry into Genoa, a large greyhound, a large stag's head, and portraits of the cardinal and a child (Deville 1850, p. 358). It is not clear that all of this commission was to be executed in stone or marble; some items were probably executed in terracotta and then gilded. The château also contained a series of portrait busts, themselves executed in terracotta, including the bust of Cardinal d'Amboise, which was perhaps the portrait cited in the aforementioned payment. The choice of terracotta is not surprising. Widely used in the sculptor's native Tuscany, it provided both rapidity of execution and economy of materials for life-size figures.

It could have been as a consequence of the Gaillon series that Antoine Juste and his brother Jean received the commission for the tomb of Louis XII, also adorned with the twelve apostles. If the figures on the tomb still show a tendency toward elongation, the heads—small in comparison to the bodies—are not really comparable to those of the Gaillon statues. The variety of hands contributing to the tomb and the premature death of Antoine Juste no doubt explain the profound originality of these terracotta statues. • GB-B

[102]

CRAFTSMEN UNDER THE DIRECTION OF NICOLAS CASTILLE
(active 1503–21)

Six Panels from the Choir Screen of the Chapel of the Château of Gaillon

Normandy, c. 1508–10

Oak; two panels: 87.6 x 21.3 cm (34½ x 8⅜ in.); four panels: 97.8 x 21.3 cm (38½ x 8⅜ in.)

The Metropolitan Museum of Art, New York, gift of J. Pierpont Morgan, 1916.32.299–304

PROVENANCE: Chapel of the château of Gaillon, until the French Revolution; Musée des Monuments Français, Paris, until 1816; transferred to Saint-Denis; Georges Hoentschel, Paris; sold to J. Pierpont Morgan, 1906; given to the museum, 1916.

BIBLIOGRAPHY: Marquet de Vasselot 1927, pp. 355–56. Rieder 1977. Bos and Dubois 2007, pp. 83–97.

THE CHAPEL of the château of Gaillon contained liturgical furnishings of particular importance and richness. Besides its choir stalls, which are partially inlayed with marquetry (housed today at the cathedral of Saint-Denis on the outskirts of Paris), a wooden enclosure separated the choir from the remainder of the chapel. This choir screen exists in a fragmentary state at the Musée national de la Renaissance at Ecouen, and some panels from the ensemble have been dispersed, notably these six preserved in New York. They were part of the lower register of the screen, which also included two upper registers of openwork. At the center was a portal giving access to the choir. The carved decoration, of extremely high quality, combined designs in a distinctly Flamboyant style on one face and Italian-influenced ornamentation on the other side, following a principle also seen, for example, in the choir screen of the church of Salles-Curan, Aveyron. These six panels are evidence of an early adoption of Italian motifs, executed at the highest level of quality. The candelabra—formed of delicate scrollwork inhabited by putti and other figures, either nude or hybrid, as well as by eagles—are characteristic of the compositions that were then beginning to be disseminated in France. In addition, one of the panels repeats an engraving from the first years of the sixteenth century attributed to Giovanni Pietro da Birago, attesting to the very rapid repetition of printed models. At their base the panels each present a sculpted medallion following a type that is commonly found on medals; their various motifs include Saint George fighting the dragon, a representation associated with Cardinal Georges d'Amboise, the patron who built the château, and a profile portrait of the cardinal himself.

The preservation of accounts for the construction and furnishing of the château of Gaillon permits us to follow, unfortunately at a substantial remove, the creation of the chapel's liturgical furnishings. A team of twelve to twenty joiners worked here under the direction of Nicolas Castille of Rouen, in collaboration with Richard Carpe, a woodworker probably of Italian origin. Furthermore, the presence of marquetry in the choir stalls clearly reveals the adoption of new techniques from the other side of the Alps. • AB

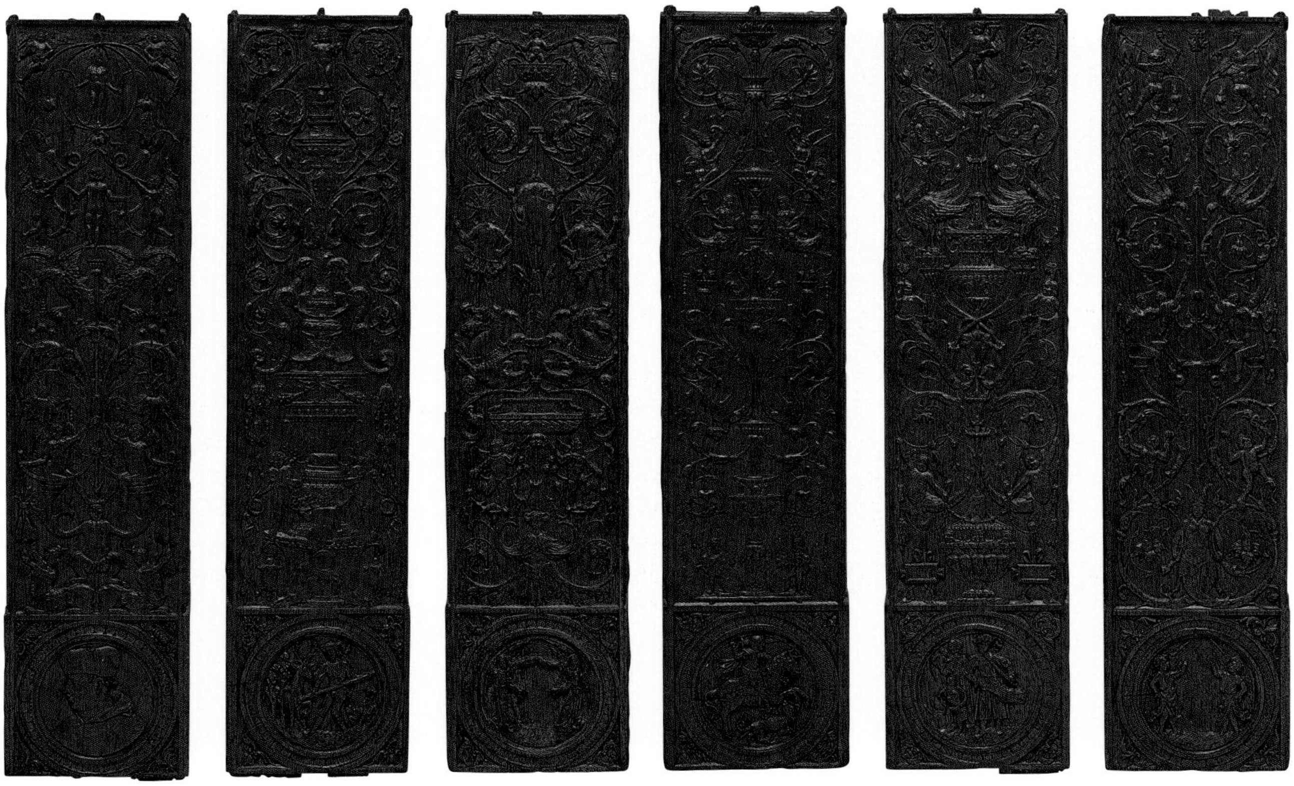

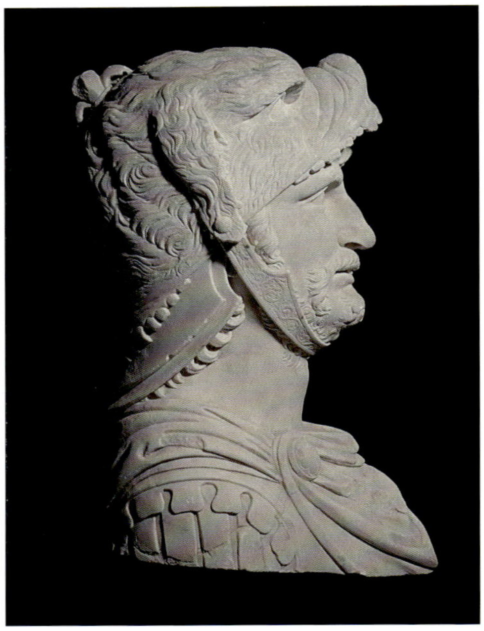

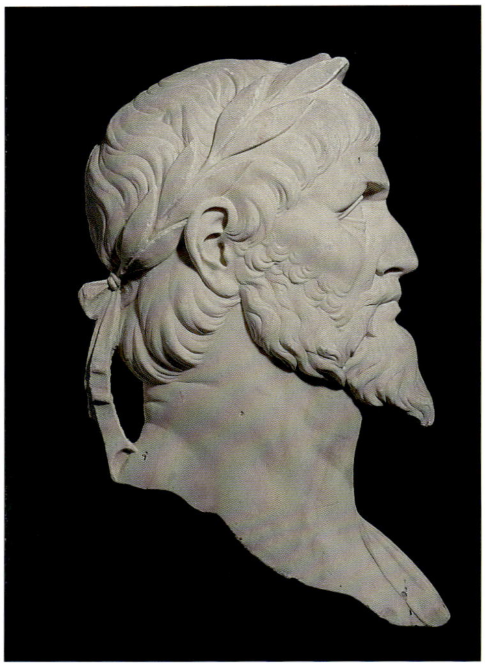

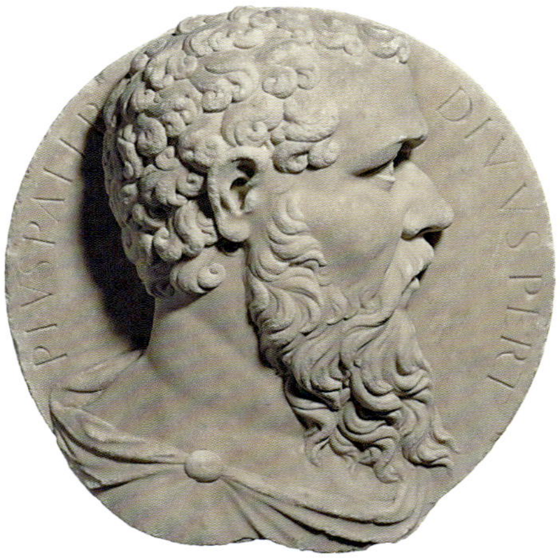

MEDALLIONS FROM THE CHÂTEAU OF GAILLON

[103]

Head with a Helmet

Northern Italy, 1506/08

Applied profile, marble; 47 x 28 x 8 cm ($18\frac{1}{2}$ x 11 x $3\frac{1}{8}$ in.)

[104]

Head of an Emperor with Laurel Crown (Pupien)

Northern Italy, 1506/08

Applied profile, marble; 50 x 32 cm ($19\frac{5}{8}$ x $12\frac{5}{8}$ in.)

[105]

Pertinax

Northern Italy, 1506/08

Medallion, marble; diam. 28 cm ($11\frac{1}{16}$ in.)

INSCRIBED: *PIVS PATER DIVVS PERTINAX*

Musée Départemental des Antiquités, Rouen, on loan from the Musée du Louvre, Ent. 1875-1721, 1875-1727, and 1875-1734

PROVENANCE: Château of Gaillon; purchased for the Musée des Monuments Français, 1802; Louvre, 1818; loaned to the Musée d'Amiens, 1875; loaned to the Musée de Rouen, 2008.

BIBLIOGRAPHY: Bresc-Bautier 2007, pp. 207, 210, 219, 222, 226. Bresc-Bautier 2008a, p. 22.

EXHIBITION: Rouen 2008.

CARDINAL GEORGES D'AMBOISE, the archbishop of Rouen, imported marble medallions representing Roman emperors and figures from antiquity to decorate his country residence at Gaillon. Twelve were sent with the sculptor Guido Mazzoni as intermediary and another nine through the lieutenant-general of the French galleys, the Knight of Saint John, Prégent de Bidoulx (1468–1528). Payments for the installation of the medallions on the walls of the château were made from April 1508 until August 1509 (Deville 1850, pp. 274, 405). There were once many more of these medallions: some forty medallions and applied marble profiles are now known to have come from Gaillon. They have sometimes been attributed to the sculptor Guillaume de Bourges, who was paid for forty-two medallions, but the size of this payment could not correspond to the execution of sculptures in marble. It is more plausible to view the medallions as imported from Italy. From July 1507 until November 1508, Pace Gagini, who had completed the large fountain in the courtyard, paid for the rental of a shed in the port of Genoa for works awaiting shipment to the cardinal.

Notable among the surviving circular medallions are those of Faustina and six emperors in the Musée de Rouen; the medallion inscribed with the fictitious name *Caldusius* (who could be Carausius, for whom no coin is currently known, but who was in fact Gordian III) in the Musée du Louvre; and those of Claudius in the École des Beaux-Arts, Paris, and of Galba at Gaillon. The other portraits are applied profiles of varied execution: the most interesting represent imaginary figures, often wearing bizarre helmets. Others show Roman emperors, not only the twelve Caesars, but also late and rarely depicted emperors such as Pertinax, who ruled for just twenty-seven days in 195. The medallions proper were displayed on the facade overlooking the Seine, their appearance enlarged by the circular settings sculpted for them by Michelet Loir and Pierre Delorme. The applied profiles were also set into large stone frames that displayed them to good effect on the walls of the château's inner courtyard. In March, Jacobo Probo d'Atri described "heads of Roman emperors, also made of marble, finely worked" in the courtyard. While the portraits in the medallions are identified by circular inscriptions modeled on antique coins, the applied profiles were identified on bronze cartouches set in stone panels beneath their frames. Two applied profiles of mythical figures still have their frames. Similar to Italian tondi, these two circular stone frames and others, now empty, remounted at Gaillon, suggest the type of ornamentation disseminated by the della Robbia workshops in glazed terracotta. With three concentric bands forming the round frame, each tondo has classical motifs (eggs, foliage) on the inner circles, contrasting with the outer circle, abundantly decorated with fruit and flowers and sometimes with dolphins or pecking birds.

Wealthy noblemen acquired medallions for themselves in Italy (Jestaz 2003). As early as 1502, the fabric of the cathedral of Milan authorized Cristoforo Solari to execute, between August and December, six marble medallions for a "marshal of France"; this could have been either Trivulzio, governor of Milan, or the Marshal de Gyé, who could have installed them at his château of Le Verger in the Loire Valley. Sixteen medallions decorated the château of Meillant, which belonged to Charles II d'Amboise, nephew of the cardinal. At least six medallions in a slightly oval format embellished the gallery of the château of Nançay, which belonged to Gabriel de La Châtre, captain of the guard for Louis XII. Four of these are now in the Musée de Bourges (*Augustus*, *Nero*, *Vespasian*, and the *King of the Moors*) and two are in the château of La Noue (*Agrippa* and *Antoniis Pius*). Twelve applied busts ornamented the Palais de Justice in Grenoble (Musée de Grenoble), of which four bear the signature of Lorenzo da Muzzano.

This list, which is not exhaustive, demonstrates the desire for imported works, which paralleled the execution of medallions in stone or terracotta in French workshops based on Italian models. The similarities between this group of French medallions and those on the facade of the charterhouse of Pavia or the Colleoni Chapel in Bergamo are striking, even though the exact types are never repeated. The group sometimes gives the impression of decorative artisanal productions intended for export, but with variations that show the effort to create an original work. Two medallions from the château of Nançay are almost identical to ones at Gaillon: one of Nero and another of a bearded subject identified at Gaillon as Pertinax and at Nançay as "the king of the Moors" (*RE DI MORI*). The model is thus the same, but the identification differs, as does the format, which is oval in Nançay and circular in Gaillon. • GB-B

MEDALLIONS FROM THE CHÂTEAU OF NANÇAY

[106]

Vespasian

Northern Italy, 1500/10

Medallion, marble; 29 x 26.2 x 10.3 cm (11 7/16 x 10 5/16 x 4 1/16 in.)

INSCRIBED: *VESPEXIAN IMPERATOR*

[107]

King of the Moors

Northern Italy, 1500/10

Medallion, marble; 30 x 28 x 11.5 cm (11 13/16 x 11 1/4 x 4 1/2 in.)

INSCRIBED: *RE DI MORI*

Musée du Berry, Bourges, 1863.19.3 and 1863.19.4

PROVENANCE: Château de Nançay; Maigny gift, 1863.

BIBLIOGRAPHY: Chancel-Bardelot 2002. Bresc-Bautier 2007, p. 211.

EXHIBITION: Bourges 2002.

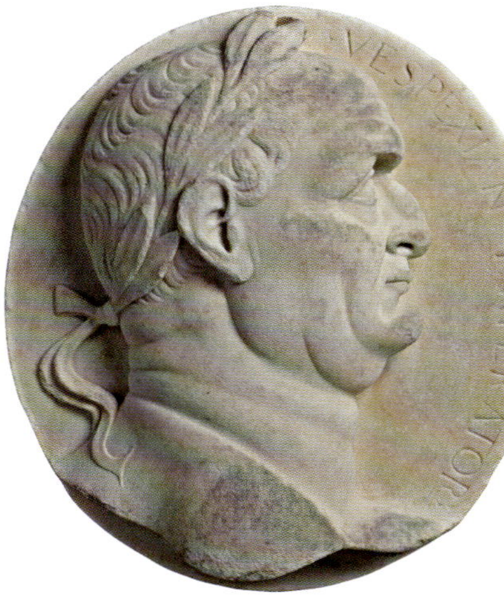

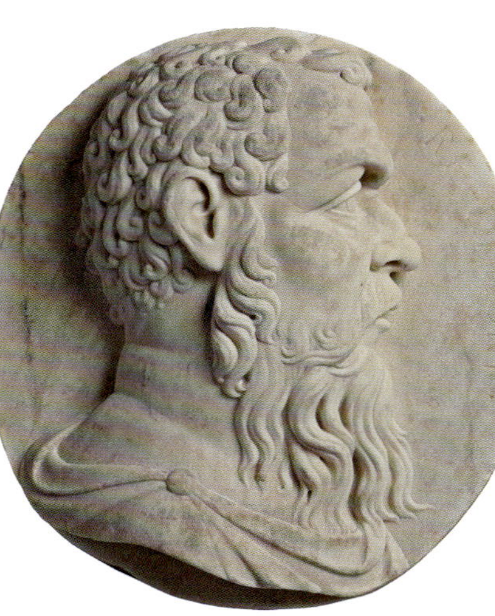

ELEMENTS FROM THE DECORATION OF THE CHÂTEAU OF GAILLON

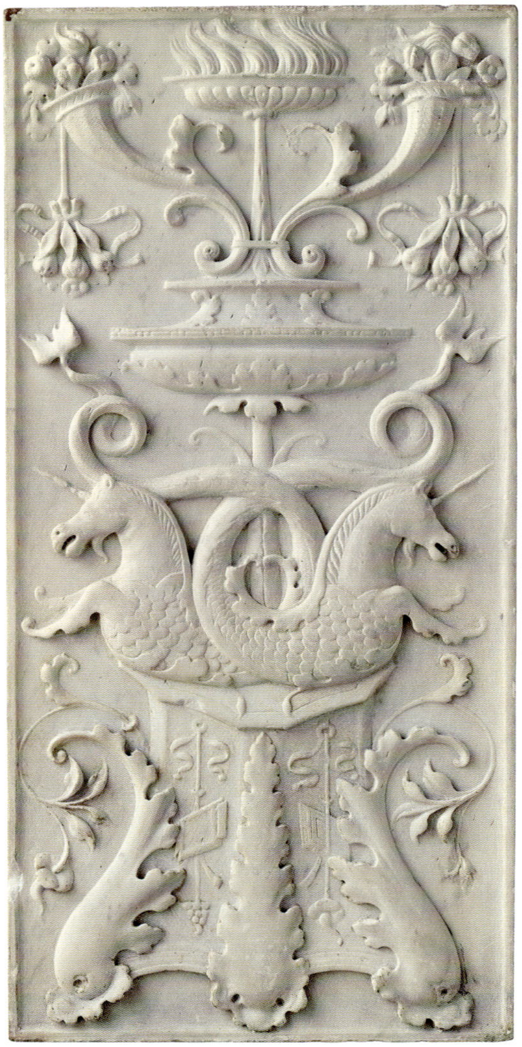

[108]

Panel

1508/10

Marble; 61 x 29 x 6 cm (24 x 11 3/8 x 2 3/8 in.)

Musée du Louvre, Paris, Department of Sculpture, MR 1662A

PROVENANCE, BIBLIOGRAPHY: See below.

[109]

Soffit

1508/10

Marble; 28.5 x 166 x 6.5 cm (11 1/4 x 65 3/8 x 2 9/16 in.)

Musée du Louvre, Paris, Department of Sculpture, MR 1661

PROVENANCE: Upper chapel of the château of Gaillon; acquired by Alexandre Lenoir for the Musée des Monuments Français, 1797 or 1801; entered the Louvre, 1818.

BIBLIOGRAPHY: Chirol 1952, pp. 190, 206. Gaborit 1998, pp. 612–13. Bottineau-Fuchs 2003a, pp. 103, 106.

EXHIBITION: Paris/Ecouen 2007–08 (the soffit only).

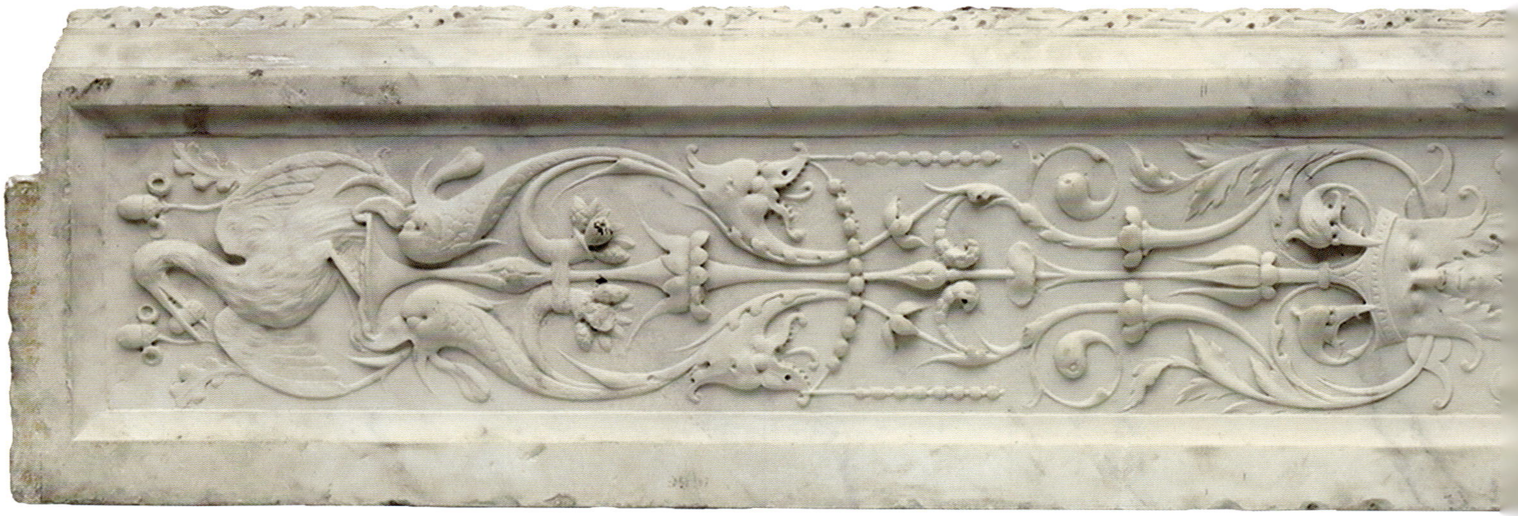

THESE TWO RELIEFS belong to a series of marble elements from the château of Gaillon, more specifically from its upper chapel. The first may be the underside of the lintel of the chapel's door and the second one of the panels decorating the altar. Cardinal Georges I d'Amboise, who wished to embellish his country palace with white marble, had it imported from Italy. He had Italian decorative sculptors working in Italy itself, paying the rent for a shed in the port of Genoa to hold the works of the sculptor Pace Gagini, a Lombard from Bissone. In 1504, Giovanni Spinola had the governor of Genoa intervene with the Marquis of Massa from Carrara to allow shipment of the marble required for the work to be executed in Genoa for the cardinal. This was how a fountain was transported to Rouen, and two large Genoese fountains were delivered to Gaillon, where they were installed by the Genoese Bertrand de Meynal. One of these fountains had been commissioned from the sculptors Agostino Solario and Antonio della Porta in association with Pace Gagini in 1506. At the same time, Italian decorative sculptors were carving raw marble at Gaillon itself. Thus, the Florentine Jérôme Pacherot, the Genoese Bertrand de Meynal, and Jean Chairsalle were paid from October 1508 until July 1509 (Deville 1850, pp. 359–60) for having worked on the "table" and pillars or on the "pierre de marbre" of the chapel. This probably refers not only to the framework of the retable with its main relief of Saint George that Michel Colombe was executing in Tours (fig. 37), but also to the other decoration of the antependium, the steps, and the pillars supporting the altar.

Among the sixteen elements that entered the collection of the Musée du Louvre in 1818, two columns, ten isolated reliefs, and three portions of the altarpiece's frame can be identified. Apparently the soffit, as well as two pilasters, framed the door of the chapel. The inscription on one of the pilasters seems to refer to the cardinal's death in 1510, which would provide a date for its execution.

The chapel's marble ornamentation shows the work of various hands, and it is difficult to distinguish those portions that were imported from those that were executed on site by several sculptors. The soffit, with its low relief, has symmetrical decoration on either side of a central star framed by leafy masks. Around this axis, scrollwork decoration is arranged head-to-tail, including opposed strands of pearls. Long-necked birds, wings outspread, one pecking, the other turning its head, flank the composition. The panel's relief is deeper. It shows a complex candelabrum, whose base, with three foliate dolphins, supports two intertwined seahorses that are surmounted by a basin from which emerge horns of plenty and a flaming vessel. Small scrolls in low relief unfurl on either side to fill the entire space. A *horror vacui* governed this decorative sculptor. It is risky to attribute any specific reliefs to known sculptors. However, it is noteworthy that Pacherot was paid 7 sols 6 deniers, Meynal 6 sols, and Chairsalle 4 sols 6 deniers, suggesting that the first was considered superior, especially as he alone received the initial payment for the work to be done. In addition, Pacherot was involved throughout the entire project and benefited from the collaboration of Meynal from October through January, then of Chairsalle from January until July, while Meynal is specified as working on his own for the three months from March until May 1509. We may therefore surmise that Pacherot played the dominant role and that a certain degree of latitude was given to this Genoese artist. One would like to know who provided the design and who was charged with its execution, because it is not at all clear that the same artist fulfilled these roles. • GB-B

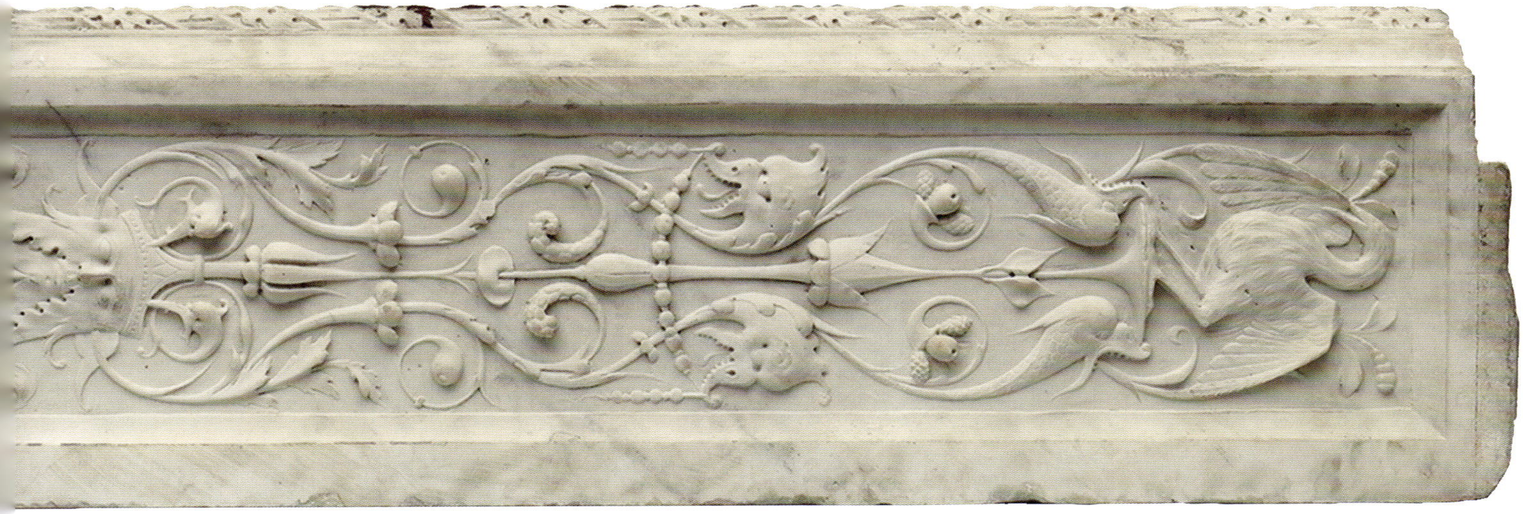

[110]

ITALIAN ILLUMINATORS

Giovanni Michele Nagonio (Nagonius), *De laudibus Galliae* (Songs in Honor of Louis XII)

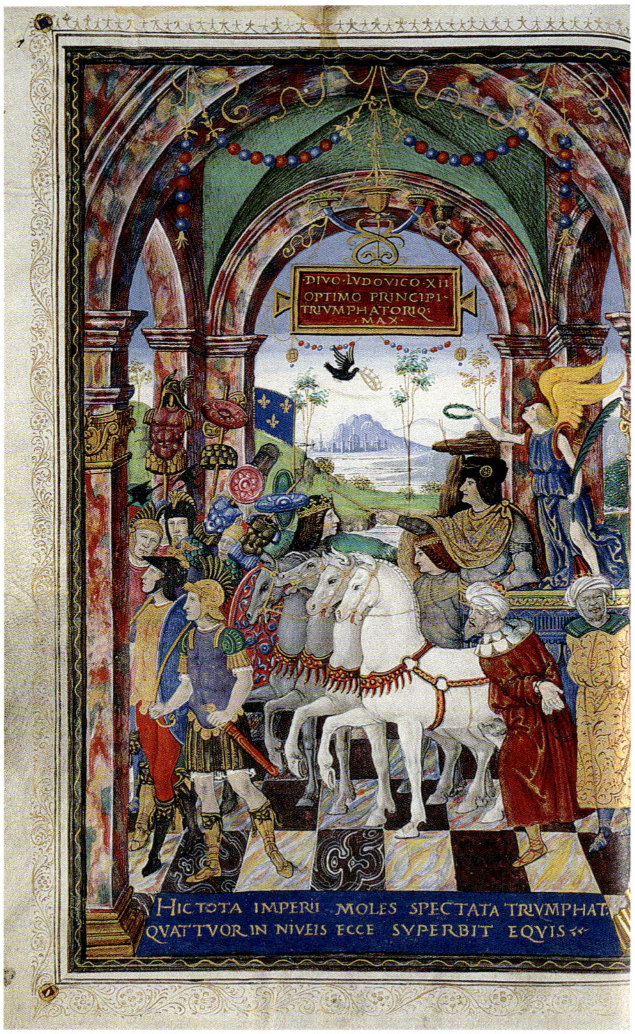

Rome, c. 1500

Tempera on parchment; calf binding with gilt and chiseled edges; VI–197 ff.; 28 x 19 cm (11 x 7½ in.)

Bibliothèque nationale de France, Paris, Department of Manuscripts, ms. lat. 8132

PROVENANCE: Copy presented to Louis XII (d. 1515); Blois, inventory of 1518 [[330] . . . *Item, les œuvres d'ung aultre poete nommé Michael Vagonius qu'ilz envoya au roy Loys XIIe escriptes toutes d'azur et de vermeillon richement historiez au commencement et bien illuminez, couvertes de drap d'or a un esmail et fermans d'argent* (Item, the works of another poet named Michael Vagonius that he sent to king Louis XII written all in blue and red richly historiated at the beginning and well illuminated, covered with cloth of gold with an enamel and silver clasps)]; Fontainebleau, inventory of 1544 [[1778] *Jo. Michaelis Hagenii, civis romani, de Laudibus Gallie; couvert de drap d'or, ferré d'argent, deux fermouers et une placque ronde esmaillee* (Joannes Michael Hagenius, Roman citizen, De Laudibus Gallie; covered with cloth of gold, edged with silver, two clasps and a round plaque enameled)]; royal collection (Rigault II 1003, Dupuy I 1365, Regius 9705).

BIBLIOGRAPHY: Scheller 1985, pp. 20-24, figs. 14–16. Hochner 2006, pp. 50–51, 98–99, 110–12, 154, fig. 13.

EXHIBITIONS: Blois 1987–88, no. 21. Blois/Paris 1992–93, no. 44.

SHOWN: *Triumph of Louis XII*, f. 8v

THE ROMAN POET Giovanni Michele Nagonio specialized in the composition of Latin panegyrics and epigrams for special occasions, in hope of attracting favor to himself. He produced such works for Henry VII of England, Ladislas of Hungary and Bohemia, Pope Julius II and his nephew Francesco Maria della Rovere, Pierre II, duke of Bourbon, and others. The most luxurious example is nevertheless this volume offered by Nagonio to Louis XII.

The six large paintings at the beginning of the manuscript were probably made by the classicizing artists who worked at the Palazzo dei Conservatori in Rome or on the frescoed wall paintings of the bishop's palace at Ostia. However, the scribe for the volume seems to have been French. The original binding was Italian, as can be deduced from the chiseling of the edges, still visible, and the presence of enamels, now vanished, on the covers, as described in early inventories (compare Bibliothèque nationale de France (BnF), ms. Italien 548).

In a scene of triumph depicted in the antique style that takes place under an arcade of multicolored marble, Louis XII is represented as an emperor entering Milan on a chariot drawn by four white horses. He wears the traditional *paludamentum* (cloak) of Roman generals, but over contemporary armor. A Winged Victory bestows a laurel crown on him, while a raven brings him a metal crown. The Saracens who follow the procession evoke the king's claims to the throne of Jerusalem. This Roman triumph recalls antique equestrian statues reinterpreted on the frontispieces of contemporaneous Italian manuscripts (for example, BnF, ms. Italien 372) and thus situates the French monarch as the worthy successor to the Roman emperors. The manuscript was originally intended to celebrate the union of Louis XII and Anne of Brittany, who were married early in 1499; her arms figured on folio 4v. The conquest of the duchy of Milan at the end of 1499 prompted an adaptation of the volume. The queen's arms were covered with those of Ludovico il Moro, the deposed duke of Milan. In the triumphal scene, which probably evokes the entry of the king of France into Milan on October 18, 1499, two crowned figures were added. Ludovico's son, Maximilian Sforza, with his red hair, appears as a captive beside Louis XII. The deposed duke himself, recognizable by his characteristic profile, stands before the chariot, as if welcoming the king of France and delivering his duchy to him. • MHt

[111]

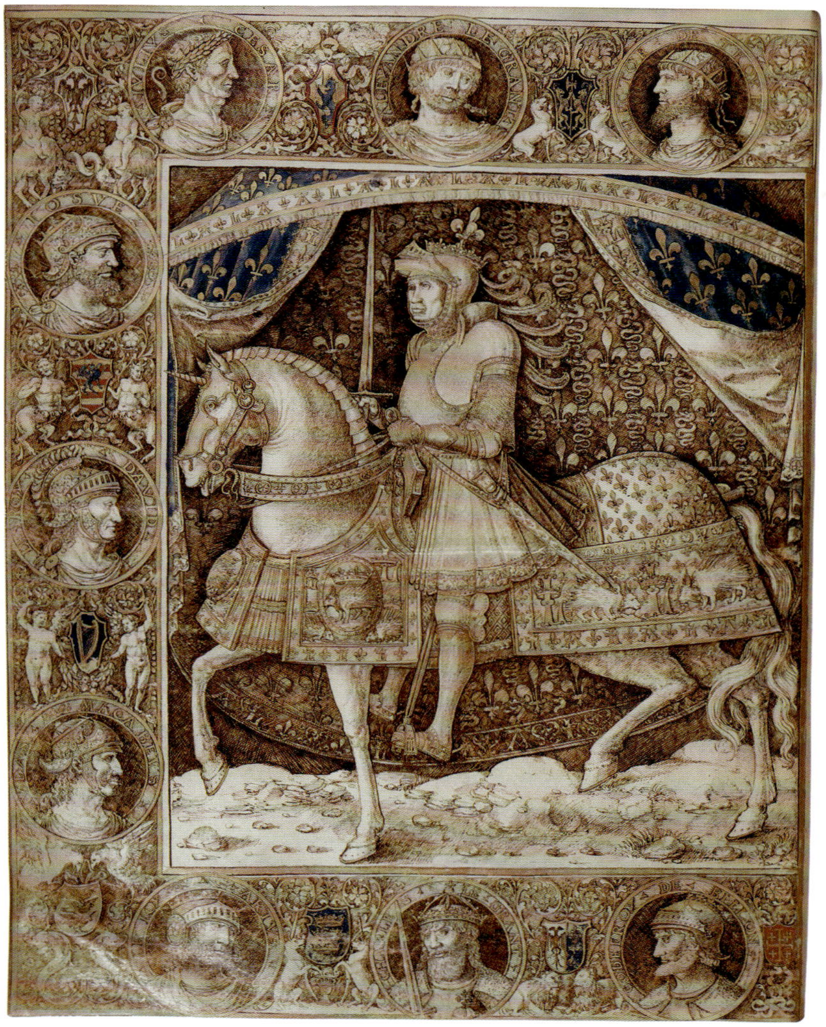

NETHERLANDISH ILLUMINATOR WORKING IN ITALY

Enguerrand de Monstrelet, *Chroniques*

Genoa, 1510

Pen and ink, with tempera and gold on parchment; 192 ff.; 39.5 x 33 x 12.5 cm (15 9/16 x 13 x 4 15/16 in.)

Bibliothèque nationale de France, Paris, Department of Manuscripts, ms. fr. 20360 (vol. 1)

PROVENANCE: François de Rochechouart (d. 1530), governor of Genoa, to 1512; Louis-Jean Gaignat; Louis-César de La Baume Le Blanc, Duke of La Vallière; purchased at the time of the sale of his collection for the royal library, 1784.

BIBLIOGRAPHY: Giordano 2003, pp. 258–59. Hochner 2006, pp. 84, 94, 106.

EXHIBITIONS: Paris 1907, no. 85. Blois 1987–88, no. 20. Paris 1991, no. 44. Paris 1993, no. 239.

SHOWN: Frontispiece, f. 1

THIS COPY OF the *Chronicles* of Enguerrand de Monstrelet (c. 1400–1453) in three volumes (ms. fr. 20360–62) provides a masterly illustration of the French elite's fascination with Italian art and with the aesthetic of Netherlandish artists at the start of the sixteenth century. The colophon inserted by the scribe François Bardin at the end of the third volume (ms. fr. 20362, f. 192) indicates that the manuscript was made at the order of François de Rochechouart, counselor and chamberlain of Louis XII, in Genoa in 1510, when this powerful nobleman was the governor of the city. Instead of approaching an Italian painter, Rochechouart gave the task of illustrating the manuscript to a Netherlandish artist, who executed seventy-four pen-and-ink drawings of great refinement, in a style close to that of contemporary prints by Lucas van Leyden and Albrecht Dürer. While illustrating Monstrelet's account of the history of France, England, and the Low Countries during the latter half of the Hundred Years War in a lively northern narrative manner, this anonymous draftsman still reveals a marked taste for the ornamental vocabulary of the Italian Renaissance.

The first volume opens with a sumptuous full-page drawing representing Louis XII on horseback (ms. fr. 20360, f. 1). The king of France appears as a military commander, his sword drawn, mounted on a steed whose caparison bears Louis's emblem, the porcupine. He is framed by a pavilion displaying a heraldic decoration composed of his initial linked with that of his wife Anne of Brittany, together with the fleurs-de-lis of France and the serpent emblem of the duchy of Milan, which Louis had reclaimed as an inheritance from the Visconti dukes. In accord with an idea pursued in contemporary propagandistic literature such as André de La Vigne's *Voyage de Naples* and Jean Marot's *Voyage de Venise*, the king is associated with the traditional Nine Worthies (*neuf preux*), who are represented here in medallions in the border. The three biblical heroes—Joshua, David, and Judas Maccabeus; the three pagan heroes, Hector of Troy, Alexander the Great, and Julius Caesar; and the three Christian champions, King Arthur, Charlemagne, and Godfrey of Bouillon, the ideal knight of the Middle Ages—are presented in the antique manner, like the profiles of Roman emperors that ornament the corresponding frontispiece of the second volume (ms. fr. 20361, f. 1). Their imaginary coats of arms are borne by centaurs, satyrs, and naked putti in a decorative fantasy that again combines medieval and classical elements. • MJ

[112]

ANDREA SOLARIO
(c. 1465–1524)

Christ Carrying the Cross

1505

Tempera and oil on panel, transferred to canvas, then to a new wood support; 51.6 x 52.1 cm (20¼ x 20½ in.)

Private collection

SIGNED AND DATED: *ĀD MEDIOLANĒS F* 1505 (upper left)

PROVENANCE: Francesco Galgani, Siena, by 1851, until c. 1890; perhaps the painting of the same theme measuring 48 x 51 cm, said to have been with the Milanese dealer Baslini, then in a Grenoble private collection, and offered to the Musée du Louvre, July 22, 1938; Heim Gallery, London, 1967; private collection, c. 1981; Jozef Grabski, Vienna, 1983; Barbara Piasecka Johnson, Princeton, N.J., 1984; sold, Sotheby's, London, July 8, 2009; private collection, United States.

BIBLIOGRAPHY: Vasari 1851, vol. 7, p. 104 n. 1. Calvi 1865, vol. 2, p. 273. Crowe and Cavalcaselle 1871, p. 54 n. 1. Morelli 1874, vol. 9, p. 252. Morelli 1880, p. 75 n. 1. Malvezzi 1882, p. 193. Morelli 1890, pp. 217, 221. Crowe and Cavalcaselle 1912, vol. 2, p. 377 n. 3. Badt 1914, pp. 37–38 n. 1, 216. Cogliati Arano 1965, p. 95. Brown 1987, pp. 86, 88, 143, no. 20, fig. 65. Brown 1990, pp. 110–17, no. 18.

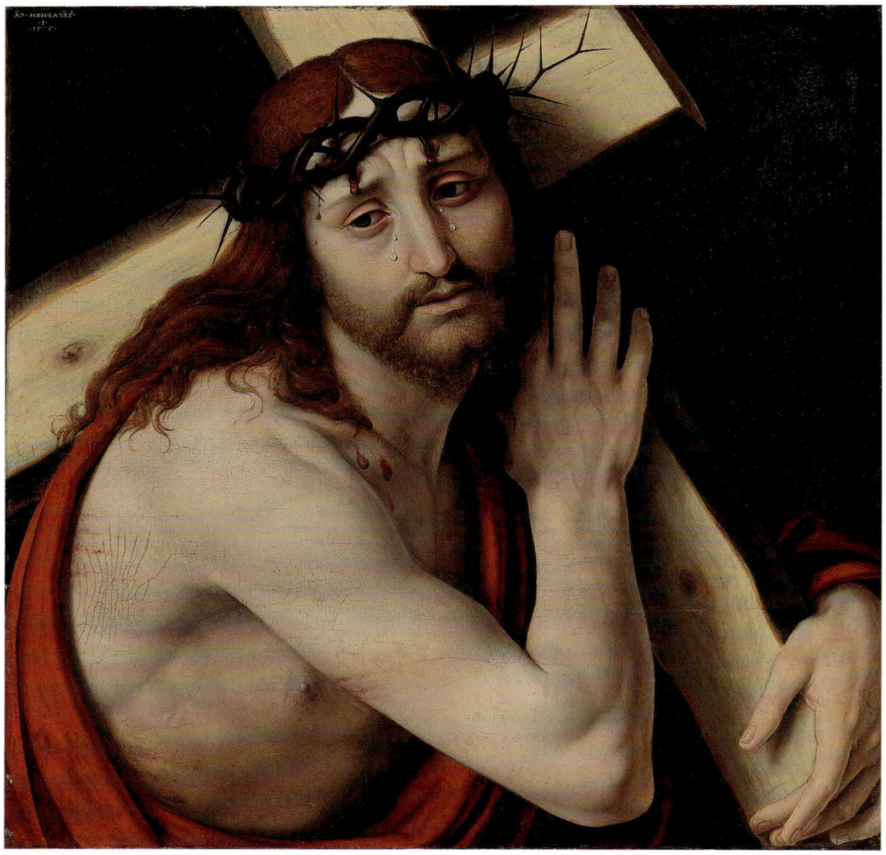

THIS EMOTIONALLY CHARGED picture depicts Christ carrying the cross upon which he will soon be crucified. Unlike scenes that are set within a larger Passion narrative, here Christ inhabits the picture alone, caught in a specific, yet timeless, moment. Around 1500, the iconography of Christ's journey to Calvary shifted from a narrative recounting to the suspended instant favored by many Italian artists. This emphasis on the isolated moment finds partial explanation in the devotional literature of the period, in which worshippers are urged to meditate on individual instances of Christ's suffering.

The panel's composition relates to a late-fifteenth-century woodcut by an anonymous artist that circulated throughout northern Italy. However, unlike this print—which shows Christ's face in profile and his body clothed in a tunic and voluminous robe—the painting by Solario depicts Christ in three-quarter view clad only in a toga, while his visage, and its attendant signs of suffering—bloodshot eyes and cascading, sculpturally rendered tears—are presented frontally. A metalpoint drawing by Leonardo (Accademia, Venice) is an early instance in which Christ is shown at this angle and probably served as a source for Solario's composition. Despite the frontal presentation of Christ's face, his oblique gaze portends his future hardship—an agony so profound that he cannot make eye contact with the viewer.

Often cited as the first artist to bring Renaissance painting to France, Solario resided there from April 19, 1507, until after August 1509. He worked for Cardinal Georges d'Amboise, and is recorded as painting decorations, now lost, for the chapel of his château at Gaillon in Normandy. He is known to have painted a series of frescoed portraits of the Amboise family (destroyed during the French Revolution), a *Nativity* (unlocated), and the *Lamentation over the Dead Christ* (possibly executed for Gaillon; Musée du Louvre), which bears the Amboise coat of arms. Ultimately, Solario's smooth surfaces—what Bernard Berenson describes as his "high porcelain finish"—would have a lasting impact on sixteenth-century French art. • ES-P

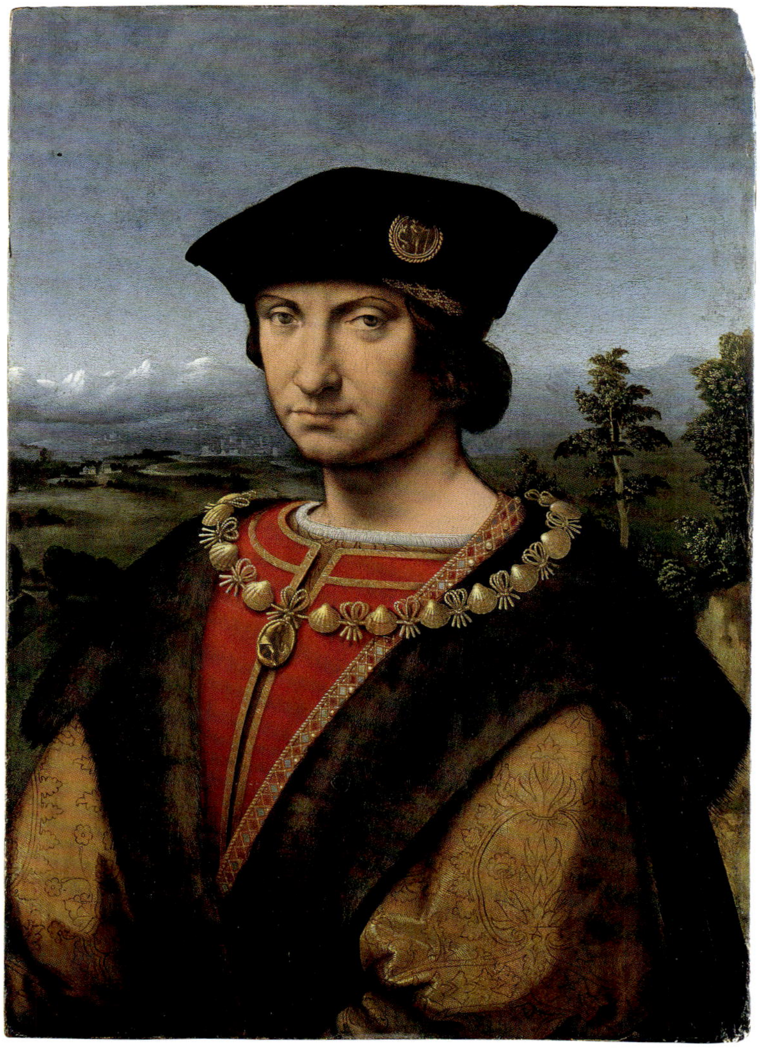

[113]

AFTER ANDREA SOLARIO
(c. 1465–1524)

Portrait of Charles II d'Amboise, Lord of Chaumont, Governor of Genoa and Milan

Oil on wood (poplar); 75 x 52 cm (29½ x 20½ in.)

Musée du Louvre, Paris, Department of Paintings, inv. 674

PROVENANCE: Mme de Palvoisin; M. de Cohade, by 1754; acquired by Louis XV in 1758.

BIBLIOGRAPHY: Brown 1987, no. 55.

EXHIBITIONS: Paris 1939, no. 427. Milan 1939, no. 8. Paris 1985, no. 21.

THE PHYSIOGNOMIC similarity to the image of Charles d'Amboise, lord of Chaumont (1473–1511), engraved in 1584 to illustrate André Thévet's *La Vie des hommes illustres*, leaves no doubt as to the identity of the subject of this portrait, although until the mid-nineteenth century it was taken to represent first Charles VIII and then Louis XII. Lieutenant general of the duchy of Milan from 1499 to 1511, Charles II d'Amboise played an essential role as ambassador for Lombard art in France, not only to his uncle, Georges I d'Amboise, but also to Florimond Robertet and to Louis XII himself. Charles d'Amboise's close connection to the Lombard milieu, and particularly the fact that he put his uncle in contact with Andrea Solario, have led to the attribution of the Musée du Louvre portrait to the latter. Yet its execution, at once impeccable and soft, does not match the density and firmness of Solario's own technique, even at its most melting. On the other hand, he must have created the original portrait that inspired Thévet, but is now lost and known only from a copy that is itself lost (last recorded in 1927; Suida 1929; Béguin in Paris 1985, pp. 47–54). In this painting in which Charles d'Amboise was apparently described more precisely, he was placed before a landscape background that was partly masked by a curtain, following a convention in use in Solario's circle. More specifically, he held the baton of a commander, as in the Thévet engraving. Moreover, the framing of the sitter in the Louvre panel—showing more of the figure than a simple bust but still omitting the hands—is awkward.

When it was assumed to depict the king, the Louvre painting carried an attribution to Perugino, which accords well with its gentle style and its reference to the convention of portraits with landscape backgrounds initiated in Bruges by Hans Memling and fully developed in Italy, particularly in Tuscany, around 1500. Solario adopted it in Milan in the first decade of the sixteenth century, while Leonardo brought it to a peak in Florence with the *Mona Lisa*. The dating for the lost original of Solario's *Charles II d'Amboise* remains hypothetical: its conception seems more evolved than that of the *Portrait of Giovanni Cristoforo Longoni* dated 1505 (National Gallery, London) and could be later than Solario's stay in France between 1507 and 1509. The influence of Leonardo, and particularly of the *Mona Lisa*, seems to argue for a date after Solario's return to Milan, probably in 1510, at a time when, in this city, Leonardo too was in contact with "Chaumont." It is interesting to note that this convention of a landscape background had no lasting influence on French portraits of the Renaissance. • CS

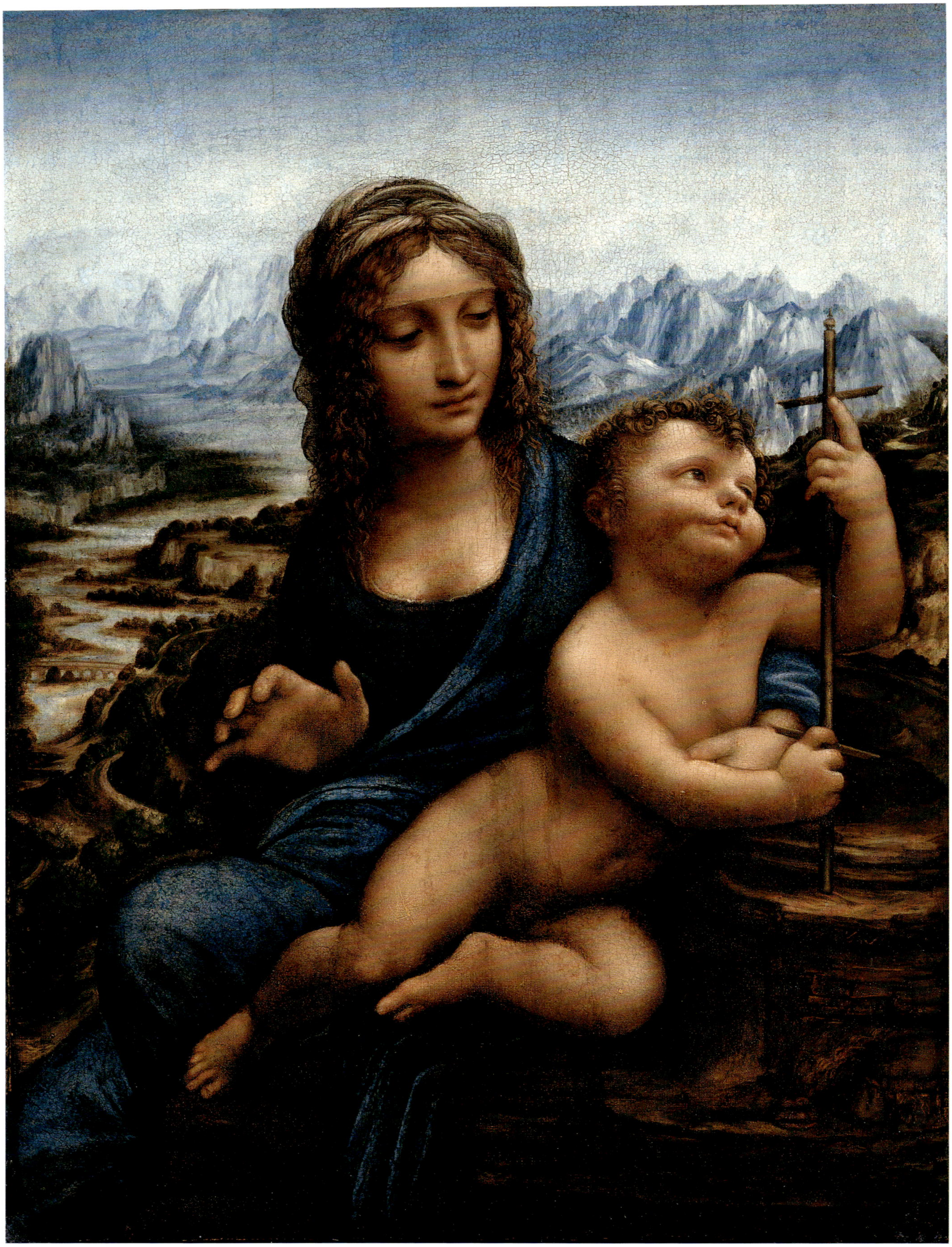

[114]

LEONARDO DA VINCI
(1452–1519), with assistance

The Madonna of the Yarnwinder (The Lansdowne Madonna)

1501/07

Oil on panel, later transferred to canvas, then mounted on panel; 50.2 x 36.4 cm (19¾ x 14⁵⁄₁₆ in.)

Private collection

PROVENANCE: Perhaps the painting made for Florimond Robertet I (d. 1527); perhaps by descent to his daughter Françoise Robertet (d. 1580), dame d'Alluye; married Jean Babou de la Bourdaisière; by descent to her daughter Isabeau Babou de la Bourdaisière, dame d'Alluye, married François d'Escoubleau; to her son, Charles d'Escoubleau, Marquis de Sourdis et d'Alluye (d. 1666), who owned the picture mentioned by André Felibien in *Entretiens sur les vies et sur les ouvrages des plus excellens peintres*, vol. 1, 1706, p. 163 ("une Vierge tenant un petit Jesus entre ses bras" by Leonardo). Henry Petty-Fitzmaurice, 3rd Marquess of Lansdowne (d. 1863), London, purchased 1809 according to catalogue of Christie's sale, 1879 (listed below); said to be presented, perhaps by Lady Lansdowne, née Louisa Emma Fox-Strangways (d. 1851), to a "Miss Giffard" [It may be the painting owned by Sir Thomas Gage Saunders Sebright (d. 1864) and seen in 1850 by Gustav Waagen, *Galleries and Cabinets of Art in Great Britain*, 1857, p. 326 (according to catalogue of Christie's sale in 1972 cited below).]. Sold, Christie's, London, July 25, 1879, no. 334 [as from a "Lady, Deceased"], to Mr. Cooper, most likely for Cyril Flower (d. 1907), later Lord Battersea, London; his widow, née Constance de Rothschild (d. 1931); sold by her to Nathan Wildenstein and René Gimpel, Paris and New York, February 1908; sold to Robert Wilson Reford (d. 1951), Montreal, 1928; by descent to his widow, Elsie Reford (d. 1967); sold, Christie's, London, December 8, 1972, no. 66, as Sodoma, to Wildenstein, New York; private collection, New York; private collection.

BIBLIOGRAPHY: Berenson 1907, p. 288 (as Sodoma). Möller 1926, pp. 61–68. Suida 1929. Vinci 1982. Kemp 1982. Naples/Rome 1983, pp. 54–69, pl. 9. Bury 1992. Penny 1992. Gould 1992. Pedretti 1992, pp. 169–75. Kemp 1994. Mayer and Bentley-Cranch 1994, p. 142. Arasse 1998, pp. 325–28. Echinger-Maurach 2000, pp. 133–36, 146–47. Zöllner 2003, pp. 148–52, 160, 180, 183, 188, 235, 238, 241. Kemp 2004. Kemp 2006, pp. xxii, 207, 209, 210–13, 218, 271, pl. 12. Universal Leonardo 2008. Kemp 2009.

EXHIBITIONS: London 1880, no. 225. London 1893, p. 37, no. 194. London 1898, no. 59. New York 1939, no. 214. Edinburgh 1992. Arezzo 2000.

EVER SINCE ITS EXHIBITION at the Burlington Fine Arts Club in London in 1898, this picture has been regarded, along with the Duke of Buccleuch's *Madonna of the Yarnwinder* (on loan to the National Gallery of Scotland, Edinburgh), as one of two primary extant versions of the subject linked to Florimond Robertet (1459–1527), secretary of state and treasurer under Charles VIII, Louis XII, and Francis I. The high level of patronage for this painting is borne out by the lapis lazuli (a costly blue pigment) employed throughout the composition. Scholarly consensus tends toward accepting both works as largely by the artist's hand, with the assistance of others, most notably in the rendering of the landscapes, of which the version shown here is more Leonardesque in style.

Since Möller singled out these two pictures in 1926 from the at least seventeen variants, copies, and replicas of the composition, much has been written on whether it was the Lansdowne or the Buccleuch version that Leonardo sent to Robertet. Documentation indicates that Leonardo was working on a picture of this subject for Robertet as early as 1501. On April 14, 1501, Fra Pietro da Novellara, head of the Carmelites in Florence, wrote to Isabella d'Este of a small picture that Leonardo was executing for Robertet: "The little picture which he is doing is of a Madonna seated as if she were about to spin yarn. The child has placed his foot in the basket of yarns and has grasped the yarnwinder and gazes attentively at the four spokes that are in the form of the cross. As if desirous of the cross he smiles and holds it firm, and is unwilling to yield it to his mother who seems to want to take it away from him" (Kemp 1989, pp. 273–75; fig. 52). Even though Novellara's description corresponds to this composition, scholars have struggled with the fact that neither this work nor the Buccleuch painting contain the basket, whereas copies of the subject do, albeit not in the aforementioned position. Kemp (2004, p. 8) contends, based on eleven non-invasive examinations of this picture undertaken at the Opificio delle Pietre Dure in Florence between November 2002 and June 2003, that: "It seems likely that the basket of spindles mentioned by Novellara was entirely painted out, leaving an area that appears unusually illegible in the examination and exhibits an unusual concentration of iron (as in brown pigments)," which would suggest that Novellara viewed the composition at a preliminary stage in its design. The picture will return to the Opificio in the second half of 2011 for further testing. In addition, the appearance in the extensive underdrawing of both the Lansdowne and Buccleuch pictures of a group of figures in the left middle ground raises the question of whether a cartoon existed for the entire composition, on which Leonardo drew for both paintings. Such a cartoon would explain the presence of this group of figures in copies or variants of the composition at Dijon and Edinburgh, to cite just two examples.

An epistle that Francesco Pandolfini, the Florentine ambassador to France, penned to the Florentine Signoria on January 12, 1507, notes that the king of France is quite fond of "a small picture" (*un piccol quadro*) by Leonardo and desires additional small panels of the Virgin. Although it cannot be determined with certainty, a number of scholars associate the small picture mentioned by Pandolfini with Robertet's *Madonna*, and the additional Virgins requested by the king as evidence that Leonardo executed multiple versions of this composition (Gould 1992; Kemp in Edinburgh 1992; see also Arezzo 2000, pp. 51–62). They conclude that Robertet's picture was finished and sent to France by 1507, hence the date 1501/07 cited here.

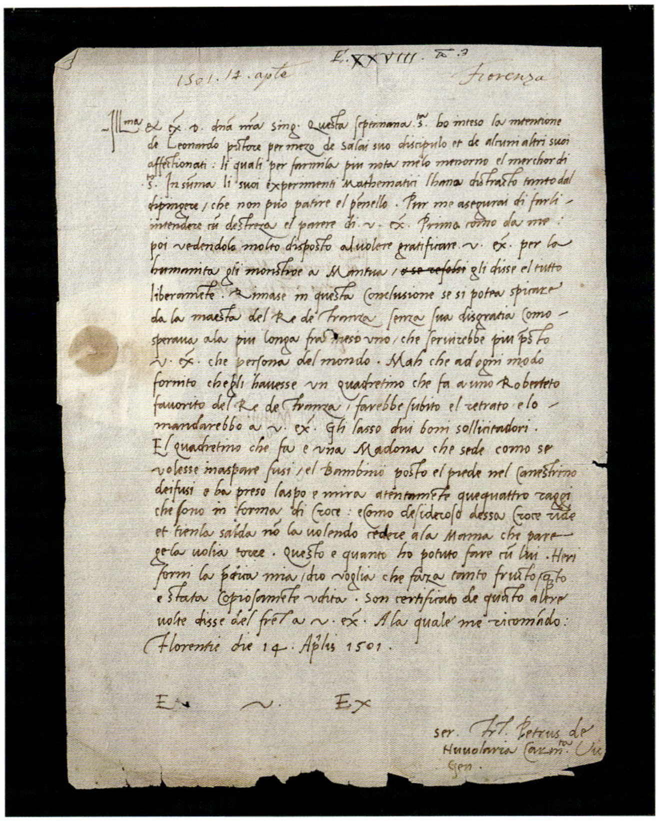
E. XXVIII.

1501. 14. aprile

Fiorenza

Ill.ma et ex.ma d.na nra sing. Questa septimana s.ta ho inteso la intentione
de Leonardo pittore per mezo de Salai suo discipulo et de alcuni altri suoi
affectionati: li quali per farmila piu nota me lo menorno el merchordi
s.to. In summa li suoi experimenti mathematici l'hanno distracto tanto dal
dipingere, che non puo patire el penello. Pur me asecurai di farli
intendere cum destrezza el parere di v. ex. prima como da me:
poi vedendolo molto disposto al volere gratificare v. ex. per la
humanita gli monstroe a Mantua, gli disse el tutto
liberamente. Rimase in questa conclusione se si potea spiccare
da la maesta del Re de Franza senza sua disgratia como
sperava ala piu longa fra mese uno, che servirebbe piu presto
v. ex. che persona del mondo. Ma che ad ogni modo
fornito ch'egli havesse un quadretino che fa a uno Robertete
favorito del Re de Franza, farebbe subito el retrato e lo
mandarebbe a v. ex. Gli lasso dui boni sollicitadori.
El quadretino che fa e una Madona che sede como se
volesse inaspare fusi, el Bambino posto el piede nel canestrino
dei fusi e ha preso l'aspo e mira attentamente quei quattro raggi
che sono in forma di croce: e como desideroso d'essa croce ride
et tienla salda no la volendo cedere ala mamma che pare
gela volia torre. Questo e quanto ho potuto fare cum lui. Heri
fornii la predica mia, dio voglia che faza tanto fructo quanto
e stata copiosamente udita. Son certificato de questo altre
volte disse del frate a v. ex. Ala quale me ricomando.
Florentie die 14. Aprilis 1501.

E. V. Ex

ser. Fr. Petrus de
Nuvolaria Carm.tum Vic.
Gen.

FIGURE 52.
Letter from Fra Pietro da Novellara to Isabella d'Este, April 14, 1501. Private collection.

The Christ Child sprawls diagonally across the Virgin's lap in a pose that would inform Raphael's *Bridgewater Madonna* of around 1507 (Duke of Sutherland, on loan to the National Gallery of Scotland, Edinburgh) and Michelangelo's *Taddei Tondo* of 1504/06 (Royal Academy, London). The painting thus establishes a new treatment of the Virgin and Child—equal parts *invenzione* and devotional image. The cross-like yarnwinder serves as both an object of playful fascination for the Christ Child and as an augur of future ill. Mary confidently and tenderly encircles his torso with her left arm, while her right hand is raised in a protective, yet cautionary, gesture. In this picture, Leonardo deftly captures the transience of time and a wide range of emotions; this would have a lasting impact on sixteenth-century painting, both in France and abroad.

Although the Lansdowne Madonna does not appear in the 1532 inventory of Robertet's collection, whose authenticity has been questioned, around 1666, a picture by Leonardo of the Virgin embracing Christ was recorded by André Felibien in the collection of Charles d'Escoubleau, Marquis de Sourdis (1588–1666), the military governor of Louis XIV in Orléans and, more importantly in this context, the great-grandson of Robertet. This suggests that Robertet's painting remained on French soil after its arrival around 1507. In addition to a picture by Leonardo, Robertet also owned a bronze *David* by Michelangelo, which was installed at the Hôtel d'Alluye, his townhouse in Blois, in 1508, and later at his château of Bury. • ES-P

[115]

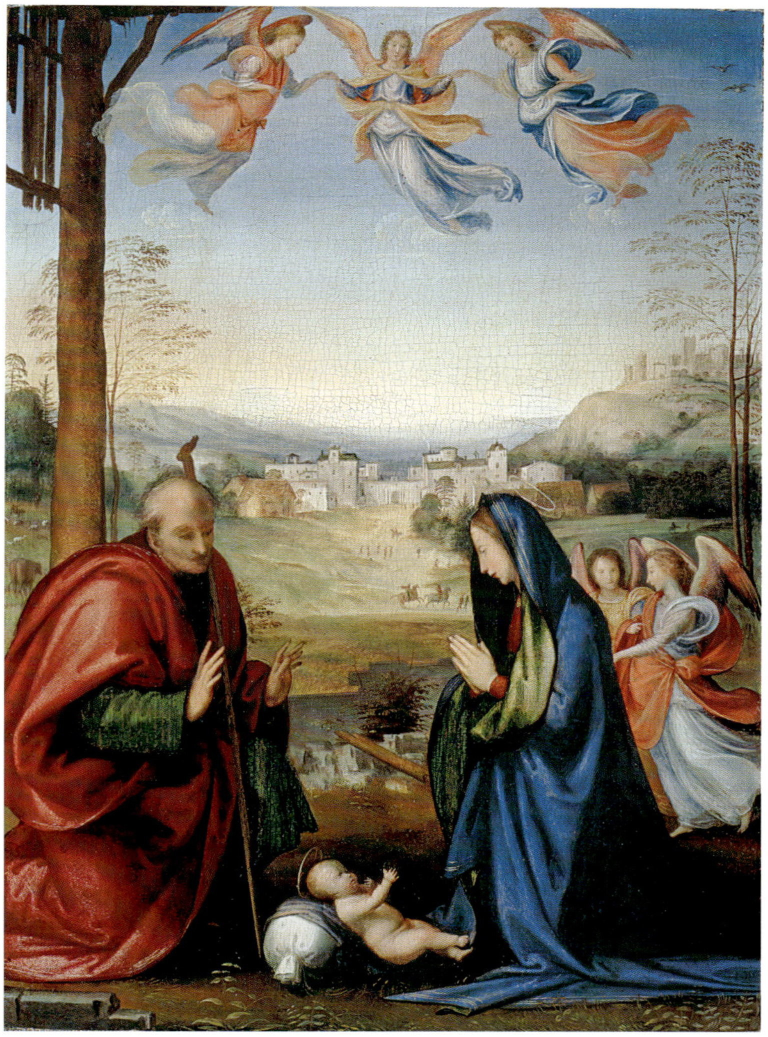

FRA BARTOLOMMEO (BACCIO DELLA PORTA) (1472–1517)

The Nativity

1504/07

Oil on panel; 34 x 24.5 cm (13 3/8 x 9 5/8 in.)

The Art Institute of Chicago, Ethel T. Scarborough Fund; L. L. and A. S. Coburn, Dr. and Mrs. William Gilligan, Mr. and Mrs. Lester King, John and Josephine Louis, Samuel A. Marx, Alexander McKay, Chester D. Tripp, and Murray Vale endowment funds; restricted gift of Marilynn Alsdorf, Anne Searle Bent, David and Celia Hilliard, Alexandra and John Nichols, Mrs. Harold T. Martin, Mrs. George B. Young in memory of her husband, and the Rhoades Foundation; gift of John Bross and members of the Old Masters Society in memory of Louise Smith Bross; through prior gift of the George F. Harding, Mr. and Mrs. W. W. Kimball, Mr. and Mrs. Martin A. Ryerson, and Charles H. and Mary F. S. Worcester collections, 2005.49

PROVENANCE: Sold through the monastery of San Marco, Florence, to Domenico Perini, April 16, 1507; sent to France (according to a list of all Fra Bartolommeo's pictures compiled in 1516) and possibly sold to King Louis XII, along with a *Noli me tangere* now in the Musée du Louvre; Bedemeau de Buxerolles, Poitou. Tabarly collection, Blois; Pierre Landry, Paris, by 1955; his heirs; sold, Christie's, London, July 11, 2001, no. 68, to Haboldt, Paris; sold to the museum, 2005.

BIBLIOGRAPHY: Ridolfi 1878, p. 122. Marchese 1879, vol. 2, p. 177. Knapp 1903, p. 271. Cox-Rearick 1972, p. 24. Fischer 1994, p. 86. Cox-Rearick 1996, pp. 168, 447. Fahy 1996, p. 85. Padovani 2002, pp. 14–16, 19.

THIS INTIMATE depiction of the Nativity is in all likelihood the latter of two works by Fra Bartolommeo that Domenico Perini purchased on April 30, 1506 and April 16, 1507, and sent to France before 1516. The other, a *Noli me tangere* (Musée du Louvre), could have joined the collection of Louis XII, even though it was not documented in the royal collection until 1625. The lapis lazuli of the Virgin's mantle and the many preparatory drawings suggest the large amount of money and attention lavished on the commission. The *Nativity* may have entered the French royal collection or the household of a prominent courtier such as Charles d'Amboise or Florimond Robertet, who both harbored considerable interest in Italian art, specifically that of Leonardo, after the French conquest of Milan in 1499.

The Virgin's delicate features and the dynamic play of her drapery folds indicate that the picture was executed between 1504, after Fra Bartolommeo ended a four-year leave from painting, and 1507, the year its payment is recorded. The palette of saturated blue, red, and green boldly announces the Holy Family, while the muted blue, pink, and yellow of the angels' garments establish an otherworldly presence. The elegantly attenuated angels demonstrate Fra Bartolommeo's knowledge of Perugino's static, celestial beings and those who inhabit Botticelli's later pictures, such as the *Mystic Nativity* (National Gallery, London). Joseph's open, reverent palms, the Virgin's hands joined in fervid prayer, and Christ's tender extension of his right arm create a compelling narrative. The strong modeling, evident in the gold thread that dances along the border of the Virgin's cloak, and the expansive sense of space, established by the hills that wend their way into the northern-inspired landscape, had much to offer artists working in France. These innovative compositional features of a central Italian painter—in addition to the Milanese pictures by Leonardo and Andrea Solario—must have influenced French painting in the first fifteen years of the sixteenth century.

The *Noli me tangere* might very well have provided inspiration for the Magdalene—likely executed by a later hand—in the picture of the same subject attributed to Jean Poyer (cat. 49). A number of additional works by Fra Bartolommeo entered France early in the sixteenth century. His altarpiece of the *Mystic Marriage of Saint Catherine of Siena* of 1511 (Louvre; fig. 51) was eventually acquired by the Signoria and sent to France as a present for Jacques Hurault, the bishop of Autun and French ambassador to Florence. Francis I acquired an *Annunciation with Six Saints* (Louvre) in 1516, and a *Saint Sebastian* (now lost), demonstrating the extent of French collectors' interest in the artist. • ES-P

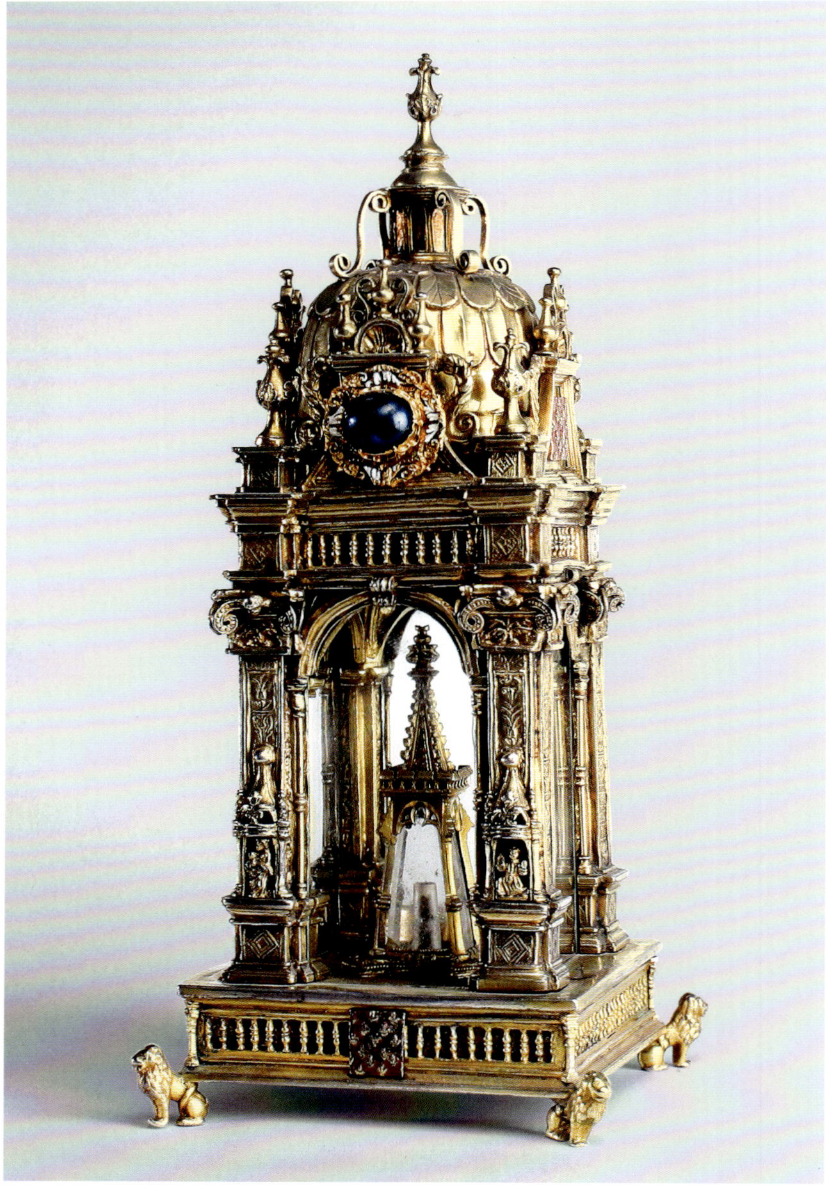

[116]

DESIGN ATTRIBUTED TO SIMON HAYENEUFVE (1455–1546)

Reliquary of the Virgin's Milk

Angers, c. 1516

Silver, gilded, chassed, and enameled; 25 x 12.5 cm. (9⅞ x 5 in.)

Basilica of Notre-Dame-de-l'Epine, Evron

MARKED: Unidentified hallmark under the base.

PROVENANCE: Offered to the abbey by François de Chateaubriand, lay abbot; supplemented by a relic of the Virgin's veil, 1836.

BIBLIOGRAPHY: Taralon 1961. Taralon 1962. Jacob 1987. Jacob 1998, pp. 330–32.

EXHIBITIONS: Paris 1965, no. 251. Paris 1995, no. 13.

OFFERED BY François de Chateaubriand, lay abbot of Evron, but also an apostolic official and dean of the chapter of Angers Cathedral, this reliquary was executed by an Angers goldsmith whose hallmark cannot be identified. Presented after the prelate's return from a journey to Rome in 1514, it takes the form of a symmetrical edifice, consisting of four columns decorated with pilasters, surmounted by a ribbed vault covered by a dome furnished with a small lantern. This design, very much influenced by Italian architecture of the period, recalls the chapel added to the cathedral of Vannes by the archdeacon Jean Daniélo starting in 1530, and especially the chapel of the episcopal palace of Le Mans, erected around 1510 by Simon Hayeneufve, cleric and architect of the cathedral chapter, who was trained in Italy. It seems entirely reasonable to attribute the design of this exceptional reliquary to Hayeneufve, whose nephews would later become goldsmiths in Angers. The presence of a gallery furnished with balusters between the pilasters, a motif found at Gaillon but also in the collegiate church of the château of Thouars as early as 1510, as well as the treatment of the dormers that crown this gallery, confirm that there was indeed the intervention of an architect. The object remains, however, a reliquary and the work of a goldsmith, on which the arms of the patron appear prominently, complemented on the principal side by the inclusion of two niches containing statuettes of the Virgin and of Saint Francis (the jewel placed above seems to date to the beginning of the seventeenth century). Documentary evidence indicates that François de Chateaubriand offered other reliquaries (now lost) to the basilica of Evron. • TC-L

BIBLIOGRAPHY AND EXHIBITIONS

BIBLIOGRAPHY

Agnew, Geoffrey. 1967. *Agnew's 1817–1967.* London.

Albanès, Joseph-Hyacinthe. 1884. "Josse Lifferin, peintre marseillais du XV° siècle," *Bulletin Archéologique du Comité des Travaux historiques et scientifiques*, pp. 245–58.

Alexander, Jonathan J. G., et al. 2005. *The Splendor of the Word: Medieval and Renaissance Illuminated Manuscripts at the New York Public Library*. New York.

Antoine, Elisabeth. 2004. "Un mystérieux livre de prières enluminé à la fin du XVe siècle Saint Germain en Laye, Bibliothèque municipale, ms. R 60732," *Art de l'enluminure* 7, pp. 20–28.

Arasse, Daniel. 1998. *Leonardo da Vinci: The Rhythm of the World*. New York.

Asselberghs, Jean-Paul. 1970. "Les Tapisseries tournaisiennes de la Guerre de Troie," *Revue belge d'archéologie et de l'histoire de l'art* 39, pp. 93–182.

———. 1974. *Les Tapisseries flamands aux Etats-unis d'Amerique*. Brussels.

Avril, François. 1977. "Pour l'enluminure provençale, Enguerrand Quarton, peintre de manuscrits?," *Revue de l'art* 35, pp. 9–40.

———. 1985a. "Le destinataire des Heures Vie à mon desir: Simon de Varie," *Revue de l'Art* 67, pp. 29–40.

———. 1985b. "Un portrait inédit de la reine Charlotte de Savoie." In *Etudes sur la Bibliothèque nationale et témoignages réunis en hommes à Thérèse Kleindienst*, edited by Michel Nortier, pp. 255–62. Paris.

———, ed. 1991. *La passion des manuscrits enluminés. Bibliophiles français: 1280–1580*. Paris.

———. 1993. "Jean Poyet." In *Les Manuscrits à Peintures en France: 1440–1520*, exh. cat., edited by François Avril and Nicole Reynaud, pp. 306–08. Paris.

———. 1995. "Die Handschrift 'De Moneta' von Nicole Oresme (BnF, Ms Latin 8733A)." In *Nicolaus Oresmius: Die Geldlehre des Spätmittelalters*, edited by Bertram Schefold et al., pp. 75–95. Düsseldorf.

———. 2003. *Jean Fouquet: Peintre et enlumineur du XVe siècle*. Paris.

———. 2007. "Les Heures de Guyot Le Peley, un chef-d'œuvre retrouvé de l'enlumineur Jean Colombe," *Art de l'enluminure* 21, pp. 2–26.

———, and Nicole Reynaud, eds. 1993. *Les Manuscrits à Peintures en France: 1440–1520*, exh. cat. Bibliothèque nationale de France, Paris.

Babelon, Ernest. 1900. *Guide illustré du Cabinet des médailles: Les antiques et les objets d'art*. Paris, 1900.

Backhouse, Janet. 1973. "Bourdichon's 'Hours of Henry VII,'" *The British Museum Quarterly* 37, 3–4, pp. 95–102.

———. 1983. "Tilliot Hours. Use of Rome; Loire School, circa 1500. Yates Thompson Ms. 5." In *Renaissance Painting in Manuscripts: Treasures from the British Library*, exh. cat., edited by Thomas Kren, pp. 175–80. New York.

———. 1987. "The Tilliot Hours: Comparisons and Relationships," *The British Library Journal* 13, pp. 211–31.

———. 1989. "Illuminated Manuscripts and the Early Development of the Portrait Miniature." In *Early Tudor England: Proceedings of the 1987 Harlaxton Symposium*, edited by Daniel Williams, pp. 1–18. Woodbridge.

———. 1996. "Jean Poyet." In *The Dictionary of Art*, edited by Jane Turner, vol. 25, pp. 405–06. New York.

Backhouse, Janet, and Yves Giraud. 1994. *Pierre Sala: Petit Livre d'Amour, Stowe MS 955, British Library, London*. Lucerne.

Badt, Kurt. 1914. *Andrea Solario: Sein Leben und Seine Werke*. Leipzig.

Baker, Christopher and Tom Henry. 1995. *The National Gallery Complete Illustrated Catalogue*. London.

Baldass, Ludwig. 1920–21. "Eine altniederländische Auferstehung Christi," *Kunstchronik*, n.s. 32, pp. 634–47.

Baluze, Etienne. 1708. *Histoire généalogique de la Maison d'Auvergne*, vol. 1. Paris.

Bande, Alexandre. 2009. *Le Cœur du roi: Les Capétiens et les sépultures multiples, XVIIIe–XVe siècles*. Paris.

Bangs, Jeremy. 1999. "The Masters of Alkmaar and Hand X: The Haarlem Painters of the Van Waterlant Family," *Wallraf-Richartz-Jahrbuch* 60, pp. 65–162.

Baratte, Sophie. 2000. *Les Émaux peints de Limoges*. Paris.

Bardati, Flaminia. 2007. "Napoli in Francia? l'arco di Afonso e i portali monumentali del primo Rinascimento francese," *I Tatti Studies: Essays in the Renaissance* 11, pp. 115–45.

Baron, Françoise. 1971. "Le maitre-autel de l'abbaye de Maubuisson au XIVe siècle," *Fondation Eugène Piot. Monuments et mémoires* 57, pp. 129–51.

Baron, Françoise. 1996. *Sculpture française, I moyen âge*. Vol. 1 of *Musée du Louvre, Département des sculptures du moyen âge, de la Renaissance et des temps modernes*. Paris.

Baron-d'Heedene, Suzanne. 1992. "Le Mécénat d'Anne de France, duchesse de Bourbon, ou la vie artistique à la cour de Moulins." Ph.D. diss., Université de Paris IV–Sorbonne.

Baudoin, Jacques. 1998. *La sculpture flamboyante en Auvergne, Bourbonnais, Forez*. Nonette.

Baurmeister, Ursula and Marie-Pierre Laffitte. 1992. *Des Livres et des Rois. La Bibliothèque Royale de Blois*, exh. cat. Paris.

Bautier, Pierre. 1926. "Deux Acquisitions nouvelles au Musée de Bruxelles," *Beaux-Arts*, pp. 60–61.

Beaulieu, Michèle. 1978. *Renaissance française*. Vol. 2 of *Description raisonnée des sculptures du musée du Louvre*. Paris.

Beaulieu, Michèle, and Victor Beyer. 1992. *Dictionnaire des sculpteurs français du Moyen Age*. Paris.

Beck, Bernard, Pierre Bouet, Clarie Etienne, and Isabelle Lettéron, eds. 2003. *L'Architecture de la Renaissance en Normandie*. 2 vols. Caen.

Becker, Philipp August. 1928. *Andry de la Vigne, c. 1475–c. 1515*. Berichte über die Verhandlungen der Sächsischen Akademie der Wissenschaften zu Leipzig, Philosophisch-Historische Klasse 80. Leipzig.

Béguerie-de Paepe, Pantxika. 1999. "Le Retable de la Vie de la Vierge: Une Oeuvre provenant de la Chartreuse Saint-Honoré de Thuison d'Abbeville." In *Célébration du 200e anniversaire de la Société d'émulation d'Abbeville*, pp. 60–72. Abbeville.

———. 2001. *La sculpture picarde à Abbeville vers 1500: autour du retable de Thuison*. Tournai.

———. 2002. "Résurrection et Assomption de la Vierge," *Revue du Louvre* 52, p. 82.

Béguin, Sylvie. 2004. "'Trésor des merveilles'" la collections peintures italiennes de François Ier." In *De l'Italie à Chambord, François I: La chevauchée des princes français*, exh. cat., edited by Catherine Arminjon, pp. 63–79.

Belozerskaya, Marina. 2002. *Rethinking the Renaissance: Burgundian Arts across Europe*, Cambridge-New York.

Bennett, Bessie. 1933. "Some Examples of French Enamel Painting," *Bulletin of the Art Institute of Chicago* 27 (November), pp. 98–99.

Benoit, Camille. 1901. "La Peinture Française à la fin du XVe siècle (1480–1501)," La Gazette des Beaux-Arts 3, 26, pp. 318–32.

Berenson, Bernard. 1907. *North Italian Painters of the Renaissance*. New York and London.

———. 1932. *Italian Pictures of the Renaissance: A List of the Principal Artists and Their Works, with an Index of Places*. Vol. 1 of *Italian Pictures of the Renaissance: Central Italian and North Italian Schools*. Repr., London, 1968.

Bernardi, Philippe. 1995. *Métiers du bâtiment et techniques de construction à Aix-en-Provence à la fin de l'époque gothique (1400–1550)*, Aix-en-Provence.

Bévotte, Marguerite de. 1936. *La Sculpture à la fin de la période gothique dans la région de Toulouse, d'Albi et de Rodez*. Paris.

———. 1982. *La "Nostre Dame de Grasse" du Musée des Augustins de Toulouse et le rayonnement de son art dans les régions voisines à la fin de l'ère gothique*. Rodez.

Białostocki, Jan. 1961. "Das Modusproblem in den bildenden Künsten: zur Vorgeschichte und zum Nachleben des Modusbriefes' von Nicolas Poussin," *Zeitschrift für Kunstgeschichte* 24, pp. 128–41.

———. 1968. "Le gothique tardi: Désaccords sur le concept," *L'information d'histoire de l'art* 13, 4 (May–June), pp. 106–28.

Bloch, Denise. 1989. "La formation de la Bibliothèque du Roi." Vol. 2 of *Histoire des Bibliothèques françaises: Les bibliothèques médiévales, du Ve siècle à 1530*, edited by André Vernet. Paris.

Blum, André. 1911. "Des rapports des miniaturistes français avec les premiers artistes graveurs," *Revue de l'art chrétien* 22, pp. 357–69. Paris.

Blum, André, and Philippe Lauer. 1930. *La miniature française aux XVe et XVIe siècles*. Paris.

Bonnaffé, E. 1887. *Le Meuble en France au xvie siècle*. Paris.

Bode, Wilhelm. 1903. "Die Anbetung der Hirten von Hugo van der Goes in der Berliner Gaerie," *Jahrbuch der Königlich Preussischen Kunstsammlungen* 24, pp. 99–102.

Boell, Charles. 1904. "Note rapportée dans le procès-verbal de la séance du 16 juin 1904," *Mémoires de la Société Eduenne* 32, pp. 438–41.

Boese, Helmut. 1966. *Die lateinischen Handschriften der Sammlung Hamilton zu Berlin*. Wiesbaden.

Boisserée, Sulpiz. 1808–54. *Tagebücher: 1808–1854*, edited by Hans-J. Weitz. 5 vols. Reprint, Darmstadt, 1978.

Bomford, David and Jo Kirby. 1977. "Two Panels by the Master of Saint Giles," *National Gallery Technical Bulletin* 1, pp. 46–56.

Bonnaffé, Edmond and Émile Molinier. 1893. *Catalogue des objets d'art et de haute curiosité antiques, du moyen-âge et de la renaissance, composant l'importante et précieuse collection Spitzer*. Paris.

Bonnet-Laborderie, Philippe. 1986. "Les Peintures sur bois de l'église St-Étienne: des primitifs beauvaisiens méconnus," *Bulletin du Groupe d'étude des monuments et oeuvres d'art du Beauvaisis* 26, pp. 20–39.

Borchert, Till-Holger. 2008. "L'an 1500 dans l'art de l'Europe du Nord," in "Périodisation et histoire de l'art," special issue, *Perspective: La Revue de l'INHA* 4, pp. 762–66.

Bos, Agnès, and Jacques Dubois. 2007. "Les boiseries de la chapelle du château de Gaillon." In *L'art des frères d'Amboise: Les chapelles de l'hôtel de Cluny et du château de Gaillon*, exh. cat., edited by Thierry Crépin-Leblond and M. Huynh, pp. 82–97. Musée national du Moyen Age—Thermes et hôtel de Cluny/Musée national de la Renaissance.

Bosseboeuf, Louis-Auguste. 1897–98. "Communication à la séance du 24 février 1897," *Bulletin de la Société archéologique de Touraine* 11, pp. 131–132.

———. 2003b. "Fécamp: l'abbatiale de la Trinité." In Beck et al. 2003, vol. 2, pp. 357–62.

Bottineau-Fuchs, Yves. 2003a. "L'ornementation 'à l'antique' en Normandie au début du XVIe siècle." In Beck et al. 2003, vol. 1, pp. 99–122.

Boucherat, Véronique. 2005. *L'art en Champagne à la fin du Moyen Âge: Productions locales et modèles étrangers, v. 1485–v. 1535*. Rennes.

Bouchot, Henri. 1887. "Les portraits peints de Charles VIII et Anne de Bretagne à la Bibliothèque nationale," *Bibliothèque de l'Ecole des Chartes* 48, 1, pp. 580–81.

———. 1888. "Charles VIII et Anne de Bretagne: Portraits peints inconnus à la Bibliothèque nationale," *Gazette Archéologique* 13, pp. 3–8, pl. 17.

———. 1902. *Les Deux Cents Incunables xylographiques du département des Estampes*. Paris.

———. 1903. "A Newly-Discovered Pack of Lyonnese Playing-Cards (1470)," *Burlington Magazine* 3, pp. 296–305.

———. 1904a. *Les Primitifs Français, 1292–1500: Complément documentaire au catalogue officiel de l'exposition*. Paris.

———. 1904b. *L'Exposition des Primitifs Français: La Peinture en France sous les Valois*. Paris.

Bousquet, Jacques. 1968. "Le problème de l'originalité de l'école des culpture languedocienne à la fin de l'époque gothique," *L'Information d'histoire de l'art* 5, pp. 208–22.

Bräm, Andreas. 1999. "Auftraggeber und Nachbesitz: Handänderungen mittelalterlicher Bilderhandschriften und deren Folgen für die Stifterbilder." In *Memory and Oblivion: Proceedings of the XXIXth International Congress of the History of Art*, edited by Wessel Reinink and Jeroen Stumpel, pp. 727–34. Amsterdam.

Bräm, Andreas. 2005. "Zum adaptierten Stifterbild in der Spätmittelalterlichen Buchmalerei." In *Manuscripts in Transition: Recycling Manuscripts, Texts, and Images. Proceedings of the International Congress*, edited by Brigitte Dekeyzer and Jan Van der Stock, pp. 253–60. Brussels.

Bramsen, Hendrik. 1957. "Attributions à Nuño Gonçalves," *Gazette des Beaux-Arts* 6, 50, pp. 311–18.

Bresc-Bautier, Geneviève. 1998. "Fontaines laïques de la première Renaissance française: les marbres de Tours, de Blois et de Gaillon." In *Sources et fontaines du Moyen Age à l'Age Baroque: Actes du colloque tenu à Université Paul Valéry*, pp. 185–201.

———. 2007. "Profils et médaillons de marbre du musée d'Amiens." In *Vases, bronzes, marbres et autres antiques: Dépôts du musée du Louvre en 1875. Etude historique et catalogue*, edited by Chantal Orgogozo and Yannick Lintz, pp. 206–31. Histoire des collections du musée du Louvre. Paris.

———. 2008a. "Médailles et profils d'applique en marbre." In *Le château de Gaillon: Fastes de la Renaissance en Normandie*, pp. 13–27.

———. 2008b. "La bataille dure encore entre les Pontifes de l'Antiquité et les Paladins du Moyen Âge: La querelle de la 'Première Renaissance' française," *Histoire de l'histoire de l'art en France au XIXe siècle*, pp. 69–93.

Brièle, Léon. 1887. *Collection de documents pour servir à l'histoire des hôpitaux de Paris*. 4 vols. Paris.

British Museum 1895. British Museum, Department of Manuscripts. 1895. *Catalogue of the Stowe Manuscripts in the British Museum*. London.

Brown, Cynthia J. 1995. *Poets, Patrons, and Printers: Crisis of Authority in Late Medieval France*. Ithaca.

———. 2005. "André de la Vigne, 'Le Sacre et couronnement d'Anne de Bretagne,'" in Pierre Gringore, *Les Entrées royales à Paris de Marie d'Angleterre (1514) and Claude de France (1517)*, edited by Cynthia J. Brown. Geneva.

———. 2006. "Books in Performance: The Parisian Entry (1504) and Funeral (1514) of Anne of Brittany," *Yale French Studies* 110, pp. 75–91.

Brown, David Allan. 1987. *Andrea Solario*. Milan.

———. 1990. "Andrea Solario." In *Opus Sacrum: Catlogue of the Exhibition from the Collection of Barbera Piasecka Johnson*, edited by Józef Grabski, pp. 110–17. Warsaw.

Bruand, Yves. 2001. "Le château ducal de Moulins." In *Le Duché de Bourbon: des origins au Connétable*, pp. 55–63.

Bruchet, Max. 1927. *Marguerite d'Autriche, duchesse de Savoie*. Lille.

Bruel, M. E. 2005. "Les vitraux historiés de la cathédrale de Moulins, mise au point chronologique et historique," *Etudes bourbonnaises* 303 (September), pp. 393–425.

Brun, Robert. 1968. "La *Mer des histoires* de Pierre Le Rouge offerte à Charles VIII," *Humanisme actif: Mélanges d'art et de littérature offerts à Julien Cain*, vol. 2, pp. 191–97. Paris.

Bruyn, Joshua. 1963. "The Master of Moulins and Hugo van der Goes," *Burlington Magazine* 105, pp. 370–71.

Buck, Stephanie. 2001. *Die Niederländischen Zeichnungen des 15. Jahrhunderts im Berliner Kupferstichkabinett: Kritischer Katalog*. Turnhout.

Bullen, J. B. 1994. *The Myth of the Renaissance in Nineteenth-Century Writing*. Oxford.

Bulletin 1916. "Notes," *Bulletin of the Chicago Art Institute* 10, 2, p. 144.

Bulliot, Jacques-Gabriel. 1840. "Croquis d'Autun vers le XVe siècle," *L'Éduen* 31, p. 1.

Burin, Elizabeth. 1998. "Pierre Sala's Pre-Emblematic Manuscripts." *Emblematica* 3, 1 (Spring), p. 30.

———. 2001. *Manuscript Illumination in Lyons: 1473–1530*. Turnhout.

Burk, Jens Ludwig. 2007. "'À l'anticque' à Nantes et 'à la moderne' à Brou: styles architecturaux et conception de la statuaire funéraire au moment du passage du gothique tardif à la Renaissance." In *Patronnes et mécènes en France à la Renaissance*, edited by Kathleen Wilson-Chevalier, pp. 225–50. Saint-Étienne.

Bury, Michael. 1992. "Leonardo/non-Leonardo: The Madonna of the Yarnwinder," *Apollo* 136, pp. 187–89.

Bussac, Georges de. 1993. "Un triptyque auvergnat de la fin du XVe siècle: L'Annonciation et les donateurs, Jean et Jeanne de Latour d'Auvergne," *Bulletin historique et scientifique de l'Auvergne* 716, pp. 283–96.

Büttner, F. O. 1983. *Imitatio Pietatis: Motive der christlichen Ikonographie als Modelle zur Verähnlichung*. Berlin.

Calvi, Girolamo Luigi. 1865. *Notizie sulla vita e sulle opere dei principali architetti scultori e pittori che fiorirono in Milano durante il governo dei Visconti e degli Sforza*, vol. 2. Milan.

Campbell, Lorne. 2002. "Review, Jean Prévost, le Maître de Moulins, by Albert Châtelet," *Burlington Magazine* 144, 1191 (June), pp. 357–59.

———. 2006. "Diptychs with Portraits." In *Essays in Context: Unfolding the Netherlandish Diptych*, edited by John Oliver Hand and Ron Spronk, pp. 33–45. New Haven and London.

Campbell, Lorne. 2009. "The Saint Giles Panels in the National Gallery of London." In *The Quest for the Original*, edited by Hélène Verougstraete and Colombe Janssens de Bisthoven, pp. 123–27. Leuven.

Caraës, J. F. 2007. "'Un cœur pour mémoire' . . . courte: A propos du reliquaire d'Anne de Bretagne," *Bulletin de la Société archéologique et historique de Nantes et de Loire-Atlantique* 142, pp. 115–22.

Caroselli, Susan L. 1993. *The Painted Enamels of Limoges: A Catalogue of the Collection of the Los Angeles County Museum of Art*. Los Angeles.

Cartier, Nicole, and Hélène Servant. 1996. "Les orfèvres à Valenciennes." In *Valenciennes au XIVe et XVe siècles: Art et Histoire*, edited by Ludovic Nys et Alain Salamagne, pp. 239–69, 392–411. Valenciennes.

Cassagnes-Brouquet, Sophie. 2007. *Louis XI ou le mécénat bien tempéré*. Rennes.

Cavallo, Adolfo Salvatore. 1993. *Medieval Tapestries in the Metropolitan Museum of Art.* New York.
Caviness, Madeline H. 1995. "Le vitrail: Recherches récentes," *Revue de l'art* 107, pp. 5–8.
Chabouillet, Anatole. 1858. *Catalogue general et raisonné des camées et pierres gravées de la Bibliothèque impériale, suivi de la description des autres monuments exposés dans le Cabinet des médailles et antiques.* Paris.
Champeaux, Alfred de. 1883. "Deux vues de la Cité de Paris au XVe siècle," *La Chronique des Arts et de la Curiosité* 23, pp. 186–87.
Chancel-Bardelot, Béatrice de. 2002. "Hommes illustres en médaillon," *Berry Magazine* 62, pp. 20–24.
Charlier, Philippe. 2009. "Etude ostéo-archéologique des restes d'Agrès Sorel." In *Actes du 2e colloque international de pathographie, Loches, April 2007,* edited by Philippe Charlier, pp. 419–525. Paris.
Charmasse, Anatole de. 1906. "La cathédrale d'Autun en 1705, d'après un manuscrit inédit de la bibliothèque de Rouen," *Mémoires de la Société Eduenne* 34, pp. 149–97.
Chartraire, Eugène. 1897. *Inventaire du Tressor de l'église Primatiale and Métropolitaine de Sens.* Sens.
———. 1925. *La Cathédrale de Sens.* Paris.
Chastel, André. 1965. *Le Grand Atelier d'Italie, 1460–1500.* Paris.
Chastel, André. 1966. *The Studios and Styles of the Renaissance: Italy 1460–1500.* Translated by Jonathan Griffin. London.
Châtelet, Albert. 1962. "A Plea for the Master of Moulins," *Burlington Magazine* 104, pp. 517–24.
———. 1970. "D'après le Maître de Moulins. 4. Le Cardinal Charles II de Bourbon." In *Chantilly—Musée Condé: Peintures de l'Ecole Française,* edited by Albert Châtelet, François-Georges Pariset, and Raoul de Broglie. Inventaire des Collections Publiques Française 16. Paris.
———. 1984. "Au temps des Jean: L'enigme du Maître de Moulins." In *Anne de Beaujeu et ses enigmes,* edited by Robert Pinet, Marc Pouget, and Mathieu Méras, pp. 110–23. Villefranche-sur-Saône.
———. 1985. "Art français et Art flamand: les Echanges dans le domaine pictural." In *La France de la fin du XVe siècle: Renouveau et apogee,* edited by Bernard Chevalier and Philippe Contamine, pp. 225–35. Paris.
———. 2001. *Jean Prévost, le Maître de Moulins.* Paris.
———. 2003. "Non, Jean Hey (Hay) n'est pas le Maître de Moulins," *Bulletin Monumental* 161, 4 (2003), pp. 353–55.
Chatenet, Monique, Krista De Jonge, Matt Kavaler, and Norbert Nussbaum. 2006. "Architecture européenne: un 'gothique de la Renaissance' autour de 1500?" *Perspective: La Revue de l'INHA* 2, pp. 280–88.
———, and Pierre-Gilles Girault. 2010. *Fastes de cour. Les enjeux d'un voyage princier à Blois en 1501.* Rennes.
Chaumet, M. P. 1998. *Sculptures gothiques.* Vol. 3 of *Toulouse, musée des Augustins: Guide des collections.* Toulouse.
Chevalier, Bernard and Philippe Contamine, eds. 1985. *La France de la fin du XVe siècle: Renouveau et apogée, économie, pouvoirs, arts, culture et conscience nationales.* nationaux? Paris.
Chirol, Elisabeth. 1952. *Un premier foyer de la Renaissance en France, le château de Gaillon.* Rouen/Paris.
Chombart de Lauwe, Marc. 1980. *Anne de Beaujeu, ou la passion du pouvoir.* Paris.
CIBN. 1981–2006. Bibliothèque Nationale de France. *Catalogue des incunables,* vol. 1, fasc. 1–3 (Xylographes et A–D), vol. 2 (H–Z and Hebraica). Paris.
Clarke, William. 1819. *Repertorium bibliographicum, or Some Account of the Most Celebrated British Libraries,* London.
Claudin, Anatole. 1900–14. *Histoire de l'imprimerie en France au XVe et au XVIe siècle.* 4 vols. Paris. Reprint, Nendeln, Lichtenstein, 1971 and 1976.
Clément de Ris, Louis. 1875. *Notice des faïences françaises: faïences dites de Henri II, faïences de Bernard Palissy, faïences diverses.* Paris.
Cogliati Arano, Luisa. 1965. *Andrea Solario.* Milan.
Colenbrander, Herman Theodoor. 1992. "Een serie de tekeningen naar Erasmus Adagia: Jean Perréal, de Maître aux Pieds-Bots en de Meester van de Legende van de H. Egidius." In *Boeken in de late Middeleeuwen: Verslag van de Groningse Codicologendagen,* edited by Joseph M. M. Hermans and Klaas Van der Hoek, pp. 211–20. Groningen.
Colenbrander, Herman Theodoor, and Pierre-Gilles Girault. 1997. "The Master of Saint Giles: A New Proposal for the Reconstruction of the London and Washington Panels," *Burlington Magazine* 139, 1135 (October), pp. 684–89.
Comblen-Sonkes, Micheline. 1988 *Les Musées de l'Institut de France: Musée Jacquemart-André et Marmottan à Paris, Musée Condé à Chantilly.* Les Primitifs Flamands. Corpus. Brussels.
Commynes, Philippe de. 1969. *Mémoires.* Edited by Sam Kinser. Translated by Isabelle Cazeaux.
———. 2007. *Mémoires,* vol. 1, edited by Joël Blanchard. Geneva.
Contamine, Philippe. 1976. "L'ordre de Saint-Michel au temps de Louis XI et Charles VIII," *Bulletin de la Société des antiquaires de France,* pp. 212–36.
———. 1988. "Les pairs de France au sacre des rois: Nature et portée d'un programme iconographique," *Bulletin de la Société nationale des antiquaires de France* 40, 3–4, pp. 321–48.
Contarini, Zaccaria. 1860. "Relazioni du Francia: Anno 1492." In *Le Relazioni degli Ambasciatori Veneti al Senato durante il Secolo Decimosest,* edited by Eugenio Albèri, , pp. 11–26. Florence.
Conway, Martin. 1915. "The Abbey of Saint-Denis and its Ancient Treasures," *Archaeologia or Miscellaneous Tracts Relating to Antiquity* 66, pp. 103–58.
Conway, Martin. 1921. *The Van Eycks and Their Followers.* London.
Corblet, Jules. 1868–75. *Hagiographie du diocèse d'Amiens,* vol. 3. Amiens.
Costa, Georges. 1971. "Une note de Prosper Mérimée sur les tapisseries de la cathédrale de Sens," *Revue de l'Art* 13, pp. 72–75.
Cottineau, Laurent Henri 1937. *Répertoire Topo-Bibliographique des Abbayes et Prieurés,* vol. 2. Maçon.
Couderc, Camille. 1908. *Album de portraits d'après les collections du Départements des Manuscrits,* Paris.
Coulet, Noël. 1986."Quelques serviteurs provençaux du roi René." In *Le Roi René: René, duc d'Anjou, de Bar et de Lorraine, roi de Sicile et de Jérusalem, roi d'Aragon, comte de Provence, 1409–1480,* pp. 42–55. Avignon.
———. 2000. "La noblesse provençale dans l'entourage du roi René." In *La Noblesse dans les territoires angevins à la fin du Moyen Age,* edited by Noël Coulet and Jean-Michel Matz, pp. 315–26. Rome.
Courajod, L. 1877. "Note sur un détail du costume de la Vierge d'Olivet," *Bulletin de la Société nationale des antiquaires de France* (1877), pp. 205–06.
———. 1888. "La polychromie dans la statuaire du Moyen Age et de la Renaissance," *Mémoires de la Société nationale des antiquaires de France* 48, pp. 193–274.
———. 1899–1903. *Leçons professées à l'École du Louvre (1887–1896),* 3 vols., edited by Henry Lemonnier and André Michel. Paris.
Courboin, François. 1923. *Des Origines à 1660.* Vol. 1 of *Histoire Illustrée de la Gravure en France.* Paris.
Courtepée, Claude. 1847. *Description générale et particulière du Duché de Bourgogne.* Dijon.
Courtillé, Anne. 1983. *Histoire de la Peinture Murale dans l'Auvergne du Moyen Age.* Brioude.
Cox-Rearick, Janet. 1972. *La Collection de François I,* exh. cat. Paris.
———. 1996. *The Collection of Francis I: Royal Treasures.* Antwerp.
Crépin-Leblond, Thierry. 2007. "Le décor peint et sculpté de la chapelle de Gaillon." In Paris/Ecouen 2007–08, pp. 100–05.
Croix, Alain and Didier Guyvarc'h. 2007. "Un cœur pour mémoire. Le reliquaire nantais d'Anne de Bretagne," *Ar Men* 157 (March–April), pp. 21–27.
Crooÿ, Fernand. 1910. *Les orfèvreries anciennes conservées au trésor de Hal.* Brussels.
Crowe, Joseph Archer and Giovanni Battista Cavalcaselle. 1857. *The Early Flemish Painters: Notices of their Lives and Works.* London.
Crowe, J. A. and G. B. Cavalcaselle. 1871. *A History of Painting in North Italy.* London.
Crowe, J. A. and G. B. Cavalcaselle. 1912. *A History of Painting in North Italy.* 2nd ed. New York.
DaCosta Kaufmann, Thomas. 2008. "Malaise dans la périodisation," in "Périodisation et histoire de l'art," special issue, *Perspective: La Revue de l'INHA* 4, pp. 597–603.
Dalas, Martine. 1991. *Les sceaux des rois et de régence.* Vol. 2 of *Corpus des sceaux français du Moyen Age.* Paris.
D'Allemagne, Henry-René. 1906. *Les cartes à jouer du XIVe au XXe siècle.* Paris.
Damianaki, Chrysa. 2000. *The Female Portrait Busts of Francesco Laurana,* pp. 188–89, 191–92. Rome.
Davies, Martin. 1957. *French School.* National Gallery Catalogues. London.
———. 1968. *Early Netherlandish School.* National Gallery Catalogues. London.
Dehaisnes, Chrétien. 1890. *L'art à Amiens vers la fin du Moyen-Âge dans les rapport avec l'école flamande primitive. III: Tableaux exécutés pour la confrérie Notre Dame du Puy.* Bruges, 1890.
Delaissé, Léon M. J., James Marrow, and John de Wit. 1977. *The James A. de Rothschild Collection at Waddesdon Manor: Illuminated Manuscripts.* London and Fribourg.
Delaunay, Isabelle. 2000. *Échanges artistiques entre livres d'heures manuscrits et imprimés produits à Paris (vers 1480–1500).* Ph.D. diss., Université de Paris IV–Sorbonne.
Delignières, Émile. 1898. *Notice sur plusieurs anciennes peintures inconnues de l'école flamande.* Paris.
———. 1905. *Souvenirs de l'exposition des Primitifs Français à Paris en 1904: la part de la Ville d'Abbeville.* Amiens.
Delisle, Léopold. 1913. *Les Grandes Heures d'Anne de Bretagne et l'atelier de Jean Bourdichon.* Paris.
De Ricci, Seymour. 1935–40. *Census of Medieval and Renaissance Manuscripts in the United States and Canada.* 3 vols. New York.
Delmarcel, Guy. 2000. *Flemish Tapestry.* New York.
D'Espézel, Pierre. 1925. "Sur un medallion de Louise de Savoie," *Arethuse: revue trimestrielle,* p. 1–10, pl. 11.
Deville, Achille. 1850. *Comptes de dépenses de la construction du château de Gaillon.* Paris.
Dhénin, Michel. 1995. "La Bulle d'or de Louis XII, roi de France, de Naples et de Jérusalem, duc de Milan." In *Mémoires et merveilles, VIIIe–XVIIIe siècle,* vol. 1 of *Trésors de la Bibliothèque nationale de France,* edited by Marie-Hélène Tesnière and Antoine Coron. Paris.
———. 2002. "La 'bulle' d'or de Louis XII, roi de France, de Naples et de Jérusalem, duc de Milan," *Bulletin de la Société française de numismatique LVII,* 6 (June), pp. 107–10.
Dijkstra, Jellie. 1997. "Enkele opmerkingen over het Retable du Parlement de Paris." In *Album Discipulorum J.R.J. van Asperen de Boer,* edited by Peter van den Brink and Liesbeth M. Helmus, pp. 53–59. Zwolle.
Dimier, Louis. 1925. *Histoire de la Peinture Française: Des Origines au retour de Vouet.* Paris.
———. 1938. "Les Primitifs Français (fin)," *La Gazette des Beaux-Arts* 20, pp. 226–36.
Dobroklonskaia, Olimpiada D. 1969. *Limozhskie raspisnye email XV I XVI vekov.* Moscow.
Douchet, Louis, ed. 1862. *Manuscrits de Jean Pagès, marchant d'Amiens, écrits de la fin du XVIIe siècle et au commencement du XVIIIe siècle sur Amiens et la Picardie,* vol. 6. Amiens.
Douët, Louis d'Arcq. 1863. *Collection de sceaux,* vol. 1. Paris.
Dumuÿs, Léon. 1909. "Séance du 19 mai," *Bulletin de la Société nationale des Antiquaires de France,* pp. 241–42.
Dumège, A. 1828. *Notice des monumens* [sic] *antiques et des objets de sculpture moderne conservés dans le musée de Toulouse.* Toulouse.
Dumège, A. 1835. *Description du musée des antiques de Toulouse.* Paris.
Dunkerton, Jill et al. 1991. *Giotto to Dürer: Early Renaissance Painting in the National Gallery.* New Haven and London.
Dupont, Jacques. 1933. "Musée de Cluny, trois peintures françaises primitives," *Bulletin des Musées de France* 5, 1 (January), pp. 6–9.
———. 1935–36. "Un triptyque de Jean Bourdichon au musée de Naples," *Monuments Piot* 35, p. 8–9, figs. 5–6.
———. 1937. *Les Primitifs Français.* Paris.
———. 1939–40. "Marie Madeleine et une donatrice, tableau du maître du Moulins au Musée du Louvre," *Bulletin de la Société nationale des Antiquaires de France,* pp. 92–93.
———. 1945–47. "Séance du 19 mars," *Bulletin de la Société nationale des Antiquaires de France,* pp. 225–27.
———. 1963. *Jean Prévost, peintre de la Cour de Moulins.* Paris.
Durand, Georges. 1911. *Tableaux et Chants Royaux de la Confrérie du Puy Notre-Dame d'Amiens reproduits en 1517 pour Louise de Savoie, duchesse d'Angoulême.* Paris.
Durin-Tercelin, Maryse. 2004. "Le Mobilier de marbre de la chapelle de Cordès, un ensemble de la Renaissance italienne," *Recherches en histoire de l'art* 3, pp. 21–46.
Durrieu, Paul. 1892. "Notes sur quelques manuscrits français ou d'origine française conservés dans des Bibliothèques d'Allemagne," Bibliothèque de l'Ecole des Chartes 53, pp. 127–29.
———. 1904. *Les Très riches heures de Jean de France.* Paris.
———. 1905. "Nouvelle miniature de Bourdichon," *Bulletin de la Société des Antiquaires de France,* p. 213.
———. 1908a. "Le peintre Jean Bourdichon et le comte Charles d'Angoulême, père de François I," *Chronique des arts,* p. 57.
———. 1908b. "Miniature de Bourdichon," *Bulletin de la Société nationale des Antiquaires de France,* pp. 112–14.
———. 1911. "La Peinture en France depuis l'avènement de Charles VII jusqu'à la fin des Valois (1422–1589)." In *Histoire de l'Art,* vol. 4, edited by André Michel, pp. 700–71. Paris.
———. 1919. "Les Relations de Leonard de Vinci avec le peintre français Jean Perréal." *Etudes Italiennes* 1, pp. 153–67.
Durville, Georges. 1915. *Etudes sur le vieux Nantes d'après les documents originaux.* Nantes.
Du Sommerard, Alexandre. 1838–46. *Les arts au moyen age.* 5 vols. Paris.
———. 1883. *Catalogue et description des objets d'art de l'Antiquité, du Moyen Age et de la Renaissance exposé au Musée des Thermes et de l'Hotel de Cluny,* exh. cat. Hotel de Cluny, 1883.
Duvanel, Maurice et al., eds. 1997. *La confrérie Notre-Dame du Puy d'Amiens.* 1997.
Echinger-Maurach, C. 2000. "'Gli occhi fissi nella somma bellezza del Figliuolo'. Michelangelo im Wettstreit Leonardos Madonnenconcetti der zweiten Florentiner Periode." In *Michelangelo: Neue Beiträge,* edited by Michael Rohlmann and Andreas Thielemann, pp. 113–50. Munich and Berlin.
Eichberger, Dagmar. 2002. *Leben mit Kunst, Wirken durch Kunst: Sammelwesen und Hofkunst unter Margarete von Österreich, Regentin der Niederlande.* Turnhout.
Edmunds, Sheila. 2009. "Catalogue des manuscrits Savoyards." In *Les Manuscrits enluminés des comtes et ducs de Savoie,* edited by A. Paravicini Bagliani, pp. 203–47. Turin.
——— and M. B. Winn. 1987. "Vérard, Meckenem and BN Fr. 1686," *Romania* 108, pp. 288–344. Turin.
Eisler, Colin. 1977. *Paintings from the Samuel H. Kress Collection: European School Including Italian.* Oxford.
Elsig, Frédéric. 2000. "Deux panneaux de Jean Poyet conservés dans l'église de Censeau?," *Bulletin monumental* 158, pp. 251–52.
———. 2002. "Un Triptyque de Jean Poyet," *Revue de l'Art* 135, pp. 107–16.
———. 2004. *La Peinture en France au XVe siècle.* Milan.
———. 2005. "Un peintre de la Renaissance en Bourgogne: le Maître du triptyque d'Autun (Grégoire Guérard ?)," *Revue de l'art ancien et moderne* 147, pp. 79–90.
Ennès, Pierre. 1983. *Céramique du Moyen Age et de la Renaissance: Département des Objets d'Art, Musée du Louvre.* Paris.
Erlande-Brandenburg, Alain. 1968. "Henri Zerner, Sharon Katic, F. Grouvel, *Le Maître de Moulins,* Paris, Hachette, 2 août 1968, 24 fig., 14 pl. en coul. (Chefs-d'oeuvre de l'Art. Grands Peintre, no. 110)," *Bulletin Monumental* 126, 2, pp. 222–23.
———, et al. 1993. *Musee national du Moyen Age: Guide des collections.* Paris.
Esquieu, Yves, ed. 2003. *Du gothique à la Renaissance: Architecture et décor en France 1470–1550.* Aix-en-Provence.
Fabia, Philippe. 1934. *Pierre Sala: Sa vie et son oeuvre avec la légende et l'histoire de L'Antiquaille.* Lyon.
Fabre, Augustin. 1834. *Histoire de Provence,* vol. 2. Marseille.
Fahy, Everett. 1996. "Fra Bartolommeo. Adorazione del Bambino." In *L'Età di Savonarola: Frà Bartolommeo e la Scuola di San Marco,* exh. cat., edited by Serena Padovani, Magnolia Scuderi, and Giovanna Damiani, pp. 84–87. Palazzo Pitti and Museo di San Marco.
Febvre, Lucien, and Henri-Jean Martin. 1958. *The Coming of the Book: The Impact of Printing 1450–1800.* Translated by David Gerard. London.
Ferré, Rose-Marie. 1957. "Le roi René peintre? Etat de la question." In *Splendeur de l'enluminure. Le roi René et les livres,* edited by Marc-Edouard Gauthier, pp. 117–21. Ville d'Angers.
Feydy, Jacques. 1957. "Le portrait du cardinal de Bourbon et le problème du Maître de Moulins," *L'information d'histoire de l'art,* pp. 164–74.
Firmin-Didot, Ambroise. 1882. *Catalogue illustré des livres précieux manuscrits et imprimés faisant partie de la bibliothèque d'Ambroise Firmin-Didot.* Paris.
Fischer, Joseph. 1932. *Claudii Ptolemaei Geographiae: Codex Urbines Graecus 82.* Leipzig.
Fischer, Chris. 1994. *Fra Bartolommeo et son Atelier: Dessins et Peintures des Collections Françaises,* exh. cat. Musée du Louvre.
Flavigny, Laurence. 1992. "Les Cerfs ailés." In *Musée des antiquités Rouen: De l'Egypte ancienne à la Renaissance rouennaise.* Rouen.
Florisoone, Michel. 1946. *Portraits français.* Paris.
Forsyth, William H. 1955. "The Trojan War in Medieval Tapestries," *Metropolitan Museum of Art Bulletin,* n.s. 14, 3, p. 79.
———. 1973. "The Biron Master and His Workshop," *Metropolitan Museum Journal* 8, pp. 105–63.
Fouquart, J. 1965. *Le Puy d'Amiens, Le seizième siècle européen: Peintures et dessins dans les collections publiques françaises.* Paris.
Fournier-Salovèze, 1909. Raymond. "Quelques Primitifs du Centre de la France," *La Revue de l'Art ancien et moderne* 25, pp.180–91.
França, José-Augusto. 1962. "Le polyptyque de Saint-Vincent-hors-les-murs à Lisbonne," *Annales, Économies, Sociétés, Civilisations* 17, 3, pp. 533–41.
Franke, Birgit. 1998. *Assuerus und Esther am Burgunderhof: Zur Rezeption des Buches Esther in den Niederlanden (1450 bis 1530).* Berlin.
Fredericksen, Burton. 1983. "A Parisian Triptych Reconstituted," *J. Paul Getty Museum Journal* 11, pp. 183–96.
Freeman, Margaret B. 1968. *The St. Martin Embroideries: A Fifteenth-Century Series Illustrating the Life and Legend of St. Martin of Tours.* Greenwich, Connecticut.

Friedländer, Max. 1900. "Ausstellungen: Die Leihausstellung des New Gallery in London, Januar-März 1900—Hauptsächlich niederländische Gemälde des XV. und XVI. Jahrhunderts," *Repertorium für Kunstwissenschaft* 23, pp. 257–58.

———. 1903. "Die Brügger Leihausstellung von 1902," *Repertorium für Kunstwissenschaft* 26, pp. 66–91, 147–75.

———. 1913. "Gemäldgalerie: Der Meister des heiligen Ägidius," *Amtliche Berichte aus den Königlichen Kunstsammlungen* 34, 10 (July), pp. 187–89.

———. 1925. "A Painting by the Maître de Moulins in the National Gallery," *Burlington Magazine* 47, 271, pp. 187–91.

———. 1926. *Die Altniederländische Malerei: Hugo Van Der Goes*. Berlin. Reprint, Brussels, 1967.

———. 1937. "Le Maître de Saint-Gilles," *La Gazette des Beaux-Arts* 17, pp. 221–31.

Friedmann, Herbert. 1966. "A Fifteenth Century French Triptych in the North Carolina Museum of Art", *North Carolina Museum of Art Bulletin*, vol. 6, no. 2–3, pp. 3–15.

Fry, Roger. 1906. "The Maître de Moulins," *Burlington Magazine* 9, 41, pp. 330–31.

Gaborit, Jean-René, ed. 1998. *Renaissance et Temps modernes*, vol. 2 of *Musée du Louvre, département des Sculptures du Moyen Age, de la Renaissance et des Temps modernes, Sculpture française*. Paris.

———. 2003a. "Une œuvre de l'atelier des Della Robbia: le tombeau de Guillaume Fillastre à l'abbaye de Saint-Bertin," *Bulletin de la société nationale des Antiquaires de France*, 2003 (2009), pp. 50–63.

———. 2003b. "Louis Courajod et l'Italie." In *Un combat pour la sculpture: Louis Courajod, 1841–1896*, edited by Geneviève Bresc-Bautier and Michèle Lafabrie, pp. 141–50. Paris.

Gaborit-Chopin, Danielle. 1994. "L'ordre du Saint-Esprit: les anges d'Anne de Bretagne," *Revue du Louvre*, pp. 29–42.

Gallissot-Ortuno, Christine. 2003. "Aux sources de la Renaissance provençale: étude des sibylles de la cathédrale Saint-Sauveur d'Aix-en-Provence." In *Du gothique à la Renaissance: Architecture et décor en France 1470–1550*, edited by Yves Esquieu, pp. 33–50. Aix-en-Provence.

Gatouillat, Françoise. 2005. "La grande verrière occidentale de Saint-Merry de Paris et ses auteurs: un cartonnier néerlandais au service d'ateliers parisiens," *Revue de l'art* 147, 1, pp. 69–78.

———, et al. 1997. "Saint-Merry de Paris: un monument daté par des vitraux," *Cahiers de la Rotonde*, 19, pp. 47–114.

Gaussen, Alfred. 1861. *Portefeuille archéologique de la Champagne*. Bar-sur-Aube.

Georgi, Katharina. 2007. "La Bethsabée des Heures de Guyot Le Peley et le traitement du thème dans l'œuvre de Jean Colombe," *Art de l'enluminure* 21 (June–August), pp. 56–61.

Giesey, Ralph E. 2007. *Le Rôle méconnu de la Loi Salique: La succession royale, XIVe–XVI siècles*. Translated by Franz Regnot. Paris.

Giogiola, K. and John Block Friedman. 2005. "Robinet Testard, Court Illuminator: His Manuscripts and His Debt to the Graphic Arts." *Journal of the Early Book Society for the Study of Manuscritps and Printing History* 8, pp. 143–88.

Giordano, Luisa. 2003. "La celebrazione della vittoria: L'esaltazione della storia contemporanea nelle terre della conquista." In *Louis XII en Milanais*, edited by Philippe Contamine and Jean Guillaume, pp. 245–71. Paris.

Gil, Marc. 2000. "La Peinture et l'enluminure à Arras au XVe siècle." In *Fragments d'une splendeur: Arras à fin du Moyen Âge*, exh. cat., edited by Annick Notter, pp. 39–70. Arras.

Girault, Pierre-Gilles. 1995. "Jean Perréal et le Maître de saint Gilles. Une contribution à l'histoire du portrait en France vers 1500," *Le Musée Condé* 48 (June), pp. 2–5.

———. 1997. "Le langage symbolique de la flore: héritage flamand et expression dynastique dans l'œuvre du Maître de saint Gilles." In *Flore et jardins: usages, savoirs et représentations du monde végétal au Moyen Age*, edited by Michel Pastoureau, pp. 145–176.

———. 2002. "De Bruges à Blois, Gauthier de Campes et le Maître de saint Gilles," *Les Amis du château et des musées de Blois* 33 (December), pp. 14–23.

———. 2007a. "Saint Julien du Mans dans un retable parisien du Maître de saint Gilles." In *L'Europe des retables: Actes du colloque du Mans (13–16 octobre 2004)*, vol. 1 (*XVe–XVIe siècles*), *Art sacré: Cahiers de Rencontre avec le patrimoine religieux* 24, pp. 160–89.

———. 2007b. "Trois 'petits maîtres': la formation du Maître de Saint-Gilles, du Maîter de sainte Lucie au Maître au Feuillage brodé." In *Le Maître au Feuillage brodé: Démarches d'artistes et méthodes d'attribution d'oeuvres à un peintre anonyme des anciens Pays-Bas du XVe siècle*, edited by Florence Gombert and Didier Martens, pp. 135–49, 217–18. Lille.

———. 2008. "Le Maître de saint Gilles et le triptyque royal de Saint-Leu-Saint-Gilles: Essai d'interprétation iconographique et historique," *Revue de l'art* 159, 1, pp. 45–58.

Girault, Pierre-Gilles, and Etienne Hamon. 2003. "Nouveaux documents sur le peintre Jean Hey et ses clients Charles de Bourbon et Jean Cueillette," *Bulletin monumental*, 161–62, pp. 117–25.

Goff, Frederick R. 1973. *Incunabula in American Libraries: A Third Census*. Reprint, Millwood, New York.

Gloton, Jean-Jacques. 1979. *Renaissance et baroque à Aix-en-Provence*. Rome.

Godwin, Molly Ohl. 1952. "Capolavori Italiani al Toledo Museum of Art," *La Vie del mondo* 14, 11 (November), pp. 1137–56.

Goldblatt, Maurice. 1948. "The 'Master of Moulins' Identified, Part I," *The Connoisseur* 121, 507, pp. 68–73.

Gonse, Louis. 1904. *Les chefs d'œuvre des musées de France: sculpture, dessins, objets d'art*. Paris.

Gothique de la Renaissance. Forthcoming. IVe rencontres d'architecture européenne.

Gould, Cecil. 1992. "Leonardo's Madonna of the Yarnwinder: Revelations of Reflectogram Photography," *Apollo* 24, 365 (July), pp. 12–16.

Gounot, Roger. 1957. *Collections lapidaires du musée Crozatier, Le Puy-en-Velay*. Le Puy.

Gozzano, Natalia. 1994. "Le origini della cultura figurativa di Josse Lieferinxe," *Ricerche di Storia dell'Arte* 62, pp. 67–80.

Grandmaison, Louis de. 1897. *Les auteurs du tombeau des Poncher (Musée du Louvre), Guillaume Regnault et Guillaume Chaleveau*. Tours.

Grasselli, Margaret Morgan. 2009. "Jean Poyet. Coronation of Solomon by the Spring of Gihon." In *Renaissance to Revolution: French Drawings from the National Gallery of Art, 1500–1800*, exh. cat., edited by Margaret Morgan Grasselli, pp. 18–19. National Gallery of Art.

Gringore, Pierre. 1858. *Les Folles Entreprises*, edited by Charles d'Héricault and Anatole de Montaiglon. Vol. 1 of *Oeuvres complètes de Gringore*.

Grodecki, Catherine. 1996. "Le 'Maître' Nicolas d'Amiens et la mise au tombeau de Malesherbes: A propos d'un document inédit," *Bulletin monumental*, 154, 4, pp. 329–34.

Grodecki, Louis. 1951. "Un panneau français au musée de Princeton et les vitraux de Riom," *Revue des arts* 4, pp. 209–21.

———. 1959. *Les vitraux de Notre-Dame et de la Sainte-Chapelle de Paris. Corpus Vitrearum*—France 1. Paris.

Grodecki, Catherine. 1996. "'Le Maître' Nicolas d'Amiens et la mise au tombeau de Malesherbes: A propos d'un document inédit," *Bulletin monumental* 154, 4, pp. 329–42.

Christa Grössinger. 1979. "The Raising of Lazarus: A French Primitive in Sherborne (Dorset)," *Journal of the British Archaeological Association* 132, pp. 1–11.

Grujic, Nada. Forthcoming. "Dialogue Gothique-Renaissance dans l'architecture ragusaine du XVe siècle." In *Gothique de la Renaissance*, forthcoming.

Guiffrey, Jules. 1886. *Histoire de la tapisserie: depuis le moyen âge jusqu'à nos jours*. Tours.

Guiffrey, Jean, and Pierre Marcel. 1912. *La Peinture Française: Les Primitifs*. Paris.

Guignard, Ph. 1849–50. "Mémoires fournis aux peintres chargés d'exécuter les cartons d'une tapisserie destinée à la collégiale Saint-Urbain de Troyes," *Mémoires de la Société d'agriculture, des sciences, arts et belles-lettres du département de l'Aube*, 2nd series, 2, pp. 421–534. Saint-Pourçain-sur-Sioule.

Guillaume, Jean. 2001. "Le portique renaissance du château de Moulins." In *Le Duché de Bourbon: des origines au Connétable*, edited by Nadine Berthelier and Jean Giono, pp. 65–70. Saint-Pourçain-sur-Sioule.

———. 2003. "Moyen Age et Renaissance, le piège des mots," in *Esquieu* 2003, pp. 313–15.

Guilhermy, F. de. 1844. *Musee de l'Hotel Cluny, Annales Archéologues* 1.

Guillot de Suduiraut, Sophie. 2004. "Les retables français de la fin du Moyen-Âge et leurs modèles des anciens Pays-Bas: quelques exemples en Picardie, Champagne et Normandie." In *L'Europe des retables*, edited by Michel Maupoix et al., pp. 109–39. Art Sacré 24. Châtillon-sur-Indre.

Hackenbroch, Yvonne. 1986. "Reinhold Vasters, Goldsmith." *Metropolitan Museum Journal* 19–2, pp. 163–268.

Hamon, Etienne. 2001. "Les architectes des ducs de Bourbon (vers 1480–1510)." In *Le Duché de Bourbon: des origines au Connétable*, edited by Nadine Berthelier and Jean Giono, pp. 122–35. Saint-Pourçain-sur-Sioule.

———. 2007. "Un aspecct du renouveau de la production dans le Paris de l'époque flamboyante: Les artsites étrangers entre 'gothique international' et seconde Renaissance (vers 1430–vers 1520)." In *Les artistes étrangers à Paris: De la fin du Moyen Age aux années 1920*, edited by Marie-Claude Chaudonneret. pp. 33–54. Bern.

———. 2008. *Documents du Minutier-central des notaries de Paris: Art et architecture avant 1515*. Paris.

———. Forthcoming. "L'étude de l'architecture flamboyante en France: entre réhabilitation et vision synthétique." In *Architecture et sculpture gothiques: renouvellement des méthodes et des regards*.

Hannema, Dirk. 1955. *Catalogue of the H. E. Ten Cate Collection*. Rotterdam.

Hans-Colas, Ilona, and Pascal Schandel. 2009. *Manuscrits de Louis de Bruges*. Vol. 1 of *Manuscrits enluminés des anciens Pays-Bas méridionaux*. Paris.

Harrouët, Roseline. 1999. "Une famille de bibliophiles au XVe siècle: les Coëtivy," *Bulletin et mémoires de la société archéologique d'Ille-et-Vilaine* 102, pp. 139–99.

Haskell, Francis. 1993. *History and Its Images: Art and the Interpretation of the Past*. New Haven and London. [French trans. L'historien et les images, Paris, 1995.]

Hébert, Michèle. 1949. "Les Monuments parisiens dans l'oeuvre du Maître de Saint-Gilles," *Mémoires de la Fédération des Sociétés historiques et archéologiques de Paris et d'Ile-de-France* 1, pp. 199–225.

———. 1976. "Un petit patron de tapisserie du XVe siecle au Cabinet des Estampes: La Commemoration de la Mort d'Hector," *Gazette des Beaux Arts* 6, 87, pp. 109–10.

Held, Julius. 1932. "Zwei Ansichten von Paris beim Meister des heiligen Ägidius," *Jahrbuch des Preuszischen Kunstsammlungen* 53, pp. 3–15.

Hérold, Michel. 1998. "Aux sources de l''invention': Gaultier de Campes peintre à Paris au début du XVIe siècle," *Revue de l'Art* 120, pp. 49–57.

Hérold, Michel, and Martine Plouvier. 1985. "L'orfèvrerie amiénoise au XVIe siècle: Jehan de Graval et la châsse de sainte Godeberthe de Noyon," *Revue de l'art* 67, pp. 77–84.

Hill, George Francis. 1930. *A Corpus of Italian Medals of the Renaissance before Cellini*. London.

Hindman, Sandra. 2008. "Gilding the Lily: Three Collections of Medieval Manuscripts in Chicago." In *To Inspire and Instruct: A History of Medieval Art in Midwestern Museums*, edited by Christina Nielsen, pp. 8–24. Newcastle.

———. 2009. *Pen to Press, Paint to Print: Manuscript Illumination and Early Prints in the Age of Gutenberg*. Paris and Chicago.

Hinkle, William M. 1965. "The Iconography of Four Panels by the Master of Saint Giles," *Journal of the Warburg and Courtauld Institutes* 28, 1965, pp. 110–44.

———.1991. *The Fleurs de lis of the Kings of France, 1285–1488*. Carbondale.

———. 2001. "Louis XII and the Porcupine: Transformations of a Royal Emblem," *Renaissance Studies* 15, pp. 17–36.

———. 2010. "Revisiting Anne of Bretagne's Queenship: On Love and Bridles." In *The Cultural and Politial Legacy of Anne de Bretagne: Negotiating Convention in Books and Documents*, edited by Cynthia J. Brown, pp. 147–62. Woodbridge, Suffolk.

Hochner, Nicole. 2006. *Louis XII: Les dérèglements de l'image royale (1498–1515)*. Seyssel.

Hoffmann, Detlef. 1972. *Die Welt der Spielkarte: Eine Kulturgeschichte*. Leipzig.

Hofmann, Mara. 2004. *Jean Poyer: Das Gesamtwerk*.Turnhout.

Hohenzollern, Johann Georg and Halldor Soehner. 1970. *Alte Pinakothek München. Katalog IV*. Französische Malerei. Munich.

Hoogewerff, Godefridus J. 1937–47. *De Noord-Nederlandsche Schilderkunst*, vol. 2. 's-Gravenhage.

Hornig, Christian. 1976. *Cavazzola*. Munich.

Hourihane, Colum, ed. 2007. *Time in the Medieval World: Occupations of the Months and Signs of the Zodiac in the Index of Christian Art*. Princeton.

Hours, Madeleine. 1963. "Le Maître de Moulins. Etude radiographique," *Art de France, Revue Annuelle de l'Art Ancien et Moderne* 3, pp. 62–74.

Huchard, Viviane et al. 1995. *Le musée de Picardie*. Paris.

Huillet d'Istria, Madeleine. 1952. "Au sujet d'articles récents sur Jean Perréal, le Maître aux Pieds-Bots," *Gazette des Beaux-Arts* 6, 40, pp. 57–63.

———. 1961. *Le Maître de Moulins*. Paris.

———. 1964. "The Problem of the Master of Moulins," *Burlington Magazine* 106, 730–41, pp. 43–44.

Hulin de Loo, Georges. 1902. *Bruges 1902: Exposition de tableaux flamands des XIVe, XVe, et XVIe siècles; Catalogue critique*. Gand.

———. 1932. "L'exposition d'Art Français, à London en 1932. Notes sur quelques tableaux du XVe siècle," *Bulletin de la Classe des Beaux-Arts, Académie Royale de Belgique* 14, pp. 57–67.

Hunter, George Leland. 1925. *The Practical Book of Tapestries*. Philadelphia.

Hutton, William. 1963. "European Glass in the Museum Collection," *Toledo Museum News*, n.s. 6, 1 (Spring), pp. 2–5.

Huyghe, René. 1935. "Dossier d'un primitif français: le Maître de Moulins," *L'Amour de l'art* 16, 2, pp. 57–62.

Huynh, Michel and Séverine Lepape. 2010. "Beau comme la recontre fortuites d'une image et d'une boîte: les coffrets à estampe," *Revue des Musées de France, Musée du Louvre* (2010) forthcoming.

Jacky, Pierre. 1992. "Jean Fouquet? Á propos d'une œuvre méconnue," *Revue du Louvre*, pp. 45–48.

———. 1993. "Un exemple du vitrail civil: un rondel de Jean Fouquet." In Paris 1993a, pp. 48–51. Paris.

Jacob, Marie. 2007. "Les *Faits des Romains*, un autre manuscrit aux armes Le Peley enluminé par Jean Colombe," *Art de l'enluminure* 21, pp. 62–67.

———. 2009. *La Représentation de l'Antiquité en France à la fin du XVe siècle: le cas de la production enluminée de l'atelier des Colombe à Bourges (1470–1500)*. Ph.D diss., Université Paris Ouest.

———. 2010. "Valeureux guerriers ou peuple vaincu: l'image des Gaulois dans les manuscrits enluminés français de la fin du XVe siècle." In *L'Antiquité entre Moyen Age et Renaissance: L'Antiquité dans les livres produits au nord des Alpes entre 1350 et 1520*, edited by Chrystèle Blondeau and Marie Jacob. Paris.

Jacob, Monique. 1987. "Les orfèvres d'Angers au XVIe siècle." In *Art, objets d'art, collections: Études sur l'art du Moyen Age et de la Renaissance, sur l'histoire du goût et des collections. Hommage à Hubert Landais*, pp. 143–50. Paris.

———. 1998. *Les Orfèvres d'Anjou et du bas Maine*. Paris.

Jacobs, Lynn F. 1993. "The Master of Getty Ms. 10 and Fifteenth-Century Manuscript Illumination in Lyons," *J. Paul Getty Museum Journal* 21, pp. 55–83.

Jacquemin, Suau, and A. Dumège. 1818 or 1820. *Notices des tableaux, statues, bustes, bas-reliefs et antiquités, composant le musée de Toulouse*. Toulouse.

Jammes, André, and Henri D. Saffrey. 1994. "Une image xylographique inconnue de la Passion de Jésus à Jérusalem," *Bulletin du bibliophile* 1, pp. 3–23.

Jestaz, Bertrand. 2003. "Les Rapports des Français avec l'art et les artistes lombards: quelques traces." In *Louis XII en Milanais: XLIe colloque international d'études humanistes*, edited by Philippe Contamine and Jean Guillaume, pp. 295–98. Paris.

Joachim, Harold. 1977. *French Drawings of the Sixteenth and Seventeenth Centuries*. Chicago.

Joly, Henri. 1925. *Un missel franciscain attribué à Jean Colombe*. Lyon.

Jones, Michael. 1978. "Les manuscrits d'Anne de Bretagne Reine de France, Duchesse de Bretagne," *Mémoires de la Société d'Histoire et d'archéologie de Bretagne* 55, pp. 43–81.

Jones, Mark. 1982. *AD 1402–1610*, vol. 1 of *A Catalogue of the French Medals in the British Museum*. London.

Jones, Susan. 2008. "Picardy (Abbeville?)." In *Northern European and Spanish Paintings before 1600 in the Art Institute of Chicago*, edited by Martha Wolff, pp. 30–42. London.

Jouanna, Arlette et al. 2001. *La France de la Renaissance, Histoire et dictionnaire*. Paris.

Joubert, Fabienne. 1999. "Nouvelles propositions sur la personnalité artistique de Pierre Spicre." In *La Splendeur des Rolin: Un mécénat privé à la cour de Bourgogne*, edited by Maurice-Chabard, pp. 169–91. Autun and Paris.

Joubert, Fabienne. 1987. *La tapisserie médiévale au musée de Cluny*. Paris.

———. 2002. *La tapisserie médiévale au musée de Cluny*. 3rd ed. Paris.

———. 2006. "Tel un prince en son diocèse, Jean Rolin, Cardinal-Evêque d'Autun." *L'Artiste et le Clerc: Commandes artistiques des grands ecclésiastiques à la fin du Moyen Âge (XIVe–XVIe siècle)*, pp. 105–32. Paris.

Kavaler, Ethan Matt. 2000. "Renaissance Gothic in the Netherlands: The Use of Ornament," *Art Bulletin* 82, 2, pp. 226–51.

Keen, Maurice. 1984. *Chivalry*. New Haven and London.

Kemp, Martin. 1982. "Review: Leonardo dopo Milano." *Burlington Magazine* 124, 957 (December), p. 788.

———, ed. 1989. *Leonardo on Painting*. New Haven.

———. 1994. "From Scientific Examination to the Renaissance Market: The Case of Leonardo da Vinci's Madonna of the Yarnwinder," *Journal of Medieval and Renaissance Studies* 24, 2 (Spring), pp. 259–74.

———. 2004. Leonardo da Vinci: The Lansdowne Madonna (The Madonna of the Yarnwinder). Overview of Present State of Research, January 2004.

———. 2006. *Leonardo da Vinci: The Marvellous Works of Nature and Man*. Oxford.

Kemp, Martin, and Thereza Wells. 2009. *The Madonna of the Yarnwinder: A Historical and Scientific Quest*. London.

Kerrebrouck, Patrick van et al. 1990. *Nouvelle histoire généalogique de l'auguste Maison de France.* Les Valois. Villeneuve d'Ascq.

King, Catherine. 1988. "Proof of Love or Proving a Will? The Historical Locations of the Love Poems Written by Pierre Sala: BL MS. Stowe 955." *Gazette des Beaux-Arts* 112, 1438, pp. 173–84.

Knapp, Fritz. 1903. *Fra Bartolommeo Della Porta und die Schule von San Marco.* Halle.

Kohler, Charles. 1896. *Catalogue des manuscrits de la Bibliothèque Sainte-Geneviève*, vol. 2. Paris.

König, Eberhard. 1978. *Das Stundenbuch des Markgrafen Christoph I. von Baden: Codex Durlach I der Badischen Landesbibliothek.* Karlsruhe.

———. 1984. *Das Vatikanische Stundenbuch Jean Bourdichons. Cod. Vat. Lat. 3781.* Zürich.

———. 1988. *Das Stundenbuch der Maria Stuart.* Darmstadt.

———. 1992. *Leuchtendes Mittelalter IV: Große Buchmalerei zwischen Rouen und Paris: Der Froissart des Kardinals Georges d'Amboise aus der Sammlung des Fürsten Pückler-Muskau mit 200 Miniaturen.* Rotthalmünster.

Kren, Thomas. 2005. "Looking at Bathsheba." In *A Masterpiece Reconstructed: The Hours of Louis XII*, exh. cat., edited by Thomas Kren, pp. 42–61. The J. Paul Getty Museum and the Victoria and Albert Museum.

Kruft, Hanno-Walter. 1995. *Francesco Laurana: ein Bildhauer der Frührenaissance.* Munich.

Krul, Wessel E. 2005. "Realism, Renaissance and Nationalism." In *Early Netherlandish Paintings: Rediscovery, Reception and Research*, edited by Bernhard Ridderbos, Anne Van Buren, and Henk Van Veen, pp. 252–89. Amsterdam.

Kurmann-Schwarz, Brigitte. 1991. "Les vitraux de la cathédrale de Moulins" in *Congrès archéologique de France* 146, pp. 21–49.

Labande-Mailfert, Yvonne. 1975. *Charles VIII et son milieu (1470–1498): La jeunesse au pouvoir.* Paris.

Laborde, Alexandre de. 1923. *La Mort chevauchant un boeuf: Origine de cette illustration de l'Office des Morts dans certains livres d'Heures de la fin du XVe siècle.* Paris.

Laclotte, Michel. 1960. *L'École d'Avignon: La Peinture en Provence aux XIVe et XVe siècles.* Paris.

———. 1966. *Primitifs Français.* Paris.

———, and Dominique Thiébaut. 1983. *L'Ecole d'Avignon.* Paris.

Laffitte, Marie-Pierre. 1997. "Les manuscripts de Louis de Bruges, chevalier de la Toison d'or." In *Le banquet du faisan*, edited by Marie-Thérèse Caron and Denis Clauzel, pp. 243–55. Arras.

———. 1998. "Premières reliures françaises realisés pour François Ier sur des manuscripts." In *Mélanges d'histoire de la reliure offerts à Georges Colin*, edited by Claude Sorgeloos, pp. 63–71. Brussels.

———. 2003. "La librairie royale de Blois." In *Actes du XVIIe congrès de l'association internationale de bibliophilie*, edited by Antoine Coron, pp. 1–38. Paris.

Lafond, Jean. 1971. "Le peintre-graveur E.-Hyacinthe Langlois, 'parrain' du style gothique flamboyant," *Bulletin de la Société nationale des antiquaires de France* 1971, pp. 313–17.

Lagabrielle, Sophie. 2006. *Vitraux: Musée national du Moyen Âge–Thermes de Cluny.* Paris.

La Guère, A. de. 1885. " Un masque de femme en marbre du XVe siècle, conservé au musée de Bourges," *Mémoires de la Société des Antiquaires du Centre* 13, 1885, pp. 167–83.

Lahondès, Jules de. 1920. *Les Monuments de Toulouse.* Toulouse.

La Nicollière-Teijeiro, S. de. 1881. "Le cœur de la reine Anne," *La Bretagne artistique, pittoresque et littéraire*, 2, pp. 97–119.

Lanmon, Dwight P. 1994. *Glass.* Vol. 1 of *The Robert Lehman Collection.* New York.

Lasteyrie, Ferdinand de. 1857. *Histoire de la peinture sur verre*, vol. 2, text. Paris.

Léandri-Morin, Marie-Pierre. 1997. "Représentations provençales et piémontaises de la vie de saint Sébastien: procédés narratifs et sources textuelles," *Mélanges de l'Ecole Française de Rome—Moyen Age* 109, 2, pp. 569–601.

Lebeuf, Jean. 1723. *Histoire de la prise d'Auxerre par les Huguenots.* Auxerre.

———. 1743. *Mémoires de l'histoire ecclésiastique et civile de la ville d'Auxerre et son encien diocese.* Auxerre. Reprint, 1848–55.

Lecoq, Anne-Marie. 1987. *François Ier imaginaire: symbolique et politique à l'aube de la Renaissance française.* Paris.

Lee, Alexander, Pit Péporté, and Harry Schnitker, eds. *Renaissance?: Perceptions of Continuity and Discontinuity in Europe, c. 1300–c. 1550.* Leiden and Boston.

Lefebvre, François. 1885. *La Chartreuse de Saint-Honoré à Thuison près d'Abbeville.* Abbeville.

Legaré, Anne-Marie. 2001. "Charlotte de Savoie's Library and Illuminators," *Journal of the Early Book Society* 4, pp. 32–87.

Lehman, Robert. 1928. *The Philip Lehman Collection, New York: Paintings.* Paris.

Lemaire, Claudine. 1981. "De Bibliotheek van Lodewijk van Gruuthuse." In *Vlaamse Kunst op Perkament. Handschriften en miniaturen te Brugge van de 12de tot de 16de eeuw*, exh. cat., pp. 207–23. Gruuthusemuseum.

Lemoisne, Paul-André. 1930. *Les Xylographies du XIVe et du XVe siècle au cabinet des estampes de la Bibliothèque nationale*, 2 vols. Paris and Brussels.

Leniaud, Jean-Michel, and Françoise Perrot. 1991. *La Sainte-Chapelle.* Paris.

Le Pogam, Pierre-Yves. 2008. *La sculpture à la lettre. Promenade épigraphique au département des Sculptures du musée du Louvre.* Paris.

Leprieur, Paul. 1892. "Correspondance d'Angleterre," *Gazette des Beaux-Arts* 8, 421, pp. 160–77.

———. 1909. "Un Portrait d'Enfant de l'Ecole Française du XVe siècle, Don de la Société des Amis du Louvre," *Bulletin des Musées de France* 8, pp. 81–82.

Leproux, Guy-Michel 2000. "Guillaume Chaleveau, le tombeau des Poncher et l'autel de Tristan de Salazar à la cathédrale de Sens," *Cahiers de la Rotonde* 22, pp. 61–70.

———. 2001. *La Peinture à Paris sous le règne de François Ier.* Paris.

Leroquais, Victor. 1927. *Les Livres d'Heures manuscrits de la Bibliothèque nationale*, vol. 1. Paris.

———. 1934. *Les sacramentaires et les missels manuscrits des bibliothèques publiques de France.* Paris.

———. 1943. *Les livres d'heures manuscrits de la Bibliothèque nationale.* 3 vols. Paris.

Leroy, Pierre. 1996. "Les Maitres de la confrerie du Puy Notre dame d'Amiens et leurs refrains," *Societe des Antiquaires de Picardie* 160, 641, pp. 228–268.

L'Estrange, Elisabeth. 2010. "Penitence, Motherhood, and Passion Devotion: Contextualizing Anne de Bretagne's Prayer Book, Chicago, Newberry Library, MS 83." In *The Cultural and Politial Legacy of Anne de Bretagne: Negotiating Convention in Books and Documents*, edited by Cynthia J. Brown, pp. 81–98. Woodbridge, Suffolk.

Lesueur, Pierre. 1937. "Remarques sur Jérôme Pacherot et sur le château de Gaillon," *Bulletin de la Société de l'histoire de l'art français*, pp. 67–87.

Limousin, R. 1954. *Jean Bourdichon.* Lyon.

Lipsius, Justus. 1605. *Diva Virgo Hallensis.* Paris and Antwerp.

Lorentz, Philippe. 1994. "Le cardinal Rolin et Jean Hey." In *La bonne étoile des Rolin: Mécénat et efflorescence artistique dans la Bourgogne du XVe siècle*, pp. 116–18. Autun.

———. 1998. "À propos du 'réalisme' flamand: la Crucifixion du Parlement de Paris et la porte du beau roi Philippe au Palais de la Cité," *Cahiers de la Rotonde* 20, pp. 101–24.

———. 1999a. "Les Rolin et les 'Primitifs Flamands,'" in *La Splendeur des Rolin: Un Mécénat privé à la Cour de Bourgogne*, edited by Brigitte Maurice-Chabard, pp. 145–62. Paris.

———. 1999b. "Quand les peintres de retables réalisaient des verrières." In *Vitrail et arts graphiques, XVe–XVIe siècle*, edited by Michel Hérold and Claude Mignot, pp. 27–39. Cahiers de l'École nationale du patrimoine 4. Paris.

———. 2002. "La France, terre d'accueil des peintres flamands." In *Le Siècle de Van Eyck: Le monde méditerranéen et les primitifs flamands 1430–1530*, edited by Till Borchert, pp. 65–71. Gand and Amsterdam.

———. 2004. *La Crucifixion du Parlement de Paris.* Paris.

———. 2005. "Children's Portraits, between Politics and Family Memories." In *Women of Distinction: Margaret of York, Margaret of Austria*, edited by Dagmar Eichberger, pp. 114–23. Turnhout.

———. 2008. "The Painter's Role in the Conception of Sculpture: Jean Hey at Chantelle." In *Invention: Northern Renaissance Studies in Honor of Molly Faries*, edited by Julien Chapuis, pp. 124–35. Turnhout.

———. 2009a. "Jean Hey." In *Dictionnaire d'histoire de l'art du Moyen Âge occidental*, edited by Pascale Charron and Jean-Marie Guillouët, pp. 491–92. Paris.

———. 2009b. "La place du peintre dans les arts visuels en France au XVe siècle." In *Renaissance en France, Renaissance française?*, edited by Henri Zerner and Marc Bayard, pp. 21–35. Collection d'Histoire de l'Art de l'Académie de France à Rome 10. Rome.

Lorentz, Philippe, and Micheline Comblen-Sonkes. 2001. *Le Musée national du Louvre, Paris*, vol. 3. Corpus de la peinture des anciens Pays-Bas méridionaux au quinzième siècle, 19. Brussels.

Lorentz, Philippe, and Annie Regond. 1990. *Jean Hey: Le Maître de Moulins.* Exposition Documentaire. Paris.

Lüdke, Dietmar. 1983. *Die Statuetten der gotischen Goldschmiede. Studien zu den "autonomen" und vollrunden Bildwerken der Goldschmiedeplastik und den Statuettenreliquiaren in Europa zwischen 1230 und 1530.* Munich.

Lugt, Frits. 1968. *Musée du Louvre. Cabinet des Dessins. Inventaire général des dessins des écoles du Nord, Maîtres des anciens Pays-Bas nés avant 1550.* Paris.

Luneau, Jean-François. 1995. "Les vitraux de la Sainte-Chapelle de Vic-le-Comte: un programme typologique original," *Revue de l'Art* 107, pp. 17–26.

MacGibbon, D. 1933. *Jean Bourdichon.* Glasgow.

Maillard, Claude. 1651. *Histoire de Notre-Dame de Hal.*

Mâle, E. 1908. *L'Art religieux en France de la fin du Moyen Age: Étude sur l'iconographie du Moyen Age et sur ses sources d'inspiration.* Paris.

Malvezzi, Luigi. 1882. *Le Glorie dell'Arte Lombarda ossia Illustrazione Storica delle Piú Belle Opere che Produssero i Lombardi.* Milan.

Marcel, Henry. 1907. "L'Exposition de portraits peints et dessinés du XIIIe au XVIIe siècle à la Bibliothèque nationale," *La Revue de l'Art Ancien et Moderne* 21 (January–June), pp. 405–16.

Marchese, Vincenzo. 1879. *Memorie dei più insigni pittori, scultori e architetti domenicani*, vol. 2. Bologna.

Marette, Jacqueline. 1961. *Connaissance des primitifs par l'étude du bois.* Paris.

Marquet de Vasselot, Jean-Joseph. 1921. *Les Émaux limousins.* Paris.

———. 1927. "Les boiseries de Gaillon au Musée de Cluny," *Bulletin monumental* 86, pp. 321–69.

Marrow, James H. 1985. "Miniatures inédites de Jean Fouquet: Les Heures de Simon de Varie." *Revue de l'Art* 67, pp. 7–32.

———. 1987. "The Book of Hours of Simon de Varie (J. Paul Getty Museum, Ms. 7): Art and Statecraft in a Newly Discovered Manuscript by Jean Fouquet." In *Transactions of the XIVth Congress of the International Association of Bibliophiles*, edited by Stephen Tabor, pp. 21–27. Los Angeles.

Marrow, James H., and François Avril. 1994. *The Hours of Simon de Varie.* Getty Museum Monographs on Illuminated Manuscripts. Malibu and The Hague.

Martens, Didier, and Claire Dumortier. 2007. "Le vitrail des Petit dé à la cathédrale de Moulins, une oeuvre de conception flamande?," *Revue Belge d'Archéologie et d'Histoire de l'art* 76, pp. 3–33.

Massing, Jean Michel. 1983. "The Influence of Erasmus: Text and Image in a French Pre-Emblematic Manuscript." In *Manuscripts in the Fifty Years After the Invention of Printing*, edited by J. B. Trapp, pp. 75–82. London.

———. 1990. *Du Texte a L'Image: La Calomine d'Apelle et son iconographie.* Strasbourg.

———. 1995. *Erasmian Wit and Proverbial Wisdom: An Illustrated Moral Compendium for Francis I.* London.

Mattéoni, Olivier. 1998. *Servir le prince: Les officiers des ducs de Bourbon à la fin du Moyen Âge (1356–1523).* Paris.

Matthews, A. 1986. "The Use of Prints in the Hours of Charles d'Angoulême," *Print Quarterly* 3 (March), pp. 4–18.

Maulde La Clavière, René. 1885. *Procédures politiques du règne de Louis XII.* Collection de documents inédits sur l'histoire de France 1. Paris.

Maulde La Clavière, René de. 1896. *Jean Perréal dit Jean de Paris: Peintre de Charles VIII, de Louis XII et de François Ier.* Paris.

Maumené, Charles and Louis d'Harcourt. 1928. *Iconographie des Rois de France de Louis IX à Louis XIII.* Archives de l'Art Français, nouvelle période, 15. Paris.

Mauger, Michel. 2002. *Bretagne chatoyante: Enluminure et histoire.* Rennes.

Maurice-Chabard, Brigitte. 1999. *La splendeur des Rolin: Un mécénat privé à la cour de Bourgogne.* Paris.

Mayer, August. 1926. "The Portrait of Suzanne de Bourbon by the Maître de Moulins," *Apollo* 3, pp. 125–26.

Mayer, Claude Albert, and Dana Bentley-Cranch. 1994. *Florimond Robertet (?–1527): Homme d'État Français.* Paris.

Mazerolle, Fernand. 1902–04. *Les Médailleurs français du XVe au milieu du XVIIe siècle.* Paris.

McKendrick, Scot. 1991. "The Great History of Troy: A Reassessment of the Development of a Secular Theme in Late Medieval Art," *Journal of the Warburg and Courtauld Institutes* 54, pp. 43–82.

McKendrick, Scot. 2003. "Painting in Manuscripts of Vernacular Texts, circa 1467–1485." In *Illuminating the Renaissance: The Triumph of Flemish Manuscript Painting in Europe*, exh. cat., edited by Thomas Kren and Scot McKendrick, pp. 223–312. The J. Paul Getty Museum and the Royal Academy of Arts.

Meiss, Millard. 1968. *French Painting in the Time of Jean de Berry: The Boucicaut Master.* London.

Mély, Fernand de. 1911. "Signature de Primitifs. L'Ecce Homo' de Jean Hey," *Revue Archéologique* 17, pp. 315–19.

Mérindol, Christian de. 1980–81. "Essai sur la signification des masques de femmes attribués à Laurana," *Bulletin de la Société nationale des Antiquaires de France*, pp. 317–34.

Meyer, Barbara Hochstetler. 1982. "Jean Perréal and Portraits of Louis XII," *Journal of the Walters Art Gallery* 40, pp. 41–56.

Michaels, Peter E. 1964–65. "Technical Observations on Early Painted Enamels of Limoges: Their Materials, Structure, Technique, and Deterioration," *Journal of the Walters Art Gallery* 27–28, pp. 21–37.

Michel, André. 1899. "Les statues de sainte Anne, saint Pierre et sainte Suzanne (musée du Louvre)," *Fondation Eugène Piot, monuments et mémoires publiés par l'Académie des Inscriptions et Belles-Lettres* 6, pp. 94–105.

Michelet, Jules. 1893. *Le XVIe siècle. La Renaissance.* Vol. 7 of *Histoire de France.* Paris.

Migeon, Gaston. [1901]. *Musée national du Louvre. Catalogue des faïences françaises et des grès allemands.* Paris.

———. 1929. *Les arts du tissu.* Paris, pp. 258–60.

Miller, Naomi. 1977. *French Renaissance Fountains.* Ph.D. diss. New York University. Garland, New York.

Millin, Albin-Louis. 1808. "Description d'un sceau d'or de Louis XII, qui appartient au Cabinet de la Bibliothèque impériale," *Magasin Encyclopédique, ou Journal des Sciences, des Lettres et des Arts* 4, pp. 5–24.

———. 1814. *Description d'un sceau d'or de Louis XII.* Paris.

Milman, Miriam. 2003. *Les Heures de la Prière: catalogue des livres d'heures de la Bibliothèque de l'Abbaye d'Einsiedeln.* Turnhout.

Mognetti, Elisabeth. 1981. "Francesco Laurana, sculpteur du roi René en Provence." In *Le Roi René en son temps 1382–1481*, exh. cat., edited by Denis Coutagne, pp. 131–82. Musée Granet.

———. 2007. "Retour sur l'œuvre de Francesco Laurana en Provence," *La scultura meridionale in età moderna nei suoi rapporti con la circolazione mediterranea*, edited by Letizia Gaerta, pp. 41–68. Lavello.

Moisy, Pierre. 1956. *Les séjours en France de Sulpice Boisserée (1820–1825).* Bibliothèque de la Société des Etudes Germaniques 10. Lyon and Paris.

Molinier, Emile. 1887. "Deux reliquaire provenant de la chapelle de l'ordre du Saint-Esprit au Musée du Louvre," *Gazette Archéologique*, pp. 94–98, pl. 12.

Möller, Emil. 1926. "Leonardo's Madonna with the Yarn Winder," *Burlington Magazine* 49, 281 (August), pp. 61–63, 66–69.

Monroe, William H. 1977. "Painted Renaissance Enamels from Limoges," *Bulletin of the Art Institute of Chicago* 71, 6, pp. 10–14.

Montaiglon, Anatole de. 1875. "La famille des Juste en France," *Gazette des Beaux-Arts* 12, pp. 385–404.

———. 1880. "Antiquités et curiosités de la ville de Sens," *Gazette des Beaux-Arts* 2, 21, pp. 5–28, 149–63, 242–61; 2, 22, pp. 125–38, 228–45.

Montesquiou-Fezensac, Blaise, and Danielle Gaborit-Chopin. 1973–77. *Le Trésor de Saint-Denis: Planches et notices*, vol. 3. Paris.

Morelli, Giovanni. 1874. "Die Galerien Roms," *Zeitschrift für bildende Kunste* 9, pp. 1–11.

———. 1880. *Die werke Italienischer Meister in den Galerien von München, Dresden, und Berlin.* Leipzig.

———. 1890. *Kunstkritische Studien über Italienische Malerei: Die Galerien Borghese und Doria Panfili in Rom.* Leipzig.

Müller, Christian. 1999. *From Schongauer to Holbein: Master Drawings from Basel and Berlin.* National Gallery of Art, Washington, D.C., and Staatliche Museen zu Berlin—Preussischer Kulturbesitz.

Müller, Theodor. 1966. *Sculpture in the Netherlands, Germany, France, Spain: 1400–1500.* Harmondsworth.

Nash, Susie. 2008. *Northern Renaissance Art.* Oxford.

Nassieu-Maupas, A. 2004. "La Vie de saint Jean-Baptiste d'Angers et la production de tapisseries à Pari sdans la première moitié du XVIe siècle," *Revue de l'Art* 145, pp. 41–53.

Naumann, Helmut. 1990. "Die Wappenzeugnisse des Kardinals Charles de Bourbon," *Archivum Heraldicum* 2, pp. 98–121.

Nettekoven, Ina. 2004. *Der Meister der Apokalypsenrose der Sainte Chapelle und die Pariser Buchkunst um 1500.* Ars nova 9. Turnhout.

Noblet, Julien, and Laurent Vissière. 2008. "Autour du Saint Sébastien d'Aigueperse: La Renaissance italienne dans l'Auvergne du XVe siècle," *Revue des musées de France* 1, pp. 34–46.

Novosselskaya, Irina. 2004. *Frantsuzskii risunok XV–XVI vekov v sobranii Ermitazha. Le dessin français des XVe et XVIe siècles dans les collections du musée de l'Ermitage.* Saint Petersburg.

Nys, Ludovic. 2006. "Par-deça et par-delà, de Tournai à Poligny: usages et functions de l'oeuvre d'art chez un grand prélat Bourguignon, Jean Chevrot." In *L'Artiste et le clerc: La commande artistique des grands ecclésiastiques à la fin du Moyen Âge (XIVe–XVIe siècle)*, edited by Fabienne Foubert, pp. 41–104. Paris, 2006.

Orth, Myra. 1999. "Louise de Savoie et le pouvoir du livre." In *Royaume de fémynie: pouvoirs, contraintes, espaces de liberté des femmes, de al Renaissance à la Fronde*, edited by Kathleen Wilson-Chevalier and Eliane Viennot, pp. 71–90. Paris.
Pächt, Otto. 1977. "René d'Anjou-Studien II," *Jahrbuch der Kunsthistorischen Sammlungen in Wien* 73, pp. 7-106.
Pächt, Otto, and Dagmar Thoss. 1977. *Die illuminierten Handschriften und Inkunabeln der Österreichischen Nationalbibliothek*, 2 vols. Vienna.
Padovani, Serena. 2002. "Il Tondo Visconti Venosta: un Capolavoro della prima maturità di Fra' Bartolommeo," in *Un Restauro per Fra' Bartolomeo*, exh cat., edited by Lavinia Galli Michero, pp. 9–19. Milan.
Page, Jutta Annette. 2006. *The Art of Glass: Toledo Museum of Art*. Toledo, Ohio.
Panofsky, Erwin. 1956. "Jean Hey's 'Ecce homo,' speculations about its author, its donor and its iconography," *Bulletin des Musées Royaux des Beaux-Arts* 5, pp. 95–138.
———. 1960. *Renaissance and Renascences in Western Art*. Stockholm.
Paris, Paulin. 1836–48. *Les Manuscrit françois de la Bibliothèque du roi*. Paris.
Parry, G. A. 1908. "Les Énigmes de L'Amour," *Revue de Philologie Française et de Littérature* 22, 3, pp. 214–20.
Parshall, Peter, and Rainer Schoch. 2005. *Origins of European Printmaking: Fifteenth Century Woodcuts and their Public*, exh. cat. National Gallery of Art, Washington, D.C., and Germanisches Nationalmuseum.
Pastoureau, Michel. 1981."Medaille ou sceau? Note sur une prétendue bulle d'or de Louis XII," *Bulletin de la Société Française de Numismatique* (January), pp. 4–6.
Pawlowski, G. 1879. *Catalogue illustré des livres précieux manuscrits et imprimés faisant partie de la bibliothèque de M. Ambroise Firmin-Didot*. Paris.
Pedretti, Carlo. 1992. "The Mysteries of a Leonardo Madonna, Mostly Unsolved," in *Achademia Leonardo Vinci: Journal of Leonardo Studies and Bibliography of Vinciana* 5, 1092, pp. 169–75.
Pèlerin, Jean (called Viator). 1510–21. *De artificiali perspectiva*. Toul, 1510 (1521, 3e ed.)
Penny, Nicholas. 1992. "Madonna of the Yarnwinder. Edinburgh. National Gallery of Scotland," *Burlington Magazine* 134, 1073 (August), pp. 542–44.
Périodisation 2008. "Périodisation et histoire de l'art," special issue, *Perspective: La Revue de l'INHA*, 4.
Perls, Klaus. 1935. "Le Maître du Charles VIII," *L'Amour de l'Art*, March, pp. 95–99.
Perrat, C. 1926. "Un livre d'heures de Marie, reine de France, et d'Henri VIII d'Angleterre." In *Documents paléographiques, typographiques, iconographiques*, edited by Henri Joly, pp. 3–15. Lyon.
Perrot, Françoise. 1970. "Un panneau de la vitrerie de la chapelle de l'hôtel de Cluny," *Revue de l'art* 10, pp. 66–72.
———. 1993–94. "Jean Fouquet et le panneau L G du musée de Cluny à Paris," "Beiträge zur mittelalterlichen Kunst, Gerhard Schmidt zum 70. Geburtstag," edited by Hans H. Aurenhammer and Michaela Krieger, special issue, *Wiener Jahrbuch für Kunstgeschichte* 46/47), pp. 549–55, 832–34.
———. 2001. *Espérance: Le mécénat religieux des ducs de Bourbon*. Souvigny.
Peters, Julie Stone. 2000. *Theatre of the Book, 1480–1880: Print, Text and Performance in Europe*. Oxford.
Phillips, John Goldsmith. 1938. "Medals from the Oppenheimer Collection." *Metropolitan Museum of Art Buleltin* 31, 12 (December), p. 273.
Poiret, Marie-Françoise. 1994. *Le monastère de Brou: Le chef-d'œuvre d'une fille d'empereur*. Paris.
Pollard, J. Graham. 1967. *Renaissance Medals from the Samuel H. Kress Collection at the National Gallery of Art*. London.
Popham, Arthur Ewart. 1935. "Style of Hugo Van Der Goes," *Old Master Drawings: A Quarterly Magazine for Students and Collectors* 9, 1935, pp. 63–64, pl. 65.
Popham, Arthur Ewart. 1938. "Mr Alfred Jowett's Collection of Drawings at Killinghall," *Apollo* 28, 159 (March), pp. 133–39.
Porcher, Jean. 1959. *L'Enluminure française*. Paris.
Pradel, Pierre. 1946. "Le sculpteur Jean de Chartres et son atelier," *Bulletin monumental* 104, pp. 48–54.
———. 1953. *Michel Colombe, le dernier imagier gothique*. Paris.
———. 1963. "Les autographes de Jean Perréal," *Bibliothèque de l'École des chartes* 121, pp. 132–86.
———. 1968. "Le premier edifice de la renaissance en France," *Mémoires de la Société nationale des antiquaires de France*, n.s. 4, pp. 243–58.
Prarond, Ernest. 1871–84. *La Topographie historique et archéologique d'Abbeville*. Paris and Abbeville.
Prietzel, Malte. 2001. *Guillaume Fillastre der Jüngere (1400/07–1473): Kirchenfürst und herzoglich-burgunischer Rat*. Stuttgart.
Prigent, Christiane. 1999. *Art et Société en France au XVe siècle*. Paris.
Prin, Maurice. 1952. "La sanctuaire de la Bienheureuse Marie de Grâce à l'église de Dominicains de Toulouse," *L'Auta* n.s. 219 (February), pp. 18–21.
———. 2001. "Nostre Dame de Grasse et un dessin conserve à Stockholm," *Mémoires de la Société archéologique du Midi de la France* 61, 2001, pp. 244–47.
Puype, Jan Piet. 1992. "Het Embleem van Lodewijk van Gruuthuse." In *Lodewijk van Gruuthuse. Mecenas en Europees Diplomaat, ca. 1427–1492*, exh. cat., edited by Maximiliaan Martens, pp. 93–102. Bruges.
Quilliet, Bernard. 1998. *La France du beau XVIe siècle*. Paris.
Rachou, Henri. 1912. *Catalogue des collections de sculpture et d'épigraphie du musée de Toulouse*. Toulouse.
Raguin, V. C., et al. 2001. *Stained Glass Before 1700 in the Collections of the Midwest States*, 2 vols. Corpus Vitrearum, United States of America, 8. London and Turnhout.
Randall, L. M. C. 1992. *France 1420–1540*, vol. 2 of *Medieval and Renaissance Manuscripts in the Walters Art Gallery*. Baltimore.
Rappé, Tamara and Larissa Boulkina. 2005. *Les emaux peints de Limoges de la collection de l'Ermitage*. St. Petersburg.
Rapp Buri, Anna and Stucky-Scürer, Monica. 2001. Burgundische Tapisserien. Munich.
Ravilly, E. 1977. "Le reliquaire." In *1477–1977: Commémoration de la naissance à Nantes de la duchesse Anne de Bretagne, reine de France*, exh. cat., edited by Jean Bruneau. Musée des Arts décoratifs, Nantes.
Réau, Louis. 1939. *French Painting in the XIVth, XVth, and XVIth Centuries*. Translated by Mary Chamot. London and New York.
———. 1955–59. *Iconographie de l'art Chrétien*. Paris.
Recht, Roland. 2008. "La périodisation, l'histoire, le style," in "Périodisation et histoire de l'art," special issue, *Perspective: La Revue de l'INHA* 4, pp. 604–20.
Reinach, Salomon. 1905–23. *Répertoire de Peintures du Moyen Age et de la Renaissance (1280–1580)*. Paris.
———. 1908. "Une miniature d'Attavante," *Académie des inscriptions et belles-lettres. Comptes-rendus* 52, pp. 543–46.
Reynaud, Nicole. 1963. "Les Portraits des Bourbons au Louvre. Reconstitution d'un panneau du Maître de Moulins," *Revue du Louvre* 4–5, pp. 159–66.
———. 1968. "Jean Hey, peintre de Moulins et son client Jean Cueillette," *La Revue de l'Art* 1–2, pp. 34–37.
———. 1973. "Un peintre français cartonnier des tapisseries au XVe siècle, Henri de Vulcop," *Revue de l'art* 22, pp. 7–21.
———. 1979. "Un Christ jardinier de l'école de Picardie," *Revue du Louvre* 29, pp. 359–61.
———. 1980. "Un Tableau du XVe siècle provenant d'Abbeville: La Translation de la Châsse de saint Foillan," *Bulletin de la Société de l'histoire de l'art français* 1980, pp. 21–27.
———. 1989. "Barthélémy d'Eyck avant 1450," *Revue de l'art* 84, pp. 22–43.
———. 1996. "Deux portraits inconnus par Jean Perréal au Louvre," *Revue du Louvre: La Revue des Musées du France* 46, 4, pp. 36–46.
———. 1997. "Une broderie de l'histoire de Saint Martin: Barthélémy d'Eyck et Pierre du Billant?" *Revue du Louvre: La Revue des Musées du France* 47, 4, pp. 37–50.
———. 2006. *Jean Fouquet: Les Heures d'Étienne Chevalier*. Dijon.
Reynolds, Catherine. 1996. "Master of Moulins." In *The Dictionary of Art*, edited by Jane Turner, vol. 20, pp. 731–34.
Rhodes, Dennis E. 1988. "La Publication des Comédies de Térence au XV Siècle." In *Le livre dans l'Europe de la Renaissance*, pp. 185–296.
Richard, Robert. 1975. "Les Puys d'Amiens et d'Abbeville," *Plaisir de France* 428 (April), pp. 28–33.
Richard, Jean. 1996. "Le role politique de l'ordre sous Philippe le Bon et Charles de Téméraire." In *L'ordre de la Toison d'or de Philippe le Bon à Philippe le Beau (1430–1505): idéal ou reflet d'une société?*, exh. cat., edited by Pierre Cockshaw and Christiane Van den Bergen-Pantens, pp. 67–70. Brussels.
Ridolfi, Enrico. 1878. "Notizie sopra varie opere di Fra da San Marco," *Giornale ligustico di Archeologica, Storia e Belle Arti* 5, pp. 81–127.
Rieder, William. 1977. "French Sixteenth-Century Boiserie and Furniture," *Apollo* 106, 89 (November), pp. 350–57.
Ring, Grete. 1949. *A Century of French Painting, 1400–1500*. London.
———. 1950. "An attempt to reconstruct Perréal," *Burlington Magazine* 92, pp. 254–61.
Riou, Charlotte. "Nostre Dame de Grasse et la sculpture à Toulouse au XVe siècle," in Toulouse 2005–06, pp. 14–40.
Roberts, Ann. 1996. "The Mocking of Elisha." In *Early Works* vol. 1 of *Drawings in Midwestern Collections*, edited by Burton Dunbar and Edward Olszewski, pp. 121–26. Columbia, Missouri.
Robiano, Maurice de. 1853. "Variétés numismatiques: II. Sceau de Louis XII comme Duc de Milan", *Revue de la Numismatique Belge* 3, pp. 32–34.
Robin, Françoise. 1985. *La Cour d'anjou-Provence: La vie artistique sous le règne de René*. Paris.
———. 1992. "L'artiste et ses modèles (retables peints et sculptés du Midi au XVe siècle)." In *De la création à la restauration: Travaux d'histoire de l'art offerts à Marcel Durliat pour son 75e anniversaire*, pp. 481–92. Toulouse.
Rochebrune, Marie-Laure de. 2004. "Venetian and Façon de Venise Glass in France in the 16th and 17th Centuries." In *Beyond Venice: Glass in Venetian Style, 1500–1750*, exh. cat., pp. 142–91. The Corning Museum of Glass, New York.
Rolfs, W. 1907. *Franz Laurana*. Berlin.
Rondot, Natalis. 1885. *La Médaille d'Anne de Bretagne et ses auteurs, Louis Lepère, Nicolas de Florence et Jean Lepère, 1494*. Lyon and Paris.
———. 1896. *Les Graveurs sur bois et les imprimeurs à Lyon au XVe siècle*. Lyon.
———. 1904. *Les Médailleurs et les graveurs de monnaies, jetons et médailles en France*. Paris.
Roschach, Ernest. 1865. *Saint Sernin: Études d'art et d'histoire. Extrait de la Revue de Toulouse*, February 1862.
Ross, Marvin Chauncey. 1941. "The Master of the Orléans Triptych, Enameler and Painter," *Journal of the Walters Art Gallery* 4, pp. 9–25.
Rouhette, Thierry, and Francesco Tuzio. 2008. *Musée des Beaux-Arts de Lyon: Médailles françaises des XVe, XVIe, et XVIIe siècles*. Lyon.
Roux-Alphéran, François-Ambroise-Thomas. 1845–47. *Les Rues d'Aix ou Recherches historiques sur l'ancienne capitale de la Provence*. Aix.
La Ruche provençale 1819. *Récueil Littéraire* 2, edited by Louis-François Jauffret.
Salet, Francis. 1996. "Les anges d'Anne de Bretagne du Trésor du Saint-Esprit," *Bulletin Monumental* 154, 2, pp. 178–79.
Samaran, Charles, and Robert Marichal. 1968. *Catalogue des manuscrits en écriture latine, portant des indications de date, de lieu ou de copistes*, vol. 6, 1, *Bourgogne, centre, sud-est et surd-ouest de la France*. Paris.
Sankovitch, Anne-Marie. 2000. "Review: L'art de la Renaissance en France: L'Invention du classicisme," *Art Bulletin* 82, 3, pp. 585–89.
Saulcy, Félicien de. 1879–92. *Recueil de documents relatifs à l'histoire des monnaies frappées par les rois de France depuis Philippe II jusqu'à François I*. Paris and Mâcon.
Saulnier-Pernuit, Lydwine. 1993. *Les Trois Couronnements: Tapisserie du trésor de la cathédrale de Sens*. Paris.
Sauzay, Alexandre. 1861. Musée impérial du Louvre. Catalogue du musée Sauvageot. Paris.
Scott, Margaret. 1980. *Late Gothic Europe, 1400–1500. The History of Dress*. London.
Schaefer, Claude. 1977. "Les débuts de l'atelier de Jean Colombe: Jean Colombe et André Rousseau," *Gazette des Beaux-Arts* 90, pp. 137–50.
———. 1994. *Jean Fouquet an de Schwelle zur Renaissance*. Basel.
Scheller, Robert W. 1981–82. "Imperial Themes in Art and Literature in the Early French Renaissance: The Period of Charles VIII," *Simiolus* 12, pp. 5–69.
———. 1985. "Gallia cisalpine: Louis XII and Italy, 1498–1508," *Simiolus* 15, pp. 5–60.
Schmidt, Gerhard. 1992. "Evrard d'Orléans und die Gräber der vier letzten Kapetinger." In *Gotische Bildwerke und ihre Meister*, pp. 59–71. Vienna.
Schmoll dit Eisenwerth, Josef Adolf. 1970. "Stilpluralismus statt Einheitszwang—Zur Kritik der Stilepochen-Kunstgeschichte," in *Argo: Festschrift für Kurt Badt zu seinem 80. Geburtstag*, edited by Martin Gosebruch and Lorenz Dittmann, pp. 77–95. Cologne.
Schreiber, Wilhelm-Ludwig. 1926–30. *Handbuch der Holz- und Metallschnitte des XV. Jahrhunderts, von W. L. Schreiber, stark vermehrte und bis zu neuesten Funden ergänzte Umarbeitung des "Manuel de l'amateur de la gravure sur bois et sur métal au XVe siècle."* 8 vols. Leipzig.
———. 1931. *Kassetten-Holzschnitte des XV. Jahrhunderts aus Sammlungen in Frankreich, Deutschland, Österreich, Schweiz, Holland, Italie, England und Amerika*. Strassburg.
———. 1937. *Die ältesten Spielkarten und die auf das Kartenspiel Bezug habenden Urkunden des 14. und 15. Jahrhunderts*. Strasbourg.
Segre, Vera. 2002–04. "L'iconografia di Enea nella miniatura francese dal XIV al XVI secolo," *Rivista di storia della miniatura* 8, pp. 107–28.
Seguin, Jean-Pierre. 1968. *Le jeu de carte*. Paris.
Seidlitz, Woldemar von. 1884. "Die illustrierten Handschriften der Hamilton-Sammlung zu Berlin," *Repertorium für Kunstwissenschaft* 7, p. 300.
Sénéchal, Philippe. 2008. "Marcel Reymond et le problème de l'antique." In *Histoire de l'histoire de l'art en France au XIXe siècle*, edited by Roland Recht, pp. 113–26. Paris.
Sénémaud, E. 1862. "La bibliothèque de Charles d'Orleans, comte d'Angoulême, au château de Cognac, en 1496." *Bulletin de la Société archéologique et historique de la Charente*, 3, 2, pp. 130–218. Paris.
Seyssel, Claude de. 2009. *Les Louenges du Roy Louys XII (1508)*, edited by Patricia Eichel-Lojkine and Laurent Vissière, pp. 216–20, 231–352. Geneva.
Shapley, Fern Rusk. 1960. "French School, Late XV Century. The Annunciation with Saints and Donors." In *The Samuel H. Kress Collection. North Carolina Museum of Art*, pp. 124–25. Raleigh.
Siefert, Helge. 2009. *Alte Pinakothek. Französische und spanische Malerei.Herausgegeben von den Bayerischen Staatsgemäldesammlungen, München*. Munich.
Siple, Ella S. 1928. "French Gothic Tapestries of about 1500," *Burlington Magazine* 53 (September), pp. 145–46.
Smital, Otto. 1930. *Handschrift 1856: Das schwarze Gebetbuch des Herzogs Galeazzo Maria Sforza*. Vienna.
Souchal, Geneviève. 1973. "Un grand peintre français de la fin du XVe siècle: le maître de la Chasse à la licorne," *Revue de l'Art* 22, pp. 22–49.
———. 1976. "Le mécénat de la famille d'Amboise," *Bulletin de la Société des antiquaires de l'Ouest* 13, pp. 485–612.
Spitzer. 1891. *Spitzer Collection Catalogue*, vol. 3, 1891, p. 101, no. 58.
Spitzer, Frédéric. 1890–93. *La Collection Spitzer: Antiquité—Moyen-Age—Renaissance*, 6 vols. Paris.
Stange, Alfred. 1935–61. *Deutsche Malerie der Gotik*, 11 vols. Berlin.
Stein, Henri. 1902. "Le sacre d'Anne de Bretagne et son entrée à Paris en 1504," *Mémoires de la Société de l'Histoire de Paris et de l'Ile de France* 29, pp. 268–304.
———. 1914. "Le Peintre Jean Hey et le Financier Jean Cueillette," *Mémoires de la Société nationale des Antiquaires de France*, pp. 1–22.
Sterling, Charles. 1938. *La Peinture Française: Les Primitifs*. Paris.
——— [Charles Jacques]. 1941. *Les Peintures du Moyen Age*. Paris.
———. 1942. "Two XV Century Provençal Painters Revived (II): The Master of St. Sebastian (Josse Lieferinxe?)," *Gazette des Beaux-Arts*, pp. 135–48.
———. 1963a. "Une peinture certaine de Perréal enfin retrouvé," *L'Œil* 103–04, pp. 2–15, 64–65.
———. 1963b. "Du nouveau sur le Maître de Moulins," *L'Œil* 107, pp. 2–15, 65–68.
———. 1964a. "Josse Lieferinxe, peintre provençal," *Revue du Louvre et des musées de France* 1, pp. 1–22.
———. 1964b. "A propos du Maître de Moulins," *L'Œil* 109, p. XXIII.
———. 1966. "Pour la Peinture en Auvergne au XVe siècle," *L'Œil*, 136, pp. 5–16.
———. 1968. "Jean Hey, le Maître de Moulins," *Revue de l'Art* 1–2, pp. 26–33.
———. 1970. "Paul Grymbault: Éminent Peintre français du XVe siècle," *Revue de l'art* 8, pp. 17–32.
———. 1979. "La peinture sur panneau picarde et son rayonnement dans le nord de la France au XVe siècle," *Bulletin de la Société de l'histoire de l'art français*, pp. 14–49. ??
———. 1981. "La peinture sur panneau picarde et son rayonnement dans le nord de la France au XVe siècle," *Bulletin de la société d'histoire de l'art français*, pp. 7–49.
———. 1983. *Enguerrand Quarton, le peintre de la Pietà d'Avignon*. Paris.
———. 1987–90. *La Peinture Médiévale à Paris 1300–1500*. Paris.
———. 1991. "Tableaux Français inédits: Langedoc et Auvergne", *L'Œil*, no. 428, 1991, pp. 28–35.
Sterling, Charles, and Hélène Adhémar. 1965. *Peintures: École Française, XIVe, XVe, et XVIe siècles*. Paris.
Sterling, Charles, and Maryan Ainsworth. 1996. "Master of Saint Giles. Virgin and Child." In *The Robert Lehman Collection*, edited by Maryan Ainsworth et al., vol. 2, pp. 11–18. Princeton.
Stieber, Joachim W. 1978. *Pope Eugenius IV, the Council of Basel and the Secular and Ecclesiastical Authorities in the Empire: The Conflict over Supreme Authority and Power in the Church. Leiden*.
String, Tatiana C., and Marcus Bull. 2008. "Entre Moyen Âge et Renaissance ? L'Angleterre vers 1500," in "Périodisation et histoire de l'art," special issue, *Perspective: La Revue de l'INHA* 4, pp. 767–71.
Suida, Wilhelm. 1931. *Leonardo und Sein Kreis*. Munich.
Taburet-Delahaye, Elisabeth. 2006. "L'orfèvre médiéval et son commanditaire: maître d'oeuvre et maître d'ouvrage?" In *Materiam superabat opus: Hommage a Alain Erlande-Brandenburg*, pp. 245–253. Paris.

Taburet-Delahaye, Elisabeth. 2006. *Thermes et Hôtel de Cluny, Musée national du Moyen âge: Oeuvres nouvelles, 1995–2005*, exh. cat. Musée national du Moyen Age—Thermes et hôtel de Cluny.
Taralon, Jean. 1961. "Le trésor d'Evron," *Congrès archéologique de France (Maine)* 119, pp. 307–11.
———. 1962. "Le trésor d'Evron," *Bulletin des monuments historiques de la France des monuments historiques de la France* 1, pp. 31–40.
Taylor, Craig. 2006. "The Salic Law, French Queenship, and the Defense of Women in the Late Middle Ages," *French Historical Studies* 29, pp. 543–64.
Tedeschi, Martha. 2009. "The Nativity and Coffer," in "Notable Acquisitions at the Art Institute of Chicago," special issue, *Art Institute of Chicago Museum Studies* 35, 2, pp. 80–81.
Ternois, David. 1962. "Autour de la Sainte Madeleine des Augustins et de Nôtre Dame de Grâce," *Revue du Louvre et des musées de France* 1, pp. 5–10.
Thibault, Pascale. 1987. "Images d'un règne: du roi très chrétien au nouveau César." In *Louis XII: Images d'un Roi. De l'Imperator au Père du Peuple*, exh. cat., edited by Pascale Thibault, pp. 29–35. Blois.
Thiébaut, Dominique. 1999. "La peinture de chevalet au XVe siècle." In *Art et société en France au XVe siecle*, edited by Christine Pringent, pp. 315–41. Paris.
———. 2008. "Deux panneaux de "l'école de Tours," *Revue des musées de France, la revue du Louvre* 2, pp. 28–30.
Thirion, Jacques. 1998. *Le Mobilier du Moyen Age et de la Renaissance en France*. Dijon.
Tilliet-Haulot, Marie-Françoise. 1982. "La collaboration pour l'exécution des broderies liturgiques à la fin du Moyen Age." In *Le dessin sous-jacent dans la peinture: Le problème de l'auteur de l'oeuvre de peinture*, edited by Dominique Hollanders-Favart and Roger van Schoute, pp. 56–65. Louvain-la-Neuve.
Thompson, H. Y. 1903. *Facsimiles of two "Histoires" by Jean Fouquet from Volumes I and II of the Anciennetés des Juifs*. London.
Thornton, Dora. 2009. "A Documentary Venetian Renaissance Dish in The British Museum," *Journal of Glass Studies* 51, p. 83.
Toledo Museum of Art. 1969. *Art in Glass: A Guide to the Glass Collections*. Toledo, Ohio.
Tolley, Thomas. 2007. "Monarchy and Prestige in France," *Viewing Renaissance Art*, edited by Kim W. Woods et al., pp. 133–67. New Haven.
Toulouse-Lautrec, Comte Raymond de. "Rapport sur l'exposition de tableaux et d'objets d'art, d'antiquités et de curiosités ouverte dans les salles du Petit Séminaire d'Autun du 29 août au 17 septembre 1876 à l'occasion de la XLIIe Session du Congrès Scientifique de France," *Congrès Scientifique de France* 42, pp. 170–201.
Trésor de numismatique. 1834. *Trésor de numismatique et de glyptique: Sceaux des rois et reines de France*. Paris.
Tricou, J. 1958. *Médailles lyonnaises du XVe au XVIII siècle*. Paris.
Tschudi, Hugo von. 1893. "London. Die Ausstellung altniederländischer Gemälde im Burlington Fine Arts Club," *Repertorium für Kunstwissenschaft* 16, pp. 100–16. Vienna.
Turner, Nancy. 2005. "The Manuscript Painting Techniques of Jean Bourdichon." In Los Angeles 2005, pp. 63–79.
Universal Leonardo. 2008. "Madonna of the Yarnwinder (The Lansdowne Madonna): As science revealed." University of the Arts, London, http://www.universalleonardo.org/scientificAnalysis.php.
Vagnon, Emmanuelle. 2002. "La réception de la Géographie de Ptolémée en Occident au XVe siècle. Un exemple de transfert culturel," *Hypothèses* 1, pp. 201–11.
Vaisse, Pierre. 2008. "Courajod et le problème de la Renaissance." In *Histoire de l'histoire de l'art en France au XIXe* siècle, edited by Roland Recht, pp. 95–112.
Valet, Paul. 1902. *Au musée de Cluny, Recherches sur le tableau catalogué sous le numero 1682*. Paris.
Vallet de Viriville, Auguste. 1850 "A Monsieur l'Editeur de la Revue Archéologique," *Revue Archéologique* 1, pp. 354–56.
Valet de Viriville, Auguste. 1852. "Notice sur Robert Blondel, poète, historien et moraliste du temps de Charles VII," *Mémoires de la Société des Antiquaires de Normandie* 19, pp. 161–26.
Vandevivere, Ignace, and Catheline Perier-d'Ieteren. 1973. *Belgique renaissante: architecture, art monumental*. Brussels.
Van Praet, Joseph Basile. 1831. *Recherches sur Louis de Bruges, Seigneur de la Gruthuyse; suivies de la notice des Manuscrits qui lui ont appartenu, et dont la plus grande partie se trouve à la Bibliothèque du Roi*. Paris.
Vasari, Giorgio.1550. *Le Vite*. Reprint, Turin, 1986.
———. 1568. *Le Vite*. Reprint, Florence, 1966–84.
———. 1851. *Le Vite*. Florence.
Vaudin, Eugène. 1882. *La Cathédrale de Sens et ses Trésors d'art. Cathédrale, archevêché et trésor*. Paris.
Vauloger, René de. 1902. "La Peinture Francaise à la fin du XVe Siècle," *Chronique des Arts et de la Curiosité* 17, pp. 131–32; no. 19, pp. 147–48, no. 20, pp. 154–56.
Velden, Hugo van der. 2000. *The Donor's Image: Gerard Loyet and the Votive Portraits of Charles the Bold*. Turnhout.
Verdier, Philippe. 1967. *The Catalogue of the Painted Enamels of the Renaissance*. Baltimore.
Verlet, Paul. 1955. "Nouvelles acquisitions du département des Objets d'art (musée de Cluny)," *Revue des arts*, pp. 53–54.
Viatte, Françoise. 1981. "Maître de Moulins (Jean Hey, peintre d'origine néerlandaise. Actif dans les dernières années du XVe siècle.) Profil de Jeune Femme," *Bulletin de la Société d'émulation du Bourbonnais* 1, pp. 186–87.
Villeneuve-Bargemon, Louis-François de. 1825. *Histoire de René d'Anjou roi de Naples, duc de Lorraine et Comte de Provence*. Paris.
Vingtrinier, A. 1896. "Les heures d'une reine de France," *Bulletin du bibliophile et du bibliothécaire*, pp. 559–64.
Wailly, Natalis de. 1838. *Eléments de paléographie*, vol. 2. Paris.
Vitry. Paul. 1901a. "Les apôtres d'Antoine Juste à la chapelle du château de Gaillon," *Bulletin monumental*.
———. 1901b. *Michel Colombe et la sculpture française*. Paris.
Vöge, Wilhel. 1908. "Konrad Meit und die Grabdenkmäler in Brou," *Jahrbuch der Preussischen Kunstsammlungen* 39, pp. 77–118.
Waagen, Gustav. 1854. *Treasures of Art in Great Britain, being an account of the Chief Collections of Paintings, Drawings, Sculptures, Illuminated Mss, etc*. London.
Warnke, Martin. 1985. *Hofkünstler: Zur Vorgeschichte des modernen Künstlers*. Cologne.
Waterhouse, Ellis. 1957. "The Manchester Exhibition 1957," *Burlington Magazine* 99, p. 415.
Weale, James. 1906. "Netherlandish Art at the Guildhall", *Burlington Magazine* 9, 39 (June), pp. 185–91.
Weigert, Roger-Armand. 1964. *La Tapisserie et le tapis en France*. Paris.
Weisinger, Herbert. 1944. "The Self-Awareness of the Renaissance as a Criterion of the Renaissance," *Papers of the Michigan Academy of Science, Arts and Literature* 19, pp. 561–67.
Wells, William. 1981. "Abbott Nicaise Delorme and Jean Perreal. Glasgow's Master of Moulins reconsidered," *Apollo* 114, 235, pp.148–55.
Wescher, Paul. 1938. "Das Französische Bildnis von Karl VII. Bis zu Franz I," *Pantheon* 11, pp. 1–11.
———. 1948. "Jean Perréal, The 'Master of Charles VIII,'" *Art Quarterly* 11, pp. 352–54.
———. "Die Kress-Schenkung für Raleigh," *Pantheon* 21, pp. 8–13.
Wheeler, Lawrence. 1998. "Master of the Latour d'Auvergne Triptych. The Annunciation with Saints and Donors, Called The Latour d'Auvergne Triptych." In *North Carolina Museum of Art: Handbook of the Collection*, edited by Rebecca Martin Nagy, pp. 72–74. New York.
Wieck, Roger S. 1988. *Time Sanctified: The Book of Hours in Medieval Art and Life*. New York.
———. 2000. "The Artist Jean Poyet and His Oeuvre." In *The Hours of Henry VIII: A Renaissance Masterpiece by Jean Poyet*, edited by Roger S. Wieck, William Voelkle, and Michelle Hearne, pp. 15–49. New York.
———. 2004. "Post Poyet." In *Excavating the Medieval Image: Manuscripts, Artists, Audiences. Essays in Honor of Sandra Hindman*, edited by D. S. Areford and N. A. Rowe, pp. 247–63. Aldershot.
———. 2007. "The Primer of Claude de France and the Education of the Renaissance Child." In *The Cambridge Illuminations: The Conference Proceedings*, edited by Stella Panayotova, pp. 267–77. London.
Wieck, Roger S., and K. Michelle Hearne. 1999. *The Prayer Book of Anne de Bretagne: MS M.50, The Pierpont Morgan Library, New York*. Lucerne.
Wieck, Roger S., W. M. Voelkle, and K. Michelle Hearne. 2000. *The Hours of Henry VIII: A Renaissance Masterpiece by Jean Poyet*. New York.
Wijsman, Hanno. 2007. "Politique et bibliophilie pendant la révolte des villes flamandes des années 1482–1492: Relations entre les bibliothèques de Philippe de Clèves et de Louis de Bruges et la Librairie des Ducs de Bourgogne." In *Entre la ville, la noblesse et l'état: Philippe de Clèves (1456–1528), homme politique et bibliophile*, edited by Jelle Haemers, Céline van Hoorebeeck, and Henri Willem Wijsman, pp. 245–78. *Burgundica* 13. Turnhout.
Winkler, Friedrich. 1932. "Der Meister von Moulins und Hugo van de Goes," *Pantheon* 5, pp. 241–48.
———. 1933. "Perréal, Jean." In *Allgemeines Lexikon der bildenden Künstler von der Antike bis zur Gegenwart*, edited by Hans Vollmer and Ulrich Thieme, vol. 26, pp. 433–35.
Winn, Mary Beth. 2007. "Louise de Savoie, ses enfants et ses livres: du pouvoir familial au pouvoir d'État." In *Pagronnes et mécènes en France à la Renaissance*, edited by Kathleen Wilson-Chevalier, pp. 251–81. Saint-Etienne.
Wolff, Martha. 1986. "Master of Saint Giles and Assistant," in *Early Netherlandish Painting*, edited by John Oliver Hand and Martha Wolff, pp. 163–76. Cambridge.
———. 2005. "Reconstitution d'une scène de la Passion peinte par le Maître de Moulins," *Revue de l'Art* 147, 1986, pp. 58–66.
———. 2008a. *Northern European and Spanish Paintings Before 1600 in the Art Institute of Chicago: A Catalogue of the Collection*. Chicago.
———. 2008b. "Observations on Underdrawings in Paintings by the Master of Moulins." In *Invention: Northern Renaissance Studies in Honor of Molly Faries*, edited by Julien Chapuis, pp. 136–51. Turnhout.
Woodner Collection. 1971. *Woodner Collection: Old Master Drawings from the XV to the XVIII Centuries*. 2 vols. New York.
Zani, V. 2000. "Lorenzo da Muzzano risarcito," *Nuovi Studi. Rivista di Arte antica e moderna* 8, pp. 35–59.
Zeman, Georg. 1997. "Review of Eberhard König, Das liebentbrannte Herz. Der Wiener Codex und der Maler Barthélémy d'Eyck," *Kunstchronik* 50, pp. 520–28.
Zerner, Henri. 1996. *L'art de la Renaissance en France. L'invention du classicisme*. Paris.
———. 2003. *Renaissance Art in France: The Invention of Classicism*. Paris.
Zerner, Henri, and Sharon Katic. 1966. *Il Maestro di Moulins*. Milan.
Zöhl, Caroline. 2004. *Jean Pichore: Buchmaler, Verleger und Graphiker in Paris um 1500*. Turnhout.
Zöhl, Caroline. 2007. "Miniaturen und Altarretabel zwischen Allegorie und Emblem: Die Chants royaux du Puy Notre-Dame d'Amiens." In *Quand la peinture était dans les livres: Mélanges en l'honneur de François Avril*, edited by Mara Hofmann and Caroline Zöhl, pp. 405–25. Turnhout.
Zöllner, Frank. 2003. *Leonardo da Vinci 1452–1519: The Complete Paintings and Drawings*. Taschen.

EXHIBITIONS

Abbeville 2001. Pantxika Béguerie-de Paepe, ed. *La sculpture picarde à Abbeville vers 1500: autour du retable de Thuison*, exh. cat., Musée Boucher-de-Perthes, Abbeville, 2001.
Aix-en-Provence 1981. Denis Coutagne, ed. *Le Roi René et son temps, 1382–1481*, exh. cat., Musée Granet, Aix-en-Provence, April–September 1981.
Amiens 1951–52. *Trois siècles de peinture en Picardie*, exh. cat., Musée de Picardie.
Amsterdam 1951. Remmet Van Luttervelt, ed. *Bourgondische Pracht van Philips De Stoute tot Philips De Schone*, exh. cat., Rijksmuseum, Amsterdam, July 28–October 1, 1951.
Arezzo 2000. *Leonardo ad Arezzo A.D. 2000: La "Madonna dei Fusi" di Leonardo da Vinci e il paesaggio del Valdarno Superiore*, exh. cat., Palazzo dei Priori, Arezzo, July 1–November 15, 2000.
Autun 1876. *Tableaux et Objets d'Art, d'Antiquité et de Curiosité*, Petit Séminaire, Autun, August 29–September 15, 1876.
Auxerre 2000. *Histoire de saint Etienne, la tenture de choeur de la cathédrale d'Auxerre*, Musées d'art et d'histoire, Auxerre.
Avignon 1981. *Le roi René en son temps: Francesco Laurana sculpteur du roi René en son temps*, Musée Granet, Aix-en-Provence, April–September 1981.
Avignon 1997. *Histoires tissées. La légende de saint Etienne: Brocarts célestes, Palais des papes et Petit-Palais*, Avignon.
Baltimore 1988. *Time Sanctified: The Book of Hours in Medieval Art and Life*, The Walters Art Gallery, April 23–July 17, 1988.
Bern 1949–50. *Kunstwerke der Münchner Museen Alte Pinakothek, Bayerisches Nationalmuseum, Glyptothek*, Berner Kunstmuseum, Bern, September 1949–February 1950.
Bern/Bruges/Vienna 2008–10. *Charles the Bold (1433–1477): The Splendor of Burgundy*, Historisches Museum Bern, April 25–August 24, 2008, Bruggemuseum and Groeningemuseum, Bruges, March 27–July 21, 2009, Kunsthistorisches Museum, Vienna, September 15–January 10, 2010.
Birmingham 1936. Kaines Smith, ed. *Heraldic Exhibition*, exh. cat., City Museum and Art Gallery, Birmingham, November 5–December 12, 1936.
Blois 1987–88. *Louis XII: Images d'un roi, de l'Imperator au Père du people*, Château de Blois, December 18, 1987–February 14, 1988.
Blois 2002. Thierry Crépin-Leblond, ed. *Parures d'or et de pourpre: Le mobilier à la cour des Valois*, exh. cat., Château de Blois, June 15–September 30, 2002.
Blois 2006. P. G. Girault, ed. *François Ier: Images d'un roi, de l'histoire à la légende*, exh. cat., Château de Blois, June–September 2006.
Blois/Paris 1992–93. Ursula Baurmeister and Marie-Pierre Lafitte. *Des livres et des rois*, exh. cat., Château de Blois, June 20–August 30, 1992, Bibliothèque Nationale de France, October 15, 1992–January 17, 1993.
Boston 1972–73. *When Tapestries Were in Flower*, Museum of Fine Arts, Boston, 1972–73.
Bourges 1951. *Chefs-d'œuvre des peintres-enlumineurs de Jean de Berry et de l'école de Bourges*, Hôtel Cujas, Bourges, June 23–Septembee 4, 1951.
Bourges 2002. *Hommes illustres en médaillon*, Hôtel Lallemand, Bourges, 2002.
Brou 1958. Françoise Baudson. *Exposition organisée par la ville de Bourg-en-Bresse en hommage à Marguerite d'Autriche, fondatrice de Brou, 1480–1530*, exh. cat., Musée de l'Ain, Salle Capitulaire, Brou, June 1–July 15, 1958.
Bruges 1902. *Exposition des primitives flamands et d'art ancien*, Hôtel de Gouvernement Provincial, Bruges, 1902.
Bruges 2002. Till-Holger Bochert, ed. *Jan van Eyck und seine Zeit: 1430–1530. Flämische Meister und der Süden*, exh. cat., Groeningemuseum, Bruges, March 15–June 30, 2002.
Brussels 1935. *Exposition Universelle et Internationale: Cinq Siècles d'Art*, Brussels, April–November 1935. (Catalogue: Paul Lambotte, *Cinq siècles d'art bruxellois, 1400–1900*, Brussels, 1935.)
Brussels 1951. *Le Siècle de Bourgogne*, Palais des Beaux-Arts, Brussels, October 13–December 16, 1951.
Brussels 1973. Claudine Lemaire, ed. *De Vijfhonderdste Verjaring van de boekdrukkunst in de Nederlanden*, exh. cat., Bibliotheque Royale Albert I, Brussels, September 11–October 27, 1973.
Brussels/Delft 1957–58. *Dieric Bouts*, Palais des Beaux-Arts, Brussels, Museum Prinsenhof, Delft.
Caen/Rouen 1999–2000. *La Normandie dans la guerre de Cent Ans 1346–1450*, Musée de Normandie, Caen, Musée départemental des Antiquités de la Seine-Maritime, Rouen, 1999–2000.
Chicago 1933. *A Century of Progress*, Art Institute of Chicago, 1933.
Chicago 1934. *A Century of Progress*, Art Institute of Chicago, 1934.
Chicago 1969. Herbert Kessler, ed. *French and Flemish Illuminated Manuscripts from Chicago Collections*, exh. cat., Newberry Library, Chicago, April 9–May 30, 1969.
Chicago 1987. *Renaissance Decorative Arts from Chicago Collections*, The Art Institute of Chicago, March 2–June 14, 1987.
Daoulas/Nantes 1991–92. M.-H. Santrot, J. Santrot, and J. Kerhervé et al. *La Bretagne au temps des ducs*, exh. cat., Abaye de Daoulas, June 15 1991–October 6, 1991, Musée Dobrée, Nantes, November 9, 1991–February 9, 1992.
Detroit 1928. *Seventh Loan Exhibition: French Gothic Art of the Thirteenth to Fifteenth Century*, Detroit Institute of Art, 1928.
Dijon 1951. Pierre Quarré, ed. *Le Grand Siècle des Ducs de Bourgogne*, Palais des Ducs de Bourgogne, Dijon, 1951.
Dijon 1952. Pierre Quarré, ed. *Musées de Bourgogne*, exh. cat. Musée des beaux-arts, Palais des États de Bourgogne, Dijon, 1952.
Dortmund 1954. *Meisterwerke alter Malerei*, Schloss Cappenberg, Dortmund, 1954.
Douai 1986. *La majolique italienne dans les musées du Nord Pas-de-Calais*, Douai, 1986.
Ecouen 1995. *Le Dressoir du prince: services d'apparat à la Renaissance*, Musée national de la Renaissance, château d'Ecouen, October 18 1995–February 19, 1996.
Ecouen 2009. *Musée national de la Renaissance. Château d'Ecouen. Album*, Paris, 2009.
Edinburgh 1992. Martin Kemp, ed. *Leonardo da Vinci, The Mystery of the Madonna of the Yarnwinder*, exh. cat., National Gallery of Scotland, Edinburgh, May 15–July 12, 1992.
Fontevraud 2001. G. Massin Le Goff, ed. *L'Europe des Anjou: aventure des princes angevins du XIIIe au XVe siècle*, exh. cat., Abbaye de Fontevraud, June–September 2001.
Ghent 1975. Miek Goossens, ed. *Duizend Jaar Kunst en Kultuur: Boekdrukkunst, boekbanden, borduurkunst, edel, edelsmeedkunst, miniatuurkunst*, exh. cat., Bijlokemuseum, Gand, June 21–August 31, 1975.
Hampstead 1997–2003. *Barlow Collection* (Prêt de longue durée), Kenwood House, Hampstead, 1997–2003.
The Hague 1966. Magdi Tóth-Ubbens, ed. *In the Light of Vermeer: Five Centuries of Painting. Jubilee-Exhibition*, exh. cat., Mauritshuis, The Hague, June 25–September 5, 1966.
The Hague 2002. Anne S. Korteweg, ed. *Splendour, Gravity, and Emotion: French Medieval Manuscripts in Dutch Collections*, Museum Meermanno-Westreenianum, The Hague, February 6–May 26, 2002.

Le Havre 2004. *Trésors du Moyen Age: livres manuscrits de bibliothèques du Havre et de Montivilliers*, Bibliothèque municipale Armand Salacrou, Le Havre, October 6–December 18, 2004.

Krefeld 1887. *Ausstellung kirchlicher Kunstwebereien und Stickereien der Vergangenheit*, Königliche Gewebesammlung, 1887.

Leuven 1998. *Dirk Bouts (ca. 1410–1475): Een Vlaams primitief te Leuven*, Sint-Pieterskerk en Predikherenkerk te Leuven, 1998.

L'Isle-Adam 2004. *De Rhodes à Malte: Le grand maitre Philippe de Villiers de L'Isle-Adam (1460–1534) et l'ordre de Malte*, Musée d'Art et d'histoire Louis-Senlecq, L'Isle-Adam, 2004.

London 1862. J. C. Robinson. *Special Exhibition of Works of Art of the Mediaeval, Renaissance, and More Recent Periods on Loan at the South Kensington Museum*, exh. cat., South Kensington Museum, London, June 1862.

London 1871. *Exhibition of the Works of the Old Masters Associated with Works of Deceased Masters of the British School: Second Winter Exhibition*, Royal Academy of Arts, London, 1871.

London 1872. *Exhibition of the Works of the Old Masters, Together with Works of Deceased Masters of the British School*, Royal Academy of Arts, London, 1872.

London 1880. *Exhibition of Works by the Old Masters and by Deceased Masters of the British School*, exh. cat., William Olowes and Sons.

London 1892a. *Exhibition of Works by the Old Masters, and by Deceased Masters of the British School: Winter Exhibition*, Royal Academy of Arts, London, 1892.

London 1892b. *Exhibition of Pictures by Masters of the Netherlandish and Allied Schools of XV. and Early XVI. Centuries*, Burlington Fine Arts Club, London, 1892.

London, 1893. *Exhibition of Early Italian Art from 1300 to 1550*, exh. cat., The New Gallery, 1893–94.

London 1894. *Exhibition of Works by the Old Masters: Winter Exhibition*, Royal Academy of Arts, London, 1894.

London 1898. *Illustrated Catalogue of Pictures by the Masters of the Milanese and Allied Schools of Lombardy*, exh. cat., Burlington Fine Arts Club, May–July 1899.

London 1899–1900. James Wheale, ed. *Exhibition of Pictures by Masters of the Flemish and British Schools Including a Selection from the Works of Sir Peter Paul Rubens*, New Gallery, London, January–May 1900.

London 1902. *Exhibition of Works by the Old Masters Winter Exhibition*, Royal Academy of Arts, London, 1902.

London 1906. *Early Flemish Art, Guildhall Art Gallery, London, 1906.* (Catalogue: Alfred Temple, *Illustrated Catalogue of the Exhibition of Works by the Early Flemish Painters*, London, 1906.)

London 1909–10. *National Loan Exhibition*, Grafton Galleries, London, 1909–10.

London 1927. *Loan Exhibition of Flemish and Belgian Art*, Royal Academy, London, 1927.

London 1932. William Constable and Paul Alfassa, eds. *French Art, 1200–1900*, exh. cat., London Royal Academy of Arts, 1932.

London 1945–46. *Exhibition in honour of Sir Robert Witt, of the Principal Acquisitions Made for the Nation Through the National Arts-Collection Fund*, National Gallery, London, November 23, 1945–January 5, 1946.

London 1952. *Paintings by Old Masters*, Colnaghi, London, 1952.

London/New York 1995. *The Painted Page: Italian Renaissance Book Illumination, 1450–1550*, Royal Academy of Arts, London, October 27, 1994–January 22, 1995, The Pierpont Morgan Library, New York, February 15–May 7, 1995.

Los Angeles/London 2005. Thomas Kren and Mark L. Evans, eds. *A Masterpiece Reconstructed: The Hours of Louis XII*, The J. Paul Getty Museum, Los Angeles, October 18, 2005–January 8, 2006, Victoria and Albert Museum, London, February 2–May 1, 2006.

Los Angeles/New York/Paris 1994–95. *The French Renaissance in Prints from the Bibliothèque nationale de France*, Armand Hammer Museum of Art and Cultural Center, Los Angeles, November 1, 1994–January 1, 1995, Metropolitan Museum of Art, New York, January 12–March 19, 1995, Bibliothèque nationale de France, Paris, April 20–July 10, 1995.

Lucerne 1949. Robert Brun and Jacques Guignard, eds. *Dix siècles de livres français*, Musée des Beaux-arts, Lucerne, 1949.

Lyon 1920. V. Leroquais. *Manuscrits à peintures du VIe au XVIIe siècle*, exh. cat., Bibliothèque municipale, Lyon, 1920.

Lyon 2002. *Manuscrits médiévaux: de l'usage au trésor,* Bibliothèque municipale, Lyon, September 21–January 4, 2002.

Madrid/Valencia 2001. Mauro Natale, ed. *El renacimiento mediterráneo: viajes de artistas e itinerarios de obras entre Francia, Italia y España en el siglo XV*, Fundación Collección Thyssen-Bornemisza, Madrid, Museo de Bellas Artes de Valencia, 2001.

Malibu/New York/London 1983–84. Thomas Kren, ed. *Renaissance Painting in Manuscripts: Treasures from The British Library*, exh. cat., The J. Paul Getty Museum, Malibu, October 6, 1983–January 8, 1984, Pierpont Morgan Library, New York, January 20, 1984–April 29, 1984, British Library, London, May 25–September 30, 1984.

Manchester 1857. G. Scharf, ed. *Art Treasures of the United Kingdom at Manchester*, exh. cat., Museum of Ornemental Art, Manchester, 1857.

Manchester 1957. Art *Treasures Centenary: European Old Masters*, City of Manchester Art Gallery, 1957.

Manchester 1968. *Paintings from Sir Thomas Barlow's Collection*, Whitworth Art Gallery, Manchester, 1968.

Milan 1939. *Mostra di Leonardo da Vinci*, Palazzo dell'Arte, Milan, 1939.

Moulins 1955. *L'Art à la cour des Bourbons*, Moulins, 1955.

Nantes 1961. *Anne de Bretagne et son temps*, Musée Dobrée, Nantes, April–June 1961. (Catalogue: Jean Porcher, *Les manuscrits d'Anne de Bretagne*, Nantes, 1961.)

Nantes 1974–75. D. Costa and C. Cosneau-Allemand. *L'Art de la vallée de la Loire du haut Moyen Age à l'époque classique*, exh. cat., Musée Dobrée, Nantes, December 1974–February 1975.

Nantes 2007. Pierre Chotard, ed. *Anne de Bretagne, une histoire, un mythe*, exh. cat., Musée du Château des ducs de Bretagne, Nantes, June 30–September 30, 2007.

Naples/Rome 1983. *Leonardo e il leonardismo a Napoli e a Roma*, Museum Nazionale di Capodimonte, Napoli, 1983, Palazzo Venezia, Roma, 1983–84.

New York 1892. *Catalogue of an Exhibition of Illuminated and Painted Manuscripts*, The Grolier Club, New York, 1892.

New York 1927. Louis Réau. *Loan Exhibition of French Primitives and Objects of Art*, Kleinberger, New York, 1927.

New York 1933–34. Bella da Costa Greene, Meta Harrsen, and Charles Rufus Morey. *Exhibition of Illuminated Manuscripts Held at the New York Public Library*. New York, November 1933–April 1934.

New York 1939. *Catalogue of Euopean Paintings and Sculpture from 1300–1800*, New York World's Fair, May–October 1939.

New York/Chicago 1957. *Treasures from the Pierpont Morgan Library: Fiftieth Anniversary Exhibition*, The Pierpont Morgan Library, New York, 1957.

New York 1959. *Enamels*, Museum of Contemporary Crafts, New York, September 18–November 29, 1959.

New York 1973–74. *Woodner Collection II: Old Master Drawings from the XV to the XVIII Century*, William H. Schab Gallery, New York, and other locations, 1973–74.

New York 1974. Geneviève Souchal. *Masterpieces of Tapestry from the Fourteenth to the Sixteenth Century: An Exhibition at the Metropolitan Museum of Art*, exh. cat., The Metropolitan Museum of Art, New York, 1974.

New York 1979. *Jean Grolier: The Man in His Time, Celebrating the 500th Anniversary of the Birth of Jean Grolier*, exh. cat., The Grolier Club, New York, October 16–December 1, 1979.

New York 1980. *Flowers in Books and Drawings Ca. 940–1840*, The Pierpont Morgan Library, New York, September 2–November 9, 1980.

New York 1982. John Plummer and Gregory Clark. *The Last Flowering: French Painting in Manuscripts, 1420–1530, from American Collections*, exh. cat. The Pierpont Morgan Library, November 18, 1982–January 30, 1983.

New York 1992–93. William Voelkle and Roger Wieck. *The Bernard H. Breslauer Collection of Manuscript Illumination*, The Pierpont Morgan Library, New York, December 9, 1992–April 4, 1993.

New York 1997. *Medieval Bestsellers: The Book of Hours*, The Pierpont Morgan Library, New York, September 17, 1997–January 4, 1998. (Catalogue: Roger Wieck, *Painted Prayers: The Book of Hours in Medieval and Renaissance Art*, New York, 1997.)

New York 2001. *Jean Poyer: Artist to the Court of Renaissance France*, The Morgan Library, New York, January 25–May 6, 2001.

New York 2002. Thomas P. Campbell, et al. *Tapestry in the Renaissance: Art and Magnificence*, exh. cat. Metropolitan Museum of Art, New York, March 12–June 19, 2002.

New York 2004. Helen C. Evans. *Byzantium: Faith and Power (1261–1557)*, exh. cat. Metropolitan Museum of Art, New York, March 23–July 4, 2004.

New York 2005–06. Jonathan Alexander, ed. *The Splendor of the Word: Medieval and Renaissance Illuminated Manuscripts at the New York Public Library*, exh. cat., New York Public Library, October 21, 2005–February 11, 2006.

New York/Fort Worth 2008–09. Andrea Bayer, ed. *Art and Love in Renaissance Italy*, exh. cat., The Metropolitan Museum of Art, New York, November 11, 2008–February 16, 2009, Kimbell Art Museum, Fort Worth, March 15–June 14, 2009.

New York/Washington 1994. S. K. Scher, ed. *The Currency of Fame: Portrait Medals of the Renaissance*, exh. cat., Frick Collection, New York, National Gallery, Washington, January–May 1994.

Nice/Sèvres 2002–03. Jean-René Gaborit, Marc Bormand, *Les Della Robbia: Sculptures en terre cuite émaillée de la Renaissance italienne*, exh. cat., Musée national Message Biblique Marc Chagall, Nice, June 29–November 11, 2002, Musée national de Céramique, Sèvres, December 10–March 10, 2003.

Paris 1878. *Exposition universelle. Exposition rétrospective*, Paris, 1878.

Paris 1900. *Exposition rétrospective de l'art français des origines à 1800*, Petit-Palais, Paris, 1900.

Paris 1904. *Les Primitifs Français au Palais du Louvre et à la Bibliothèque nationale*, Musée du Louvre, Pavillon de Marsan, et Bibliothèque nationale de France, Paris, 1904 (Catalogue: Henri Bouchot, *La Peinture en France sous les Valois*, Paris, 1904.)

Paris 1907. François Courboin, ed. *Exposition de portraits peints et dessinés du XIIIe au XVIIe siècle*, exh. cat., Bibliothèque nationale de France, Paris, April–June 1907.

Paris 1926. *Catalogue de l'Exposition du Moyen Âge. Catalogue des manuscrits, estampes, médailles et objets d'art imprimés*, Bibliothèque nationale de France, Paris, January 28–February 28, 1926.

Paris 1928. *La Tapisserie gothique*, Manufacture nationale des Gobelins, Paris, June 1928.

Paris 1935. Jacques Dupont and Jacqueline Bouchot-Saupique, eds. *De Van Eyck à Bruegel*, Musée de l'Orangerie, Paris, 1935.

Paris 1937. Henri Focillon, Georges Huisman, et Jean Zay, eds. *Chefs-d'Oeuvre de l'Art Français: Exposition Internationale des Arts et des Techniques appliqués à la Vie Moderne*, Palais National des Arts, Paris, 1937.

Paris 1939. *Exposition de l'art italien du Cimabue à Tiepolo*, Paris, Musée du Petit Palais, 1939.

Paris 1946. *La tapisserie française du Moyen Age à nos jours*, Paris, Musée national d'Art moderne, 1946.

Paris 1955. *Jean Porcher, ed. Les Manuscrits à Peintures en France du XIIIe au XVIe siècle.* Bibliothèque nationale de France, Paris, December 17, 1955–September 20, 1956.

Paris 1956. *De Giotto à Bellini: les primitifs italiens dans les musées de France*, Orangerie des Tuileries, Paris, 1956.

Paris 1957. Charles Sterling, ed. *La Collection Lehman de New York*, Musée de l'Orangerie, Paris, 1957.

Paris 1963. Jean-Pierre Seguin and Cécile de Jandin, eds. *Cinq siècles de cartes à jouer en France*, Bibliothèque nationale, Paris, September–October 1963.

Paris 1964. F. Baron and M. Beaulieu. *Huit siècles de sculpture française: chefs-d'œuvre des musées de France*, Musée du Louvre, Paris, May–June 1964.

Paris 1965. *Trésors des églises de France*, exh. cat., Musée des Arts décoratifs, Paris, 1965.

Paris 1966. Ary Bob de Vries, ed. *Dans la lumière de Vermeer: cinq siècles de peinture*, Musée de l'Orangerie, Paris, September 24–November 28, 1966.

Paris 1968. *L'Europe Gothique, XIIe–XIVe siècle*, Musée du Louvre, Pavillon de Flore, Paris, April 2–July 1, 1968.

Paris 1971. P. Dehaye, ed. *Les Graveurs d'acier et la médaille de l'Antiquité à nos jours*, Hôtel de la Monnaie, Paris, June–October 1971.

Paris 1972. Roger Pierrot and Marcel Thomas. *Le Livre*, Bibliothèque nationale de France, Paris, May 17–Otober 31, 1972.

Paris 1973–74. Geneviève Souchal. *Chefs d'œuvre de la tapisserie médiévale*, Grand-Palais, Paris, October 26, 1973–January 7, 1974.

Paris 1977. Jean Adhémar. *Collections de Louis XIV*, Orangerie des Tuileries, Paris, October 7, 1977–January 9, 1978.

Paris 1985. *Andrea Solario en France*, Musée du Louvre, Paris, November 15, 1985–March 3, 1986.

Paris 1991. François Avril, ed. *La Passion des Manuscrits enluminés. Bibliophiles Français: 1280–1580*, Bibliothèque nationale de France, Paris, September 2–21.

Paris 1993b. Guy-Michel Leproux, ed. *Vitraux parisiens de la Renaissance*, Rotonde de la Villette and Mairie of the Fifth Arrondissement, Paris, 1993.

Paris 1993b. *Quand la peinture était dans les livres*, Bibliothèque nationale, Paris, October 16, 1993–January 16, 1994. (Catalogue: François Avril and Nicole Reynaud, eds., *Les Manuscrits à Peintures en France: 1440–1520*, Paris, 1993.)

Paris 1995. M. Bimbenet-Privat, ed. *L'Orfèvrerie parisienne de la Renaissance: Trésors dispersés,* Centre culturel du Panthéon, Paris, September 15–December 15, 1995.

Paris 2002a. *Sur la terre comme au ciel: Jardins d'Occident à la fin du Moyen Age*, Musée de Cluny, Paris, 2002.

Paris 2002b. Isabelle de Conihout and Christian Péligry. *Le cardinal, la Fronde et le bibliothècaire: les trente plus beaux livres de Mazarin*, Bibliothèque nationale de France, Paris, October 25, 2002–January 12, 2003.

Paris 2003. François Avril, ed. *Jean Fouquet, peintre et enlumineur du XVe siècle*, Bibliothèque nationale de France, site Richelieu, galerie Mazarine, Paris, March 25–June 22, 2003.

Paris 2004. Dominique Thiébaut, Philippe Lorentz, François-René Martin. *Primitifs français: Découvertes et redécouvertes*, exh. cat., Musée du Louvre, Paris, February 27–May 17, 2004.

Paris 2006. *Oeuvres nouvelles, 1995–2005*, Musée national du Moyen Âge—Thermes et hôtel de Cluny, May 10–September 25, 2006.

Paris/Ecouen 2007–08. Thierry Crépin-Leblond and M. Huynh, eds. *L'art des frères d'Amboise, les chapelles de l'hôtel de Cluny et du château de Gaillon*, exh. cat., Musée national du Moyen Âge—Thermes et hôtel de Cluny, Paris, Musée national de la Renaissance, Ecouen, October 3, 2007–January 14, 2008.

Paris/Mont-Saint-Michel 1966. F. Enaud, ed. *Millénaire du Mont-Saint-Michel: 966–1966*, exh. cat., Palais de justice, Paris, March 18–May 15, 1966, Mont-Saint-Michel, May 28–October 1, 1966.

Pau 1876. *Catalogue abrégé des tableaux exposés dans les salons de l'ancien Asile de Pau, appartenant aux héritiers de feu Mgr l'Infant Don Sébastien Gabriel de Bourbon et Bragance*, Pau, September 1876.

Pittsburgh 1951. *French Painting, 1100–1900*, Carnegie Institute, Department of Fine Arts, Pittsburgh, October 18–December 2, 1951.

Poligny et al. 1972. *L'art sacré dans le Jura du Moyen-âge au XVIIIe siècle*, Poligny, Baume-les-Messieurs, and Saint-Claude, June–September 1972.

Pontarlier 1949. *La Passion selon les artistes comtois.* Pontarlier, 1949.

Prague/Bratislava 1978–79. *Umení Francouzského Stredoveku*, exh. cat., Národní galerie, Prague, December 13, 1978–January 2, 1979, Slovenská národná galleria, Bratislava, February 6–March 3, 1979.

Rodez 1979. *VIIe centenaire de la cathédrale de Rodez, 1277–1977*, exh. cat., Rodez, 1979.

Rouen 1980–81. *La Renaissance à Rouen*, Musée des Beaux-arts, Rouen, November 28, 1980–February 28, 1981.

Rouen 2008. *Le château de Gaillon. Fastes de la Renaissance en Normandie*, Musée départemental des antiquités, Rouen, February 27–May 12, 2008.

Saint-Omer 1992. G. Blazy, ed. *Trésors des églises de l'arrondissement de Saint-Omer*, exh. cat., Musée de l'hôtel Sandelin, Saint Omer, September 26–December 13, 1992.

Sèvres 1973. *La Céramique du Beauvaisis du Moyen-Age au dix-huitième siècle*, Musée national de céramique, Sèvres, May 4–September 3, 1973.

Tokyo/Auckland 1972–73. *Medieval Arts in France*, exh. cat., Museum of Western Art, Tokyo, October 12–November 30, 1972, City Art Gallery, Auckland, 1972–73.

Toledo 1935. *French and Flemish Primitive Exhibition*, Toledo Museum of Art, 1935.

Toulouse 2005. *Polychromies secrètes. Autour de la restauration de deux œuvres majeures du XVe siècle toulousain*, Musée des Augustins, Toulouse, December 2005–April 2006.

Tours 1952. Julien Cain, ed. *L'Art du Val de Loire de Jean Fouquet à Jean Clouet. 1450–1540. Exposition organisée à l'occasion du cinquième centenaire de la naissance de Léonard de Vinci*, exh. cat., Musée des Beaux-Arts, Tours, July 9–September 30, 1952.

Tours/Angers 1975. D. Costa, C. Cosneau-Allemand, and V. Huchard. *L'Art de la vallée de la Loire du XVe siècle à l'époque classique*, exh. cat., Musée des Beaux-Arts, Tours, Musée des Beaux-Arts, Angers, February–June 1975.

Vinci 1982. *Leonardo dopo Milano: La Madonna dei fusi (1501)*, Castello dei Conti Guidi, Vinci, May 16–September 30, 1982.

Washington 1961. *Art Treasures for America from the Samuel H. Kress Collection*, National Gallery of Art, Washington, D.C., December 1961–February 4, 1962.

Washington 1995. M. H. Tesnière and P. Gifford. *Creating French Culture: Treasures from the Bibliothèque nationale de France*, exh. cat., Library of Congress, Washington, D.C., September–December 1995.

Washington 2009. Margaret Morgan Grasselli, ed. *Renaissance to Revolution: French Drawings from the National Gallery of Art, 1500–1800*, exh. cat., National Gallery of Art, Washington, D.C., October 1, 2009–January 31, 2010.

Washington/Antwerp 2006–07. John O. Hand, Catherine A. Metzger, and Ron Spronk, eds. *Prayers and Portraits: Unfolding the Netherlandish Diptych*, exh. cat., National Gallery of Art, Washington, D.C., November 12, 2006–February 4, 2007, Koninklijk Museum voor Schone Kunsten, Antwerp, March 3–May 27, 2007.

Kings, Queens, and Courtiers: Art in Early Renaissance France was published in conjunction with an exhibition organized by the Art Institute of Chicago and the Réunion des musées nationaux, Paris, and realized with the collaboration of the Musée du Louvre, Paris, the Musée de Cluny—Musée national du Moyen Age, Paris, and the Musée national de la Renaissance, Château d'Ecouen. It was presented at the Art Institute from February 27 to May 30, 2011. Under the title *France 1500: Entre Moyen Age et Renaissance*, it was shown at the Galeries nationales, Grand Palais, Paris, from October 6, 2010, to January 10, 2011.

Major funding is generously provided by Paul and Melinda Sullivan and the Eloise W. Martin Legacy Fund.

Lead individual sponsorship is generously provided by Scott, Lynda, Jonathan, and Lindsey Canel.

Additional support is provided by the Chauncey and Marion Deering McCormick Foundation and the Prince Charitable Trusts.

This exhibition is also supported by an award from the National Endowment for the Arts, which believes a great nation deserves great art.

Generous support is provided by the Exhibitions Trust: Kenneth and Anne Griffin, Thomas and Margot Pritzker, the Earl and Brenda Shapiro Foundation, Donna and Howard Stone, Mr. and Mrs. Paul Sullivan, and an anonymous donor.

First edition
Printed in Canada
Library of Congress Control Number: 2010918540
ISBN 978-0-300-17025-2 (cloth)
ISBN 978-0-86559-244-5 (paper)

Published by
The Art Institute of Chicago
111 South Michigan Avenue
Chicago, Illinois 60603-6404
www.artic.edu

Distributed by
Yale University Press
302 Temple Street
New Haven, Connecticut 06520-9040
www.yalebooks.com/art

Produced by the Publications Department of the Art Institute of Chicago
Robert V. Sharp, Executive Director
Edited by Amy R. Peltz
Production by Sarah Guernsey and Clo Pazera
Photography research by Joseph Mohan
Designed and typeset by The Grillo Group, Inc., Chicago, Illinois
Separations by Professional Graphics, Inc., Rockford, Illinois
Printing and binding by Friesens Corporation, Altona, Manitoba, Canada

Translations from the French and German by the Art of Translation: Nicholas Elliott, Elizabeth G. Heard, John Paul McDonald, Kenneth McKerrow, Molly Stevens, and Diana C. Stoll. Translation managed by Molly Stevens.

Map by Mapping Specialists, Ltd., Fitchburg, Wisconsin

Front cover: Jean Hey, *Madeleine of Burgundy Presented by Saint Mary Magdalene* (detail), c. 1490, Musée de du Louvre, Paris (see page 127, cat. 58).

Back cover: *Narcissus at the Fountain*, c. 1500, Museum of Fine Arts, Boston (see pages 150–51, cat. 77).

Frontispiece: Jean Hey, *The Annunciation* (detail), 1490/95, the Art Institute of Chicago (see pages 128–29, cat. 60).

Photography Credits

Images of objects in the collection of the Art Institute of Chicago were produced by its Department of Imaging, Christopher Gallagher, Director.

Unless otherwise noted, all photographs of artworks from public and private collections appear by permission of those institutions. Every effort has been made to contact and acknowledge copyright holders for all reproductions. The following credits apply to all images for which separate acknowledgment is due.

Figs. 1, 3, 6, 16, 17, 20, 31, 38, 44, 46; cats. 13, 19, 22, 27, 28, 35, 54, 72, 91, 110, 111: Bibliothèque nationale de France. Figs. 2, 4, 11, 30: Giraudon / The Bridgeman Art Library International. Figs. 5, 43; cat. 68: © Michel Hérold. Fig. 7: © Delphine Cingal. Figs. 8, 39: The Art Archive / Cathédrale de Moulins / Alfredo Dagli Orti. Fig. 10: © M. Rosso, Service Patrimoine et inventaire, Région de Bourgogne, 1992. Fig. 12: © David Bordes. Fig. 13: © Centre des monuments nationaux, Paris, Marc Tulane. Fig. 14: Erich Lessing / Paris, akg-images. Fig. 15; cat. 116: P. Giraud / Région des Pays de la Loire, Inventaire general, ADAGP. Figs. 18, 51; cats. 58, 99, 113: Gérard Blot / Réunion des musées nationaux, Paris. Fig. 19; cat. 34: Waddesdon Manor, The Rothschild Collection (The National Trust). Fig. 21; cats. 4, 12: Thierry Le Mage / Réunion des musées nationaux, Paris. Fig. 22; cat. 11: Erich Lessing / Art Resource, NY. Fig. 24; cats. 75, 78: Jean-Gilles Berizzi / Réunion des musées nationaux, Paris. Cats. 2, 44, 46, 53, 70: photography, Graham Haber, 2010. Cats. 5, 14, 38, 42, 74, 94; figs. 29, 45, 50: Réunion des musées nationaux / Art Resource, NY. Fig. 26; cat. 89: © The British Library Board. Fig. 27: V&A Images / Art Resource, NY. Fig. 28: Scala / White Images / Art Resource, NY. Cat. 16: Le Puy-en-Velay Musée Crozatier. Cat. 17: Trésor de la Cathédrale de Sens. Cat. 18: Saint-Omer, Musée de l'Hôtel Sandelin / Ph. Beurtheret. Cats. 20, 21: Daniel Martin. Figs. 32, 48; cat. 36: Franck Raux / Réunion des musées nationaux, Paris. Fig. 33; cats. 83, 108: Rene-Gabriel Ojeda / Réunion des musées nationaux, Paris. Cats. 26, 96, 97, 102: image copyright © The Metropolitan Museum of Art, New York / Art Resource, NY. Cats. 29, 70, 90: courtesy of the Library of Congress. Cats. 32, 33, 51, 98: image courtesy of the Board of Trustees, National Gallery of Art, Washington, D. C. Figs. 34, 35; cat. 59: © National Gallery, London / Art Resource, NY. Cat. 37: Tim Thayer, Oak Park, Michigan. Fig. 36: Jacques Philippot © Région Picardie—Inventaire général/Ministère de la Culture et de la Communication. Fig. 37; cats. 47, 101, 109: Herve Lewandowski/Réunion des musées nationaux, Paris. Fig. 40: © Daniel TARDIF. Cat. 43: Teylers Museum Haarlem Netherland. Cat. 45: Bibliothèque municipale de Lyon, Didier Nicole. Cat. 52: Patrick Boyer / Musée des Beaux-Arts, Tours. Cat. 63: Culture and Sport Glasgow. Cat. 64: © Royal Museums of Fine Arts of Belgium, Brussels. Cat. 66: Stephane Marechalle / Réunion des musées nationaux, Paris. Cat. 69: North Carolina Museum of Art, Raleigh, Gift of the Samuel H. Kress Foundation, GL.60.17.61. Fig. 41: © Centre des monuments nationaux, Paris, Bernard Acloque. Cat. 77; fig. 47: photograph © 2011 Museum of Fine Arts, Boston. Cats. 84, 85: The Philadelphia Museum of Art / Art Resource, NY. Cat. 87: digital image © 2009 Museum Associates / LACMA / Art Resource, NY. Cat. 95: Christian Jan / Réunion des musées nationaux, Paris. Fig. 49: Tours, Cathédrales Saint-Gatien, ministère de la culture et de la communication. Cat. 100: Réunion des musées nationaux, Paris.

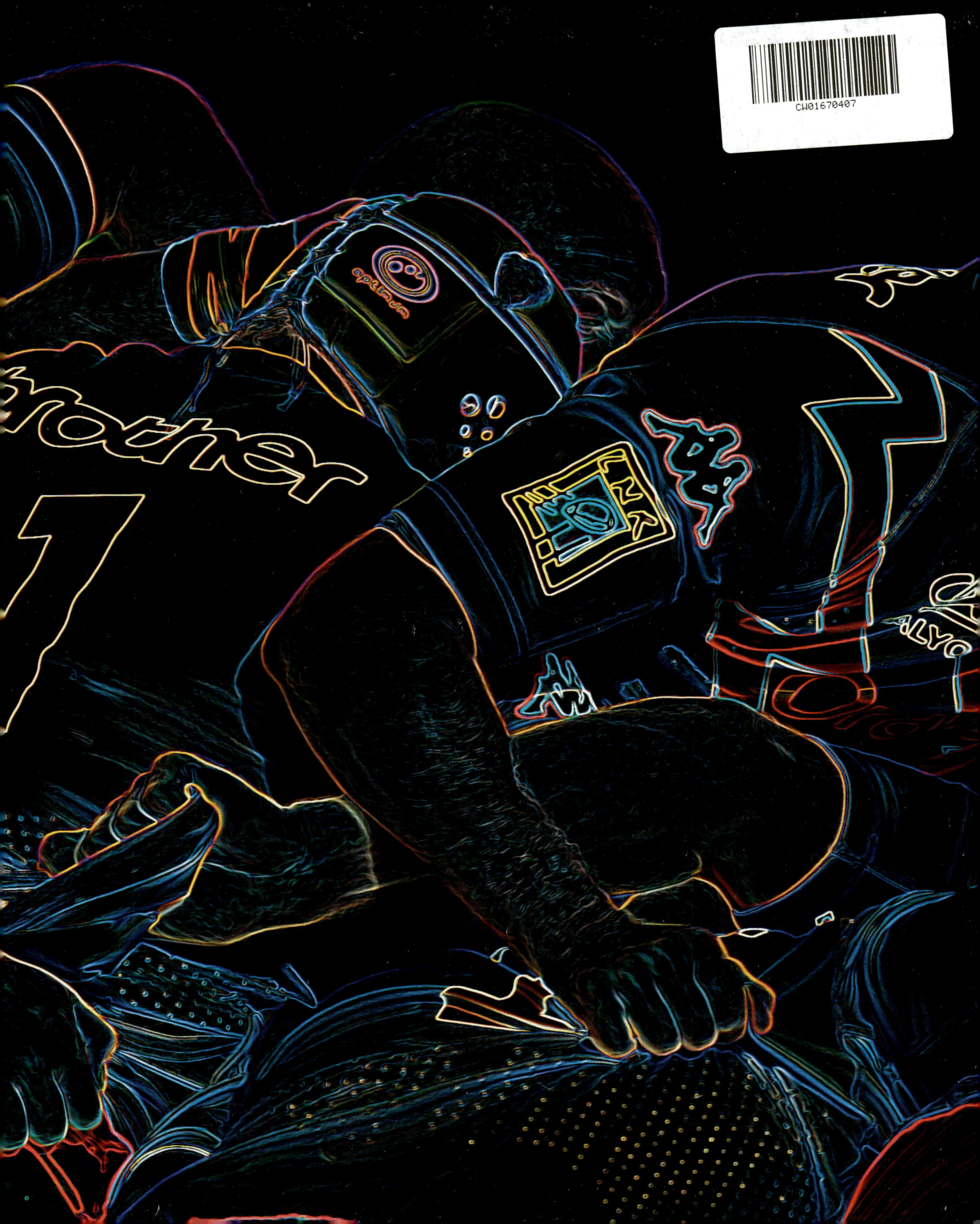

LE RUGBY

raconté aux enfants

RICHARD ESCOT

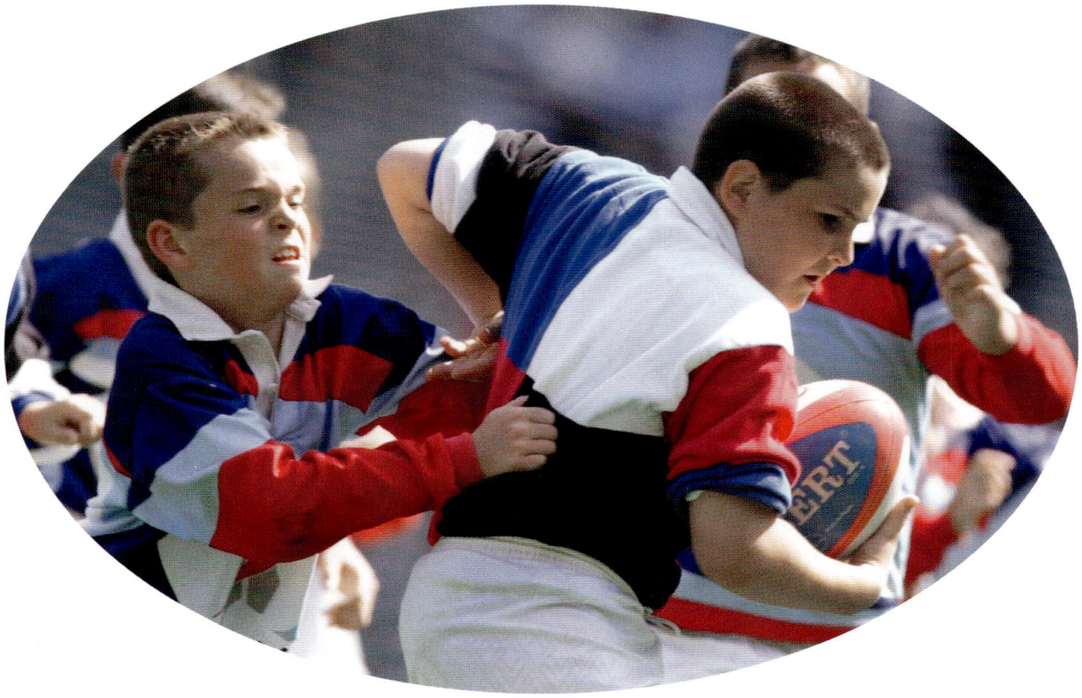

De La Martinière
Jeunesse

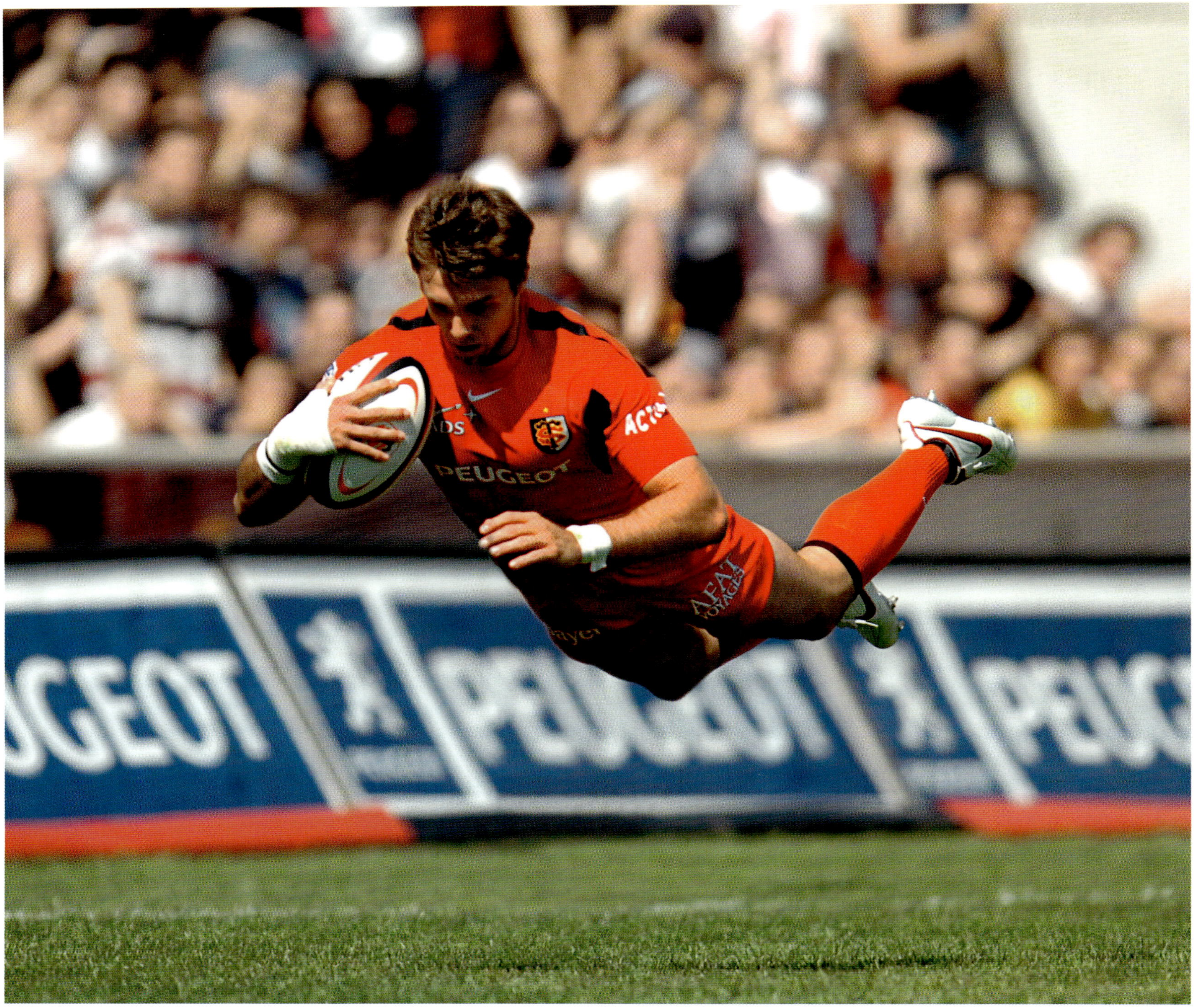

Deux actions parmi les plus spectaculaires du rugby :
L'ailier Vincent Clerc, sous le maillot du Stade Toulousain, plonge dans l'en-but avec style.
Bataille des airs entre le Biarrot Imanol Harinordoquy et le Toulousain Jean Bouilhou.

Écriture visuelle et mise en page : Benoit Nacci

Connectez-vous sur :
www.lamartinierejeunesse.fr

Sommaire

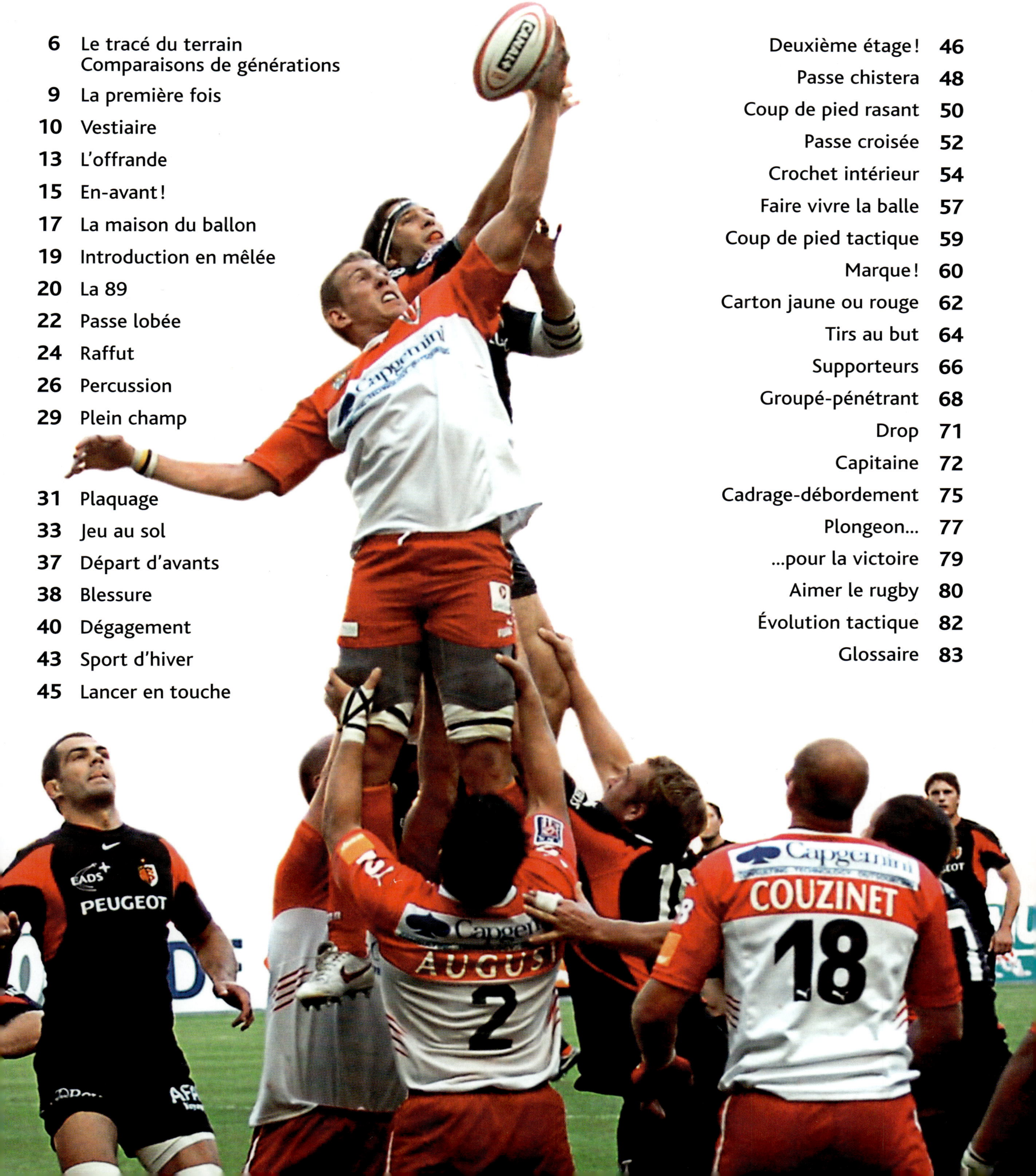

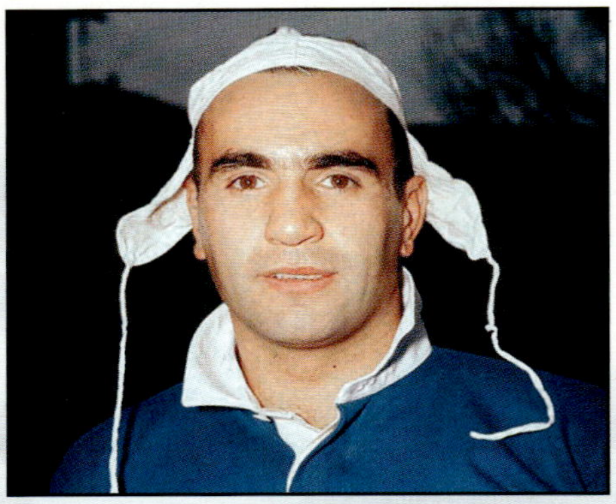

Jean Barthe, années 50

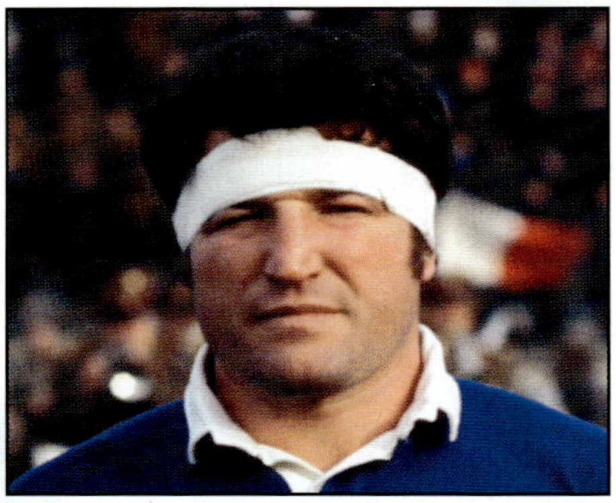

Jean Iraçabal, années 70

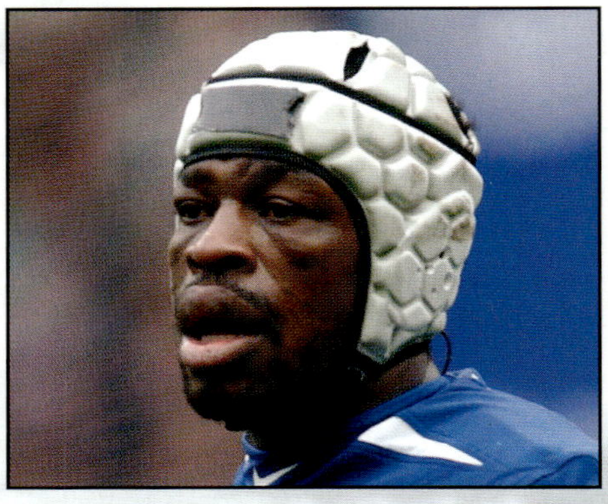

Serge Betsen, aujourd'hui

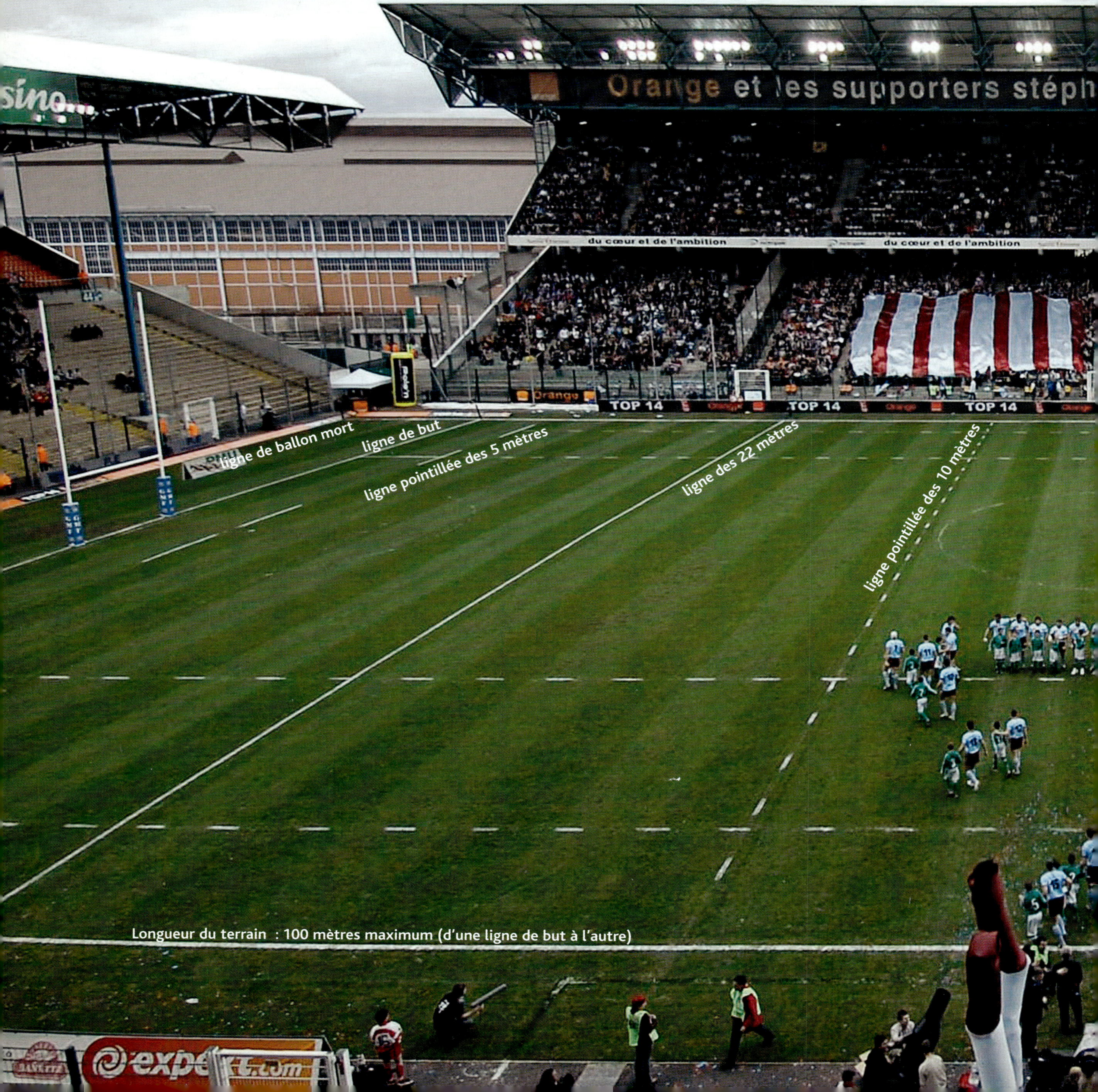

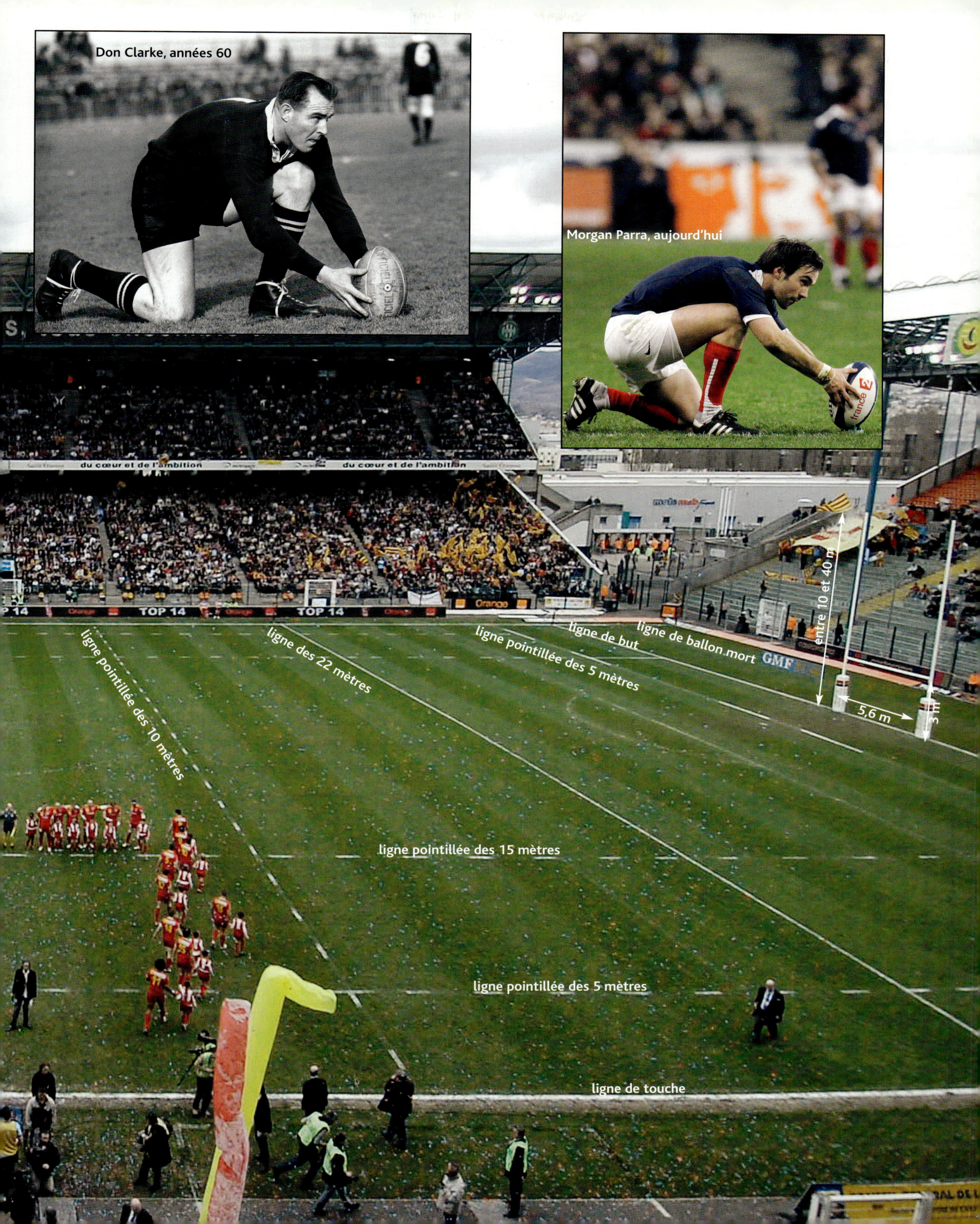

Don Clarke, années 60

Morgan Parra, aujourd'hui

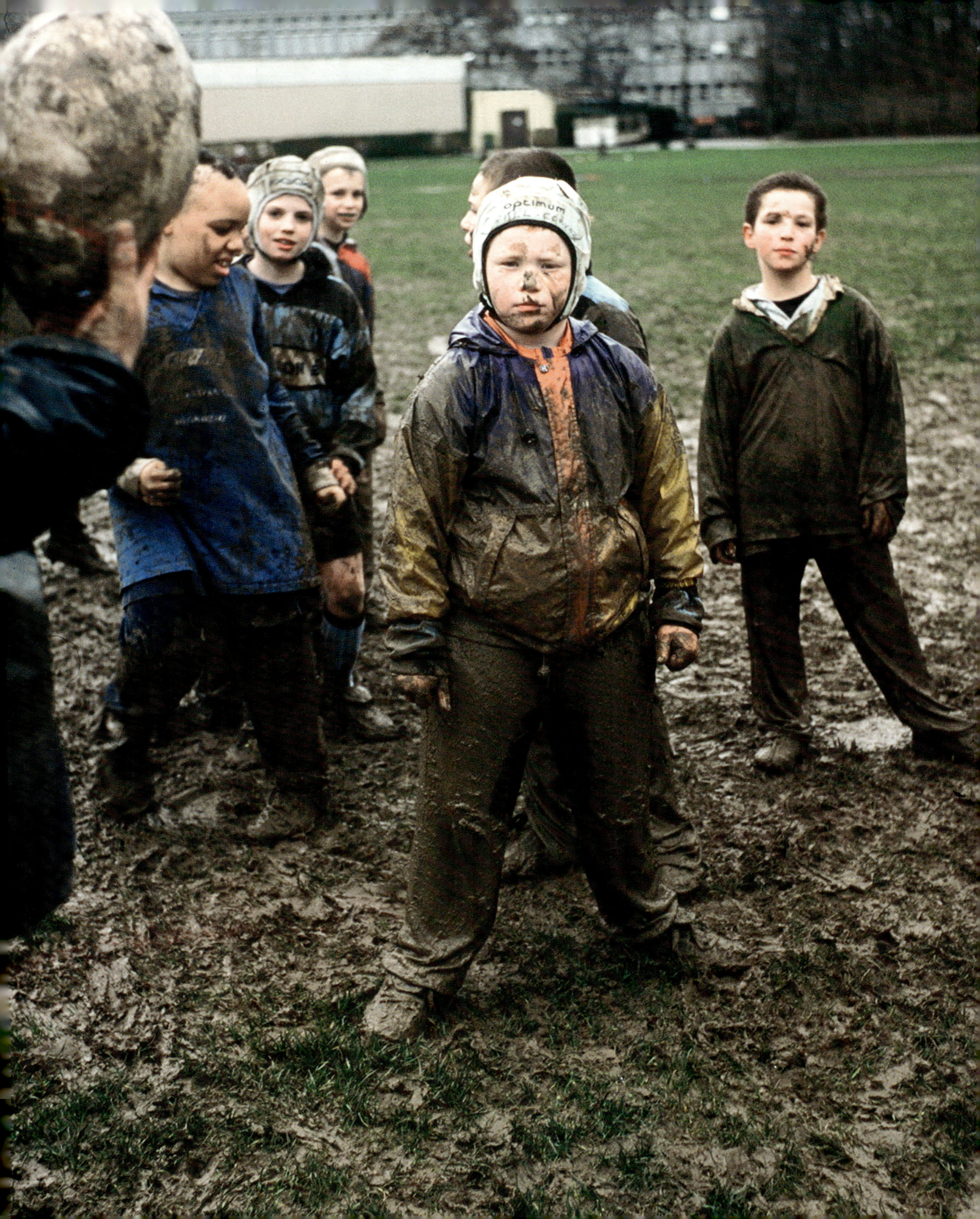
optimum

LA PREMIÈRE FOIS

Frédéric Michalak, Serge Blanco, Jean-Pierre Rives, Philippe Sella, Abdelatif Benazzi, Jean-Baptiste Elissalde, Dimitri Yachvili ou Yannick Nyanga, que j'ai la chance de côtoyer, se souviennent de leurs premiers pas, ballon en main, de leurs premières passes, et gardent intacte cette intense émotion. Qu'ils soient originaires d'Afrique ou d'Atlantique, de l'Est ou des Îles, les grands champions français n'ont pas oublié l'enfant qu'ils étaient. Rien ne pourra effacer de leur mémoire ce qu'ils ont ressenti le jour où ils découvrirent cet œuf de pack devenu, depuis, leur complice. Pour nous, les héros modernes du Quinze de France sont devenus des personnages de conte. Ils ont accepté de descendre à hauteur d'enfant pour montrer aux filles et aux garçons à quoi ressemble le rugby, si riche, si complexe. Voilà qu'ils s'élancent, feintent, percent, poussent, sautent et marquent, et nous les suivons, calés dans le sillage de leurs exploits.

Cet ouvrage, inscrit dans une riche collection qui balaie l'histoire de la terre et de l'humanité, je voulais qu'il ressemble à une main tendue. Et je me souviens des instants privilégiés où, après m'avoir accompagné au stade, mon père Jean-Claude me laissait avec des éducateurs attentionnés dont le nom m'est toujours familier. C'est aussi en pensant à vous, messieurs Bas, Courthès et Puyfourcat, aux mots que vous prononciez, aux regards que vous portiez sur les jeunes pousses que ce livre a été imaginé.

Plus d'un siècle après son entrée dans le concert international, la France se rendra en Nouvelle-Zélande, à l'autre bout de la planète, pour y disputer la septième Coupe du monde. Jamais elle n'a remporté le trophée Webb-Ellis. Elle mettra tout en œuvre, son énergie, sa volonté, pour vaincre. Car le destin du Quinze de France n'est pas tant d'être sacré champion du monde que d'offrir à ses supporteurs l'image d'une équipe solidaire et enthousiaste.

Bon match !

RICHARD ESCOT

Vestiaire

Notre équipe, c'est une bande de copains. On se connaît depuis toujours, c'est-à-dire depuis les premiers entraînements à l'école de rugby. Dans le vestiaire, l'entraîneur nous tend, à chacun, l'un après l'autre, nos maillots. Aujourd'hui, nous allons disputer un match important. De toute façon, tous nos matches sont importants. Il n'y a rien à gagner, pas de coupe, pas de trophée, juste le plaisir de jouer et, si possible, de vaincre. J'aime cet endroit. Simple, dépouillé. Nous y sommes assis les uns à côté des autres. Serrés. Il sent la pommade chauffante et l'huile camphrée, qui font luire nos muscles. Il nous reste encore quelques minutes pour nous échauffer. Elles paraissent longues, et il faut les savourer. Le vestiaire, c'est toujours un moment particulier, avec un peu de crainte et de bonheur mêlés. La peur de ne pas être à la hauteur, et le plaisir d'être ensemble. L'entraîneur nous rappelle une dernière fois les consignes de jeu mais déjà nos crampons griffent le sol en ciment. D'un coup de sifflet strident, l'arbitre nous invite à sortir. Là-bas, au bout du couloir, le terrain nous appelle.

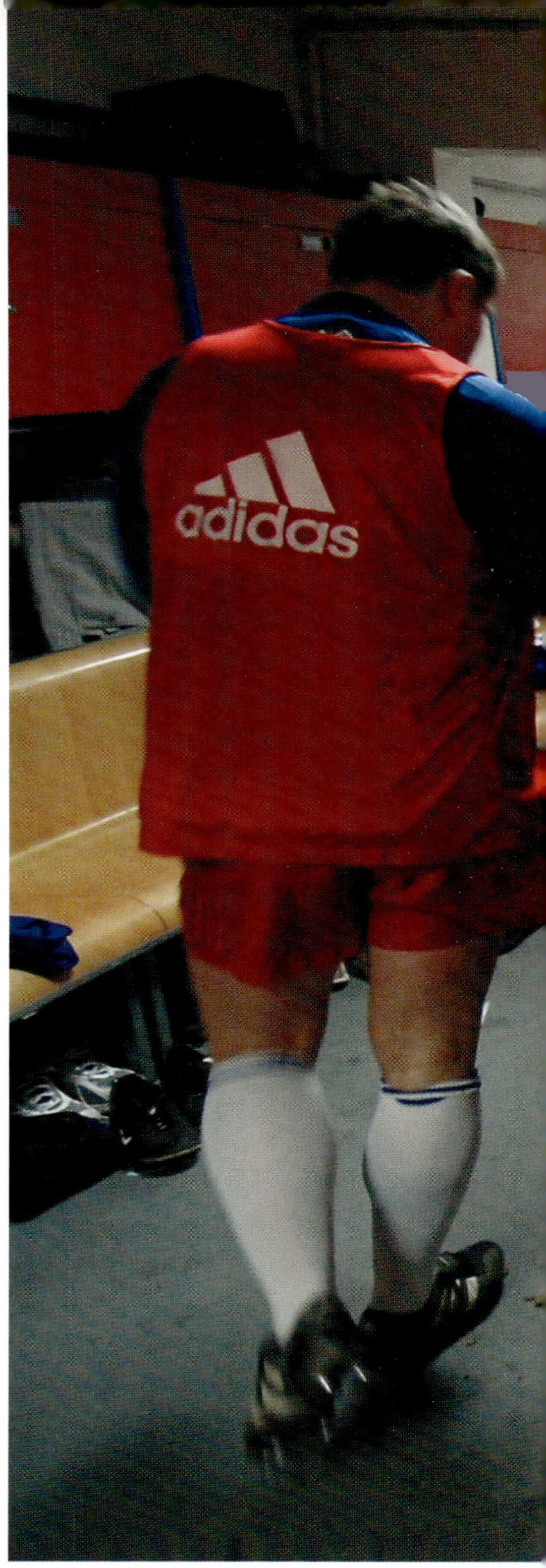

Les photographes pénètrent rarement dans le vestiaire des équipes professionnelles juste avant une rencontre de rugby. C'est l'endroit où les joueurs vivent leurs derniers moments d'intimité avant d'aller affronter l'adversaire. Soudés, ils s'encouragent, se promettent de rester unis et solidaires, de faire corps et de vaincre, comme ici ceux du Stade Français, dans le sous-sol du stade Jean-Bouin.

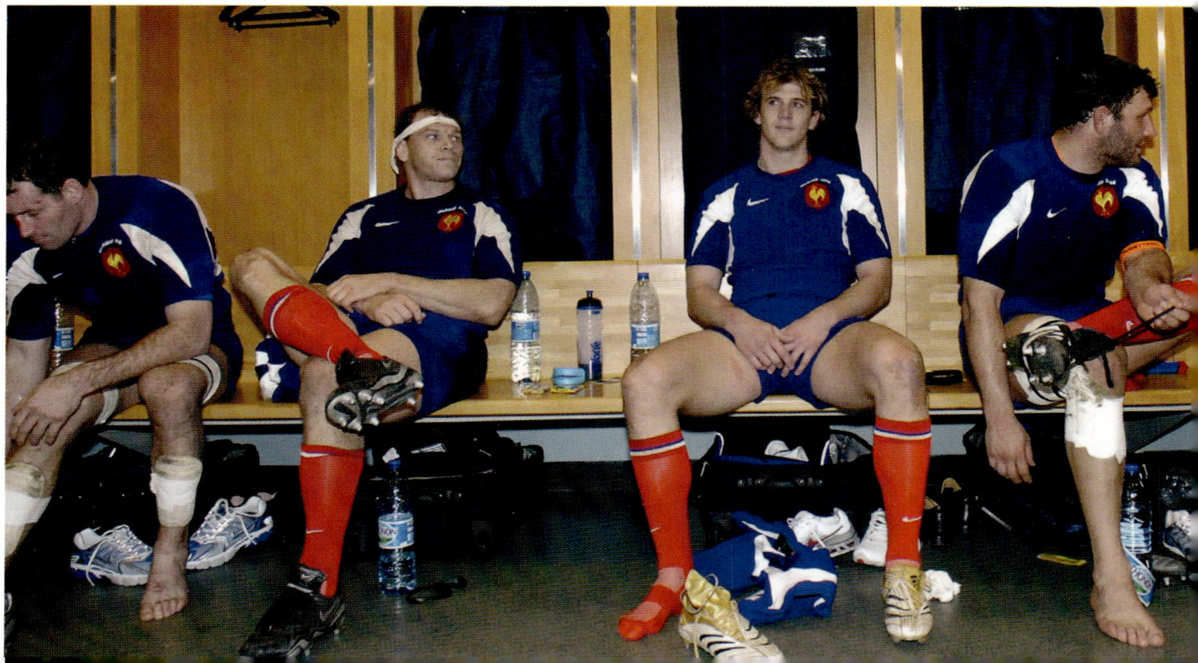

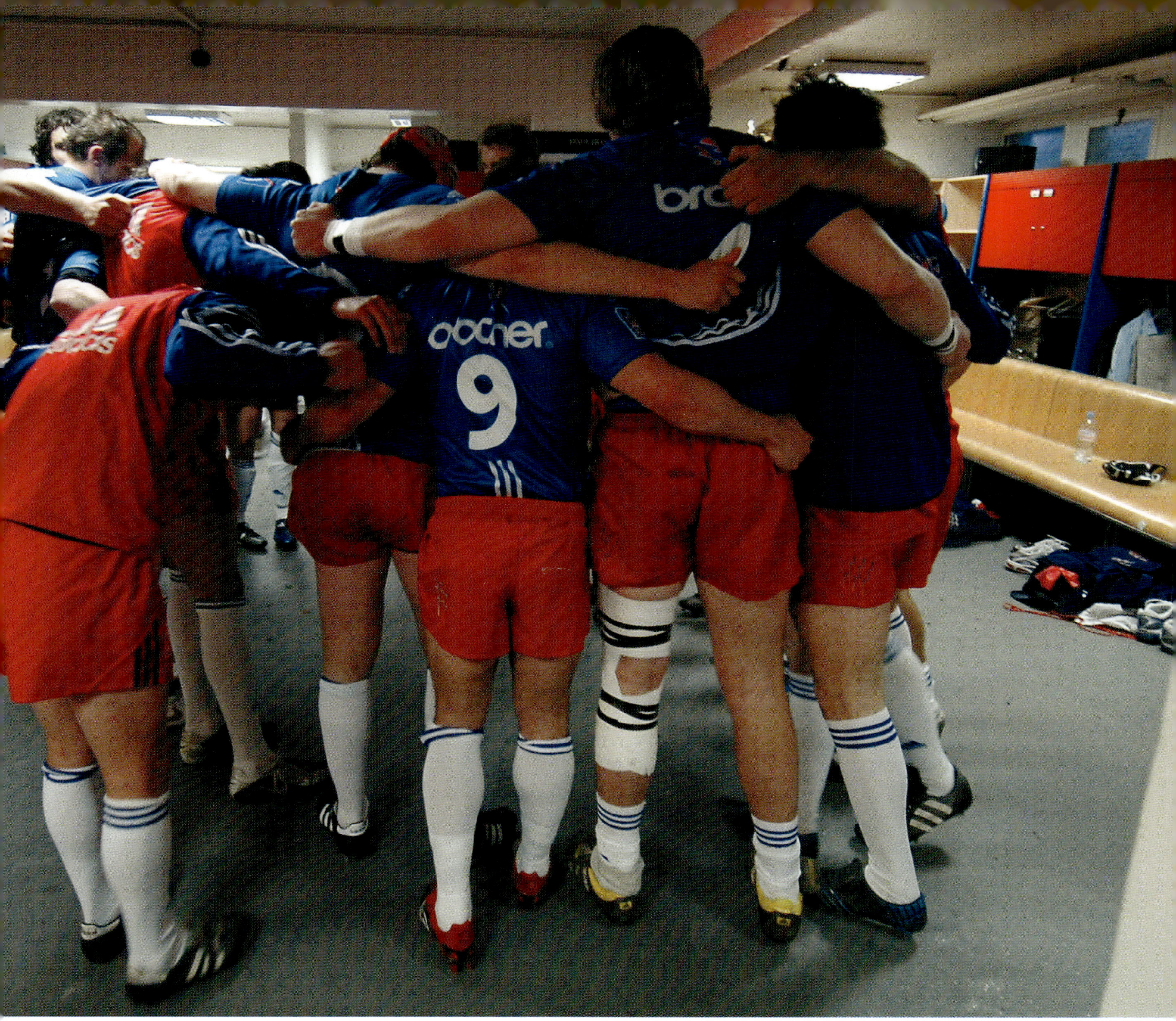

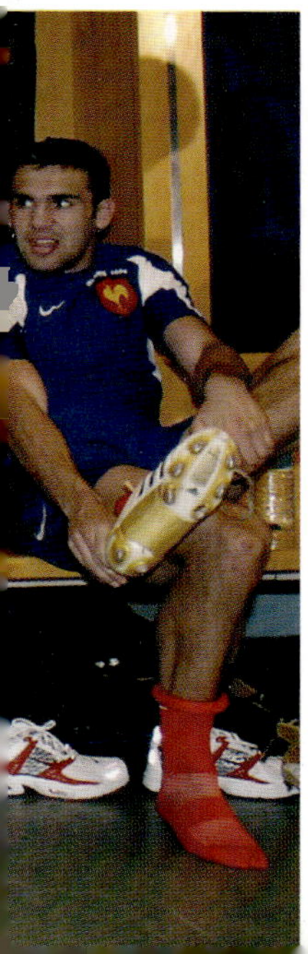

Olivier Magne, Pieter De Villiers, Aurélien Rougerie, Lionel Nallet et David Marty, fourbus mais heureux à l'issue d'une rencontre internationale au Stade de France. À noter que les footballeurs et les rugbymen de l'équipe de France partagent le même vestiaire.

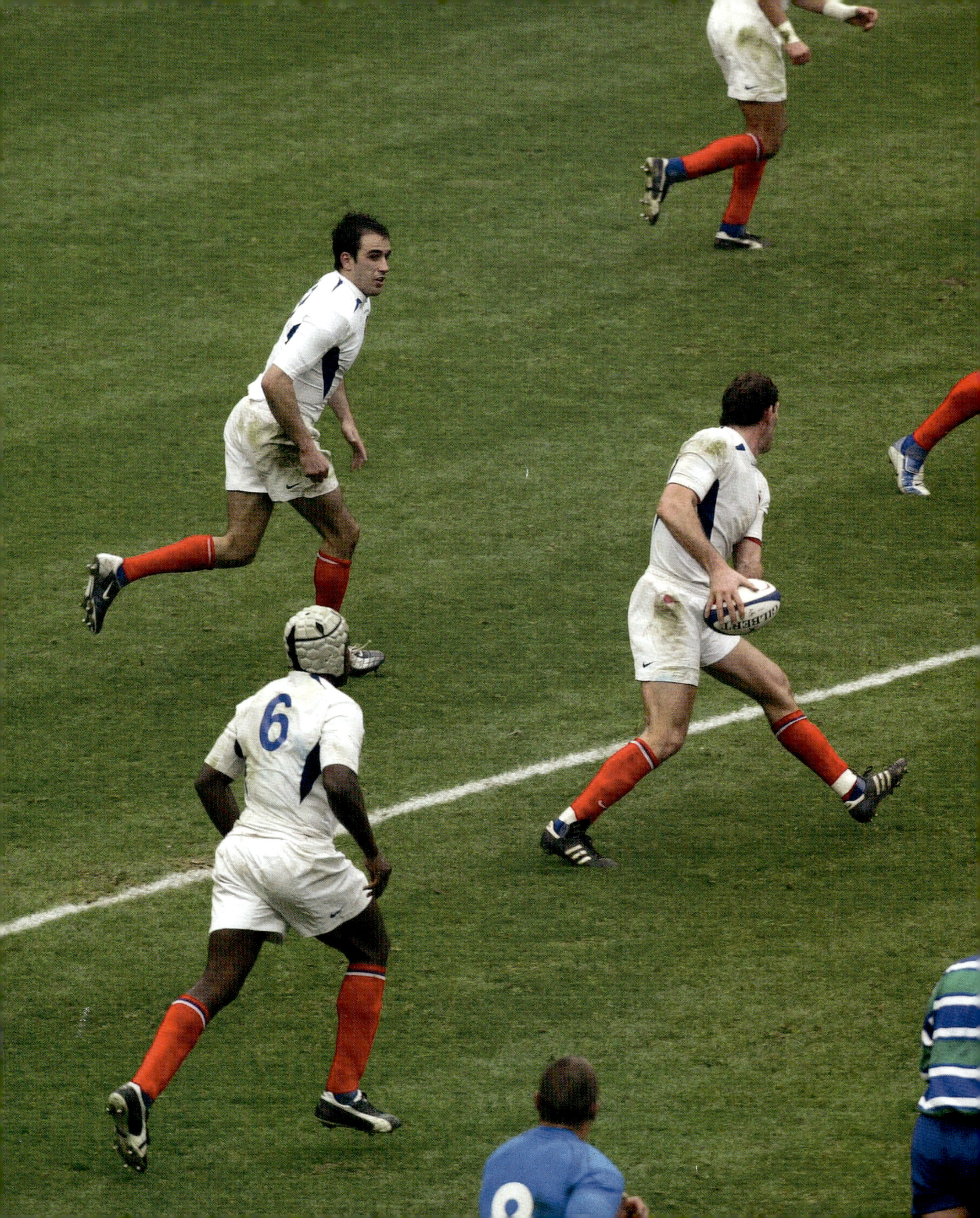
6

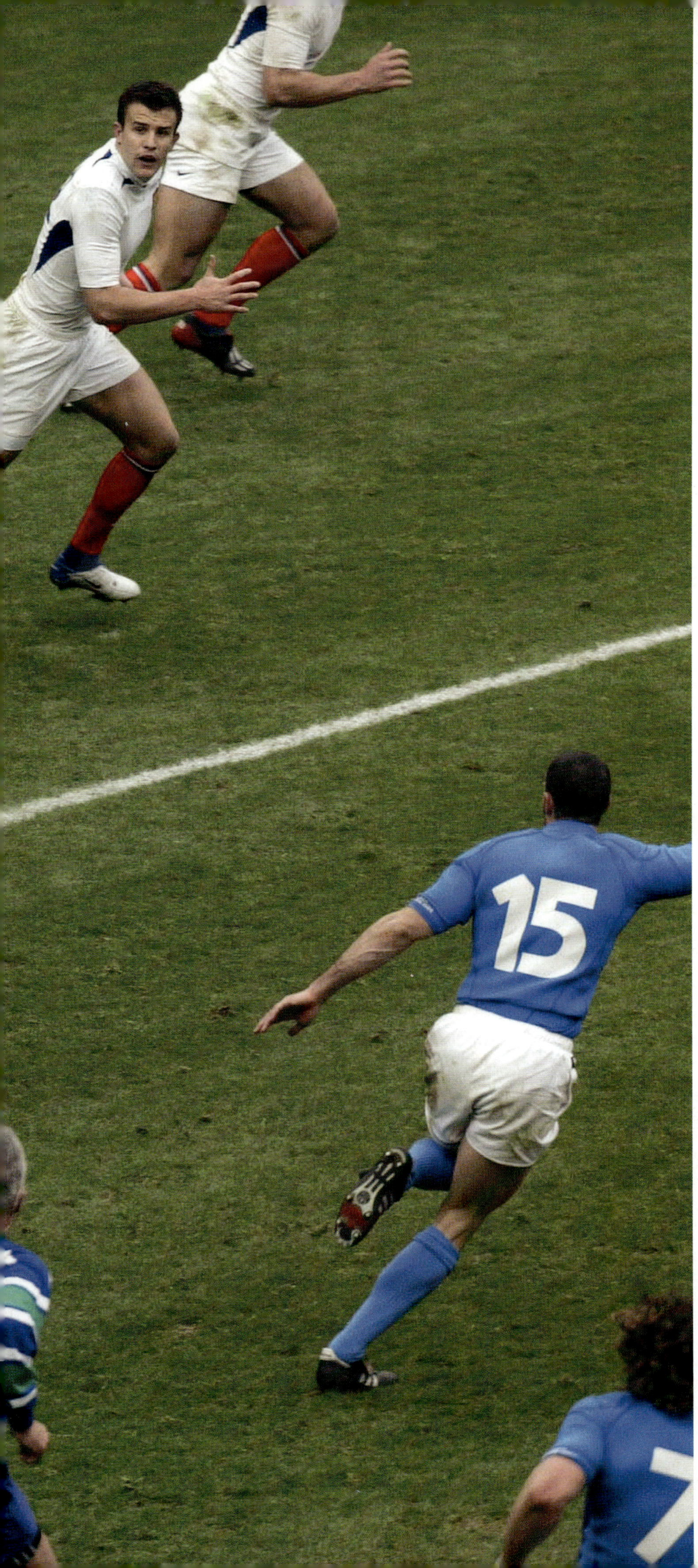

L'offrande

« Petit, c'est un cadeau que tu fais... Applique-toi ! » Mon éducateur - il n'aime pas qu'on l'appelle entraîneur - nous a d'abord fait sentir le ballon. Avec les mains. Et si possible du bout des doigts. Comme une caresse. Il ne veut pas qu'on l'attrape en le faisant claquer. Le ballon, on doit l'apprivoiser, le poser au creux des paumes, délicatement, et ensuite, dans un mouvement de balancier, l'offrir au partenaire qui se tient à côté de nous, pas trop loin. La passe, c'est une façon de donner le meilleur de soi pour que le ballon continue de vivre, continue de voler au-dessus du sol, hors de portée des adversaires. Il est tellement difficile à gagner qu'il ne faut pas le gâcher. Passer, c'est le transmettre avec précision à un coéquipier démarqué, sans précipitation, bien en arrière, afin que le jeu ne s'arrête pas. Cette balle, il ne faut surtout pas s'en débarrasser. Si je la passe, ce n'est pas parce que je n'en veux plus ; au contraire, j'aimerais bien la garder encore pour moi. Mais le rugby ne se joue pas tout seul. Il faut penser aux autres, aux copains. Ils voudraient bien la tenir, eux aussi, et courir avec.

Ballon en mains, buste tourné, le regard précédant la passe, le flanker Olivier Magne ouvre sur les trois-quarts, Damien Traille en l'occurrence. Serge Betsen (n°6) et Julien Peyrelongue assurent le soutien de l'action.

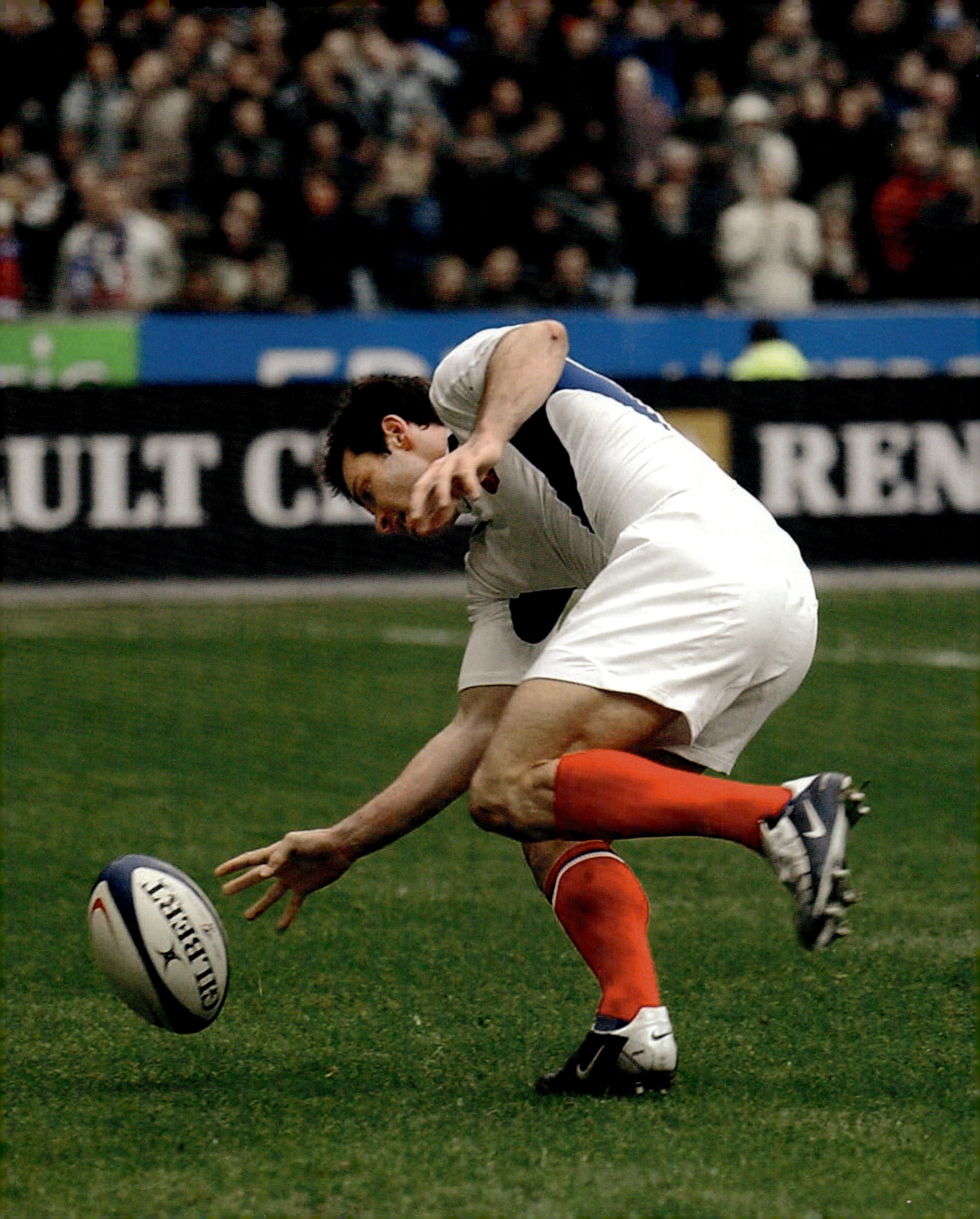
GILBERT

En-avant!

Je ne l'ai pas vu venir. Il m'a foncé dessus sans crier gare et m'a bousculé. Il est plus petit que moi, mon adversaire, mais ça ne l'a pas empêché de me faire tomber. Et à ce moment-là, j'ai senti le ballon m'échapper des mains. Au dernier moment, j'ai voulu le passer, mais c'était trop tard : il a glissé devant moi, sans que je puisse le rattraper. En-avant ! En rugby, quand

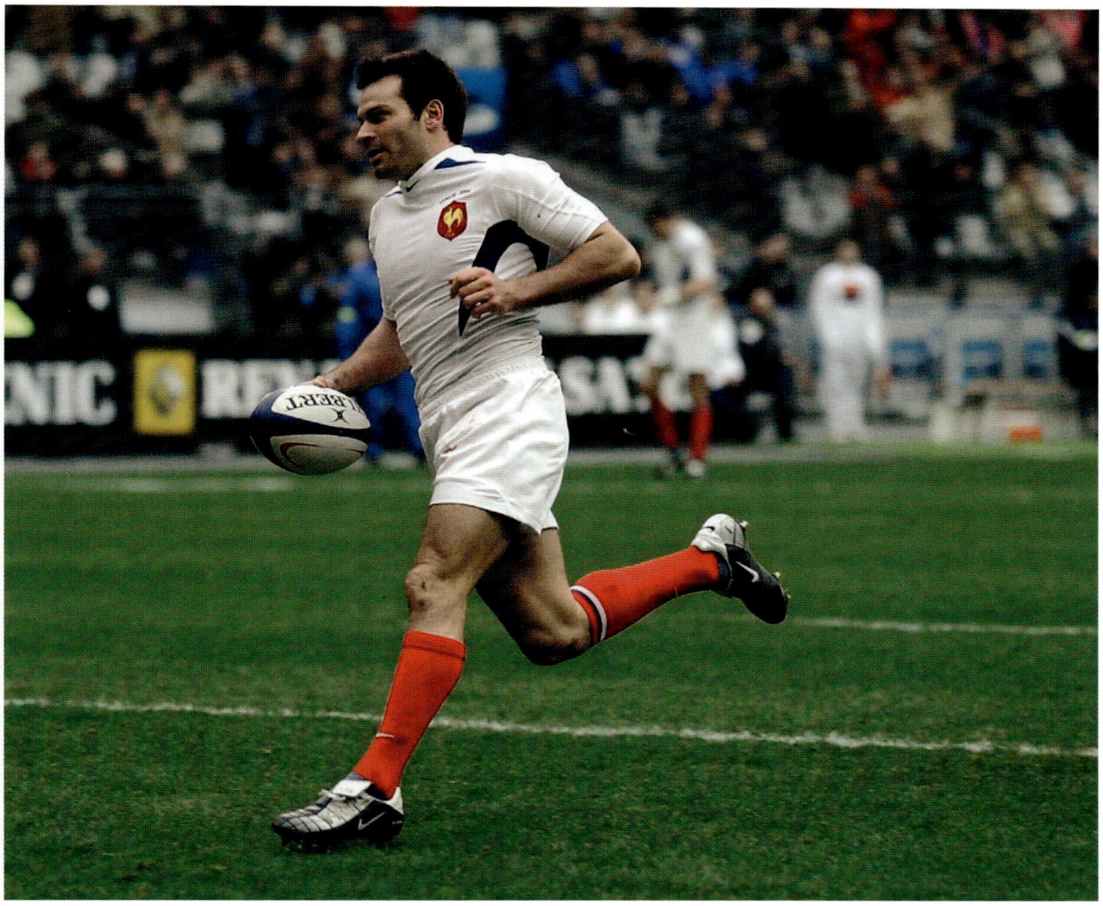

Il faut savoir respecter le ballon et pour cela, éviter de le tenir négligemment d'une seule main. Voyez la mésaventure survenue à l'ailier Christophe Dominici… Au moment d'aller sans opposition aplatir l'essai dans l'en-but, le ballon glisse de sa main et tombe au sol avant qu'il puisse le rattraper. L'essai, bien sûr, lui sera refusé. En rugby, on paye souvent très cher les excès de suffisance.

on veut le passer, le ballon doit toujours aller derrière, c'est la règle de base. Et quand il tombe au sol en nous échappant des mains, ou bien lorsque l'on n'ajuste pas très bien sa passe et que le ballon part devant, le jeu s'arrête et l'arbitre indique qu'il faudra disputer une mêlée. L'en-avant, c'est un peu comme une vilaine faute d'orthographe, une tache d'encre sur la feuille de papier Canson ou un gros mot qui nous échappe dans la discussion : ça fait désordre. Mais je n'y peux rien, le ballon m'a échappé des mains…

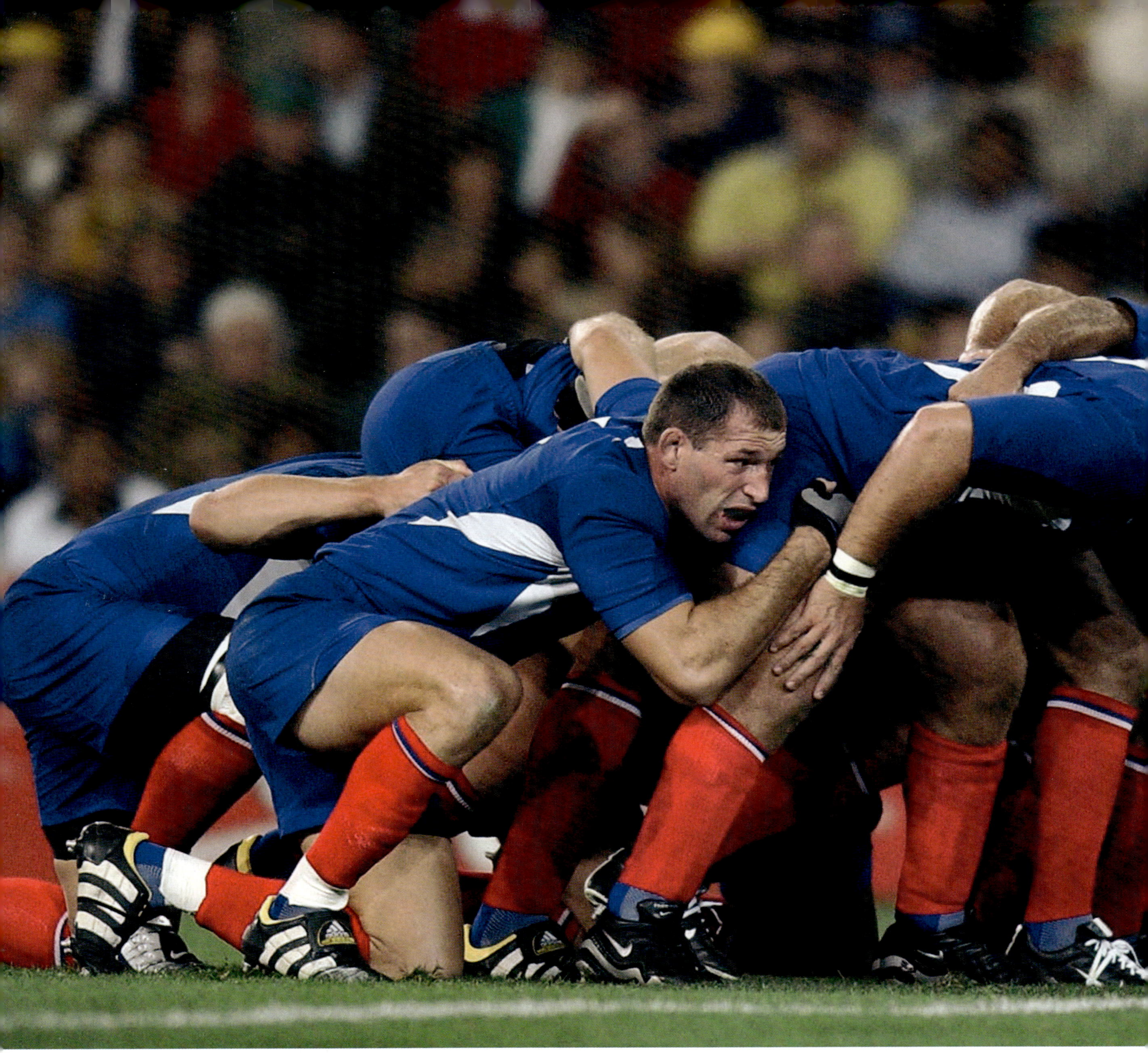

Le moment, juste avant l'entrée en mêlée, où les hommes se jaugent du regard. Sur le flanc, Olivier Magne cale avec l'épaule le pilier droit Jean-Baptiste Poux. On reconnaît aussi en première ligne le talonneur Raphaël Ibanez et le pilier gauche Jean-Jacques Crenca.

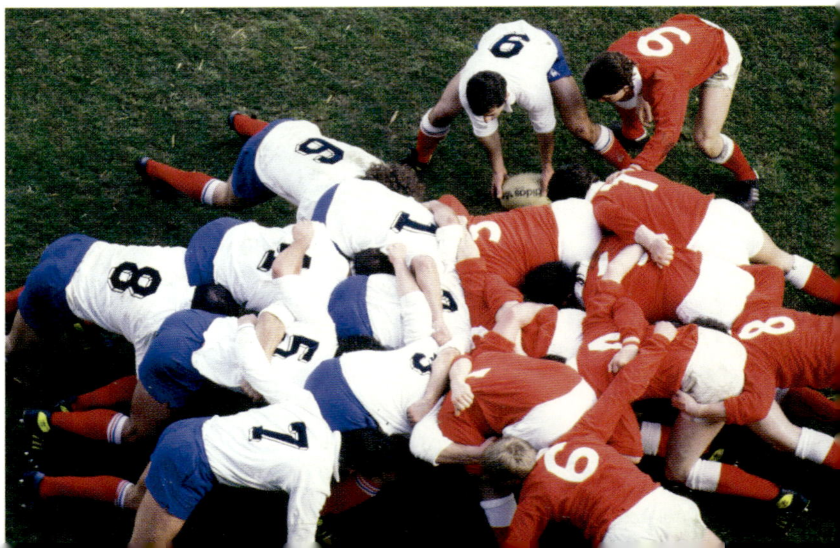

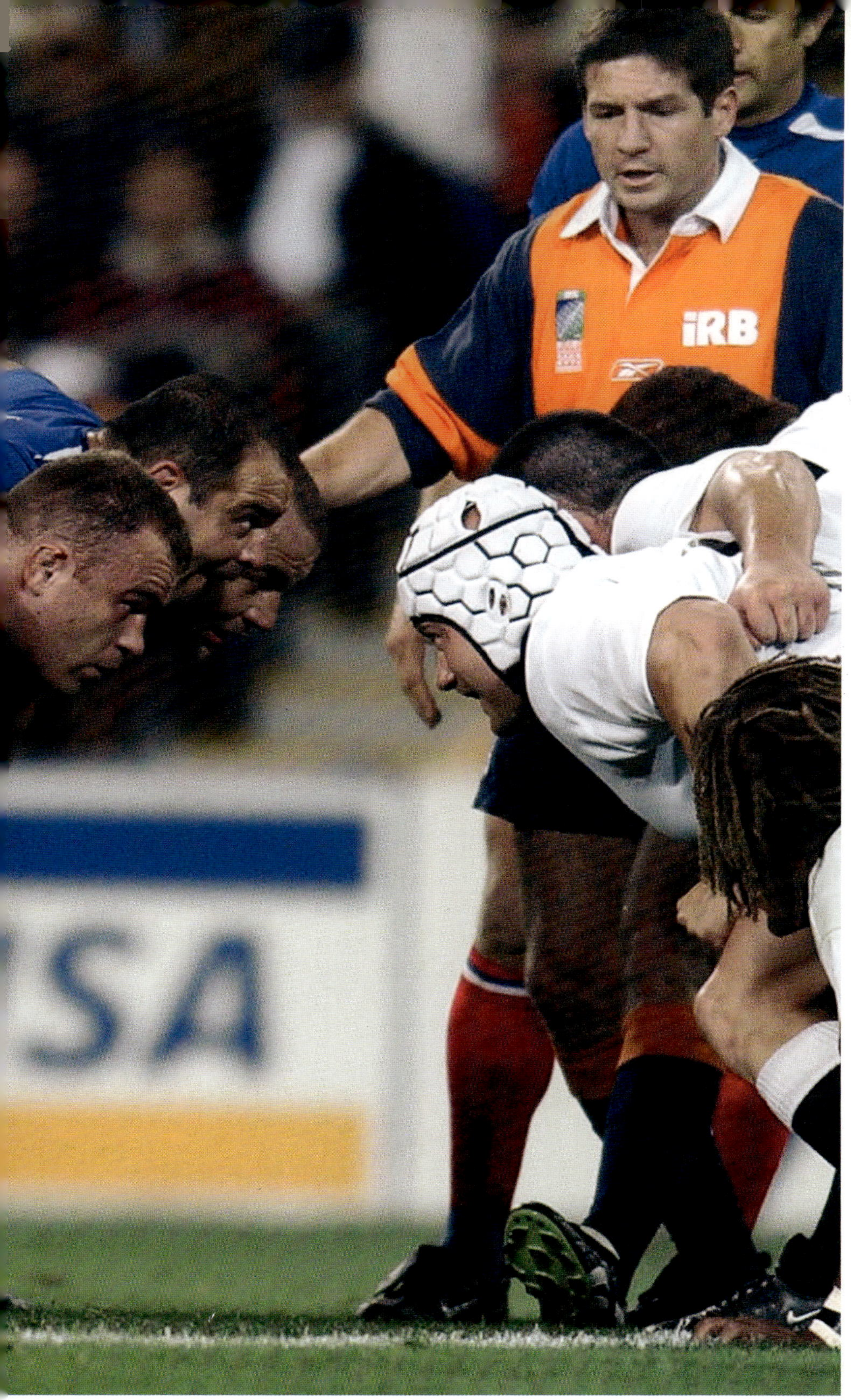

Ci-contre, une mêlée constituée : en ce qui concerne cette phase statique, les positions des joueurs sont immuables. La première ligne est composée, de gauche à droite, des joueurs porteurs des maillots n° 1, 2 et 3. Viennent ensuite les deuxièmes lignes, n° 4 et 5. Puis la troisième ligne prend place autour de cette structure : le n° 6 sur le flanc gauche, le n°7 sur le flanc droit et le troisième ligne centre, n° 8, dans l'axe. On voit le demi de mêlée, n° 9, introduire la balle, qui va être talonnée puis dirigée vers le n° 8. Récupérée par le demi de mêlée, elle pourra être passée vers les joueurs des lignes arrière.

La maison du ballon

Là, nous entrons dans une zone réservée. La mêlée, c'est le domaine des gros, pardon, je veux dire des costauds. Car n'est pas pilier qui veut. Il faut du coffre et de larges épaules, un cou de taureau et un mental de fer. Ce sont des rocs, les trois joueurs de la première ligne. Ils se soudent comme s'ils ne faisaient qu'un. Eux, c'est sûr, ils jouent avec leurs têtes, front contre front. Ils n'ont pas peur des bosses et, au bout d'un moment, leurs oreilles enflent et deviennent aussi grosses que des choux-fleurs. Les piliers disent que c'est une façon pour eux de se reconnaître sans avoir à se présenter. De toute façon, les piliers et les talonneurs n'aiment pas beaucoup parler. Ils préfèrent se baisser, entrer en mêlée, pousser et se frictionner avec leurs adversaires. Ça leur brûle le dos, les oreilles et les cuisses, mais ils aiment ça. Et ne se plaignent jamais. Des mêlées, il y en a plusieurs dizaines par match. Chez les jeunes, le règlement interdit de pousser, afin d'éviter les accidents, aux vertèbres cervicales surtout, mais chez les grands, c'est autre chose. Les poussées sont telluriques et les huit avants de chaque équipe, liés, sont obligés de rester placés en mêlée et d'attendre que le ballon sorte pour se mêler au jeu. On dit de la mêlée qu'elle est la maison du ballon. J'aime assez l'image car c'est un mot d'enfant. Et si c'est une maison, alors ce sont les piliers qui en assurent les fondations.

Introduction en mêlée

Demi de mêlée, j'ai pour mission d'extraire la balle gagnée par mes avants. Mais avant cela, je dois l'introduire. Elle sera immédiatement déviée par le pied droit du talonneur, enjambée par les deuxièmes lignes placés juste derrière lui, puis délicatement guidée par le troisième ligne centre, un peu comme une note de musique qui descendrait la gamme d'une ligne à une autre, jusqu'en bas de la portée. J'attends donc qu'elle soit lentement digérée par le pack, jusqu'à moi. Protégé, je l'attrape alors et, d'une passe, l'envoie à mon demi d'ouverture chargé d'orienter le jeu. On nous appelle les demis, car à nous deux nous ne faisons qu'un, moi près de la mêlée avec les avants, lui auprès des arrières. Cette passe est notre trait d'union. Bien campé sur mes jambes, à moi de choisir : plonger pour passer ou bien armer ma passe, dans un mouvement de balancier. Mais l'important, c'est bien que le ballon puisse s'éloigner rapidement de la fournaise des mêlées pour s'en aller au large, naviguer de mains en mains.

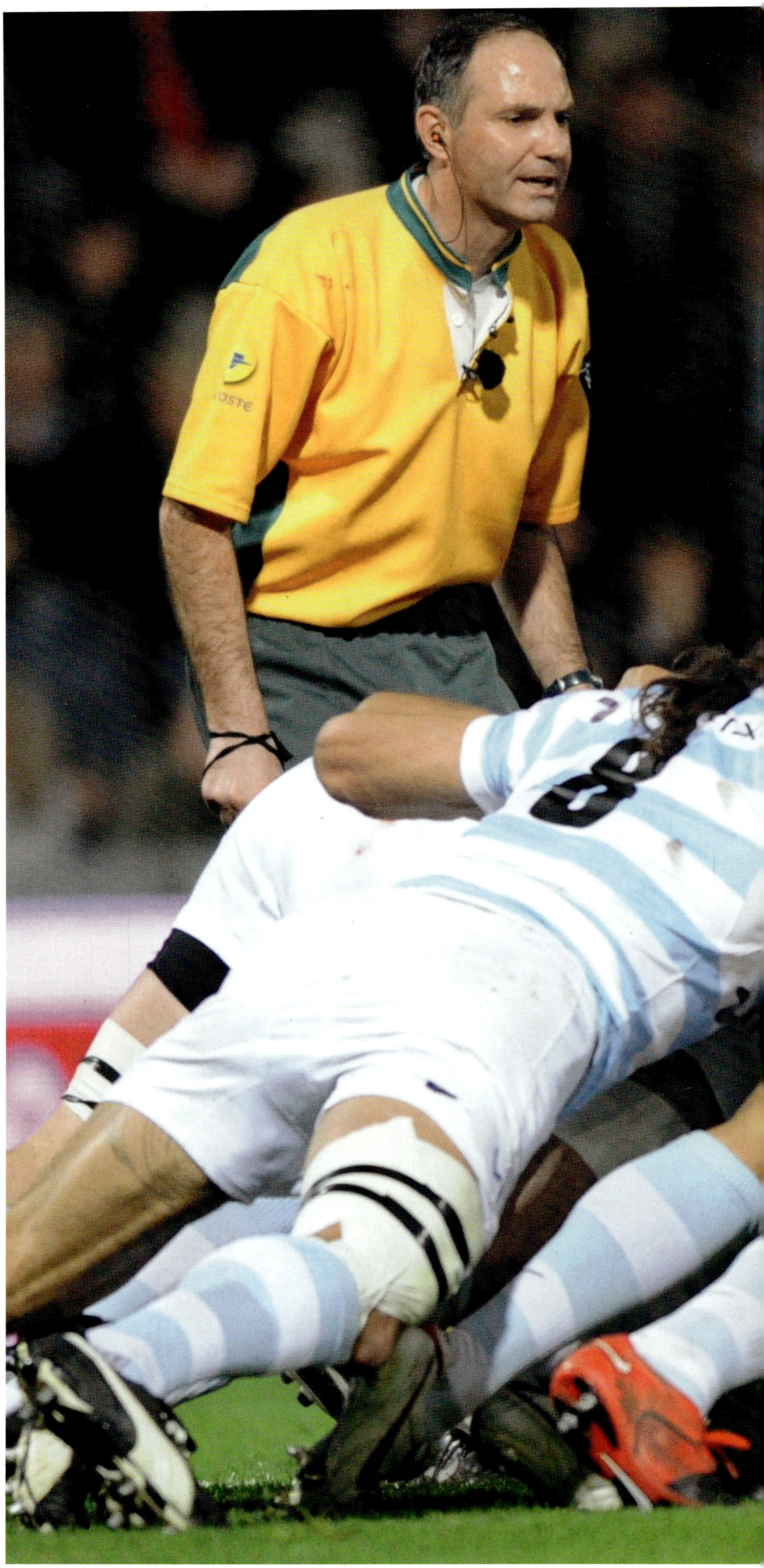

Bras levé, le talonneur du Biarritz Olympique indique à son demi de mêlée le moment précis où celui-ci doit introduire. Le ballon va rouler et sera dévié par le pied droit du talonneur. Remarquez les jambes fléchies des avants, en appuis sur le bout de leurs chaussures à crampons, prêts à exercer une poussée au moment où le ballon va passer devant eux. Le demi de mêlée, ici Dimitri Yachvili, n'aura plus ensuite qu'à le prendre dans les pieds du dernier participant de cette mêlée, pour lancer le jeu.

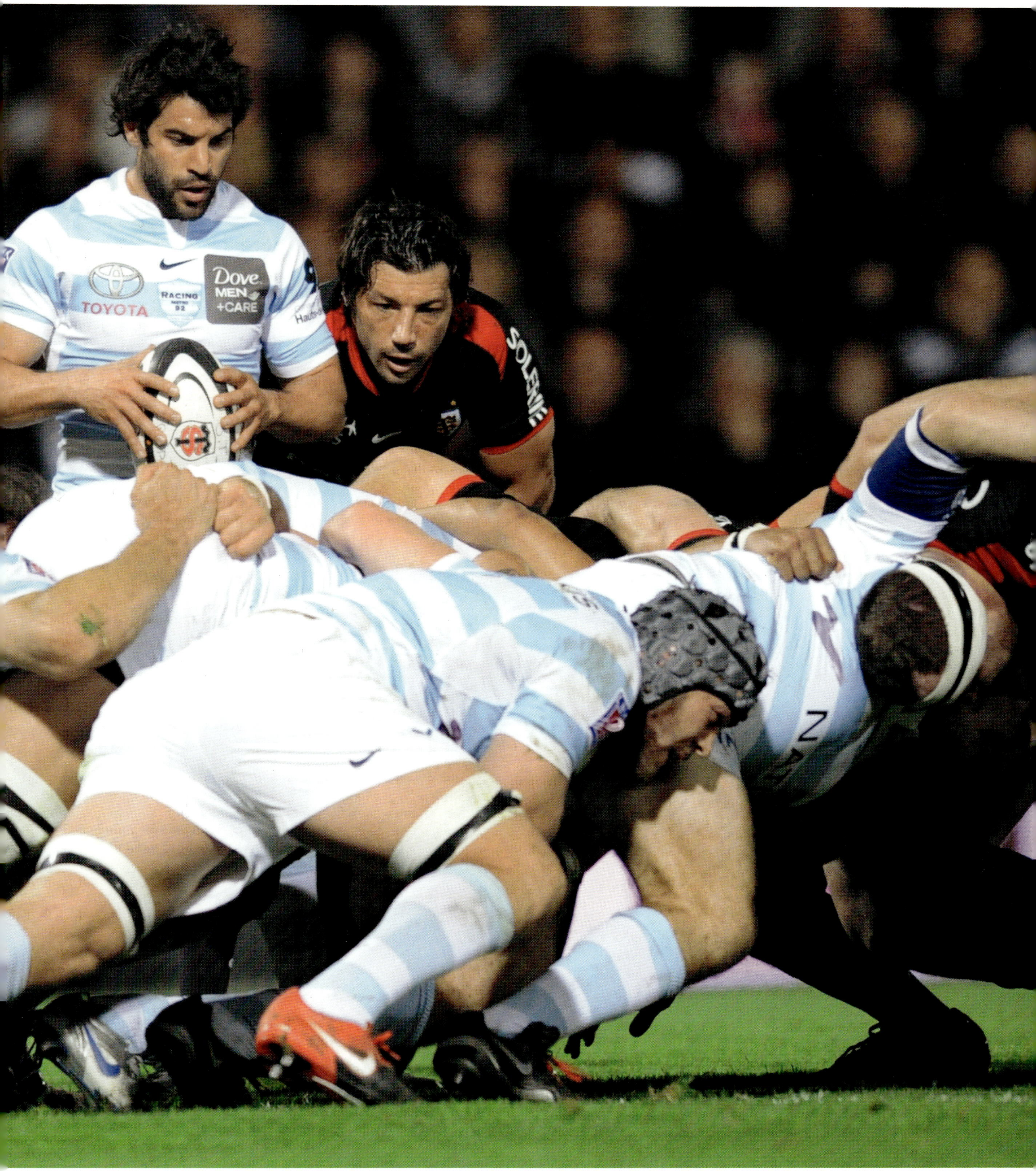
TOYOTA
RACING
92
Dove
MEN
+CARE

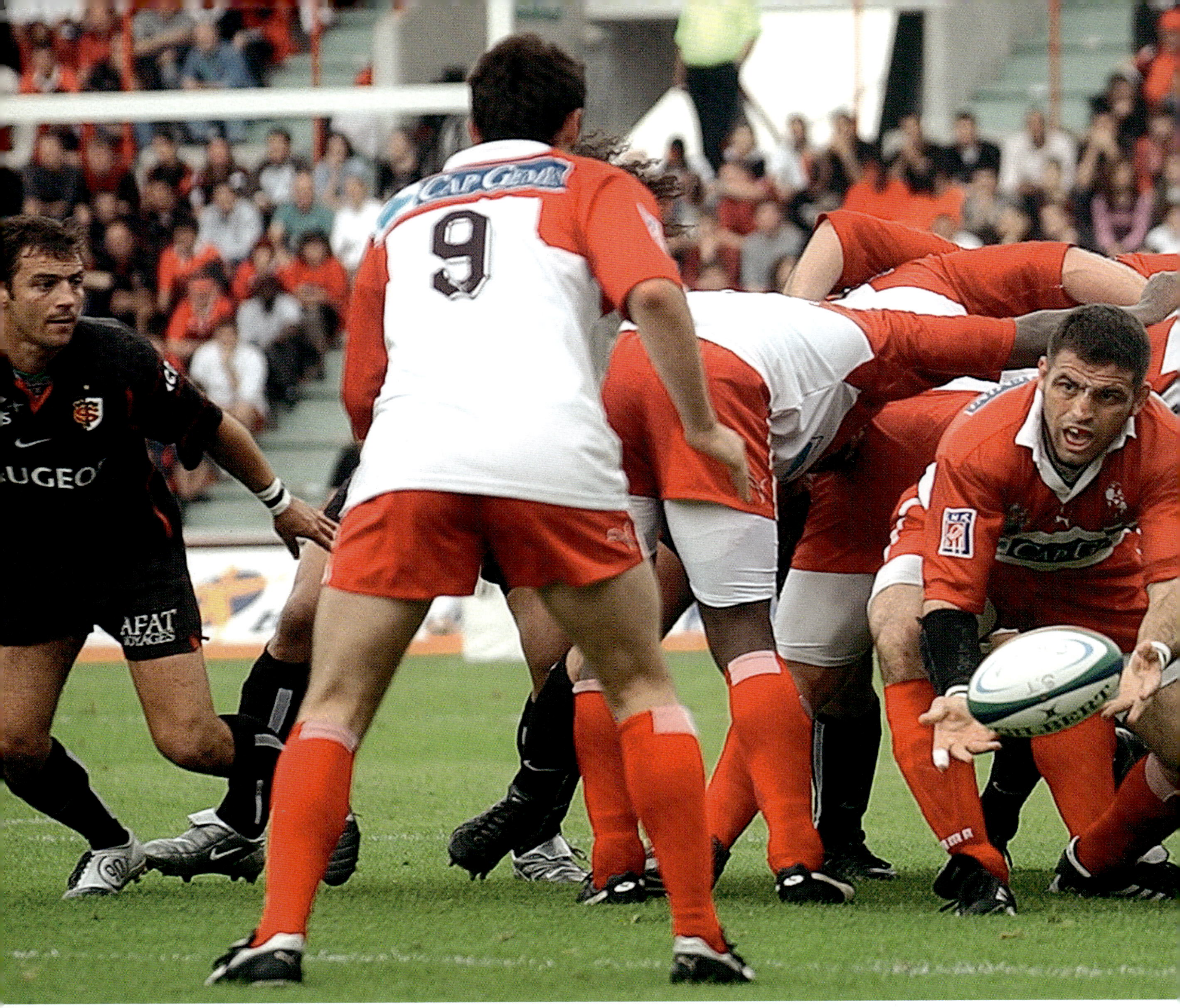

La 89

Thomas Lièvremont passe à Dimitri Yachvili… La mêlée du Biarritz Olympique, légèrement désaxée, décale les défenseurs toulousains, comme ici, à droite, Jean Bouilhou et William Servat. Seul le demi de mêlée Jean-Baptiste Elissalde a le droit de suivre la progression du ballon. Il s'apprête à monter sur son vis-à-vis biarrot (n° 9), lequel est confortablement placé pour diriger le jeu à sa guise.

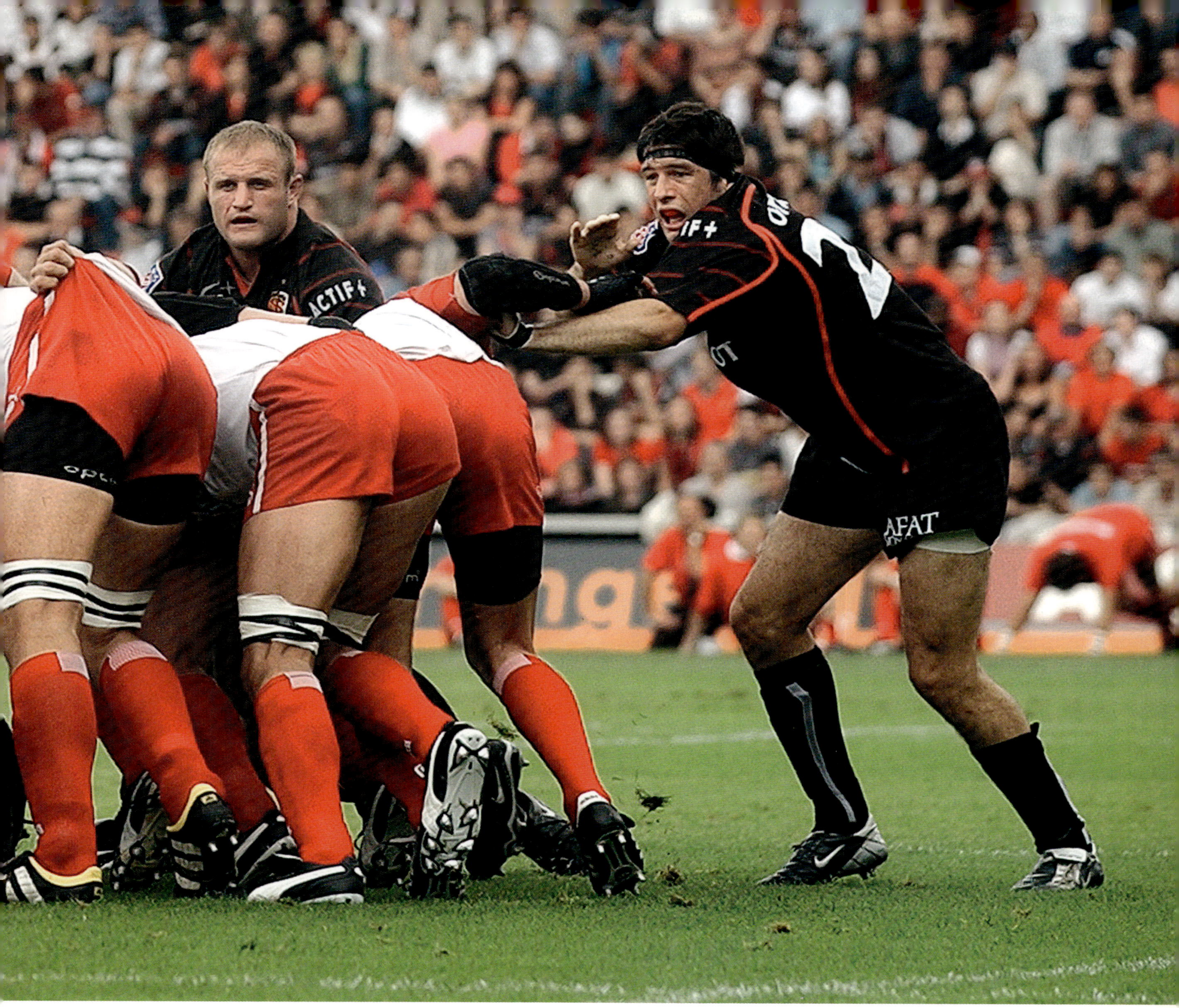

Comme son nom l'indique, le demi de mêlée est placé au plus près des zones de conquêtes et de combat : il surveille la touche et la mêlée. Heureusement, parmi les combinaisons qu'il doit maîtriser, il en est une, conçue à son profit, qui lui permet de s'évader. « Quatre-vingt-neuf ». Le mouvement est discrètement annoncé afin que l'adversaire n'ait pas le temps de s'organiser. Huit plus neuf égale quatre-vingt-neuf. CQFD. Derrière la mêlée, le numéro huit, aussi appelé troisième ligne centre, prend le ballon, s'avance de quelques pas et le passe à son demi de mêlée, le numéro neuf. Avec ce simple déplacement latéral de deux joueurs, le jeu devient limpide. Les défenseurs sont fixés autour de la mêlée. Cette petite passe, effectuée dans le bon tempo, va permettre à l'attaque d'occuper l'espace et surtout de gagner en vitesse, à l'image d'une fusée intersidérale qui perd son premier étage et, boostée, traverse de plus en plus vite l'atmosphère. En effet, la « 89 » oblige la défense adverse à marquer un temps d'arrêt et suffit à créer un déséquilibre, un décalage et, peut-être, là-bas, tout au bout, une occasion d'essai.

Passe lobée

Devant moi, les adversaires forment un mur de bras et d'épaules. Impossible de les éviter. Ils coupent les trajectoires, bloquent les issues. Pourtant, je dois passer. À moi de les lober en faisant passer la balle par-dessus, comme au basket ou au hand-ball. Ça n'a rien d'académique, mais qu'importe !

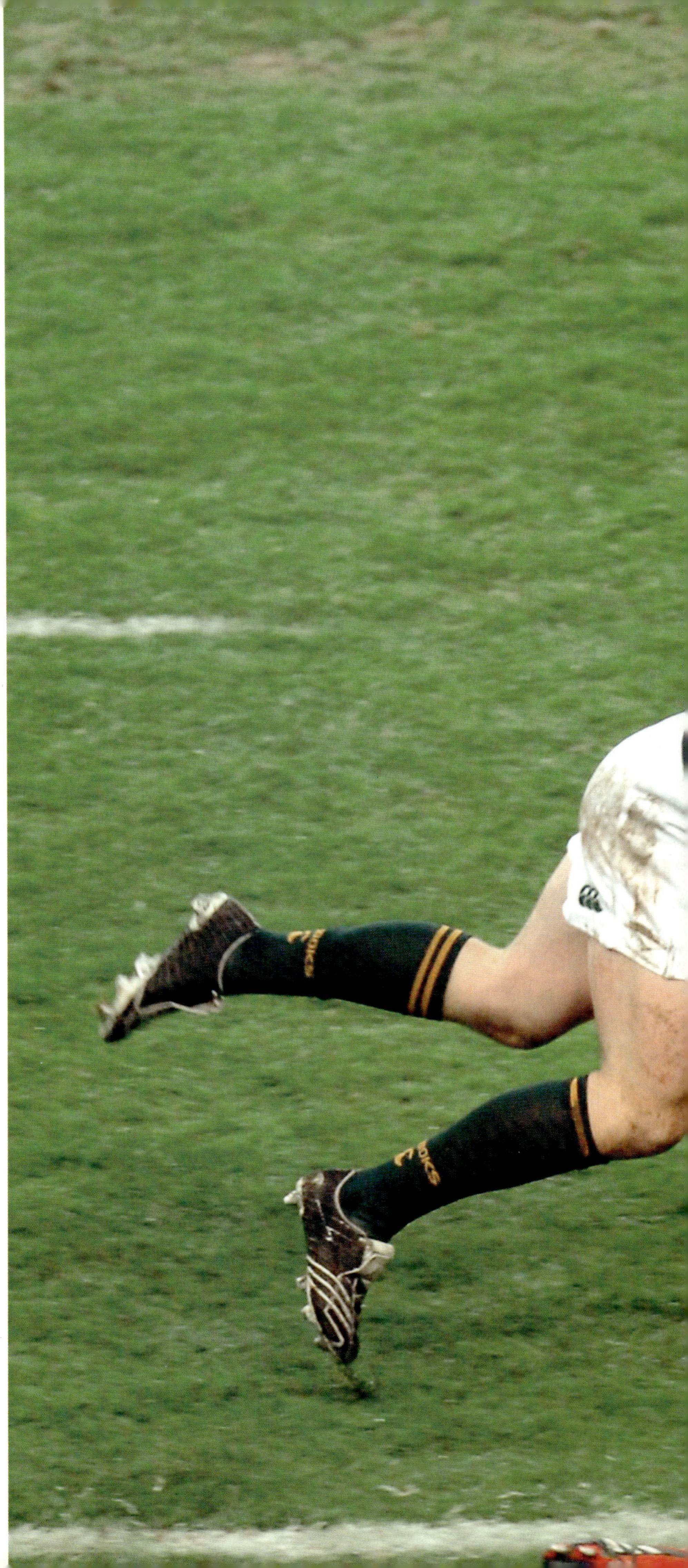

Cerné par trois Sud-Africains, au Stade de France, le troisième ligne aile Yannick Nyanga illumine le match par ce geste inattendu, une passe lobée qui mystifie les défenseurs et amènera l'essai de son ami Dimitri Szarzewski.

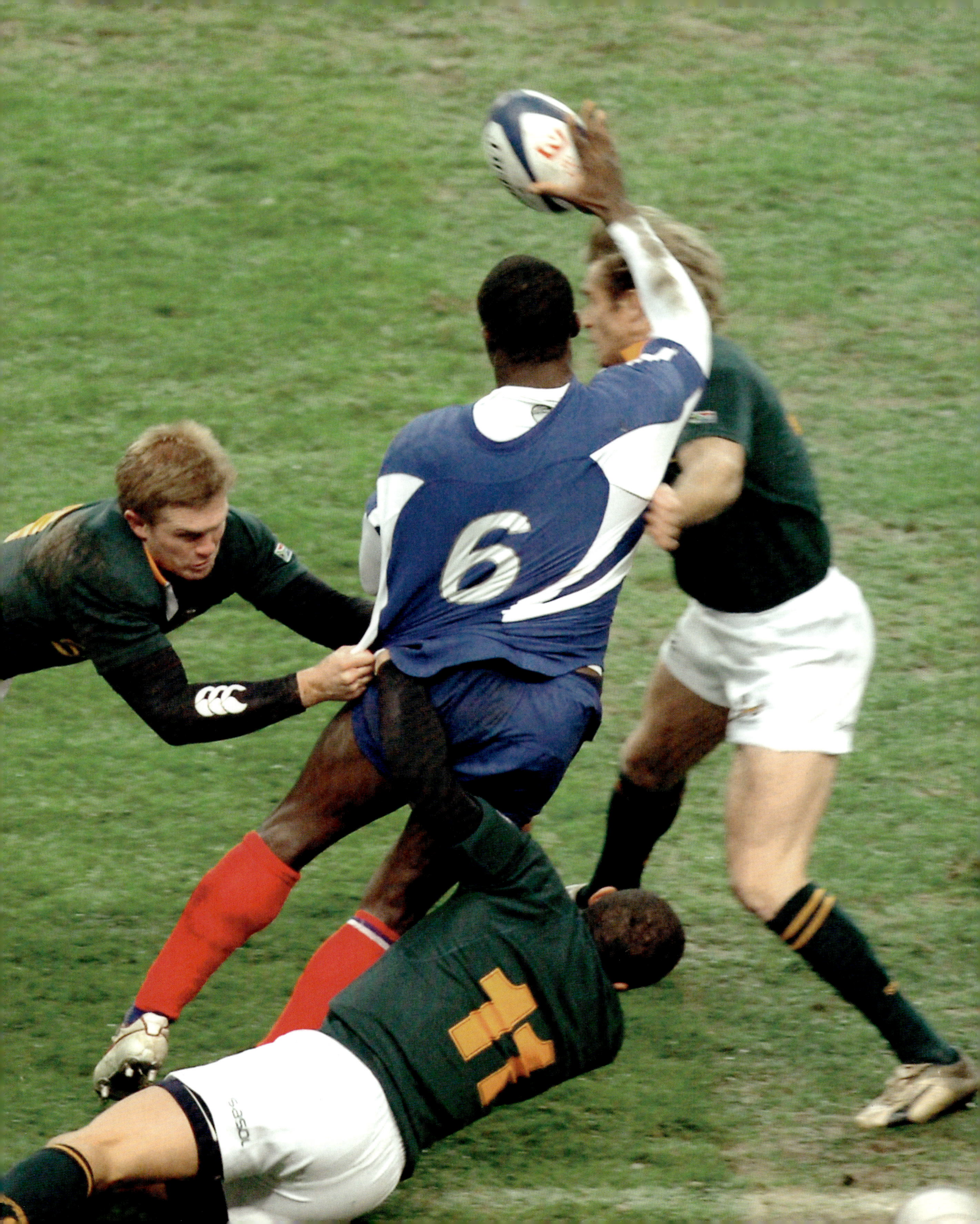
6

Raffut

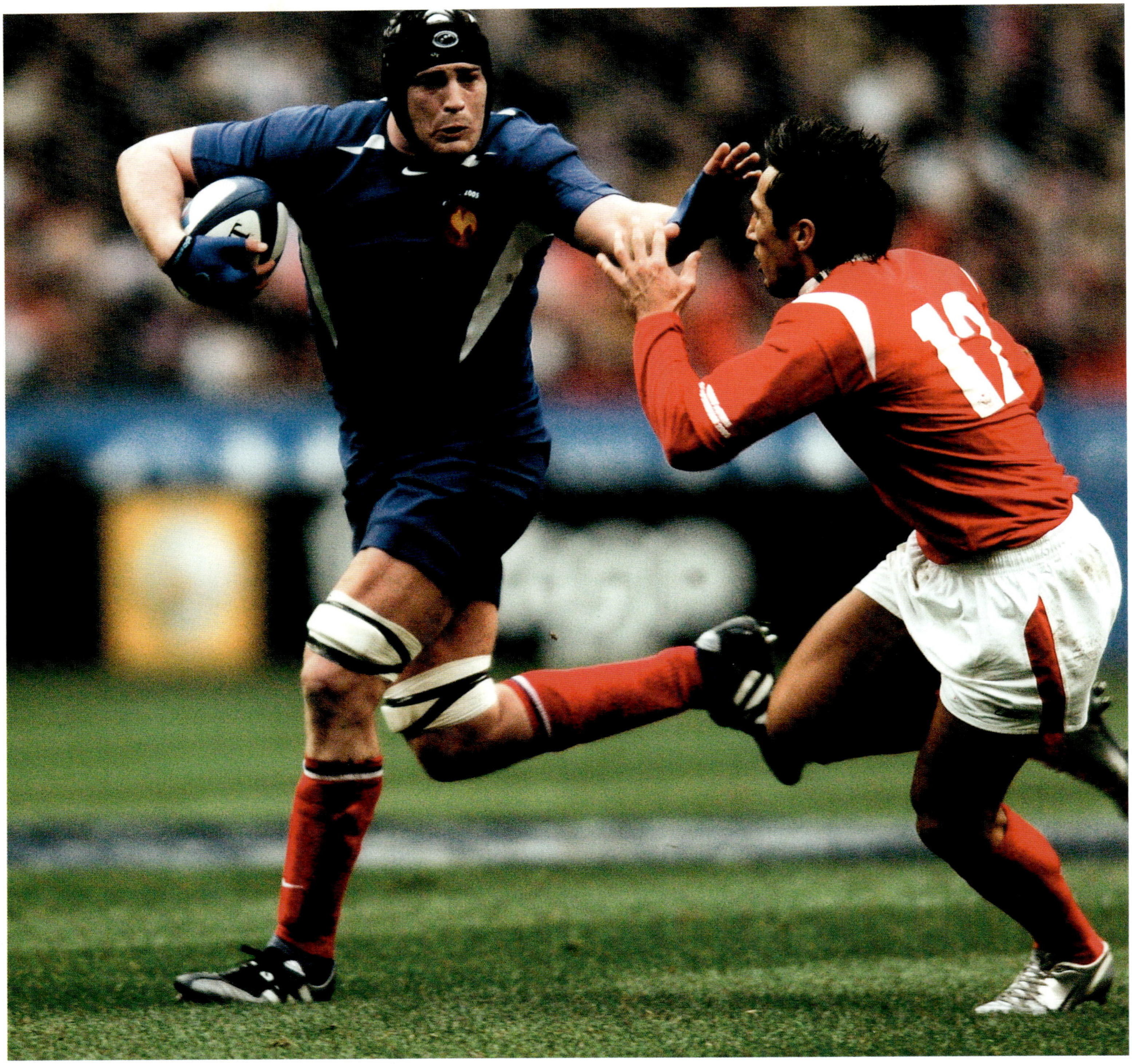

Tel un taureau qui charge le matador, le plaqueur baisse la tête au moment de stopper l'attaquant. Durant une fraction de seconde, il ne voit plus ce qui se passe autour de lui, aveuglé par son geste défensif. C'est alors que sa proie va le repousser d'un geste vif et précis. La paume ouverte, le bras tendu, l'attaquant effectue un raffut. Il se sert de l'adversaire comme d'un appui pour ré-accélérer, tout en éloignant la menace du plaquage. Pas besoin d'être un monstre physique pour appliquer cette méthode : tout est question de coordination.

Le deuxième ligne Jérôme Thion (ci-dessus) et l'arrière Thomas Castaignède (à droite), deux gabarits différents mais une même façon d'effacer l'adversaire, qu'il soit gallois ou italien.

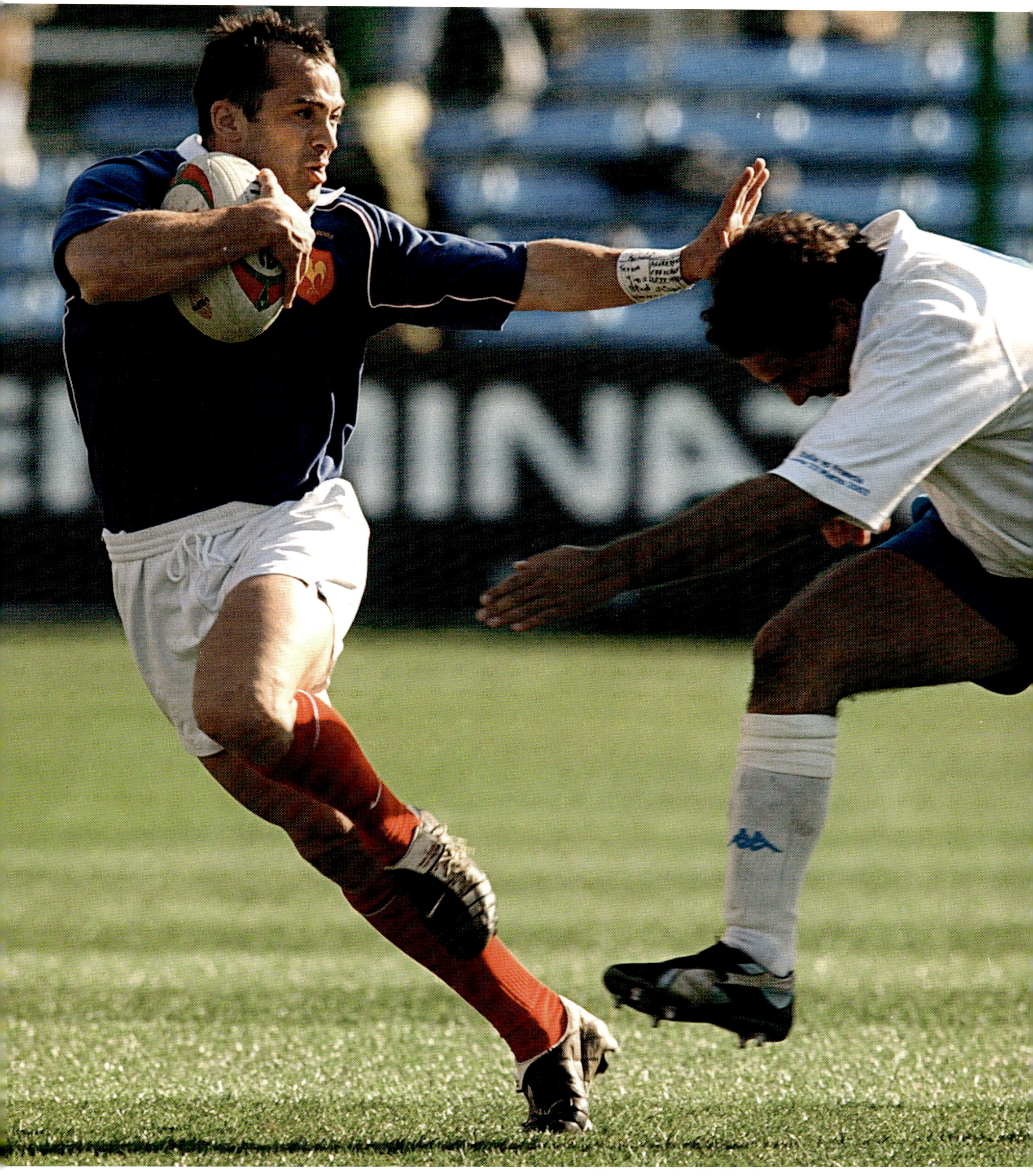

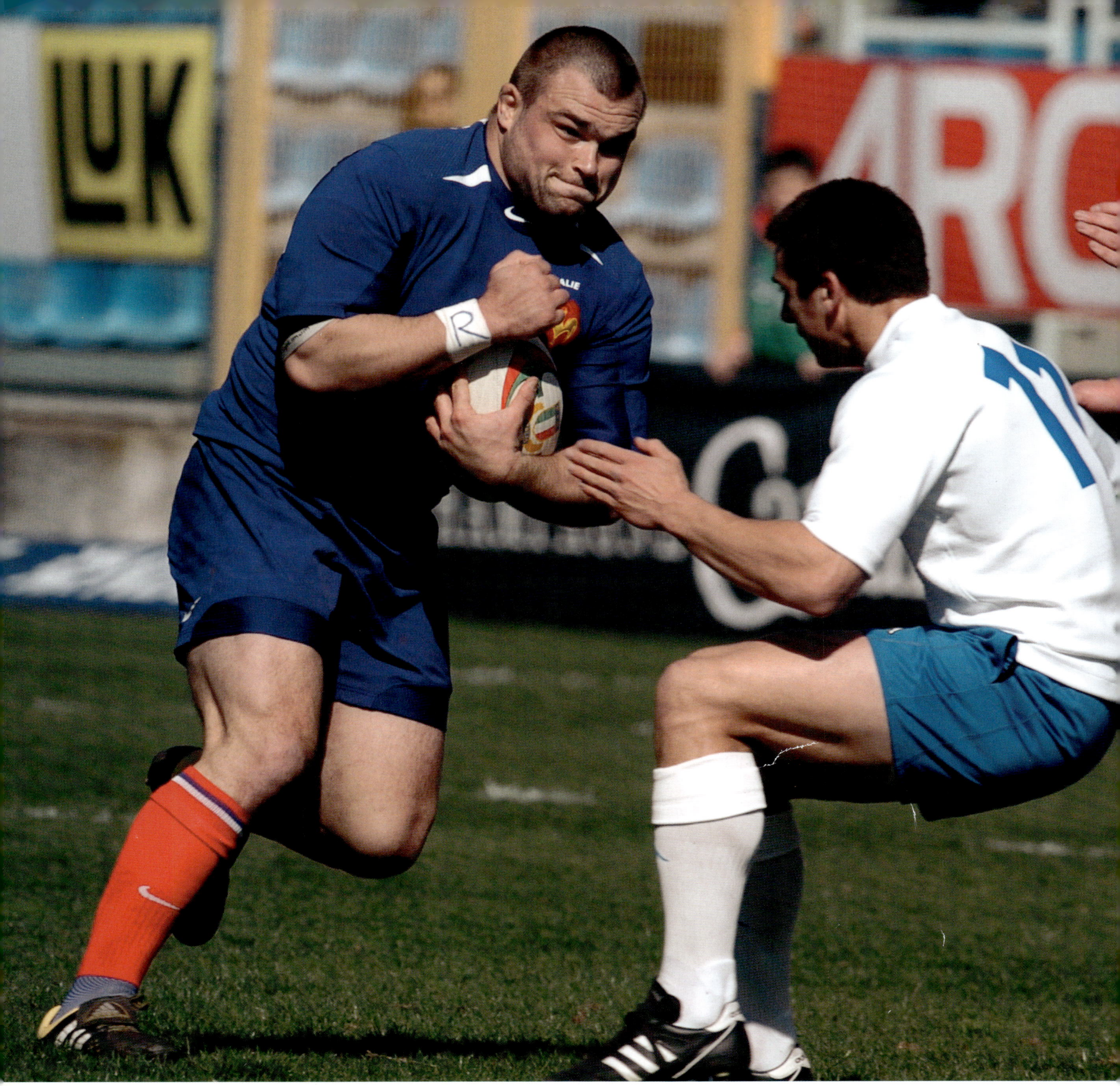

Percussion

Le rugby est un sport de contact. Épaules rentrées, muscles bandés, le regard planté droit sur l'adversaire, l'attaquant provoque un défi. C'est aussi une façon de se faire respecter. Ceux d'en face savent alors qu'il ne craindra personne. Percuter le défenseur permet de gagner quelques mètres par le plus court chemin qui soit : la ligne droite ! Le porteur de la balle exerce

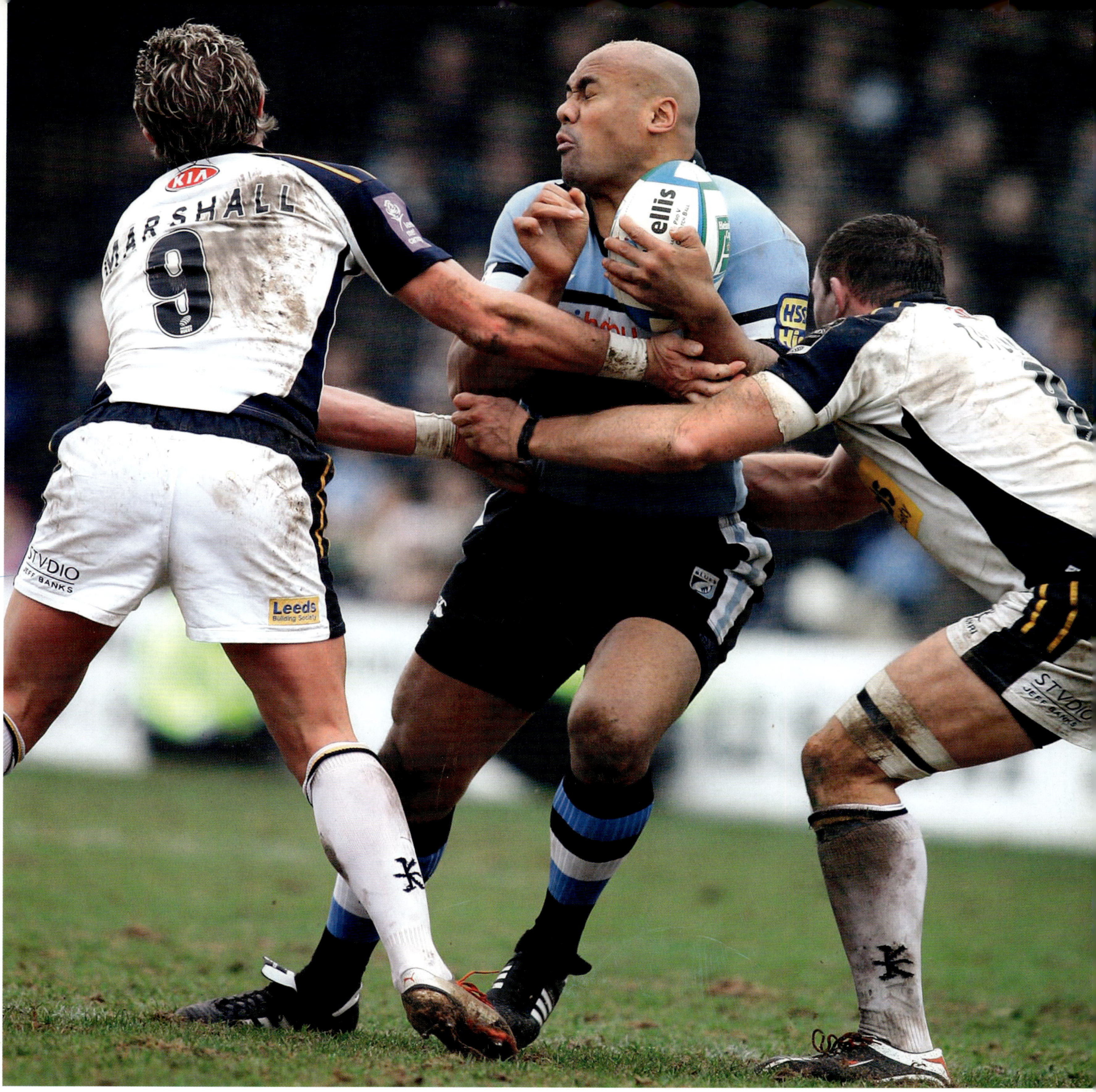

ainsi sa volonté pour devenir le maître du jeu. Sa détermination et l'énergie qu'il dégage obligent parfois l'adversaire à reculer. Ces mètres, gagnés à l'impact, valent de l'or. On voit ici en action *(page de gauche)* le pilier tricolore Nicolas Mas face à l'Italie, dans le Tournoi, et l'ailier néo-zélandais Jonah Lomu *(ci-dessus)*, sous le maillot de Cardiff, en Coupe d'Europe, face à Leeds. Depuis une dizaine d'années, les entraîneurs des grandes équipes nationales et internationales ont fait de la percussion un des plus sûrs moyens d'assurer le gain du terrain en forçant l'équipe adverse à se mobiliser pour plaquer, et encore plaquer, jusqu'à ce qu'une brèche se crée dans la défense harassée. Il s'agit là d'une des clés du rugby moderne.

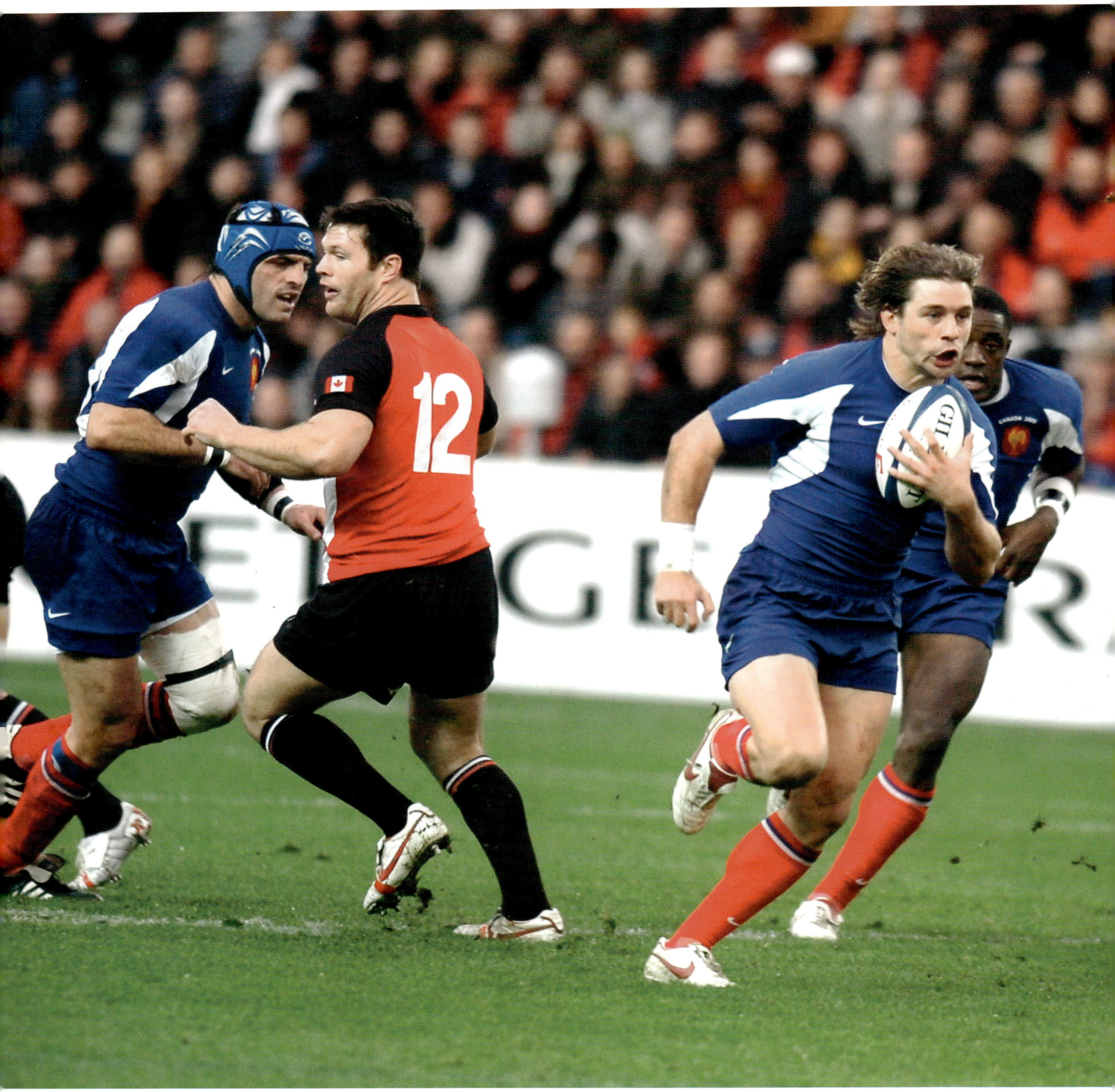
12

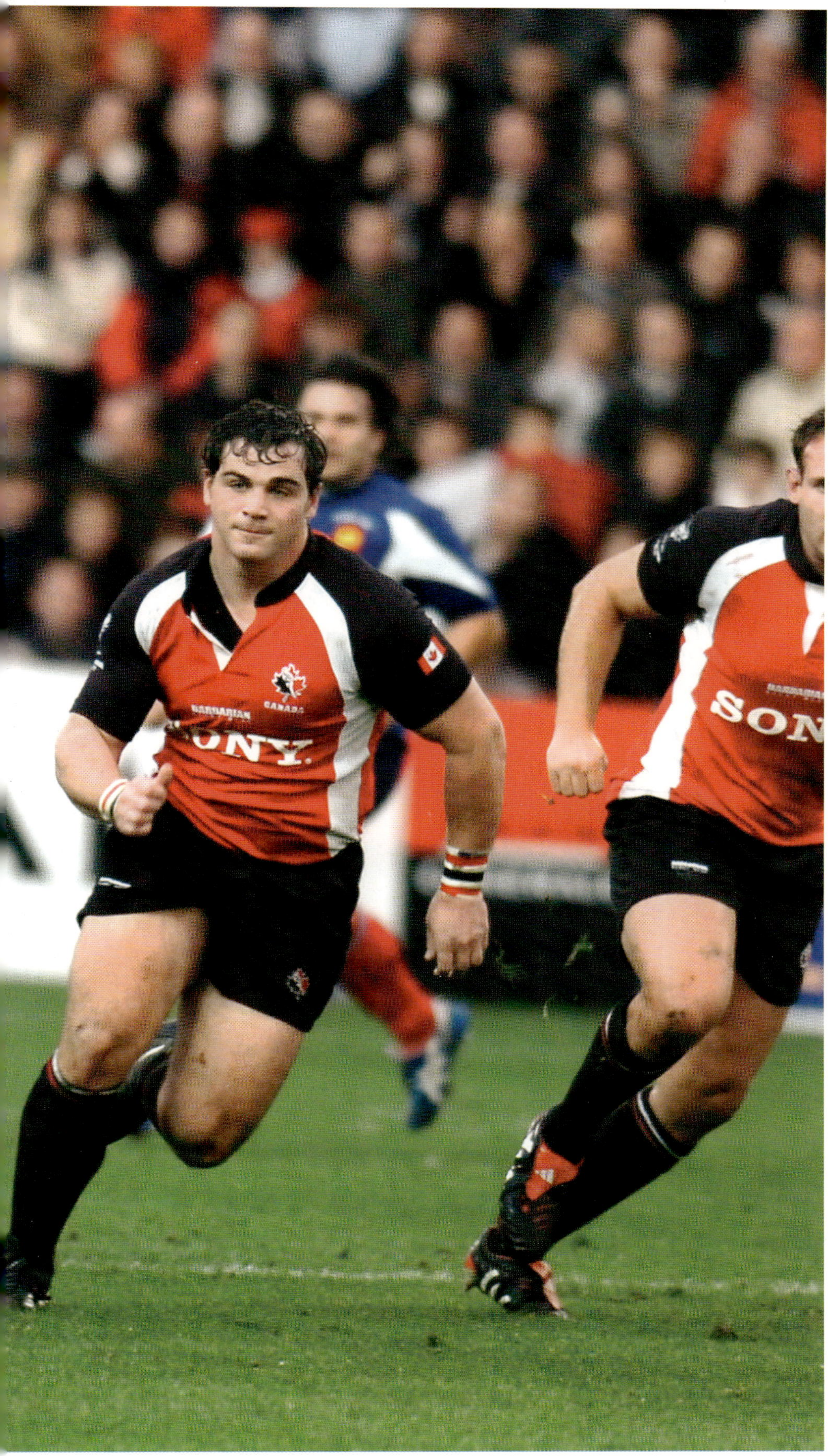

Plein champ

L'ivresse du jeu pourrait se résumer dans une percée qui nous vient des origines, quand un élève du collège de Rugby, William Webb Ellis, décida de courir avec le ballon dans les mains pour échapper à ses adversaires. D'essence, la percée symbolise ce jeu inventé en Angleterre, il y a deux siècles, afin de permettre aux enfants des écoles de se dépenser tout en respectant quelques règles simples. Percer, c'est se libérer des pesanteurs, goûter la liberté, s'enivrer. Elle naît à la fin d'un long travail tactique de préparation, ou s'inscrit dans le prolongement d'une envie buissonnière. C'est un instant magique fait d'inspiration, de naturel et de grâce que seuls les plus grands joueurs peuvent porter à son paroxysme, ou tout simplement faire partager.

L'ailier tricolore Cédric Heymans vient de se frayer un passage entre les trois-quarts canadiens et s'échappe, ballon sur le cœur, soutenu par le troisième ligne aile Yannick Nyanga. On peut noter que le troisième ligne centre Thomas Lièvremont, casqué, a servi de leurre et bloqué le centre canadien (n°12).

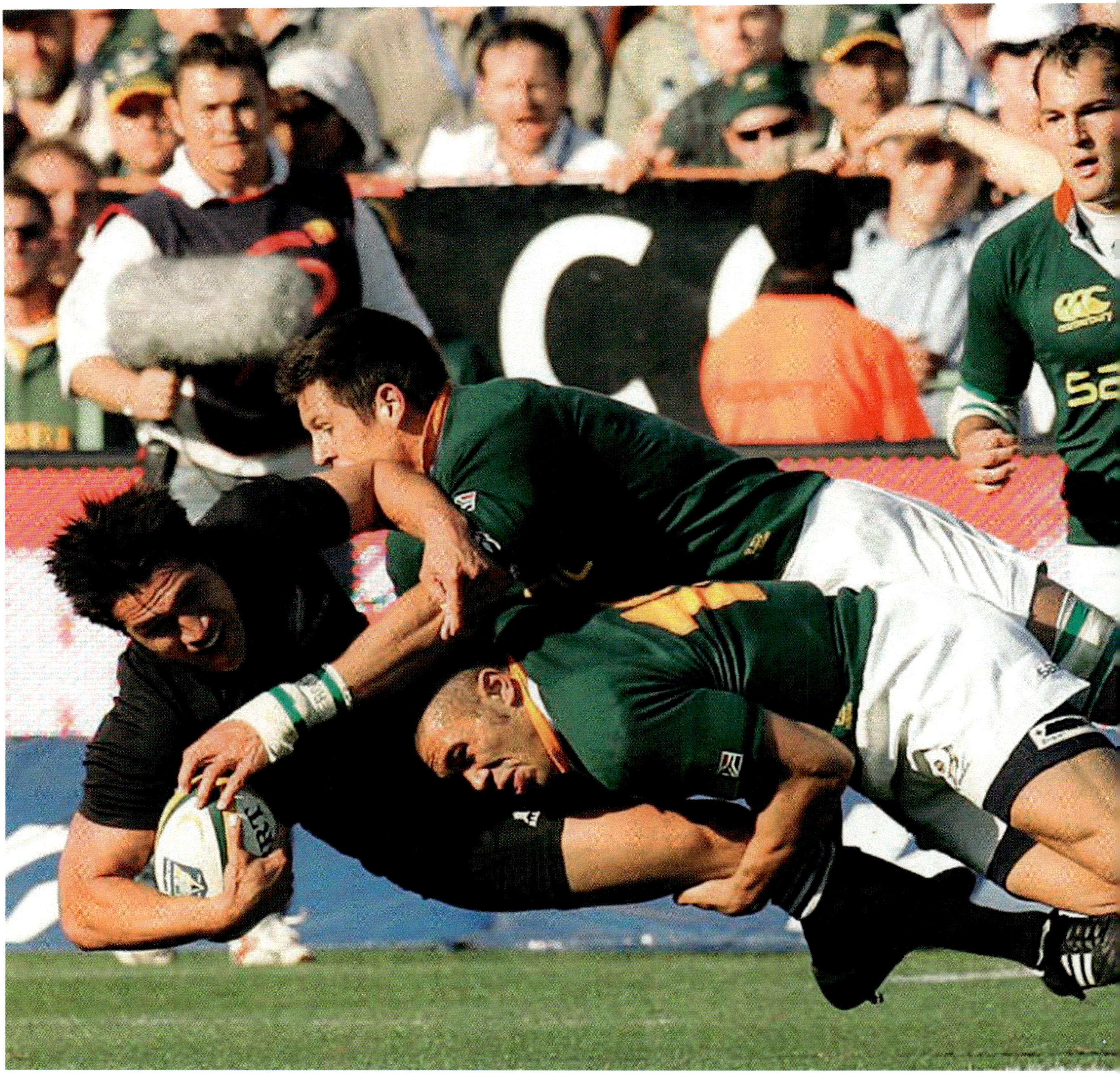

Gros chocs durant les rencontres de Tri-Nations qui opposent les trois grandes nations de l'hémisphère Sud, Afrique du Sud, Nouvelle-Zélande et Australie. Ci-dessus, les Springboks s'y mettent à deux pour stopper net l'arrière des All Blacks, Mils Muliaina. Le premier enserre les jambes, le second percute le haut du corps et cherche à mettre la main sur le ballon. Page de droite, le flanker et capitaine néo-zélandais Richie McCaw illustre parfaitement l'art du plaquage face à l'ailier australien Wendell Sailor.

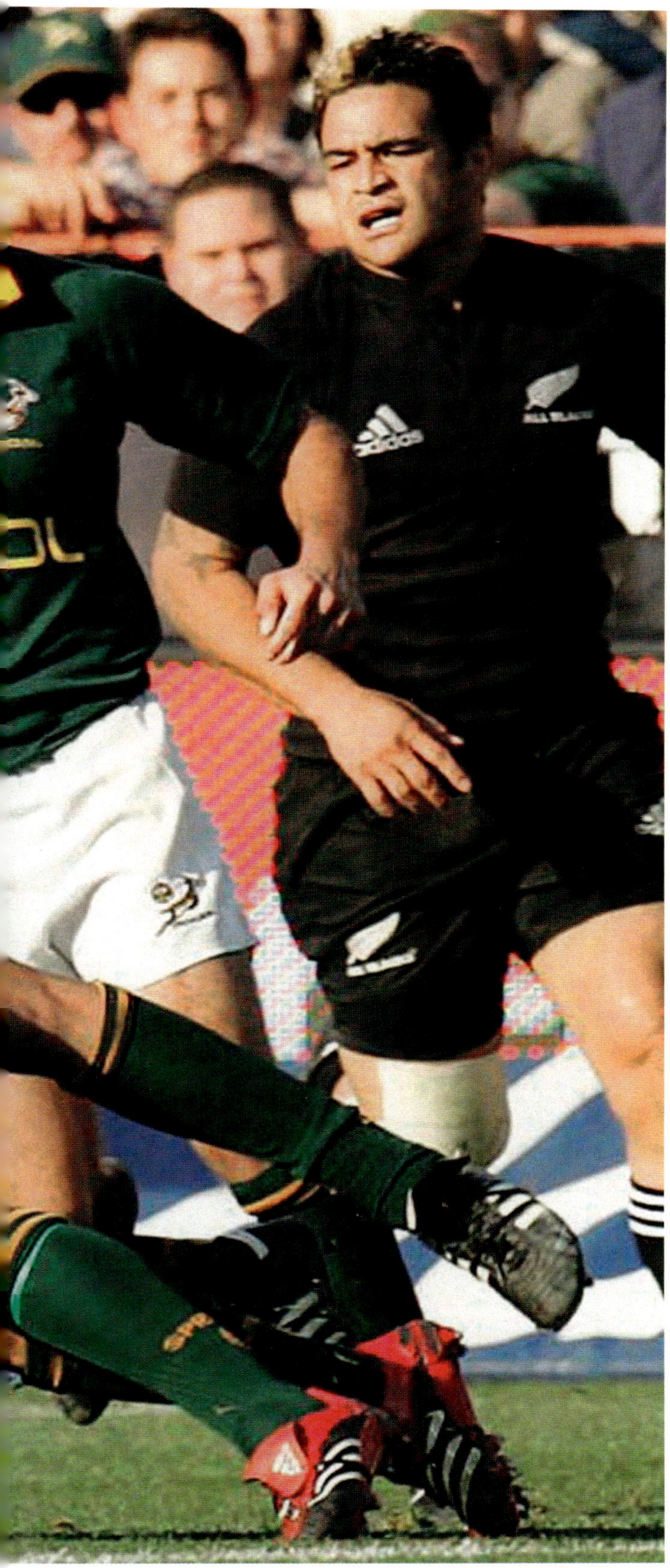

Plaquage

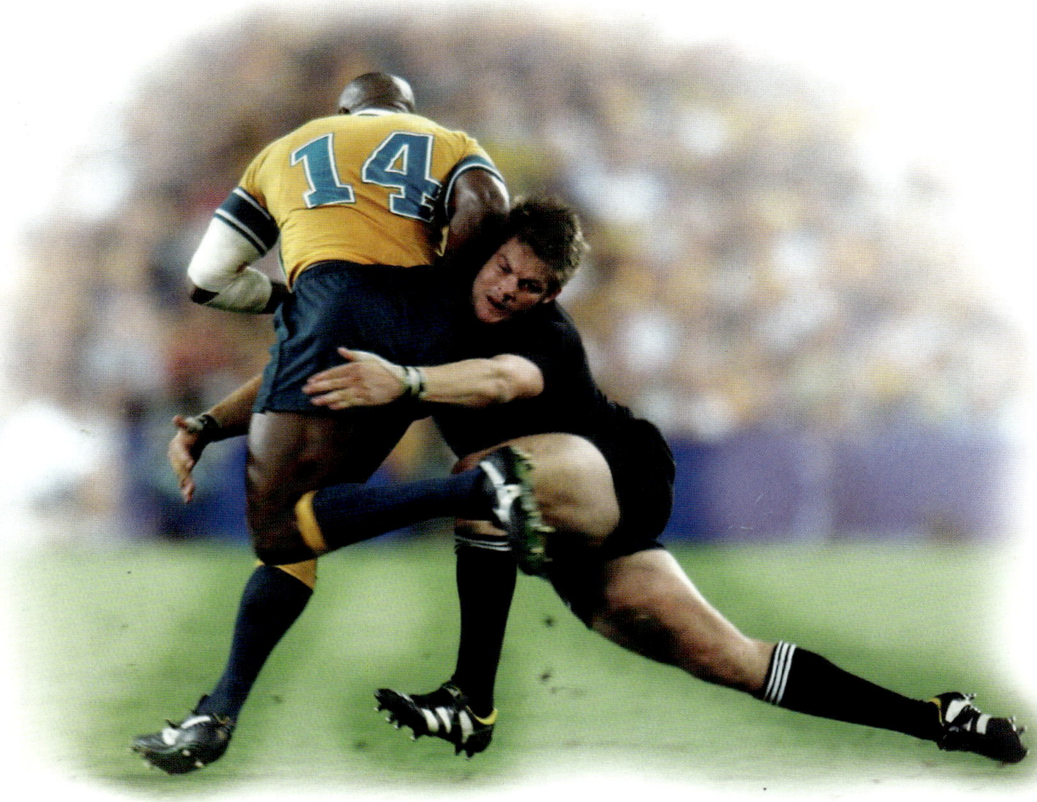

Il existe plusieurs façons d'arrêter le joueur porteur de la balle, mais le meilleur moyen reste encore le plaquage aux jambes. Au moment où mon adversaire s'approche, il me suffit de me baisser, d'écarter les bras et, en m'avançant vers lui, d'enserrer ses jambes avant de me laisser glisser au sol. Gros ou grands, tous tombent. Effectué selon les règles, c'est-à-dire sous la ligne des épaules, en évitant de viser la tête et le cou, il n'est dangereux ni pour l'attaquant ni pour le défenseur. Chez les jeunes qui débutent, plaquer n'est pas naturel. Il y a parfois de l'appréhension au moment de se jeter dans les pieds d'un adversaire. Mais les premières craintes surmontées, on trouve beaucoup de fierté à faire tomber son vis-à-vis et, ainsi, à couper l'élan de l'équipe adverse.

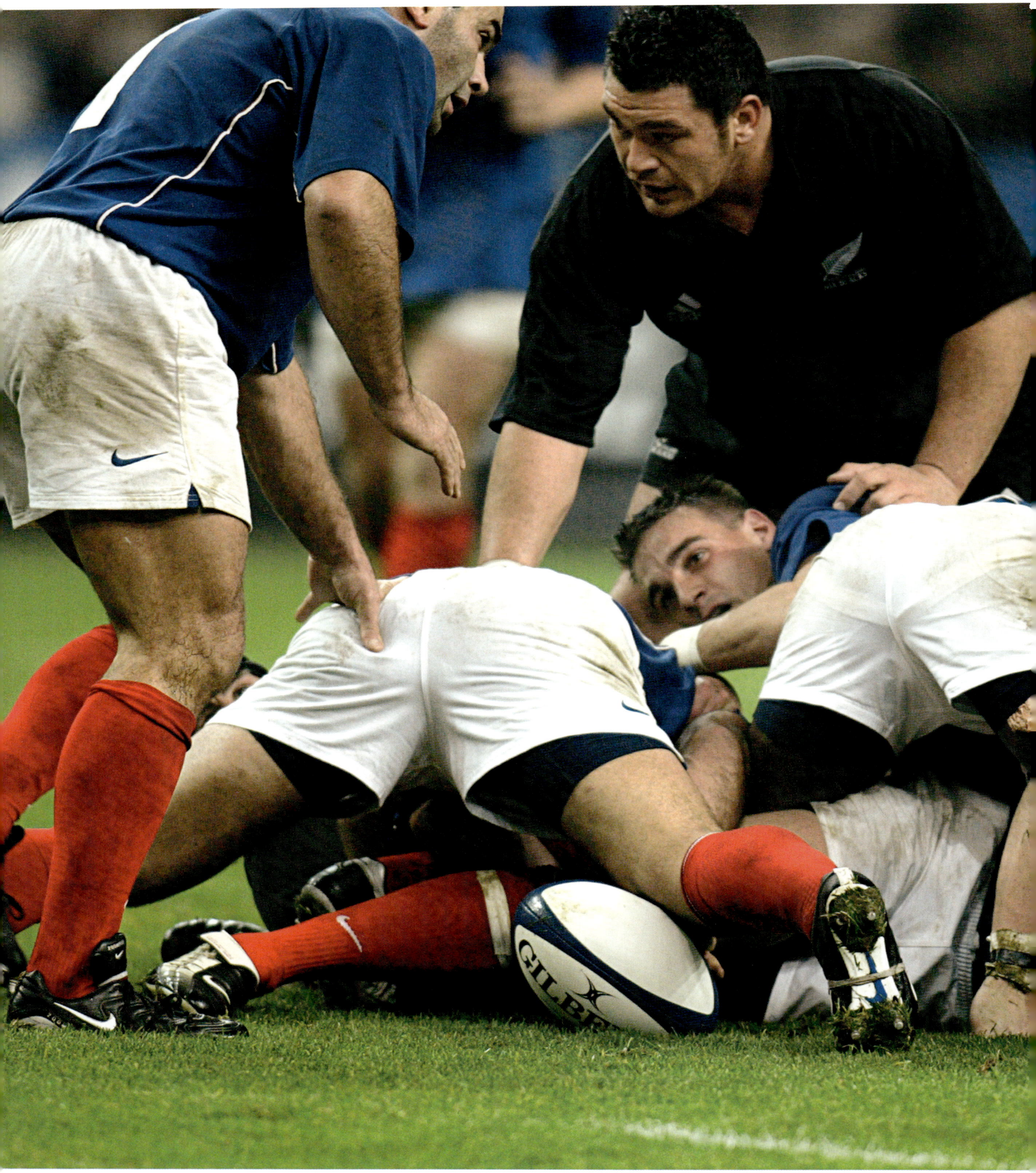

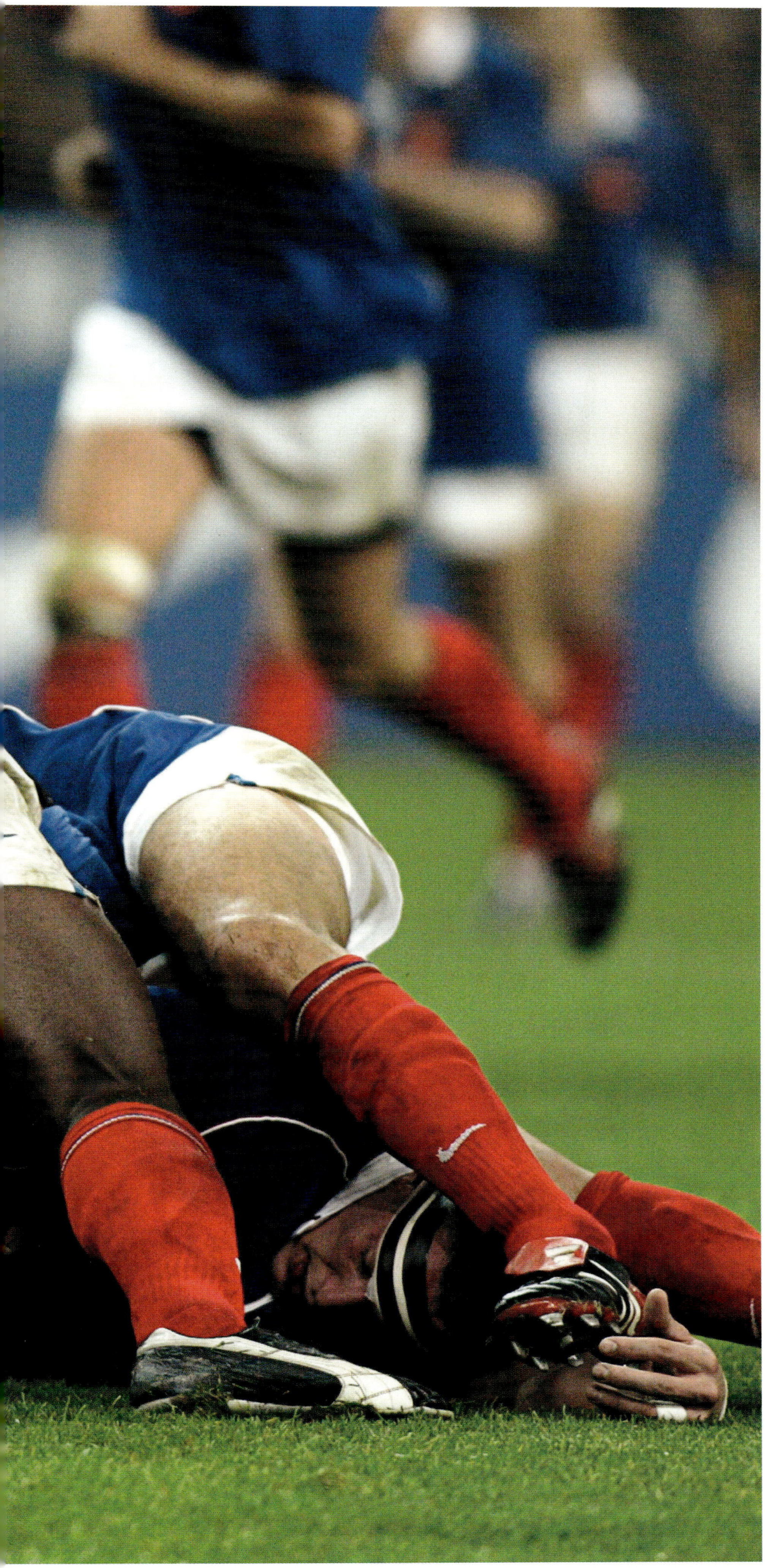

Jeu au sol

Depuis 1997, la règle permet au joueur plaqué au sol d'offrir la balle à ses partenaires en se retournant vers son camp et en éloignant le ballon de ses bras tendus, tandis qu'il met son corps en barrage. Bien entendu, les premiers partenaires qui se portent au soutien du plaqué, comme ceux qui viennent aider le plaqueur, sont déterminants. Ils font la différence pour un camp ou pour l'autre en arrivant rapidement sur les lieux de l'action, les uns essayant de protéger ce ballon en formant un mur, les autres tentant de le récupérer au sol. Tous doivent néanmoins rester debout sur leurs appuis. Pas question de plonger ou de se coucher pour bloquer la sortie du ballon. Cette action, qui va de la tombée au sol du plaqué jusqu'à l'extraction de la balle, doit normalement durer quatre secondes, pas plus. Au-delà, on considère que le jeu s'est ralenti, ce dont profite toujours le camp adverse pour se replacer et dresser une nouvelle ligne de défense hermétique.

Imanol Harinordoquy, plaqué et mis au sol, s'est allongé de tout son long pour faire écran. Trois de ses partenaires se sont immédiatement placés au-dessus de lui afin de protéger le ballon et interdire aux Néo-Zélandais de s'en approcher. Leurs pieds sont en contact avec le sol. Ils forment une barrière que l'adversaire n'a pas le droit de franchir sous peine d'être pénalisé. Le pilier Jean-Jacques Crenca peut alors se saisir de la balle sans être gêné et assurer la continuité du jeu d'une passe ou en allant défier les défenseurs all blacks.

Pages suivantes :
Et toujours le désir de faire vivre le ballon, de le laisser à la disposition des partenaires. Afin d'assurer la continuité du jeu, le Biarrot Thomas Lièvremont, enfoui sous un regroupement, parvient à offrir, d'une main, la balle à son demi de mêlée. Bel exemple d'altruisme.

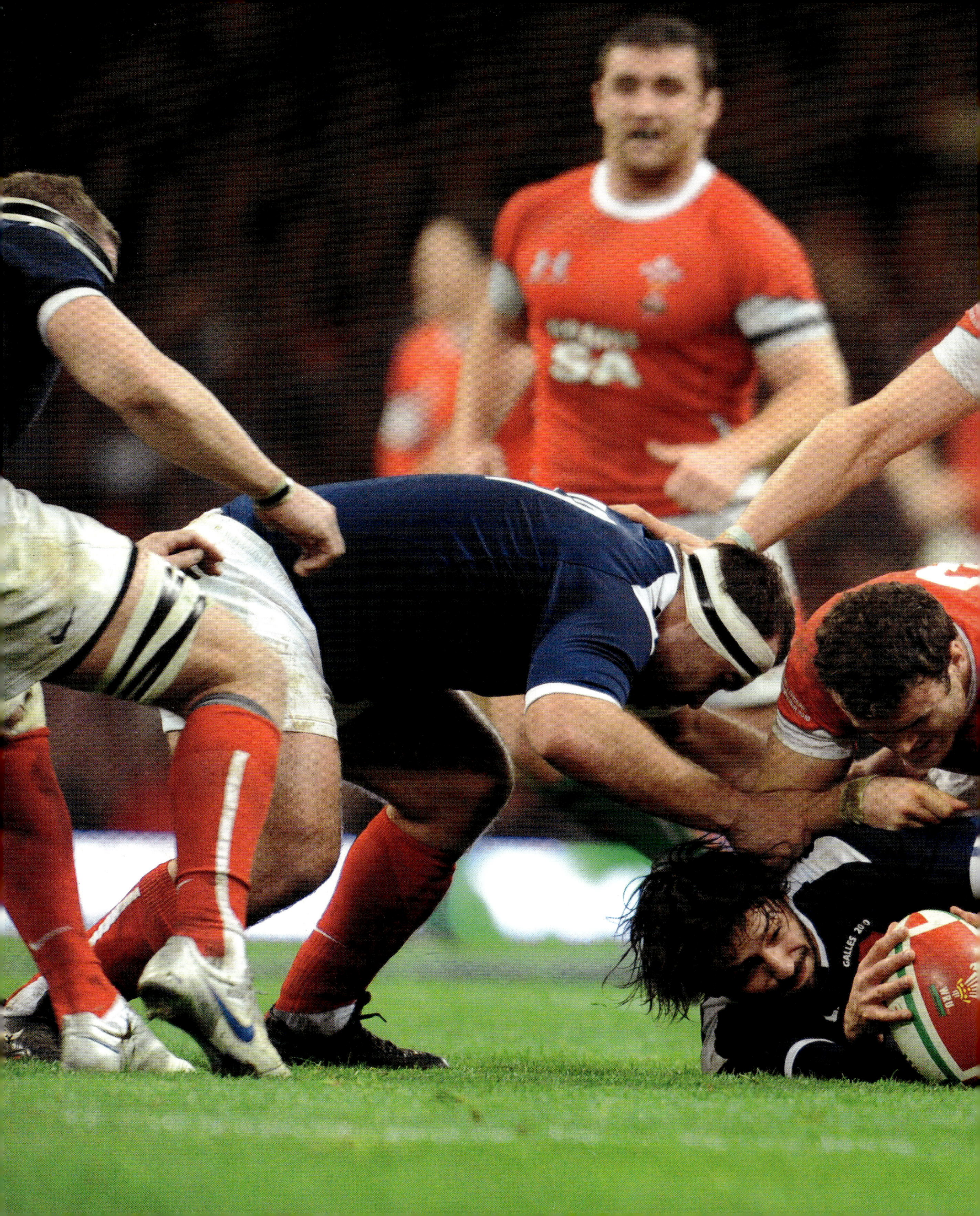
SA
GALLES 200
WRU

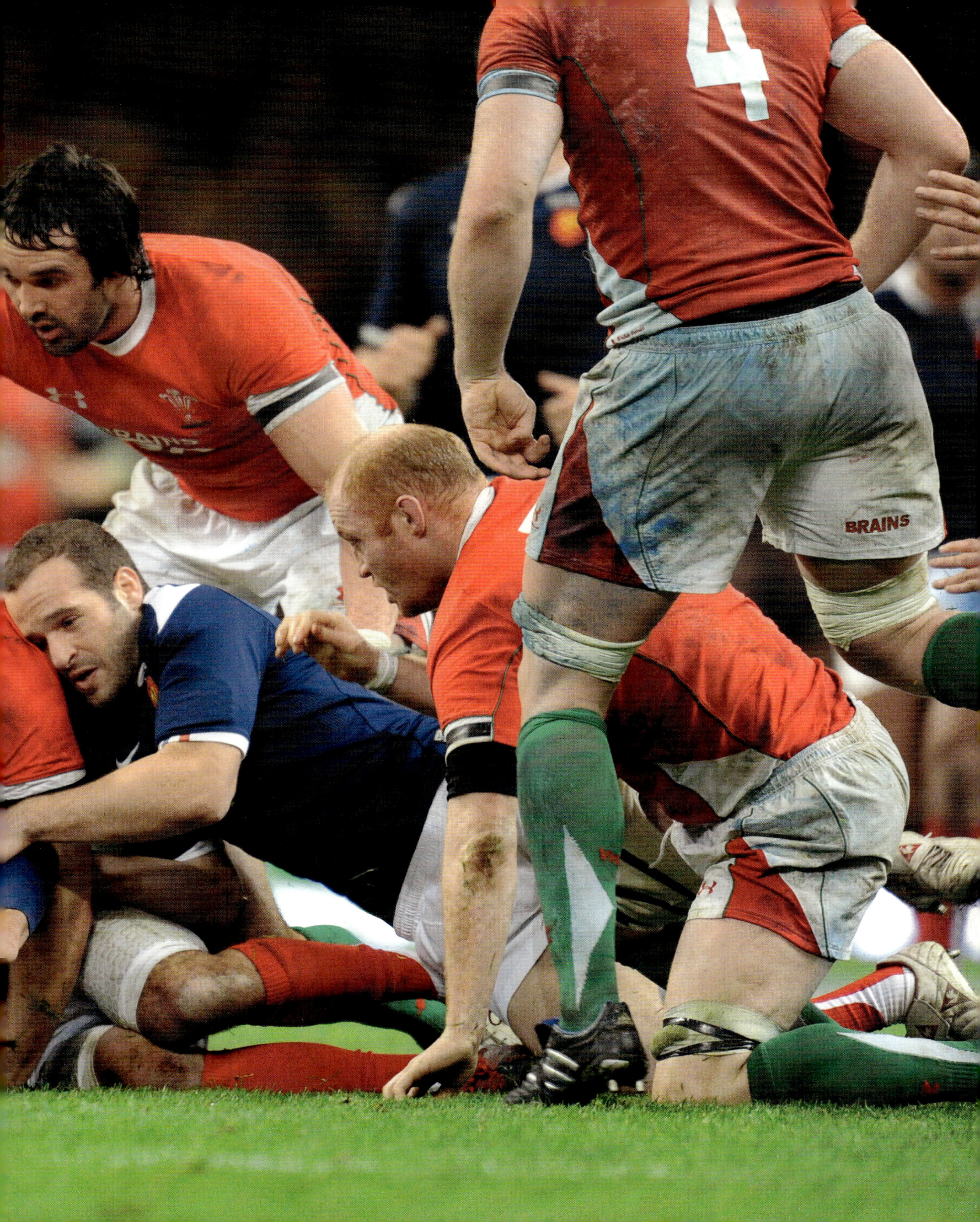
4
BRAINS

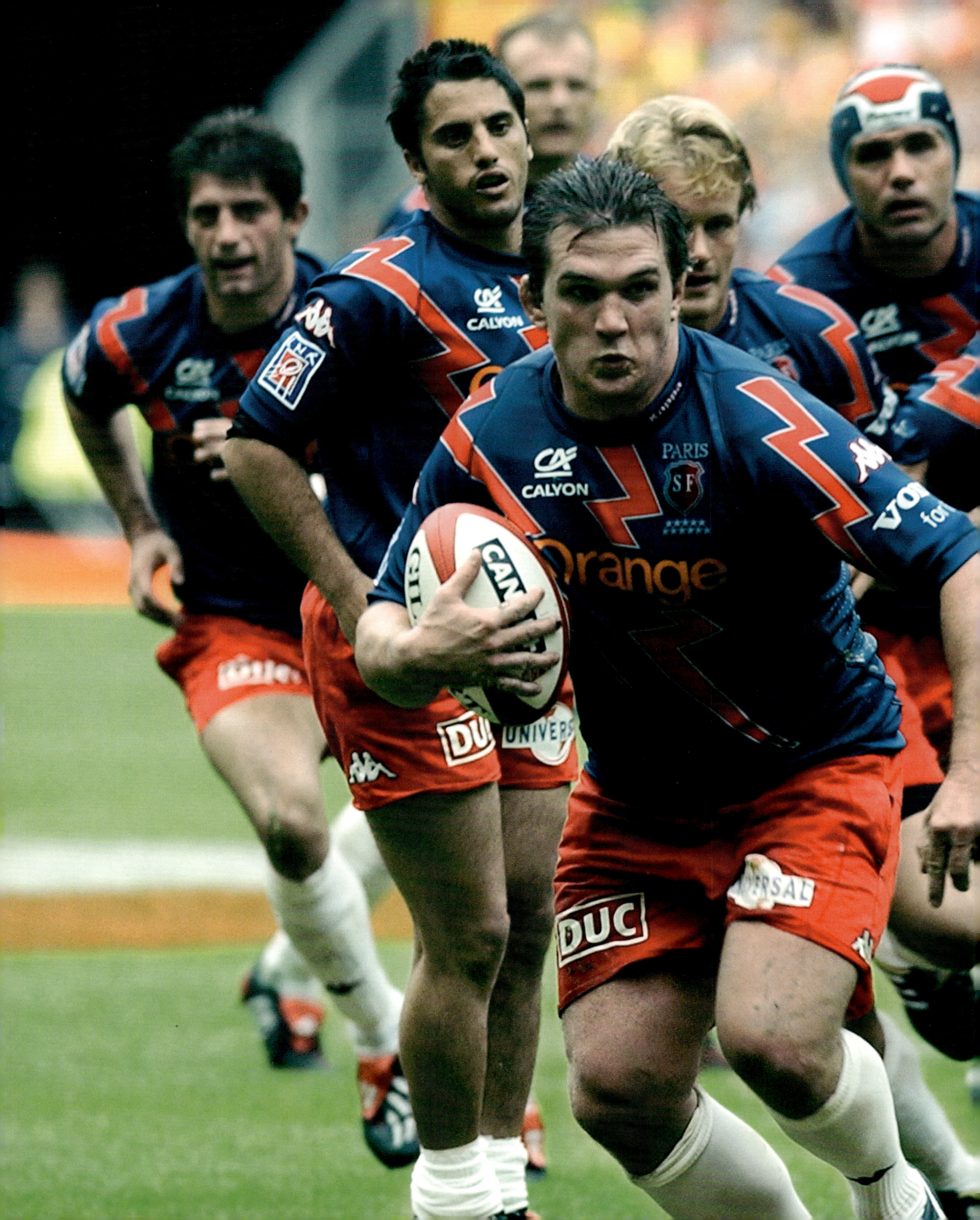
CALYON
CALYON
PARIS
SF
Orange
DUC
DUC

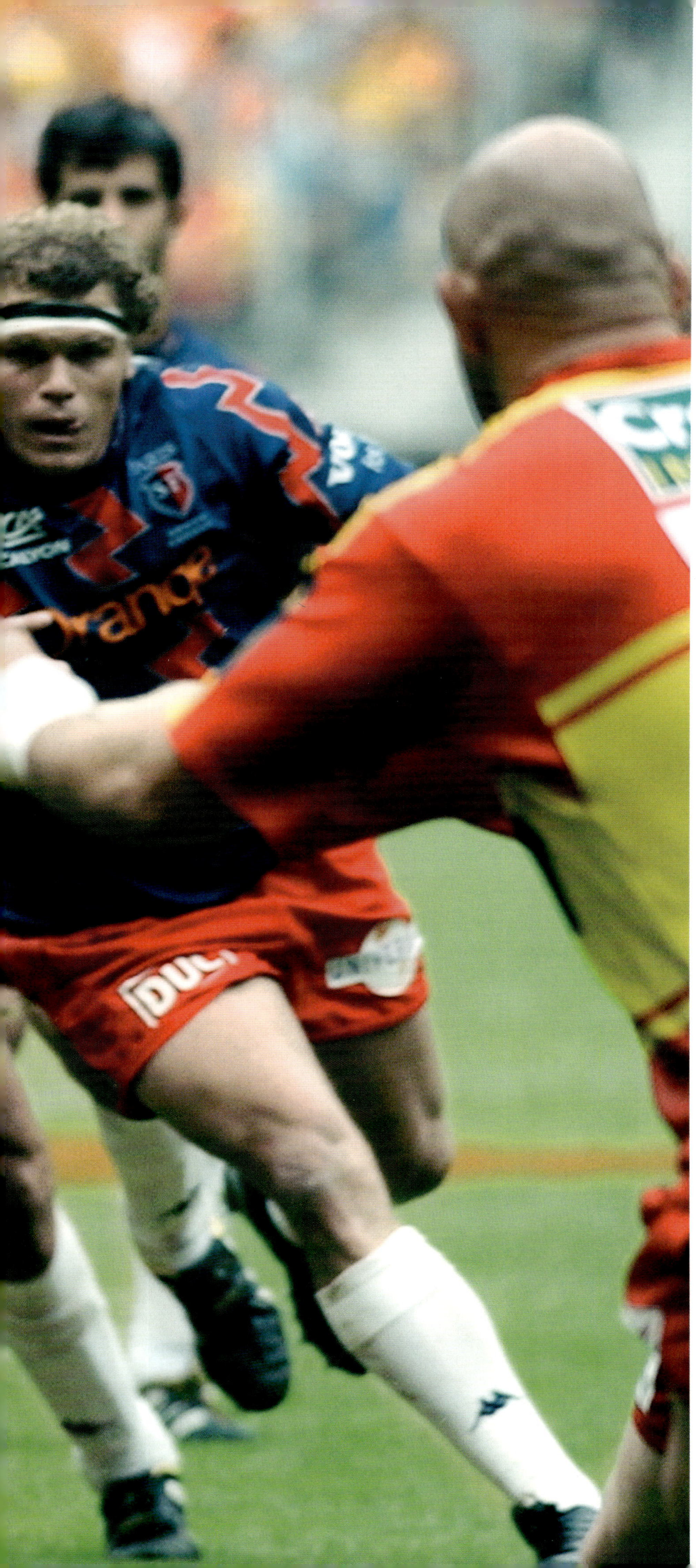

Départ d'avants

Parmi les actions les plus impressionnantes, celle où les avants décident d'attaquer en ordre serré, les uns derrière les autres, s'inscrit dans la logique de combat. La plupart du temps confinés aux phases de conquête, les huit avants montent parfois ensemble à l'assaut de l'adversaire. Et il est difficile de les arrêter quand ils décident de prendre de cette façon les choses en main. À grands coups d'épaules, tête la première, ils percutent, cherchant à tout dévaster sur leur passage. En passes courtes, ils vont tenter de progresser sans perdre le ballon. En rugby, le meilleur moyen d'avancer reste la ligne droite. Les avants aiment le prouver.

Le pilier international du Stade Français, Sylvain Marconnet, sonne la charge face à Perpignan, en finale du championnat de France. Tout le pack s'est engouffré dans son sillage. On reconnaît de gauche à droite, Pierre Rabadan, Agustin Pichot, Patrick Tabacco, Mike James, David Auradou, Pieter De Villiers et Mathieu Blin.

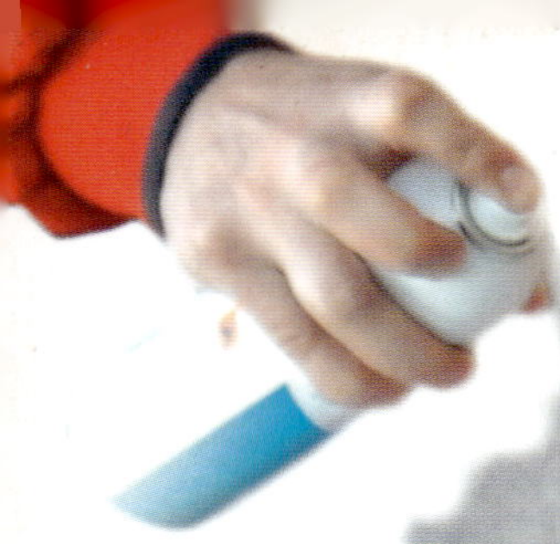

Blessure

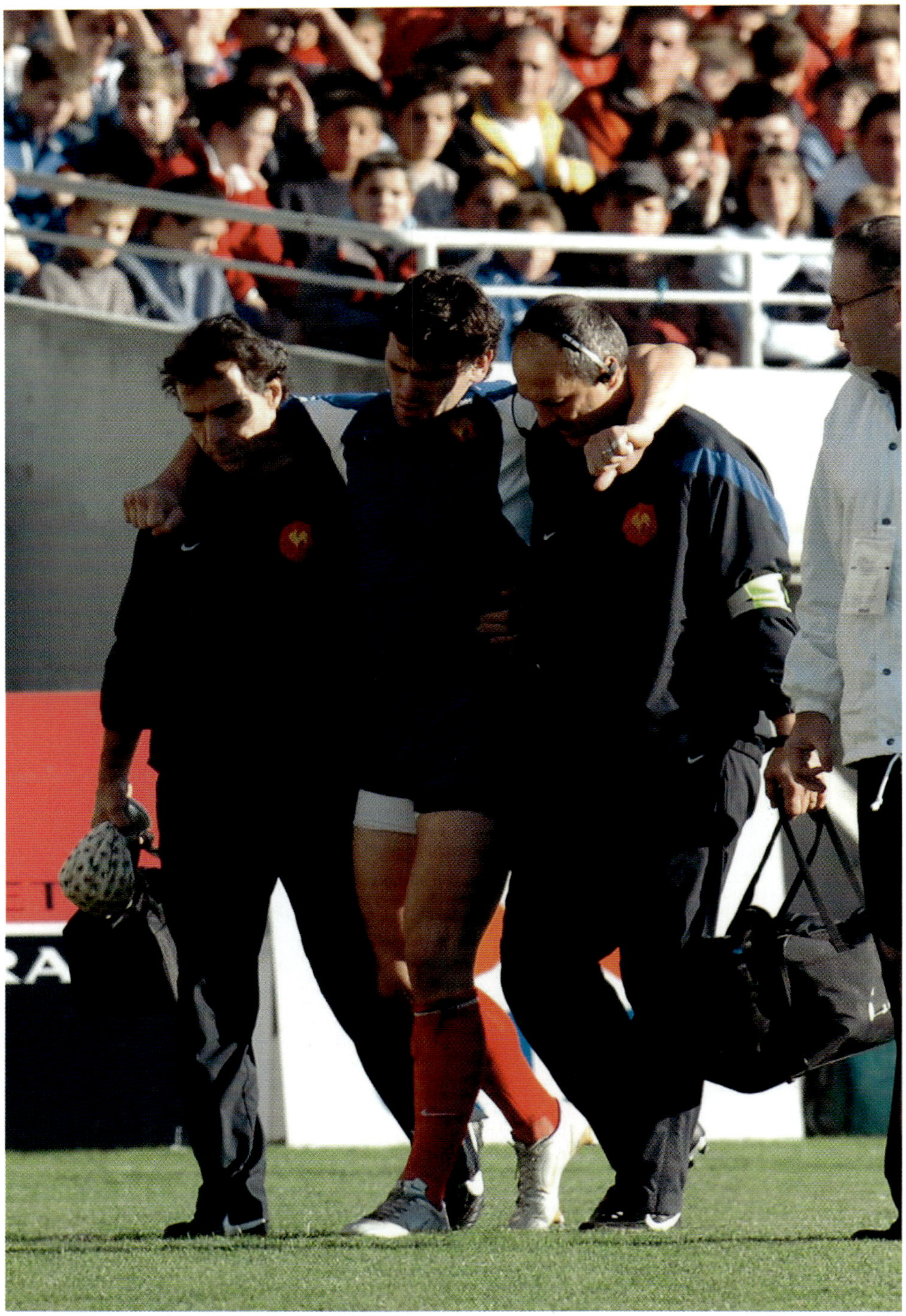

Elle nécessite l'arrêt du match, ordonné par l'arbitre. Valises à la main, une kyrielle de soigneurs entre précipitamment sur le terrain. Il y a les blessures bénignes qu'un coup d'éponge fait disparaître comme par enchantement et celles, plus graves, qui nécessitent la sortie sur civière. Avec son engagement physique sans concession, le rugby fait naître des chocs et des douleurs. Mais rien n'arrête les joueurs, en tout cas certainement pas les entailles et les hématomes. Se faire soigner, d'accord, mais surtout reprendre le match. À un arbitre qui lui enjoignait de quitter le terrain, l'international français Jean-Pierre Rives, titubant, le front ceint d'un bandage après avoir heurté de plein front les « buffles » sud-africains, répondit : « Quitter le terrain ? Mais pour aller où ? »

L'arrière Julien Laharrague, soutenu par Xavier Gousse et Thierry Hermerel, respectivement kinésithérapeute et médecin de l'équipe de France, quitte le terrain du Stadium de Toulouse, touché aux ligaments du genou. Pour lui l'indisponibilité sera de plusieurs mois.

La blessure de l'international biarrot Imanol Harinordoquy, elle, est moins grave. Un coup de bombe réfrigérante et le coup qu'il a pris dans les reins ne sera bientôt plus qu'un souvenir.

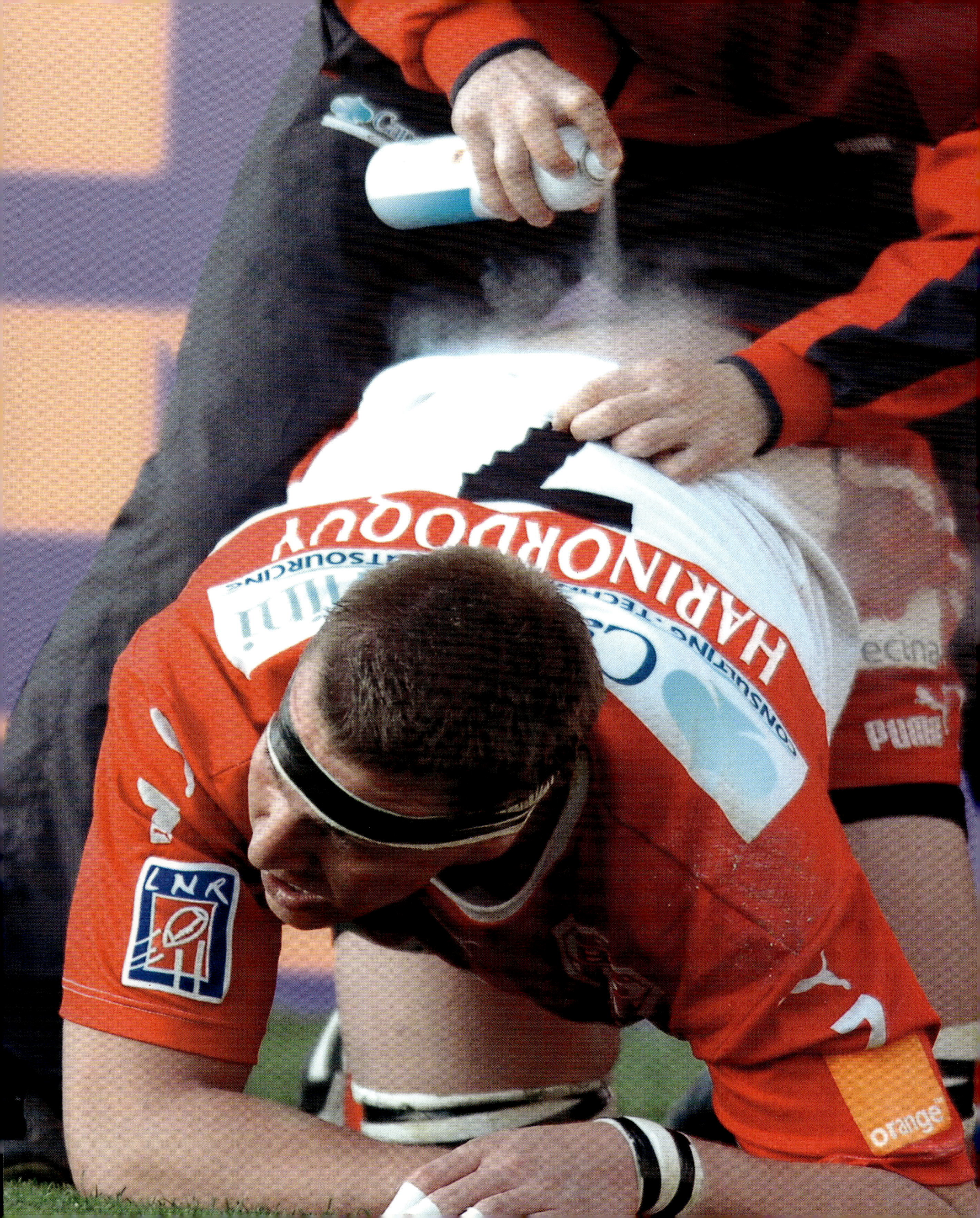
HARINORDOQUY
LNR
PUMA
orange

Dégagement

Un grand souffle de soulagement parcourt les tribunes au moment où l'arrière dégage loin et fort le ballon, repoussant d'un majestueux coup de pied la menace de l'équipe adverse. Depuis ses propres vingt-deux mètres, il a le droit de taper directement en touche. C'est d'ailleurs le seul endroit du terrain où un joueur est autorisé à le faire. Partout ailleurs, la balle doit rebondir dans l'aire de jeu avant de franchir la ligne de touche. Dans le cas contraire, l'arbitre indiquera la sortie de balle à l'endroit où se trouvait celui qui vient de frapper la balle.

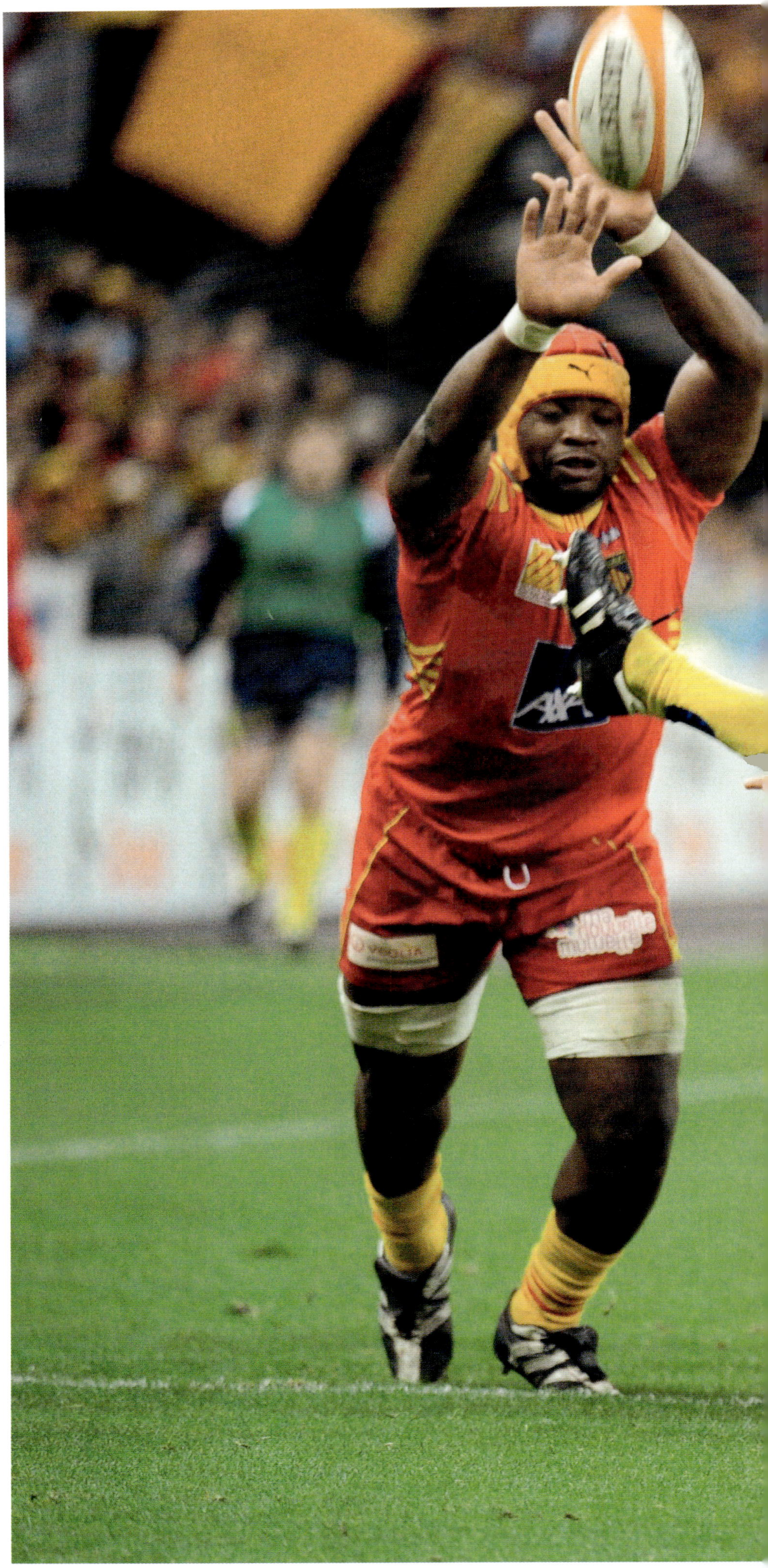

L'arrière n'est pas le seul à pouvoir repousser le danger d'un long coup de pied en touche. Ici, lors d'une rencontre entre Brive et Bourgoin, le deuxième ligne berjallien (n°4) contourne le regroupement et court en levant les bras pour tenter de contrer le dégagement du demi de mêlée briviste.

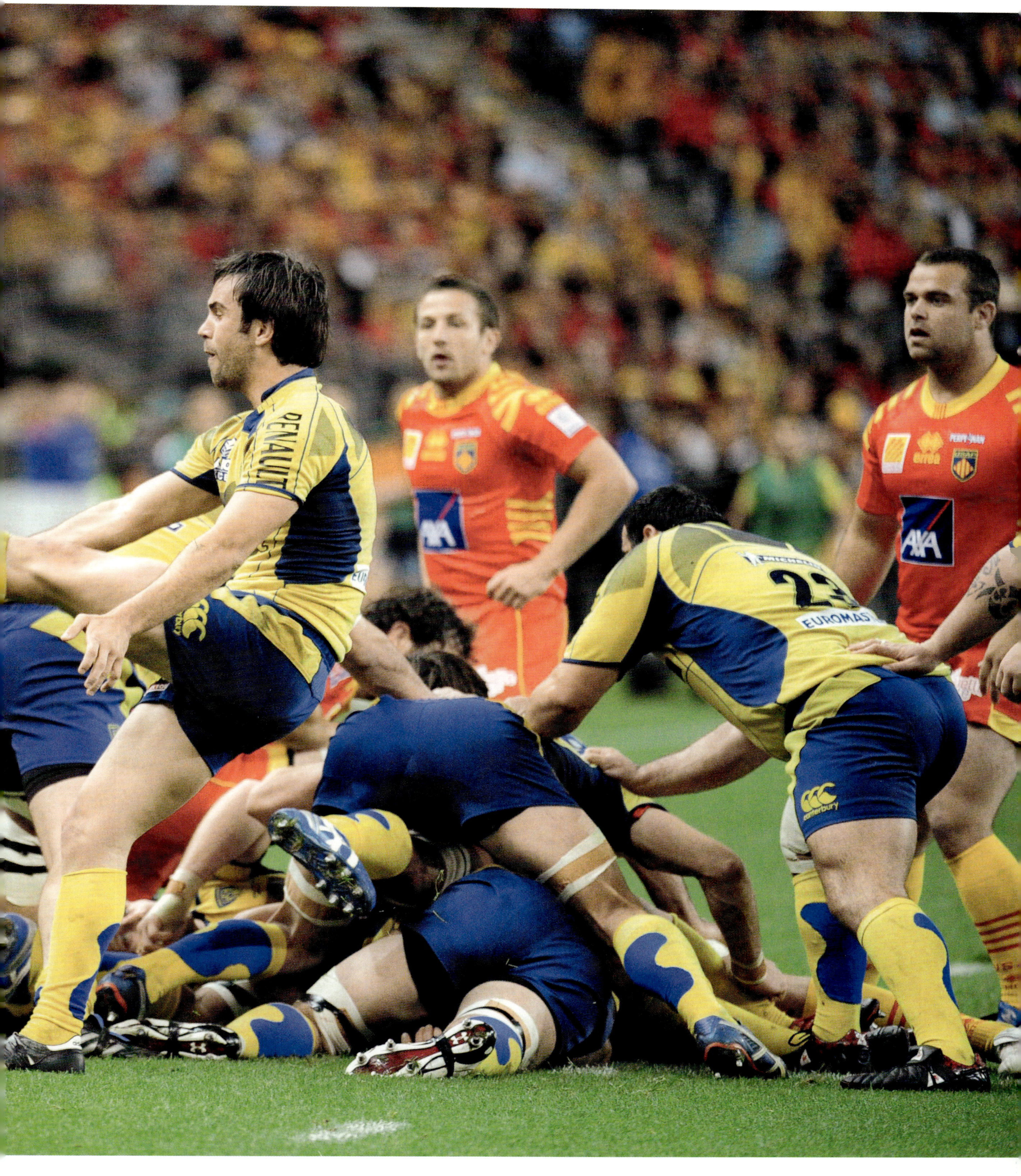
RENAULT
AXA
AXA
23
EUROMAST
canterbury

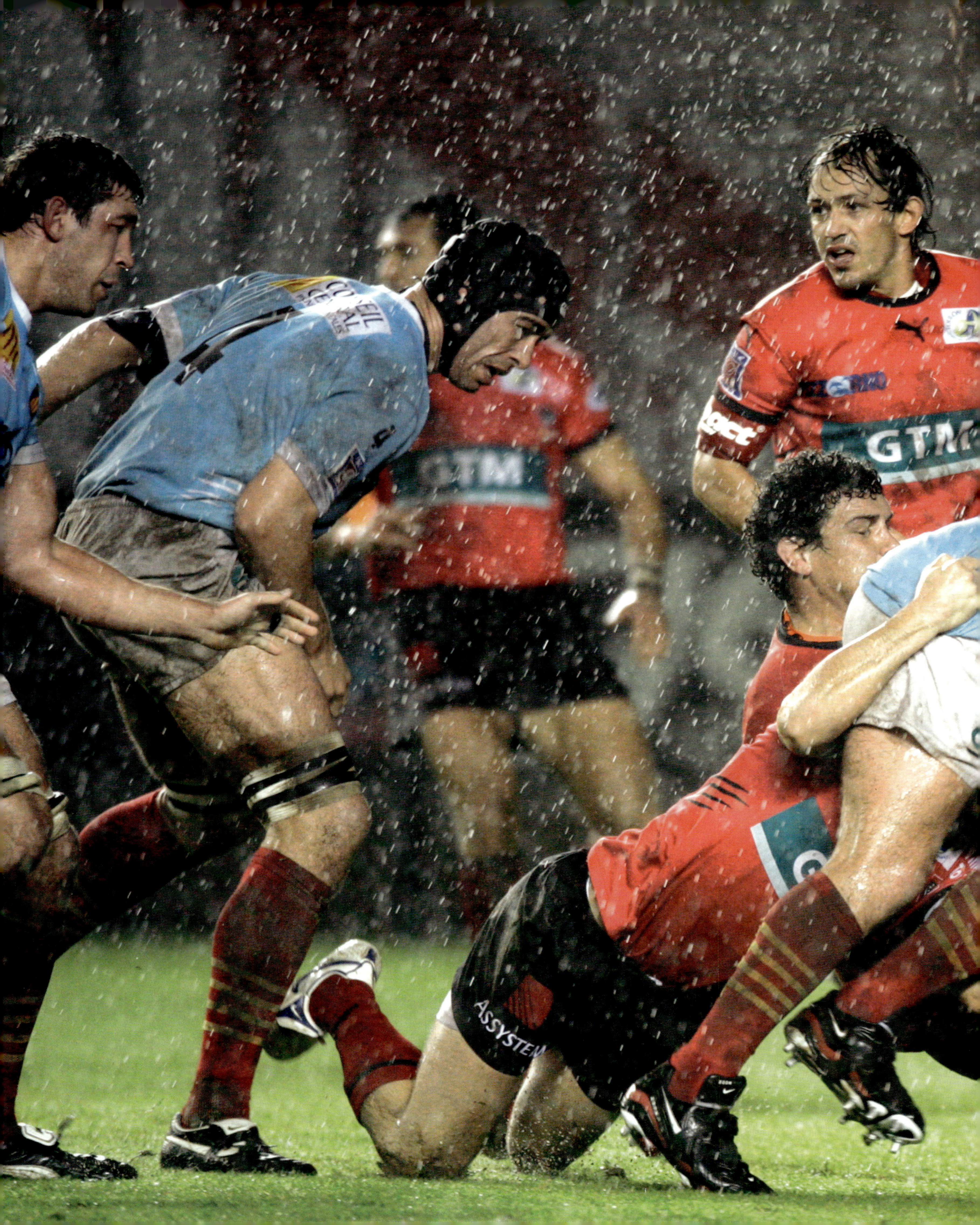
GTM
GTM
ASSYSTEM

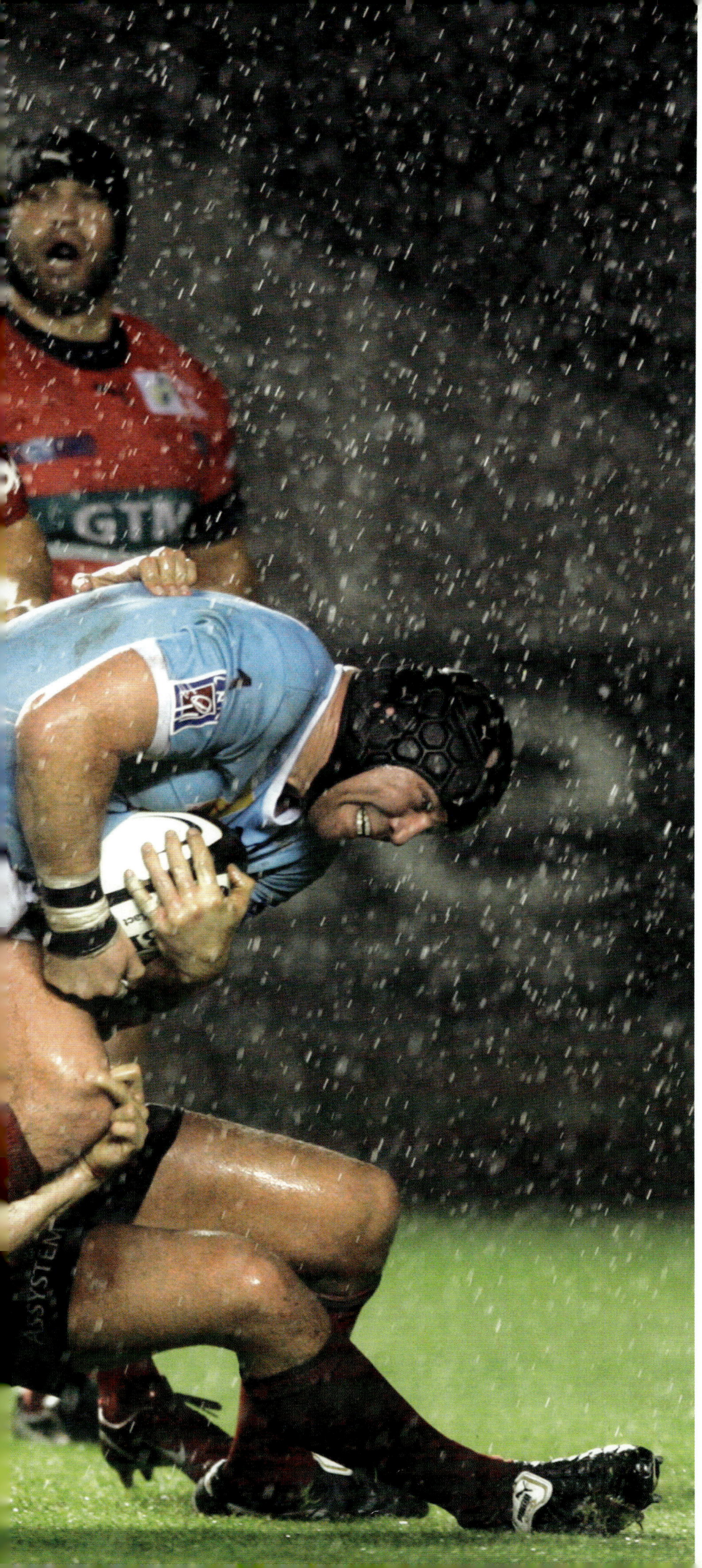

Sport d'hiver

Mis à part ceux qui ont la chance de jouer sur le continent africain, toute l'année au soleil, les joueurs de rugby évoluent d'ordinaire sous la pluie, sur des terrains lourds et gras. Le rugby n'est pas un sport de plage, encore moins une activité de gymnase. Considérons-le comme une authentique discipline hivernale, soumise aux intempéries, aux morsures du froid et aux caprices du vent. De quoi forger les corps et le caractère.

Même si les villes de Toulon et Perpignan se trouvent au bord de la Méditerranée, les conditions climatiques ne sont pas toujours clémentes. Sous une pluie diluvienne, Varois (maillot rouge) et Catalans (maillot bleu ciel) s'engagent sans retenue. À noter la longueur des crampons (18 mm), maximum autorisé par le règlement.

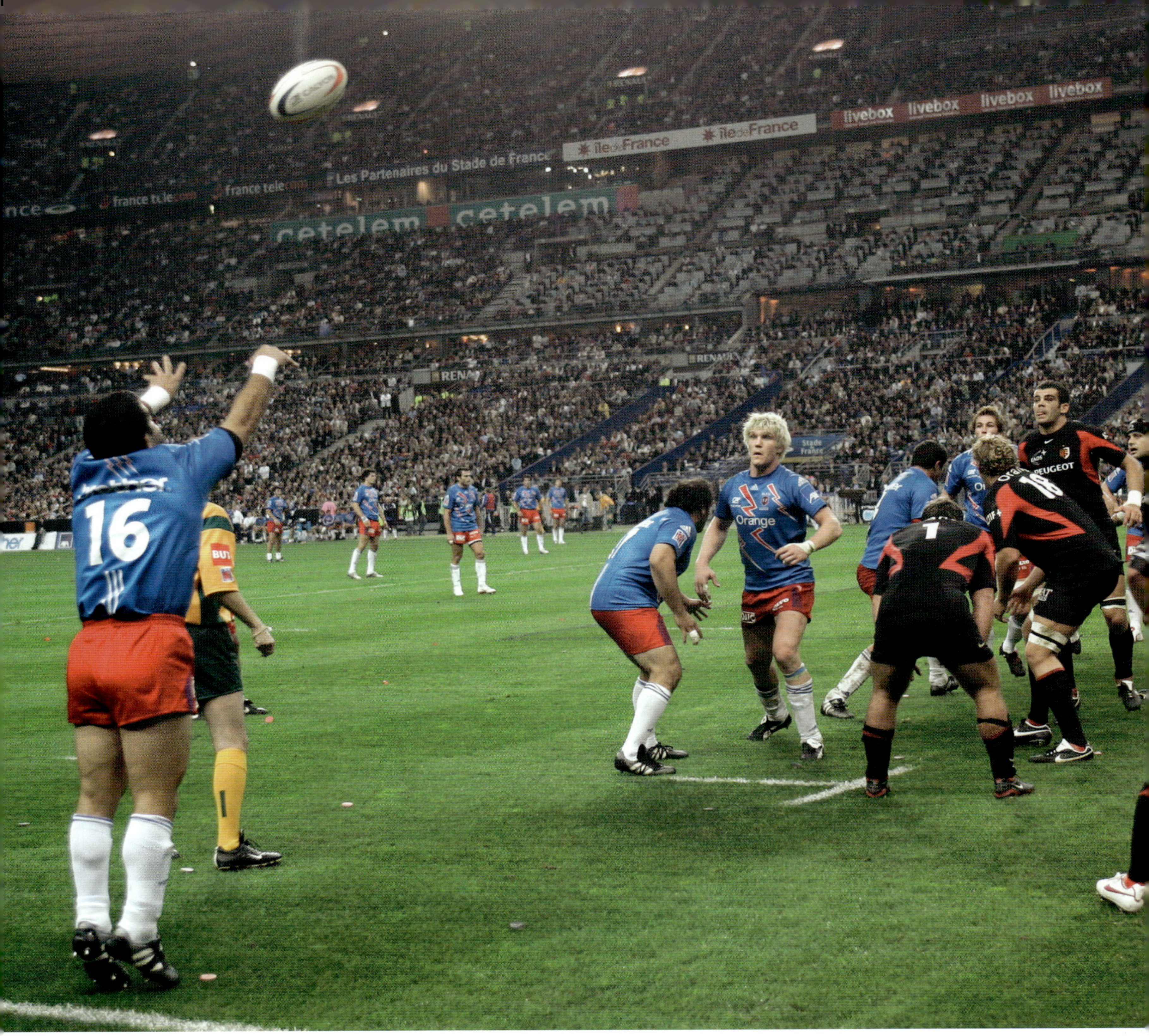

Une fois l'alignement formé, les joueurs peuvent changer de position avant que la balle soit lancée. D'où l'importance de la communication entre le lanceur et le sauteur. Il existe une série de signaux et de codes qui permettent aux joueurs de se comprendre sans avoir besoin de se parler. Un mouvement des doigts, une position des pieds, des clins d'œil : tout est bon pour distiller des informations que l'adversaire ne pourra pas décrypter. Plusieurs types de lancers sont utilisés, courts, tendus, longs, lobés : ils prennent en compte la position des adversaires, la vivacité du sauteur, son sens du timing et la qualité des soutiens qui peuvent le maintenir en l'air plus ou moins longtemps après l'avoir fait décoller du sol. Tel un *quaterback* de football américain, le lanceur est parfois amené à envoyer la balle avec précision à plus de vingt-cinq mètres de distance et, là comme ailleurs, la différence entre une touche gagnée ou perdue se joue à quelques centimètres près.

Lancer en touche

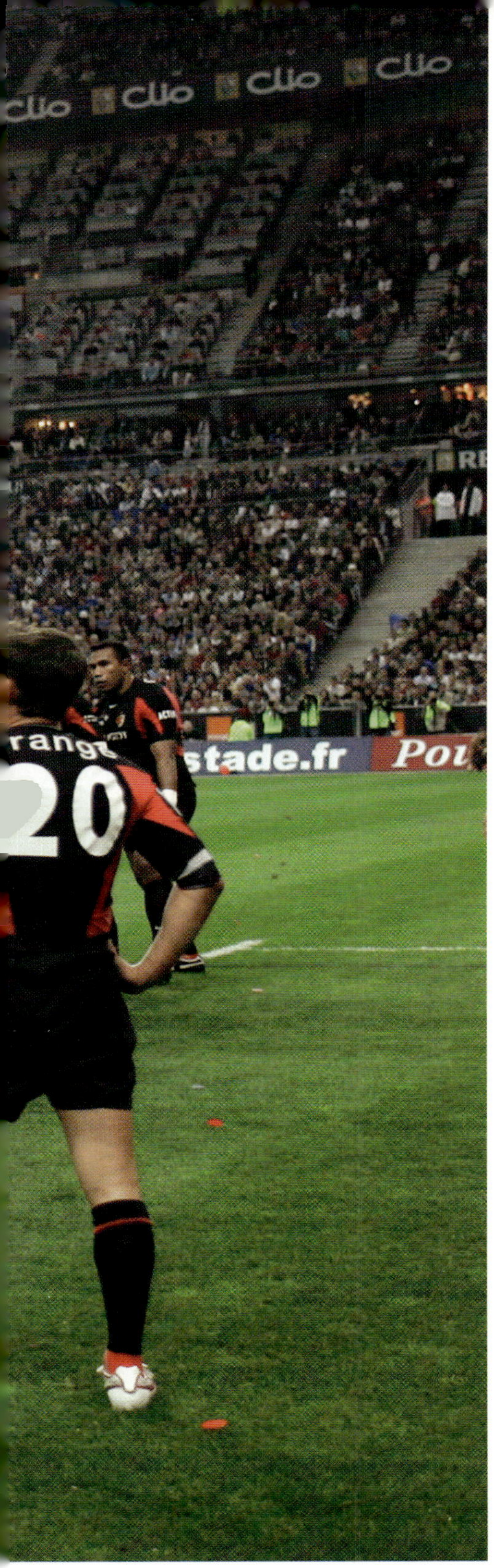

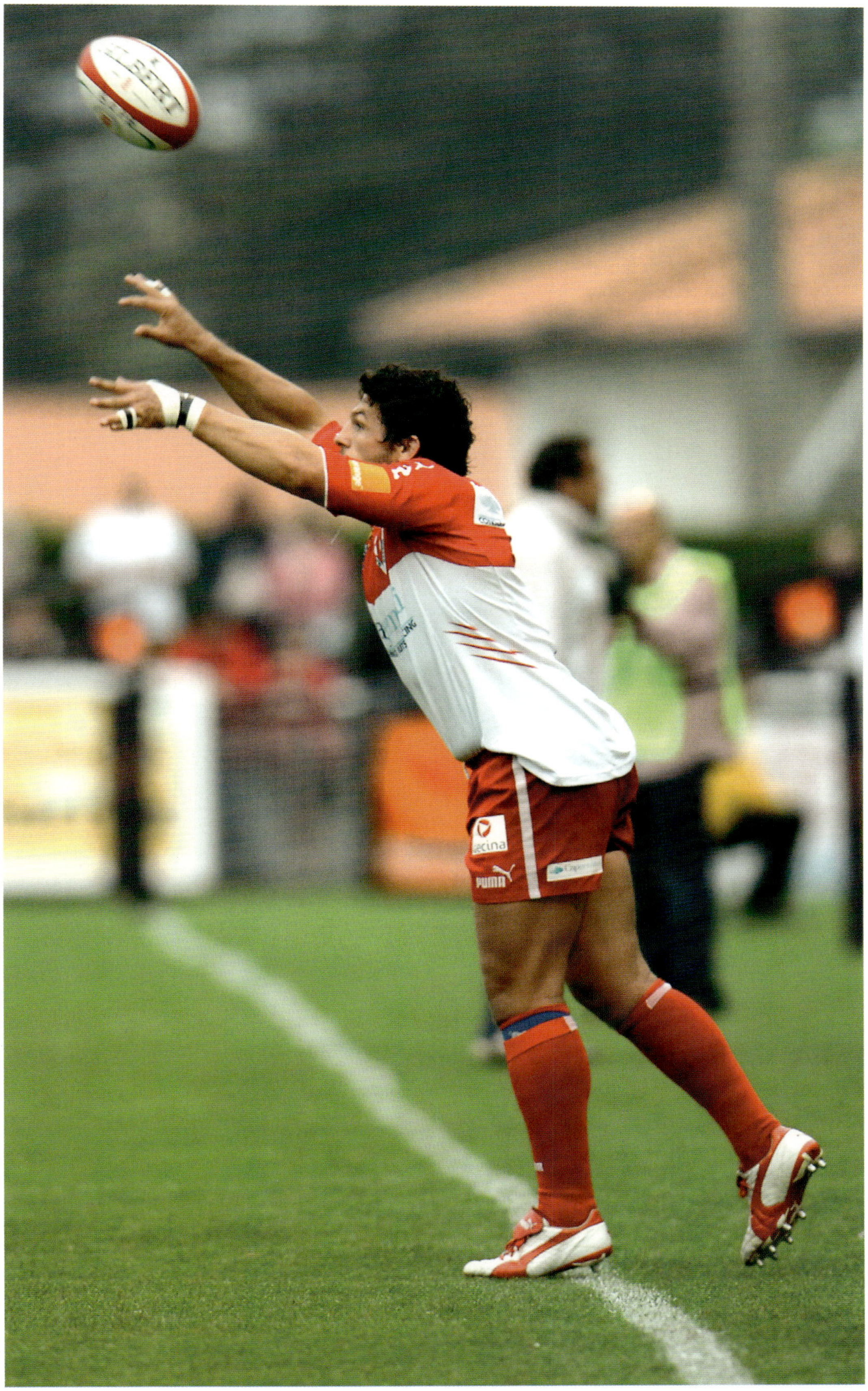

Ci-dessus, première rencontre de championnat de France organisée au Stade de France. Parisiens et Toulousains s'affrontent en touche. Le ballon vient de quitter les mains du talonneur remplaçant Mathieu Blin (n° 16) et se dirige vers un des sauteurs parisiens. Ci-contre, même attitude chez le talonneur biarrot Benoît August.

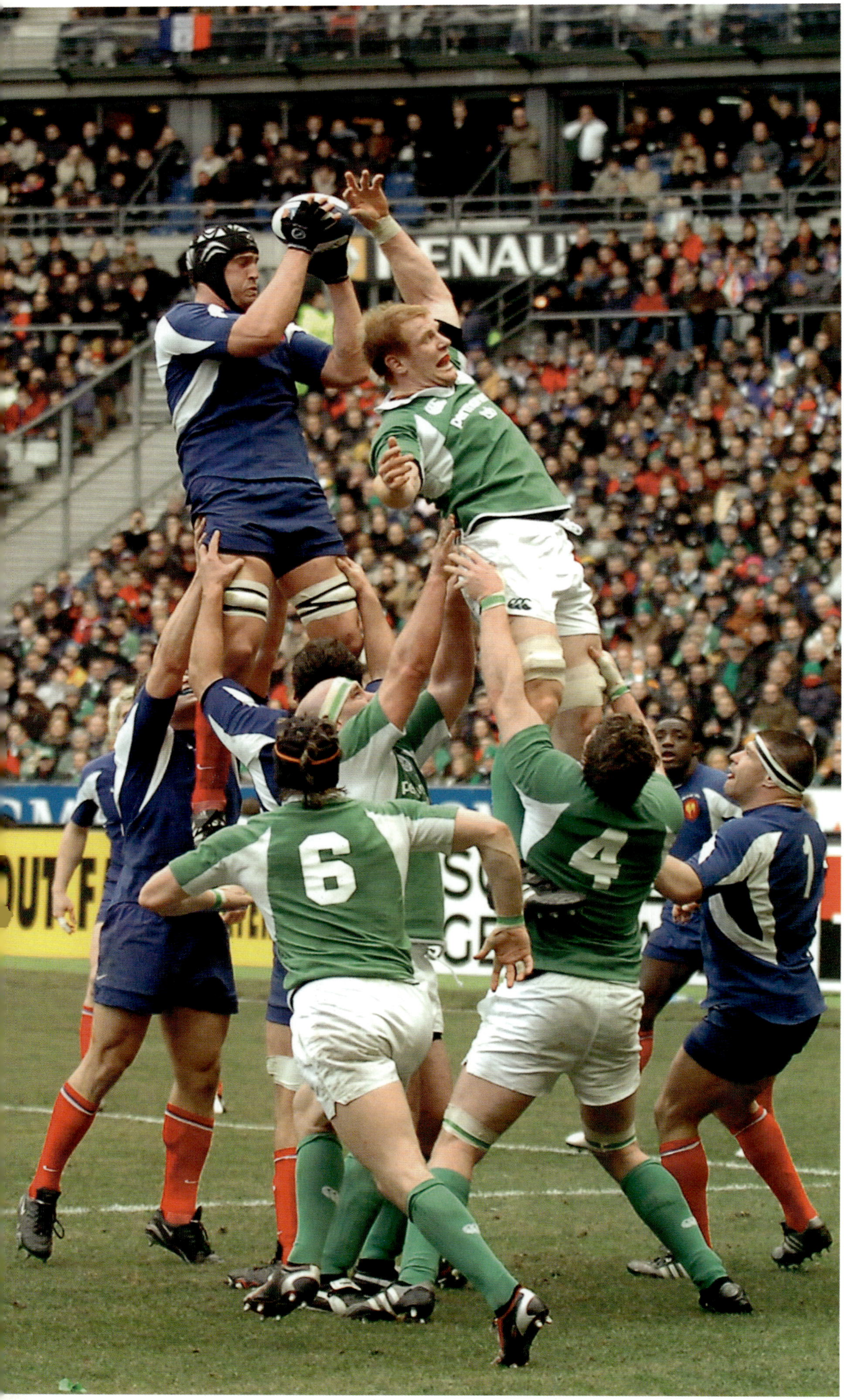

Deuxième étage!

Capter une balle en touche, c'est jouer au poker à cinq mètres d'altitude. Depuis que le législateur a décidé d'autoriser le saut assisté, c'est-à-dire la possibilité pour le sauteur d'être aidé par deux partenaires, la touche a changé radicalement d'allure. À la foire d'empoigne, guerre des coudes, bousculades et intimidations, succède désormais une phase de jeu épurée, subtile et spectaculaire ; une bataille aérienne à des hauteurs d'homme vertigineuses, combat qui mêle adresse, stratégie, ruse, technique collective et anticipation. Situation clé, la touche favorise l'attaque et le mouvement général. En effet, dans le prolongement de l'alignement des avants, les lignes arrière des deux équipes sont obligées de laisser un espace de vingt mètres de profondeur, véritable *no man's land* qui incite au jeu à la main et donne donc à la touche toute son importance tactique.

À gauche, Jérôme Thion fait la loi dans les airs face à l'Irlandais Paul O'Connell.

Quant à Yannick Nyanga,à droite, son adresse lui permet de jouer les trouble-fêtes en gênant l'alignement italien. À noter la structure en triptyque, c'est-à-dire un sauteur et deux soutiens, qui permet au preneur de balle de s'élever à presque cinq mètres de hauteur.

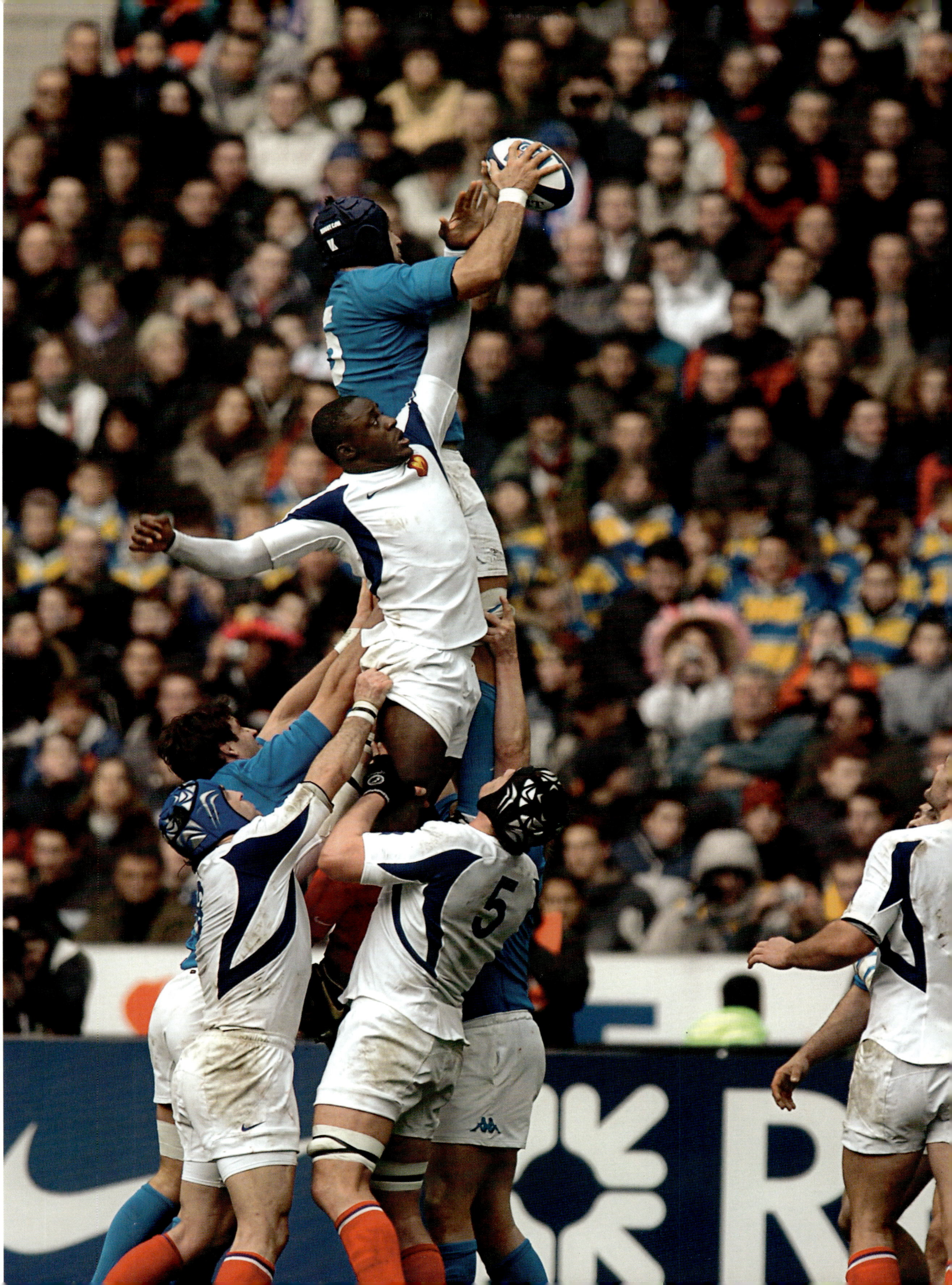

Passe chistera

On dit du jeu d'attaque spontané et instinctif qu'il est un « rugby en sandales ». Ce sont les clubs basques, Bayonne en particulier, qui le mirent à la mode il y a un demi-siècle de cela. Chorégraphiée comme une danse, l'attaque dite « à la bayonnaise » a adapté le coup de chistera que l'on retrouve dans la pelote basque. Il s'agit d'une passe retournée et vrillée qui, à l'aide d'un ample mouvement de revers et d'une rotation du bassin, permet au joueur, le plus souvent le demi de mêlée, de propulser le ballon vite et loin en faisant écran de son corps afin que l'adversaire ne puisse pas gêner la transmission. Extrêmement spectaculaire, cette passe s'est exportée un peu partout dans le monde.

Le Rochelais Jean-Baptiste Elissalde, Basque d'origine par ses grands-pères, est issu d'une lignée de demis de mêlée. Arnaud, l'aïeul, fut le cornac du Stade Rochelais dans les années 50 et 60. Son père Jean-Pierre, international, porta lui aussi les couleurs noir et jaune du club maritime. La passe chistera n'a donc aucun secret pour le numéro neuf de l'équipe de France.

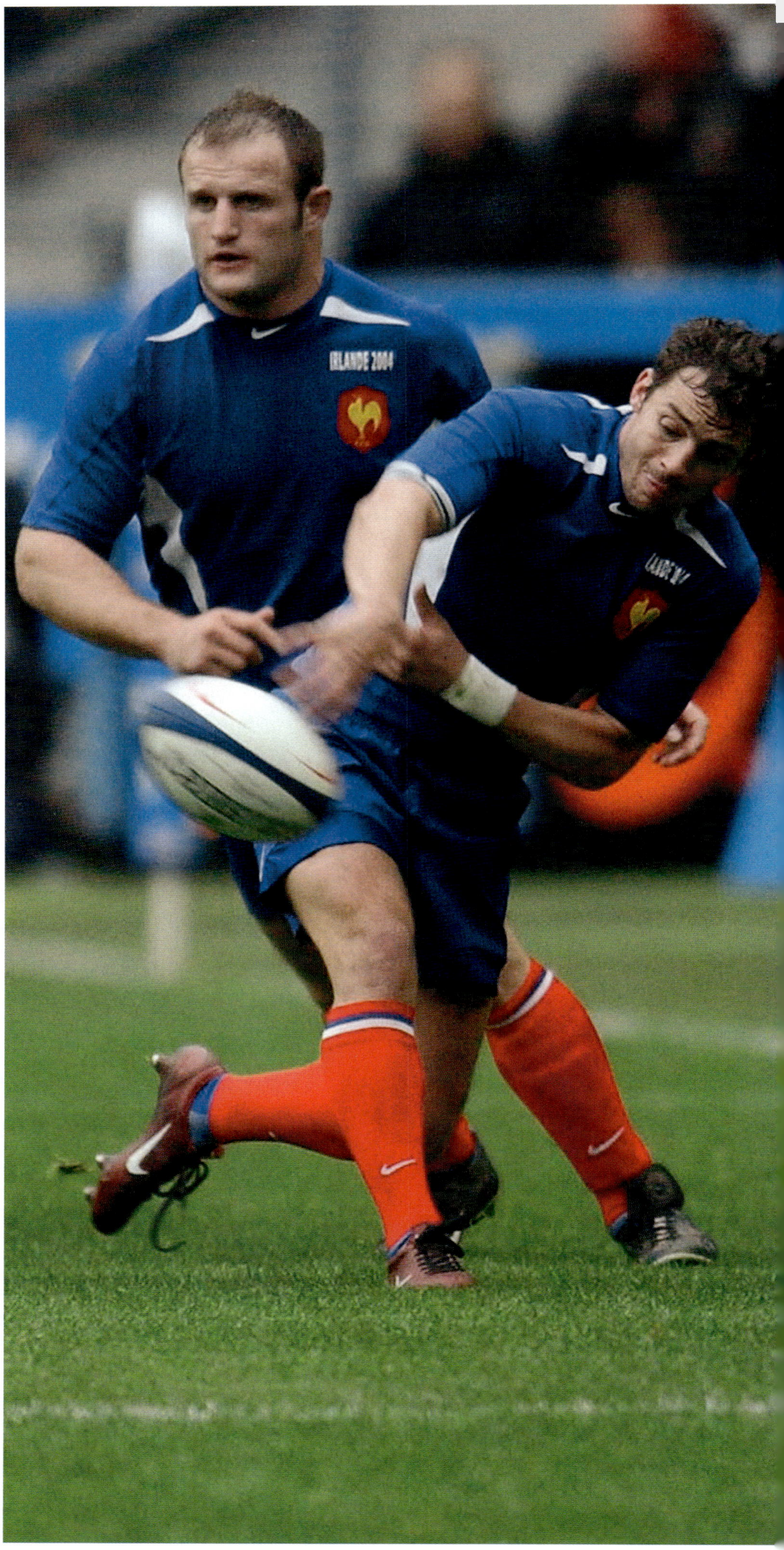

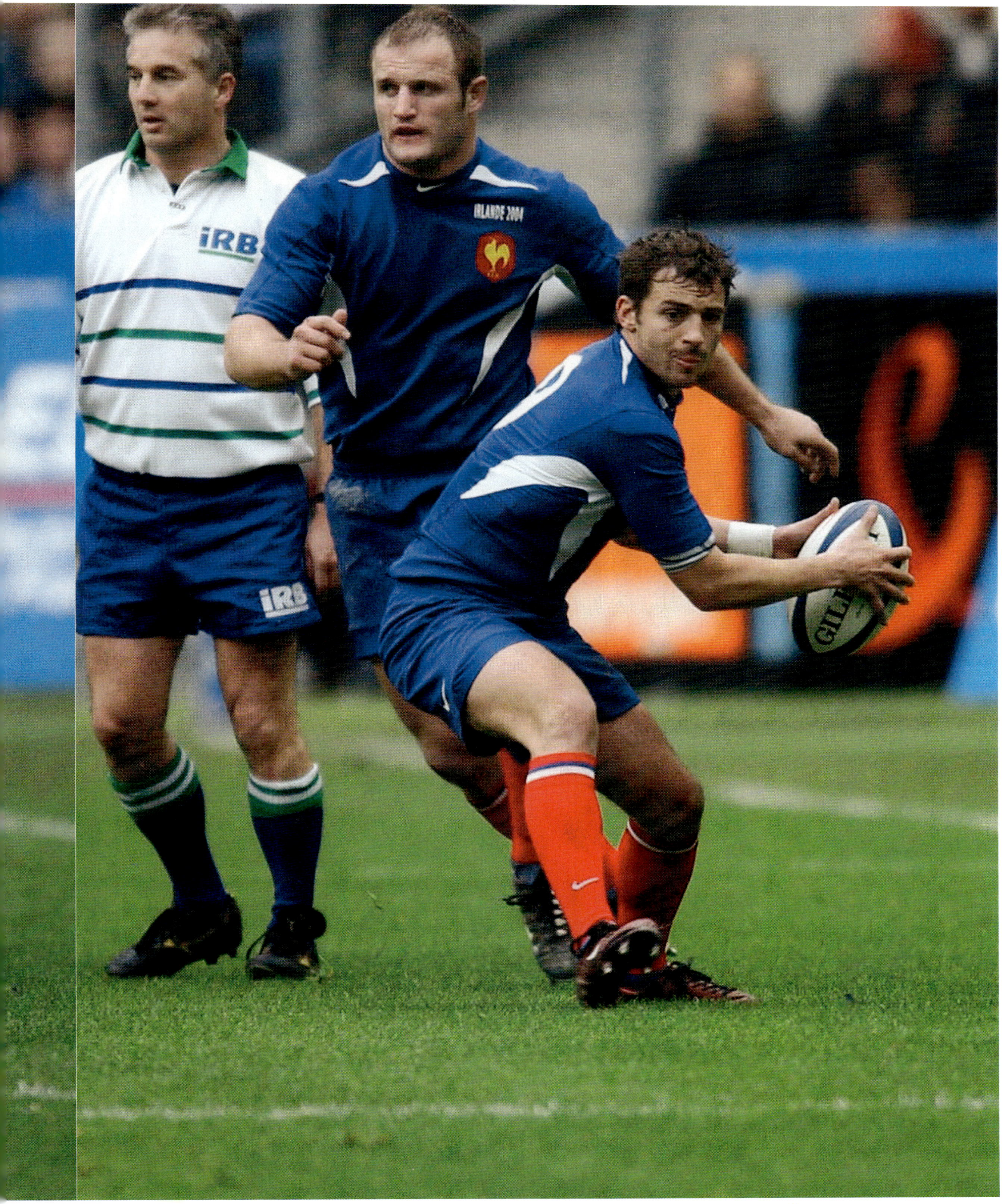
iRB
IRLANDE 2004
iRB

Coup de pied rasant

Au football, on appellerait ça une passe dans le dos du défenseur. Subtilement distillé à pleine vitesse, le coup de pied rasant est une arme offensive redoutable qu'utilisent les joueurs des lignes arrière, du demi de mêlée au trois-quarts aile. De l'intérieur du pied et en pleine course, il s'agit de glisser la balle entre deux adversaires afin qu'elle rebondisse au bout de quelques mètres, assez haut pour qu'un partenaire puisse s'en saisir dans le dos des défenseurs. Il est impossible de contrer ce coup de pied, sauf à avoir des talents innés de footballeur. On s'en sert aussi pour envoyer le ballon en touche le plus près possible de la ligne d'en-but afin de mettre l'équipe adverse sous pression. Le plus bel exemple de coup de pied rasant est l'œuvre du demi de mêlée tricolore Dimitri Yachvili effectuant au Stade de France un grand pont sur les défenseurs anglais, dans le Tournoi 2004, avant d'attraper la balle au rebond et s'en aller marquer seul.

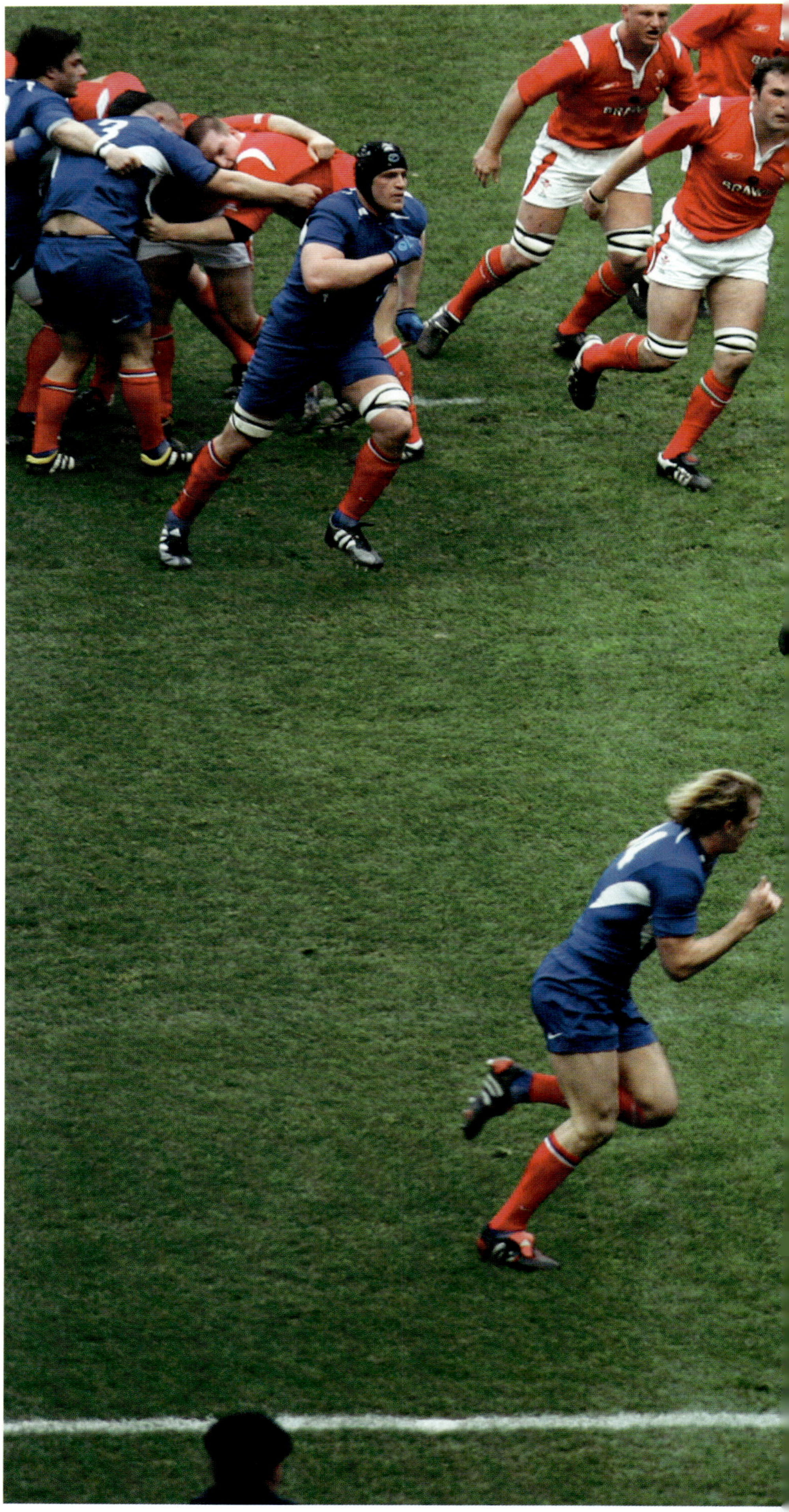

Ancien footballeur de l'OGC Nice, Dimitri Yachvili glisse subtilement le ballon au pied dans le dos de la défense galloise. Son ailier Aurélien Rougerie, démarqué le long de la ligne de touche, va chercher à s'en saisir. Yannick Nyanga et Julien Bonnaire se portent rapidement au soutien de leurs partenaires.

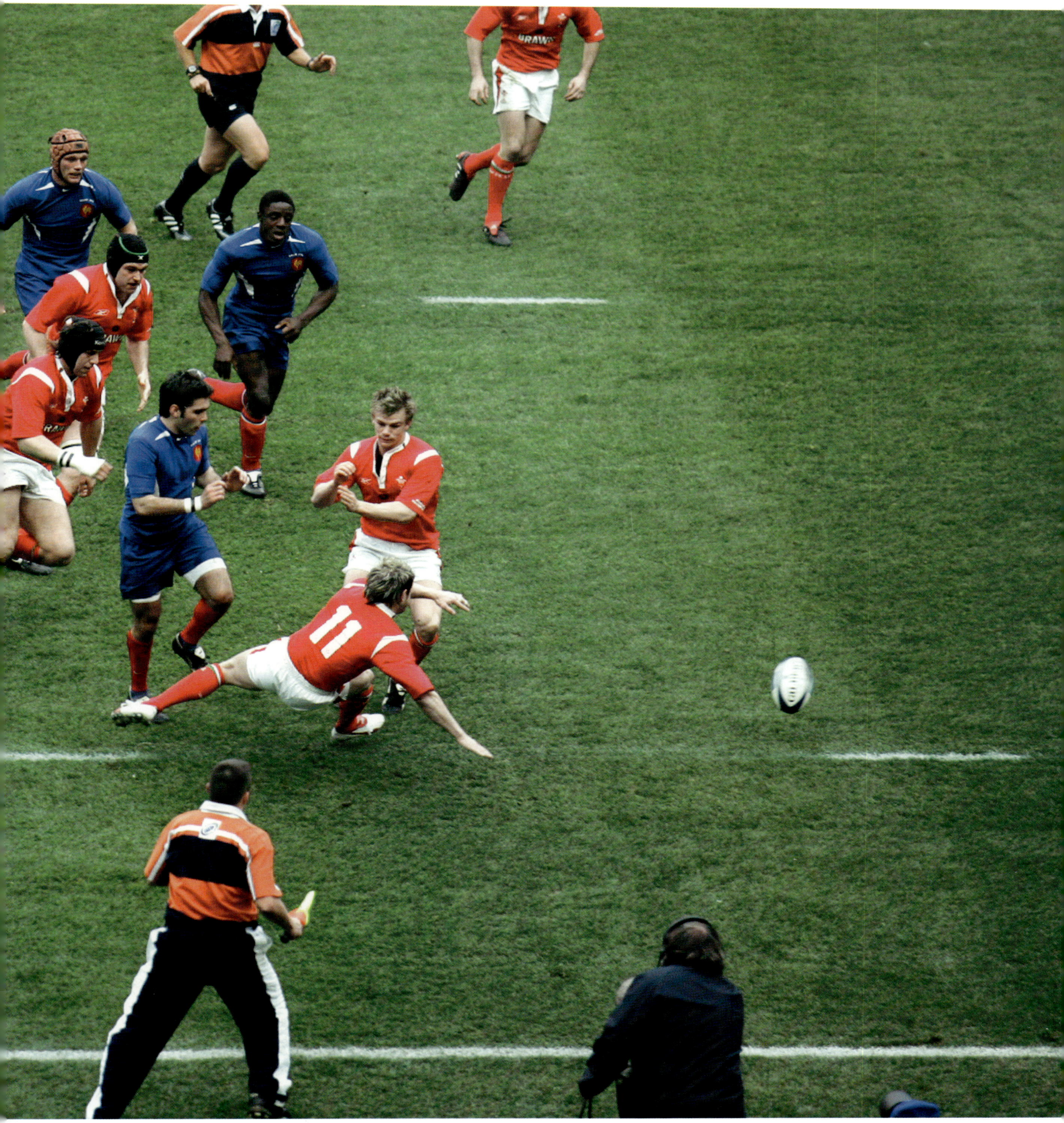

Passe croisée

Inventée par les frères Boniface à Mont-de-Marsan, reprise par Jo Maso et Jean Trillo en équipe de France, puis aujourd'hui par des joueurs du talent de Thomas Castaignède, Yannick Jauzion et Damien Traille, la passe croisée est l'expression ultime de l'art français qui consiste à mystifier les défenses. Les centres vont par paire. Ainsi le premier centre attaquant, balle en main, fait mine

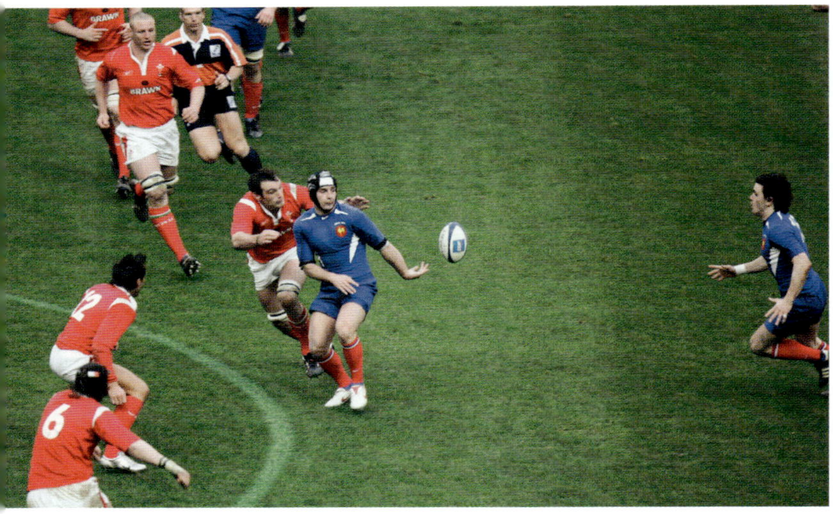

de vouloir contourner son vis-à-vis placé en défense et, dans sa course, attire le deuxième centre adverse. Son partenaire, lui, croise sa course et n'a plus qu'à tendre les bras pour recevoir la passe. Cette manœuvre demande une grande complicité, un parfait timing et une technique irréprochable. Le résultat est saisissant : l'attaquant, ainsi démarqué, perce plein champ, au milieu du terrain, comme une dague dans le dos de la défense arrêtée. Attention toutefois à bien ajuster la passe et à ne pas laisser tomber le ballon, car derrière cette combinaison à haut risque, le contre peut être dévastateur...

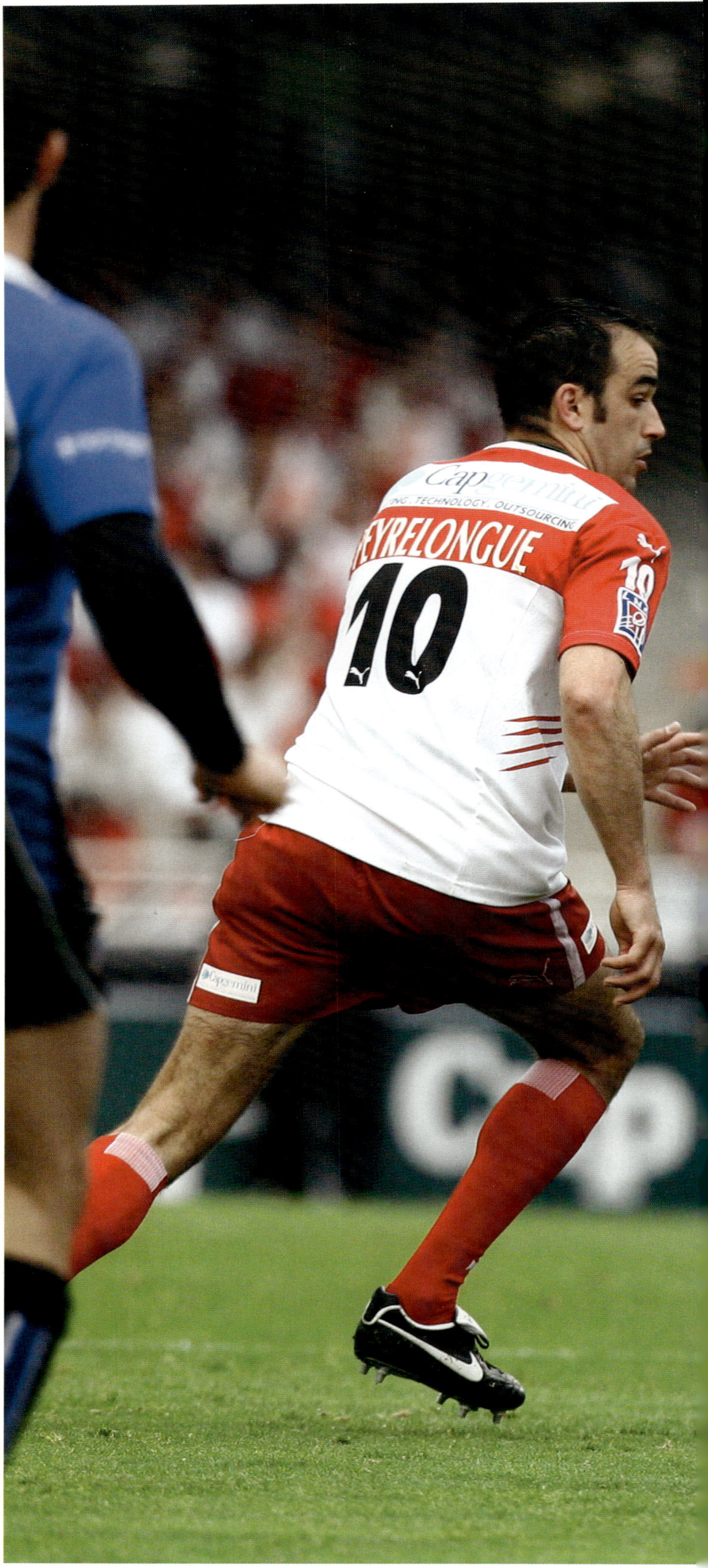

Les centres ne sont pas seuls à aimer croiser la passe. Les demis d'ouverture, eux aussi, excellent dans cet art très français. Yann Delaigue (ci-dessus) pour Julien Laharrague, ou bien encore Julien Peyrelongue (n°10, maillot rouge et blanc) sous les couleurs de Biarritz, redouble avec son centre Damien Traille et plante la défense adverse.

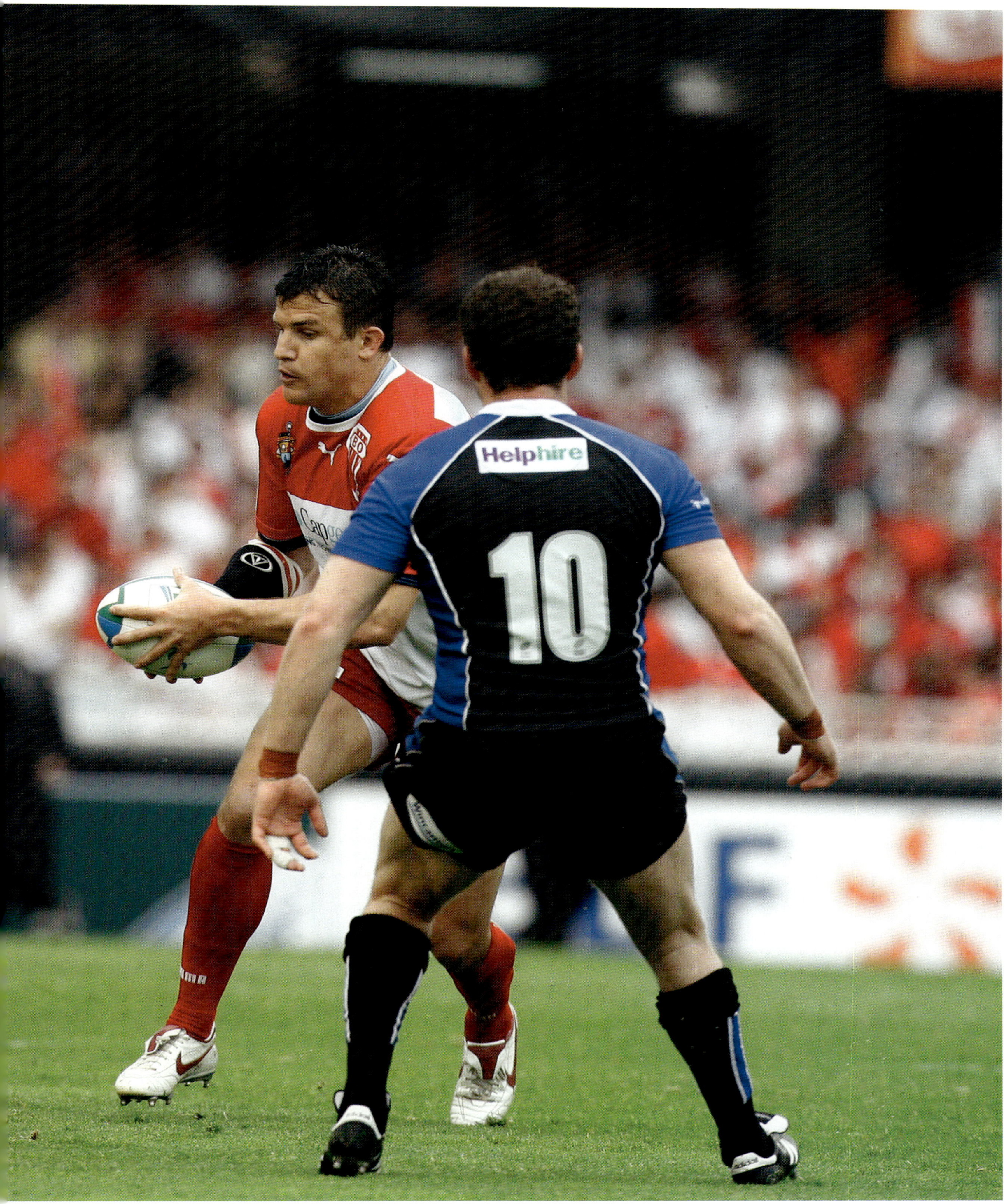
Helphire
10

Crochet intérieur

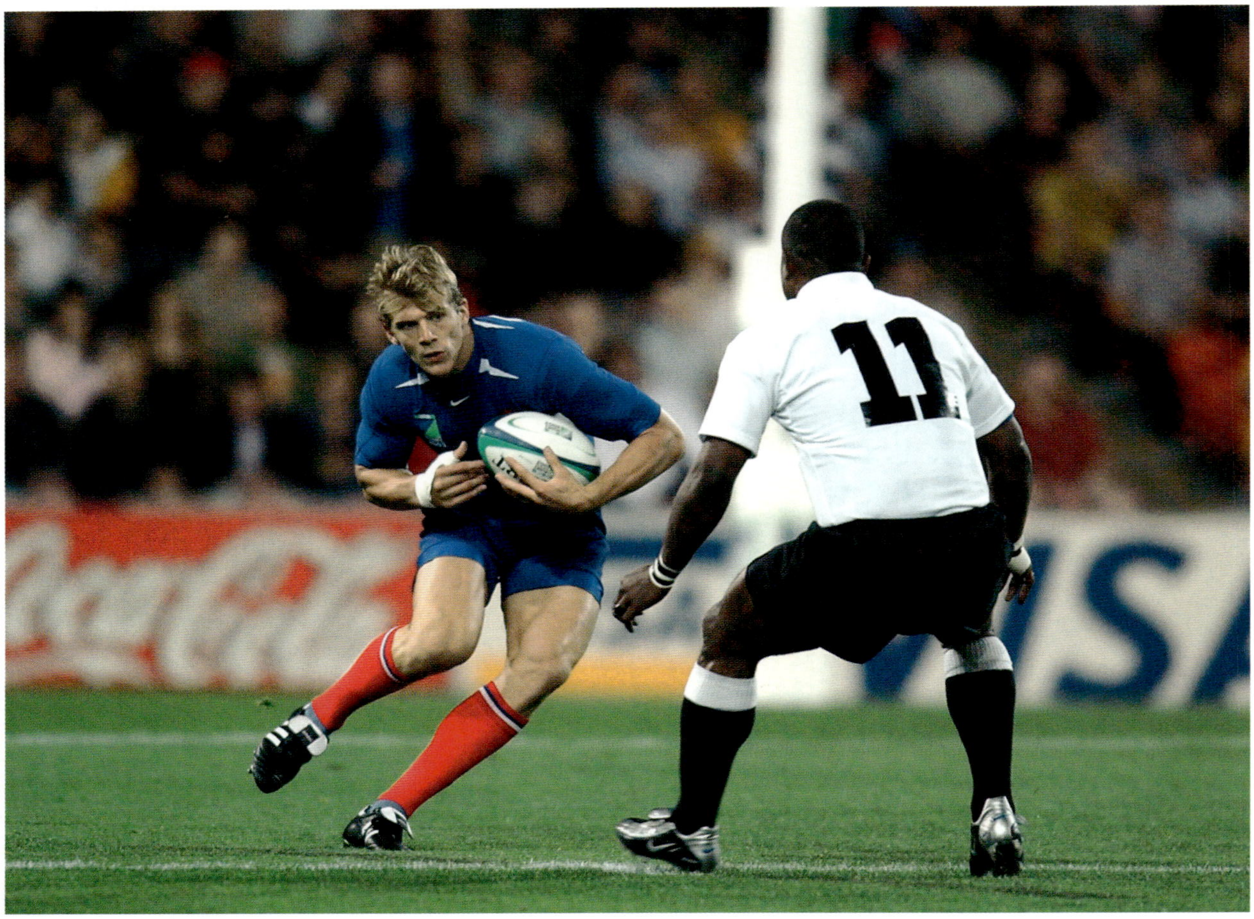

Si la passe croisée implique une parfaite liaison entre deux attaquants, le crochet intérieur, lui, illustre l'inspiration individuelle. Il s'agit d'un changement de direction brutal, un contre-pied. Pour avoir côtoyé de près, à l'entraînement et en match, la plupart des très grands joueurs de rugby de ces vingt-cinq dernières saisons, j'avoue que personne ne m'a autant impressionné que l'ouvreur du Racing Club de France des années 90, Franck Mesnel, quand il arrachait d'énormes mottes sur la pelouse du stade Yves Du-Manoir de Colombes à chacun de ses crochets. Il possédait des appuis de sprinter sous des cuisses d'haltérophile, et la puissance dégagée par ses foulées n'avait d'égal que son engagement physique au plus près des défenses.

Lors de la Coupe du monde 2003, l'ailier tricolore Aurélien Rougerie, ci-dessus, tente de feinter son vis-à-vis fidjien Rupeni Caucaunibuca, lequel ne mord pas au piège et reste bien campé sur ses appuis. En revanche, photo de droite, l'ailier namibien (n° 11) est battu par le contre-pied de l'Australien Lote Tuquiri.

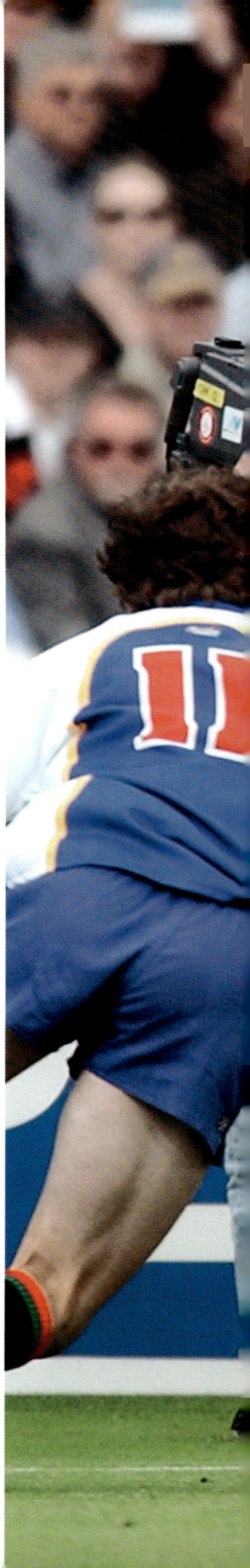

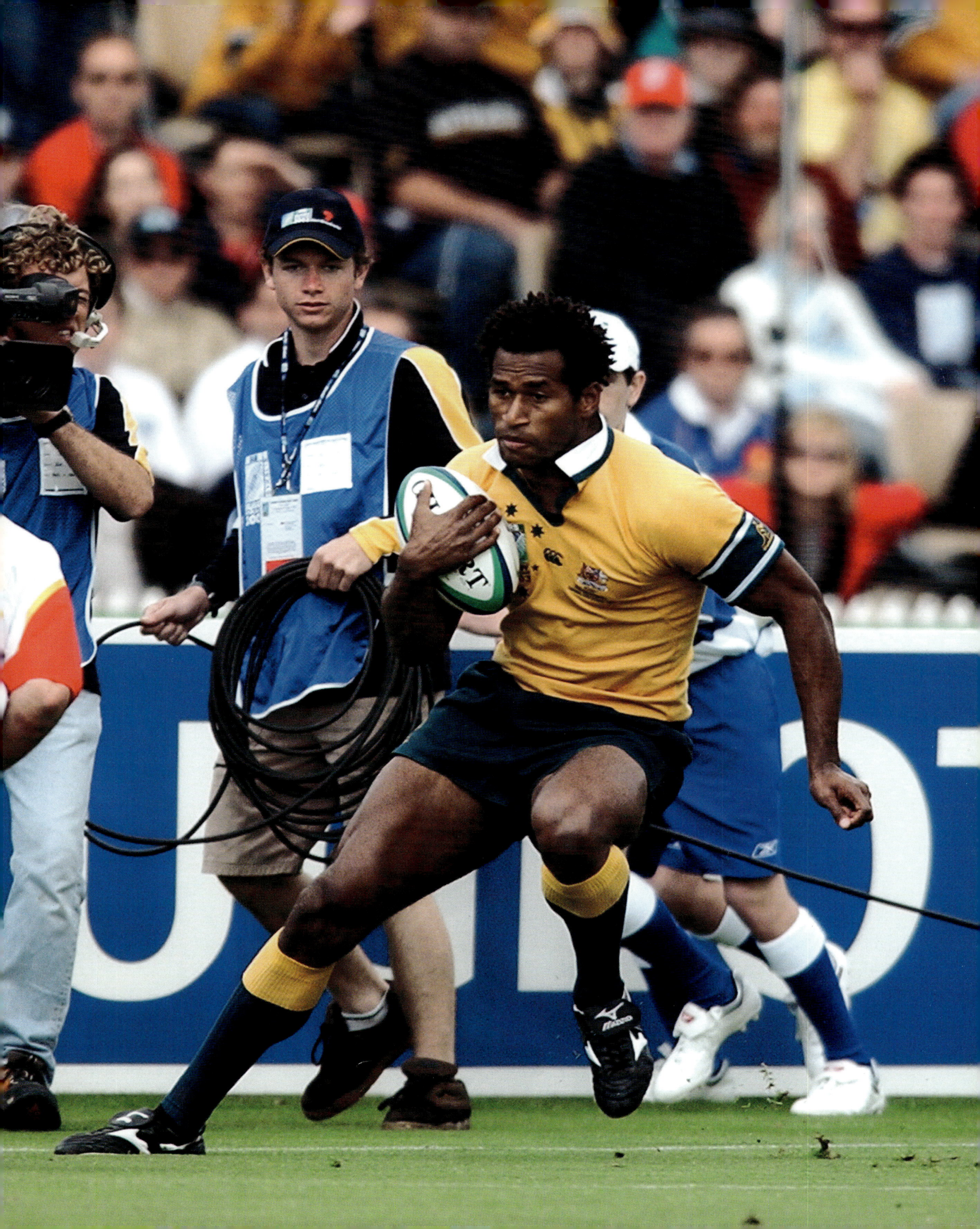

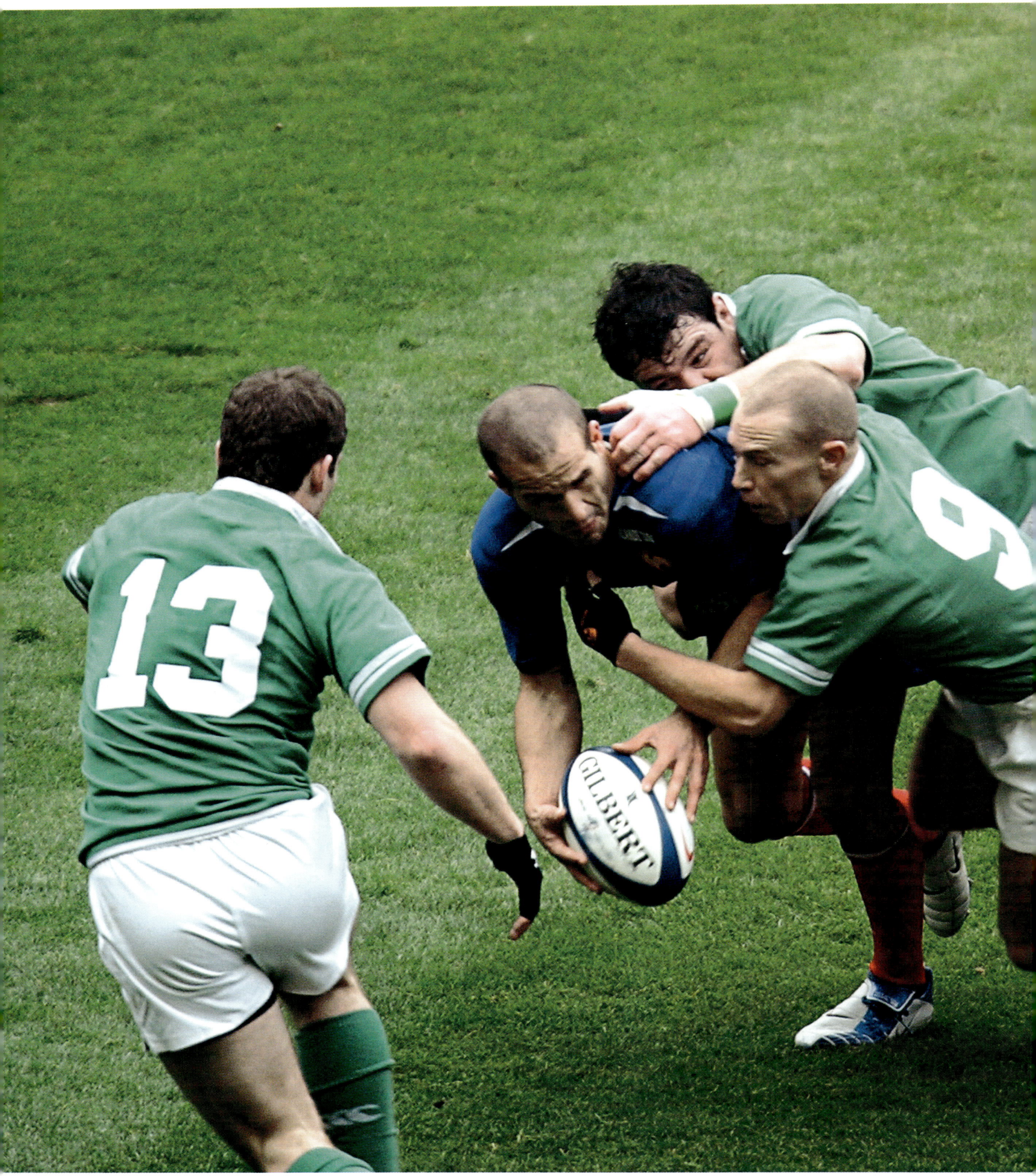
13
9
GILBERT

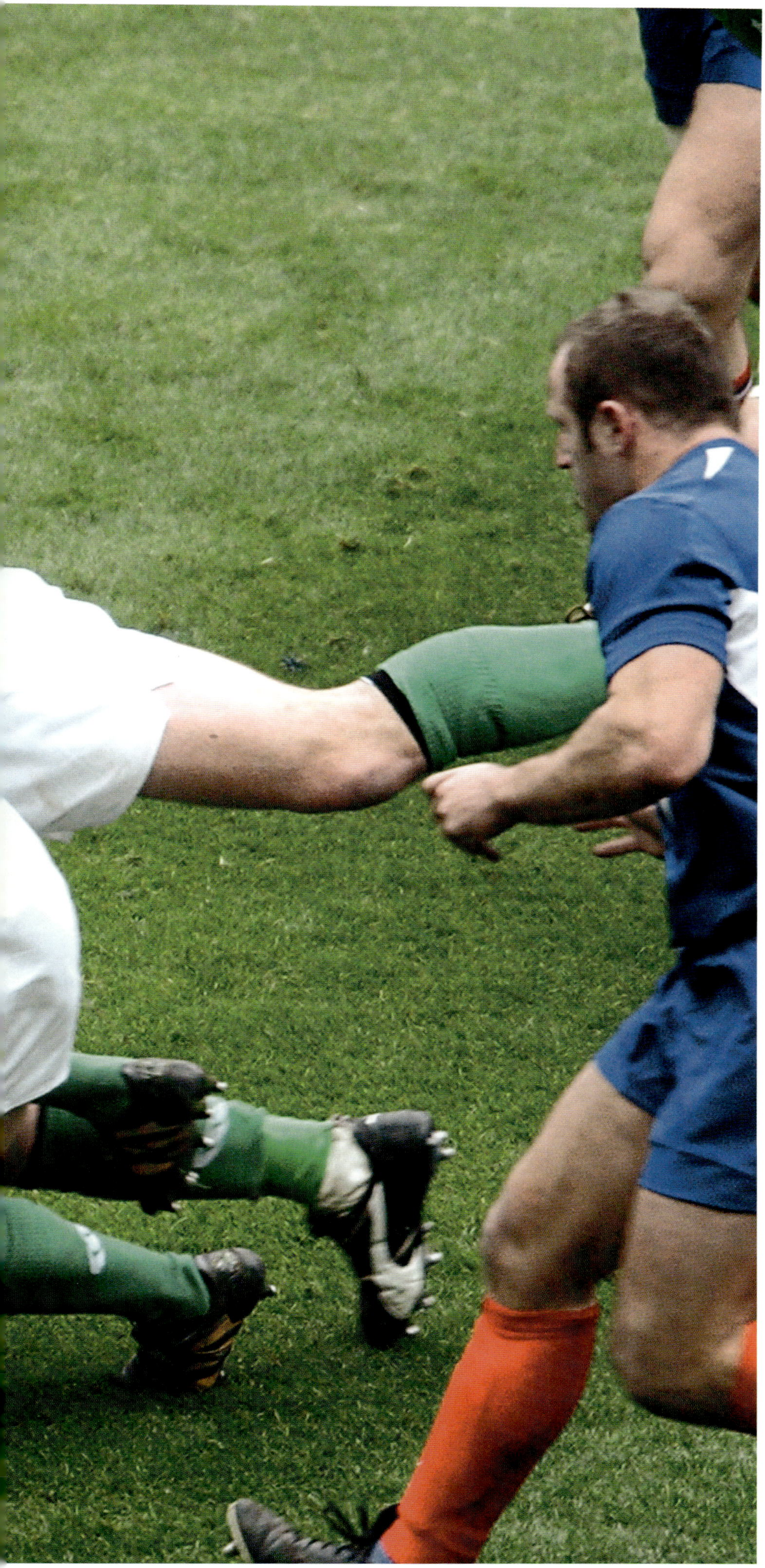

Faire vivre la balle

On peut dater la naissance du rugby moderne à la capacité qu'eurent les attaquants, à partir des années 80, à venir jouer dans les défenses, c'est-à-dire provoquer le plaquage et, en dégageant les bras pour s'offrir au contact, faire vivre la balle en la passant malgré la violence du choc et de l'impact. Longtemps, le plaquage fut considéré comme un obstacle à la continuité du jeu dans la mesure où il bloquait les velléités offensives. Mais en parvenant à passer la balle au contact, les attaquants se mirent en position d'aller défier les défenseurs sans arrêter le jeu, et ce fut une vraie révolution technique et tactique. Jeu d'évitement où il était impensable de se faire plaquer balle en mains, le rugby est donc devenu une science de l'affrontement, une façon de défier les défenses en perforant au cœur des dispositifs les plus hermétiques. Conséquence de cette propension récente à annihiler le plaquage en allant le provoquer, les lignes se sont ainsi resserrées, les joueurs aussi, qu'ils soient partenaires ou adversaires.

Le demi d'ouverture Frédéric Michalak, malgré le plaquage de deux Irlandais, parvient à faire vivre le ballon en le passant à son partenaire, le talonneur William Servat.

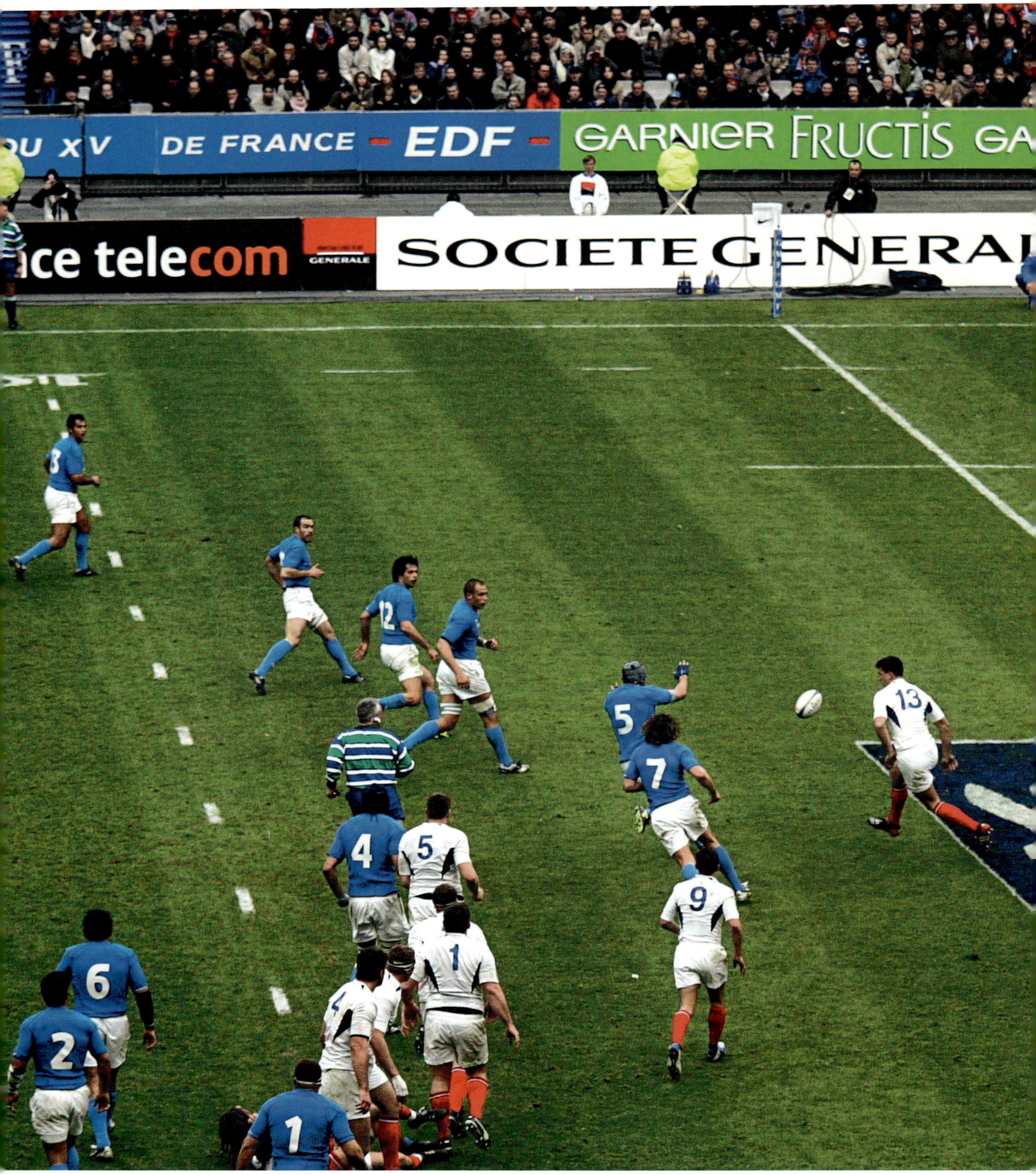
DU XV
DE FRANCE
EDF
GARNIER FRUCTIS
ce telecom
SOCIETE GENERAL

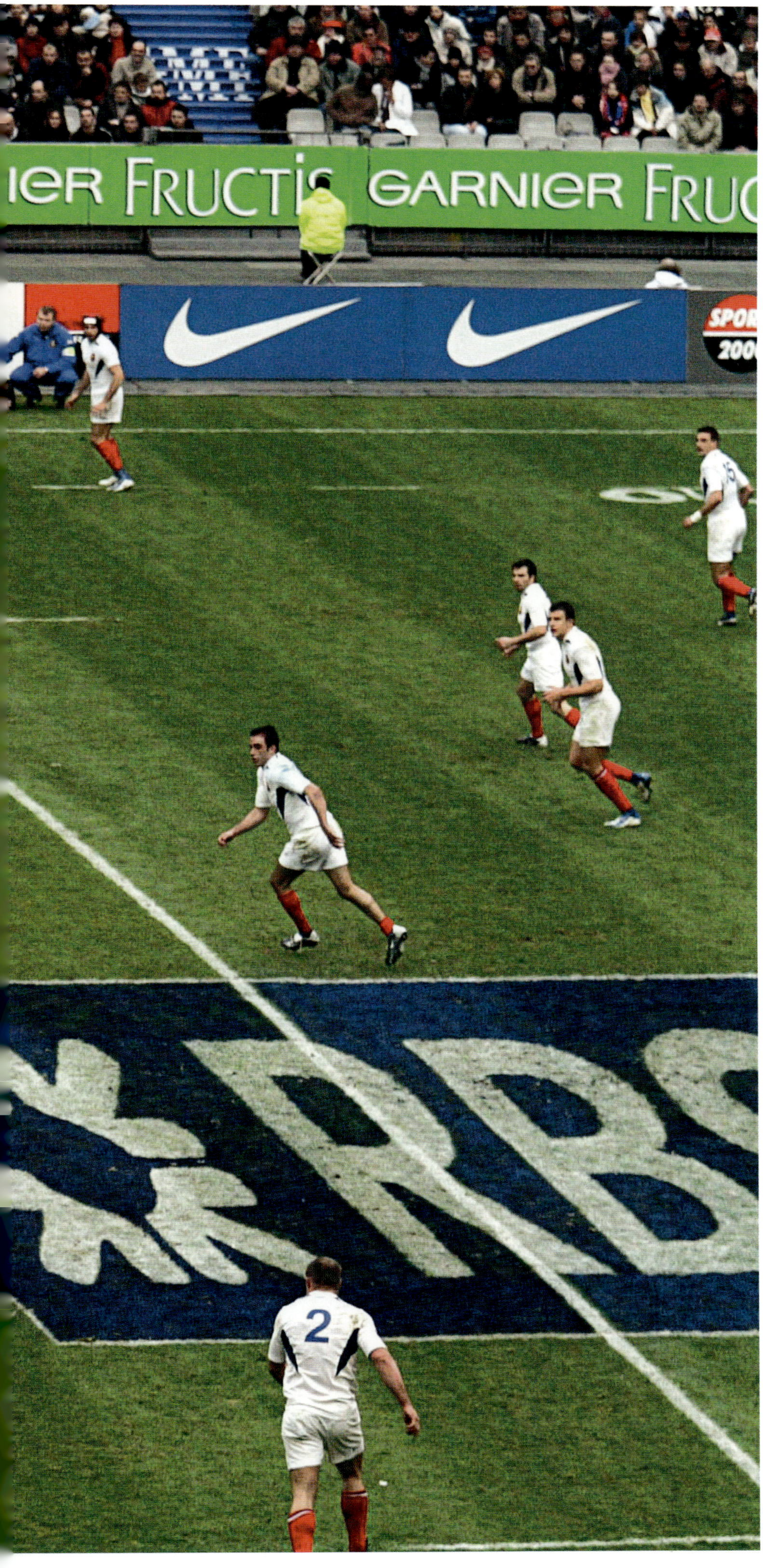

Coup de pied tactique

Grand stratège du rugby gallois au faîte de sa gloire, l'ouvreur Barry John aimait répéter qu'« une belle attaque à la main se prépare toujours au pied », ce qui n'est pas aussi paradoxal qu'il n'y paraît. En effet, avant de se risquer à passer le ballon jusqu'à l'aile, il vaut mieux au préalable faire reculer les défenseurs, les obliger à couvrir leur base arrière. Pour cela, rien de mieux qu'une bonne série de coups de pieds tactiques, de transversales dosées dans le dos des ailiers, de tirs croisés qui incitent l'arrière à veiller sur son en-but. Qui dit coup de pied tactique dit précision du tir, maîtrise de l'effet donné au ballon, et surtout connivence de toute l'équipe afin d'exercer une pression sur le réceptionnaire, l'obligeant à se débarrasser de la balle au plus vite. Aujourd'hui, les grands stratèges au poste de demi d'ouverture, comme l'étaient Pierre Albaladejo, Jean-Patrick Lescarboura ou Thierry Lacroix, sont rares dans le rugby français. Citons Yann Delaigue, dont la carrière touche à sa fin, et le jeune Lionel Beauxis, champion du monde en 2006 avec l'équipe de France des moins de vingt et un ans, qui ne devrait pas tarder à se faire un nom.

France-Italie, au Stade de France. Le trois-quarts centre Yannick Jauzion tente un lob, petit coup de pied dosé qu'il va essayer de récupérer derrière la défense. Ses partenaires sont placés en profondeur pour attaquer à la main et son coup de pied tactique prend les défenseurs à contre-pied.

Marque!

Il n'y a plus beaucoup de points communs entre le jeu tel qu'il était pratiqué en 1871 lors du premier test-match international et la discipline sportive que nous apprécions aujourd'hui dans le Tri-Nations et le Tournoi. Un geste, pourtant, nous rappelle l'ère antédiluvienne : le coup de pied à suivre tapé haut dans le ciel et ponctué à sa chute d'un cri : « marque ! » pour signaler qu'il est en possession de cette balle bottée. À ce moment, il est protégé par la règle qui veut qu'on ne plaque pas un joueur qui vient de crier « marque ! » J'aime l'idée qu'à la montée de balle, on puisse imaginer le premier rugbyman, les yeux rivés sur la balle, s'engager dans l'espace après s'être échappé du magma. Il profite, nez au vent, de cet instant de liberté où le temps est suspendu. En rugby, opter pour la verticalité, c'est se libérer des pesanteurs à moindres frais. À la chute du ballon, l'ultime défenseur ose l'arrêt de volée, protégé par la règle qui veut que personne ne puisse le déséquilibrer lorsqu'il monte en l'air pour capter l'objet de tous les désirs.

Entouré de ses partenaires Yannick Nyanga (n °6) et Damien Traille, l'arrière Thomas Castaignède effectue un arrêt de volée, c'est-à-dire qu'il décolle du sol pour attraper le ballon avant les Anglais et crie en même temps : « marque ! » De cette façon, l'adversaire ne peut pas le plaquer. Devenu intouchable, il peut alors relancer ou dégager en touche, afin de repousser le danger.

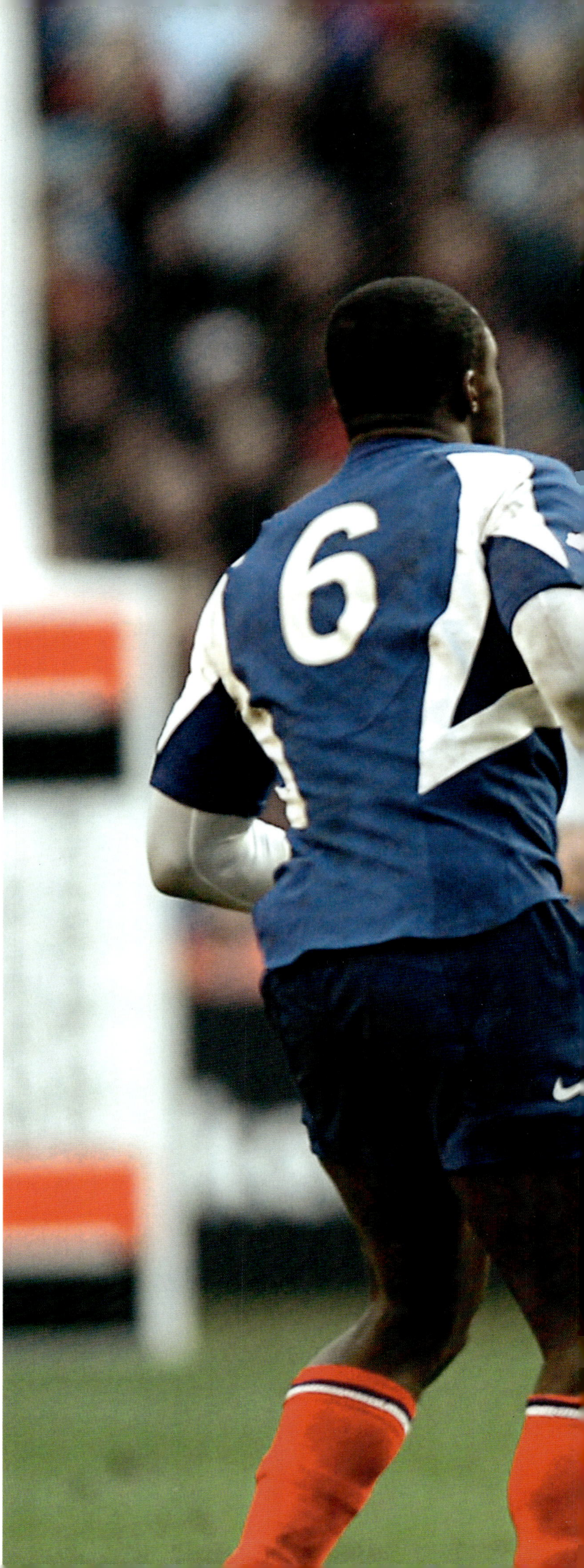

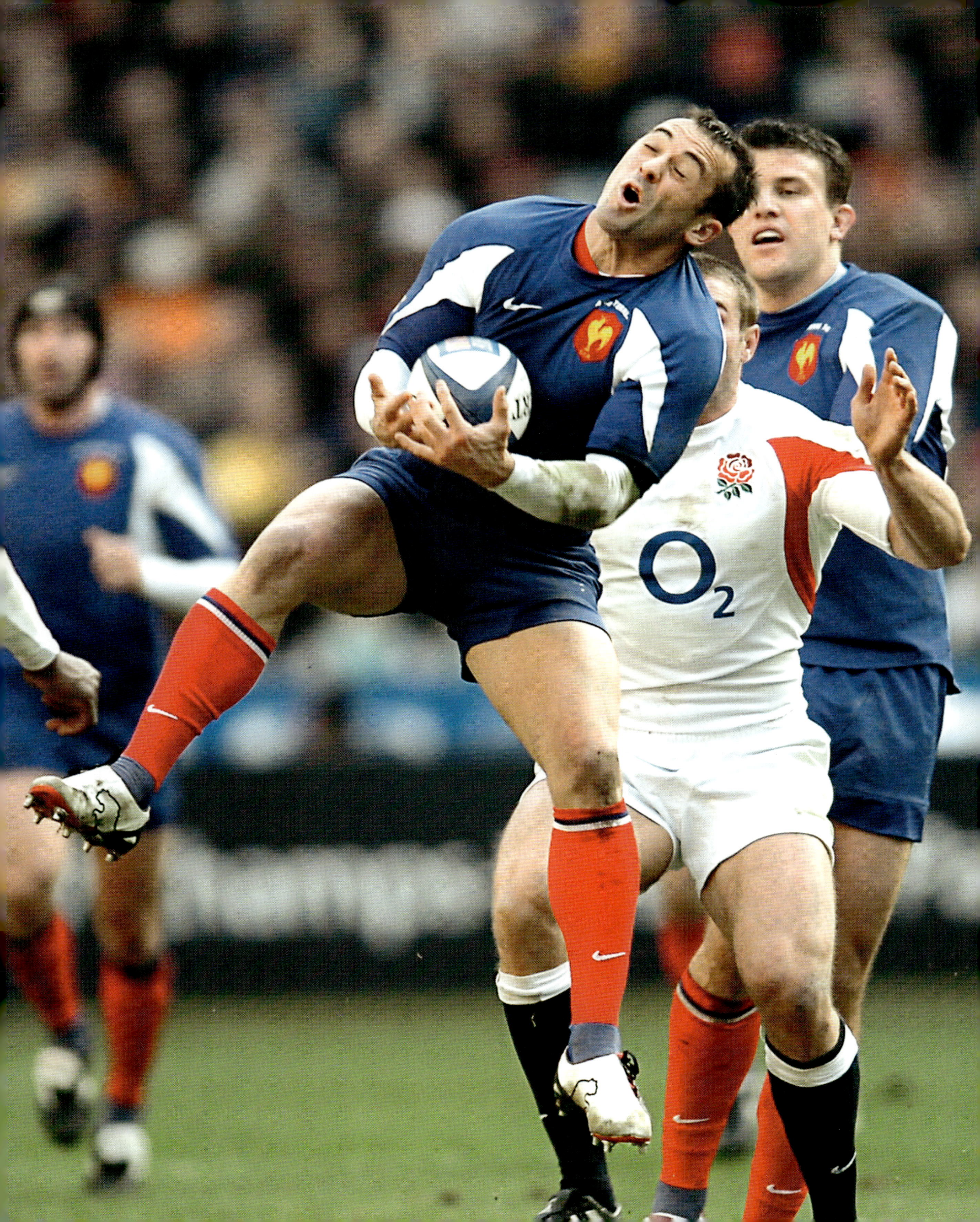
O2

Carton jaune ou rouge

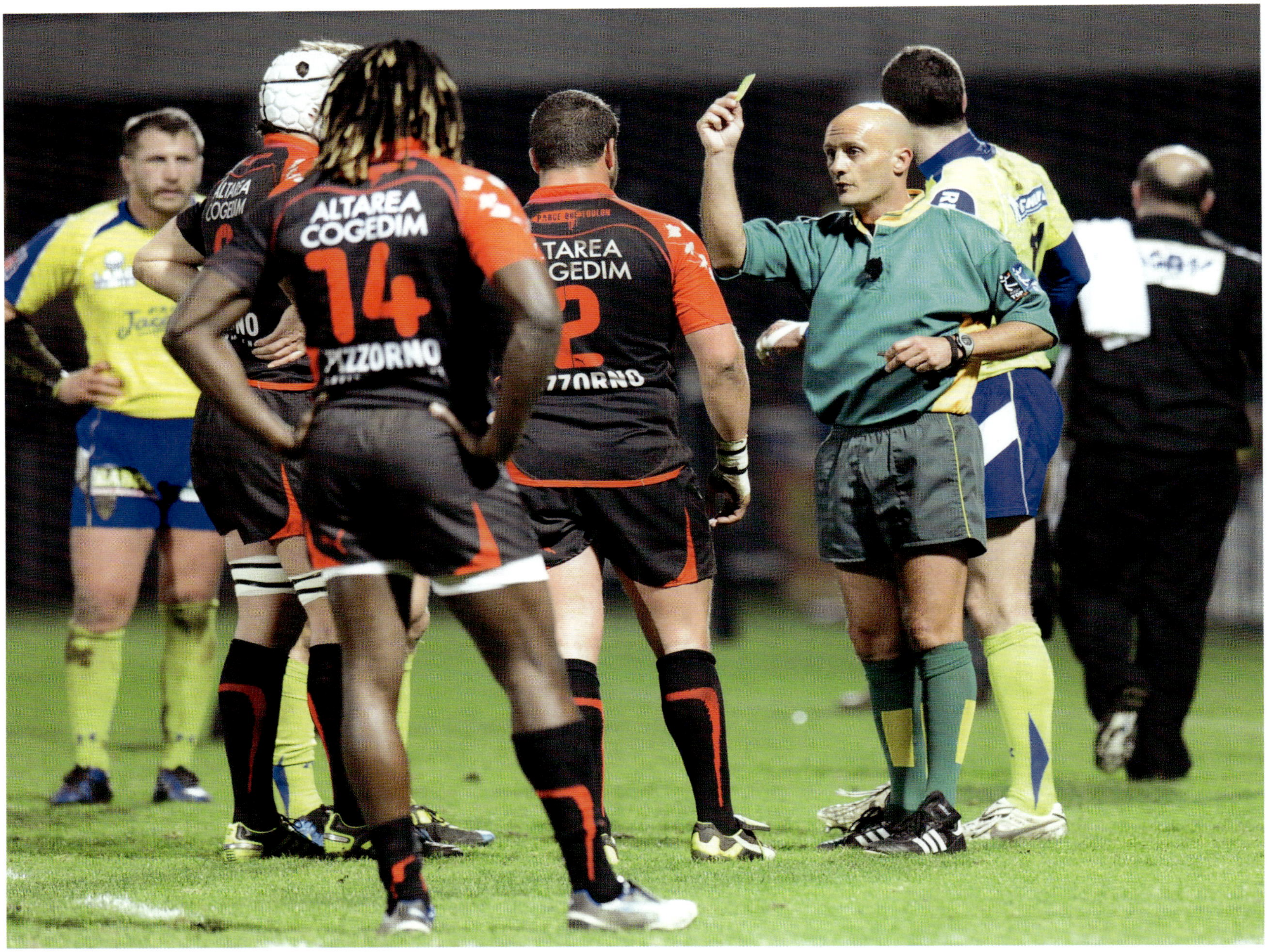

Peut être exclu du terrain temporairement, c'est-à-dire pendant dix minutes, un joueur coupable d'une action d'anti-jeu, d'une brutalité, d'une action dangereuse ou d'une faute technique intentionnelle. L'arbitre lui adresse alors un carton jaune et il ne peut pas être remplacé, sauf s'il s'agit d'un joueur de la première ligne. Dans ce cas, son entraîneur fera sortir un joueur et entrer un pilier remplaçant afin que les mêlées puissent se disputer. L'exclusion définitive, elle, est signalée par un carton rouge qui sanctionne un geste interdit, un acte déloyal ou un second carton jaune. Ces décisions, prises en cours de match par l'arbitre, sont extrêmement pénalisantes : en effet, l'équipe du joueur fautif se retrouve à quatorze joueurs, au lieu de quinze. De triste mémoire, on se souvient, par exemple, qu'en demi-finale de la Coupe du monde 2003, les exclusions temporaires successives de Christophe Dominici et de Serge Betsen avaient coûté la victoire au Quinze de France, face à l'Angleterre, à Sydney.

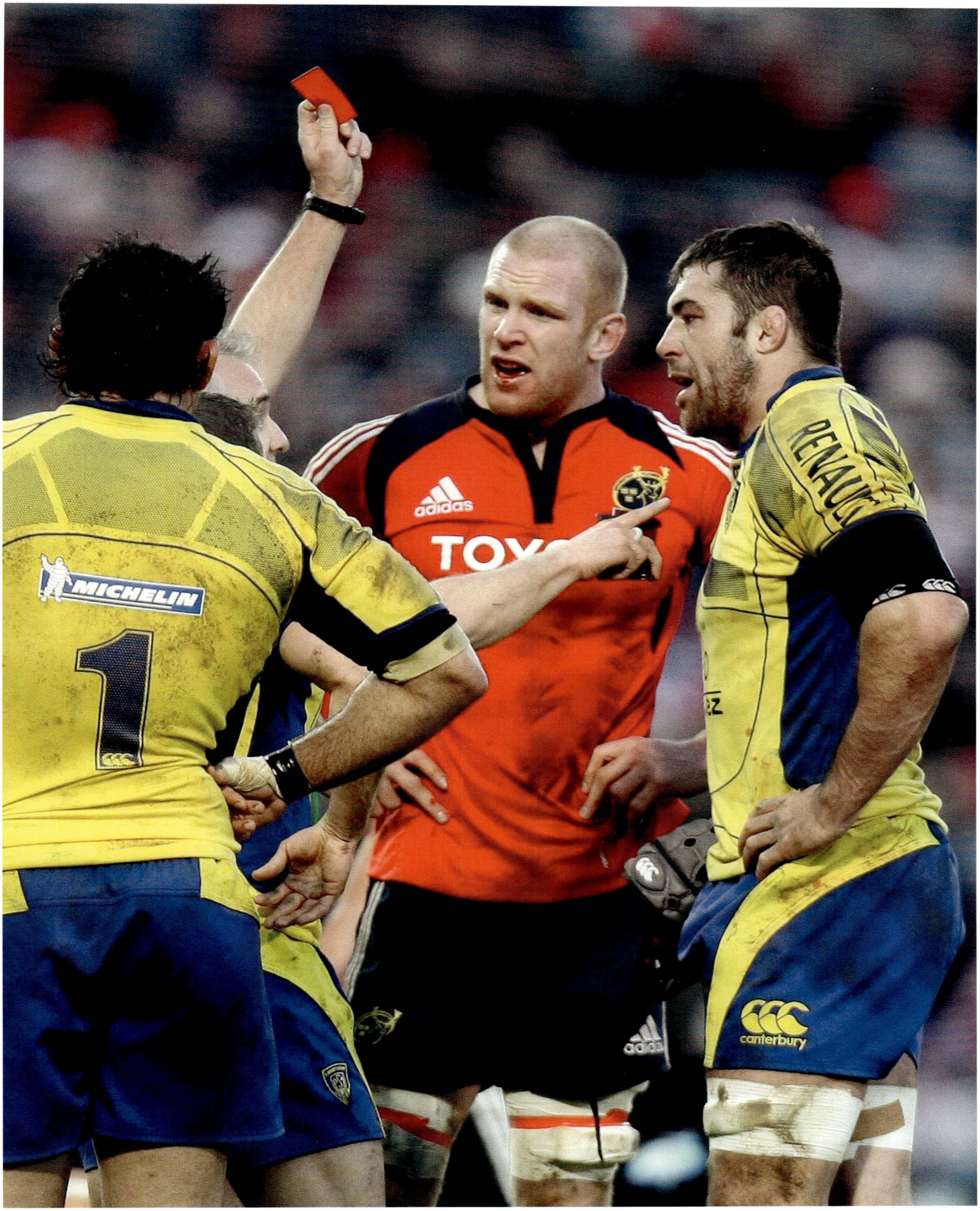
MICHELIN
1
adidas
canterbury

Tirs au but

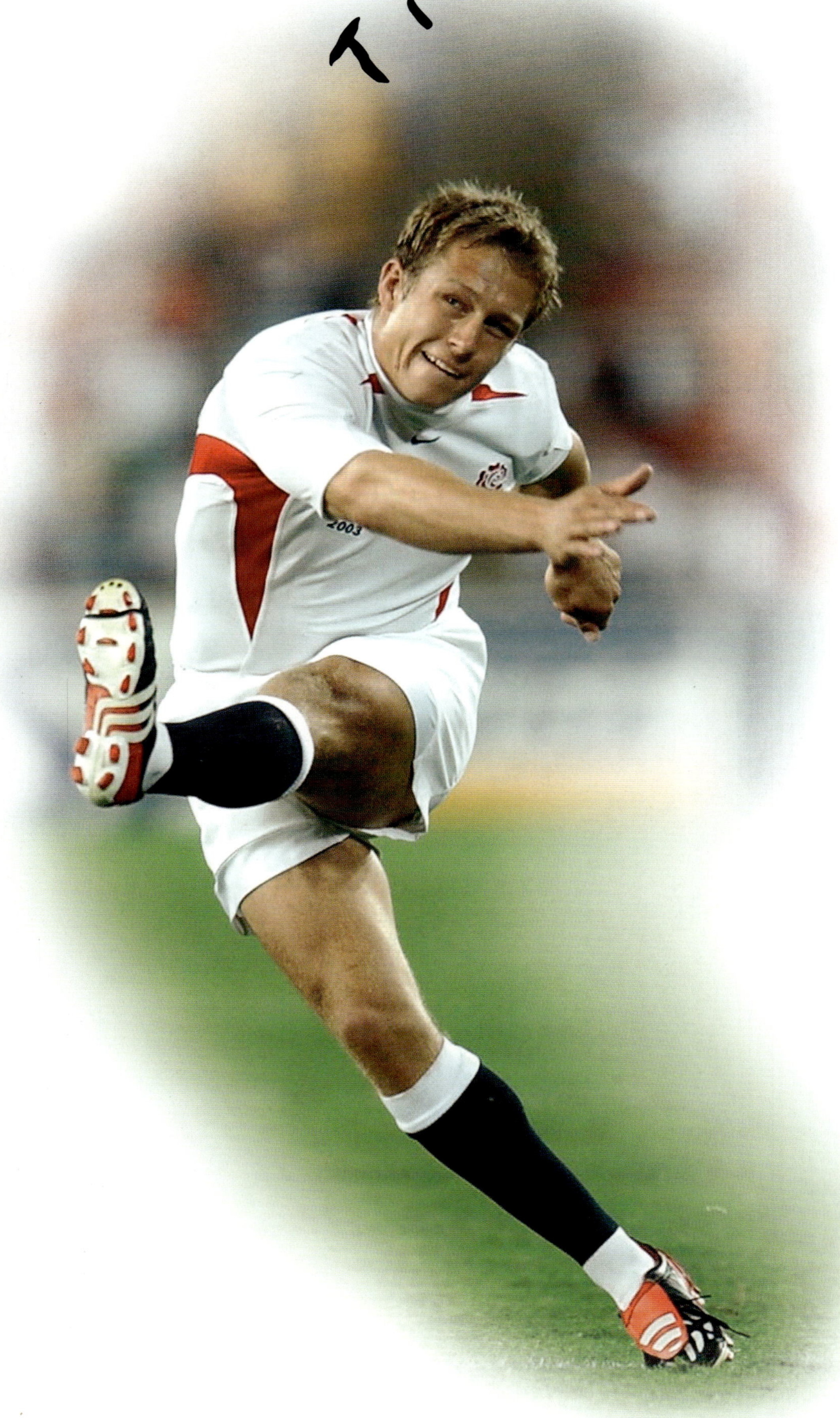

Il faut po-si-ti-ver ! Surtout quand le poids d'un but de pénalité dans le destin d'un match pèse entièrement sur les épaules du buteur. Tirer au but est une question d'état d'esprit, de mental, de concentration, et pas seulement de technique. Seul dans sa bulle, un buteur travaille sa respiration afin d'évacuer la fatigue et se relâche le plus possible. Il fixe les poteaux, puis le ballon, ce qui lui permet de se focaliser sur son geste et de ne pas se laisser distraire. Il apprécie ainsi la distance qui sépare la balle des poteaux et se prépare à doser son coup de pied. Il sent le vent, sa force et sa direction, et mesure si la brise sera un frein ou un allié. Chaque buteur a ses propres marques, sa routine, ses habitudes. Aujourd'hui, il tape en fauchant, comme un footballeur. Mais il se sert aussi d'éléments techniques propres au golf : le regard fixé sur le point d'impact après la frappe, les bras écartés en recherche d'équilibre, la jambe de frappe qui reste en suspens pour mieux diriger la balle, le bassin placé parallèlement aux poteaux pour éviter la rotation et l'effet de balancier.

Le but de pénalité vaut trois points, tandis que la transformation, effectuée après qu'un joueur de l'équipe a marqué un essai, ne procure que deux points.

Un gaucher, l'ouvreur anglais Jonny Wilkinson, héros de la Coupe du monde 2003, et un droitier, le Français Frédéric Michalak, dans l'exercice du tir au but. Le ballon est posé sur un tee *afin que le buteur puisse frapper l'ovale par en dessous et le faire monter haut pour qu'il passe au-dessus de la barre transversale. Le regard du buteur est d'abord fixé sur le ballon puis suit sa trajectoire. Noter la position des bras, qui maintiennent le joueur en équilibre.*

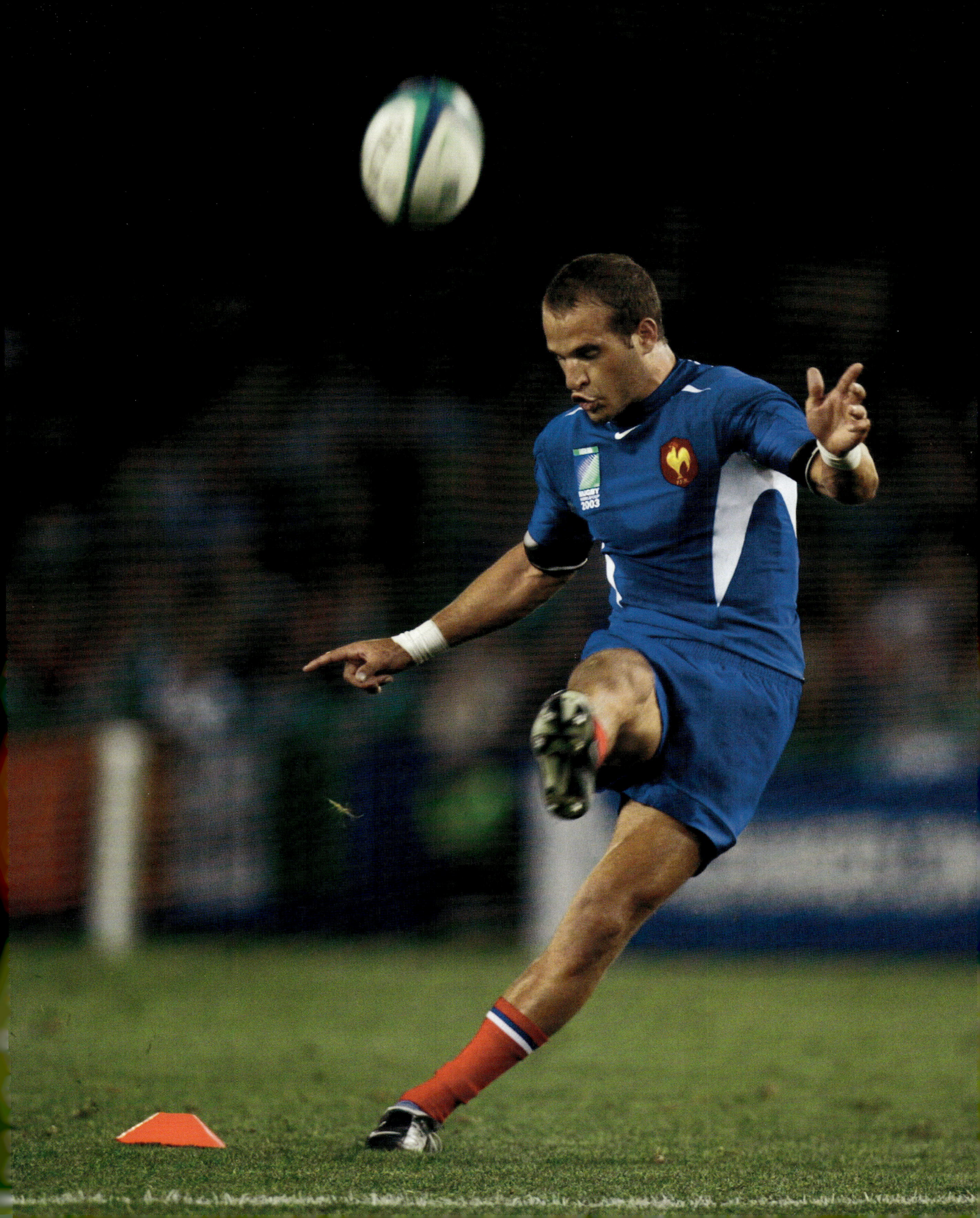
RUGBY
2003

Supporteurs

Une famille élargie, qui peut être touchante quand elle déborde d'émotion mais aussi franchement désagréable quand elle conspue sans discernement. Aux connaisseurs fidèles qui suivent leur équipe partout où elle se déplace et respectent l'adversaire, s'ajoutent désormais des sympathisants occasionnels qui viennent voir un match comme on va au spectacle, c'est-à-dire en exigeant d'en avoir pour leur argent. Les arènes bétonnées remplies d'un public hétéroclite succèdent maintenant aux tribunes de bois garnies de passionnés. Mais dans son ensemble, mis à part quelques excités plus bêtes que méchants, le supporteur de rugby sait reconnaître la valeur de l'adversaire, encourager les siens, relativiser la défaite comme la victoire. À l'issue des grands matches de championnat de France ou des rencontres du Tournoi des Six Nations, il n'est pas rare de voir les supporteurs des deux équipes fraterniser. Et c'est bien là où se situe la beauté de ce sport.

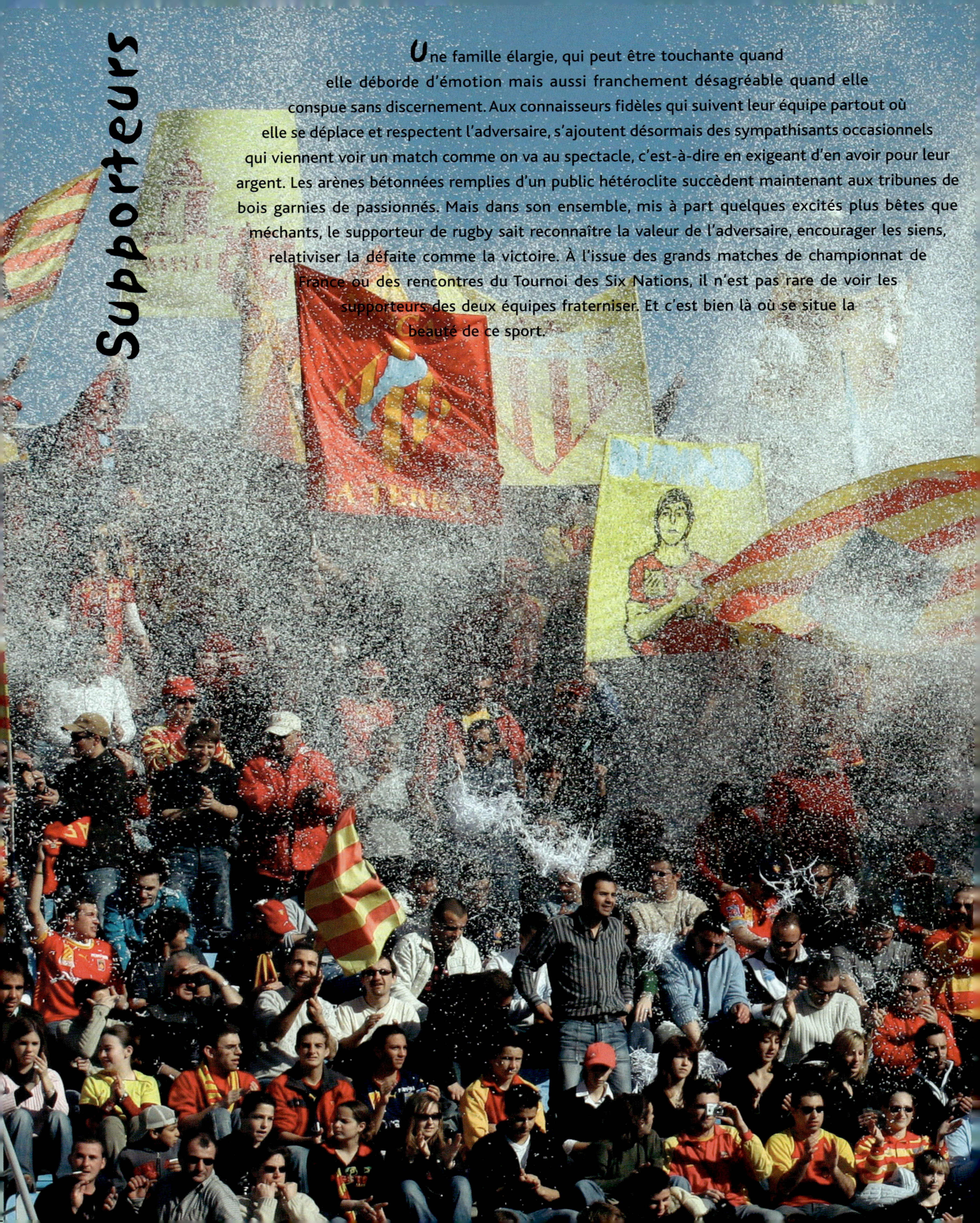

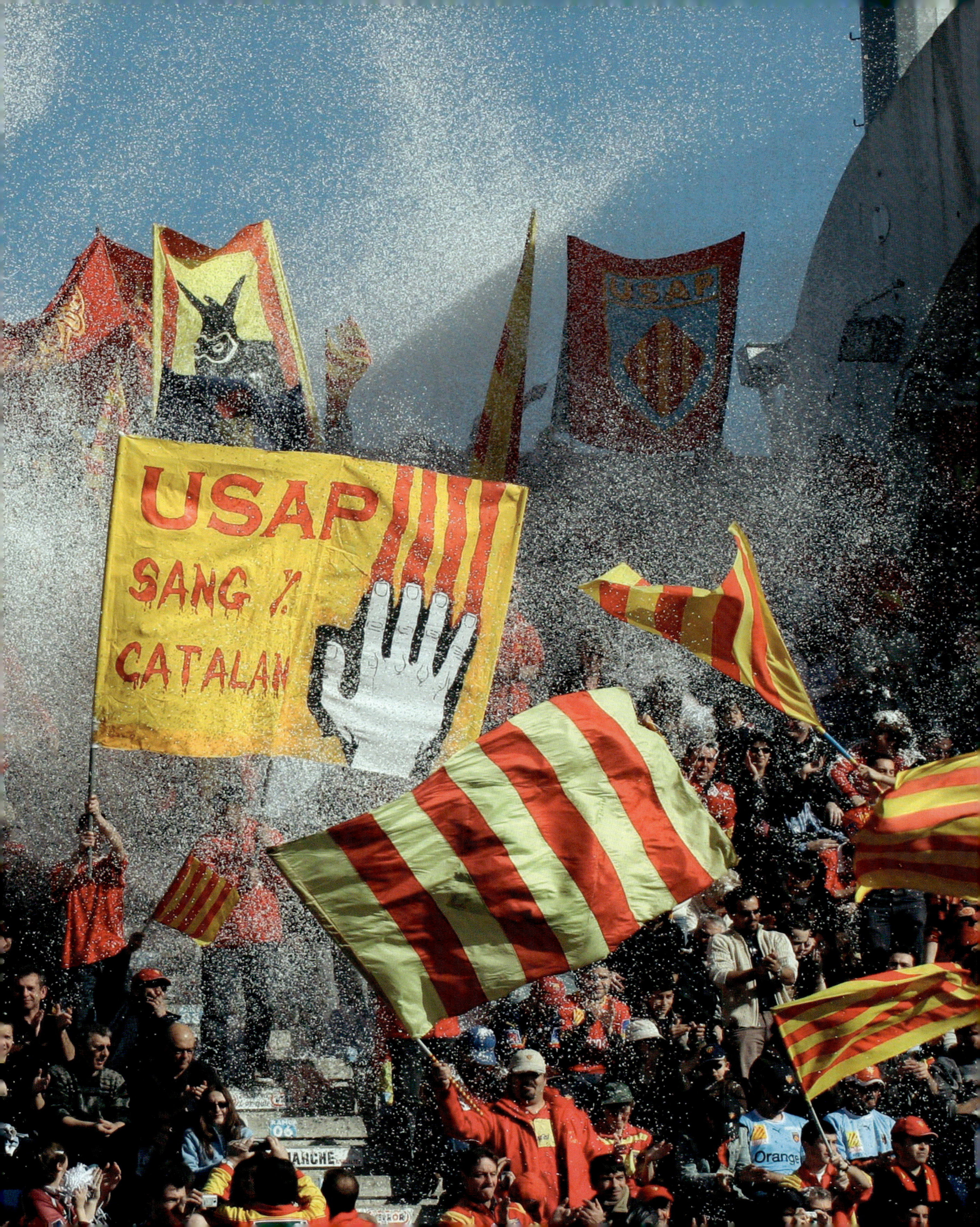
USAP
USAP
SANG %
CATALAN
Orange

Groupé-pénétrant

Construction particulièrement technique, où les participants sont obligés de rester liés, le groupé-pénétrant est un art qui consiste à cacher le ballon au cœur d'un paquet d'avants en mouvement. Il oblige souvent l'adversaire à commettre une faute : en effet, il est impossible d'arrêter un groupé-pénétrant sans l'écrouler, ce qui est formellement interdit et suivi d'une pénalité sifflée par l'arbitre. Si les Toulonnais et les Béglais le mirent à la mode il y a vingt ans, le groupé-pénétrant est aujourd'hui l'une des phases de jeu les plus prisées. Il permet de gagner un maximum de terrain sans avoir à effectuer une seule passe. Il est aussi appelé « tortue » en référence aux phalanges de l'armée romaine qui avançaient groupées, protégées de toutes parts par leurs boucliers.

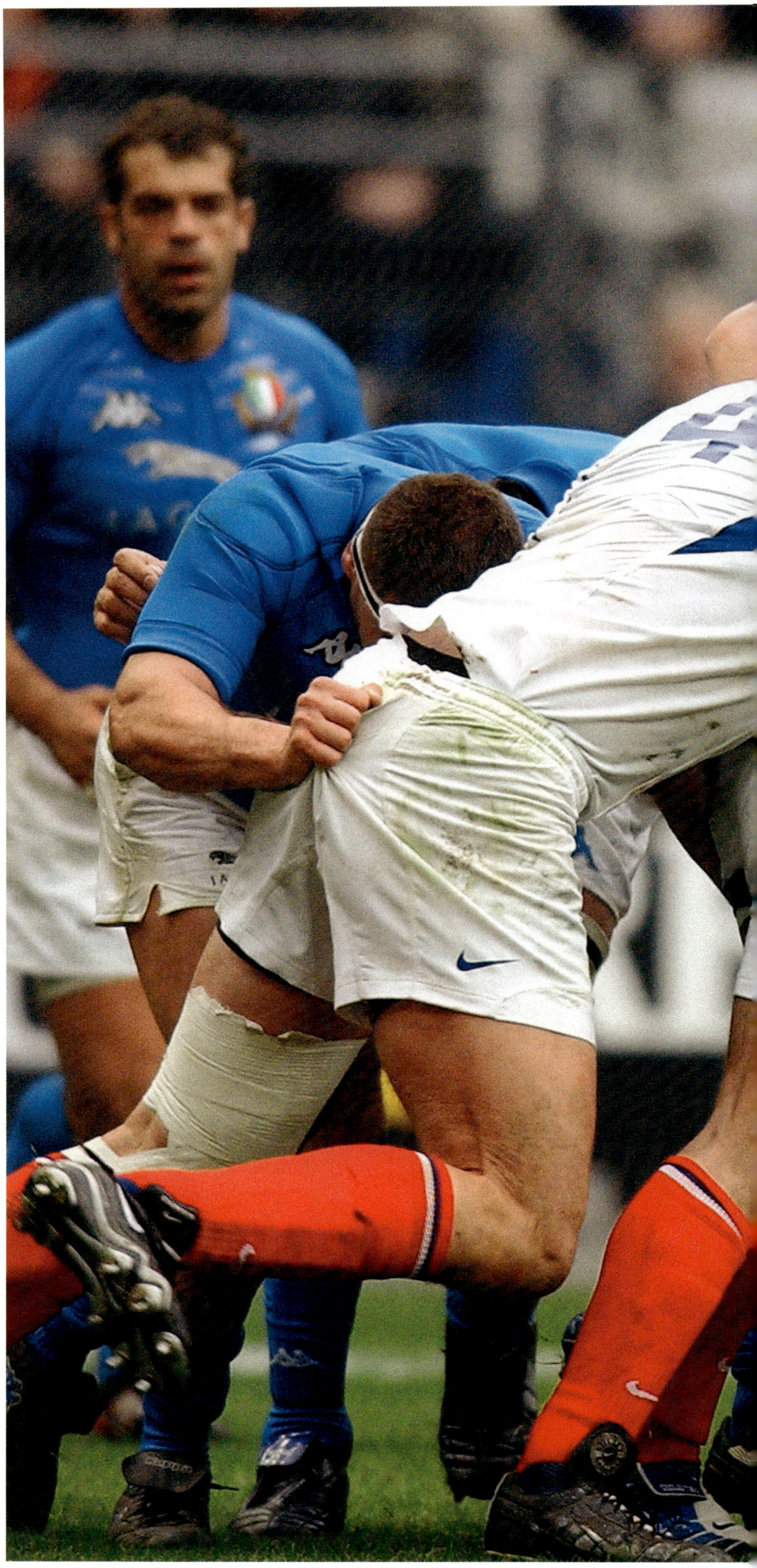

Porteur de la balle, Jean-Jacques Crenca avance vers le camp italien, remarquablement protégé par ses coéquipiers de l'équipe de France. De gauche à droite, on reconnaît Fabien Pelous (n°4), Imanol Harinordoquy, Pieter De Villiers, Pascal Papé et Olivier Magne.

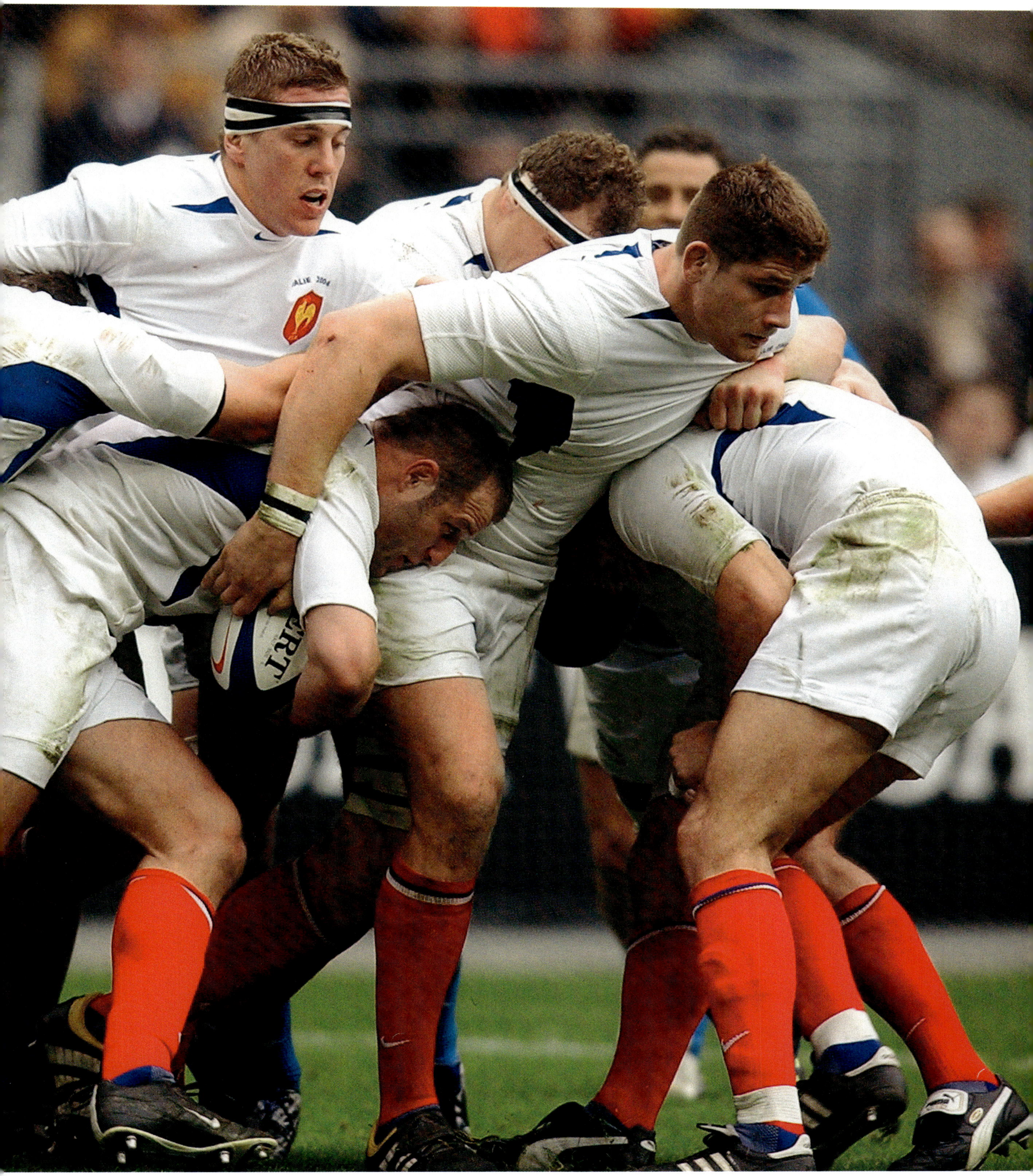

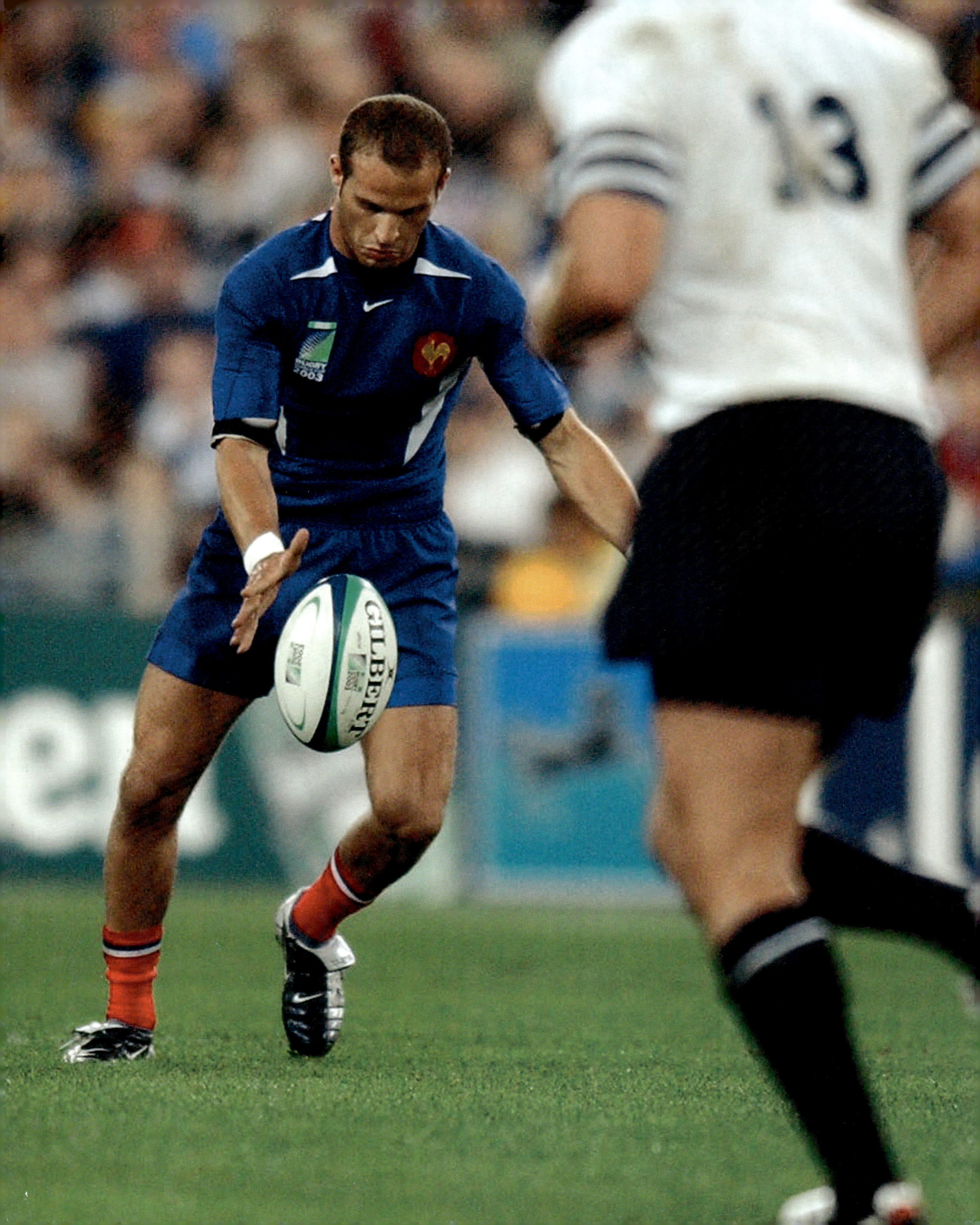
2003
GILBERT

Drop

Laisse tomber ! *To drop*, en anglais. Le drop-goal est traduit par l'expression « coup de pied tombé ». Mais pas perdu pour tout le monde. Le botteur, comme ici à gauche Frédéric Michalak avec l'équipe de France et Alain Penaud sous les couleurs du Stade Français, fait tomber le ballon devant lui et le laisse rebondir avant de frapper dedans. Exercice particulièrement difficile, le drop rapporte autant qu'un but de pénalité, à savoir trois points, et sans coup férir. On a tort de le décrier : il permet à une équipe qui domine de remporter une rencontre dans les dernières secondes. Comme le tir de loin des footballeurs qui finit sa course dans la lucarne, le drop-goal offre un plaisir limpide et instantané. Parmi les artistes remarquables, citons les deux ouvreurs Joel Stransky et Jonny Wilkinson : lorsque, avec la précision de l'archer zen qui lâche sa flèche les yeux fermés, ils décochèrent leurs drop-goals durant la prolongation des finales de Coupes du monde 1995 et 2003, l'Afrique du Sud et l'Angleterre se retrouvèrent instantanément au paradis.

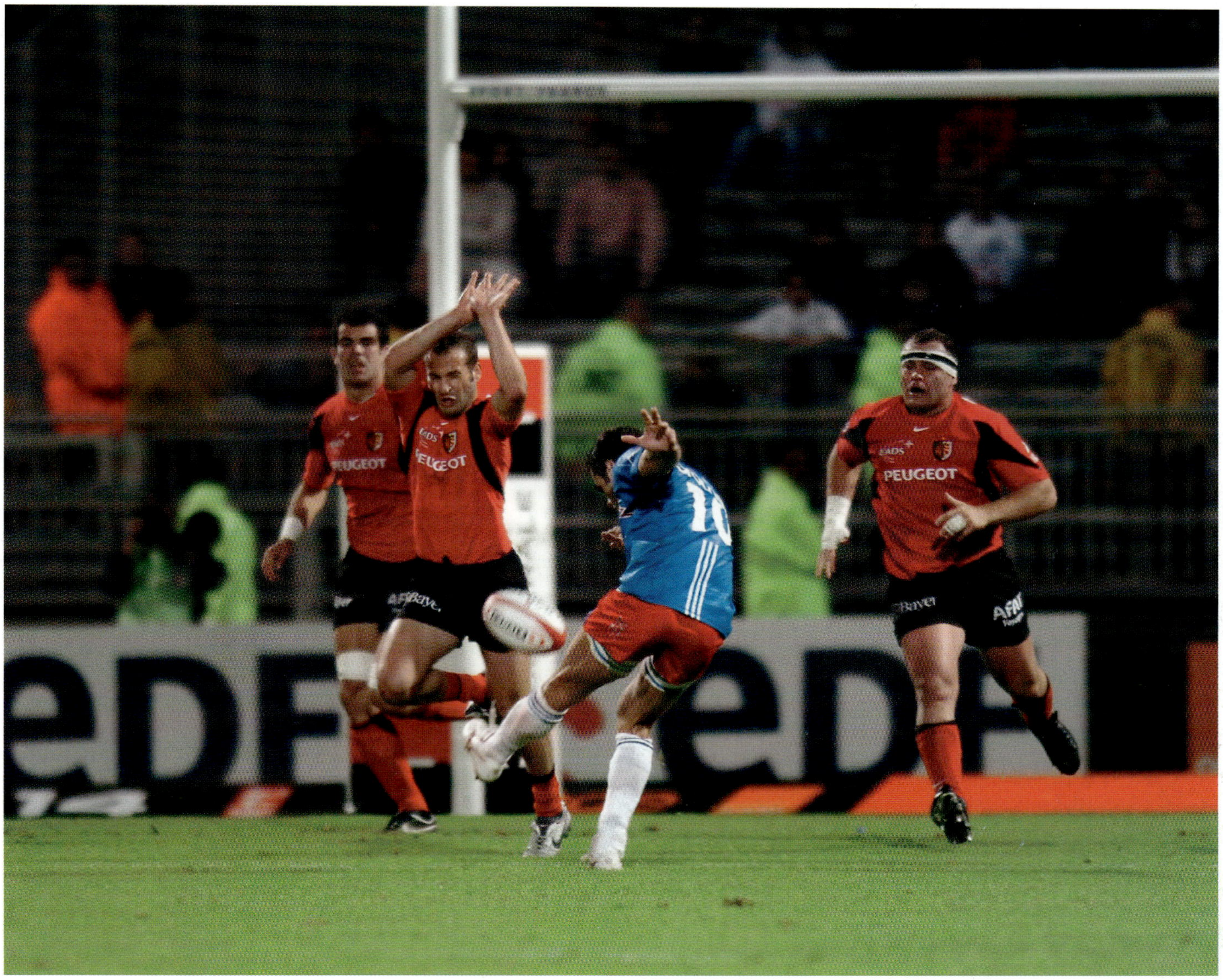

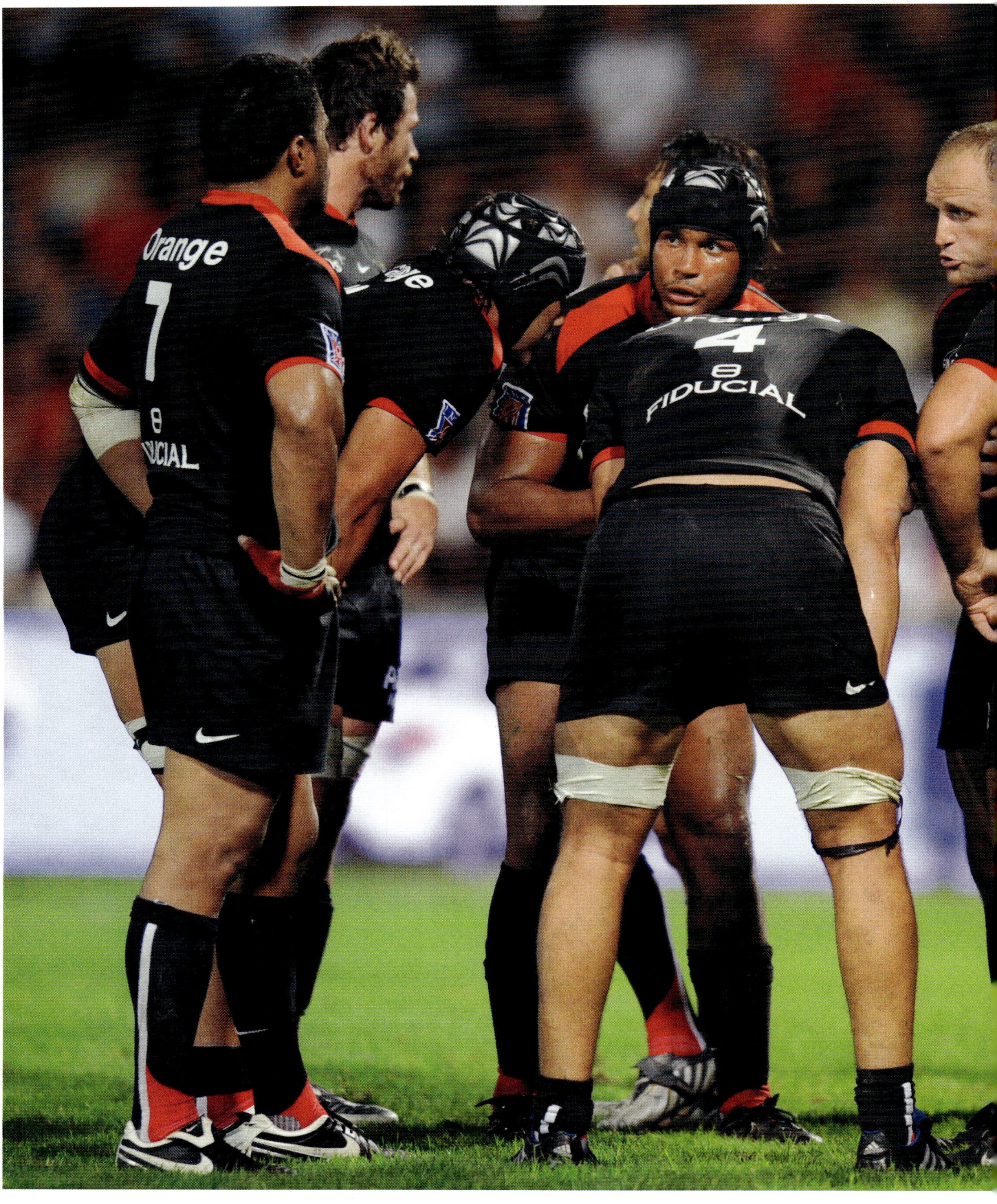
Orange
7
4
FIDUCIAL

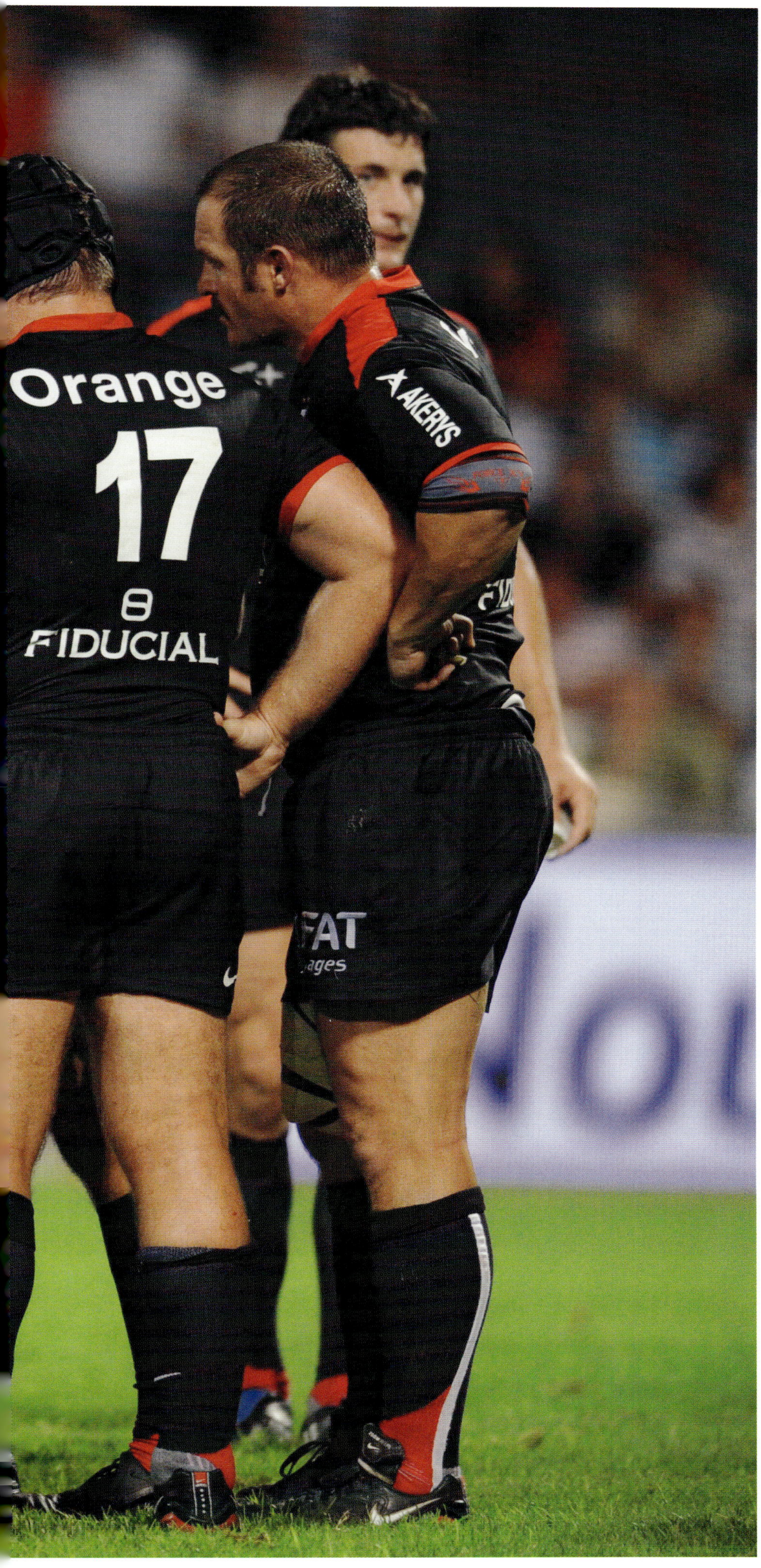

Capitaine

« Le rugby ne s'emploie pas à la première personne : il se conjugue à quinze », répétait Jean-Pierre Rives, soucieux de relativiser son rôle de leader. La plupart du temps choisi par ses partenaires pour son charisme à la fois sur et hors du terrain, et nommé officiellement par l'entraîneur, le capitaine ne dirige pas simplement le jeu, il est un véritable guide spirituel pour ses coéquipiers. À travers la grande aventure du Quinze de France, des personnages d'envergure comme Jean Prat, Lucien Mias, Michel Crauste, Christian Carrère, Jacques Fouroux, Philippe Saint-André et Raphaël Ibanez, possédaient eux aussi les qualités de cœur et les vertus sans lesquelles il n'y a pas de grand capitaine. Humble mais habité, comme ici Thierry Dusautoir au milieu de ses troupes, il est d'abord un homme de valeurs. Au pluriel.

Durant un arrêt de jeu, entouré de ses avants (on reconnaît entre autres Sowerby, Albacete (casqué), Maestri (n°4), Servat et Human), le troisième ligne aile toulousain Thierry Dusautoir précise certains points tactiques et redonne les consignes. Il est tout à son rôle.

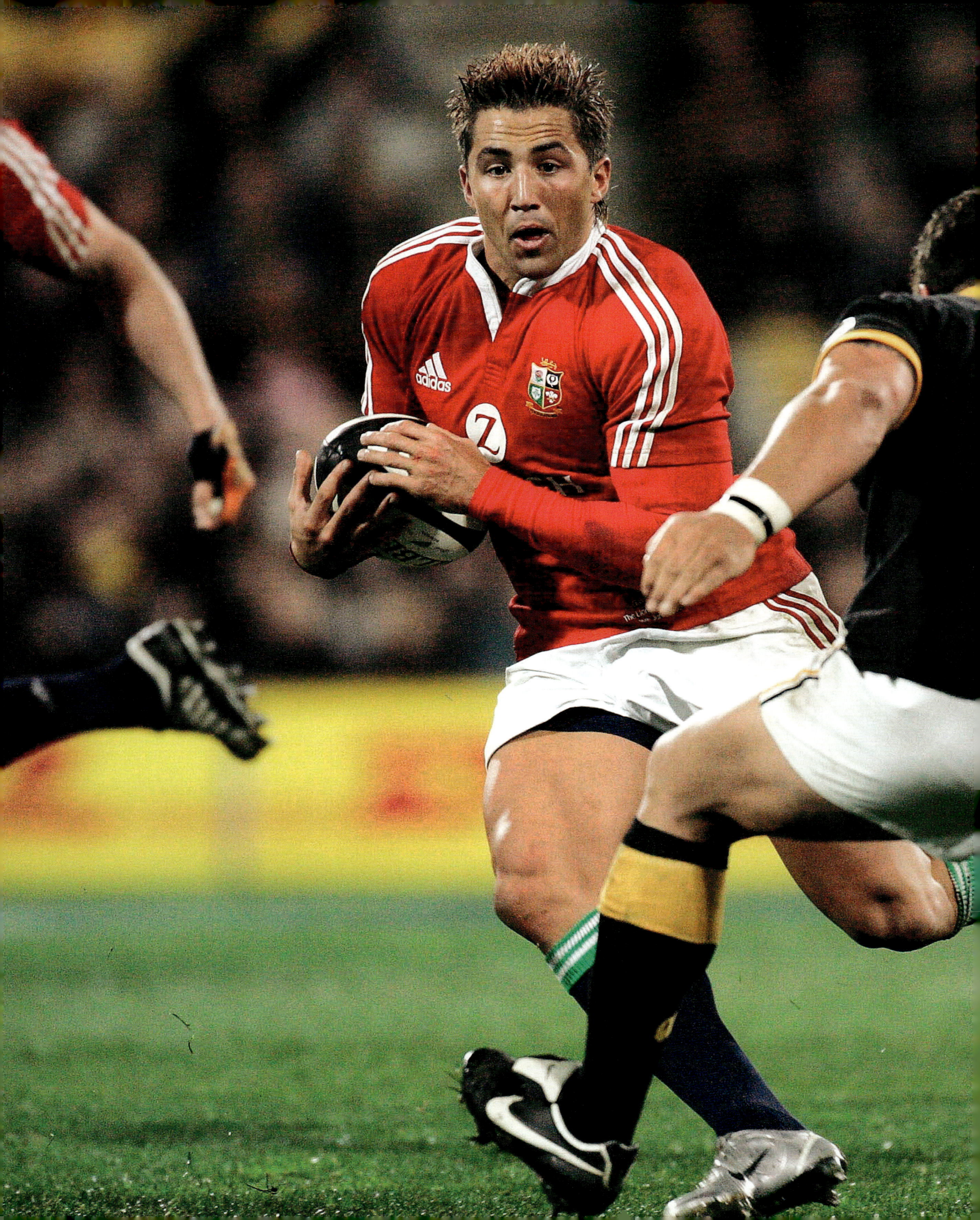
adidas

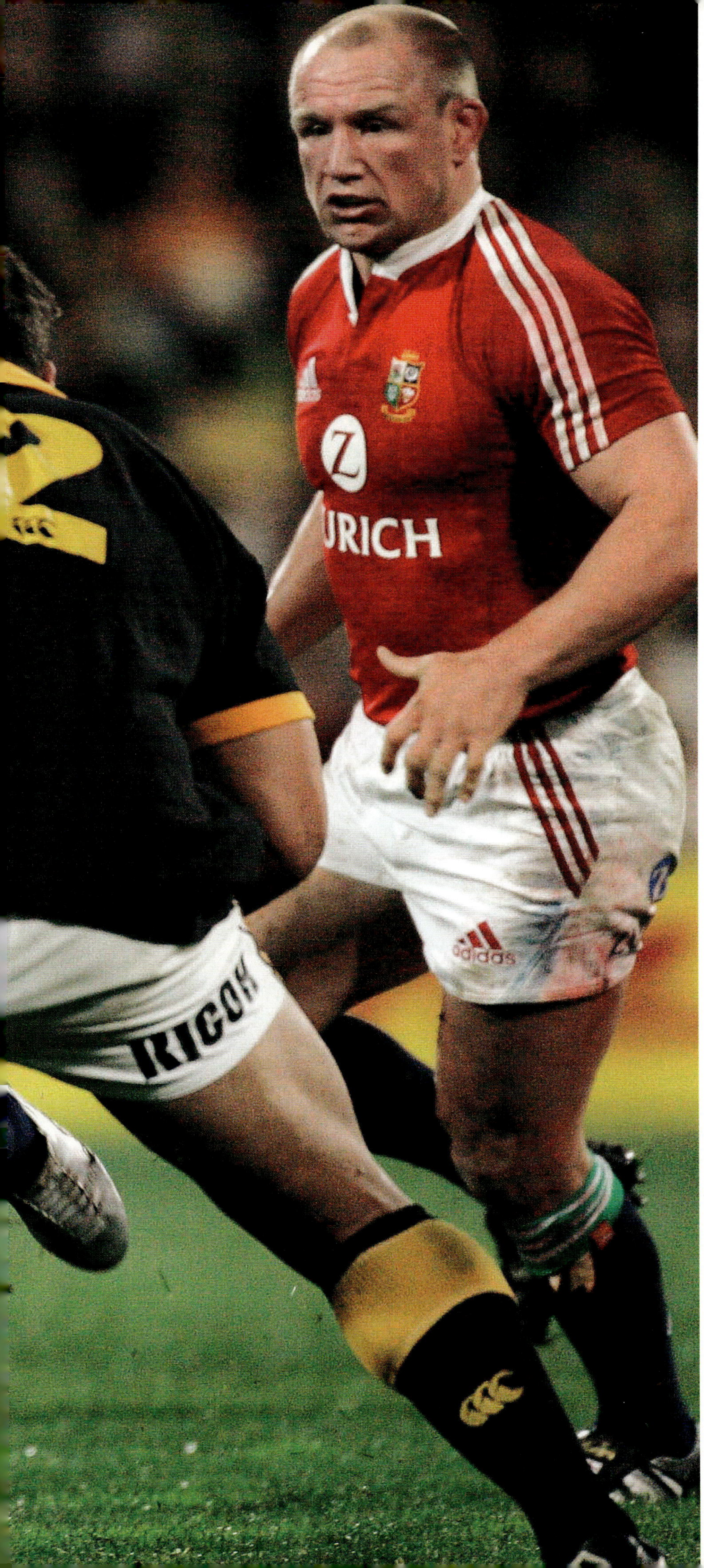

Cadrage-débordement

Cadrer et déborder. Rien de plus simple à décrire, rien de plus difficile à réaliser. Dans un premier temps, le joueur, ouvreur, centre ou ailier, fixe son vis-à-vis à cinq mètres de distance en allant droit sur lui, puis il incurve légèrement sa course vers l'intérieur. Au moment où il sent le défenseur ferré, l'attaquant change alors violemment sa course de direction et file vers l'extérieur. Il contourne alors le défenseur en le prenant de vitesse. Ce débordement, comme un arc de cercle, correspond à une explosion physique intense qui permet à l'attaquant d'avoir un dixième de seconde d'avance sur le défenseur à l'arrêt. Cela suffit pour ne pas être attrapé. Tout l'art du « un contre un » tel que le pratiquent les lignes arrière est contenu dans ce geste hautement technique.

Face à Wellington, Gavin Henson, le trois-quarts centre gallois des Lions Britanniques, sélection des meilleurs joueurs britanniques, effectue un cadrage-débordement sur le talonneur de la province néo-zélandaise, sous le regard du troisième ligne aile Neil Back. Le défenseur, pris sur son appui intérieur, c'est-à-dire planté sur le pied droit, ne pourra pas plaquer l'attaquant qui le défie à pleine vitesse.

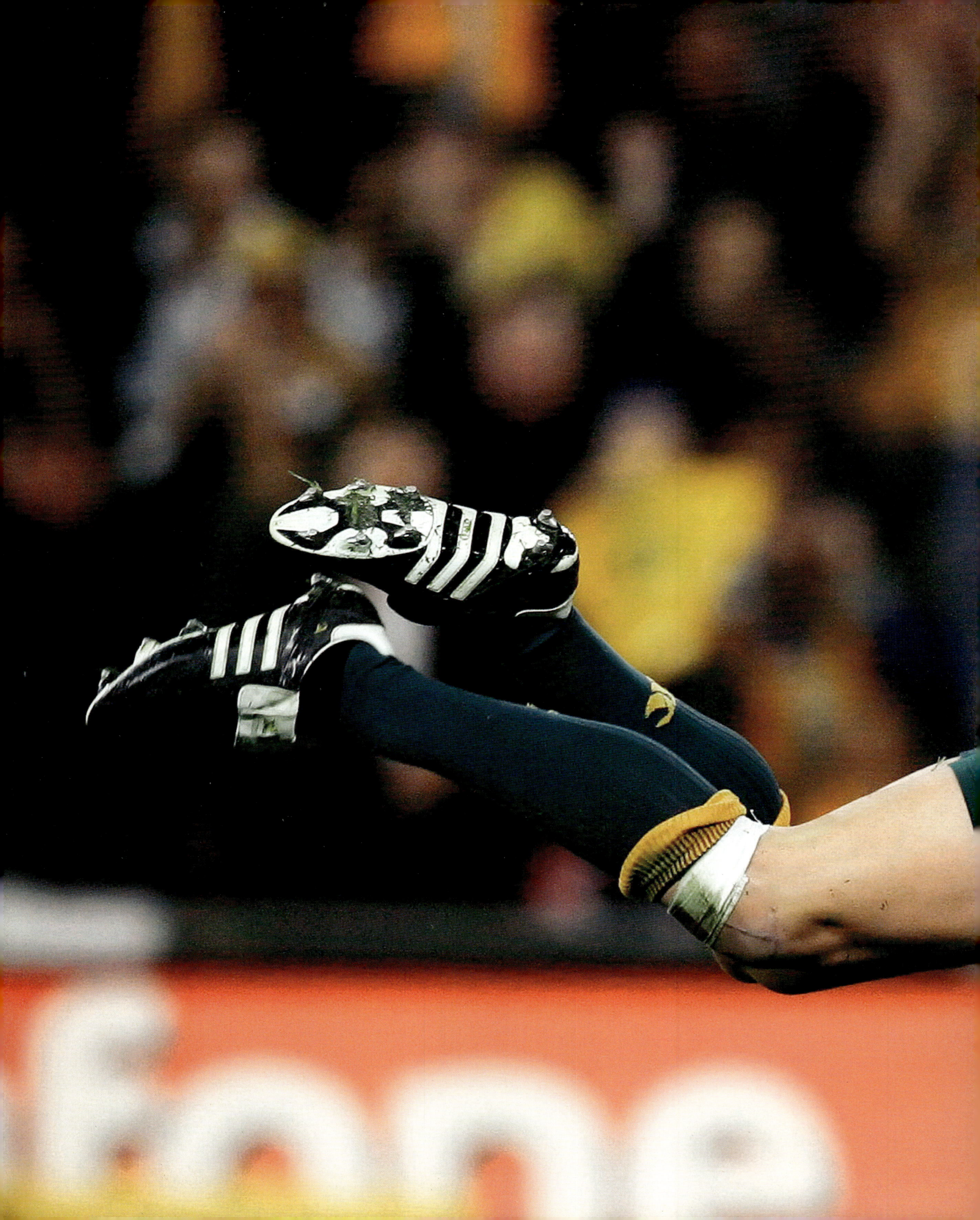

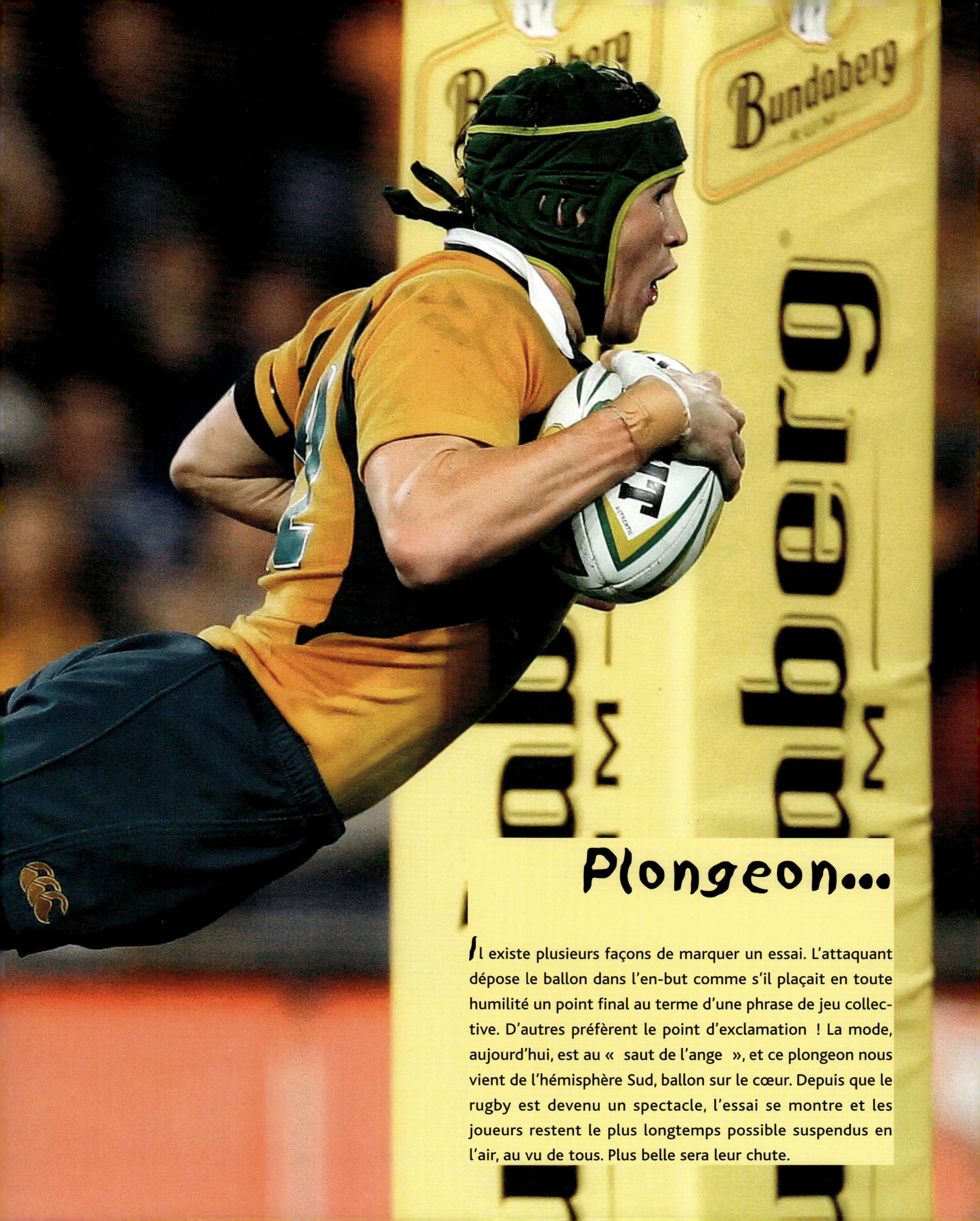

Plongeon...

Il existe plusieurs façons de marquer un essai. L'attaquant dépose le ballon dans l'en-but comme s'il plaçait en toute humilité un point final au terme d'une phrase de jeu collective. D'autres préfèrent le point d'exclamation ! La mode, aujourd'hui, est au « saut de l'ange », et ce plongeon nous vient de l'hémisphère Sud, ballon sur le cœur. Depuis que le rugby est devenu un spectacle, l'essai se montre et les joueurs restent le plus longtemps possible suspendus en l'air, au vu de tous. Plus belle sera leur chute.

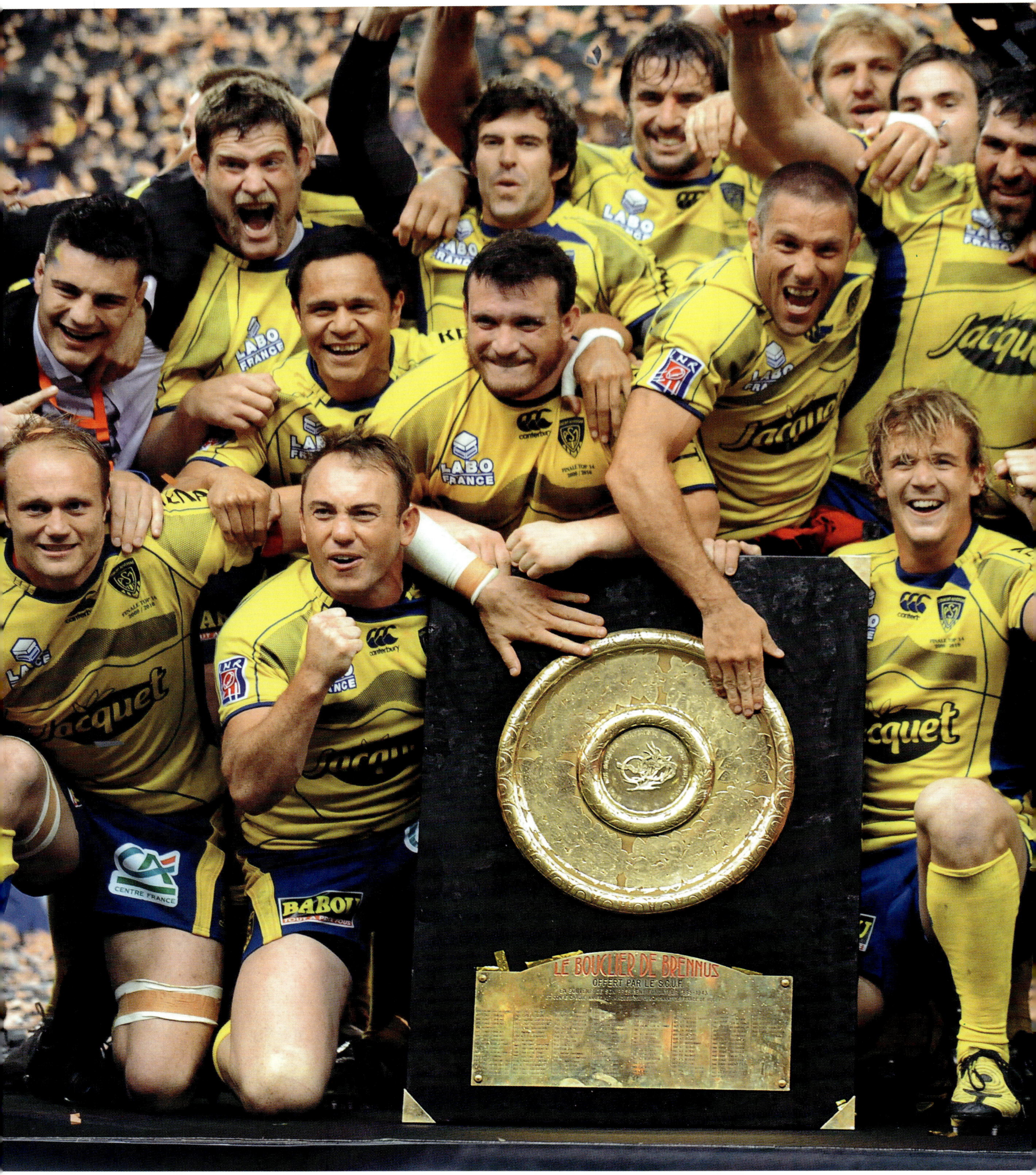
LE BOUCLIER DE BRENNUS
OFFERT PAR LE S.C.U.F.
LABO FRANCE
Jacquet
CENTRE FRANCE

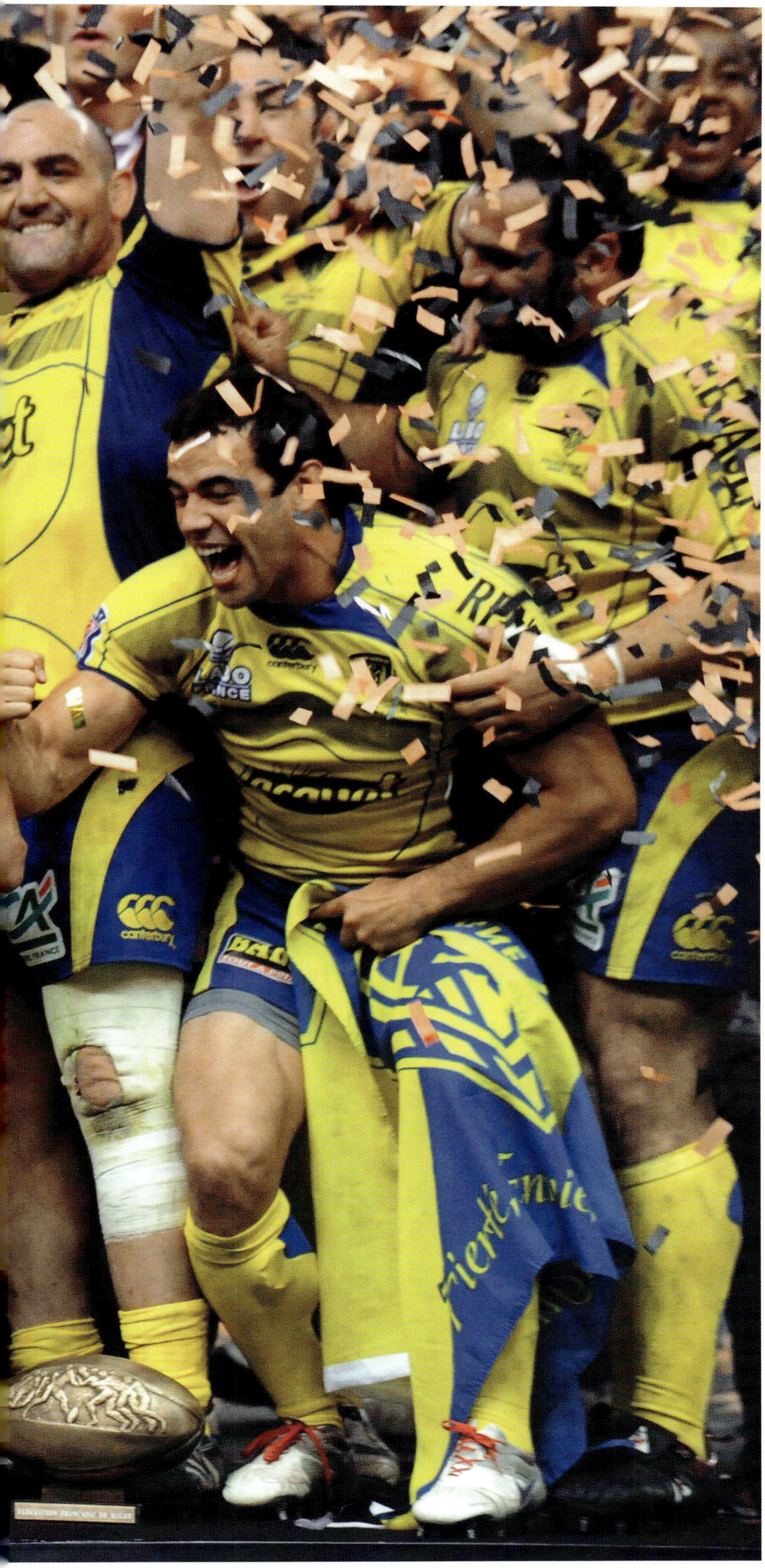

...pour la victoire

Gagner, c'est prendre le dessus, s'imposer, surclasser l'adversaire, marquer l'histoire. Dans le championnat de France, la meilleure équipe de club est sacrée à l'issue de la finale, au Stade de France, et remporte le Bouclier de Brennus. Un cran au-dessus, les grandes équipes nationales disputent plusieurs compétitions : le Tournoi des Six Nations en Europe et le Tri-Nations dans l'hémisphère Sud. Tous les quatre ans, les vingt meilleures nations du monde s'affrontent pour avoir l'honneur de soulever le trophée Webb-Ellis. Mais toutes ces coupes ne représentent pas à elles seules l'essence du jeu. L'important, en sport, n'est pas de vaincre mais de donner le meilleur de soi-même.

Où que l'on joue, d'où que l'on soit, la joie de gagner demeure la même. Comme ici celle que l'on partage avec le Biarritz Olympique qui célébrait, en 2006, à Saint-Denis, le cinquième titre de champion de France de son histoire.

Aimer le rugby

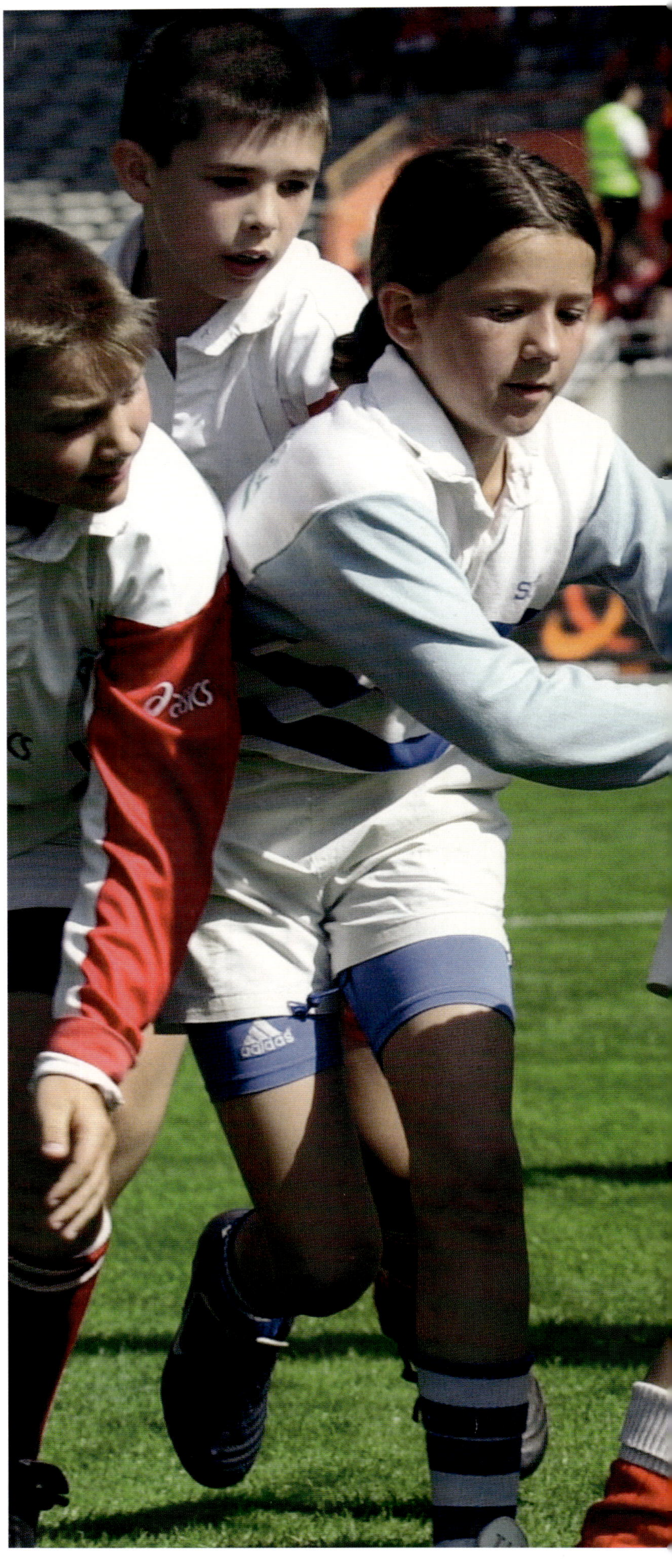

Pour soi

Du pilier à l'arrière, une équipe de rugby est formée par quinze joueurs différents, de tous les gabarits et de tous les caractères. Qu'il soit gros, grand ou mince, vif ou calme, téméraire ou réfléchi, un enfant trouvera toujours sa place au milieu de ses partenaires. Certains se complaisent dans l'anonymat, au cœur du paquet d'avants, d'autres utilisent leurs qualités naturelles pour briller. Il faut le savoir quand on débute : le profil type du joueur de rugby n'existe pas. Au contraire, une équipe puise sa force dans la différence et dans la complémentarité. Il ne faut donc nourrir aucun complexe : tel écart de poids ou de taille, qui peut paraître au départ un handicap, ou plus simplement une gêne, se révèle vite un atout. L'exemple du gros patapouf Benazzi devenu l'international français le plus percutant, ou de l'intenable Benetton transformé en modèle de sérénité dans son rôle de capitaine puis d'entraîneur quelques années plus tard, sont des exemples parmi d'autres qui illustrent la façon dont le rugby accueille ses enfants, filles et garçons.

Pour les autres

On dit de ce jeu qu'il est une école de la vie : aucune autre image ne sert mieux les desseins de cette activité née dans un collège anglais en 1823 et créée par les élèves eux-mêmes pour se défouler tout en respectant quelques règles. Dans ce sport collectif de combat et de contact, un joueur seul ne peut rien. Il n'existe qu'avec les autres. Même le plus doué des sujets, comme l'était Serge Blanco il y a vingt ans, ou comme l'est aujourd'hui Frédéric Michalak, ne peut tenir à lui seul le destin d'une rencontre. Gagner la balle, la conserver, la distribuer, la transmettre, la botter, la récupérer… Les actions, comme les rôles, sont multiples. En ce sens, le rugby n'est pas un sport individuel. En tant que discipline sportive collective, il demande d'abord à chaque individu de se mettre au service d'un collectif. Appartenir à une équipe, c'est apprendre à connaître les autres, accepter leurs différences, trouver en chaque partenaire un allié, un complice, et parfois un ami.

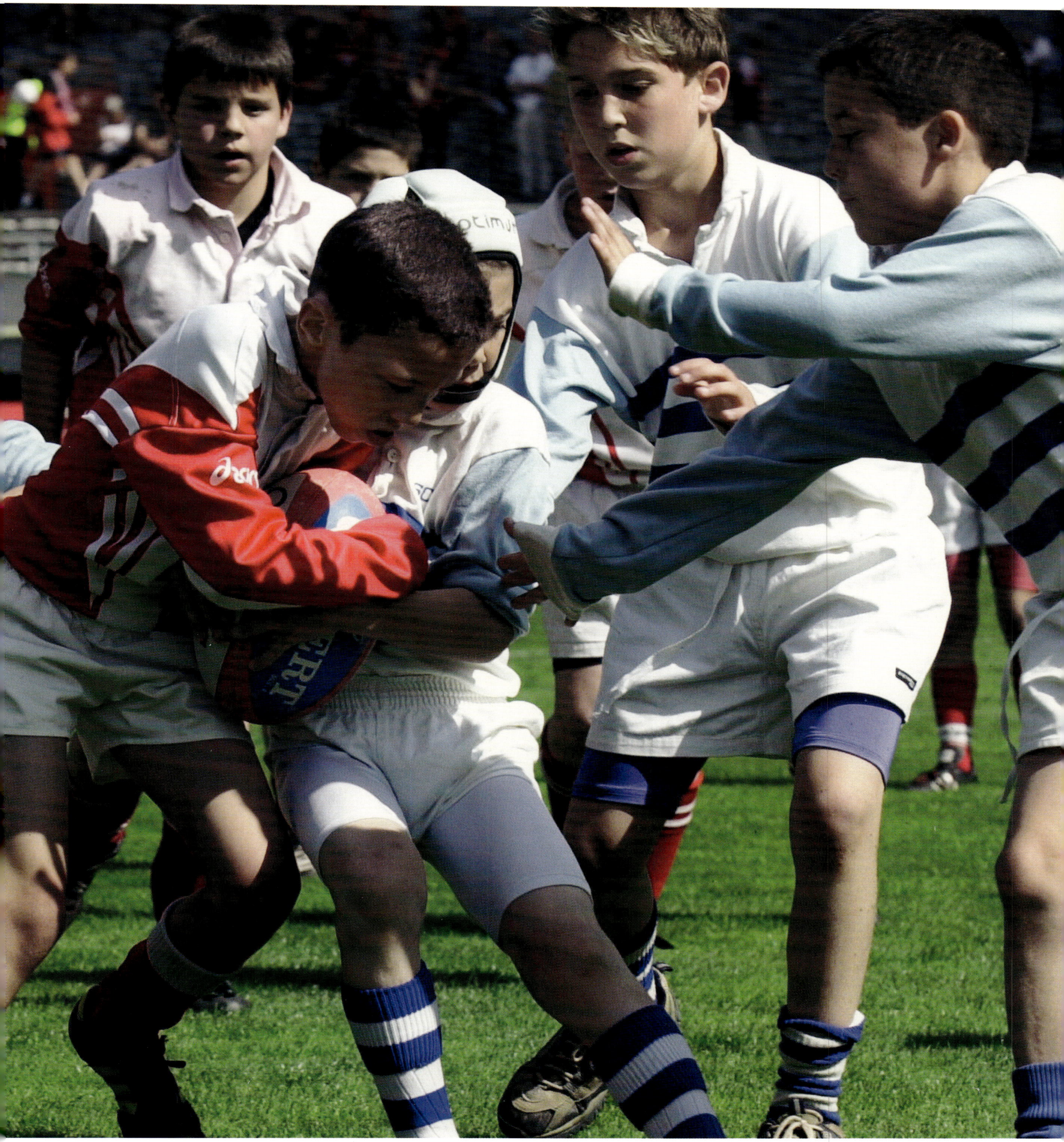

Évolution tactique

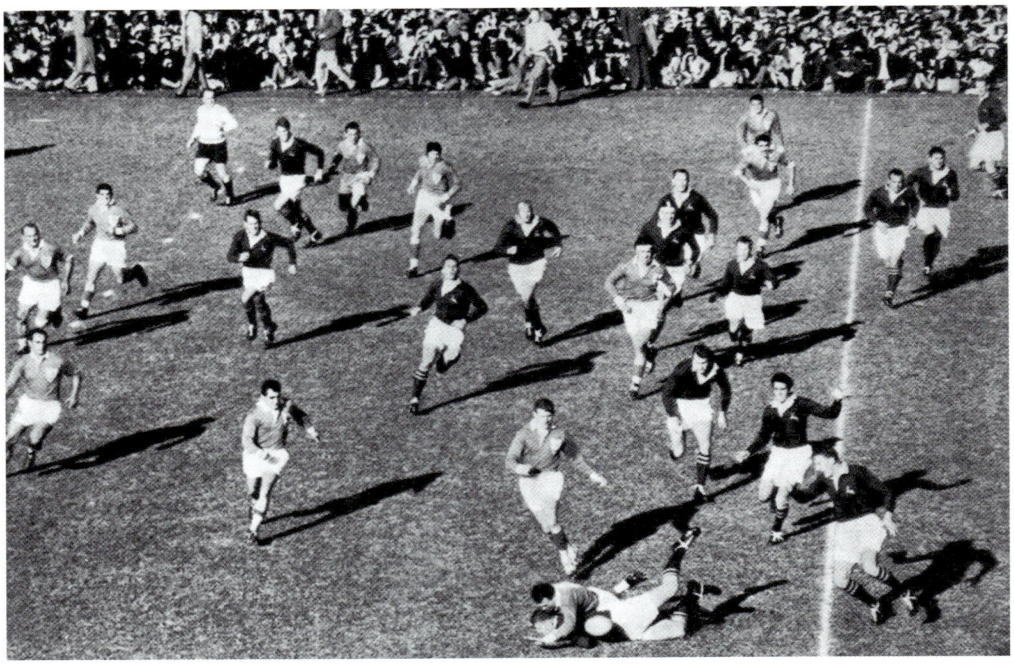

Années 50

Quand les deux meilleures équipes de l'époque, la France et l'Afrique du Sud, s'affrontent, le terrain est quadrillé au hasard des différents déplacements de joueurs. Un Sud-Africain, porteur de la balle, est plaqué (au premier plan), mais six de ses coéquipiers sont placés devant lui. La défense française, elle, n'est absolument pas en ligne.

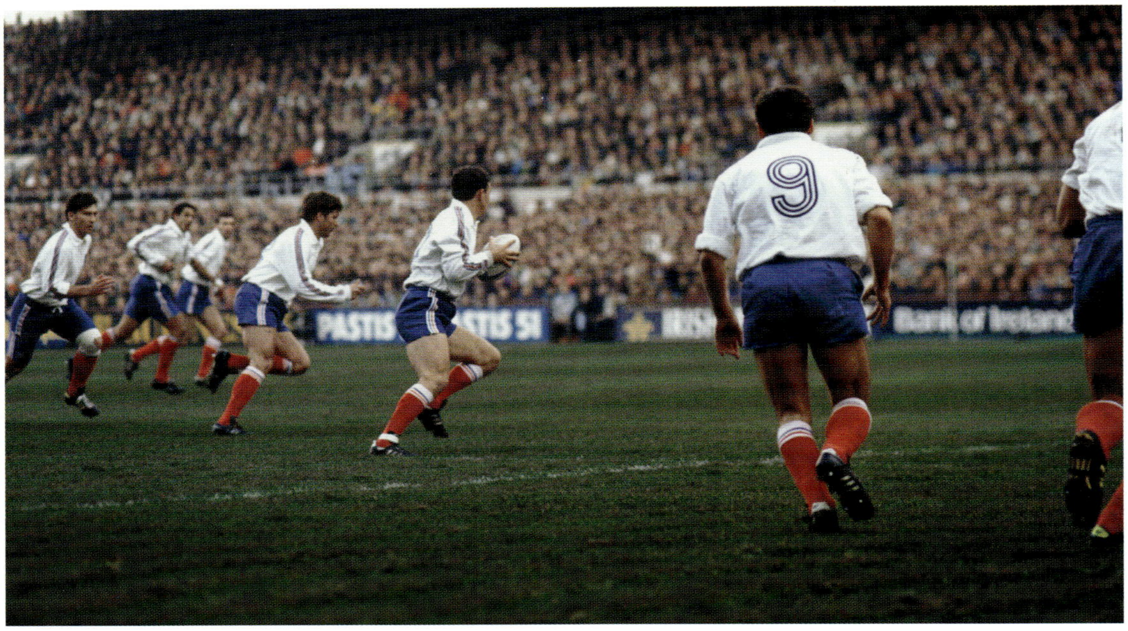

Années 80

L'une des meilleures attaques tricolores en position. Pierre Berbizier (n° 9) a ouvert sur Didier Camberabero. On reconnaît Denis Charvet, Franck Mesnel, Serge Blanco et Patrice Lagisquet. L'époque est au jeu de ligne, ordonné et classique, les arrières cherchant à faire fructifier par un jeu de passes les ballons gagnés par les avants.

Aujourd'hui

Le demi de mêlée australien George Gregan, recordman du monde des sélections, joue dans l'intervalle et passe les bras devant le Sud-Africain Jean De Villiers (n° 12). Ses partenaires Lote Tuquiri et Phil Waugh vont intervenir dans son sillage pour recueillir la passe. Le rugby moderne est fait de défis physiques et de polyvalence technique.

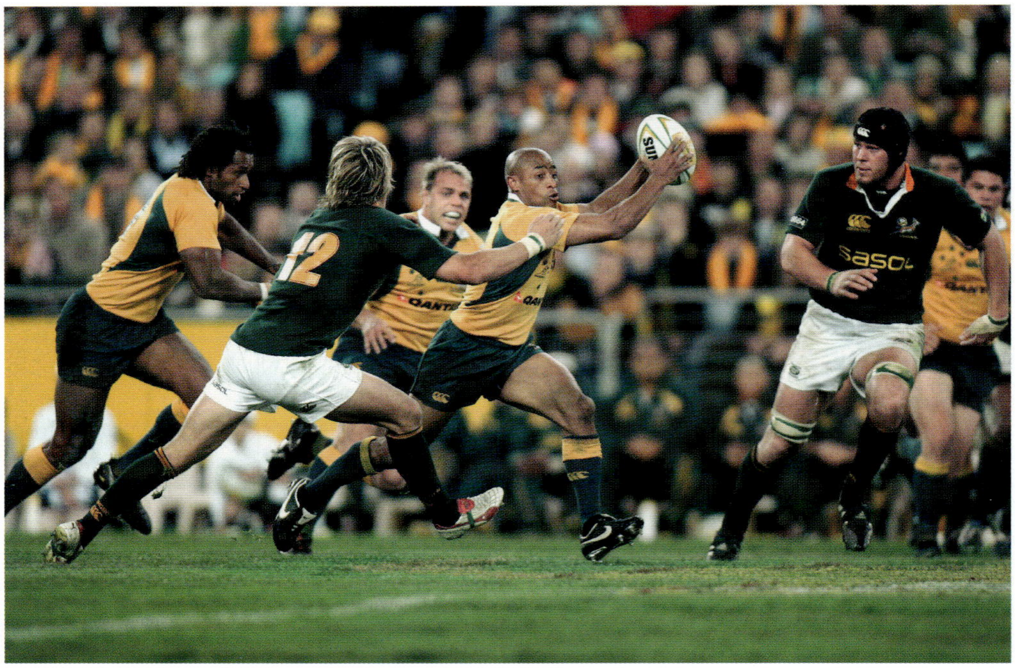

Glossaire

ARRIÈRE : appelé aussi « dernier défenseur ». Il est chargé de récupérer les ballons joués au pied par l'adversaire et de repousser le danger soit en dégageant en touche, soit en relançant à la main. En attaque, il s'intercale dans la ligne de trois-quarts pour créer un surnombre. Porte le numéro 15.

TROIS-QUARTS AILE : le monumental Néo-Zélandais Jonah Lomu (1,96 m, 118 kg) est mondialement connu. D'habitude, les joueurs situés en bout d'attaque, le long de la ligne de touche, sont d'un gabarit plus ordinaire. Rapides, vifs, crocheteurs, on les appelle « les finisseurs » : ils sont censés marquer au terme de l'offensive lancée par leurs partenaires. Portent les numéros 11 et 14.

TROIS-QUARTS CENTRE : placés dans l'axe du terrain, ils créent le jeu, c'est-à-dire qu'ils libèrent par leurs courses et leurs passes millimétrées l'espace dont ont besoin leurs partenaires. Les Français sont passés maîtres pour éviter les défenseurs, un art que nos adversaires appellent le « French Flair ». Portent les numéros 12 et 13.

DEMI D'OUVERTURE : à la charnière des avants et des arrières, il est le chef d'orchestre de l'équipe. Il décide s'il faut jouer au pied ou à la main, annonce les combinaisons, organise la montée défensive et, souvent, occupe la fonction de buteur. Porte le numéro 10.

DEMI DE MÊLÉE : il choisit s'il faut attaquer avec les avants ou avec les arrières. Toutes les balles passent par lui. Avec le demi d'ouverture, il forme la charnière chargée de diriger le jeu. Porte le numéro 9.

TROISIÈME LIGNE CENTRE : rien n'échappe à cette tour de contrôle. Athlétique, il rayonne sur le terrain. Son rôle est complexe : preneur de balle en touche, il distille les ballons derrière la mêlée et couvre les arrières en assurant un repli défensif. Porte le numéro 8.

TROISIÈME LIGNE AILE : installé sur l'un des flancs de la mêlée, le « flanker » est l'homme à tout faire du rugby moderne : attaquant supplémentaire, mais aussi défenseur intraitable dont les plaquages sont craints. Résistant, endurant, il colle au ballon. Portent les numéros 6 et 7.

DEUXIÈME LIGNE : joueur de devoir, il est chargé d'assurer la poussée en mêlée. Allant toujours par paire, les deuxièmes lignes sont les poutres maîtresses de l'équipe. Leur gabarit impressionne : 2 mètres et 125 kilos en moyenne. Portent les numéros 4 et 5.

PILIER : les épaules carrées, le cou épais, il encaisse le poids de la mêlée. L'homme fort du pack, taillé comme un lutteur, est aujourd'hui extrêmement impliqué dans le jeu et doit se déplacer avec vivacité. En touche, il soutient les sauteurs le plus longtemps possible en l'air. Portent les numéros 3 et 1.

TALONNEUR : à la fois électron libre et libero, il est aux avants ce que l'arrière est aux trois-quarts : celui qui comble les espaces en défense et joue le surnombre en attaque. Son rôle est capital dans les phases de conquêtes : il talonne la balle en mêlée pour la ramener dans son camp, et la lance en touche. Avec les deux piliers, il forme la première ligne. Porte le numéro 2.

ATTAQUE : pas besoin d'être dans le camp adverse pour attaquer. Il faut simplement que toute l'équipe soit sur la même longueur d'onde. Il s'agit de fixer le maximum de défenseurs par des passes afin de démarquer un partenaire qui pourra filer vers l'en-but inscrire l'essai.

DÉFENSE : ce n'est pas simplement plaquer un adversaire ; la défense est une organisation collective. Son but ? Arrêter les attaquants.

POLYVALENCE : depuis vingt ans, il est demandé aux joueurs, quels que soient les postes qu'ils occupent, d'être capables de réagir avec les gestes appropriés aux situations de jeu qui se présentent. C'est ainsi qu'un pilier moderne doit pouvoir jouer comme un ouvreur si le jeu le commande.

PREMIÈRE MAIN : se dit de l'attaque où le ballon part d'une phase statique, touche ou mêlée, et traverse en quelques passes le terrain vers l'ailier mis en débordement.

TEMPS DE JEU : on parle d'un temps de jeu chaque fois qu'un attaquant est plaqué, le ballon touchant le sol, mais qu'il parvient à le libérer pour un partenaire qui peut s'en saisir, et jouer à son tour. Il n'est pas rare aujourd'hui de compter dix temps de jeu sur une même action.

RUGBY : petite ville située dans le centre de l'Angleterre, entre Northampton, au sud, et Leicester, au nord. C'est dans l'établissement scolaire de Rugby, qui regroupe collège et lycée, que fut pratiqué en 1823 le jeu de balle ovale. Le rugby est le seul sport qui porte le nom de la ville où il a été inventé.

TOURNOI : entre 1883 et 1909, le Tournoi était joué uniquement par les nations britanniques, Angleterre, Irlande, Écosse et Pays de Galles. La France fut invitée à partir de 1910. L'Italie a ensuite rejoint cette compétition en 2000.

TRI-NATIONS : compétition internationale créée à Johannesburg, basée sur des matches aller-retour et disputée par l'Afrique du Sud, la Nouvelle-Zélande et l'Australie. Le premier Tri-Nations date de 1996.

INTERNATIONAL BOARD : organisme international fondé en 1886 qui gère le rugby sur toute la planète. Réservé aux nations anglo-saxonnes jusqu'en 1978, il s'est ouvert aux Français, puis au reste du monde à partir de 1992. On compte aujourd'hui presque cent nations membres.

COUPE DU MONDE : créée en 1985 à Paris, à l'initiative du président de la FFR, Albert Ferrasse. Elle se dispute tous les quatre ans. La première édition, en 1987, s'est tenue en Australie et en Nouvelle-Zélande.

Toutes les photographies de cet ouvrage
proviennent de l'agence Presse Sports / *l'Équipe*

Page de titre : Bardou - 4 Francotte - 5 Rondeau - 6hg Presse Sports - 6hc Presse Sports - 6hd Francotte
7hg Presse Sports - 7hd Mons - 6-7 Mantey - 8 Gripe Patrick - 10-11h Deschamps - 10-11b De Martignac
12-13 Boutroux - 14-15 Papon - 16-17 Papon - 16b Caron - 18-19 Rondeau
20-21 Francotte - 22-23 Presse Sports - 24 De Martignac - 25 Papon - 26 De Martignac
27 Mark Leech - 28-29 De Martignac - 30 Duif du Toit/Touchline
31 Papon - 32-33 Lablatinière - 34-35 Alain Mounic - 36-37 Presse Sports - 39 Luttiau
40-41 Mantey - 42-43 Lahalle - 44 Lahalle - 45 Fel
46 Rondeau - 47 De Martignac - 48-49 Presse Sports - 50-51 Boutroux - 52 Boutroux
53 Lahalle - 54 Papon - 55 Luttiau - 56-57 De Martignac - 58-59 Boutroux
60-61 Francotte - 62 Fel - 63 James Crombie/Inpho/Presse Sports - 64 Luttiau - 65 De Martignac - 66-67 Éric Bouvet
68-69 Papon - 70 Papon - 71 Papon - 72-73 Rondeau -
74-75 Offside/Presse Sports - 76-77 Sport the library - 78-79 Mantey
80-81 Fablet - 82h Presse Sports - 82c Clément - 82b Paul Seiser - 84 Martin
Pages de gardes : d'après Mantey - Couverture plat 1 : Mark Leech - plat 4 : Francotte

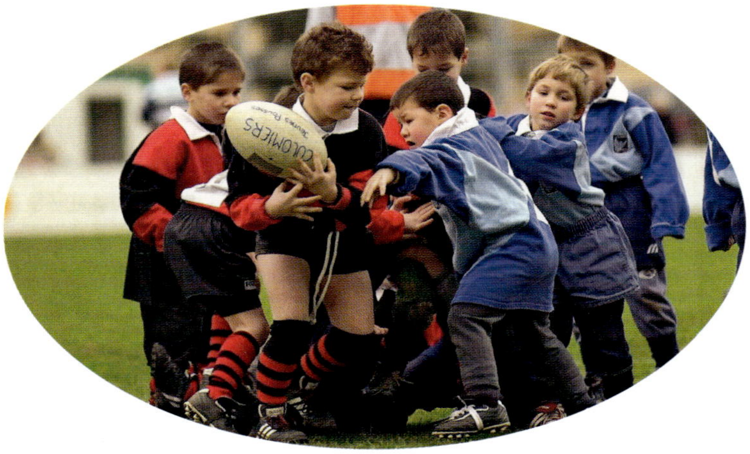

Conforme à la loi n°49-956 du 16 juillet 1949 sur les publications destinées à la jeunesse

ISBN : 978-2-7324-4821-3
Dépôt légal : août 2011
Achevé d'imprimé : juin 2011

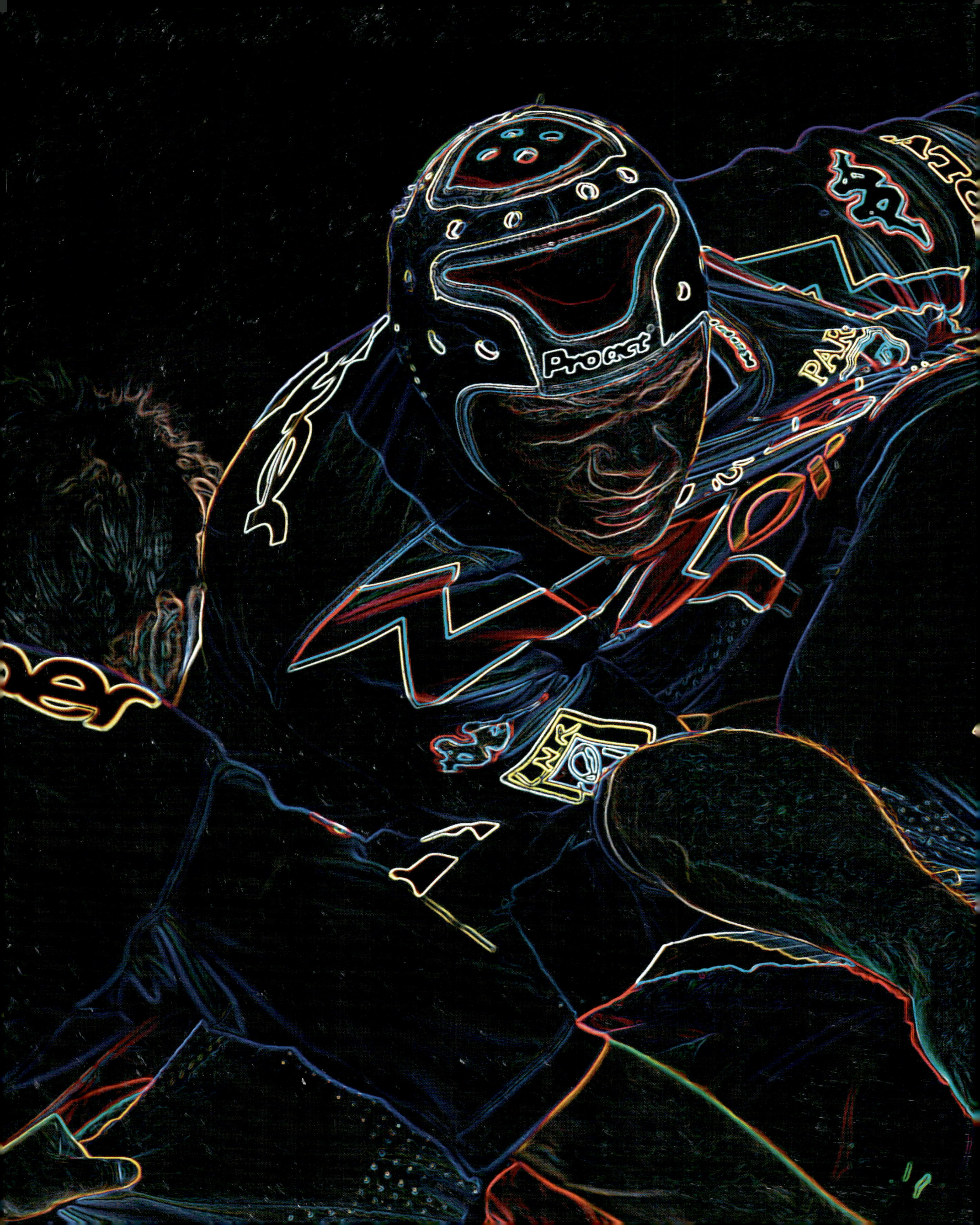